African American Classics in

CRIMINOLOGY & CRIMINAL JUSTICE

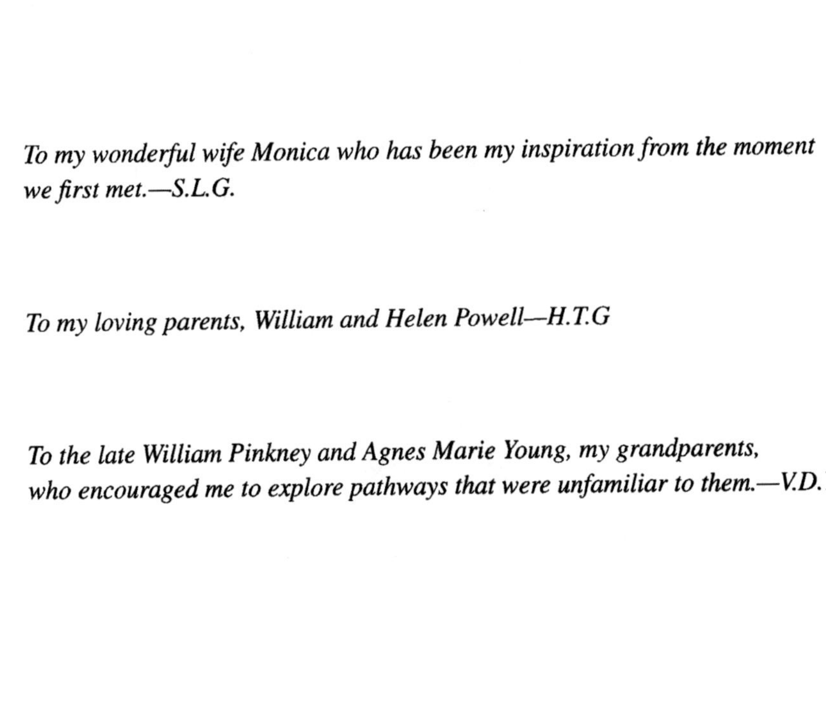

To my wonderful wife Monica who has been my inspiration from the moment we first met.—S.L.G.

To my loving parents, William and Helen Powell—H.T.G

To the late William Pinkney and Agnes Marie Young, my grandparents, who encouraged me to explore pathways that were unfamiliar to them.—V.D.Y.

African American Classics in CRIMINOLOGY & CRIMINAL JUSTICE

SHAUN L. GABBIDON
Pennsylvania State University—Capital College
HELEN TAYLOR GREENE
Old Dominion University
VERNETTA D. YOUNG
Howard University
Editors

Sage Publications
International Educational and Professional Publisher
Thousand Oaks ▪ London ▪ New Delhi

For information:

Sage Publications, Inc.
2455 Teller Road
Thousand Oaks, California 91320
E-mail: order@sagepub.com

Sage Publications Ltd.
6 Bonhill Street
London EC2A 4PU
United Kingdom

Sage Publications India Pvt. Ltd.
M-32 Market
Greater Kailash I
New Delhi 110 048 India

Printed in the United States of America

Library of Congress Cataloging-in-Publication Data

African American classics in criminology and criminal justice / edited
by Shaun Gabbidon, Helen Taylor Greene, Vernetta D. Young.
p. cm.
Includes bibliographical references and index.
ISBN 0-7619-2432-9 (cloth : acid-free paper)
ISBN 0-7619-2433-7 (pbk. : acid-free paper)
1. Crime and race—United States. 2. African American criminals.
3. Discrimination in criminal justice administration—United States.
4. Criminology—United States. 5. African Americans—Social conditions.
6. United States—Race relations. I. Gabbidon, Shaun L., 1967–
II. Greene, Helen Taylor, 1949– III. Young, Vernetta D. IV. Title.
HV6197.U5 A38 2001
364'.089'96073—dc21

Cover photos, left to right: E. Franklin Frazier, Coramae Richey Mann, and W.E.B. Du Bois.
Coramae Richey Mann photo used with permission.

01 02 03 04 05 06 07 7 6 5 4 3 2 1

Acquiring Editor: Jerry Westby
Editorial Assistant: Vonessa Vondera
Production Editor: Denise Santoyo
Editorial Assistant: Kathryn Journey
Copy Editor: Gillian Dickens
Typesetter: Tina Hill
Indexer: Teri Greenberg
Cover Designer: Michelle Lee

Contents

FOREWORD

The works included herein are classics. The writings are elegant conversations in motion, moving lockstep with us across the past century. They are remarkably adaptive to our ever-changing times, as are our descriptions of criminal conduct and our interpretations of the U.S. Constitution. The piquancy and enduring value of these works and their current applicability are quite evident. W. E. B. Du Bois was perspicacious in his prognostication nearly 100 years ago that the inexorable effects of racism would surely journey with us throughout the entire 20th century.

At the dawn of a new millennium, still firmly shackled are we to the enormously heavy weight of this nation's 400-year-old shameful history of race-based slavery and discrimination. Here now, we wonder not whether race matters when crime and its control are considered. The questions before us are the extent to which race matters, how far into the future institutionalized racism will travel with us, and when race-based discrimination no longer will be intricately woven into the very fabric of all aspects of American life.

This volume of classic writings is, in part, a chronicle of the continual struggle against racism, the constant challenge to define *criminal,* and the seemingly futile search for the illusive concept we call justice. When considering the historical context in which each work was completed, we find each is even more brilliant than initially thought.

For example, W. E. B. Du Bois's "The Negro Criminal" emerged at the height of the industrial revolution. Sociology was just getting its footing in academic circles.

Lomboroso's "born criminal" theory was being passionately debated. Most prison inmates were White.

As E. Franklin Frazier prepared "Rebellious Youth," our nation still was suffering from its Great Depression. Robert Merton's theory of anomie was being hailed. The theoretically proposed relationship between social class and crime was widely accepted as truth. Most prison inmates were White.

As Earl R. Moses drafted "Differentials in Crime Rates Between Negroes and Whites Based on Comparisons of Four Socio-Economically Equated Areas," World War II had just ended. Edwin Sutherland's theory of differential association was in its second stage of development. Most prison inmates were White.

And by the time Coramae Richey Mann wrote "Minority and Female: A Criminal Justice Double Bind," criminal justice was firmly entrenched as the new academic discipline studying crime. The war on drugs was continuing in earnest. The empirically suggested relationship between race and crime was accepted as truth. The face of "the criminal" was African American and male. Most prison inmates were people of color.

This collection of writings is crucially important, in part, because it reminds us that the theoretical paradigms of these and other African American scholars are excluded when crime, its causes, and its control are discussed by criminologists, criminal justice practitioners, and policymakers. To understand crime fully, the perspectives advanced by these scholars must become an integral part of discussions about who is criminal and which public policies will best control crime.

—Anne Thomas Sulton

INTRODUCTION

So he grew, and brought within his wide influence all that was best of those who walk within the Veil. They who live without knew not nor dreamed of that full power within, that mighty inspiration which the dull gauze of caste decreed that most men should not know.

—W. E. B. Du Bois (1903/1994, p. 139)

This quote is part of a tribute by Du Bois to Alexander Crummell, a Negro priest who met with considerable rejection from the Episcopalian church in America during the 19th century. Throughout *The Souls of Black Folk,* Du Bois uses the term *veil* to refer to how Negroes were separated from the rest of America. He wrote this semi-autobiographical book in an effort to lift the veil and provide an overview of the history, culture, and contributions of Negroes to America.

Like Du Bois, we believe there is a veil under which the contributions of African Americans to criminology and criminal justice exist. Although certainly not as detrimental as the type of veil that existed a century ago, the criminological veil has lasted too long. More important, the perspectives of African Americans remain on the periphery of the discipline. For more than 20 years, African American criminologists have striven to lift the veil. Although considerable progress has been made, their contributions continue to be excluded from textbooks and course material (Free, 1999).

We have produced *African American Classics in Criminology and Criminal Justice* to give students, faculty, and others the opportunity to explore the unique contributions of Black scholars to criminological theories and research.[1] The volume is a reflection of the interdisciplinary nature of the discipline and includes research and writings by criminologists, geographers, historians, jurists, and sociologists. After the introduction and first chapter by Young and Taylor Greene, the remainder of the book is separated into two parts. Part I includes reprints of historical Black "classics" published prior to 1950. The historical "classics" begin with *Southern Horrors* (1892) by Ida B. Wells-Barnett, which is the first of three radical publications based on her research on the hate crime of lynching. Following Ms. Wells-Barnett's publication, we present "The Negro Criminal" from W. E. B. Du Bois's landmark urban ethnography, *The Philadelphia Negro* (1899), which paints one of the earliest portraits of crime in an urban Black community. In his next chapter, Du Bois's (1901) article, titled "The Spawn of Slavery," reviews the notorious convict-lease system, a tool used in the criminal justice process to criminalize many African Americans in the years following emancipation. While Du Bois was steadily developing the Atlanta School of Social Scientific Research at Atlanta University (Gabbidon, 1999), Monroe Work, the first African American graduate of the University of Chicago, was already at work investigating crime in the Black community of Chicago, which resulted in "Crime Among the Negroes of Chicago" (Work, 1900). After graduation, Work moved South, where the conditions he observed led him to write "Negro Criminality in the South," which reviews crime among African Americans before and after slavery (Work, 1913).

The next three chapters feature articles written by two more University of Chicago graduates. The first, "Rebellious Youth," from the highly acclaimed book, *The Negro Family in the United States* (1939), was written by E. Franklin Frazier, the first African American to be elected president of the American Sociological Association. The next chapter, "Community Factors in Negro Delinquency," was authored by Earl Moses, and was based on his master's thesis and a later study, *The Negro Delinquent in Chicago* (1936). In 1947, Moses returned to the issue of crime and produced, "Differential in Crime Rates Between Negroes and Whites, Based on Four Socio-Equated Areas" (Moses, 1947); this is the last chapter in the historical section.

Part II includes articles written by Blacks after 1950. The first selection in the contemporary section is the classic work of the late jurist A. Leon Higginbotham, Jr., who researched and wrote on the ills of the American criminal justice system for more than 30 years (Higginbotham, 1996). In this article, Higginbotham examines the role that the state judicial system played in enforcing racial inferiority through both formal and informal means. In Chapter 11, Robert Staples focuses on the internal colonial model and its potential for explaining race and crime. Chapter 12 presents the connections between women, race, and crime that first appeared in an article by Vernetta D. Young. During the 1980s, one of the leading Black theorists was Darnell Hawkins, who produced several pioneering articles, two of which are presented in Chapters 13 and 14 (Hawkins, 1987a, 1987b). In Chapter 13, Hawkins provides a critical review of conflict theory that is often used to explain crime in the Black community. Chapter 14 examines the impact of stereotypes on Black families.

The 1980s also saw Lee P. Brown (now Mayor Brown of Houston) forging new ground in the field of policing. Brown served in several positions of police leadership, including chief of police in Atlanta, New York, and Houston. Chapter 15 presents one of his important articles on community policing, which provided a model for police departments nationwide (Brown, 1989). In 1989, Daniel Georges-Abeyie presented a unique perspective for explaining Black crime (Georges-Abeyie, 1989). Rooted in the ecological approach, this perspective is presented in Chapter 16. William Oliver, a graduate of the State University of New York at Albany, is one of very few scholars to address Afrocentricity in criminology. Chapter 17 explores his work stressing the importance of Afrocentric socialization in the prevention of crime and other major social problems in the Black community. Chapter 18 presents a classic by Coramae Richey Mann, titled "Minority and Female: A Criminal Justice Double Bind."

At the start of the last decade of the 20th century, Katheryn Russell (1992) argued for the development of a subfield within criminology to be called "Black Criminology." Chapter 19 presents her article, which suggests that this subfield would set the stage for the development of more useful theories to explain Black criminality. Chapter 20 presents the pioneering ethnographic work of Elijah Anderson. A veteran of the streets of Philadelphia, Anderson provides an in-depth look at the so-called "Code of the Streets" (Anderson, 1994). Some 20 years after Staples's (1975) classic formulation of the colonial model, in Chapter 21, Becky Tatum presents a contemporary version, noting its strengths and weaknesses in explaining crime among minorities (Tatum, 1994). Chapter 22 presents Paul Butler's controversial position on jury nullification that first appeared in an article published in the *Yale Law Journal.* In the final chapter, we present another of Katheryn Russell's articles. Chapter 23 presents "The Racial Hoax as Crime: The Law as Affirmation" (Russell, 1996), and it shows the wide-ranging impact of crime-related racial hoaxes on the Black community.

Our selection of the above scholarship was based on the selected work's adherence to one of the following criteria. First, we included some of the earliest pioneering research written on the subject by Blacks. Another criterion, particularly for the early works, is that the authors must have been discussing an important issue of the decade in which their work appeared. For this criteria, we also considered the results of a recent citation analysis of Black scholarship in early criminology texts (see Gabbidon & Taylor Greene, 2000). Third, the author presents a unique perspective in the study of criminology, criminal justice, or both. Finally, we drew on our combined 50 years of researching and writing on Black perspectives on crime. Yet even with these criteria, we recognize that there will certainly be debate surrounding our selections. In fact, we debated among ourselves about the final content. Undoubtedly, there will be expanded and revised volumes in future years.

Although there are an abundance of readers on criminological "classics" (see, e.g., Cullen & Agnew, 1999; Horton, 2000; Jacoby, 1994; Scarpitti & Nielson, 1999;

Williams & McShane, 1998), very few include more than one article written by Blacks.[2] Furthermore, considering that mainstream authors have generally shown a lack of serious appreciation for Black perspectives (see Barak, 1991; Caldwell & Greene, 1980; Gabbidon, 1996; LaFree & Russell, 1993; Taylor Greene, 1979; Young & Sulton, 1991; Young & Taylor Greene, 1995), we felt it important to create a volume to fill this void in the literature.

In light of the exclusion of Black scholarship in readers purporting to present "classic" publications in criminology and criminal justice, the definition of the word *classic* becomes important. According to *Webster's Ninth New Collegiate Dictionary* (1983), the word *classic* has many meanings, including something of recognized value, serving as a standard of excellence, and being a work of enduring excellence. In the past, because the authors of these types of readers were not exposed to a substantial body of Black scholarship, they naturally did not see the work of Black scholars as being of value. Similarly, an unknown or minimally cited article by a Black scholar would not be seen as a "standard of excellence" or as "an enduring work of excellence." Many of the authors of these texts have likely selected their "classics" based on their individual intellectual heritages, which, in most cases, would not originate with a Black scholar or in an environment where there was an emphasis on Black scholarship. Hence, the "classics" presented in many of these texts have been determined by White males, who have historically produced mostly White male protégés, which results in a cycle in which the prevailing "classics" will undoubtedly, in their minds, be produced by themselves. It is within this context that much Black scholarship (particularly historical work) has been neglected.

Given the cyclical pattern described earlier, without a volume such as this, the contributions of African Americans might remain under the veil. Unfortunately, we are well aware that those vested in both the cycle and the veil will likely buy this book yet ignore it, whereas others will buy it but continue to think of its contents as "that Black stuff." We are also aware of the slight progress that has been made during the past two decades that has contributed to an increasing number of our colleagues who are more than willing to include African American scholarship in their courses. Although the articles included here are not yet a part of criminological core knowledge, that does not diminish their importance. Rather, we hope the volume will continue to stimulate interest in the study of crime and justice.

Acknowledgments

This project began in 1996, as part of our desire to create a volume that contained both historical and unique contributions by African Americans to the study of criminology and criminal justice. Its completion is the result of the assistance of numerous individuals. First are those persons who assisted in the preparation of the manuscript. At

Pennsylvania State University, Capital College, those persons include Dr. Bob Munzenrider, Jennifer Bonger, and Rosalie Salim. A special thanks to Drs. Patti Mills and Steve Peterson for ensuring that secretarial assistance was available to complete the manuscript on schedule. We would also like to acknowledge our universities for providing subventions to cover some of the copyright expenses. At Howard University, Dr. Florence Bonner approved the funds for the project. Drs. Howard Sachs and Steve Peterson of Pennsylvania State University, Capital College, similarly valued the project and approved a portion of the required funds. Dr. Karen Gould at Old Dominion University also provided funds for the copyright expenses.

We would also like to express our appreciation to Jerry Westby, senior acquisitions editor for Sage Publications. Jerry's strong support for the project translated into an extremely positive publication experience. He also provided timely information and assistance in our completion of the project. His assistant, Vonessa Vondera, was also most helpful.

A special thank you to Dr. Darnell Hawkins for waiving the copyright fee for his article titled "Beyond Anomalies: Rethinking the Conflict Perspective on Race and Criminal Punishment." We also thank Dr. Anne T. Sulton for agreeing to write the foreword to this volume.

Finally, we thank our families for their support and encouragement of our scholarly endeavors.

Notes

1. For more information on the scholars included in this volume, see Taylor Greene and Gabbidon (2000). Their volume provides detailed biographical information on many of the authors selected for this volume.
2. A recent notable exception to this trend is Baker and Davin (2000).

References

Anderson, E. (1994, May). The code of the streets. *The Atlantic Monthly,* pp. 80-94.

Baker, D. V., & Davin, R. P. (2000). *Notable selections in crime, criminology and criminal justice.* Guilford, CT: McGraw-Hill/Dushkin.

Barak, G. (1991). Cultural literacy and a multicultural inquiry into the study of crime and justice. *Journal of Criminal Justice Education, 2*(2), 173-192.

Brown, L. P. (1989, August). Community policing: A practical guide for police officials. *The Police Chief,* pp. 72-82.

Caldwell, L., & Taylor Greene, H. (1980). Implementing a Black perspective in criminal justice. In A. Cohn & B. Ward (Eds.), *Improving management in criminal justice* (pp. 143-156). Beverly Hills, CA: Sage.

Cullen, F. T., & Agnew, R. (Eds.). (1999). *Criminological theory: Past to present.* Los Angeles: Roxbury.

Du Bois, W. E. B. (1899). The Negro criminal. In *The Philadelphia Negro* (pp. 235-268). Philadelphia: University of Pennsylvania.

Du Bois, W. E. B. (1901). The spawn of slavery: The convict-lease system in the South. *The Missionary Review of the World, 14,* 737-745.

Du Bois, W. E. B. (1994). *The souls of Black folk.* New York: Dover. (Original publication 1903)

Frazier, E. F. (1939). *The negro family in the United States*. Chicago: The University of Chicago Press.

Free, M. D. (1999). Racial issues in contemporary criminology textbooks: The case of African Americans. *Contemporary Justice Review, 1*, 429-466.

Gabbidon, S. L. (1996). An argument for the inclusion of W. E. B. Du Bois in the criminology/criminal justice literature. *Journal of Criminal Justice Education, 7*(1), 99-112.

Gabbidon, S. L. (1999). W. E. B. Du Bois and the Atlanta School of Social Scientific Research: 1897-1913. *Journal of Criminal Justice Education, 10*(1), 21-38.

Gabbidon, S. L., & Taylor Greene, H. (2000, March). *Toward African American literacy in criminology and criminal justice: The study of criminological theory.* Paper presented at the meeting of the Academy of Criminal Justice Sciences, New Orleans, LA.

Georges-Abeyie, D. E. (1989). Race, ethnicity, and the spatial dynamic: Toward a realistic study of Black crime, crime victimization, and criminal justice processing of Blacks. *Social Justice, 16*(4), 35-54.

Hawkins, D. (1987a). Beyond anomalies: Rethinking the conflict perspective on race and criminal punishment. *Social Forces, 65*(3), 719-745.

Hawkins, D. (1987b). Devalued lives and racial stereotypes: Ideological barriers to the prevention of family violence among Blacks. In R. L. Hampton (Ed.), *Violence in the Black family* (pp. 189-205). New York: Wiley and Sons.

Higginbotham, A. L. (1996). *Shades of freedom*. New York: Oxford University Press.

Horton, D. M. (2000). *Pioneering perspectives in criminology.* Incline Village, NV: Copperhouse.

Jacoby, J. E. (1994). *Classics in criminology* (2nd ed.). Prospect Heights, IL: Waveland.

LaFree, G., & Russell, K. K. (1993). The argument for studying race and crime. *Journal of Criminal Justice Education, 4*(2), 273-289.

Moses, E. R. (1936). Community factors in Negro delinquency. *Journal of Negro Education, 5*(2), 220-227.

Moses, E. R. (1947). Differentials in crime rates between Negroes and Whites based on comparisons of four socio-economically equated areas. *American Sociological Review, 12*, 411-420.

Russell, K. K. (1992). Development of a Black criminology and the role of the Black criminologist. *Justice Quarterly, 9*(4), 667-683.

Russell, K. K. (1996). The racial hoax as crime: The law as affirmation. *Indiana Law Journal, 71*(3), 594-621.

Scarpitti, F. R., & Nielson, A. L. (1999). *Crime and criminals: Contemporary and classic readings.* Los Angeles: Roxbury.

Staples, R. (1975). White racism, Black crime and American justice: An application of the colonial model to explain crime and race. *Phylon, 36*, 14-22.

Tatum, B. (1994). The colonial model as a theoretical explanation of crime and delinquency. In A. T. Sulton (Ed.), *African American perspectives on crime causation, criminal justice administration and crime prevention* (pp. 32-52). Boston: Butterworth-Heinemann.

Taylor Greene, H. (1979). *A comprehensive bibliography of criminology and criminal justice literature by Black authors from 1895-1978.* College Park, MD: Ummah.

Taylor Greene, H., & Gabbidon, S. L. (2000). *African American criminological thought.* Albany: State University of New York Press.

Webster's ninth new collegiate dictionary. (1983). Springfield, MA: Merriam-Webster.

Wells-Barnett, I. B. (1892). *Southern horrors: Lynch law in all its phases.* New York: The New York Age Print.

Williams, F. P., & McShane, M. D. (1998). *Criminological theory: Selected classic readings* (2nd ed.). Cincinnati, OH: Anderson.

Work, M. (1900). Crime among the Negroes of Chicago. *American Journal of Sociology, 6*, 204-223.

Work, M. (1913). Negro criminality in the South. *Annals of the American Academy of Political and Social Sciences, 49*, 74-80.

Young, V. D., & Sulton, A. T. (1991). Excluded: The current status of African American scholars to the field of criminology and criminal justice. *Journal of Research in Crime and Delinquency, 28*, 101-116.

Young, V. D., & Taylor Greene, H. (1995). Pedagogical reconstruction: Incorporating African American perspectives into the curriculum. *Journal of Criminal Justice Education, 6*(1), 85-104.

1

INTRODUCTION

Vernetta D. Young and Helen Taylor Greene have each made important contributions to the study of Blacks, crime, and justice. They first met at the University of Maryland, College Park, where Dr. Young was a faculty member and Dr. Taylor Greene was a doctoral student. Young is one of the first African American females to receive a doctorate in criminology. Her research on several topics—including African American women, crime, and victimization as well as the exclusion of African American contributions in the discipline—is well known. Most recently, she has been examining the history of juvenile institutions and incarcerated women in Maryland. In the late 1970s, Taylor Greene compiled one of the first bibliographies of writings and research on Blacks, crime, and justice. Her most recent writings focus on police brutality and women in policing. After several discussions in the early 1990s about how the contributions of Black scholars were still marginalized in the discipline, they decided to collaborate on this article. Shortly after its publication, they were invited to conduct a workshop on the topic at the annual meeting of the Academy of Criminal Justice Sciences.

Although written in 1995, Young and Taylor Greene's article is first in this reader for several reasons. First, the article summarizes the cultural literacy debate within the study of criminology and criminal justice. Although race and crime have been an issue in the discipline for more than 100 years, until very recently, it has often been omitted from the discipline's "core" knowledge. Second, the article provides a historical overview of the contributions of African Americans to understanding crime and justice. Third, it summarizes the issues and themes presented in many of the other articles in the reader. Thus, this article gives the reader an overview of African American contributions in criminology and criminal justice.

PEDAGOGICAL RECONSTRUCTION

Incorporating African American[1] Perspectives Into the Curriculum

 VERNETTA D. YOUNG
HOWARD UNIVERSITY
HELEN TAYLOR GREENE
OLD DOMINION UNIVERSITY

> *In sum, I would say that we are at a very difficult crossroads, where it will be easy to go backwards, hard and complex to move ahead. . . . A multiculturalism that goes beyond cosmetics requires rethinking the paradigms that we use in order to understand the relational aspects of ethnicity. . . . Once multiculturalism is unleased in the classroom, it creates new relations of pedagogy. . . . (Platt 1993:1, 22).*

The race of the offender has been a leading question in discussions and comments on crime by the media and the public. Also, although the academic discipline of criminal justice and criminology has long dealt with the issue of race and crime, members of the field have often approached the topic with much trepidation, evasion, and confusion. According to Young (1989), most discussions of crime statistics repeatedly underscore the fact that African Americans are arrested disproportionately in comparison with whites, whereas in etiological discussions there seems to be an effort not to discuss race specifically. Yet since the turn of the century, a body of work by African American scholars has examined race and crime in a social, economic, and political context. Unfortunately, most of these works have not filtered into mainstream criminology/criminal justice (C/CJ), and often are omitted from textbooks and classroom discussions. As a result, any contributions that these works could have made to the discussion of race and crime/criminal justice issues have been ignored (Young and Sulton 1991).

From Young, V.D., & Taylor Green, H. (1995). Incorporating African American perspectives into the curriculum. *Journal of Criminal Justice Education*, 6(1), 85-104. Reprinted with permission of the Academy of Criminal Justice Sciences. The authors would like to thank Dr. Julius Debro for pioneering this research and our African American students for challenging traditional criminological thought. We would also like to thank the anonymous reviewers for their helpful comments and criticisms.

The purpose of this article is twofold: 1) to analyze historical and contemporary works by African Americans on race and crime, and 2) to begin integrating these works into the criminology/criminal justice curriculum. We view this paper as part of an ongoing process of pedagogical reconstruction that we deem necessary for creating a multicultural curriculum. First we discuss African American perspectives in the context of the ongoing cultural literacy/multiculturalism debate. Then we review selected African American scholarly works published between 1899 and 1989. Finally, we recommend strategies for incorporating these materials into existing undergraduate and graduate courses.

African American Perspectives, Cultural Literacy, and Multiculturalism in Criminology/Criminal Justice

Cultural literacy and multiculturalism have received considerable attention in this journal (Barak 1991; Siegel and Zalman 1991; Thornberry 1990). Thornberry and Siegel and Zalman have attempted to identify core knowledge, or cultural literacy in C/CJ. Others (Barak 1991) argue for multiculturalism, or inclusion of race and crime (LaFree and Russell 1993), in the study of C/CJ. Although there is no consensus about inclusion of race and crime in cultural literacy in C/CJ, the issue frequently arises in both undergraduate and graduate courses. Therefore it is important to analyze both race and crime and African American perspectives on race and crime in the context of cultural literacy and multiculturalism.

Hirsch identified the need to determine the common information that must be delivered in schools to impart American literacy (1987: 94). Hirsch's concept of cultural literacy was applied to criminology by Thornberry (1990), who identified core historical, empirical, and theoretical ideas specific to criminology and essential for a full understanding of contemporary topics (1990:46). Race and crime was not part of this core.

According to one possible explanation for this omission,

> [c]ultural literacy argues that all knowledge is not equally important or equally valued. In every culture some things are more central than others; for that reason they serve as basic building blocks for a general understanding of thought and action in that culture (Thornberry 1990:34).

Siegel and Zalman (1991) noted that Hirsch excluded specialized knowledge from his concept of cultural literacy. Nevertheless, they agreed that identifying core knowledge in criminal justice is important, especially for graduate education. Their lists of central CJ works include only two items that specifically address race and crime (Petersilia 1983; Wilbanks 1987). Neither is by an African American.

Although Hirsch emphasized core knowledge, he recognized that diversity in teaching and learning is inevitable. Hirsch stated that

> cultural literacy requires a two-part school curriculum which contains an extensive and intensive curriculum (1987:127).

Thus, although race and crime is not a part of the core curriculum (for some scholars), it would be placed in what Hirsch labels the intensive curriculum. This curriculum

> encourages a fully developed understanding of a subject, making one's knowledge of it integrated and coherent . . . it is the more pluralistic element of my proposal, because it ensures that individuals, students, teachers, and schools can work intensively with materials that are appropriate for their diverse temperaments and aims (Hirsch 1987:128).

Unlike Thornberry or Siegel and Zalman, other criminologists argue that race and crime belongs in the C/CJ curriculum (Barak 1991;

LaFree and Russell 1993). In fact, this topic has been a critical issue in the origins of criminological thought, the measurement of crime, and criminological theories. Throughout this century numerous African American and white scholars in the discipline have written on race.[2] How can an issue that has sparked scholarly research and debate within the discipline for more than 90 years be excluded from the cultural literacy core? Barak suggested

> that the culturally white and male bias in criminal justice/criminology has had the effect of suppressing the understanding of important historical and social contexts for making sense of African American (or other ethnic) and female-based experiences in relation to the vagaries of crime and justice . . . these omissions are dangerous (1991:174).

Though cultural literacy and multiculturalism are often viewed as competing paradigms, they are not. Both general (core) and specialized knowledge have always existed within the discipline. The cultural literacy/multiculturalism debate focuses on which topics will constitute each type of knowledge. Depending on one's perspective, race and crime can be viewed as general knowledge, specialized knowledge, or both. Most criminologists, however, probably do not view the issue as core knowledge deemed necessary for cultural literacy.

Although the study of crime in America was undertaken at the same time by African American and by white scholars, most works by the former remain unknown. The historical marginalization of those works is tied inextricably to issues of race. Barak (1991) and Young and Sulton (1991) correctly surmised the damage that such omissions caused, and will continue to cause within the discipline. Barak argued for the development of an African American literacy or perspective within the discipline; he listed books, articles, chapters, and papers identified in a survey of contemporary African American criminologists. The number of works excluded from the list highlights a historical pattern of marginalization of early works by African Americans in the study of crime.[3]

To clarify the issues related specifically to African Americans and crime, we believe that the works excluded until now must be integrated into the C/CJ curriculum. Both race and crime and African American perspectives should be part of what Barak calls the mainstream study of the field (1991:183). Like Platt (1993), we recognize that integrating these works into the C/CJ core is a challenge. Thus we leave it to academicians to place these works in either an extensive or an intensive curriculum, if not in both.

Our goal is to continue diversifying the C/CJ curriculum by cataloging and bringing some historical perspective to African American works on race and crime. We provide a review of both classical and contemporary literature related to crime and justice, and suggest ways to incorporate these works into the C/CJ curriculum. It is impossible to review here all the available African American literature. Instead we have selected some works that we view as representative of African American perspectives on race and crime, which appeared between 1899 and 1989.

Review of the Literature

Most writings by African American scholars have been characterized as attributing crime to many different causes including social, economic, and political conditions, racism, and oppression (Taylor Greene 1979; Young and Sulton 1991). A number of themes run through these scholars' works, such as social disorganization, the impact of the administration of justice on crime, black criminals as a special group of blacks, the use of statistics, and economics and crime. Like other early American sociologists and criminologists, African American scholars were influenced greatly by Emile Durkheim and by the "Chicago School." Consequently, their works included early sociological conceptualizations including social disorganization, anomie, and the ecology of crime. We briefly describe some of these ideas below to contextualize African American writings.

Durkheim ([1893] 1933) introduced the concept of anomie in *The Division of Labor in Society.* This concept has been important to the theoretical development of both sociology and C/CJ. Durkheim defined anomie as a pathological state of rapidly changing society characterized by societal disharmony and individual pathology. African American scholars (Du Bois [1899] 1987; Work [1913] 1987) focused on anomie and other concepts associated with Durkheim at least two decades before early mainstream sociologists.[4]

In the "Chicago School," as the group of sociologists living in Chicago came to be known, social disorganization was used to explain increasing criminality. One criminology textbook explains:

> The Chicago School believed that the core areas of major cities—highly populated . . . with recently relocated and diverse European immigrants and black migrants, both often unemployed—were characterized by a high degree of cultural heterogeneity . . . these diverse groups had not yet been able to incorporate the values and behaviors that made up the indigenous American culture (Eitzen and Timmer 1985:24).

Another Chicago School concept found frequently in the early writings is the ecological approach. Shaw and McKay (1942) used this approach to describe the distribution of delinquency rates in Chicago and other cities: they reported that official delinquency rates declined as one moved away from the center of the city. These authors used the theory of social disorganization to explain why delinquency was distributed as it was in urban areas (Shoemaker 1990).

The application of these concepts to the peculiar position of blacks in America is evident in the review of the literature presented below. In addition, however, many of the themes introduced by these scholars seem to stem from their unique analyses of race and crime in America.

Early Writings

The earliest group of scholars includes two eminent African American sociologists, William Edward Burghardt Du Bois (1868-1963) and Monroe Work (1866-1945).[5] Du Bois was trained at Fisk University and received his PhD from Harvard University in 1895. He taught at Atlanta University from 1897 to 1910, and was influential in organizing the university's annual conferences and editing its publications (Broderick 1968:304-305). Du Bois ([1899] 1987) was one of the earliest academicians to make empiricism central to the study of Negro life: he devoted two chapters to a discussion of the history of Negroes and crime in Philadelphia between 1600 and 1896, using primary and secondary data (Caldwell and Taylor Greene 1980:146).

Monroe Work studied under William Graham Taylor at the Chicago Theological Seminary, in the Department of Christian Sociology. Later he enrolled in the sociology department at the University of Chicago, where he completed his master's degree in 1903. At the turn of the century, a close connection existed between the Seminary, the sociology department, and the divinity school at the University of Chicago. Taylor later taught part-time in the sociology department at the University of Chicago. Work, through his association with the Seminary and the sociology department, was able to work closely with both Taylor and Albion Small, the founder of the department. He was the first African American (Work 1900) to have an article published in the *American Journal of Sociology* (McMurry 1985:19). He was affiliated later with Georgia State Industrial College (Savannah State) and Tuskegee Institute. While at Tuskegee, Work edited the *Negro Year Book* between 1912 and 1920 (Guzman, Jones, and Hall 1952).

For a brief period, Du Bois and Work studied Negro crime and presented their findings at Atlanta University's annual conferences on

Negro life. Myers (1987) included reprints of original articles by Du Bois ([1899] 1987), the Ninth Annual Atlanta Conference ([1906] 1987) and Monroe Work ([1913] 1987) in a special issue of *The Journal of Black Political Economy.* According to Myers, these scholars were more intent on explaining why so many persons involved in the criminal justice system were black than why blacks were criminal. They analyzed the increase in crime among blacks as measured by arrest and incarceration after the Civil War.

In the social disorganization tradition of the Chicago School, Du Bois, Work, and the members of the Atlanta Conference focused on the change of environment experienced by Negroes, particularly the change from slavery to emancipation. Du Bois suggested that

> if men are suddenly transported from one environment to another, the result is lack of harmony with the new conditions, lack of harmony with the new physical surroundings leading to disease and death or modification of physique, lack of harmony with social surroundings, leading to crime ([1899] 1987:17).

Members of the Ninth Annual Atlanta Conference, held in 1906, argued that with emancipation, "the freedman was in an anomalous situation" (1906] 1987:48). They concluded:

> Such a period of change involves physical strain, mental bewilderment and moral weakness. Such periods of stress have among all people given rise to crime and a criminal class (p. 60).

Work ([1913] 1987:63), writing on Negro criminality in the south, added that "confusion and disorder" resulted from the removal of old forms of social control.

Du Bois and the members of the Ninth Annual Atlanta Conference differed in their views on the normality of crime. Du Bois, like Durkheim, suggested that crime was normal. He argued that it was

> . . . a phenomenon of organized social life, and . . . the open rebellion of an individual against his social environment ([1899] 1987:17).

In contrast, members of the 1906 Ninth Annual Atlanta Conference stated:

> Above all, we must remember that crime is not normal, that the appearance of crime among Southern Negroes is a symptom of wrong social conditions—of a stress of life greater than a large part of the community can bear ([1906] 1987:54).

A second theme common to these scholars was the view that the manner in which justice was administered contributed to crime. Work and the members of the Ninth Annual Atlanta Conference suggested that the method of social control introduced after the Civil War, namely the convict-lease system, served to link "crime and slavery indissolubly in their minds (in the minds of Negroes) as simply forms of the white man's oppression" ([1906] 1987:50). As a result, the criminal justice system lost its legitimacy. The Conference held this view:

> Punishment, consequently, lost the most effective of its deterrent effects, and the criminal gained pity instead of disdain. The Negroes lost faith in the integrity of courts and the fairness of juries ([1906] 1987:50).

Work ([1913] 1987:66) argued that the number of convicts increased because of the financial benefits of the convict-lease system. He implied that the criminalization of Negroes, the major contributors to the convict-lease system, and their movement into the system in large numbers could be attributed to more than their behavior. (Later we discuss the consequences of this pattern of behavior on statistics on race and crime.)

A third theme that these scholars seem to have shared was the view that Negro criminals were a special class of Negroes. According to Du Bois,

> The better class of colored citizens felt that accusation and held a meeting to denounce crime and take a firm stand against their own criminal class ([1899] 1987:19).

Members of the Ninth Annual Atlanta Conference (1987:51) reported that after the war "a class of criminals, loafers, and ne'er do wells who were a menace to fellows, both Negro and white" were responsible for the crime problem. According to Work ([1913] 1987:63), enfranchisement for most of the freedmen meant a continuation of restraint; for others, however, "freedom meant the license to do what they pleased." According to Work, this group was the criminal class. Davis (1976:8), however, reported that at the Ninth Conference, members appealed to whites to recognize that "ignorant, underpaid serfs" were the "class that breeds dangerous crime."

On the surface these sentiments appear to be consistent with the "kind of people" paradigm found in early mainstream sociology/criminology (Quinney 1970). These African American scholars, however, did not attribute the criminality of this group to any biologically inherent inadequacy. Rather, they recognized the differential effects of slavery and emancipation on various segments of the population.

Another common element was the use of statistics. Du Bois stressed the importance of avoiding the mistakes and exaggerations of others who had studied race and crime. He accomplished this by looking at "the number of prisoners received at different institutions and not the prison population at particular times" ([1899] 1987:31). Du Bois also addressed the issue of disproportionality when he reported that

> the problem of Negro crime in Philadelphia from 1830 to 1850 arose from the fact that less than one-fourteenth of the population was responsible for nearly a third of the serious crimes committed ([1899] 1987:19).

Du Bois ([1899] 1987:20), however, cautioned readers to remember that Negroes were discriminated against, often were "arrested for less cause" than whites, and were sentenced for longer periods. The Conference members ([1906] 1987:51) added that Negroes were convicted readily.

Work ([1913] 1987:63) noted that before the Civil War, Negroes were underrepresented in the crime statistics because the system of slavery handled social control. After the War, however, "Negro crime" increased. Work attributed this increase to the fact that the law responded to freedmen by focusing on "punishment and restraint rather than protection" and by "imposing severe sanctions and sometimes unjust sentences for misdemeanors, petty offenses, and for vagrancy" ([1913] 1987:69). Like Du Bois, Work pointed out the importance of how one viewed the prison population: he observed that counting only those who had been committed to prison in a given year rather than all persons in prison on a particular date was much more favorable to Negroes because of the disparity in sentence length.

Finally, these scholars focused on economics and crime. Du Bois ([1899] 1987:29) presented a complicated picture of the relationship between the two. He noted the psychological impact of color prejudice in terms of ridicule and oppression and observed its effect on social conditions, but he focused on the practical impact of prejudice in closing the paths of advancement for Negroes by institutionalizing a system of economic exclusion. He argued that as a result of color prejudice, Negroes were 1) hampered in their ability to obtain a skilled job or enter a profession; 2) prevented from keeping work by whim, accident, or group label; 3) prevented from entering new lines of work; and 4) faced with a situation in which their money bought less food, shelter, and other necessities. Du Bois suggested that as a result of these encumbrances, some Negroes demonstrated bitterness, discouragement, oversensitiveness, or recklessness. Myers (1987:8) characterized the Du Bois work as a "landmark piece which tied together thinking about crime and economics."

These scholars make some additional points as well. Du Bois added that in addition to prejudice, Negro crime was caused by the "violent economic and social changes . . . [and] the sad social history that preceded [emancipation]" ([1899] 1987:30). Members of the Atlanta Conference attributed "Negro crime" to the faults of both Negroes and whites. The faults of Negroes included both individual personality factors, such as unreliability and lack of proper self-respect, and structural factors such as poverty and low wages ([1906] 1987:54). The faults of whites were related primarily to the administration of the criminal justice system. These faults, for example, included the attempt to enforce a double standard of justice, a system in which judges were subservient to the public opinion, and the use of the law to enforce a caste system and to criminalize Negroes (Ninth Annual Atlanta Conference [1906] 1987:56).

Finally, Work ([1913] 1987) argued that the difference between the crime rates of Negroes in the north and in the south was explained largely by the patterns of migration; Negroes in the north were more likely to live in urban areas and to be in the age group most likely to be involved in criminal behavior. In summary, the increase in crime among Negroes after the Civil War was attributed to the differential impact of the abolition of slavery on Negroes and on whites. Moreover, Negroes were attempting to adjust to a new status, while whites were trying to maintain the status quo.

Later Writings

These early writers gave way to a second group of scholars who wrote after the development of the Chicago School (1930-1949) and during the civil rights era (1950-1969). Among these scholars one can see several patterns or approaches. One was to review the works of earlier African American scholars who examined race and crime. Another was the continued application of Chicago School concepts, including social disorganization and ecological theory, to African Americans. Many black scholars elaborated on the earlier themes; they examined the impact of racial prejudice on educational, occupational, and economic opportunities and the resulting consequences of the denial of these opportunities. These works led us closer to a structural explanation of criminal behavior.

Because it is impossible to focus on all contributors in this group, we have selected six African American scholars whose works made a significant contribution to understanding African Americans and crime: John T. Blue, Lee P. Brown, E. Franklin Frazier, Mozell Hill, Earl R. Moses, and Gwynne Peirson.

E. Franklin Frazier (1894-1962) graduated with honors from Howard University, received his master's degree from Clark University, and completed his PhD in sociology at the University of Chicago in 1931. As a graduate student, he worked closely with Robert Park. He was affiliated with the Department of Sociology at Howard University from 1934 until his death. In 1948 he served as president of the American Sociological Society. Frazier is known widely for his scholarly works on race and culture (Edwards 1968).

Earl R. Moses, John T. Blue, and Mozell Hill belonged to the second generation of black sociologists, described as unheralded professionals who nourished the sociological tradition in the black colleges (Conyers and Epps 1974; Jones 1974). Earl Moses completed his PhD in sociology at the University of Pennsylvania in 1948 and was affiliated with Morgan State University. Mozell Hill received his master's degree from the University of Kansas, and completed his PhD at the University of Chicago in 1946. He taught at Langston University in Oklahoma from 1937 to 1946, and was chair of the department of sociology at Atlanta University from 1948 to 1958. He also served as editor of *Phylon* during this period. Professor Hill later taught at Columbia University (Low and Clift 1981). John T. Blue received his master's degree from the University of Michigan in 1946 and his PhD in sociology from American University in 1958. He taught at D.C. Teachers College from 1957 to 1958, the Norfolk division of Virginia State College from 1958 to 1965, and Shaw University from 1969 to 1970. He returned to D.C. Teachers College in the 1970s (Cattell 1978).

Moses (1947) and Frazier (1949) applied the theory of social disorganization to blacks. Moses compared the crime rates among blacks and among whites in four socioeconomically equated areas in Baltimore and found greater criminality in the black population. He attributed the differences to blacks' and whites' relative buying power and to the fact that whites in these areas had "longer residence, wider occupational opportunities, (and) easier financing of purchasing homes" (1947:439) than blacks. These views are similar to those of Du Bois on the impact of color prejudice. Frazier (1949) compiled one of the most comprehensive literature reviews of the problem of race and crime; he surveyed literature by African American and white scholars including Hoffman (1896), Du Bois (1904), McCord (1914), Sellin (1928), Reid (1931), Johnson (1941), and Myrdal (1944). Frazier (1949) specifically examined crime among blacks, and noted the following causes cited by earlier authors: social disorganization, physical and moral deficiency, poverty, ignorance, urbanization, and the effects of subordinate status (1949:653). He also devoted considerable attention to the problem of delinquency among African Americans.

In an examination of delinquency in New York City, Frazier reported an inverse relationship between the rate of juvenile delinquency and diminishing social disorganization. Many of the same factors as those introduced by Shaw and McKay were evident. For example, Frazier stated that

> the diminishing social disorganization was indicated by an increase in homeownership, a decrease in the number of adult criminals, and a decrease in family dependency, desertion, and illegitimacy (1949:652).

Continuing the tradition of Shaw and McKay, Blue (1948) examined the rates of juvenile delinquency for each of 363 tracts in the city of Detroit, and concluded that economic status was related more closely to juvenile delinquency than was race. According to Blue (1948:473), "race, at least in part, determines economic status and thus affects delinquency rates." His presentation is similar to Du Bois' discussion of the relationship between color prejudice and crime.

Hill (1959) examined the relationship between race, crime, and social disorganization, and considered the applicability of social disorganization and anomie to juvenile delinquency among blacks. He rejected the idea that black communities were "inevitably disorganized" and argued instead that most black communities were highly organized (1959:282-83). Hill attributed the increase in the rate of delinquency among blacks to the "systematic and persistent segregation of Negroes into so-called 'natural areas' of the metropolis." He concluded by suggesting that anomie more aptly explained delinquency among black juveniles, arguing that

> access to the success-goals by legitimate means is seldom available to Negro youth in cities. . . . On the other hand, illegal means are readily accessible in most metropolitan areas, especially in the neglected, poorly-schooled, and poorly-policed sections (1959:284).

Hill's article, along with many others, was published in a special issue of *The Journal of Negro Education* devoted to the problem of juvenile delinquency among blacks in the United States.

The 1960s provided an impetus to the study of crime and the administration of justice. African Americans continued to write on earlier themes but tended to focus more on the criminal justice process (Brown 1968, 1969; Bullock 1961; DaCosta 1968; Williams 1960) than on causal factors. During the mid-1960s, civil unrest in communities across the country prompted the federal government to appoint two commissions to study this social problem: The President's Commission on Law Enforcement and the Administration of Justice (1967) and The National Advisory Commission on Civil Disorders (1968), hereafter called the Kerner Commission. The Kerner Commission, which consisted of "representatives of the moderate and 'responsible' Establishment (1968:v)," attributed the civil disorders to pervasive discrimination and segregation, especially in employment and education; to black migration and white exodus; and to black ghettos, which were fertile ground for poverty. Members of the Kerner Commission also cited frustrated hopes, the legitimation of violence, and feelings of powerlessness as the "catalyst" for the riots (1968:204). This report supported the earlier works that also attributed the increase in crime and delinquency among blacks to discrimination and segregation.

As a result of the recommendations and findings of the President's Commission, Congress passed the Omnibus Crime Control and Safe Streets Act in 1968. This legislation created the Law Enforcement Assistance Administration (LEAA), responsible for directing federal funds to state and local law enforcement agencies. Through its Law Enforcement Education Program (LEEP) LEAA also allocated funds for law enforcement officers to continue their education at the college level.

With the assistance of LEEP, black officers pursued college degrees and were among the first black doctoral candidates in criminology. This group included former California police officers Lee Brown and Gywnne Peirson. During the late 1960s, Brown (1968, 1969) wrote articles, as well as his dissertation, on police-community relations.[6] Peirson wrote a dissertation on institutional racism in law enforcement. Both were academicians at Howard University and worked with LEAA's National Minority Advisory Council (NMAC) during the 1970s. Most of their scholarly works were written during the contemporary period described below.

Contemporary Writings

During the latter part of the contemporary period (1970-1989), an unprecedented number of African Americans began to study C/CJ as a direct result of increased educational opportunities. Consequently, research conducted by African American criminologists, sociologists, psychologists, economists, and political scientists became more readily available. In discussing these more recent writings, we will focus on major themes and contributions by black criminologists.[7] Unlike the work of earlier periods, the writings produced since 1970 deal with more specific crime issues including violence (Bell 1987; Pinkney 1972; Staples 1974), internal colonialism (Tables 1974), homicide (Hawkins 1986; Poussaint 1972), crime in the black community (Bell and Joyner 1977; Perry 1989), institutional racism (Debro 1977; Peirson 1977a, 1977b), and gender and crime (Mann 1984; Young 1980).

The first edited volumes by African Americans on blacks, crime, and criminal justice did not appear until the late 1970s (Bryce 1977; Gary and Brown 1976; Georges-Abeyie 1984; Hawkins 1986; Owens and Bell 1977; Woodson 1977). African American scholars also began to address the omission of black perspectives from criminology (Caldwell and Taylor Greene 1980; Taylor Greene 1979; Woodson 1977). Several scholars reviewed and critiqued some mainstream works on causes of crime (Austin 1978; Covington 1986; Myers and Sabol 1987; Young 1980). Others continued to study the extent of crime, using both official and victimization data (Georges-Abeyie 1984; Peirson 1977a, 1977b; Young 1980).

As in the earlier periods, crime among blacks received considerable attention. During the contemporary period, however, African American researchers focused more strongly on intraracial violence (Perry 1989; Pinkney 1972; Staples 1974). After the civil disturbances of the 1960s, many Americans believed that young black males were among the most violent members of our society. Pinkney was one of the first African Americans to refute this position and to suggest that young black men were more likely than others to be the victims of violence by state and local police. He described the United States as an unusually violent society, both domestically and in its relations with other countries.

According to Pinkney, violence, including violence toward racial minorities, has a long-standing history in America. He attributed violence in America to several factors, including social values that condone it. Pinkney believed, however, that violent behavior was not inherent but learned.

Perry (1989) attributed black-on-black crime to conflict resulting from the civil rights movement, ghettoization, migration, alcohol, and drugs. Borrowing from the African scholar Frantz Fanon, Staples (1974) used the concept of internal colonialism to explain black violence. According to this theoretical framework, such violence reflects colonial relationships, characterized as a social order in which race defines life chances, opportunities for subsistence, social rewards, and access to social position. Staples emphasized that violence is dichotomous in a colonial context: it is used both as a tool of oppression and as an instrument of liberation.

Directly related to violence is the issue of homicide among blacks, which received considerable attention during the contemporary period. Darnell Hawkins (1986) argued that the widely used "subculture of violence" theory, presented to explain the high rates of homicide among blacks, was theoretically inadequate and empirically limited. Using slavery as a starting point, Hawkins presented a supplementary or alternative causal model that attributed the high rates of black criminal homicide to 1) the legal and social devaluing of black life; 2) racialist patterns of law enforcement and punishment; and 3) economic deprivation, which creates a climate of powerlessness in which individual acts of violence are likely to take place. Hawkins maintained that the study of racial discrimination and bias in the criminal justice system is linked inextricably to the study of homicide among blacks.

Unlike earlier writers, Peirson (1977a, 1977b) attributed the overrepresentation of blacks in crime statistics to institutional racism in policing. In his view, criminal justice practitioners are guilty of perpetuating the belief that blacks are prone to crime. They do so by relying too heavily on the FBI's *Crime in the United States,* commonly known as the Uniform Crime Reports.

> The manner in which the Uniform Crime Report itself contributes to this belief is shown by the way in which they cease to measure disposition of persons arrested by race past the point of arrest. . . . If we were to measure disposition of criminal offenses by race at each stage of the criminal justice process, rather than merely at the point of arrest, a fair approximation of the degree to which race is a determining factor throughout the criminal justice system would be available (1977b:109-10).

Peirson believed that the pattern of using arrest statistics and prison commitments to "prove" blacks' criminality was neither accidental nor naive, but an intentional result of systematic and extensive manipulation of crime statistics.

By the 1980s, gender, race, and crime had become the focus of African American female criminologists (Mann 1984; Young 1980). Young (1980, 1986) compared the patterns of black males' and females' crime with those of white males and females, and examined the impact of race-specific gender role expectations on black females. She argued that the intersection of race and gender was important in explaining both the patterns of behavior and the treatment of victims and offenders by criminal justice system personnel. Mann (1984:xi) noted that "crime has rather myopically been seen as a 'male' problem." She examined women's contribution to the crime problem and explored the consequences of discriminatory treatment and neglect.

TABLE 1 Early Writings

Author	*Date of Publication*	*Issues/Themes*
W.E.B. Du Bois	([1899] 1987)	Negro crime in Philadelphia (1600-1896) Social disorganization as a result of slavery and emancipation The Negro criminal class Crime statistics Economics and crime
Ninth Annual Atlanta Conference	([1906] 1987)	Crime among southern Negroes The Negro criminal class Criminalization of Negroes through use of the convict-lease system
Monroe Work	([1913] 1987)	Negro criminality in the South Slavery as a form of social control Patterns of migration and crime Social disorganization The Negro criminal class

Several contemporary African American scholars examined race and crime in the context of other earlier themes, including the ecological tradition and unemployment and crime. Daniel Georges-Abeyie (1989) wrote on the spatial distribution of crime and the relationship between ethnic/racial heterogeneity and elevated black crime rates. He challenged sociological and criminological theories and research that treat black ghettos and slum ghettos as monolithic ethnic or racial entities.

Myers and Sabol (1987) examined unemployment and crime in an effort to explain the causal relationship between labor and penal practices. They applied Rusche and Kirsheimer's argument that every system of production tends to discover punishments that correspond to productive relations.

> Thus, crime is best understood by investigating the relationship between labor markets, systems of punishment and variations in levels of production (1987:192).

These authors found support for their structural model, which linked black imprisonment to manufacturing output and black unemployment.

During the contemporary period, research and publications by African Americans on race and crime increased dramatically. Yet, like the writings of earlier African American scholars, their works remain unknown to many contemporary criminologists and criminal justice practitioners. Consequently this material still needs to be incorporated into C/CJ courses.

Incorporating African American Perspectives Into the C/CJ Curriculum

Pedagogical reconstruction requires strategies for including African American perspectives in the C/CJ curriculum. As stated above, we believe they should be included in both the extensive (core) and the intensive (specialized) curriculum. To this end, Tables 1-3 provide summaries of the African American works presented here. Authors, dates, and issues/themes are presented for early (Table 1), later (Table 2), and contemporary writings (Table 3). Strategies for incorporating these materials into C/CJ courses include

TABLE 2 Later Writings

Author	*Date of Publication*	*Issues/Themes*
John T. Blue	1948	Juvenile delinquency The ecological approach Economic status
Lee P. Brown	1968, 1969	Police community relations
E. Franklin Frazier	1949	Review of race and crime literature Juvenile delinquency Social disorganization
Mozell Hill	1959	Race, crime, and social disorganization
Earl R. Moses	1947	Social disorganization Crime rates of blacks and whites in Baltimore

TABLE 3 Contemporary Writings

Author	*Date of Publication*	*Issues/Themes*
Julius Debro	1977	Institutional racism in corrections
Daniel Georges-Abeyie	1989	Spatial distribution Racial/ethnic heterogeneity
Darnell Hawkins	1986	Black criminal homicide
Coramae Mann	1984	Women and crime
Samuel Myers and William Sabol	1987	Unemployment and crime
Gywnne Peirson	1977	Institutional racism in policing
Robert Perry	1989	Black-on-black crime
Alphonso Pinkney	1972	History of violence in America
Robert Staples	1974	Internal colonialism Black violence
Vernetta D. Young	1980	Women, race, and crime
	1986	Gender, race, and crime

Making the African American works required course readings;

Assigning descriptive and evaluative critiques of specific readings;

Assigning comparative analyses of mainstream and the African American works;

Requiring oral presentations (group or individual) on selected works; and

Requiring term projects on African American perspectives on race and crime.

The choice of strategy will depend on the subject and the level of a course. African American perspectives, however, should be included in all courses where criminological theories, the extent of crime, and race and crime are central issues. The historical African American perspectives are integrated most easily into upper-level and graduate topic courses that examine race and crime issues. They are advantageous in discussions relating social

TABLE 4 Strategies for Incorporating Black Perspectives Into Graduate Courses

Course	*Topic/Issue*	*African American Sources*
Administration of Justice	Extent of crime	Du Bois Ninth Annual Atlanta Conference Work
Criminological Theory	History of criminological thought Crime and social disorganization	Frazier Du Bois Ninth Annual Atlanta Conference Work Frazier Hill Moses
	Ecological approach Economics and crime	Blue Du Bois Ninth Annual Atlanta Conference Work Myers and Sabol
Corrections	History Convict-lease system	Du Bois Ninth Annual Atlanta Conference Work
Policing	Institutional racism Institutional racism Police-community relations	Debro Peirson Brown

economic, and political conditions to race and crime.

We believe that graduate programs should include both historical and contemporary African American perspectives on race and crime as general (core) knowledge. The works discussed here can be integrated into several graduate courses including administration of justice, criminological theory, corrections, and policing (see Table 4). In addition, graduate courses should include background biographical information on African American scholars.

CONCLUSION

It is important to view this paper as a work in progress that provides material for future research and dialogue. We have presented only a sample of the available writings. Our intent is to continue the dialogue begun in earlier works by acknowledging African Americans' contributions to the study of C/CJ. It should be clear that 1) African Americans' works have a history that parallels mainstream works; 2) along with perspectives that support mainstream criminology, these works include those that differ from the mainstream; and 3) there is no monolithic "African American perspective." Additional studies are needed 1) to identify and catalogue writings since 1989; 2) to reconstruct specific C/CJ topics (criminological thought, measurement of crime, law enforcement, corrections, courts, criminal law, and victimization); 3) to conduct content analyses of existing course materials; 4) to determine current knowledge about African American research and writings by surveying faculty members and students; and 5) to add to the body of knowledge by African American scholars.

Culturally literate criminologists, responsible for imparting core knowledge, can no longer sit idly and ignore the relevance of historical and contemporary African American perspectives on race and crime. The field of criminal justice and criminology may face a serious problem of credibility if it continues to ignore these perspectives. Before and since 1989, some journals have published special issues on race and crime, providing a bridge to works by African American scholars. Also, some academicians have incorporated African American scholars' works into textbooks and undergraduate and graduate courses. We believe that pedagogical reconstruction requires even more effort in this direction.

REFERENCES

Austin, R.L. (1978) "Race, Father-Absence, and Female Delinquency." *Criminology* 15:487-504.

Barak, G. (1991) "Cultural Literacy and a Multicultural Inquiry into the Study of Crime and Justice." *Journal of Criminal Justice Education* 2:173-92.

Bell, C.C. (1987) "Preventive Strategies for Dealing with Violence among Blacks." *Community Mental Health Journal* 23:217-27.

Bell, J. and I. Joyner (1977) "Crime in the Black Community." In C.E. Owens and J. Bell (eds.), *Blacks and Criminal Justice*, pp. 69-74. Lexington, MA: Lexington Books.

Blue, J.T. (1948) "The Relationship of Juvenile Delinquency, Race, and Economic Status." *Journal of Negro Education* 17:469-77.

Broderick, F. (1968) "W.E.B. Du Bois." In D.L. Sills (ed.), *International Encyclopedia of the Social Sciences*, pp. 304-305. New York: Macmillan.

Brown, Lee P. (1968) "Handling Complaints against the Police." *Police* 12:74-81.

——— (1969) "Evaluation of Police-Community Relations Programs." *Police* 16:27-31.

Bryce, H.J. (1977) *Black Crime: A Police View.* Washington, DC: Joint Center for Political Studies.

Bullock, H.A. (1961) "Significance of the Racial Factor in the Length of Prison Sentences." *Journal of Criminal Law, Criminology and Police Science* 52: 411-17.

Caldwell, L. and H. Taylor Greene (1980) "Implementing a Black Perspective in Criminal Justice." In A. Cohn and B. Ward (eds.), *Improving Management in Criminal Justice*, pp. 143-56. Beverly Hills: Sage.

Cattell, J. ed. (1978) *American Men and Women of Science: The Social and Behavioral Sciences.* 13th ed. New York: Bowker.

Conyers, J. and E. Epps (1974) "A Profile of Black Sociologists." In J. Blackwell and M. Janowitz (eds.), *Black Sociologists: Historical and Contemporary Perspectives*, pp. 231-52. Chicago: University of Chicago Press.

Covington, J. (1986) "Self-Esteem and Deviance: The Effects of Race and Gender." *Criminology* 24:105-38.

DaCosta, F.A. (1968) "Disparity and Inequality of Criminal Sentences: Constitutional and Legislative Remedies." *Howard Law Journal* 14:29-59.

Davis, L. (1976) "Historical Overview of Crime and Blacks since 1876." In L. Gary and L. Brown (eds.), *Crime and Its Impact on the Black Community*, pp. 3-11. Washington, DC: Howard University Institute for Urban Affairs and Research.

Debro, J. (1977) "Institutional Racism within the Structure of American Prisons." In R. Woodson (ed.), *Black Perspectives on Crime and the Criminal Justice System*, pp. 143-60. Boston: G.K. Hall.

Du Bois, W.E.B. ([1899] 1987) "The Negro Criminal." *Review of Black Political Economy* 16(1-2):17-32.

——— (1899) *The Philadelphia Negro.* Philadelphia: University of Pennsylvania Press.

——— (1904) *Some Notes on Crime.* Atlanta: Atlanta University Press.

Durkheim, E. ([1893] 1933) *The Division of Labor in Society.* Glencoe, IL: Free Press.

Edwards, G.F. (1968) "E. Franklin Frazier." In D.L. Sills (ed.), *International Encyclopedia of the Social Sciences*, pp. 553-54. New York: Macmillan.

Eitzen, D.S. and D.A. Timmer (1985) *Criminology: Crime and Criminal Justice.* New York: Wiley.

Frazier, E.F. (1949) *The Negro in the United States.* New York: Macmillan.

Gary, L. and L. Brown (1976) *Crime and Its Impact on the Black Community.* Washington, DC: Howard University Institute for Urban Affairs and Research.

Georges-Abeyie, D. (1984) *The Criminal Justice System and Blacks.* New York: Clark Boardman.

——— (1989) "Race, Ethnicity, and the Spatial Dynamic, Toward a Realistic Study of Black Crime, Crime Victimization, and Criminal Justice Processing of Blacks." *Social Justice* 16:35-54.

Guzman, J.P., L.W. Jones, and W. Hall (1952) *1952 Negro Year Book.* New York: Wide.

Hawkins, D. (1986) *Homicides among Black Americans.* Lanham, MD: University Press of America.

Heard, C.A. and R.L. Bing (1993) *African American Criminology & Criminal Justice Directory.* Arlington: University of Texas at Arlington.

Hill, M. (1959) "The Metropolis and Juvenile Delinquency among Negroes." *Journal of Negro Education* 28:277-85.

Hirsch, E.D., Jr. (1987) *Cultural Literacy.* Boston: Houghton Mifflin.

Hoffman, F.L. (1896) *Race Traits and Tendencies of the American Negro.* New York.

Johnson, G.B. (1941) "The Negro and Crime." *Annals of the American Academy of Political and Social Science* 271:93-104.

Jones, B.A. (1974) "The Tradition of Sociology Teaching in Black Colleges: The Unheralded Professionals." In J. Blackwell and M. Janowitz (eds.), *Black Sociologists: Historical and Contemporary*

Perspectives, pp. 121-163. Chicago: University of Chicago Press.

LaFree, G. and K.K. Russell (1993) "The Argument for Studying Race and Crime." *Journal of Criminal Justice Education* 4:273-89.

Low, W.A. and V. Clift (1981) *Encyclopedia of Black America.* New York: McGraw-Hill.

Mann, C.R. (1984) *Female Crime and Delinquency.* Alabama: University of Alabama Press.

Marable, M. (1986) *W.E. Du Bois: Black Radical Democrat.* New York: MacMillan.

McCord, C.H. (1914) *The American Negro as a Dependent, Defective and Delinquent.* Nashville: Press of Benton Printing Company.

McMurry, L.O. (1985) *Recorder of the Black Experience: A Biography of Monroe N. Work.* Baton Rouge: Louisiana State University Press.

Merton, R.K. (1938) "Social Structure and Anomie." *American Sociological Review* 3:672-82.

Moses, E.R. (1947) "Differentials in Crime Rates between Negroes and Whites Based on Comparisons of Four Socio-Economically Equated Areas." *American Sociological Review* 12:411-20.

Myers, S.L. (1987) "Introduction." *Review of Black Political Economy* 6(1-2):5-16.

Myers, S.L. and W.J. Sabol (1987) *Review of Black Political Economy* 6(1-2):189-210.

Myrdal, G. (1944) *An American Dilemma.* New York: Harper.

National Advisory Commission on Civil Disorders (1968) *Report of the National Advisory Commission on Civil Disorders.* New York: Dutton.

Ninth Annual Atlanta Conference ([1906] 1987) "Negro Crime." *Review of Black Political Economy* 6(1-2):47-62.

Owens, C. and J. Bell (1977) *Blacks and Criminal Justice.* Lexington, MA: Lexington Books.

Peirson, G.W. (1977a) "An Introductory Study of Institutional Racism in Police Law Enforcement." Doctoral dissertation, University of California, Berkeley.

——— (1977b) "Institutional Racism and Crime Clearance." In R. Woodson (ed.), *Black Perspectives on Crime and the Criminal Justice System,* pp. 107-22. Boston: G.K. Hall.

Perry, R.L. (1989) "Re-Examining the Black on Black Crime Issue: A Theoretical Essay." *Western Journal of Black Studies* 13:66-71.

Petersilia, J. (1983) *Racial Disparities in the Criminal Justice System.* Santa Monica, CA: Rand.

Pinkney, A. (1972) *The American Way of Violence.* New York: Random House.

Platt, A. (1993) "Beyond the Canon, with Great Difficulty." *ACJS Today* 12:1, 22.

Poussaint, A. (1972) *Why Blacks Kill Blacks.* New York: Emerson Hall.

President's Commission on Law Enforcement and the Administration of Justice (1967) *The Challenge of Crime in a Free Society.* Washington, DC: U.S. Government Printing Office.

Quinney, R.P. (1970) *The Problem of Crime.* New York: Dodd, Mead.

Reid, I. (1931) "Notes on the Negro's Relation to Work and Law." In *Report on Causes of Crime, Vol. 1,* Part 3, pp. 221-55. Washington, DC: U.S. Government Printing Office.

Sellin, T. (1928) "The Negro Criminal." *Annals of the American Academy of Political and Social Science* 140:52-64.

Shaw, C. and H. McKay (1942) *Juvenile Delinquency and Urban Areas: A Study of Rates of Delinquency in Relation to Differential Characteristics of Local Communities in American Cities.* Chicago: University of Chicago Press.

Shoemaker, D. (1990) *The Theories of Delinquency: An Examination of Explanations of Delinquent Behavior.* New York: Oxford University Press.

Siegel, L.J. and M. Zalman (1991) " 'Cultural Literacy' in Criminal Justice: A Preliminary Assessment." *Journal of Criminal Justice Education* 2:15-44.

Staples, R. (1974) "Internal Colonialism and Black Violence." *Black World* 23:16-34.

Taylor Greene, H. (1979) *A Comprehensive Bibliography of Criminology and Criminal Justice Literature by Black Authors from 1895 to 1978.* College Park, MD: Ummah Publications.

Thornberry, T.P. (1990) "Cultural Literacy in Criminology." *Journal of Criminal Justice Education* 1: 33-49.

Wilbanks, W. (1987) *The Myth of a Racist Criminal Justice System.* Monterey, CA: Brooks-Cole.

Williams, F.H. (1960) "The Death Penalty and the Negro." *Crisis* 67:501-12.

Woodson, R.L. (1977) *Black Perspectives on Crime and the Criminal Justice System.* Boston: G.K. Hall.

Work, M. (1900) "Crime among the Negroes of Chicago." *American Journal of Sociology* 6:204-23.

——— ([1913 1987) "Negro Criminality in the South." *Review of Black Political Economy* 6(1-2):63-70.

Young, V.D. (1980) "Women, Race, and Crime." *Criminology* 18:26-34.

——— (1986) "Gender Expectations and Their Impact on Black Female Offenders and Victims." *Justice Quarterly* 3:305-27.

——— (1989) "Criminal Justice in the Twenty-First Century: The Removal of the Mantle of Silence Surrounding Race." Presented at the Twentieth Anniversary Conference School of Criminal Justice, Albany.

Young, V.D. and A.T. Sulton (1991) "Excluded: The Current Status of African American Scholars in the Field of Criminology and Criminal Justice." *Journal of Research in Crime and Delinquency* 28:101-16.

NOTES

1. The history of Africans in America is captured in the names that have been used to identify them. In this paper we will use *negro, black,* and *African American.* The idea is to remain faithful to the acceptable usage current in each historical period. Consequently, in general discussion we will use the contemporary term *African American.*

2. See Frazier (1949) for a review of the early literature.

3. For a more complete listing of African American perspectives on crime, see Taylor Greene (1979).

4. For example, Merton's seminal work on the topic was not published until 1938.

5. For more detailed biographical information on W.E.B. Du Bois, see Marable (1986); for more information on Monroe Work, see McMurry (1985).

6. Today Brown serves as President Clinton's drug czar.

7. Biographical sketches of contemporary African American criminologists are not included here. For that information we recommend Heard and Bing (1993).

PART I

HISTORICAL CLASSICS

2

INTRODUCTION

Ida B. Wells-Barnett (1862-1931) was an outspoken anti-lynching crusader of the late 19th and early 20th centuries. She was born in Holly Springs, Mississippi, and later lived in Memphis and Chicago. She was a teacher, newspaper publisher, and activist involved in the anti-lynching movement, politics, and the Negro women's clubs movement. She also traveled extensively both in the United States and abroad in her efforts to promote a more realistic understanding of the problem of lynching in the United States. In March 1892, three of her close friends were lynched in Memphis. Ms. Wells wrote several controversial editorials in *Free Speech,* a newspaper she owned with a pastor and another journalist. Her writings inflamed the Whites in Memphis, who in May 1892 destroyed the *Free Speech* office. Ida B. Wells, who was vacationing in New York City at the time, was warned not to return to Memphis.

Southern Horrors, originally published in 1892, is the first of Wells-Barnett's writings on the problem of lynching. Written in New York City shortly after she was exiled from Memphis, this article includes the editorials that appeared in the Black and White newspapers prior to the destruction of the *Free Speech* office. Wells-Barnett also explained how rapes that often resulted in lynchings were often not rapes but rather efforts to cover up relationships between White women and African American men. She also noted how White men who perpetrated rapes against Black girls and women were rarely punished. Wells-Barnett called for the law to punish lynchers. More important, she encouraged African Americans to boycott business establishments in communities where lynchings occurred and to arm themselves! After the lynchings, she encouraged Negroes to leave Memphis and continued to criticize lynchers and their beliefs.

Southern Horrors

Lynch Law in All Its Phases

Ida B. Wells-Barnett

To the Afro-American women of New York and Brooklyn, whose race love, earnest zeal and unselfish effort at Lyric Hall, in the City of New York, on the night of October 5th, 1892,—made possible its publication, this pamphlet is gratefully dedicated by the author.

Preface

The greater part of what is contained in these pages was published in the New York *Age* June 25, 1892, in explanation of the editorial which the Memphis whites considered sufficiently infamous to justify the destruction of my paper, *The Free Speech.*

Since the appearance of that statement, requests have come from all parts of the country that "Exiled," (the name under which it then appeared) be issued in pamphlet form. Some donations were made, but not enough for that purpose. The Noble effort of the ladies of New York and Brooklyn Oct 5 have enabled me to comply with this request and give the world a true, unvarnished account of the causes of Lynch law in the South.

This statement is not a shield for the despoiler of virtue, nor altogether a defense for the poor blind Afro-American Sampsons who suffer themselves to be betrayed by white Delilahs. It is a contribution to truth, an array of facts, the perusal of which it is hoped will stimulate this great American Republic to demand that justice be done though the heavens fall. It is with no pleasure I have dipped my hands in the corruption here exposed. Somebody must show that the Afro-American race is more sinned against than sinning, and it seems to have fallen upon me to do so. The awful death-roll that Judge Lynch is calling every week is appalling, not only because of the lives it takes, the rank cruelty and outrage to the victims, but because of the prejudice it fosters and the stain it places against the good name of a weak race. The Afro-American is not a bestial race. If this work can contribute in any way toward proving this, and at the same time arouse the conscience of the American people to a demand for justice to every citizen, and punishment by law for the lawless, I shall feel I have done my race a service. Other considerations are of minor importance.

—IDA B. WELLS

HON. FRED. DOUGLASS'S LETTER.

Dear Miss Wells:

Let me give you thanks for your faithful paper on the lynch abomination now generally practiced against colored people in the South. There has been no word equal to it in convincing power. I have spoken, but my word is feeble in comparison. You give us what you know and testify from actual knowledge. You have dealt with the facts with cool, painstaking fidelity and left those naked and uncontradicted facts to speak for themselves.

Brave woman! you have done your people and mine a service which can neither be weighed nor measured. If American conscience were only half alive, if the American church and clergy were only half Christianized, if American moral sensibility were not hardened by persistent infliction of outrage and crime against colored people, a scream of horror, shame and indignation would rise to Heaven wherever your pamphlet shall be read.

But alas! even crime has power to reproduce itself and create conditions favorable to its own existence. It sometimes seems we are deserted by earth and Heaven—yet we must still think, speak and work, and trust in the power of a merciful God for final deliverance.

Very truly and gratefully yours,

FREDERICK DOUGLASS.

CHAPTER I: THE OFFENSE

Wednesday evening May 24th, 1892, the city of Memphis was filled with excitement. Editorials in the daily papers of that date caused a meeting to be held in the Cotton Exchange Building; a committee was sent for the editors of the "Free Speech" an Afro-American journal published in that city, and the only reason the open threats of lynching that were made were not carried out was because they could not be found. The cause of all this commotion was the following editorial published in the "Free Speech" May 21st, 1892, the Saturday previous.

"Eight Negroes lynched since last issue of the "Free Speech" one at Little Rock, Ark., last Saturday morning where the citizens broke into the penitentiary and got their man; three near Anniston, Ala., one near New Orleans; and three at Clarksville, Ga., the last three for killing a white man, and five on the same old racket—the new alarm about raping white women. The same programme of hanging, then shooting bullets into the lifeless bodies was carried out to the letter.

Nobody in this section of the country believes the old thread bare lie that Negro men rape white women. If Southern white men are not careful, they will over-reach themselves and public sentiment will have a reaction; a conclusion will then be reached which will be very damaging to the moral reputation of their women."

"The Daily Commercial" of Wednesday following, May 25th, contained the following leader:

"Those Negroes who are attempting to make the lynching of individuals of their race a means for arousing the worst passions of their kind are playing with a dangerous sentiment. The negroes may as well understand that there is no mercy for the negro rapist and little patience with his defenders. A negro organ printed in this city, in a recent issue publishes the following atrocious paragraph: 'Nobody in this section of the country believes the old thread-bare lie that negro men rape white women. If Southern white men are not careful they will over-reach themselves, and public sentiment will have a reaction; and a conclusion will be reached which will be very damaging to the moral reputation of their women.'

The fact that a black scoundrel is allowed to live and utter such loathsome and repulsive calumnies is a volume of evidence as to the wonderful patience of Southern whites. But we have had enough of it. There are some things that the Southern white man will not tolerate, and the obscene intimations of the foregoing have brought the writer to the very outermost limit of public patience. We hope we have said enough."

The "Evening Scimitar" of same date, copied the "Commercial's" editorial with these words of comment: "Patience under such circumstances is not a virtue. If the negroes themselves do not apply the remedy without delay it will be the duty of those whom he has attacked to tie the wretch who utters these calumnies to a stake at the intersection of Main and Madison Ste., brand him in the forehead with a hot iron and perform upon him a surgical operation with a pair of tailor's shears."

Acting upon this advice, the leading citizens met in the Cotton Exchange Building the same evening, and threats of lynching were freely indulged, not by the lawless element upon which the deviltry of the South is usually saddled—but by the leading business men, in their leading business centre. Mr. Fleming, the business manager and owning a half interest in the "Free Speech," had to leave town to escape the mob, and was afterwards ordered not to return; letters and telegrams sent me in New York where I was spending my vacation advised me that bodily harm awaited my return. Creditors took possession of the office and sold the outfit, and the "Free Speech" was as if it had never been.

The editorial in question was prompted by the many inhuman and fiendish lynchings of Afro-Americans which have recently taken place and was meant as a warning. Eight lynched in one week and five of them with rape! The thinking public will not easily believe freedom and education more brutalizing than slavery, and the world knows that the crime of rape was unknown during four years of civil war, when the white women of the South were at the mercy of the race which is all at once charged with being a bestial one. Since my business has been destroyed and I am an exile from home because of that editorial, the issue has been forced, and as the writer of it I feel that the race and the public generally should have a statement of the facts as they exist. They will serve at the same time as a defense for the Afro-Americans Sampsons who suffer themselves to be betrayed by white Delilahs.

The whites of Montgomery, Ala., knew J. C. Duke sounded the keynote of the situation—which they would gladly hide from the world, when he said in his paper, "The Herald," five years ago: "Why is it that white women attract negro men now more than in former days? There was a time when such a thing was unheard of. There is a secret to this thing, and we greatly suspect it is the growing appreciation of white Juliets for colored Romeos." "Mr. Duke, like the "Free Speech" proprietors, was forced to leave the city for reflecting on the "honah" of white women and his paper suppressed; but the truth remains that Afro-American men do not always rape (?) white women without their consent.

Mr. Duke, before leaving Montgomery, signed a card disclaiming any intention of slandering Southern white women. The editor of the "Free Speech" has no disclaimer to enter, but asserts instead that there are many white women in the South who would marry colored men if such an act would not place them at once beyond the pale of society and within the clutches of the law. The miscegenation laws of the South only operate against the legitimate union of the races; they leave the white man free to seduce all the colored girls he can, but it is death to the colored man who yields to the force and advances of a similar attraction in white women. White men lynch the offending Afro-American, not because he is a despoiler of virtue, but because he succumbs to the smiles of white women.

Chapter II: The Black and White of It

The "Cleveland Gazette" of January 16, 1892, publishes a case in point. Mrs. J. S. Underwood, the wife of a minister of Elyria, Ohio, accused an Afro-American of rape. She told her husband that during his absence in 1888, stumping the State for the Prohibition Party, the man came to the kitchen door, forced his way in the house and insulted her. She tried to drive him out with a heavy poker, but he overpowered and chloroformed her, and when she revived her clothing was torn and she was in a horrible condition. She did not know the man but could identify him. She pointed out William Offett, a married man, who was arrested and, being in Ohio, was granted a trial.

The prisoner vehemently denied the charge of rape, but confessed he went to Mrs. Underwood's residence at her invitation and was criminally intimate with her at her request. This availed him nothing against the sworn testimony of a minister's wife, a lady of the highest respectability. He was found guilty, and entered the penitentiary, December 14, 1888, for fifteen years. Some time afterwards the woman's remorse led her to confess to her husband that the man was innocent.

These are her words: "I met Offett at the Post Office. It was raining. He was polite to me, and as I had several bundles in my arms he offered to carry them home for me, which he did. He had a strange fascination for me, and I invited him to call on me. He called, bringing chestnuts and candy for the children. By this means we got them to leave us alone in the room. Then I sat on his lap. He made a proposal to me and I readily consented. Why I did so, I do not know, but that I did is true. He visited me several times after that and each time I was indiscreet. I did not care after the first time. In fact I could not have resisted, and had no desire to resist."

When asked by her husband why she told him she had been outraged, she said: "I had several reasons for telling you. One was the neighbors saw the fellow here, another was, I was afraid I had contracted a loathsome disease, and still another was that I feared I might give birth to a Negro baby. I hoped to save my reputation by telling you a deliberate lie." Her husband, horrified by the confession, had Offett, who had already served four years, released and secured a divorce.

There are thousands of such cases throughout the South, with the difference that the Southern white men in insatiate fury wreak their vengeance without intervention of law upon the Afro-Americans who consort with their women. A few instances to substantiate the assertion that some white women love the company of the Afro-American will not be out of place. Most of these cases were reported by the daily papers of the South.

In the winter of 1885-6 the wife of a practicing physician in Memphis, in good social standing whose name has escaped me, left home, husband and children, and ran away with her black coachman. She was with him a month before her husband found and brought her home. The coachman could not be found. The doctor moved his family away from Memphis, and is living in another city under an assumed name.

In the same city last year a white girl in the dusk of evening screamed at the approach of some parties that a Negro had assaulted her on the street. He was captured, and tried by a white judge and jury that acquitted him of the charge. It is needless to add if there had been a scrap of evidence on which to convict him of so grave a charge he would have been convicted.

Sarah Clark of Memphis loved a black man and lived openly with him. When she was indicted last spring for miscegenation, she swore in court that she was *not* a white woman. This she did to escape the penitentiary and continued her illicit relation undisturbed. That she is of the lower class of whites, does not disturb the fact that she is a white woman. "The leading citizens" of Memphis are defending the "honor" of *all* white women, *demi-monde* included.

Since the manager of the "Free Speech" has been run away from Memphis by the guardians of the honor of Southern white women, a young girl living on Poplar St., who was discovered in intimate relations with a handsome mulatto young colored man, Will Morgan by name, stole her father's money to send the young fellow away from that father's wrath. She has since joined him in Chicago.

The Memphis "Ledger" for June 8th has the following; "If Lillie Bailey, a rather pretty white girl seventeen years of age, who is now at the City Hospital, would be somewhat less reserved about her disgrace there would be some very nauseating details in the story of her life. She is the mother of a little coon. The truth might reveal fearful depravity or it might reveal the evidence of a rank outrage. She will not divulge the name of the man who has left such black evidence of her disgrace, and, in fact, says it is a matter in which there can be no interest to the outside world. She came to Memphis nearly three months ago and was taken in at the Woman's Refuge in the southern part of the city. She remained there until a few weeks ago, when the child was born. The ladies in charge of the Refuge were horrified. The girl was at once sent to the City Hospital, where she has been since May 30th. She is a country girl. She came to Memphis from her father's farm, a short distance from Hernando, Miss. Just when she left there she would not say. In fact she says she came to Memphis from Arkansas, and says her home is in that State. She is rather good looking, has blue eyes, a low forehead and dark red hair. The ladies at the Woman's Refuge do not know anything about the girl further than what they learned when she was an inmate of the institution; and she would not tell much. When the child was born an attempt was made to get the girl to reveal the name of the Negro who had disgraced her, she obstinately refused and it was impossible to elicit any information from her on the subject."

Note the wording. "The truth might reveal fearful depravity or rank outrage." If it had been a white child or Lillie Bailey had told a pitiful story of Negro outrage, it would have been a case of woman's weakness or assault and she could have remained at the Woman's Refuge. But a Negro child and to withhold its father's name and thus prevent the killing of another Negro "rapist." A case of "fearful depravity."

The very week the "leading citizens" of Memphis were making a spectacle of themselves in defense of all white women of every kind, an Afro-American, M. Stricklin, was found in a white woman's room in that city. Although she made no outcry of rape, he was jailed and would have been lynched, but the woman stated she bought curtains of him (he was a furniture dealer) and his business in her room that night was to put them up. A white woman's word was taken as absolutely in this case as when the cry of rape is made, and he was freed.

What is true of Memphis is true of the entire South. The daily papers last year reported a farmer's wife in Alabama had given birth to a Negro child. When the Negro farm hand who was plowing in the field heard it he took the mule from the plow and fled. The dispatches also told of a woman in South Carolina who gave birth to a Negro child and charged three men with being its father, every one of whom has since disappeared. In Tuscumbia, Ala, the colored boy who was lynched there last year for assaulting a white girl told her before his accusers that he had met her there in the woods often before.

Frank Weems of Chattanooga who was not lynched in May only because the prominent citizens became his body guard until the doors of the penitentiary closed on him, had letters in his pocket from the white woman in the case, making the appointment with him. Edward Coy who was burned alive in Texarkana, January 1, 1892, died protesting his innocence. Investigation since as given by the Bystander in the Chicago Inter-Ocean, October 1, proves:

"1. The woman who was paraded as a victim of violence was of bad character; her husband was a drunkard and a gambler.

2. She was publicly reported and generally known to have been criminally intimate with Coy for more than a year previous.

3. She was compelled by threats, if not by violence, to make the charge against the victim.

4. When she came to apply the match Coy asked her if she would burn him after they had 'been sweethearting' so long.

5. A large majority of the 'superior' white men prominent in the affair are the reputed fathers of mulatto children.

These are not pleasant facts, but they are illustrative of the vital phase of the so-called 'race question,' which should properly be designated an earnest inquiry as to the best methods by which religion, science, law and political power may be employed to excuse injustice, barbarity and crime done to a people because of race and color. There can be no possible belief that these people were inspired by any consuming zeal to vindicate God's law against miscegenationists of the most practical sort. The woman was a willing partner in the victim's guilt, and being of the 'superior' race must naturally have been more guilty."

In Natchez, Miss., Mrs. Marshall, one of the *creme de la creme* of the city, created a tremendous sensation several years ago. She has a black coachman who was married, and had been in her employ several years. During this time she gave birth to a child whose color was remarked, but traced to some brunette ancestor, and one of the fashionable dames of the city was its godmother. Mrs. Marshall's social position was unquestioned, and wealth showered every dainty on this child which was idolized with its brothers and sisters by its white papa. In course of time another child appeared on the scene, but it was unmistakably dark. All were alarmed, and "rush of blood, strangulation" were the conjectures, but the doctor, when asked the cause, grimly told them it was a Negro child. There was a family conclave, the coachman heard of it and leaving his own family went West, and has never returned. As soon as Mrs. Marshall was able to travel she was sent away in deep disgrace. Her husband died within the year of a broken heart.

Ebenezer Fowler, the wealthiest colored man in Issaquena County, Miss., was shot down on the street in Mayeraville, January 30, 1865, just before dark by an armed body of white men who filled his body with bullets. They charged him with writing a note to a white woman of the place, which they intercepted and which proved there was an intimacy existing between them.

Hundreds of such cases might be cited, but enough have been given to prove the assertion that there are white women in the South who love the Afro-American's company even as there are white men notorious *for* their preference for Afro-American women.

There is hardly a town in the South which has not an instance of the kind which is well-known, and hence the assertion is reiterated that "nobody in the South believes the old thread bare lie that negro men rape white women." Hence there is a growing demand among Afro-Americans that the guilt or innocence of parties accused of rape be fully established. They know the men *of* the section of the country who refuse this are not so desirous of punishing rapists as they pretend. The utterances of the leading white men show that with them it is not the crime but the *class*. Bishop Fitzgerald has become apologist for lynchers of the rapists of *white* women only. Governor Tillman, of South Carolina, in the month of June, standing under the tree in Barnwell, S. C., on which eight Afro-Americans were hung last year, declared that he would lead a mob to lynch a *negro* who raped a *white* woman." So say the pulpits, officials and newspapers of the South. But when the victim is a colored woman it is different.

Last winter in Baltimore, Md., three white ruffians assaulted a Miss Camphor, a young Afro-American girl, while out walking with a young man of her own race. They held her escort and outraged the girl. It was a deed dastardly enough to arouse Southern blood, which gives its horror of rape as excuse for lawlessness, but she was an Afro-American. The case went to the courts, an Afro-American lawyer defended the men and they were acquitted.

In Nashville, Tenn., there is a white man, Pat Hanifan, who outraged a little Afro-American girl, and, from the physical injuries received, she has been ruined for life. He was jailed for six months, discharged, and is now a detective in that city. In the same city, last May, a white man outraged an Afro-American girl in a drug store. He was arrested, and released on bail at the trial. It was rumored that five hundred Afro-Americans had organized to lynch him. Two hundred and fifty white citizens armed themselves with Winchesters and guarded him. A cannon was placed in front of his home, and the Buchanan Rifles (State Militia) ordered to the scene for his protection. The Afro-American mob did not materialize. Only two weeks before Eph. Grizzard, who had only been *charged* with rape upon a white woman, had been taken from the jail, with Governor Buchanan and the police and militia standing by, dragged through the streets in broad daylight, knives plunged into him at every step, and with every fiendish cruelty a frenzied mob could devise, he was at last swung out on the bridge with hands cut to pieces as he tried to climb up the stanchions. A naked, bloody example of the blood-thirstiness of the nineteenth century civilization of the Athens of the South! No cannon or military was called out in his defense. He dared to visit a white woman.

At the very moment these civilized whites were announcing their determination "to protect their wives and daughters," by murdering Grizzard, a white man was in the same jail for raping eight-year-old Maggie Reese, an Afro-American girl. He was not harmed. The "honor" of grown women who were glad enough to be supported by the Grizzard boys and Ed Coy, as long as the liaison was not known, needed protection; they were white. The outrage upon helpless childhood needed no avenging in this case; she was black.

A white man in Guthrie, Oklahoma Territory, two months ago inflicted such injuries upon another Afro-American child that she died. He was not punished, but an attempt was made in the same town in the month of June to lynch an Afro-American who visited a white woman.

In Memphis, Tenn., in the month of June, Ellerton L. Dorr, who is the husband of Russell Hancock's widow, was arrested for attempted rape on Mattie Cole, a neighbor's cook; he was only prevented from accomplishing his purpose, by the appearance of Mattie's employer. Dorr's friends say he was drunk and not responsible for his actions. The grand jury refused to indict him and he was discharged.

Chapter III: The New Cry

The appeal of Southern whites to Northern sympathy and sanction, the adroit, insiduous plea made by Bishop Fitzgerald for suspension of judgment because those "who condemn lynching express no sympathy for the *white* woman in the case," falls to the ground in the light of the foregoing.

From this exposition of the race issue in lynch law, the whole matter is explained by the well-known opposition growing out of slavery to the progress of the race. This is crystalized in the oft-repeated slogan: "This is a white man's country and the white man must rule." The South resented giving the Afro-American his freedom, the ballot box and the Civil Rights Law. The raids of the Ku-Klux and White Liners to subvert reconstruction government, the Hamburg and Ellerton, S. C., the Copiah County Miss., and the Layfayette Parish, La., massacres were excused as the natural resentment of intelligence against government by ignorance.

Honest white men practically conceded the necessity of intelligence murdering ignorance to correct the mistake of the general government, and the race was left to the tender mercies of the solid South. Thoughtful Afro-Americans with the strong arm of the government withdrawn and with the hope to stop such wholesale massacres urged the race to sacrifice its political rights for sake of peace. They honestly believed the race should fit itself for government, and when that should be done, the objection to race participation in politics would be removed.

But the sacrifice did not remove the trouble, nor move the South to justice. One by one the Southern States have legally (?) disfranchised the Afro-American, and since the repeal of the Civil Rights Bill nearly every Southern State has passed separate car laws with a penalty against their infringement. The race regardless of advancement is penned into filthy, stifling partitions cut off from smoking cars. All this while, although the political cause has been removed, the butcheries of black men at Barnwell, S. C., Carrolton, Miss., Waycross, Ga., and Memphis, Tenn., have gone on; also the flaying alive of a man in Kentucky, the burning of one in Arkansas, the hanging of a fifteen-year-old girl in Louisiana, a woman in Jackson, Tenn., and one in Hollendale, Miss., until the dark and bloody record of the South shows 728 Afro-Americans lynched during the past 8 years. Not 50 of these were for political causes; the rest were for all manner of accusations from that of rape of white women, to the case of the boy Will Lewis who was hanged at Tullahoma, Tenn., last year for being drunk and "sassy" to white folks.

These statistics compiled by the Chicago "Tribune" were given the first of this year (1892). Since then, not less than one hundred and fifty have been known to have met violent death at the hands of cruel bloodthirsty mobs during the past nine months.

To palliate this record (which grows worse as the Afro-American becomes intelligent) and excuse some of the most heinous crimes that ever stained the history of a country, the South is shielding itself behind the plausible screen of defending the honor of its women. This, too, in the face of the fact that only *one-third* of the 728 victims to mobs have been *charged* with rape, to say nothing of those of that one-third who were innocent of the charge. A white correspondent of the Baltimore Sun declares that the Afro-American who was lynched in Chestertown, Md., in May for assault on a white girl was innocent; that the deed was done by a white man who had since disappeared. The girl herself maintained that her assailant was a white man. When that poor Afro-American was murdered, the whites excused their refusal of a trial on the ground that they wished to spare the white girl the mortification of having to testify in court.

This cry has had its effect. It has closed the heart, stifled the conscience, warped the judgment and hushed the voice of press and pulpit on the subject of lynch law throughout this "land *of* liberty." Men who stand high in the esteem of the public for christian character, for moral and physical courage, for devotion to the principles of equal and exact justice to all, and for great sagacity, stand as cowards who fear to open their mouths before this great outrage. They do not see that by their tacit encouragement, their silent acquiescence, the black shadow of lawlessness in the form of lynch law is spreading its wings over the whole country.

Men who, like Governor Tillman, start the ball of lynch law rolling for a certain crime, are powerless to stop it when drunken or criminal white toughs feel like hanging an Afro-American on any pretext.

Even to the better class of Afro-Americans the crime of rape is so revolting they have too often taken the white man's word and given lynch law neither the investigation nor condemnation it deserved.

They forget that a concession of the right to lynch a man for a certain crime, not only concedes the right to lynch any person for any crime, but (so frequently is the cry of rape now raised) it is in a fair way to stamp us a race of rapists and desperadoes. They have gone on hoping and believing that general education and financial strength would solve the difficulty, and are devoting their energies to the accumulation of both.

The mob spirit has grown with the increasing intelligence of the Afro-American. It has left the out-of-the-way places where ignorance prevails, has thrown off the mask and with this new cry stalks in broad daylight in large cities, the centres of civilization, and is encouraged by the "leading citizens" and the press.

Chapter IV: The Malicious and Untruthful White Press

The "Daily Commercial" and "Evening Scimitar" of Memphis, Tenn., are owned by leading business men of that city, and yet, in spite of the fact that there had been no white woman in Memphis outraged by an Afro-American, and that Memphis possessed a thrifty law-abiding, property owning class of Afro-Americans the "Commercial" of May 17th, under the head of "More Rapes, More Lynchings" gave utterance to the following:

The lynching of three Negro scoundrels reported in our dispatches from Anniston, Ala., for a brutal outrage committed upon a white woman will be a text for much comment on "Southern barbarism" by Northern newspapers; but we fancy it will hardly prove effective for campaign purposes among intelligent people. The frequency of these lynchings calls attention to the frequency of the crimes which causes lynching. The "Southern barbarism" which deserves the serious attention of all people North and South, is the barbarism which preys upon weak and defenseless women. Nothing but the most prompt, speedy and extreme punishment can hold in check the horrible and beastial propensities of the Negro race. There is a strange similarity about a number of cases of this character which have lately occurred.

In each case the crime was deliberately planned and perpetrated by several Negroes. They watched for an opportunity when the women were left without a protector. It was not a sudden yielding to a fit of passion, but the consummation of a devilish purpose which has been seeking and waiting for the opportunity. This feature of the crime not only makes it the most fiendishly brutal, but it adds to the terror of the situation in the thinly settled country communities. No man can leave his family at night without the dread that some roving Negro ruffian is watching and waiting for this opportunity. The swift punishment which invariably follows these horrible crimes doubtless acts as a deterring effect upon the Negroes in that immediate neighborhood for a short time. But the lesson is not widely learned nor long remembered. Then such crimes, equally atrocious, have happened in quick succession, one in Tennessee, one in Arkansas, and one in Alabama. The facts of the crime appear to appeal more to the Negro's lustful imagination than the facts of the punishment do to his fears. He sets aside all fear of death in any form when opportunity is found for the gratification of his bestial desires.

There is small reason to hope for any change for the better. The commission of this crime grows more frequent every year. The generation of Negroes which have grown up since the war have lost in large measure the traditional and wholesome awe of the white race which kept the Negroes in subjection, even when their masters were in the army, and their families left unprotected except by the slaves themselves. There is no longer a restraint upon the brute passion of the Negro.

What is to be done? The crime of rape is always horrible, but the Southern man there is nothing which so fills the soul with horror, loathing and fury as the outraging of a white woman by a Negro. It is the race question in the ugliest, vilest, most dangerous aspect.

The Negro as a political factor can be controlled. But neither laws nor lynchings can subdue his lusts. Sooner or later it will force a crisis. We do not know in what form it will come."

In its issue of June 4th, the Memphis "Evening Scimitar" gives the following excuse for lynch law:

"Aside from the violation of white women by Negroes, which is the outcropping of a bestial perversion of instinct, the chief cause of trouble between the races in the South is the Negro's lack of manners. In the state of slavery he learned politeness from association with white people, who took pains to teach him. Since the emancipation came and the tie of mutual interest and regard between master and servant was broken, the Negro has drifted away into a state which is neither freedom nor bondage. Lacking the proper inspiration of the one and the restraining force of the other he has taken up the idea that boorish insolence is independence, and the exercise of a decent degree of breeding toward white people is identical with servile submission. In consequence of the prevalence of this notion there are many Negroes who use every opportunity to make themselves offensive, particularly when they think it can be done with impunity.

We have had too many instances right here in Memphis to doubt this, and our experience is not exceptional. *The white people won't stand this sort of thing, and whether they be insulted as individuals are as a race, the response will be prompt and effectual.* The bloody riot of 1866, in which so many Negroes perished, was brought on principally by the outrageous conduct of the blacks toward the whites on the streets. It is also a remarkable and discouraging fact that the majority of such scoundrels are Negroes who have received educational advantages at the hands of the white taxpayers. They have got just enough of learning to make them realize how hopelessly their race is behind the other in everything that makes a great people, and they attempt to "get even" by insolence, which is ever the resentment of inferiors. There are well bred Negroes among us, and it is truly unfortunate that they should have to pay, even in part, the penalty of the offenses committed by the baser sort, but this is the way of the world. The innocent must suffer for the guilty. If the Negroes as a people possessed a hundredth part of the self-respect which is evidenced by the courteous bearing of some that the "Scimitar" could name, the friction between the races would be reduced to a minimum. It will not do to beg the question by pleading that many white men are also stirring up strife. The Caucasian blackguard simply obeys the promptings of a depraved disposition, and he is seldom deliberately rough or offensive toward strangers or unprotected women.

The Negro tough, on the contrary, is given to just that kind of offending and he almost invariably singles out white people as his victims."

On March 9th, 1892, there were lynched in this same city three of the best specimens of young since-the-war Afro-American manhood. They were peaceful, law-abiding citizens and energetic business men.

They believed the problem was to be solved by eschewing politics and putting money in the purse. They owned a flourishing grocery business in a thickly populated suburb of Memphis, and a white man named Barrett had one on the opposite corner. After a personal difficulty which Barrett sought by going into the "People's Grocery" drawing a pistol and was thrashed by Calvin McDowell, he (Barrett) threatened to "clean them out." These men were a mile beyond the city limits and police protection; hearing that Barrett's crowd was coming to attack them Saturday night, they mustered forces and prepared to defend themselves against the attack.

When Barrett came he led a *posse* of officers, twelve in number, who afterward claimed to be hunting a man for whom they had a warrant. That twelve men in *citizen's* clothes should think it necessary to go in the night to hunt one man who had never before been arrested, or made any record as a criminal has never been explained. When they entered the back door the young men thought the threatened attack was on, and fired into them. Three of the officers were wounded, and when the *defending* party found it was officers of the law upon whom they had fired, they ceased and got away.

Thirty-one men were arrested and thrown in jail as "conspirators," although they all declared more than once they did not know they were firing on officers. Excitement was at fever heat until the morning papers, two days after, announced that the wounded deputy sheriffs were out of danger. This hindered rather than helped the plans of the whites. There was no law on the statute books which would execute an Afro-American for wounding a white man, but the "unwritten law" did. Three of these men, the president, the manager and clerk of the grocery—"the leaders of the conspiracy"—were secretly taken from jail and lynched in a shockingly brutal manner. "The Negroes are getting too independent," they say, "we must teach them a lesson."

"What lesson! The lesson of subordination. Kill the leaders and it will cow the Negro who dares to shoot a white man, even in self-defense."

Although the race was wild over the outrage, the mockery of law and justice which disarmed men and locked them up in jails where they could be easily and safely reached by the mob—the Afro-American ministers, newspapers and leaders counselled obedience to the law which did not protect them.

Their counsel was heeded and not a hand was uplifted to resent the outrage; following the advice of the "Free Speech," people left the city in great numbers.

The dailies and associated press reports heralded these men to the country as "toughs," and "Negro desperadoes who kept a low dive." This same press service printed that the Negro who was lynched at Indianola, Miss., in May, had outraged the sheriff's eight-year-old daughter. The girl was more than eighteen years old, and was found by her father in this man's room, who was a servant on the place.

Not content with misrepresenting the race, the mob-spirit was not to be satisfied until the paper which was doing all it could to counteract this impression was silenced. The colored people were resenting their bad treatment in a way to make itself felt, yet gave the mob no excuse for further murder, until the appearance of the editorial which is construed as a reflection on the "honor" of the Southern white women. It is not half so libelous as that of the "Commercial" which appeared four days before, and which has been given in these pages. They would have lynched the manager of the "Free Speech" for exercising the right of free speech if they had found him as quickly as they would have hung a rapist, and glad of the excuse to do so. The owners were ordered not to return, "The Free Speech" was suspended with as little compunction as the business of the "People's Grocery" broken up and the proprietors murdered.

Chapter V: The South's Position

Henry W. Grady in his well-remembered speeches in New England pictured the Afro-American as incapable of self-government. Through him and other leading men the cry of the South to the country has been "Hands off! Leave us to solve our problem." To the Afro-American the South says, "the white man must and will rule." There is little difference between the Ante-bellum South and the New South.

Her white citizens are wedded to any method however revolting, any measure however extreme, for the subjugation of the young manhood of the race. They have cheated him out of his ballot, deprived him of civil rights or redress therefore in the civil courts, robbed him of the fruits of his labor, and are still murdering, burning and lynching him.

The result is a growing disregard of human life. Lynch law has spread its insiduous influence till men in New York State, Pennsylvania and on the free Western plains feel they can take the law in their own hands with impunity, especially where an Afro-American is concerned. The South is brutalized to a degree not realized by its own inhabitants, and the very foundation of government, law and order, are imperilled.

Public sentiment has had a slight "reaction" though not sufficient to stop the crusade of lawlessness and lynching. The spirit of christianity of the great M. E. Church was aroused to the frequent and revolting crimes against a weak people, enough to pass strong condemnatory resolutions at its General Conference in Omaha last May. The spirit of justice of the grand old party asserted itself sufficiently to secure a denunciation of the wrongs, and a feeble declaration of the belief in human rights in the Republican platform at Minneapolis, June 7th. Some of the great dailies and weeklies have swung into line declaring that lynch law must go. The President of the United States issued a proclamation that it be not tolerated in the territories over which he has jurisdiction. Governor Northern and Chief Justice Bleckley of Georgia have proclaimed against it. The citizens of Chattanooga, Tenn., have set a worthy example in that they not only condemn lynch law, but her public men demanded a trial for Weems, the accused rapist, and guarded him while the trial was in progress. The trial only lasted ten minutes, and Weems chose to plead guilty and accept twenty-one years sentence than invite the certain death which awaited him outside that cordon of police if he told the truth and shown the letters he had from the white woman in the case.

Col. A. S. Colyar, of Nashville, Tenn., is so overcome with the horrible state of affairs that he addressed the following earnest letter to the Nashville "American." "Nothing since I have been a reading man has so impressed me with the decay of manhood among the people of Tennessee as the dastardly submission to the mob reign. We have reached an unprecedented low level; the awful criminal depravity of substituting the mob for the court and jury, of giving up the jail keys to the mob whenever they are demanded. We do it in the largest cities and in the country towns; we do it in midday; we do it after full, not to say formal, notice, and so thoroughly and generally is it acquiesced in that the murderers have discarded the formula of masks. They go into the town where everybody knows them, sometimes under the gaze of the governor, in the presence of the courts, in the presence of the sheriff and his deputies, in the presence of the entire police force, take out the prisoner, take his life, often with fiendish glee, and often with acts of cruelty and barbarism which impress the reader with a degeneracy rapidly approaching savage life. That the State is disgraced but faintly expresses the humiliation which has settled upon the once proud people of Tennessee. The State, in its majesty, through its organized life, for which the people pay liberally, makes but one record, but one note, and that a criminal falsehood, 'was hung *by* persons to the jury unknown.' The murder at Shelbyville is only a verification of what every intelligent man knew would come, because with a mob a rumor is as good as a proof."

These efforts brought forth apologies and a short halt, but the lynching mania raged again through the past three months with unabated fury.

The strong arm of the law must be brought to bear upon lynchers in severe punishment, but this cannot and will not be done unless a healthy public sentiment demands and sustains such action.

The men and women in the South who disapprove of lynching and remain silent on the perpetration of such outrages, are particeps criminis, accomplices, accessories before and after the fact, equally guilty with the actual law-breakers who would not persist if they did not know that neither the law nor militia would be employed against them.

Chapter VI: Self Help

In the creation of this healthier public sentiment, the Afro-American can do for himself what no one can do for him. The world looks on with wonder that we have conceded so much and remain law abiding under such great outrage and provocation.

To Northern capital and Afro-American labor the South owes its rehabilitation. If labor is withdrawn capital will not remain. The Afro-American is thus the backbone of the South. A thorough knowledge and judicious exercise of this power in lynching localities could many times effect a bloodless revolution. The white man's dollar is his god, and to stop this will be to stop outrages in many localities.

The Afro-Americans of Memphis denounced the lynching of three of their best citizens, and urged and waited for the authorities to act in the matter and bring the lynchers to justice. No attempt was made to do so, and the black men left the city by the thousands, bringing about great stagnation in every branch of business. These who remained so injured the business of the street car company by staying off the cars, that the superintendent, manager and treasurer called personally on the editor of the "Free Speech," asked them to urge our people to give them their patronage again. Other business men became alarmed over the situation and the "Free Speech" was run away that the colored people might be more easily controlled. A meeting of white citizens in June, three months after the lynching, passed resolutions for the first time, condemning it. *But they did not punish the lynchers.* Every one of them was known by name, because they had been selected to do the dirty work, by some of the very citizens who passed these resolutions. Memphis is fast losing her black population, who proclaim as they go that there is no protection for the life and property of any Afro-American citizen in Memphis who is not a slave.

The Afro-American citizens of Kentucky whose intellectual and financial improvement has been phenomenal have never had a separate car law until now. Delegations and petitions poured into the Legislature against it, yet the bill passed and the Jim Crow Car of Kentucky is a legalized institution. Will the great mass of Negroes continue to patronize the railroad? A special from Covington, Ky., says:

Covington, June 13th.—The railroads of the State are beginning to feel very markedly, the effects of the separate coach bill recently passed by the Legislature. No class of people in the State have so many and so largely attended excursions as the blacks. All these have been abandoned, and regular travel is reduced to a minimum. A competent authority says the loss to the various roads will reach $1,000,000 this year.

A call to a State Conference in Lexington, Ky., last June had delegates from every county in the State. Those delegates, the ministers, teachers, heads of secret and other orders, and the head of every family should pass the word around for every member of the race in Kentucky to stay off railroads unless obliged to ride. If they did so, and their advice was followed persistently the convention would not need to petition the Legislature to repeal the law or raise money to file a suit. The railroad corporations would be so effected they would in self-defense lobby to have the separate law repealed. On the other hand, as long as the railroad can get Afro-American excursions they will always have plenty of money to fight all the suits brought against them. They will be aided in so doing by the same partisan public sentiment which passed the law. White men passed the law, and white judges and juries would pass upon the suits against the law, and render judgement in line with their prejudices and in deference to the greater financial power.

The appeal to the white man's pocket has ever been more effectual than all the appeals ever made to his conscience. Nothing, absolutely nothing, is to be gained by a further sacrifice of manhood and self-respect. By the right exercise of his power as the industrial factor of the South the Afro-American can demand and secure his rights, the punishment of lynchers, and a fair trial for accused rapists.

Of the many inhuman outrages of this present year, the only case where the proposed lynching did *not* occur, was where the men armed themselves in Jacksonville, Fla., and Paducah, Ky., and prevented it. The only times an Afro-American who was assaulted got away has been when he had a gun and used it in self-defense.

The lesson this teaches and which every Afro-American should ponder well, is that a Winchester rifle should have a place of honor in every black home, and it should be used for that protection which the law refuses to give. When the white man who is always the aggressor knows he runs as great a risk of biting the dust every time his Afro-American victim does, he will have greater respect for Afro-American life. The more the Afro-American yields and cringes and begs, the more he has to do so, the more he is insulted, outraged and lynched.

The assertion has been substantiated throughout these pages that the press contains unreliable and doctored reports of lynchings, and one of the most necessary timings for the race to do is to get these facts before the public. The people must know before they can act, and there is no educator to compare with the press.

The Afro-American papers are the only ones which will print the truth, and they lack means to employ agents and detectives to get at the facts. The race must rally a mighty host to the support of their journals, and thus enable them to do much in the way of investigation.

A lynching occurred at Port Jarvis, N. Y., the first week in June. A white and colored man were implicated in the assault upon a white girl. It was charged that the white man paid the colored boy to make the assault, which he did on the public highway in broad day time, and was lynched. This, too was done by "parties unknown." The white man in the case still lives. He was imprisoned and promises to fight the case on trial. At the preliminary examination, it developed that he had been a suitor of the girl's. She had repulsed and refused him, yet had given him money, and he had sent threatening letters demanding more.

The day before this examination she was so wrought up, she left home and wandered miles away. When found she said she did so because she was afraid of the man's testimony. Why should she be afraid of the man's testimony? Why should she yield to his demands for money if not to prevent exposing something he knew? It seems explainable only on the hypothesis that a *liaison* existed between the colored boy and the girl, and the white man knew of it. The prose is singularly silent. Has it a motive? We owe it to ourselves to find out.

The story comes from Larned, Kansas, Oct. 1st, that a young white lady held at bay until daylight, without alarming any one in the house, "a burly Negro" who entered her room and bed. The "burly Negro" was promptly lynched without investigation or examination of inconsistent stories.

A house was found burned down near Montgomery, Ala., in Monroe County, Oct. 13th, a few weeks ago; also the burned bodies of the owners and melted piles of gold and silver.

These discoveries led to the conclusion that the awful crime was not prompted by motives of robbery. The suggestion of the whites was that "brutal lust was the incentive, and as there are nearly 200 Negroes living within a radius of five miles of the place the conclusion was inevitable that some of them were the perpetrators."

Upon this "suggestion" probably made by the real criminal, the mob acted upon the "conclusion" and arrested ten Afro-Americans, four of them, they tell the world, confessed to the deed of murdering Richard L. Johnson and outraging his daughter, Jeanette. These four men, Berrell Jones, Moses Johnson, Jim and John Packer, none of them 25 years of age, upon this conclusion, were taken from jail, hanged, shot, and burned while yet alive the night of Oct. 12th. The same report says Mr. Johnson was on the best of terms with his Negro tenants.

The race thus outraged must find out the facts of this awful hurling of men into eternity on supposition, and give them to the indifferent and apathetic country. We feel this to be a garbled report, but how can we prove it?

Near Vicksburg, Miss., a murder was committed by a gang of burglars. Of course it must have been done by Negroes, and Negroes were arrested for it. It is believed that 2 men, Smith Tooley and John Adams belonged to a gang controlled by white men and, fearing exposure, on the night of July 4th, they were hanged in the Court House yard by those interested in silencing them. Robberies since committed in the same vicinity have been known to be by white men who had their faces blackened. We strongly believe in the innocence of these murdered men, but we have no proof. No other news goes out to the world save that which stamps us as a race of cut-throats, robbers and lustful wild beasts. So great is Southern hate and prejudice, they legally (?) hung poor little thirteen-year-old Mildrey Brown at Columbia, S. C., Oct. 7th, on the circumstantial evidence that she poisoned a white infant. If her guilt had been proven unmistakably, had she been white, Mildrey Brown would never have been hung.

The country would have been aroused and South Carolina disgraced forever for such a crime. The Afro-American himself did not know as he should have known as his journals should be in a position to have him know and act.

Nothing is more definitely settled than he must act for himself. I have shown how he may employ the boycott, emigration and the press, and I feel that by a combination of all these agencies can effectually stamp out lynch law, that last relic of barbarism and slavery. "The gods help those who help themselves."

3

INTRODUCTION

Born 5 years after the end of slavery in the small town of Great Barrington, Massachusetts, William Edward Burghardt Du Bois rose to become one of the leading intellectuals of the 20th century. Among African American scholars, he is affectionately known as "the Prophet." This title was given to him because of his keen insights into the African American experience, many of which manifested themselves decades after he articulated them. His work continues to astound those who take the time to read them because of their relevancy to current social issues. Nearly 40 years after his death in 1963, criminology and criminal justice have slowly begun to take notice of his contributions to the discipline, with the National Institute of Justice creating the W. E. B. Du Bois Fellowship Program (Dr. Becky Tatum, whose work is profiled in Chapter 21, was the inaugural recipient) and the Western Society of Criminology creating an award bearing Du Bois's name to be given annually to an outstanding scholar (from the West Coast) in the area of race, crime, and ethnicity.

With the recent reissue of *The Philadelphia Negro* by the University of Pennsylvania Press, Du Bois's pioneering urban ethnography has experienced a renaissance within the social science. In his introduction to the new edition, Elijah Anderson (1996) shows the eerie contemporary relevance of Du Bois's 100-year-old pioneering study of the African American community in Philadelphia's Seventh Ward. Although the entire book is laced with crime-related analyses, presented here is "The Negro Criminal," which represents the only chapter exclusively devoted to crime in a ward populated by a large number of recent African American migrants from southern states. As a part of his comprehensive study of the ward, Du Bois's focus on crime yielded insights on the disproportionate representation of African Americans in the arrest and prison statistics. However, unlike his contemporaries, Du Bois explains away much of the disproportionality with sociological explanations vis-à-vis biological determinism. Present within the chapter are analyses suggesting that Du Bois was astutely aware of criminological concepts such as white-collar crime, recidivism, discriminatory enforcement, and sentencing disparities between Whites and African Americans.

THE NEGRO CRIMINAL

W. E. B. DU BOIS

37. History of Negro Crime in the City.[1]— From his earliest advent the Negro, as was natural, has figured largely in the criminal annals of Philadelphia. Only such superficial study of the American Negro as dates his beginning with 1863 can neglect this past record of crime in studying the present. Crime is a phenomenon of organized social life, and is the open rebellion of an individual against his social environment. Naturally then, if men are suddenly transported from one environment to another, the result is lack of harmony with the new conditions; lack of harmony with the new physical surroundings leading to disease and death or modification of physique; lack of harmony with social surroundings leading to crime. Thus very early in the history of the colony characteristic complaints of the disorder of the Negro slaves is heard. In 1693, July 11, the Governor and Council approved an ordinance, "Upon the Request of some of the members of Council, that an order be made by the Court of Quarter Sessions for the Countie of philadelphia, the 4th July instant (proceeding upon a presentment of the Grand Jurie for the bodie of the sd countie), agt the tumultuous gatherings of the Negroes of the towne of Philadelphia, on the first dayes of the weeke, ordering the Constables of philadelphia, or anie other person whatsoever, to have power to take up Negroes, male or female, whom they should find gadding abroad on the said first dayes of the weeke, without a ticket from their Mr. or Mris., or not in their Compa, or to carry them to gaole, there to remain that night, and that without meat or drink, and to Cause them to be publickly whipt next morning with 39 Lashes, well Laid on, on their bare backs, for which their sd. Mr. or Mris. should pay 15d. to the whipper," etc.[2]

Penn himself introduced a law for the special trial and punishment of Negroes very early in the history of the colony, as has been noted before.[3] The slave code finally adopted was mild compared with the legislation of the period, but it was severe enough to show the unruly character of many of the imported slaves.[4]

Especially in Philadelphia did the Negroes continue to give general trouble, not so much by serious crime as by disorder. In 1732, under Mayor Hasel, the City Council "taking under Consideration the frequent and tumultuous meetings of the Negro Slaves, especially on Sunday, Gaming, Cursing, Swearing, and committing many other Disorders, to the great Terror and Disquiet of the Inhabitants of this city," ordered an ordinance to be drawn up against such disturbances.[5] Again, six years later, we hear of the draft of another city ordinance for "the more Effectual suppressing Tumultuous meetings and other disorderly doings of the Negroes, Mulattos and Indian servts. and slaves."[6] And in 1741, August 17, "frequent complaints having been made to the Board that many disorderly persons meet every ev'g about the Court house of this city, and great numbers of Negroes and others sit there with milk pails and other things late at night, and many disorders are there committed against the peace and good government of this city," Council ordered the place to be cleared "in half an hour after sunset."[7]

Of the graver crimes by Negroes we have only reports here and there which do not make it clear how frequently such crimes occurred. In 1706 a slave is arrested for setting fire to a dwelling; in 1738 three Negroes are hanged in neighboring parts of New Jersey for poisoning people, while at Rocky Hill a slave is burned alive for killing a child and burning a barn. Whipping of Negroes at the public whipping post was frequent, and so severe was the punishment that in 1743 a slave brought up to be whipped committed suicide. In 1762 two Philadelphia slaves were sentenced to death for felony and burglary; petitions were circulated in their behalf but Council was obdurate.[8]

Little special mention of Negro crime is again met with until the freedmen under the act of 1780 began to congregate in the city and other free immigrants joined them. In 1809 the leading colored churches united in a society to suppress crime and were cordially endorsed by the public for this action. After the war immigration to the city increased and the stress of hard times bore heavily on the lower classes. Complaints of petty thefts and murderous assaults on peaceable citizens now began to increase, and in numbers of cases they were traced to Negroes. The better class of colored citizens felt the accusation and held a meeting to denounce crime and take a firm stand against their own criminal class. A little later the Negro riots commenced, and they received their chief moral support from the increasing crime of Negroes; a Cuban slave brained his master with a hatchet, two other murders by Negroes followed, and gambling, drunkenness and debauchery were widespread wherever Negroes settled. The terribly vindictive insurrection of Nat Turner in a neighboring State frightened the citizens so thoroughly that when some black fugitives actually arrived at Chester from Southampton County, Virginia, the Legislature was hastily appealed to, and the whole matter came to a climax in the disfranchisement of the Negro in 1837, and the riots in the years 1830 to 1840.[9]

Some actual figures will give us an idea of this, the worst period of Negro crime ever experienced in the city. The Eastern Penitentiary was opened in 1829 near the close of the year. The total number of persons received here for the most serious crimes is given in the next table. This includes prisoners from the Eastern counties of the State, but a large proportion were from Philadelphia (see Table 1).[10]

Or to put it differently the problem of Negro crime in Philadelphia from 1830 to 1850 arose from the fact that less than one-fourteenth of the population was responsible for nearly a third of the serious crimes committed.

These figures however are apt to relate more especially to a criminal class. A better measure of the normal criminal tendencies of the group would perhaps be found in the statistics of Moyamensing, where ordinary cases of crime and misdemeanor are confined and which contains only county prisoners. The figures for Moyamensing prison are found in Table 2.

Here we have even a worse showing than before; in 1896 the Negroes forming 4 per cent of the population furnish 9 per cent of the arrests, but in 1850 being 5 per cent of the

TABLE 1

Years	*Total Commitments*	*Negroes*	*Per Cent of Negroes*	*Per Cent of Negroes of Total Population*
1829-34	339	99	29.0	8.27 (1830)
1835-39	878	356	40.5	7.39 (1840)
1840-44	701	209	29.8	7.39 (1840)
1845-49	633	151	23.8	4.83 (1850)
1850-54	664	106	16.0	4.83 (1850)

TABLE 2

Years	*Total White Prisoners Received*	*Total Negro Prisoners Received*	*Per Cent of Negroes of Total Prisoners*	*Per Cent of Negroes of Total Population*
1836-45	1164	1087	48.29	7.39 (1840)
1846-55	1478	696	32.01	4.83 (1850)
Total	2642	1783		

population they furnished 32 per cent of the prisoners received at the county prison. Of course there are some considerations which must not be overlooked in interpreting these figures for 1836-55. It must be remembered that the discrimination against the Negro was much greater then than now: he was arrested for less cause and given longer sentences than whites.[11] Great numbers of those arrested and committed for trial were never brought to trial so that their guilt could not be proven or disproven; of 737 Negroes committed for trial in six months of the year 1837, it is stated that only 123 were actually brought to trial; of the prisoners in the Eastern Penitentiary, 1829 to 1846, 14 per cent of the whites were pardoned and 2 per cent of the Negroes. All these considerations increase the statistics to the disfavor of the Negro.[12] Nevertheless making all reasonable allowances it is undoubtedly true that the crime of Negroes in this period reached its high tide for this city.

The character of the crimes committed by Negroes compared with whites is shown by the following table, which covers the offences of 1359 whites and 718 Negroes committed to the Eastern Penitentiary, 1829-1846. If we take simply petty larceny we find that 48.8 per cent of the whites, and 55 per cent of the Negroes were committed for this offence (Table 3).[13]

38. Negro Crime Since the War.—Throughout the land there has been since the war a large increase in crime, especially in cities. This phenomenon would seem to have sufficient cause in the increased complexity of life, in industrial competition, and the rush of great numbers to the large cities. It would therefore be natural to suppose that the Negro would also show this increase in criminality and, as in the case of all lower classes, that he would show it in greater degree. His evolution has, however, been marked by some peculiarities. For nearly two decades after emancipation he took little part in many of the great social movements about him for obvious reasons. His migration to city life, therefore, and his sharing in the competition of modern industrial life, came later than was the case with the mass of his fellow citizens. The Negro began to rush to the cities in large numbers after 1880 and consequently the phenomena attendant on that momentous change of life are tardier in his case. His rate of criminality has in the last two decades risen rapidly, and this is a parallel phenome-

TABLE 3

	Whites		Negroes	
Kinds of Crime	*Number*	*Per Cent*	*Number*	*Per Cent*
Offences *vs.* the person	166	11.4	89	12.4
Offences *vs.* property with violence	191	13.1	165	22.9
Offences *vs.* property without violence	873	59.8	432	60.2
Malicious offences *vs.* property	22	1.5	14	2.0
Offences *vs.* Currency and forgery	167	11.5	7	1.0
Miscellaneous	40	27.0	11	1.5
All offences	1359	100	718	100

non to the rapid rise of the white criminal record two or three decades ago. Moreover, in the case of the Negro there were special causes for the prevalence of crime: he had lately been freed from serfdom, he was the object of stinging oppression and ridicule, and paths of advancement open to many were closed to him. Consequently the class of the shiftless, aimless, idle, discouraged and disappointed was proportionately larger.

In the city of Philadelphia the increasing number of bold and daring crimes committed by Negroes in the last ten years has focused the attention of the city on this subject. There is a widespread feeling that something is wrong with a race that is responsible for so much crime, and that strong remedies are called for. One has but to visit the corridors of the public buildings, when the courts are in session, to realize the part played in lawbreaking by the Negro population. The various slum centres of the colored criminal population have lately been the objects of much philanthropic effort, and the work there has aroused discussion. Judges on the bench have discussed the matter. Indeed, to the minds of many, this is the real Negro problem.[14]

That it is a vast problem a glance at statistics will show;[15] and since 1880 it has been steadily growing. At the same time crime is a difficult subject to study, more difficult to analyze into its sociological elements, and most difficult to cure or suppress. It is a phenomenon that stands not alone, but rather as a symptom of countless wrong social conditions.

The simplest, but crudest, measure of crime is found in the total arrests for a period of years. The value of such figures is lessened by the varying efficiency and diligence of the police, by discrimination in the administration of law, and by unwarranted arrests. And yet the figures roughly measure crime. The total arrests and the number of Negroes is given in the next table for thirty-two years, with a few omissions (see Table 4).

We find that the total arrests in the city per annum have risen from 34,221 in 1864 to 61,478 in 1894, an increase of 80 per cent in crime, parallel to an increase of 85 per cent in population. The Negroes arrested have increased from 3114 in 1864 to 4805 in 1894, an increase of 54 per cent in crime, parallel to an increase of 77 per cent in the Negro population of the city. So, too, the percentage of Negroes in the total arrests is less in 1894 than in 1864. If, however, we follow the years between these two dates we see an important development: 1864 was the date bounding the ante-bellum period of crime; thereafter the proportion of Negro arrests fell steadily until, in 1874, the Negroes came as nearly as ever furnishing their normal quota of arrests, 3.9 per cent from 3.28 per cent (1870) of the population. Then slowly there came a change. With the Centennial Exposition in 1876 came

TABLE 4 Arrests in Philadelphia, 1864-96

Date	*Total Number Arrested*	*Total Negroes Arrested*	*Percentage of Negroes*
1864	34,221	3,114	9.1
1865	43,226	2,722	6.3
1869	38,749	2,907	7.5
1870	31,717	2,070	6.5
1873	30,400	1,380	4.5
1874	32,114	1,257	3.9
1875	34,553	1,539	4.5
1876	—	—	—
1877	44,220	2,524	5.7
1879	40,714	2,360	5.8
1880	44,097	2,204	4.98
1881	45,129	2,327	5.11
1882	46,130	2,183	4.73
1883	45,295	2,022	4.46
1884	49,468	2,134	4.31
1885	51,418	2,662	5.11
1886	—	—	—
1887	57,951	3,256	5.61
1888	46,899	2,910	6.20
1889	42,673	2,614	6.10
1890	49,148	3,167	6.44
1891	53,184	3,544	6.66
1892	52,944	3,431	6.48
1892	52,944	3,431	6.48
1893	57,297	4,078	7.11
1894	61,478	4,805	7.81
1895	60,347	5,137	8.5
1896	58,072	5,302	9.1

a stream of immigrants, and once started the stream increased in speed by its own momentum. With this immigration the proportion of Negro arrests arose rapidly at first as a result of the exposition; falling off a little in the early eighties, but with 7885 rising again steadily and quickly to over 6 per cent in 1888, 6.4 per cent in 1890, 7 per cent in 1893, 8.5 per cent in 1895, 9 per cent in 1896. This is, as has been said before, but a rough indication of the amount of crime for which the Negro is responsible; it must not be relied on too closely, for the number of arrests cannot in any city accurately measure wrongdoing save in a very general way; probably increased efficiency in the police force since 1864 has had large effect; and yet we can draw the legitimate conclusion here that Negro crime in the city is far less, according to population, than before the war; that after the war it decreased until the middle of the seventies and then, coincident with the beginning of the new Negro immigration to cities,[16] it has risen pretty steadily.

These same phenomena can be partially verified by statistics of Moyamensing prison. If we take the tried and untried prisoners committed to this county prison from 1876 to 1895 we find the same gradual increase of crime (see Table 5).

TABLE 5 Moyamensing Prison: Both Tried and Untried Prisoners

Date	*Total Receptions*	*Negroes*	*Per Cent of Negroes*
1876	21,736	1,530	7.8
1877	22,736	1,460	6.44
1878	22,147	1,356	6.12
1879	20,736	1,136	5.48
1880	22,487	1,030	4.58
1881	22,478	1,168	5.19
1882	24,176	1,274	5.27
1883	23,245	1,175	5.05
1884	25,081	1,218	4.86
1885	24,725	1,427	5.77
1886	27,286	1,708	6.26
1887	28,964	1,724	5.97
1888	21,399	1,399	6.54
1889	18,476	1,338	7.24
1890	20,582	1,611	7.83
1891	22,745	1,723	7.57
1892	22,460	1,900	8.46
1893	25,209	2,234	8.86
1894	25,777	2,452	9.51
1895	22,584	2,317	10.26
Total	464,959	31,180	6.70
1976-1885	229,477	12,774	5.57
1886-1895	235,482	18,406	7.81

TABLE 6

Year	*Total Receptions*	*Negroes*	*Per Cent of Negroes*
1891	5907	274	4.6
1892	5297	254	4.8
1893	—	—	—
1894	6579	1055	16.0
1895	7548	672	8.9

If we compare in this table the period 1876-85 with that of 1886-95 we find that the proportion of Negro criminals in the first period was 5.6 per cent, in the second 7.8 per cent.

The statistics of inmates of the House of Correction, where mild cases and juveniles are sent, for the last few years go to tell the same tale (see Table 6).

Gathering up the statistics presented let us make a rough diagram of some of the results. First let us scan the record of the Negro in serious crime, such as entails incarceration in the Eastern Penitentiary. In these figures the Philadelphia convicts are not separated from those in the eastern counties of the state prior to 1885. A large proportion of the prisoners however are from Philadelphia; perhaps the net result of the error is somewhat to reduce

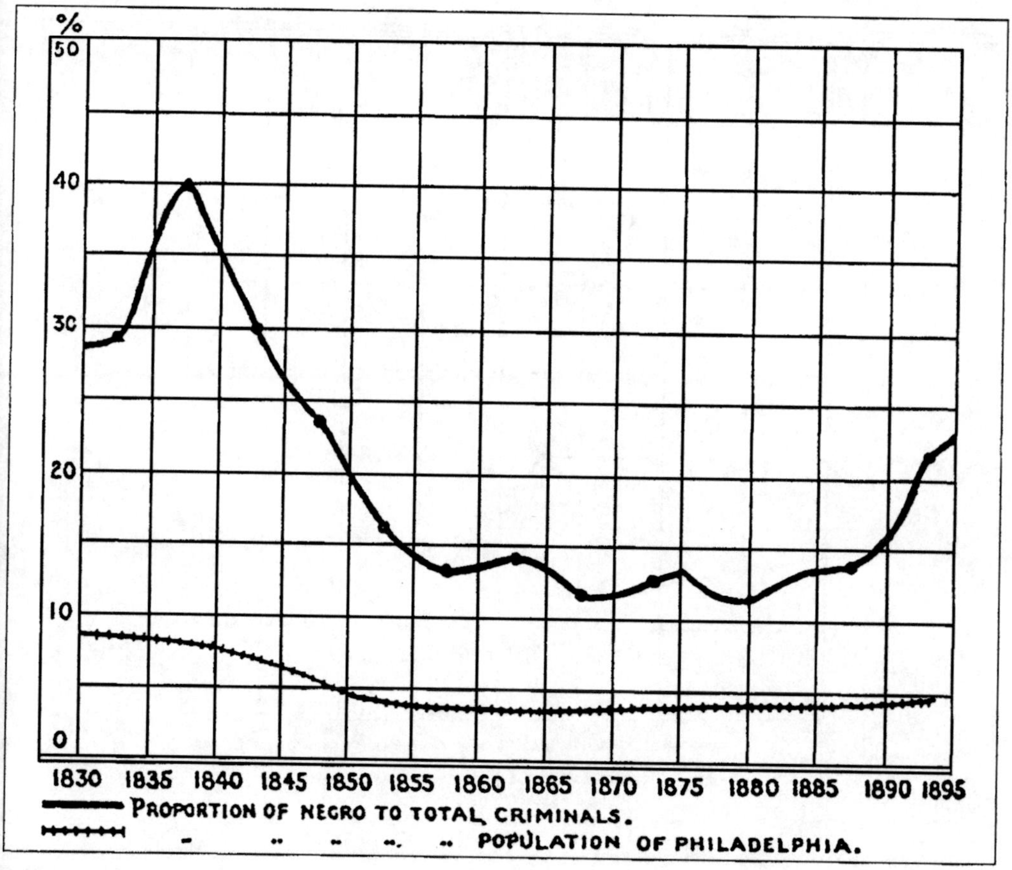

Figure 1 Proportion of Negroes to Total Convicts Received at the Eastern Penitentiary, 1829-1895

the apparent proportion of Negroes in the earlier years. Taking then the proportion of Negro prisoners received to total receptions since the founding of the Penitentiary we have the diagram in Figure 1.

The general rate of criminality may be graphically represented from the proportion of Negroes in the county prison, although changes in the policy of the courts make the validity of this somewhat uncertain (see Figure 2).

It thus seems certain[17] that general criminality as represented by commitments to the county prison has decreased markedly since 1874, and that its rapid increase since 1880 leaves it still far behind the decade 1830 to 1840. Serious crime as represented by commitments to the penitentiary shows a similar decrease but one not so marked indicating the presence of a pretty distinct criminal class (see Table 7).

The record of arrests per 1000 of Negro population 1864 to 1896 seems to confirm these conclusions for that period (see Figure 3).

The increase in crime between 1890 and 1895 is not without pretty adequate explanation in the large Negro immigration cityward and especially in "the terrible business depression of 1893" to which the police bureau attributes the increase of arrests. The effect of this would naturally be greater among the economic substrata.

This brings us to the question, Who are the Negro criminals and what crimes do they commit? To obtain an answer to this query let us make a special study of a typical group of criminals.

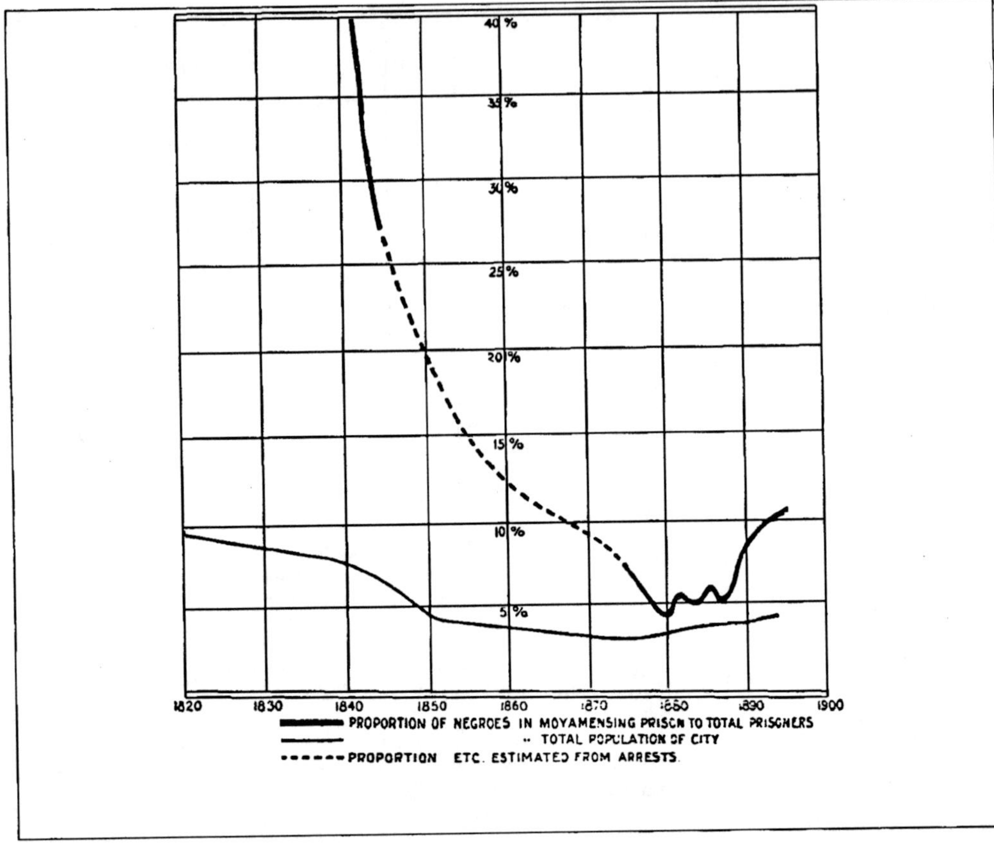

Figure 2

TABLE 7 Convicts Committed to the Eastern Penitentiary

Years	*Total Commitments*	*Negroes*	*Per Cent of Negroes*
1835-39	878	356	40.5
1855-59	941	126	13.4
1860-64	909	129	14.2
1865-69	1474	179	12.1
1870-74	1291	174	13.4
1875-79	2347	275	11.7
1880-84	2282	308	13.5
1885-89*	1583	223	14.09
1890-95*	1418	318	22.43

* Only convicts from Philadelphia; the statistics for the year 1891 are not available and are omitted.

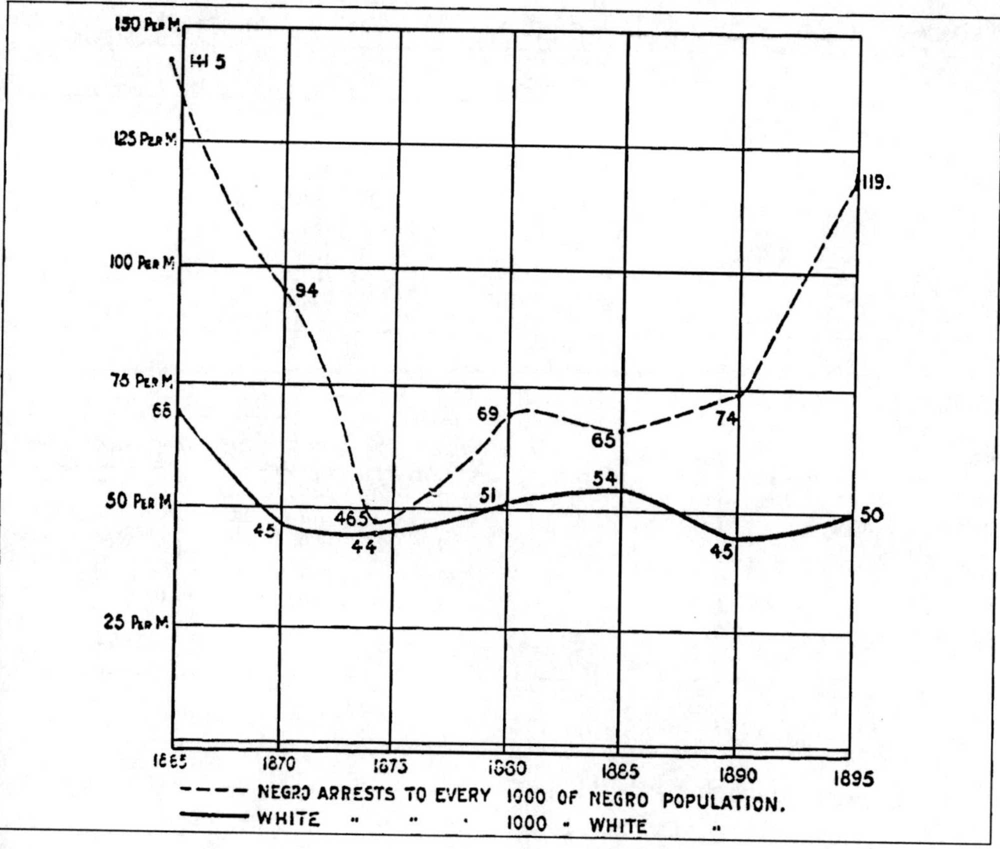

Figure 3

TABLE 8 Philadelphia Whites and Negroes Committed to the Eastern Penitentiary

Date	*Total Commitments*	*Negroes*	*Per Cent of Negroes*	
1885	313	40	12.78	
1886	347	45	12.97	
1887	363	53	14.60	14.9
1888	269	39	14.49	
1889	291	46	15.81	
1890	271	63	23.25	
1891*	—	—	—	
1892	213	42	19.71	
1893	320	74	23.13	22.43
1894	329	69	20.97	
1895	285	70	24.56	
Total	3,001	541	18.2 average	

* Statistics for this year were not available. Throughout this section, therefore, this year is omitted.

TABLE 9

Crime	
Theft	243
Serious assaults on persons	139
Robbery and burglary	85
Rape	24
Other sexual crime	23
Homicide	16
All other crime	11
Total	541

TABLE 10

Crime	*1885*	*1886*	*1887*	*1888*	*1889*	*1890*	*1892*	*1893*	*1894*	*1895*	*Total*
Theft, etc.	20	21	23	13	24	39	20	32	23	28	243
Robbery and burglary	2	8	8	5	5	9	7	14	19	8	85
Serious assaults	10	9	11	15	9	12	9	19	18	27	139
Homicide	—	—	3	2	5	—	2	1	1	2	16
Sexual crimes	6	7	7	4	4	4	4	5	3	3	47
All others	2	—	1	1	—	—	—	2	3	2	11
Total	40	45	53	40	47	64	42	73	67	70	541

39. A Special Study in Crime.[18]—During ten years previous to and including 1895, there were committed to the Eastern Penitentiary, the following prisoners from the city of Philadelphia, indicated in Table 8.

Let us now take the 541 Negroes who have been the perpetrators of the serious crimes charged to their race during the last ten years and see what we may learn. These are all criminals convicted after trial for periods varying from six months to forty years. It seems plain in the first place that the 4 per cent of the population of Philadelphia having Negro blood furnished from 1885 to 1889, 14 per cent of the serious crimes, and from 1890 to 1895, 22½ per cent. This of course assumes that the convicts in the penitentiary represent with a fair degree of accuracy the crime committed. The assumption is not wholly true; in convictions by human courts the rich always are favored somewhat at the expense of the poor, the upper classes at the expense of the unfortunate classes, and whites at the expense of Negroes. We know for instance that certain crimes are not punished in Philadelphia because the public opinion is lenient, as for instance embezzlement, forgery, and certain sorts of stealing; on the other hand a commercial community is apt to punish with severity petty thieving, breaches of the peace, and personal assault or burglary. It happens, too, that the prevailing weakness of ex-slaves brought up in the communal life of the slave plantation, without acquaintanceship with the institution of private property, is to commit the very crimes which a great centre of commerce like Philadelphia especially abhors. We must add to this the influences of social position and connections in procuring whites' pardons or lighter sentences. It has been charged by some Negroes that color prejudice plays some part, but there is no tangible proof of this, save perhaps that there is apt to be a certain presumption of guilt when a Negro is accused, on the part of police, public and judge.[19] All these considerations modify somewhat our judgment of the moral status of the mass of Negroes. And yet, with all allowances, there remains a vast problem of crime.

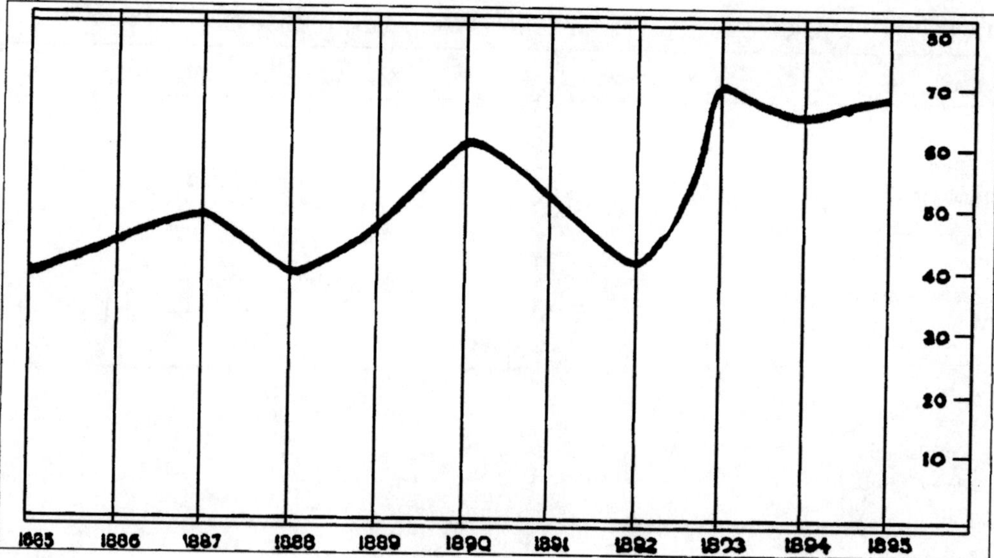

Figure 4

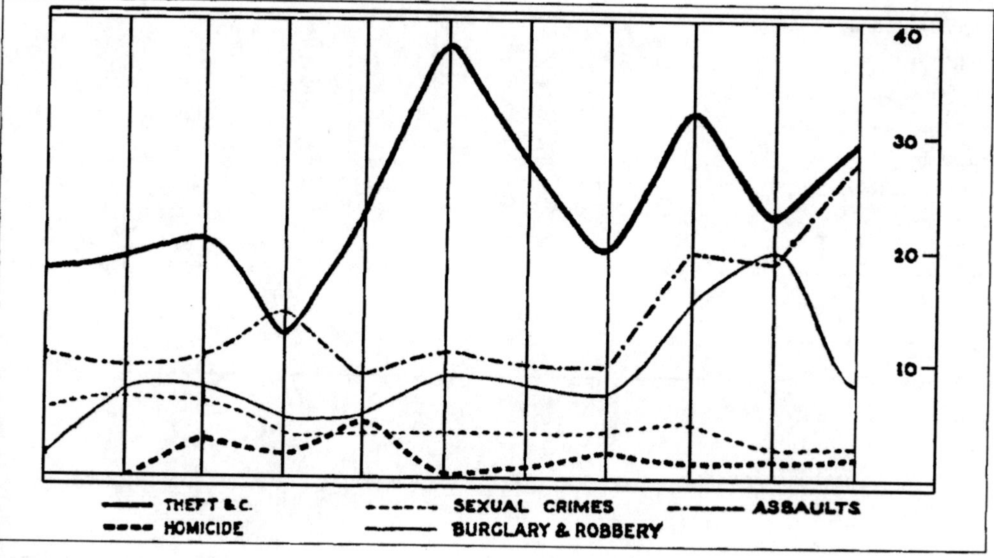

Figure 5

The chief crimes for which these prisoners were convicted are noted in Table 9. Following these crimes from year to year we have the results documented in Table 10.

The course of the total serious crime for this period may be illustrated by the diagram shown in Figure 4. Drawing a similar diagram for the different sorts of crime we have the graph shown in Figure 5.

In ten years convictions to the penitentiary for theft have somewhat increased, robbery, burglary and assault have considerably increased, homicide has remained about the same, and sexual crimes have decreased. De-

TABLE 11 Crimes of 541 Convicts in Eastern Penitentiary, 1885-1895

Crimes	*1885*	*1886*	*1887*	*1888*	*1889*	*1890*	*1892*	*1893*	*1894*	*1895*
Assault and battery	3	—	1	2	—	1	—	—	—	—
Aggravated assault and battery	3	3	3	7	3	6	3	6	6	9
Assault to kill	4	6	7	6	6	5	4	13	11	17
Manslaughter	—	—	—	1	3	—	1	1	—	1
Murder	—	—	3	1	2	—	1	—	1	1
Assault to murder	—	—	1	—	—	—	—	—	—	—
Assault to steal	—	—	—	—	—	—	2	—	1	1
Larceny	20	21	23	13	24	39	17	27	22	28
Robbery	2	3	3	1	—	4	3	5	9	6
Burglary	—	5	5	4	5	5	4	9	10	2
Embezzlement	—	—	—	—	—	—	—	1	—	—
Sodomy	2	1	1	3	2	3	2	—	—	1
Abortion	1	—	—	—	—	—	1	—	—	—
Rape	1	—	—	—	—	—	—	2	1	—
Attempt to rape	1	6	1	1	1	1	1	3	2	1
Incest	1	—	—	—	—	—	—	—	—	—
Keeping bawdy house	—	—	4	—	—	—	—	—	—	1
Enticing female child	—	—	1	—	1	—	—	—	—	—
Carrying concealed weapons	1	—	—	—	—	—	—	1	—	—
Forgery	1	—	—	—	—	—	—	—	1	1
False pretence	—	—	—	1	—	—	1	—	1	—
Receiving stolen goods	—	—	—	—	—	—	2	4	1	—
Mayhem	—	—	—	—	—	—	—	1	—	—
Indecent exposure	—	—	—	—	—	—	—	—	—	1
Conspiracy	—	—	—	—	—	—	—	—	1	—
Total	40	45	53	40	47	64	42	73	67	70

TABLE 12

Crimes against property	328	60.63 per cent
Crimes against persons	157	29.02 per cent
Crimes against persons and property	8	1.48 per cent
Sexual crimes	48	8.87 per cent
	541	100 per cent

tailed statistics are given in Table 11. The total crime can be classified also as indicated in Table 12.

Let us now turn from the crime to the criminals. 497 of them (91.87 per cent) were males and 44 (8.13 per cent) were females. 296 (54.71 per cent) were single, 208 (34.45 per cent) were married, and 37 (6.84 per cent) were widowed. In age they were divided as shown in Table 13.

The mass of criminals are, it is easy to see, young single men under thirty. Detailed

TABLE 13

Age	*Number*	*Percentage*	
15-19	58	10.73	66.92
20-24	170	56.19	
25-29	132		
30-39	132	24.03	34.08
40-49	34	6.29	
50-59	10	1.85	
60 and over	5	.91	
Total	541	100	

TABLE 14 Age and Sex of Convicts in Eastern Penitentiary Negroes, 1885-1895

Ages	*Males*	*Females*	*Totals*
15-19	53	5	58
20-24	153	17	170
25-29	119	13	132
30-34	80	5	85
35-39	45	2	47
40-44	21	1	22
45-49	11	1	12
50-59	3	—	3
60 and over	15	—	15
Total	497	44	541

TABLE 15 Conjugal Condition of Convicts in Eastern Peniitentiary

	Males			*Females*		
Age	*Single*	*Married*	*Widowed*	*Single*	*Married*	*Widowed*
15-19	48	5	0	4	1	0
20-24	117	35	0	7	9	1
25-29	59	54	8	3	10	0
30-34	30	38	6	0	4	1
35-39	11	30	4	0	0	2
40-49	8	16	8	0	2	0
50-59	3	3	4	0	0	0
60 and over	0	2	3	0	0	0

TABLE 16

Philadelphia	114	New York	11
Other parts of Pennsylvania	48	South Carolina	9
New Jersey	21	Georgia	8
Maryland	99	Other parts of the North	13
Virginia	77	Other parts of the South	22
Delaware	37	The West	13
District of Columbia	35	Foreign countries	15
North Carolina	19		541

TABLE 17 Illiteracy of Convicts in the Eastern State Penitentiary

	Read and Write		*Read and Write Imperfectly*		*Totally Illiterate*	
Year	*Number*	*Per Cent*	*Number*	*Per Cent*	*Number*	*Per Cent*
1885	20	50.0	6	15.0	14	35.0
1886	25	55.55	4	8.88	16	35.55
1887	27	50.94	13	24.53	13	24.53
1888	25	64.10	6	15.38	8	20.51
1889	26	56.52	10	21.74	10	21.74
1890	43	68.25	3	4.76	17	21.43
1892	33	78.57	0	0	9	21.43
1893	55	74.32	0	0	19	25.68
1894	49	71.01	0	0	20	28.99
1895	55	78.57	0	0	15	21.43
Total	358	66.17	42	7.76	141	26.06

statistics of sex and age and conjugal condition are given in the next tables (Tables 14 and 15).

The convicts were born in the states listed in Table 16.

Altogether 21 per cent were natives of Philadelphia; 217 were born in the North, and 309, or 57 per cent, were born in the South. Two-thirds of the Negroes of the city, judging from the Seventh Ward, were born outside the city, and this part furnishes 79 per cent of the serious crime; 54 per cent were born in the South, and this part furnishes 57 per cent of the crime, or more, since many giving their birthplace as in the North were really born in the South.

The total illiteracy of this group reaches 26 per cent or adding in those who can read and write imperfectly, 34 per cent compared with 18 per cent for the Negroes of the city in 1890. In other words the illiterate fifth of the Negro population furnished a third of the worst criminals (Table 17).

Naturally as the general intelligence of a community increases the general intelligence of its criminals increases, though seldom in the same proportion, showing that some crime may justly be attributed to pure ignorance. The number of criminals able to read and write has increased from 50 per cent in 1885 to 79 per cent in 1895. The number of colored men from fifteen to thirty who can read and write was about 90 per cent in the Seventh Ward in 1896. This shows how little increased intelligence alone avails to stop crime in the face of other powerful forces. It would of course be illogical to connect these phenomena directly as cause and effect and make Negro crime the result of Negro education—in that case we should find it difficult to defend the public schools in most modern lands. Crime comes either in spite of intelligence or as a result of misdirected intelligence under severe economic and moral strain. Thus we find here, as is apparently true in France, Italy and Germany, increasing crime and decreasing illiteracy as concurrent phenomena rather than as cause and effect. However the rapid increase of intelligence in Negro convicts does point to some grave social changes: first, a large number of young Negroes are in such environment that they find it easier to be rogues than honest men; secondly, there is evidence of the rise of more intelligent and therefore more dangerous crime from a trained criminal class, quite different from the thoughtless, ignorant crime of the mass of Negroes.

TABLE 18 Criminals in Eastern State Penitentiary—Females, by Age and Crime

	Crimes							
Ages	*Larceny*	*Assault and Battery*	*Aggravated Assault*	*Assault to Kill*	*Murder*	*Bawdy and Disorderly Houses*	*Accessory to Murder*	*Abduction*
15-19	5	—	—	—	—	—	—	—
20-24	10	1	3	2	1	—	—	—
25-29	11	—	1	—	—	1	—	—
30-34	3	—	—	—	—	—	1	1
35-39	1	—	—	—	—	1	—	—
40-44	1	—	—	—	—	—	—	—
45-49	1	—	—	—	—	—	—	—

TABLE 19

Whole number of male convicts, 15-19 years of age	53
Convicted for larceny	27
Convicted for assault and fighting	8
Convicted for sexual crimes	5
Convicted for burglary	5
Convicted for other crimes	8
	53

TABLE 20

Men, 22-24 Years		*Men, 25-29 Years*	
Larceny	62	Larceny	45
Assault	41	Assault	33
Burglary and robbery	30	Burglary and robbery	22
Sexual crimes	6	Sexual crimes	13
Other crimes	14	Homicide	4
		Other crimes	3
	153		119

A separation of criminals according to sex and age and the kind of crime is of interest (Table 18). (See p. 256 for males.)

The women are nearly all committed for stealing and fighting. They are generally prostitutes from the worst slums. The boys of fifteen to nineteen are sentenced largely for petty thieving (Table 19).

Making a similar table for two other age periods we have the data given in Tables 20 and 21.

TABLE 21 Criminals in Eastern State Penitentiary—Males, by Age and Crime

	Crimes																							
Ages	*Larceny*	*Assault & Battery*	*Receiving Stolen Goods*	*Assault to Steal*	*Concealed Weapons*	*Aggravated Assault & Battery*	*Assault to Kill*	*Burglary*	*Robbery*	*Sodomy*	*Assault to Rape*	*Rape*	*Manslaughter*	*Forgery*	*Murder*	*Conspiracy*	*False Pretense*	*Embezzlement*	*Mayhem*	*Bawdy houses*	*Enticement to Rape*	*Indecent Exposure*	*Incest*	*Abortion*
15-19	27	1	2	1	1	2	4	5	—	1	3	1	1	1	3	—	—	—	—	—	—	—	—	—
20-24	62	4	2	1	1	16	24	14	16	4	1	1	1	—	1	1	2	1	1	—	—	—	—	—
25-29	45	1	1	2	—	9	22	12	10	3	3	4	1	—	3	—	—	—	—	1	2	—	—	—
30-34	23	1	1	—	—	6	17	12	9	3	2	—	1	1	2	—	—	—	—	1	—	1	—	—
35-39	23	—	1	—	—	6	3	3	—	—	4	—	1	1	—	—	1	—	—	1	—	—	1	—
40-44	9	—	—	—	—	4	2	1	1	—	2	—	1	—	—	—	—	—	—	—	—	—	—	1
45-49	3	—	—	—	—	2	2	1	—	1	1	—	1	—	—	—	—	—	—	—	—	—	—	—
50-59	2	—	—	—	1	—	1	2	1	3	—	—	—	—	—	—	—	—	—	—	—	—	—	—
60 and over	3	—	—	—	—	—	1	—	—		—	—	—	—	—	—	—	—	—	—	—	—	—	1
Total	197	7	7	4	3	45	76	50	37	15	16	6	7	3	9	1	3	1	1	3	2	1	1	2

TABLE 22

Twice	105	46.5 per cent
Three times	60	26.5 per cent
Four times	24	11.0 per cent
Five times	19	8.0 per cent
Six times	9	4.0 per cent
Seven times	4	1.8 per cent
Nine times	1	2.2 per cent
Ten times	1	2.2 per cent
Eleven times	2	2.2 per cent
Twelve times	1	2.2 per cent
	226	100 per cent

There is here revealed no especial peculiarity: stealing and fighting are ever the besetting sins of half-developed races.

It would be very instructive to know how many of the 541 criminals had been in the hands of the law before. This is however very difficult to ascertain correctly since in many, if not the majority of cases, the word of the prisoner must be taken. Even these methods however reveal the startling fact that only 315 or 58 per cent of these 541 convicts are reported as being incarcerated for the first time. 226 or 42 per cent can be classed as habitual criminals, who have been convicted as listed in Table 22.

When we realize that probably a large number of the other convicts are on their second or third term we begin to get an idea of the real Negro criminal class.[20]

A few other facts are of interest: if we tabulate crime according to the illiteracy of its perpetrators, we have Table 23.

Or in other words, the more serious and revolting the crime the larger part does ignorance play as a cause. If we separate prisoners convicted for the above crimes according to length of sentence, we have Table 24.

Of the 49 sentenced for 5 years and over, 18 or 37 percent were illiterate; of those sentenced for less than 5 years 160 or 35 per cent were illiterate.

TABLE 23

Larceny	31 per cent of illiteracy
Assault, burglary and homicide	34 per cent of illiteracy
Sexual crimes	55 per cent of illiteracy

TABLE 24

Under five years	464	90.5 per cent
Five and under ten years	40	8.0 per cent
Ten years and over	9	1.5 per cent
	513	

From this study we may conclude that young men are the perpetrators of the serious crime among Negroes; that this crime consists mainly of stealing and assault; that ignorance, and immigration to the temptations of city life, are responsible for much of this crime but not for all; that deep social causes underlie this prevalence of crime and they have so worked as to form among Negroes since 1864 a distinct class of habitual criminals; that to this criminal class and not to the great mass of Negroes the bulk of the serious crime perpetrated by this race should be charged.

40. Some Cases of Crime.—It is difficult while studying crime in the abstract to realize just what the actual crimes committed are, and under what circumstances they take place. A few typical cases of the crimes of Negroes may serve to give a more vivid idea than the abstract statistics give. Most of these cases are quoted from the daily newspapers.

First let us take a couple of cases of larceny:

Edward Ashbridge, a colored boy, pleaded guilty to the larceny of a quart of milk, the property of George Abbott. The boy's mother said he was incorrigible, and he was committed to the House of Refuge.

William Drumgoole, colored, aged thirty-one years, of Lawrenceville, Va., was shot in the back and probably fatally wounded late yesterday afternoon by William H. McCalley, a detective, employed in the store of John Wanamaker, Thirteenth and Chestnut streets. Drumgoole, it is alleged, stole a pair of shoes from the store, and was followed by McCalley to the corner of Thirteenth and Chestnut streets, where he placed him under arrest. Drumgoole broke away from the detective's grasp, and running down Thirteenth street turned into Drury street, a small thoroughfare above Sansom street. McCalley started in pursuit, calling upon him to stop, but the fugitive darted into an alleyway, and when his pursuer came up within a few yards of him, he threatened to "do him up" if he followed him any further. McCalley drew his revolver from his pocket, and as Drumgoole again broke into a run he pointed the weapon at his legs and fired. Drumgoole fell to the ground, and when McCalley came up to him he was unable to rise. McCalley saw at a glance that, instead of wounding him in the leg, as he had intended, the bullet had lodged in the man's back. He hurriedly sought assistance, and had the wounded man taken to the Jefferson Hospital. McCalley then surrendered himself to Reserve Policeman Powell, and was taken to the Central Station.

Fighting and quarreling among neighbors and associates is common in the slum districts:

Etta Jones, colored, aged twenty-one years, residing on Hirst street, above Fifth, was stabbed near her home last night, it is alleged, by Lottie Lee, also colored, of Second and Race streets. The other woman was taken to the Pennsylvania Hospital, where her injuries were found to consist of several cuts on the left shoulder and side, none of which are dangerous. Her assailant was arrested later by Policeman Dean and locked up in the Third and Union streets station house. The assault is said by the police to have been the outcome of an old grudge.

Joseph Cole, colored, aged twenty-four years, residing in Gillis' alley, was dangerously stabbed shortly before midnight on Saturday, as is alleged, by Abraham Wheeler, at the latter's house, on Hirst street. Cole was taken to the Pennsylvania Hospital, where it was found the knife had penetrated to within a short distance of the right lung. Wheeler fled from the house after the cutting and eluded arrest until yesterday afternoon, when he was captured by Policeman Mitchell, near Fifth and Lombard streets. When brought to the station house Wheeler denied having cut Cole, but acknowledged having struck him because he was insulting his wife. He was locked up, however, to await the result of Cole's injuries.

Sometimes servants are caught pilfering:

Theodore Grant, colored, residing on Burton street, attempted to pledge a woman's silk dress for $15 at McFillen's Seventeenth and Market streets, several days ago. The pawnbroker refused, under his rule, to take women's raiment from a man, and told Grant to bring the owner. Grant went away and returned with Ella Jones, a young colored woman, who consented to take $7 for the dress. Since that time C. F. Robertson, residing at Sixtieth and Spruce streets, made complaint to the police of the loss of the dress, and as the result of an investigation made by Special Policemen Gallagher and Ewing, Grant and Ella Jones were arrested yesterday charged with the larceny of the silk dress, which was recovered. Grant admitted to the special policemen that Ella had given him the dress to pawn, but asserted that he had nothing to do with the matter except to offer to pledge the article. At a hearing before Magistrate Jermon, at the City Hall, yesterday, Mr. Robertson stated that the girl had made a statement to him, saying that Grant had induced her to take the dress. He said the girl had been perfectly trustworthy up to the time of her acquaintance with Grant, and had been left in full charge of the house, and that nothing was ever missed. He said he also expected to show that Grant had been concerned in two or three robberies. Ella Jones, a neatly dressed girl, who said she came from Maryland, stated to the magistrate that Grant had been coming to see her for about a year past. She said he had been importuning her to take something and let him pawn it, so that he could raise some money, until she finally consented. After she started to go to her mistress' room to get the dress her heart failed and she turned back, but he persuaded her, telling her that Mrs. Robertson would not miss it, and then she took the dress. Mr. Robertson informed the magistrate, and Ella assented to the statement, that Grant had taken every cent of her earnings from her for weeks past and had also pawned all of her clothing, so that at the present time she was penniless and had not a single garment except what she wore. The magistrate said it was undoubtedly a hard case, but he would have to hold Grant and Ella on the charge of larceny, and Grant under additional bail for a further hearing next Thursday on the charges referred to by Mr. Robertson. The police say that Grant, who is a smooth-faced, cross-eyed mulatto, is a "crap fiend," and that whatever money he has managed to obtain by threats and cajolery from his victim, Ella Jones, has gone into the pockets of the small-fry gamblers.

There is growing evidence of the appearance of a set of thieves of intelligence and cunning: sneak thieves, confidence-men, pickpockets, and "sharpers." Some typical cases follow:

Marion Shields and Alice Hoffman, both colored and residing on Fitzwater street, above Twelfth, had a further hearing yesterday before Magistrate South, at the City Hall, and were held for trial on the charge of pilfering wearing apparel, money, vases, umbrellas, surgical instruments, and other portable property from physicians' offices and houses, where they had made visits, under the pretence of desiring to hold consultations with the doctors. The Magistrate said there were ten cases against Marion Shields individually on which she would be placed under $2500 bail, and six cases against both women on which the bail would be $1500. For her frankness, Marion Shields was given the lighter sentence, one year in the Eastern Penitentiary, and Alice Hoffman was sentenced to eighteen months in the same institution.

Two daring thieves yesterday entered the jewelry store of Albert Baudschopfs', 468½ North Eighth street, and secured a number of articles of jewelry from under the very eyes of the proprietor. They had left the store and proceeded leisurely down the street before the jeweller discovered his loss, with the result that before an alarm could be given the thieves had traveled a considerable distance. One of the men was captured after a long chase, but the other's whereabouts is unknown. About half-past one o'clock two colored men entered the store and upon their request were shown trays of various articles. One of the men engaged the proprietor in conversation while the other continued to inspect the jewelry. They said they did not intend buying then and would call again and opening the door walked hurriedly down the street. Mr. Baudschopfs says the men got away with a gold-filled watch case, a silver watch, three gold lockets, each set with a small diamond; two dozen ladies' gold rings, not jewelled; a gold scarf pin and a man's gold watch.

A crime for which Negroes of a certain class have become notorious is that of snatching pocketbooks on the streets:

While passing down Eleventh street, near Mount Vernon, shortly after nine o'clock, Mrs. K. Nichun, of 1947 Warnock street, was approached from behind by a Negro, who snatched a pocketbook containing $2 from her hand and ran down a small thoroughfare towards Tenth street. Very few pedestrians were upon the street at the time, but two men, who were attracted by the woman's scream, started in pursuit of the thief. The latter had too much of a start, however, and escaped.

William Williams, colored, of Dayton, O., was locked up in the Central Station yesterday, by Reserve Policeman A. Jones, on the charge of snatching a pocketbook from the hands of Mrs. Diary Tevis, of 14, Mifflin street. The theft occurred at Eighth and Market streets. After securing the pocketbook Williams ran until he reached the old office of the city solicitor, at Sixth and Locust streets. He was followed by Reserve Jones, who captured him in the cellar of the building. Williams was taken to Eighth and Sansom streets to await the arrival of the patrol wagon, and while getting into the vehicle the pocketbook dropped from out of his trousers.

Detectives Bond and O'Leary and Special Policeman Duffy, of the Eighth and Lombard streets station, arrested last night Sylvester Archer, of Fifth street, below Lombard, William Whittington, alias "Piggy," of Florida street, and William Carter, of South Fifteenth street, all colored and about twenty-one years of age, on the charge of assault upon and robbery of Mrs. Harrington Fitzgerald, wife of the editor of the *Evening Item.* The assault occurred on Monday at noon. As Mrs. Fitzgerald was passing Thirteenth and Spruce streets, a purse which she carried in her hand, and which contained $20, was snatched from her by one of three colored men. They took advantage of the crowd to strike her after the robbery had been perpetrated and escaped before her outcry was heard. When the men were brought to the Central Station last night and questioned by Captain of Detectives Miller, Whittington, it is said, confessed complicity in the crime. He told the captain that they had been following a band up Thirteenth street, and as they reached Spruce street Carter said, "There's a pocketbook; I'm going to get it." "All right; get it," came the response. Carter ran up to Mrs. Fitzgerald and in a moment shouted, "I've got it!" Then he and Archer ran up Thirteenth street. Each man has a criminal record, and the picture of each is in the Rogues' Gallery. Carter has just completed a six months' sentence for purse-snatching, while Williams and Archer have each served time for larceny.

So frequent have these crimes become that sometimes Negroes are wrongfully suspected; whoever snatches a pocketbook on a dark night is supposed to be black.

A favorite method of stealing is to waylay and rob the frequenters of bawdy houses; very little of this sort of crime, naturally, is reported. Here are some cases of such "badger thieves," as they are called:

William Lee, colored, and Kate Hughes, a white woman, were convicted of robbing Vincenzo Monacello of $10. Lee was sentenced to three years and three months in the Eastern Penitentiary and his accomplice to three years in the county prison. Mary Roach, jointly indicted with them, was acquitted. Monacello testified that, while walking along Christian street between Eighth and Ninth streets, on Thursday night of last week, he was accosted by Mary Roach and accompanied her to her home on Essex street. Here he met Lee and Kate Hughes and they all drank considerable beer. Later in the night he started with Kate Hughes, at her suggestion, to a house further up the street. While on their way the prosecutor said he was struck in the face with a brick by Lee, after which the money was stolen from him. Mary Roach took the stand against the other two defendants and the case against her was abandoned.

Ella Jones, colored, claiming to be from Baltimore, was arrested yesterday by Policeman Dean on the charge of the larceny of a $10 bill from Joseph Gosch, a Pole, who came from Pittsburg on Sunday, and claims that while he was looking for lodging he was taken to the woman's house and robbed.

From pocketbook snatching to highway robbery is but a step:

Before Judge Yerkes, in Court No. 1 Samuel Buckner, a young colored man, was convicted of robbing George C. Goddard of a gold watch and chain and a pocketbook containing $3. He was sentenced to ten years in the Eastern Penitentiary. Mr. Goddard, with his head swathed in bandages, was called to the stand. He said that a few minutes past midnight of November 28 he was returning to his home, No. 1220 Spruce street, after a visit. He placed his hand in his pocket, drew out his key and was about to mount the steps when a dark form appeared from Dean street, a small, poorly-lighted thoroughfare, next door but one to his home, and at the same instant he was struck a violent blow full in the face with a brick. He sank to the pavement unconscious. When he recovered his senses he was in the Pennsylvania Hospital. There was a long, deep cut on his right cheek, another across the forehead, both eyes were blackened and swollen, and his nose was also bruised. At the same time he discovered the loss of his pocketbook and jewelry. Judge Yerkes reviewed the facts of the case, and in imposing sentence said: "When you committed this offence you were absolutely indifferent as to the consequences of your cowardly attack. You rifled this man's person of all his valuables and left him lying unconscious on the pavement, and for aught you knew he might have been dead. It is necessary not only that society be protected from the depredations of such fiends as you, but also that an example be made of such ruffians. The sentence of the Court is that you undergo an imprisonment of ten years at labor in the Eastern Penitentiary, and stand committed until this sentence shall be complied with." The official record shows that Buckner was arrested on December 11, 1893, by policeman Logan, of the Lombard street station, on the charge of the larceny of a purse from Mrs. Caroline Lodge, of 2416 North Fifteenth street, on the street, and was sentenced December 14, 1893, by Judge Biddle, to one year's imprisonment.

Cases of aggravated assaults, for various reasons, are frequent:

Rube Warren, colored, thirty years, of Foulkrod and Cedar streets, was held in $1000 bonds, by Magistrate Eisenbrown, for an alleged aggravated assault and battery on Policeman Haug, of the Frankford station, during a dog fight about a month ago. The policeman attempted to stop the fight when Warren, it is charged, assisted by several companions, assaulted him, broke his club and took away his revolver. During the free fight that followed, in which other policemen took part, Warren escaped and went to Baltimore. There, it is said, he was sent to prison for thirty days. As soon as he was released he went back to Frankford, where he was arrested on Saturday night.

William Braxton, colored, aged twenty-eight years, of Irving street, above Thirty-seventh, was yesterday held in $800 bail for a further hearing, charged with having committed an aggravated assault on William Keebler, of South Thirtieth street. The assault occurred about three o'clock yesterday morning on Irving street, near Thirty-seventh, where the colored folks of the neighborhood were having a party. Keebler and two friends, none of whom were colored, forced their company on the invited guests, it is said, and a fight ensued. Keebler was found a short time afterward lying in the snow with one eye almost gouged out. He was conveyed to the University Hospital and the police of the Woodland avenue station, under Acting Sergeant Ward, upon being notified of the affair, hurried to the Irving street house and arrested twenty of the guests just in the height of their merrymaking. All of them, however, were discharged at the hearing, upon Braxton's being recognized as the man who struck Keegler. The physician at the hospital says that the injured man will very likely lose the sight of one eye.

Gambling goes on almost openly in the slum sections and occasions, perhaps, more quarreling and crime than any other single cause. Reporters declared in 1897 that—

"Policy playing is rampant in Philadelphia. Under the very noses of the police officials and, it is safe to say, with the knowledge of some of them, policy shops are conducted openly and with amazing audacity. They are doing a 'land office' business. Hundreds of poor people every day place upon the infatuating lottery money that had better be spent for food and clothing. They actually deny themselves the necessaries of life to gamble away their meagre income with small chance of getting any return. Superintendent of Police Linden, discussing the general subject of policy playing with a *Ledger* reporter, said: 'There are not words enough in the dictionary to express my feelings upon this matter. I regard policy as the worst evil in a large city among the poor people. There are several reasons for this. One is that women and children may play. Another is that players may put a few cents on the lottery. Policy may do more harm than all the saloons and "speak easies" in the city. The price of a drink of liquor is five or ten cents and the cost of a "growler" is ten cents, but a man or a woman can buy two cents' worth of policy. The effect of this is obvious. Persons who have not the price of a drink may gamble away the few pennies they do possess in a policy shop. Then the drain is constant. Policy "fiends" play twice a day, risking from two cents to a dollar upon the chance. They become so infatuated with the play that they will spend their last cent upon it in the hope of making a "hit." Many children go hungry and with insufficient clothing as a result of policy playing. I have heard of young children engaging in this sort of gambling. Of course the effect of this is very bad. The policy evil is, to my mind, the very worst that exists in our large cities as affecting the poorer classes of people.' "[21]

Once in a while gambling-houses are raided:

> Twenty-three colored men, who were arrested in a raid of the police on an alleged gambling house, on Rodman street, above Twelfth, had a hearing yesterday, before Magistrate South, at the City Hall. One man, residing on Griscom street, testified that the house was supposed to be a "club," and that it was customary to pay a dollar before admission could be secured, and that he had been gambling at "crap" and a card game known as "five-up," and had lost $18. He said there was a president, marshal and sergeant-at-arms. He pointed out Bolling, Jordan and Phillips as the principals. Special Policeman Duffy testified that the crowd was playing "crap" with dice on the floor when he headed the raid on Monday night. He said he had notified Bolling, as the head of the house, three months ago, wizen he had heard that gambling was going on there, to stop it. On cross-examination the witness said he did not know that it was a social club called the "Workingmen's Club." Patrolman William Harvey testified that he went to the house on last Saturday night and got in readily, and was not called on to pay a dollar initiation fee, as had been claimed was the rule. He said he played "sweat" and lost twenty-five cents, but did not win anything. He said Bolling was running the game. He said that when he entered the house somebody called out "Sam's got a new man," and that was all that was said.

More and more frequently in the last few years, have crime, excess, and disappointment led to attempted suicide:

> Policeman Wynne, of the Fifth and Race streets station, last evening found an unknown colored woman lying unconscious in an alleyway at Delaware avenue and Race street. Beside the woman was an empty bottle labeled benzine. Wynne immediately summoned the patrol wagon and had the woman removed to the Pennsylvania Hospital, where her condition was said to be critical. The physicians said there was no doubt the woman had drunk the contents of the bottle, and narcotics were at once administered to counteract the effect of the poison. At midnight the woman showed signs of returning consciousness and it was thought that she would recover. The police have no clue to her identity, as she could not tell her name, and the alleyway where she was found is surrounded by business houses, and no one could be found who knew her.

It is but fair to add that many unsustained charges of crime are made against Negroes, and possibly more in proportion than against other classes. Some typical cases of this sort are of interest:

> W. M. Boley, colored, thirty years old, who said he resided in Mayesville, South Carolina, was a defendant before Magistrate Jermon, at the City Hall, yesterday, on the charge of as-

sault with intent to steal. Detective Gallagher and Special Policeman Thomas testified that their attention was attracted to the prisoner by his actions in a crowd at the New York train gate at Broad street station on Saturday. He had with him several parcels which he laid on the floor near the gate, and they said they saw him make several attempts to pick women's pockets, and arrested him. The man however proved by documentary evidence that he was a clergyman, a graduate of Howard University, and financial agent of a Southern school. He was released.

Under instructions from Judge Finletter, a jury rendered a verdict of not guilty in the case of George Queen, a young colored man, charged with the murder of Joseph A. Sweeney and John G. O'Brien. Dr. Frederick G. Coxson, pastor of the Pitman Methodist Episcopal Church, at Twenty-third and Lombard streets, testified that on the night in question he was about to retire, when he heard a disturbance on the street. Upon going out he saw three young men, two of whom were leading the other and persuading him to come with them. At the same time the prisoner, Queen, came along in the middle of the street, walking leisurely. Immediately upon seeing him the three men attacked him, and were shortly afterward joined by three others, and the entire crowd, among whom were Sweeney and O'Brien, continued beating and striking the colored man. Suddenly the crowd scattered and Queen was placed under arrest; he had fatally stabbed two of his assailants. This testimony showed that the accused was not the aggressor, and without hearing the defence Judge Finletter ordered the jury to render a verdict of not guilty. The case, he said, was one of justifiable homicide, the defendant having a right to resist the attack by force. The judge further said he thought the case would have a tendency to repel the brutal attacks made on inoffensive persons in the community, and to make the streets safe for every man to walk on at any hour without fear.

Leaving for a moment the question of the deeper social causes of crime among Negroes, let us consider two closely allied subjects, pauperism and the use of alcoholic liquors.

Notes

1. Throughout this chapter the basis of induction is the number of prisoners received at different institutions and *not* the prison population at particular times. This avoids the mistakes and distortions of the latter method. (Cf. Falkner: "Crime and the Census;" Publications of the American Academy of Political and Social Science, No. 190). Many writers on Crime among Negroes, as *e. g.*, F. L. Hoffman, and all who use the Eleventh Census uncritically, have fallen into numerous mistakes and exaggerations by carelessness on this point.

2. "Pennsylvania Colonial Records," I, 380-81.

3. See Chapter III, and Appendix B.

4. Cf. "Pennsylvania Statutes at Large," Ch. 56.

5. "Watson's Annals," I, 62.

6. *Ibid.*

7. *Ibid.*, pp. 62-63.

8. "Pennsylvania Colonial Records," II, 275; IX, 6; "Watson's Annals," I, 309.

9. Cf. Chapter IV.

10. Reports Eastern Penitentiary.

11. Average length of sentences for whites in Eastern Penitentiary during nineteen years, 2 years 8 months 2 days; for Negroes, 3 years 3 months 14 days. Cf. "Health of Convicts" (pam.), pp. 7, 8.

12. *Ibid.*, "Condition of Negroes," 1838, pp. 15-18; "Condition," etc., 1848, pp. 26, 27.

13. "Condition of Negroes," 1849, pp. 28, 29. "Condition," etc., 1838, pp. 15-18.

14. "The large proportion of colored men who, in April, had been before the criminal court, led Judge Gordon to make a suggestion when he yesterday discharged the jurors for the term. 'It would certainly seem,' said the Court, 'that the philanthropic colored people of the community, of whom there are a great many excellent and intelligent citizens sincerely interested in the welfare of their race, ought to see what is radically wrong that produces this state of affairs and correct it, if possible. There is nothing in history that indicates that the colored race has a propensity to acts of violent crime; on the contrary, their tendencies are most gentle, and they submit with grace to subordination.' " Philadelphia *Record*, April 29, 1893; Cf. *Record*, May 10 and 12; *Ledger*, May 10, and *Times*, May 22, 1893.

15. Except as otherwise noted, the statistics of this section are from the official reports of the police department.

16. Cf. Chapters IV and VII.

TABLE 25 Crimes of Negroes Arrested by Detectives, 1878-1892

Crimes	*1887*	*1888*	*1889*	*1890*	*1891*	*1892*
Fugitives from justice	—	10	2	4	4	9
Larceny	10	19	17	19	18	29
Pickpocket	7	4	1	—	—	13
Burglary	1	—	2	—	2	4
Professional thief	1	4	2	1	2	3
Sodomy	—	—	—	—	—	1
Misdemeanor	—	1	—	1	—	1
Absconding	—	—	—	—	—	1
Assault to kill	5	6	1	1	4	4
Stabbing	—	—	—	—	—	1
False pretense	—	2	—	1	—	1
Forgery	—	—	—	—	—	1
Receiving stolen goods	1	4	8	—	3	—
Murder	3	2	1	3	2	—
Abortion	—	—	—	1	1	—
Breach of peace	—	—	—	2	—	—
Abandonment	—	—	1	1	—	—
Gambling house	—	4	—	5	—	—
Fornication and adultery	—	—	1	—	—	—
Infanticide	—	1	—	—	—	—
House robbery	—	1	—	—	—	—
Lottery	1	8	—	—	—	—
Embezzlement	—	1	—	—	—	—
Perjury	—	1	—	—	—	—
Seduction	1	—	—	—	—	—
Bawdy house	1	—	—	—	—	—

17. The chief element of uncertainty lies in the varying policy of the courts, as for instance, in the proportion of prisoners sent to different places of detention, the severity of sentence, etc. Only the general conclusions are insisted on here.

18. For the collection of the material here compiled, I am indebted to Mr. David N. Fell, Jr., a student of the Senior Class, Wharton School, University of Pennsylvania, in the year '96-'97. As before noted the figures in this Section refer to the number of prisoners received at the Eastern Penitentiary, and not to the total prison population at any particular time.

19. Witness the case of Marion Stuyvesant accused of the murder of the librarian, Wilson, in 1897.

20. The following Negroes were measured by the Bertillon system in Philadelphia during the last three years:

1893 64 (Whites 101)
1984 66 (Whites 248)
1895 56 (Whites 267)
1896 75 (Whites 347)

The arrests by detectives for five years are given in Table 25.

20. Although the police lieutenants have reported to the Superintendent that few policy shops exist, the *Ledger* has information which leads it to state that such is not the fact. Many complaints against the evil have been received at this office. A reporter found it easy to locate and gain admittance to a number of houses where policy is written. A policy writer who is thoroughly informed as to the inside working of the system is authority for the statement that at no time in recent years has policy playing been so prevalent or the business carried on as openly as it is now.

While the locations of the policy shops are well known and the writers familiar to many persons, the backers, who, after all, are the substantial part of the system, are hard to reach, for they exercise an unusual cunning in the direction of the business. There are several backers in Philadelphia of greater or less pretensions, but a young man who resides uptown and operates principally in the territory north of Girard avenue, is said to be the heaviest backer of the game in this city. He owns sixty or seventy "books," and his income from their combined receipts is sufficient to support himself and several relatives in magnificent style.

A *Ledger* reporter spent one day last week looking up the policy shops in one of the sections where this backer operates. He found, in addition to several places where policy is written, the rendezvous of the writers and the headquarters of the policy king himself.

The writers who hold "books" from the backer in question meet twice every day, Sundays excepted, in a mean, dirty little house overlooking the Reading tracks, just below Montgomery avenue. They enter by the rear through a narrow alley leading off Delhi street, several yards below Montgomery avenue. At noon and at 6 o'clock in the evening the writers hurry to this rendezvous.

The unusual number of men gathering at this point at regular intervals, and the business-like manner in which they go through the alley and back gate is enough to attract the attention of the Twelfth District policeman on this beat and arouse his suspicions. Whether he notices it or not, these proceedings have been going on for months.

Each writer, when he reaches this central point, turns in his "book" and receipts. There are two drawings daily, hence the two meetings. Two relatives of the backer receive the "books" and the money. A copy of each writer's "book" and all the money are carried by one of these men to the house of an ex-special policeman, a few squares away, and there turned over to the backer, who has received a telegram from Cincinnati stating the numbers that have come out at that drawing.

The "books" are carefully gone over, to see if there are any "hits." If there are they are computed, and the backer sends to each writer the amount necessary to pay his losses. The numbers that appear at each drawing are printed with rubber stamps in red ink, on slips of white paper and given to the writers to distribute among the players.

These drawings are usually carried to the rendezvous by the ex-policeman. The backer pockets the half day's receipts, mounts his bicycle and rides away.

To establish beyond a doubt the character of the building in which the writers meet, the reporter made his way into it on the afternoon in question. It is a well-known policy shop, conducted by a colored man, who has been writing policy for years. He is president of a colored political club, with headquarters near by. On the occasion of the visit the back gate was ajar. Pushing it open, the reporter walked in without challenge.—From the *Public Ledger,* December 3, 1897.

INTRODUCTION

Monroe Nathan Work was one of the first African Americans to complete a master's degree in sociology at the University of Chicago. In the early 1900s, Work taught at Georgia State Industrial College (Savannah State) for 5 years. In 1908, he was hired by Booker T. Washington at Tuskegee Normal and Industrial Institute to establish a research program. Gradually, the Department of Records and Research became a national and international clearinghouse for information on African Americans. The most well-known publication of the department was the *Negro Year Book: An Annual Encyclopedia of the Negro.* It provided information on a wide range of crime-related topics, including lynchings, race riots, and African Americans employed in criminal justice, juvenile delinquents, and prisoners.

This article originated as a term project when Work was enrolled in a course in Christian sociology, taught by Graham Taylor at the Chicago Theological Seminary. Later, it appeared in the *American Journal of Sociology.* In this article, Work presents facts about the Negro population in Chicago in the late 1800s and includes information on arrests and prisoners. When the study began in 1897, Chicago, the second largest city in the country, was at the center of industry and trade. His sources include the Eleventh Census of the United States, police records of arrests, data from the Chicago House of Correction, and the Cook County Jail. This article provides one of the first descriptive studies of the social conditions of Negroes in Chicago and includes information on their occupations, nativity, church organizations, slum populations, and crime. The main focus of the article is describing arrests in Chicago from 1872 to 1898, with emphasis on arrests for 10 days in January and 16 days in May 1897 for the slum districts of the city. Unlike most of the early writings, this article includes information on both women and men. The article concludes with a discussion of the cause of the excess of crime among Negroes.

Crime Among the Negroes of Chicago

A Social Study

Monroe N. Work

This study was begun in the month of November, 1897, and was carried on during the month of December, 1897, and the months of January, February, and May, 1898. The writer has endeavored to ascertain the facts, and to present those facts in such a way that we may be able to see from them the trend of crime among the negroes of Chicago, *i.e.*, whether it is increasing or decreasing, and how this crime compares with the crime among the other peoples of the city, and of the country in general.

The Negro and Crime in the United States

Before taking up the study of crime among the negroes of Chicago, it is perhaps best to notice briefly their crime for the entire United States. From the census reports we see that the total number of prisoners in the United States in 1890 was 82,329; of these 24,277 were negroes. The negro prisoners were 29.49 per cent, of the entire number. When the different nationalities are considered, the negroes are found to be the third highest.

A further fact that the Eleventh Census shows in respect to negro crime is that there is a greater number of negro prisoners, in proportion to the negro population, in the northern than in the southern states. The Eleventh Census gives the ratio of prisoners in the United States by division of states. From this we see that the ratio of negro prisoners for the United States in 1890 was three times as great as that of the whites; also that the highest ratio of the negro prisoners was in the western division—9,527 to the million of negro population. Further we see that in the south central, north Atlantic, and western divisions the ratio of negro prisoners is four times as great as that of the white. In the south Atlantic the ratio is six times as great, and in the north central the ratio of negro prisoners is eight times as great as that of the white. This would seem to indicate that in the north central states there is a greater difference in the proportion of crime among the whites and negroes than in any other part of the United States.

A study of the Eleventh Census tables shows that the ratio of negro prisoners to the negro population is greatest in the northern and western states; also that the greatest difference in the proportion of crime between the whites and negroes is in the northern and western states; this seems to indicate that in these states the negro is more given to crime than in the southern states. When we come to notice the criminality of the negroes of Chicago, we shall see whether or not this is true.

Increase of Crime From South Toward the North

Another fact that is shown by the Eleventh Census reports on crime is that, taking the states from the south toward the north, there is a gradual increase in the proportion of negro prisoners to the negro population. It appears from this that from the south toward the north there is a corresponding increase of crime among the negroes.

Taking Mississippi in the south central states for one starting-point, and South Carolina in the south Atlantic states for another, and going toward the north from these two points, we have in each case a gradual increase in the ratio of negro prisoners to the negro population as we go from state to state. It is further seen that this gradual increase of crime has followed certain natural and well-defined lines of travel. This increase is along the two natural highways from the south toward the north, viz., the Mississippi valley and the Atlantic seaboard.

The Negro Population of Chicago

Chicago, situated on Lake Michigan at the intersection of the great inland arteries of trade and travel, is one of the foremost industrial and commercial centers of the world. It is the second largest city in the United States, and had, according to the school census of 1896, a population of 1,616,635. The negro population has during the last thirty-six years increased in the city in about the same proportion as the total population. The Chicago river and its north branch divide the city into three sections or divisions, known as the north, west, and south divisions. The negro population in 1896 was divided among these three sections as follows: north division, 700; west division, 2,606; south division 19,436.

Occupation

The majority of the men are employed as railroad porters, waiters, janitors, elevator and bell boys, saloon porters, dock laborers, foundrymen, house servants, and coachmen. There are a few in the trades as carpenters, painters, etc., but these are decreasing. Several are in the employ of the United States government as clerks and carriers in the post-office. A few hold political appointments in the various departments of the county and city government. In the professions are found several doctors, dentists, lawyers, teachers, and clergymen. The women are with few exceptions engaged in domestic service.[1] There is a large class of unemployed negroes in the city, numbering several hundreds. Could a careful census of this class be taken, it would no doubt be found to reach into the thousands. From this class the ranks of the criminals are recruited. Mention of this class will be made later on in this study.

Nativity

The negroes of Chicago are from all parts of the United States; but the majority are from the middle west and south central states, Kentucky, Tennessee, and, Missouri furnishing the largest number.

Church

There are in the city twenty-four negro church organizations, scattered among the following denominations: Baptist, Catholic, Episcopal, Methodist Episcopal, African Methodist Episcopal, African Methodist Episcopal Zion, Free Methodist, and Presbyterian. Of these different church organizations, ten own their property and worship in their own edifices. The others are what are popularly known as mission churches. These twenty-four places of worship have an approximate seating capacity of 10,000 persons. The membership is about 6,500 persons. The church attendance, including all casual attendants at funerals and like occasions, is about 12,000. This would leave some 10,000 non-churchgoers among the negroes, out of a total population of 22,742, or 44 per cent.

In all social studies of the negro the church must be considered, for it is one of the greatest factors in his social life. It is not only the religious, but also the moral, intellectual, and social center of his community. When the church removes from a district inhabited by negroes, nothing else comes in to take its place. Hence in this study we must notice the relation of the negro churches to the negro slum population.

The proximity of the negro churches to the negro slum population.—The negro slum population of Chicago may be said to be comprised within two districts, viz., the levee district in the south division, and the seventeenth and eighteenth wards in the west division, or that part of them that is bounded on the east by Jefferson street, on the north by Grand avenue, on the west by Ann street, and on the south by Madison street. These two wards had in 1896 a negro population of 895. About 800 of these are found within the limits just defined.

The negro slum population of the levee district is comprised within the following boundaries, viz.: Michigan avenue on the east, Van Buren street on the north, the Chicago river on the west as far south as Sixteenth street; from this point by Clark street to Twenty-second street; on the south by Twenty-second street. This district had in 1896 a negro population of 4,900. Adding to this the 800 in the west division, we have a total of about 5,700 negro persons living in the slums of Chicago in 1896.

In the districts mentioned above there are no negro churches excepting one or two struggling missions. These 5,700 persons are practically outside the influence of the church. Of the numerous social settlements located in Chicago, none are in localities where the negroes dwell in any large numbers; so that the negroes of the slum districts are practically untouched by the social settlements. Of all the peoples dwelling in Chicago's slums the negroes are the most neglected. They are the ones that need the most done for them; for it is among them, as we shall see, that the largest proportion of crime is found.

The Negro Slum Population and the Total Negro Population

The negro slum population, as we have seen, is about 5,700. The total negro population of the city is seen to be 22,742; 25 per cent, or one-fourth of the entire number, live within the slum districts. It is to be noticed, however, that there is a large migration of the negroes from the slum districts toward the more respectable parts of the city; *e. g.*, the first ward of the city, which is comprised within the district mentioned as the levee, had in 1890 a negro population of 3,381; in 1896 the negro population of this ward was 1,983, a decrease of 1,398.

The total population of the first, second, seventeenth, and eighteenth wards of the city, which comprise within their boundaries the districts mentioned as slums, was 106,527. The negro population of these wards was 7,052. Of the entire population of these wards the percentage of negroes was 6.62. Of the city at large we have seen that in 1896 it was 1.40. From this it appears that Chicago has a very large negro slum population when compared with the total number of negroes living in the city. The Seventh Special Report of the Commissioner of Labor, 1894, *Slums of Great Cities,* p. 27, shows that Chicago has a larger negro slum population than either Baltimore, New York, or Philadelphia.

It is to be remembered that not all the negroes living in the districts which have been designated as slums in this work are disreputable or criminal. Many of the best negro fam-

TABLE 1 Ratio of Negro Arrests to the Total Number of Arrests

Year	*Ratio*	*Year*	*Ratio*	*Year*	*Ratio*	*Year*	*Ratio*
1872	1 to 33	1882	1 to 22	1892	1 to 8	1897	1 to 11

TABLE 2 Ratio of Negro Population to Total Population, Compared With the Ratio of Negro Arrests to Total Arrests

Year		
1872	Ratio of negro population to total population	1 to 81
	Ratio of negro arrests to total arrests	1 to 33
1880	Ratio of negro population to total population	1 to 77
	Ratio of negro arrests to total arrests	1 to 17
1890	Ratio of negro population to total population	1 to 77
	Ratio of negro arrests to total arrests	1 to 11
1892	Ratio of negro population to total population	1 to 72
	Ratio of negro arrests to total arrests	1 to 8
1894	Ratio of negro population to total population	1 to 63
	Ratio of negro arrests to total arrests	1 to 11
1896	Ratio of negro population to total population	1 to 71
	Ratio of negro arrests to total arrests	1 to 10

ilies of the city live within these districts. But in speaking of the population of the slums, all persons living therein must be included.

Crime of Negroes in Chicago

Police arrests.—The arrests made from year to year in the police departments of great cities may be regarded as an approximately true indicator of the criminal tendencies of the times; for almost all the inmates of prisons have passed through the hands of the police. On the records of the police department are placed data relating to the individual arrested and the nature of his crime. Because of the data thus obtainable the writer has made a special study of the police records of the city. The period covered by this study is the past twenty-six years, *i. e.,* from 1872 to 1898. The police records of arrests in the city were not obtainable for an earlier period than 1872. The yearly reports back to this time were obtainable with the exception of the year 1873 and a part of the report for 1874.

By this comparison it is seen that during the past twenty-six years there has been a very large increase in the number of negro arrests in proportion to the whole number of arrests.

By this comparison we see that in 1872 the ratio of negro arrests to total arrests was two and a half times as great as the ratio of the negro population to the total population; in 1880 the ratio of arrests was four and a half times as great; in 1890 the ratio of arrests was seven times as great; in 1892 the ratio of arrests was nine times as great; in 1894 the ratio of arrests was five and three-fourths times as great; and in 1896 the ratio of negro arrests to the total arrests was seven times as great as the ratio of the negro population to the total population.

TABLE 3 Ratio of Negro Arrests to the Negro Population, Compared With the Ratio of Total Arrests to the Total Population

Year	*Ratio of Negro Arrests*	*Ratio of total arrests*	*Year*	*Ratio of Negro Arrests*	*Ratio of total arrests*
1872	1 to 5.6	1 to 13	1892	1 to 1.9	1 to 16
1880	1 to 4.7	1 to 19	1894	1 to 3	1 to 17
1890	1 to 2.6	1 to 17	1896	1 to 2.4	1 to 16

From this table we see that the ratio of negro arrests to the negro population is from three to nine times as great as the ratio of total arrests to the total population.

The ratio of negro arrests to the negro population, compared with the ratio of foreign arrests to the foreign population, shows that the ratio of arrests for the foreign population and the ratio of arrests for the total white population is about the same. The proportion of arrests among the negroes is about six times as great as the proportion of arrests among the total foreign population.

With the exception of the Chinese, Greeks, and Mexicans, the proportion of arrests among the negroes to the negro population is from two to eighteen times as great as the proportion of arrests among the different foreign peoples of the city.

A comparison of the negro arrests, 1890-97, in Chicago with the negro arrests in New York city, Washington, D. C., Richmond, Va., and Charleston, S. C., shows that the ratio of negro arrests in Charleston is but slightly greater than the ratio of negroes in the total city population; in Richmond the ratio of negro arrests to the total arrests is one and one-fourth times greater than the ratio of the negro population to the total population; in Washington and New York the ratio is one and a half times as great; while in Chicago the ratio of negro arrests to the total arrests is seven times as great as the ratio of the negro population to the total population.

The negro arrests in these cities compared with the negro population show that the proportion of negro arrests in Chicago is from two to five times as great as the proportion of negro arrests to negro population in these cities; *e. g.*, in 1890 the ratio of negro arrests to negro population was: in New York, 1 to 12; Washington, 1 to 6; Richmond, 1 to 8; Charleston, 1 to 13.5; Chicago, 1 to 2.6. In 1897 the ratio of negro arrests to negro population was: in New York (1896), 1 to 7; Washington, 1 to 6.3; Richmond, 1 to 9.7; Chicago, 1 to 3. In New York, during 1890, the ratio of negro arrests to the negro population was one and a half times as great as the ratio of white arrests to the white population; in Washington, Richmond, and Charleston the ratio of negro arrests was twice as great as the ratio of white arrests; in Chicago the ratio of negro arrests to the negro population was six times as great as the ratio of white arrests to the white population.

Chicago house of correction.—The proportion of negro prisoners sent each year to the Chicago house of correction has increased during the past twenty-five years; the proportion sent from 1890 to 1898 is from two to three times as great as the proportion sent each year from 1873 to 1890. From a comparison of the proportion of negroes in the city's population with the proportion of negroes confined in the house of correction we see that in 1873 the proportion of negro prisoners confined in the Chicago house of correction was 2.7 as great as the proportion of the negro population to the total population of the city; in 1880 the proportion of negro prisoners was 2.5 times as great; in 1890 it was 6 times as great; in 1892 it was 8 times as great; in 1894 it was 9 times as great; and in 1896 the proportion of negro prisoners confined in the Chicago house of correction to the total number of prisoners confined therein was 8 times as great as the proportion of negroes in the total population of the city.

Cook county jail.—The city of Chicago is in Cook county, Ill. The jail for the county is located in this city. The United States census for 1890 showed that there were at that time 279 prisoners in the Cook county jail, of whom 31 were negroes. The writer visited the jail February 3, 1898. On that day there were 400 prisoners, of whom 45 were negroes. The writer also visited the same institution May 23, 1898. At this time there were 431 prisoners, of whom 50 were negroes.

From these figures we see that on the day the census for the Cook county jail was taken in 1890 one-ninth of the prisoners were negroes. On the days that the writer visited the jail in February and May of this year about one-ninth of the prisoners were negroes. These facts would seem to indicate that about one-ninth of the prisoners confined in the Cook county jail during the past eight years have been negroes.

The population of Cook county in 1890 was 1,191,222. The negro population of the county was 14,910. The ratio of negro population in the county to total population was 1 to 79. The ratio of negro prisoners in the jail total prisoners was 1 to 9 in 1890 and 1898. Therefore we can conclude that the proportion of prisoners furnished to the county jail by the negro population of Cook county during the past eight years was from eight to nine times as great as it should have been according to the number of the negroes in the county.

Social relations.—The writer was permitted to have access to the records of the police arrests of the city. From them he selected the records for the months of January and May, 1897. The reports of the second, third, and fourth police precincts were examined. These precincts are in the slum districts of the city, and within their boundaries the majority of negro arrests are made. The records for sixteen days in May and ten days in January were gone over, *i. e.*, from May 15-30 and January 1-10. The negro arrests for these periods were picked out and classified according to sex, age, occupation, conjugal relation, and the nature of the complaints lodged against them. Four hundred and twenty-seven negro arrests were thus examined; 272 from May 15-30, and 155 from January 1-10.

The writer was also allowed to have access to the records of criminals as kept in the Bureau of Identification of Criminals. Here he was enabled to examine the records of negro persons who had been classed as criminals. The writer examined 217 identifications of negroes, and noted the age, sex, occupation, nativity, complexion, and crime of the persons thus recorded.

At the county jail he was unable to obtain anything except the number and sex of negro prisoners and the charges for which they were held. At the house of correction he was also unable to secure any data relative to the social relations of the negro prisoners.

Sex.—Of the 427 negro arrests examined for the months of May, and January, 1897, 242 were males and 185 were females. Of the arrests made during the sixteen days of May, 128 were of males and 144 of females. Of the arrests made during the ten days of January, 114 were of males and 41 of females. From this we see that in May the arrests among the females exceeded those among the males, while in January the arrests among the males were almost three times as many as those among the females. This would seem to indicate that the proportion of female arrests to the male arrests is greatest in the warmer months. The largest number of all arrests is made in the warm months of spring and summer, *e. g.*, the greatest number of arrests made during 1897 was in the month of May—9,620; the smallest number made during any one month was in February—4,000. This is true of all years.

The ratio of negro female arrests to the total negro arrests is 1 to 2.3. The total arrests for the city for 1897 were 83,680 female arrests, 17,624, or 1 to 4. From this we may infer that the proportion of female arrests among the negro population is about twice as great as the proportion of female arrests among the total population of the city.

An examination of the police reports of the city of New York from 1889 to 1896 shows that the average ratio of yearly negro female arrests to total yearly negro arrests is 1 to 2. Therefore we may conclude that the proportion of negro female arrests is about the same in the two cities. In Charleston, S. C., the ratio of negro female arrests to the total yearly negro arrests is as follows: 1890, 1891, 1896, and 1897, 1 to 5; during 1892,1893, 1894, and 1895, 1 to 6. From this we see that the proportion of negro female arrests to the total negro arrests is from two to three times as great in Chicago as in Charleston.

Of the total number of prisoners in the county jail at the time of the taking of the United States census in 1890, 1 in every 10 was a female. Of the negro prisoners at this time 1 in every 3 was a female. On May 23, 1898, 1 in every 16 of the total number of prisoners was a female, and 1 in every 4.5 of the negro prisoners was a female. From this we may conclude that the proportion of female negro prisoners is greatly in excess of the proportion of total female prisoners confined in the county jail.

Age

Ages of negroes under general police arrests.—The average age of the 427 negro persons arrested by the police in May, and January, 1897, was twenty-six years. The average age of the males was 25.29; females, 26.70. The largest number of arrests is of persons from twenty to twenty-five years of age. From a comparison of the total arrests for 1897 with the negro arrests for January and May it would appear that the proportion of arrests for the total population and the negro population is about the same for persons between the ages of ten and twenty; that the proportion of negro arrests is greater for persons between the ages of twenty and thirty than the proportion of total arrests for persons of that age; and that the proportion of total arrests is greater for all persons over thirty years of age than the proportion of negro arrests for negro persons over that age.

Classification of ages by sex.—Classified by sex it is seen that the largest number of male arrests among the negroes was of persons from twenty to twenty-five years of age, and that the majority of male arrests were of persons less than twenty-five years of age. Also that there was a larger percentage of negro male arrests between the ages of ten and twenty than the percentage of total arrests between those ages.

Comparing the male and female arrests of negroes, we see that there is a less proportion of female arrests under the age of twenty years than of males, the percentage of female arrests under twenty years of age being 10, male 22; also that there is a greater proportion of arrests among the females from twenty to twenty-five years of age than among the males for that period, the percentage of female arrests for that period being 41 per cent, male 30 per cent; from twenty-five to thirty years of age the proportion of female arrests is also greater than the males, the percentage of arrests of females from twenty-five to thirty being 29 per cent, males 22 per cent; after thirty years of age the proportion of arrests is greater among the males than among the females. Twenty-four per cent of the male arrests were of persons over thirty years of age, 19 per cent of the female arrests were of persons above that age.

Ages of negro criminals.—The persons whose ages we have been considering come under the head of general police arrests, *i. e.,* those arrested for all causes. We will now notice those classed as criminals.

The ages here given are of persons who have been recorded in the Bureau of Identification of Criminals, and are therefore said to belong to the criminal class. The records of 217 negro persons were examined; 120 were males and 97 were females. The average age of these 217 negro persons was twenty-four years; average age of males was 25.74; females, 22.63. From a classification of ages it appears that the majority of negro persons classed as criminals are between the ages of fifteen and twenty-five years; that the largest proportion of persons is between the ages of twenty and twenty-five. Taking the percentages, we see that 64 per cent are between the ages of fifteen and twenty-five years, and that 43 per cent are between the ages of twenty and twenty-five years, and that only 36 per cent are above twenty-five years of age.

From the classification of ages under general negro arrests we see that 52 per cent of the negro arrests were of persons between the ages of fifteen and twenty-five years, 35 percent between the ages of twenty and twenty-five years, and 48 per cent beyond the age of twenty-five years. From the ages under general arrests we have seen that the average age of negro persons thus arrested was twenty-six years; the average age of males was 25.29 years, females 26.70 years. From the classification just considered we see that the average age of negro persons classed as criminals was twenty-four, males 25.74, females 22.63 years. This would seem to indicate that the proportion of negro persons, between the ages of fifteen and twenty-five years, classed as criminals, to the total number so classed, is greater than the proportion of negroes of this same age in the general negro arrests to the total general negro arrests of the city.

Classification of ages by sex.—Classified by sex it appears that the majority of negro criminals are between the ages of fifteen and twenty-five years, and that the largest number of these are between the ages of twenty and twenty-five; also that there is a larger percentage of negro females between the ages of fifteen and twenty-five classed as criminals, to the total number of negro females so classed, than of negro males between the ages of fifteen and twenty-five, classed as criminals, to the total number of negro males so classed. We see further that 90 per cent of the negro females classed as criminals, and 71 per cent of the males so classed, are between the ages of fifteen and thirty.

This would seem to indicate that negro female criminals become so at an earlier age than negro male criminals, and that criminality among the negro females decreases after the age of twenty-five years. Criminality among the negro males decreases after the age of thirty years. From this we may conclude that the tendency to crime among the negroes decreases with advancing age. This same fact is noted in the United States census reports on *Crime, Pauperism, and Benevolence,* Part I, "Analysis of Statistics," p. 167.[2]

Marital relations.—The writer was unable to ascertain the marital relations of any class of negroes connected with crime, except those coming under the head of general police arrests. Of the 427 general negro arrests made by the police of the city in January and May of 1897, 60 were of married persons and 367 were of single. The percentage of married persons was 14. Of the total arrests of the city for 1897, 24,608 were of married and 59,072 were of single; 29 per cent of the total arrests of the city were of married persons. This would seem to indicate that the proportion of single negro persons arrested to the total negro arrests is much greater than the proportion of single persons arrested for the total arrests of the city. The United States Census Reports on Crime for 1890 give the following percentages for the marital relations of negro prisoners: single, 62.43; married, 33.51. The percentage for the marital relation for the total prisoners of all nationalities was: single, 63.68; married, 30.04. The percentage for the whites was: single, 64.25; married, 28.54. From these percentages it is seen that the negroes had the largest percentage of married persons. The small percentage of married persons among the arrests of negroes in Chicago is probably accounted for by the fact that there is an ever-increasing number of young and unmarried negro persons coming into the large cities from the country and small towns.

Occupations.—Of the 427 negro persons under general arrests, 329, or 75 per cent, had, or gave, no occupation. Of the total arrests of the city, 83,680, for the year 1897, 32,158, or 38 per cent, were arrests of persons without occupations. This great difference in the percentage of persons arrested without occupations would seem to indicate that the proportion of negroes in Chicago without occupation or unemployed is greater than the proportion of unemployed in the total population of the city.

From the list of occupations given by those classed as criminals it is seen that a greater number had an occupation of some sort than those under the head of general police arrests. Also that there is a more varied list of occupations. Comparing those without occupations, classed as criminals, with those without occupations in the total general arrests in the city, we see that the negroes still have a larger number without occupations. Thirty-eight per cent of the total arrests were of persons without occupations; 42 per cent of negro criminal arrests were of persons without occupations. Previous mention has been made of the large number of unemployed negroes in the city, and it is now seen that from this class comes a large part of the negro arrests and crimes.

Nativity.—The 217 persons classed as criminals were from twenty-seven different states of the United States, and two foreign countries. This is due to the fact, which has already been noted, that the negro population of Chicago is made up of negroes from all parts of the United States. The largest number of criminals are from Kentucky, Tennessee, and Missouri. It is from these states, as has already been stated, that the largest number of negroes in Chicago has come.

Offenses

Offenses of negro persons under the head of general arrests.—Comparing offenses for May and January with offenses of total arrests, we see that the proportionate number of negroes arrested for assault and burglary is less than the proportionate number of total arrests for these offenses; that for larceny and vagrancy the proportionate number of negroes arrested is about the same as the proportionate number of total arrests for these offenses; and that the proportionate number of negroes arrested for disorderly conduct and robbery is greater than the proportionate total arrests for these offenses.

Classification of offenses.—Eighty per cent of offenses were against society; 74 per cent of the offenses against society were offenses against public peace; 11 per cent of the offenses were against property, and 7 per cent against the person.

Offenses of negro persons classed as criminals.—The three offenses of larceny, burglary, and robbery predominate; the largest number of persons, as would be expected, committed larceny; 42 per cent of all offenses were larceny; 16 per cent of all persons committed or attempted burglary, and 18 per cent committed or attempted robbery. From the Census Reports on Crime for 1890 it is seen that 28 per cent of all negro persons then confined in prison had been committed for larceny, 11 per cent for burglary, and 2.38 per cent for robbery.

Offenses by sex.—Burglary, it appears, is an offense committed almost entirely by the males; also that the tendency to commit larceny and robbery is greater among the females than among the males. Fifty-eight per cent of the total offenses committed by the females were of larceny, against 26 per cent of the males for this same offense; 24 per cent of the females committed robbery, against 12 per cent of the males for this offense. It is further seen that 5.15 per cent of the females committed murder, against 1.66 per cent of the males.

Classification of offenses.—All the offenses come under the two groups of offenses against the person and against property; 84 per cent of the offenses are against property.

Classification by sex.—The majority of both male and female offenses are against property. But there is a larger percentage of female offenses against property than of male offenses against property. Eighty-seven per cent of the total female offenses are against property, and 81 per cent of the male offenses.

Jail offenses.—Negroes confined in jail May 23, 1898. Thirty-six per cent of the offenses were larceny, 24 per cent were for murder or attempted murder, 16 per cent were for robbery. This high percentage of homicides or attempted homicide is to be noticed.

Offenses by sex.—The largest number of males committed larceny—38 per cent; 27 per cent of the females committed larceny. The largest number of the females committed robbery—36 per cent; 10 per cent of the male offenses were of robbery. Eighteen per cent of the females were held for murder, and 5 per cent of the males. We have already seen under the head of negroes classed as criminals that there was a larger percentage of females charged with robbery and murder than of males; therefore we may conclude that the negro females of Chicago have more of a tendency for robbery and homicide than the males.

Classification of offenses.—The largest percentage of offenses is against property—68 per cent; 28 per cent of the offenses are against the person, and 4 per cent against society.

Comparing this classification with the classification of offenses under negroes classed as criminals, and with the census report on crime (1890), it is seen that there is a larger percentage of offenses against property than of any other offenses among the negroes of the United States. It is also seen that this tendency is more manifested among the negroes of Chicago than of the country at large.

Classification by sex.—Classified by sex, all the offenses of negro females examined under jail arrests fall under the head of person and property; the offenses against the person, 36 per cent, is greater than the per cent of male offenses against the person, 25 per cent. An examination of negro female offenses under general arrests and of those classed as criminals shows that all the female offenses considered come under the head of person and property. For the country at large one-third of all offenses of negro females are against society. It is also seen that there is a larger per cent of male offenses against society in the country at large than in Chicago; that there is a larger percentage of offenses against the person among the negroes of the country at large than of Chicago, and that offenses against property predominate among both male and female negroes in Chicago.

Complexion and offenses.—Of the 217 records examined it was found that 72 were of persons of black complexion, *i. e.,* the negro blood predominated; 145 were of light complexion or of mixed blood, *i. e.,* Caucasian blood predominated. As to the crimes committed by these different-complexioned criminals, the blacks committed more of the offenses against the person and the mulattoes against property. Of the four cases of rape that have been noted two were by blacks and two were by mulattoes; of the seven murder cases noted six were by black persons, five females and one male.

Age and offenses.—Under the head of negroes classed as criminals there were thirty-seven persons between the ages of fifteen and twenty years. Considering the offenses of these persons, it is seen that larceny offenses have the largest percentage—43 per cent robbery comes next, 30 per cent; then burglary, 21 per cent; and assaults, 6 percent. We may then conclude that with negro criminals under twenty years of age the tendency to commit offenses is in the following order: the greatest tendency is to commit larceny, then robbery, burglary, and assaults.

By sex it is seen that the tendency to larceny and assault is greatest among the females under twenty years of age; that the tendency to robbery is about the same in each sex; and that burglary is exclusively confined to the males.

Classifying the offenses, it is seen that 94.59 per cent of the offenses are against property and 5.41 per cent against the person; therefore we may say that the offenses of negro criminals under twenty years of age are very largely against property. By sexes it is seen that 100 per cent of the male offenses were against property and 89 per cent of the female are against property. We see that 11 per cent of the female offenses are against the person; therefore we may conclude that the tendency to crime against the person is much stronger in negro females under twenty years of age than in negro males under that age.

Of the seven murder cases noted under the head of negroes classed as criminals it was seen that five were by females and two by males. The ages of the females were respectively 22, 26, 27, 30, and 34 years. The ages of the males were 29 and 31 years. The average age of females is seen to be 27.80 years. The average age of the males is 30 years. This, with what we have already seen in connection with offenses committed by persons under twenty years of age, would seem to indicate that murder is not committed at as early an age as larceny, burglary, and robbery; it also appears that the females committed murder at an earlier age than the males.

Habits.—The writer was unable to collect any data relative to the habits of negro criminals, beyond the fact that the opium habit is quite prevalent among them and is increasing.

Literacy and illiteracy.—Of the literacy and illiteracy of the negro criminals of Chicago no data were collected. It is to be presumed, however, because of the general educational advancement of the negro, and the fact that the majority of them are less than twenty-five years of age, that the greater number of the negro criminals of Chicago are literate.

Is Crime Increasing?

During the past twenty-five years there has been a very great increase in the proportion of negroes arrested in the city, and the numbers confined in the jail and house of correction, to the proportion of negroes in the city's population. The per cent of negro arrests in the total arrests has increased slightly in the past five years, from 1893-7, over the previous five years, from 1888-92. The average per cent of negro arrests in the total arrests of the city 1888-92 was 9.41; 1893-7 the average percentage was 9.50. The average percentage 1893-7 was 6.42. Judging from this, crime among the negroes of Chicago appears to be on the increase at the present time.

The Cause of This Excess of Crime

The question now arises: Why this excess of crime among the negroes of Chicago and of the United States in general? Are they advancing or retrograding? F. L. Hoffman, in *Race Traits and Tendencies of the American Negro,* "Publication of American Economic Association," Vol. XI, 1896, takes the position that the negro is retrograding. Since his emancipation he has made no real advancement in a moral or social way. The fact that his tendency is downward accounts for a large part of his excess of crime.

If the American negro is degenerating, then his degeneracy does, in a large measure, account for his excess of crime. On the other hand, if he is not degenerating, but making progress in civilization, then his excess of crime must be accounted for on other grounds. Going on the hypothesis of his social advancement, may we not say that, since his emancipation, he has been in a transitional state—a transition from a state of slavery to one of freedom? During all these years he has been endeavoring to adjust himself to his new environment. He has had to endure the economic stress and strain attendant upon this transition. The fact that he is in this transitional state from a lower to a higher plane of development accounts for a part, at least, of his excess of crime. Within this transition the economic stress under which he has labored appears to be the main factor. In the South his economic condition is better in many ways than in the North. In those places where his economic condition is the best his rate of crime is the lowest. The reverse is also true: where his economic condition is poorest his rate of crime is the highest. His economic condition is poorer in Chicago than in the southern cities noted.

There are other causes common to all races that enter into the life of the negro and tend to increase his criminality. These should not be overlooked. There are race characteristics peculiar to him that also help. But it appears to the writer that the fact of the negro being in a transitional state, and the economic phase of this transition, accounts for a large part of the excess of negro crime in the United States.

Notes

1. The writer has not had opportunity to make a careful and systematic study of the industrial condition of the negroes of the city, and does not claim that the foregoing classification of occupations is correct in all its details. He feels safe, however, in saying that in the main it is correct.

2. The facts here shown of the tendency to crime at an early age, the proportion of crime between the males and females, and the ages of negro criminal, are found to agree essentially with what is said in the same connection in the United States census report on *Crime, Pauperism and Benevolence,* Part 1, "Analysis of Statistics," p. 155-67.

5

INTRODUCTION

With *The Philadelphia Negro* completed, Du Bois accepted an appointment at Atlanta University, where he established the "Atlanta School" of social scientific research. The critically acclaimed research program included an annual study on a topic of relevance to the African American community. Along with this annual focus, he regularly published on other pressing topics. Around the turn of the century, he was quite concerned about crime and subsequently focused on related issues. Two of those related issues were the convict-lease and crop-lien systems in the South. In 1901, Du Bois addressed both of these concerns, one with a public testimony before the Industrial Committee, where he spoke of the criminalizing effect of the crop-lien system. He addressed the former concern in the form of a pioneering analysis of the convict-lease system.

Unlike his chapter from *The Philadelphia Negro,* this article focuses on Du Bois's views on the South, where he believed the convict-lease system was criminalizing African Americans. The system allowed states to lease out the labor of convicts to southern landowners who had lost their slave labor with the recent abolition of slavery. Du Bois's analysis points to the strategic enactment of an assortment of vagrancy laws (a.k.a.

Black Codes) to secure the African American labor required to keep the South afloat after the Civil War. This analysis shows his strong leanings toward the conflict perspective. Moreover, he reiterates his conviction that crime in the African American community was not normal. In his view, crime was a result of the dire social conditions that were present in far too many African American communities.

THE SPAWN OF SLAVERY

The Convict-Lease System in the South

W. E. B. Du Bois

A modified form of slavery survives wherever prison labor is sold to private persons for their pecuniary profit.—Wines.

Two systems of controlling human labor which still flourish in the South are the direct children of slavery, and to all intents and purposes are slavery itself. These are the crop-lien system and the convict-lease system. The crop-lien system is an arrangement of chattel mortgages so fixed that the housing, labor, kind of agriculture and, to some extent, the personal liberty of the free black laborer is put into the hands of the landowner and merchant. It is absentee landlordism and the "company-store" systems united and carried out to the furthest possible degree. The convict-lease system is the slavery in private hands of persons convicted of crimes and misdemeanors in the courts. The object of the present paper is to study the rise and development of the convict-lease system, and the efforts to modify and abolish it.

Before the Civil War the system of punishment for criminals was practically the same as in the North. Except in a few cities, however, crime was less prevalent than in the North, and the system of slavery naturally modified the situation. The slaves could become criminals in the eyes of the law only in exceptional cases. The punishment and trial of nearly all ordinary misdemeanors and crimes lay in the hands of the masters. Consequently, so far as the state was concerned, there was no crime of any consequence among Negroes. The system of criminal jurisprudence had to do, therefore, with whites almost exclusively, and as is usual in a land of scattered population and aristocratic tendencies, the law was lenient in theory and lax in execution.

Reprinted from *The Missionary Review of the World* (New York), 14 (October 1901): 737-745.

On the other hand, the private well-ordering and control of slaves called for careful cooperation among masters. The fear of insurrection was ever before the South, and the ominous uprising of Cato, Gabriel, Vesey, Turner, and Toussaint made this fear an ever-present nightmare. The result was a system of rural police, mounted and on duty chiefly at night, whose work it was to stop the nocturnal wandering and meeting of slaves. It was usually an effective organization, which terrorized the slaves, and to which all white men belonged, and were liable to active detailed duty at regular intervals.

Upon this system war and emancipation struck like a thunderbolt. Law and order among the whites, already loosely enforced, became still weaker through the inevitable influence of conflict and social revolution. The freedman was especially in an anomalous situation. The power of the slave police supplemented and depended upon that of the private masters. When the masters' power was broken the patrol was easily transmuted into a lawless and illegal mob known to history as the Ku Klux Klan. Then came the first, and probably the most disastrous, of that succession of political expedients by which the South sought to evade the consequences of emancipation. It will always be a nice question of ethics as to how far a conquered people can be expected to submit to the dictates of a victorious foe. Certainly the world must to a degree sympathize with resistance under such circumstances. The mistake of the South, however, was to adopt a kind of resistance which in the long run weakened her moral fiber, destroyed respect for law and order, and enabled gradually her worst elements to secure an unfortunate ascendency. The South believed in slave labor, and was thoroughly convinced that free Negroes would not work steadily or effectively. The whites were determined after the war, therefore, to restore slavery in everything but in name. Elaborate and ingenious apprentice and vagrancy laws were passed, designed to make the freedmen and their children work for their former masters at practically no wages. Some justification for these laws was found in the inevitable tendency of many of the ex-slaves to loaf when the fear of the lash was taken away. The new laws, however, went far beyond such justification, totally ignoring that large class of freedmen eager to work and earn property of their own, stopping all competition between employers, and confiscating the labor and liberty of children. In fact, the new laws of this period recognized the Emancipation Proclamation and the Thirteenth Amendment simply as abolishing the slave-trade.

The interference of Congress in the plans for reconstruction stopped the full carrying out of these schemes, and the Freedmen's Bureau consolidated and sought to develop the various plans for employing and guiding the freedmen already adopted in different places under the protection of the Union army. This government guardianship established a free wage system of labor by the help of the army, the striving of the best of the blacks, and the cooperation of some of the whites. In the matter of adjusting legal relationships, however, the Bureau failed. It had, to be sure, Bureau courts, with one representative of the ex-master, one of the freedman, and one of the Bureau itself, but they never gained the confidence of the community. As the regular state courts gradually regained power, it was necessary for them to fix by their decisions the new status of the freedmen. It was perhaps as natural as it was unfortunate that amid this chaos the courts sought to do by judicial decisions what the legislatures had formerly sought to do by specific law—namely, reduce the freedmen to serfdom. As a result, the small peccadillos of a careless, untrained class were made the excuse for severe sentences. The courts and jails became filled with the careless and ignorant, with those who sought to emphasize their new-found freedom, and too often with innocent victims of oppression. The testimony of a Negro counted for little or nothing in court, while the accusation of white witnesses was usually decisive. The result of this was a sudden large increase in the apparent criminal population of the Southern states—an increase so large that there was no way for the state to house it or watch it even had the state wished to. And the state did not wish to. Throughout the South laws were immediately passed authorizing public officials to lease the labor of convicts to the highest bidder. The lessee then took charge of the convicts—worked them as he wished under the nominal control of the state. Thus a new slavery and slave-trade was established.

The Evil Influences

The abuses of this system have often been dwelt upon. It had the worst aspects of slavery without any of its redeeming features. The innocent, the guilty, and the depraved were herded together, children and adults, men and women, given into the complete control of practically irresponsible men, whose sole object was to make the most money possible. The innocent were made bad, the bad worse; women were outraged and children tainted; whipping and torture were in vogue, and the death-rate from cruelty, exposure, and overwork rose to large percentages. The actual bosses over such leased prisoners were usually selected from the lowest classes of whites, and the camps were often far from settlements or public roads. The prisoners often had scarcely any clothing, they were fed on a scanty diet of corn bread and fat meat, and worked twelve or more hours a day. After work each must do his own cooking. There was insufficient shelter; in one Georgia camp, as late as 1895, sixty-one men slept in one room, seventeen by nineteen feet, and seven feet high. Sanitary conditions were wretched, there was little or no medical attendance, and almost no care of the sick. Women were mingled indiscriminately with the men, both in working and sleeping, and dressed often in men's clothes. A young girl at Camp Hardmont, Georgia, in 1895, was repeatedly outraged by several of her guards, and finally died in childbirth while in camp.

Such facts illustrate the system at its worst—as it used to exist in nearly every Southern state, and as it still exists in parts of Georgia, Mississippi, Louisiana, and other states. It is difficult to say whether the effect of such a system is worse on the whites or on the Negroes. So far as the whites are concerned, the convict-lease system lowered the respect for courts, increased lawlessness, and put the states into the clutches of penitentiary "rings." The courts were brought into politics, judgeships became elective for shorter and shorter terms, and there grew up a public sentiment which would not consent to considering the desert of a criminal apart from his color. If the criminal were white, public opinion refused to permit him to enter the chain-gang save in the most extreme cases. The result is that even today it is very difficult to enforce the laws in the South against whites, and red-handed criminals go scot-free. On the other hand, so customary had it become to convict any Negro upon a mere accusation, that public opinion was loathe to allow a fair trial to black suspects, and was too often tempted to take the law into their own hands. Finally the state became a dealer in crime, profited by it so as to derive a new annual income for her prisoners. The lessees of the convicts made large profits also. Under such circumstances, it was almost impossible to remove the clutches of this vicious system from the state. Even as late as 1890 the Southern states were the only section of the Union where the income from prisons and reformatories exceeded the expense.[1] Moreover, these figures do not include the county gangs where the lease system is today most prevalent and the net income largest.

The effect of the convict-lease system on the Negroes was deplorable. First it linked crime and slavery indissolubly in their minds as simply forms of the white man's oppression. Punishment, consequently, lost the most effective of its deterrent effects, and the criminal gained pity instead of disdain. The Negroes lost faith in the integrity of courts and

TABLE 1 Income and Expense of State Prisons and Reformatories, 1890

	Earnings	*Expense*	*Profit*
New England	$299,735	$1,204,029	—
Middle States	71,252	1,850,452	—
Border States	597,898	962,422	—
Southern States[2]	938,406	890,452	$47,974
Central States	624,161	1,971,795	—
Western States	378,036	1,572,316	—

the fairness of juries. Worse than all, the chain-gangs became schools of crime which hastened the appearance of the confirmed Negro criminal upon the scene. That some crime and vagrancy should follow emancipation was inevitable. A nation can not systematically degrade labor without in some degree debauching the laborer. But there can be no doubt but that the indiscriminate careless and unjust method by which Southern courts dealt with the freedmen after the war increased crime and vagabondage to an enormous extent. There are no reliable statistics to which one can safely appeal to measure exactly the growth of crime among the emancipated slaves. About seventy per cent of all prisoners in the South are black; this, however, is in part explained by the fact that accused Negroes are still easily convicted and get long sentences, while whites still continue to escape the penalty of many crimes even among themselves. And yet allowing for all this, there can be no reasonable doubt but that there has arisen in the South since the war a class of black criminals, loafers, and ne'er-do-wells who are a menace to their fellows, both black and white.

The appearance of the real Negro criminal stirred the South deeply. The whites, despite their long use of the criminal court for putting Negroes to work, were used to little more than petty thieving and loafing on their part, and not to crimes of boldness, violence, or cunning. When, after periods of stress or financial depression, as in 1892, such crimes increased in frequency, the wrath of a people unschooled in the modern methods of dealing with crime broke all bounds and reached strange depths of barbaric vengeance and torture. Such acts, instead of drawing the best opinion of these states and of the nation toward a consideration of Negro crime and criminals, discouraged and alienated the best classes of Negroes, horrified the civilized world, and made the best white Southerners ashamed of their land.

What Has Been Done

Nevertheless, in the midst of all this a leaven of better things had been working and the bad effects of the epidemic of lynching quickened it. The great difficulty to be overcome in the South was the false theory of work and of punishment of wrong-doers inherited from slavery. The inevitable result of a slave system is for a master class to consider that the slave exists for his benefit alone—that the slave has no rights which the master is bound to respect. Inevitably this idea persisted after emancipation. The black workman existed for the comfort and profit of white people, and the interests of white people were the only ones to be seriously considered. Consequently, for a lessee to work convicts for his profit was a most natural thing. Then, too, these convicts were to be punished, and the slave theory of punishment was pain and intimidation. Given these ideas, and the convict-lease system was inevitable. But other ideas were also prevalent in the South; there were in slave times plantations where the well-being of the slaves was considered, and where punishment meant the correction of the fault rather than brute discomfort. After the chaos of war and reconstruction passed, there came from the better conscience of the South a growing demand for reform in the treatment of crime. The worst horrors of the convict-lease system were attacked persistently in nearly every Southern state. Back in the eighties George W. Cable, a Southern man, published a strong attack on the system. The following decade Governor Atkinson, of Georgia, instituted a searching investigation, which startled the state by its revelation of existing conditions. Still more recently Florida, Arkansas, and other states have had reports and agitation for reform. The result has been marked improvement in conditions during the last decade. This is shown in part by the statistics of 1895; in that year the prisons and reformatories of the far South cost the states $204,483 more than they earned, while before this they had nearly always yielded an income. This is still the smallest expenditure of any section, and looks strangely small beside New England's $1,190,564. At the same time, a movement in the right direction is clear. The laws are being framed more and more so as to prevent the placing of convicts altogether in private control. They are not, to be sure, always enforced, Georgia having several hundreds of convicts so controlled in 1895 despite the law. In nearly all the Gulf states the convict-lease system still has a strong hold, still debauches public sentiment and breeds criminals.

The next step after the lease system was to keep the prisoners under state control, or, at least, regular state inspection, but to lease their labor to contractors, or to employ it in some remunerative labor for the state. It is this stage that the South is slowly reaching today so far as the criminals are concerned who are dealt with directly by the states. Those whom the state still unfortunately leaves in the hands of county officials are usually leased to irresponsible parties. Without doubt, work, and work worth the doing—*i.e.*, profitable work—is best for prisoners. Yet there lurks in this system a dangerous temptation. The correct theory is that the work is for the benefit of the criminal—for his correction, if possible. At the same time, his work should not be allowed to come into unfair competition with that of honest laborers, and it should never be an object of traffic for pure financial gain. Whenever the profit derived from the work becomes the object of employing prisoners, then evil must result. In the South today it is natural that in the slow turning from the totally indefensible private lease system, some of its wrong ideas should persist. Prominent among these persisting ideas is this: that the most successful dealing with criminals is that which costs the state least in actual outlay. This idea still dominates most of the Southern states. Georgia spent $2.38 per capita on her 2,938 prisoners in 1890, while Massachusetts spent $62.96 per capita on her 5,227 prisoners. Moreover, by selling the labor of her prisoners to the highest bidders, Georgia not only got all her money back, but made a total clear profit of $6.12 on each prisoner. Massachusetts spent about $100,000 more than was returned to her by prisoners' labor. Now it is extremely difficult, under such circumstances, to prove to a state that Georgia is making a worse business investment than Massachusetts. It will take another generation to prove to the South that an apparently profitable traffic in crime is very dangerous business for a state; that prevention of crime and the reformation of criminals is the one legitimate object of all dealing with depraved natures, and that apparent profit arising from other methods is in the end worse than dead loss. Bad public schools and profit from crime explain much of the Southern social problem. Georgia, Florida, and Louisiana, as late as 1895, were spending annually only $20,799 on their state prisoners, and receiving $80,493 from the hire of their labor.

Moreover, in the desire to make the labor of criminals pay, little heed is taken of the competition of convict and free laborers, unless the free laborers are white and have a vote. Black laborers are continually displaced in such industries as brick-making, mining, road-building, grading, quarrying, and the like, by convicts hired at $3, or thereabouts, a month.

The second mischievous idea that survives from slavery and the convict-lease system is the lack of all intelligent discrimination in dealing with prisoners. The most conspicuous and fatal example of this is the indiscriminate herding of juvenile and adult criminals. It need hardly be said that such methods manufacture criminals more quickly than all other methods can reform them. In 1890, of all the Southern states, only Texas, Tennessee, Kentucky, Maryland, and West Virginia made any state appropriations for juvenile reformatories. In 1895 Delaware was added to these, but Kentucky was missing. We have, therefore:

	1890	1895
New England	$632,634	$854,581
Border States	233,020	174,781
Southern States	10,498	33,910

And this in face of the fact that the South had in 1890 over four thousand prisoners under twenty years of age. In some of the Southern states—notably, Virginia—there are private associations for juvenile reform, acting in cooperation with the state. These have, in some cases, recently received state aid, I believe. In other states, like Georgia, there is permissive legislation for the establishment of local reformatories. Little has resulted as yet from this legislation, but it is promising.

I have sought in this paper to trace roughly the attitude of the South toward crime. There is in that attitude much to condemn, but also something to praise. The tendencies are today certainly in the right direction, but there is a long battle to be fought with prejudice and inertia before the South will realize that a black criminal is a human being, to be punished firmly but humanely, with the sole object of making him a safe member of society, and that a white criminal at large is a menace and a danger. The greatest difficulty today in the way of reform is this race question. The movement for juvenile reformatories in Georgia would have succeeded some years ago, in all probability, had not the argument been used: it is chiefly for the benefit of Negroes. Until the public opinion of the ruling masses of the South can see that the prevention of crime among Negroes is just as necessary, just as profitable, for the whites themselves, as prevention among whites, all true betterment in courts and prisons will be hindered. Above all, we must remember that crime is not normal; that the appearance of crime among Southern Negroes is a symptom of wrong social conditions—of a stress of life greater than a large part of the community can bear. The Negro is not naturally criminal; he is usually patient and law-abiding. If slavery, the convict-lease system, the traffic in criminal labor, the lack of juvenile reformatories, together with the unfortunate discrimination and prejudice in other walks of life, have led to that sort of social protest and revolt which we call crime, then we must look for remedy in the sane reform of these wrong social conditions, and not in intimidation, savagery, or the legalized slavery of men.

Notes

1. Bulletin No. 8, Library of State of New York. All figures in this article are from this source.

2. South Carolina, Georgia, Alabama, Mississippi, Louisiana, Texas, and Arkansas.

INTRODUCTION

Monroe Nathan Work (see Chapter 4) was dedicated to providing accurate facts about the Negro. Discouraged with teaching, he assumed his position at Tuskegee Institute under the leadership of one of the most influential African Americans of the time, Booker T. Washington. During his 30 years as director of research work, he was able to document the achievements of Negroes in the United States and abroad. Thus, Work was a pioneer in African American studies who contributed to the advancement of knowledge not only at the research department but also by participating in conferences and publishing extensively on a wide array of topics, including African civilization, crime, health, and the race problem.

This article is a classic in the study of crime among African Americans because of its historical focus. It originally appeared in the *Annals of the American Academy of Political and Social Sciences* in 1913. Work provided information on prisoners in northern and southern states between 1870 and 1904. Unlike most contemporary scholars, Work included the nationality of White persons committed to prisons for comparative purposes. Work also discussed several factors that contributed to the Negro crime rate, including the convict-lease system, migration to the North, and unfairness of the law. At the time the article was written, very little attention was devoted to understanding how social conditions during emancipation, Reconstruction, and post-Reconstruction contributed to crime among African Americans. Rather, the dominant ideology of the time emphasized what it believed to be the inferiority and criminal tendencies of Negroes.

NEGRO CRIMINALITY IN THE SOUTH

MONROE N. WORK

Prior to the Civil War there was not, in the South, the problem of Negro crime such as now exists. Although at that time each of the slave states had elaborate and severe laws for dealing with Negro criminals, they were, in proportion to the total number of Negroes, comparatively few. Immediately following emancipation, however, their numbers increased. This was inevitable; for many of the restraints that had been about the slaves were suddenly removed and much of the machinery for state and local government had broken down. As a result there was confusion and disorder. Many of the slaves left the plantations. There was the beginning of the migration from section to section from the rural districts to the cities and from the South to the North. Under all these circumstances it was not surprising that there should be an increase in Negro crime. The wonder is that there was not more confusion, disorder and rapine. The great majority of the freedmen did not attempt to be lawless. They exercised the same restraint that they had exercised during the four years that their masters had been away on the field of battle. But to some of the newly enfranchised, freedom meant the license to do what they pleased. It was from this class that the majority of the criminals came.

As an example of the increase in the number of Negro criminals, we will take the state of Georgia. In 1858, there were confined in the Georgia penitentiary 183 prisoners, all of whom were apparently white. Twelve years later, in 1870, there were 393 prisoners in this penitentiary, of whom 59 were white and 334 colored.

According to the United States census, the total number of Negroes confined in Southern prisons in 1870 was 6,031; ten years later, the number, 12,973, had more than doubled; twenty years later, the number, 19,244, was three times as great; thirty-four years later, however, that is in 1904, the number of Negroes confined in Southern prisons was 18,550. This would appear to indicate that, so far as prison population is an index, Negro criminality in the South in recent years has not increased. It is probable that there is some decrease, for a study of criminal statistics of cities North and South, indicates that between 1890 and 1904 Negro criminality, which up to this time had seemed to be steadily increasing, reached its highest point and began to

From Work, M. (1939). Negro criminality in the south. *Annals of the American Academy of Political and Social Sciences*, 49, 74-80. Reprinted with permission of the Annals of the American Academy of Political and Social Sciences.

decrease. It appears that the decrease began about 1894-1895.

The number of prisoners per 100,000 of Negro population also appears to bear out this conclusion. It also shows that there is a much higher rate of crime among Negroes in the North than in the South. This is to a large extent due to the fact that seven-tenths of the Negroes in the North, as against one-tenth in the South, live in cities and are of an age when persons have the greatest tendency to crime.

In the following table the number of Negro prisoners in Northern and Southern states is compared.

TABLE 1 Negro Prisoners

Year	*Northern States*	*Southern States*
1870	2,025	6,031
1880	3,774	12,973
1890	5,635	19,244
1904	7,527	18,550
Prisoners per 100,000 of Negro Population		
1870	372	136
1880	515	221
1890	773	284
1904	765	220

It is significant that the number of lynchings reached its highest point about the same period that Negro crime reached its highest point. From 1882 to 1892 the number of persons lynched annually in the United States increased from 114 to 255. From that time on the number decreased. In 1912, there were 64 lynchings in the United States. The total number of lynchings during the thirty years from 1882 to 1912 were 4,021. Of this number, 1,231 were whites and 2,790 were Negroes. The average per year for Negroes was 93, for whites, 41. From 80 to 90 per cent of the lynchings are in the South. Less than one-fourth of the lynchings of Negroes is due to assaults upon women; in 1912 only one-fifth was for this cause. The largest per cent of lynchings is for murder or attempted murder. Over 10 per cent is for minor offenses.

It is of still greater interest to compare the commitments for rape. In 1904, the commitments for this crime per 100,000 of the total population were: all whites, 0.6; colored, 1.8; Italians; 5.3; Mexicans, 4.8; Austrians, 3.2; Hungarians, 2.0; French, 1.9; Russians, 1.9. Of those committed to prison for major offenses in 1904 the per cent committed for rape was, for colored, 1.9; all whites, 2.3; foreign white, 2.6; Irish, 1.3; Germans, 1.8; Poles, 2.1; Mexicans, 2.7; Canadians, 3; Russians, 3; French, 3.1; Austrians, 4.2; Italians, 4.4; Hungarians, 4.7. The commitments for assaults upon women are low in the Southern States. In the south Atlantic division the rate per 100,000 of the population in 1904, was 0.5; in the south central division it was 0.7. Some would suppose that the low rate of commitments for rape in the South is due to the fact that the most of the perpetrators of these crimes are summarily lynched; but if, however, all the Negroes who were lynched for rape in the South were included, the rate for colored would be changed less than one-fourth of 1 per cent.

The report of the immigration commission in 1911 on *Immigration and Crime* gives the following concerning the per cent that rape forms of all offenses by Negroes and whites: of convictions in the New York City court of general sessions for nine months of 1908-1909, Negro, 0.5; foreign white, 1.8; native white, 0.8. Chicago police arrests from 1905-1908, Negro, 0.34; foreign white, 0.35; native white, 0.30; of alien white prisoners, 1908, in the United States, 2.9.

Both North and South the crime rate for Negroes is much higher than it is for whites. In 1904 the commitments per 100,000, in the entire country, were, for whites, 187; for Negroes, 268. In the Southern States, Negro crime compared with white is in the ratio of 34 to 1. On the other hand it is interesting to find that the Negro has a relatively lower crime rate than several of the emigrant races

TABLE 2

Nationality	Number in United States according to Census 1900	Prison commitments in 1904	Commitments per 1,000 of each nationality
Mexicans	103,410	484	4.7
Italians	484,207	2,143	4.4
Austrians	276,249	1,006	3.6
French	104,341	358	3.4
Canadians	1,181,255	3,557	3.0
Russians	424,096	1,222	2.8
Poles	383,510	1,038	2.7
Negroes	8,840,789	23,698	2.7

who are now coming to this country. Table 2 shows the commitments to prison, in 1904, per 1,000, of certain nationalities.

As a result of emancipation and the increase in Negro crime, great changes were brought about in the prison systems of the South. Before the war the states of the South operated their prisons on state accounts and they were generally a burden on the states. After the close of the war the states found themselves with an increasing prison population and no resources from which to make appropriations for the support of these prisons. Throughout the South there was great demand for labor. Inside the prisons were thousands of able-bodied Negroes. Offers were made to the states by those needing labor to lease these prisoners, and so it was discovered that what had been an expense could be converted into a means of revenue and furnish a source from which the depleted state treasuries could be replenished. Thus it came about that all the Southern state prisons were either by the military governments or by the reconstruction governments, put upon lease.

The introduction of the convict lease system into the prisons of the South, thereby enabling the convicts to become a source of revenue, caused each state to have a financial interest in increasing the number of convicts. It was inevitable, therefore, that many abuses should arise. In his report for 1870, less than a year after the Georgia lease had been effected, the principal keeper of the penitentiary complained about the treatment of the convicts by the lessees. An investigation in 1875 of the Texas system revealed a most horrible condition of affairs. From time to time in other states there were attacks on the systems and legislative investigations. The better conscience of the South demanded reform in the treatment of criminals for it was found that "the convict lease system had made the condition of the convict infinitely worse than was possible under a system of slavery in which the slave belonged to his master for life." In recent years there has been much improvement in the condition of convicts in the South. Five states, Louisiana, Mississippi, Georgia, Oklahoma and Texas have abolished the lease, contract, and other hiring systems. All the other Southern states still sell convict labor to some extent, but in each of these strong movements are on foot to abolish the custom.

After the close of the war and as a part of the reconstruction of the South there had to be some readjustment of court procedure with reference to Negroes. Hitherto they had been dealt with as slaves or as free persons of color. After the adoption of the war amendments, they came before the courts as full citizens of the United States. From now on, much of the time, in many sections, the major part of the time of the criminal courts has been taken up with trying cases where Negroes were concerned.

Before emancipation the Negro had noted that wherever the law had been invoked with reference to a Negro that it was generally to punish or to restrain. Thus he came to view the law as something to be feared and evaded but not necessarily to be respected or to be sought as a means of protection. Under freedom the Negro's experience with the law was much the same as it had been in slavery. He found that the courts were still used as a means of punishment and restraint and that generally they were not the place to seek for protection. Another cause of the Negroes regarding the courts unfavorably was the stringent laws relating to labor contracts. These laws imposed severe penalties upon the laborer who violated his contract and often reduced him to peonage. The result is that at present the attitude of the Negroes toward the law is that many still associate laws with slavery and look upon courts as places where punishment is meted out rather than where justice is dispensed.

This brings us to the question whether the Negroes are fairly tried in the courts. Judge W. H. Thomas, of Montgomery, Ala., after an experience of ten years as a trial judge, in an address before the Southern Sociological Congress, at Nashville, in 1912, said:

> My observation has been that courts try the Negro fairly. I have observed that juries have not hesitated to acquit the Negro when the evidence showed his innocence. Yet, honesty demands that I say that justice too often miscarries in the attempt to enforce the criminal law against the native white man. It is not that the Negro fails to get justice before the courts in the trial of the specific indictment against him, but too often it is that the native white man escapes it. It must be poor consolation to the foreign born, the Indian, the Negro and the ignorant generally to learn that the law has punished only the guilty of their class or race, and to see that the guilty of the class, fortunate by reason of wealth, learning or color, are not so punished for like crime. There must be a full realization of the fact that if punishments of the law are not imposed on all offenders alike, it will breed distrust of administration.

Hon. William H. Sanford, also of Montgomery, Ala., in an address before the same congress on "Fundamental Inequalities of Administration Of Laws," further illuminated this question. He pointed out that the real population of the South is made up of three distinctive communities:

> First where the population is composed largely of Negroes, sometimes in the ratio of as many as ten to one. Second, where the population is largely white, usually at a ratio of about two to one. Third, where the population is almost entirely white.
>
> In the first of these, in the administration of the criminal law, the Negro usually gets even and exacts justice, sometimes tempered with mercy. The average white man who serves on the juries in these counties, in his cooler moments and untouched by racial influences, is a believer in fair play, and for the most part is the descendant of the men who builded the foundation of our states. But in these communities, a white man rarely, if ever, gets a fair and an impartial trial, and, if indeed he is indicted by a grand jury, his conviction or acquittal is determined more upon his family connections, his business standing or his local political influence than upon the evidence in the case as applied to the law.
>
> In the second of these communities the law is more nearly enforced as to both classes, and except in cases where the rights of the one are opposed to those of the other, convictions may be had, and indeed are often had, against the members of both races for offenses of the more serious nature.
>
> In the third of these communities the white man usually gets a fair trial and is usually acquitted or convicted according to the evidence under the law, while the Negro, the member of an opposite race, has scant consideration before a jury composed entirely of white men, and is given the severest punishments for the most trivial offenses.

In conclusion what are some of the principal factors of Negro criminality in the South? The convict lease system has already been indicated as one of these factors. Another factor is the imposing of severe and sometimes unjust sentences for misdemeanors, petty offenses and for vagrancy. Still another factor is the lack of facilities to properly care for Negro juvenile offenders. Ignorance is, by some, reckoned as one of the chief causes of Negro crime. The majority of the serious offenses, such as homicide and rape, are committed by the ignorant. It appears to be pretty generally agreed that one of the chief causes of Negro crime in the South is strong drink. Attention was called to this fact by the great falling off in crime in those sections of the South where the prohibition law was put into effect. The general testimony is that where prohibition has really prohibited the Negro from securing liquor, the crime rate has decreased; where, however, the prohibition law has not prevented the Negro from securing liquor, there has been no decrease in the crime rate, but, instead, the introduction of a cheaper grade of liquor peddled about in the city and in the country districts, appears to have tended to increase crime.

One of the most significant and hopeful signs for the satisfactory solution of the race problem in the South is the attitude that is being taken towards Negro crime. The Negroes themselves are trying to get at the sources of crime and are making efforts to bring about better conditions. In some sections they have law and order leagues working in cooperation with the officers of the law. The white people are also giving serious consideration to Negro crime. Its sources, causes and effects upon the social life of the South are being studied. Movements are on foot for bettering conditions. Under the leadership of the late ex-Governor W. J. Northern, of Georgia, Christian civic leagues, composed of colored and white persons, were organized in that and other states for the purpose of putting down mob violence. The Southern Sociological Congress is taking the lead for the abolition of the convict lease and contract systems and for the adoption, in the South, of modern principles of prison reform.

7

INTRODUCTION

E. Franklin Frazier is one of the most influential African American sociologists of the 20th century. In 1931, he completed his dissertation at the University of Chicago. Like most other early Black scholars, Frazier taught at predominantly Black colleges, including Morehouse College, Fisk University, and Howard University. Unlike others, during his career, he also taught at many predominantly White institutions, including Columbia University, New York University, and the University of California at Berkeley. During his career, he served in several leadership positions, including the following: director of the Atlanta School of Social Work; chair of the Department of Sociology at Howard; head of the Applied Social Science Division of the United Nations Educational, Scientific, and Cultural Organization; and president of the American Sociological Society (predecessor of the American Sociological Association) in 1948. He also received numerous awards, including scholarships, fellowships, and honorary degrees.

This article first appeared in Frazier's book, *The Negro Family in the United States.* In the book, Frazier analyzed how social conditions shaped Negro families more than race or African survivals as was customary of the time period. The book is considered to be Frazier's most important work and won the Anisfield Award as the most significant book on race relations published in 1939. Unlike previous studies of the Negro family, Frazier described the impact of slavery, emancipation, and urbanization on the family unit. "Rebellious Youth" is a chapter in Part 4 of the book, titled "In the City of Destruction." Frazier argues that family disorganization in the urban environment contributes to delinquency among Negro youth. In this chapter, he provides descriptive details about male and female Negro delinquents that are rarely seen in either past or contemporary studies. He also provides detailed information about Negro boys and girls who were arrested because of delinquency and neglect between 1930 and 1934 in Harlem and compares them to Negro youth arrested in Nashville and Chicago.

Rebellious Youth

E. Franklin Frazier

The disorganization of Negro family life in the urban environment, together with the absence of communal controls, results in a high delinquency rate among Negro boys and girls. However, among Negroes, as among whites, boys are much more frequently brought before the courts than girls. For example, in 1933 there were 9,864 Negro boys compared with 1,803 Negro girls dealt with in delinquent cases disposed of by sixty-seven courts in the United States[1] not including the 283 boys and 8 girls whose cases were disposed of by federal authorities.[2] Since the misconduct of Negro girls has been considered to some extent in connection with the problem of unmarried motherhood, our attention here will be directed mainly to the misconduct of Negro boys which may be dealt with under the law.[3]

Negro boys and girls are younger on the whole than white boys and girls handled by the courts. In the sixty-seven courts for which we have records in 1933, 87 per cent of the Negro boys and 84 per cent of the Negro girls compared with 79 per cent of the white boys and 69 the white girls were under sixteen years of age.[4] Moreover, available studies indicate that the rates of delinquency for both Negro boys and Negro girls are distinctly higher than for white boys and girls. For example, in New York City the Negro rate is about three times the white rate, while in Baltimore it is more than four times the white rate.[5] Then, if we view the situation from the standpoint of the Negro alone, we find that in three southern cities—Richmond, Memphis, and Charleston—the proportion of Negro cases has been about one and a half times their relative numbers in the population of these cities, while in Indianapolis, Gary, and Dayton, the proportion has reached three or four times their relative numbers.[6]

It is difficult to detect any significant trend in juvenile delinquency among Negroes for the country as a whole. However, in certain localities one may find fairly definite indications that the rates have mounted or declined over a period of years.[7] In the District of Columbia the rate has declined from 922 per 10,000 boys of juvenile court age in 1927 to 737 in 1933. During the same period the rate in Hudson County, New Jersey, declined from 698 to 263; and in Fulton County, Georgia, from 644 to 496 for the years 1930-33. On the

From Frazier, E. F. (1939). Rebellious youth. *The Negro Family in the United States.* Chicago: Universtiy of Chicago Press.

TABLE 1 Number of Negro Boys and Girls Brought Before the Juvenile Court, Nashville, Tennessee, 1925-29

	1925	*1926*	*1927*	*1928*	*1929*
Boys	210	169	186	200	176
Girls	98	96	95	84	68

other hand, in Baltimore from 1930-1933 the rate rose from 672 to 962, and in New York City it leaped from 170 in 1927 to 342 in 1928 and remained close to the latter rate until 1933. But even the trends observable in the various cities throw little or no light on the problem of Negro delinquency. In order to get an understanding it is necessary to study the delinquent boy or girl in relation to his or her family and community setting.

The facts brought out in a study of Negro juvenile delinquency in Nashville, Tennessee, during recent years will enable us to get some understanding of the social factors which are responsible for delinquency in southern cities.[8]

During the period from 1925 to 1929, the number of Negro boys brought into the juvenile court in Nashville fluctuated considerably, whereas the number of Negro girls declined from 98 to 68 (see Table 1). The number of Negro delinquents brought to court during this period was only slightly in excess of their relative numbers in the population of the city.[9] In 1929 about 70 percent of the boys and 63 percent of the girls were from twelve to fifteen years of age. Nearly a half of the boys were charged with stealing; whereas the majority of the girls were charged with incorrigibility and disorderly conduct. It should be added that these Negro delinquents were apprehended as ordinary criminals and brought to court by the police much more frequently than the white delinquents.

The complaint of a deputy sheriff against a ten-year-old offender gives some notion of the demoralization of childhood represented in these delinquency cases:

> This boy was brought in on a state warrant charging tippling and boy admits that he sold a pint of whisky for the people for whom he was working, to some man he did not know, for $1.50 and gave the money to the people for whom he worked. H. made an investigation of the boy's home and found conditions deplorable. The boy's mother does not live there but at the place where she works. The boy lives with a married sister whose home is filthy and unsanitary and an unfit place to live. The boy does not have supervision. He will not tell the truth and is badly in need of supervision.[10]

In the charges brought by police officers against a fifteen-year-old boy, who was sentenced to the Children's Detention Home for a year, one can see to what extent these homeless children in the slum areas of southern cities are subjected to all types of vicious influences:

> The proof is that he, S. P., A. W., and two other men were all in one bed together on Sunday morning, March 3, and were engaged in lewdness. The boy is not going to school and has not been at home in weeks. He lives in this room where the officer caught all the lewdness at 7 A.M. The boy has heretofore been at the C.D.H. for larceny. He is delinquent and a truant.[11]

But more often these boys are picked up for acts of theft ranging from petty stealing to burglaries. The record of a boy only eleven years of age charged with larceny states:

> The boy's father came in court and made complaint that the boy would not work or go to school but was stealing all around the neighborhood and was teaching the small boys with whom he associates to steal. His mother brought him to court this day and made the same complaint and both request that he be committed to the S.T.A. From the statements of both parents and after talking to the boy the court is satisfied that he is a truant and delinquent and is stealing.

Often these young lawbreakers are schooled in crime by older boys or men or even members of their families. This was evident in the case of the eight-year-old boy charged in housebreaking and larceny:

> Policeman B found a raincoat and two pairs of shoes in the home of this boy and arrested him. The boy admits that he and his uncle C.B. went to the home of F. about 12 o'clock at night and the uncle took a watch and chain and the boy a raincoat and the shoes home with him. The boy says that they broke in the house. The boy's uncle got away and he does not know where he is.

Sometimes boys as young as eleven or twelve are apprehended as members of criminal gangs engaging regularly in housebreaking and thefts. The extreme youth of the boys caught in such delinquencies is indicative of the general lack of parental control among some elements of the Negro population. In the complaint of the aunt against her wayward twelve-year-old nephew we get a hint of the broken homes from which so many of these delinquents come:

> This boy was brought into court by his aunt; she states that the boy's mother is dead, that his father does not provide for the boy, that she has reared him since he was one year old, that he will not work nor go to school and associates with bad company and she can no longer control him and wants the court to take the custody of him. She promises to clothe him.

In fact, only 67 of the 176 delinquent Negro boys brought into court in 1929 came from families in which both parents were living together. In 37 other cases, although both parents were living, they were separated, chiefly because of the desertion of the father. Fifty-nine boys came from homes where either the mother or the father was dead. The home situation was even worse in the case of the 68 delinquent girls; only 15 of them came from normal families.

The charge of incorrigibility against 50 of these girls involved five specific offenses: sex delinquency, truancy, ungovernability, running away, and continued association with vicious companions.[12] In 27 cases there was sex delinquency ranging from initial sex experiences to promiscuous relations and prostitution. Truancy, which was often associated with sex delinquency, was found in 23 cases. Although ungovernability was found as the sole offense in 7 cases, in 9 others it was associated with sex delinquency, truancy, and running away. Fourteen of the 15 girls who were charged with running away were most frequently guilty of sex offenses, while the 5 girls charged with association with vicious companions were generally guilty of the other four offenses. A view of the type of family background from which some of these girls come is given us in the following excerpt from the story given by a girl charged with incorrigibility:

> I never want nor expect to return home again, never. I guess I haven't a home anyway. I asked my adopted father to never come out here to see me. He wouldn't get me any clothes then because I didn't want to see him. He said if I didn't want to see him I sure couldn't have any of his money or anything his money bought. When I left home to come here I told that woman he lived with that the last thing I intended to do was to poison both of them. I might change my mind though.
>
> My own mother and father are dead. I liked my adopted father all right while my adopted mother was living. They were like parents to me. When my adopted mother got sick and

stayed for a while papa began running around with this woman that he is living with. One of my chums put me on to it. This woman lived next door to her and she used to see him going there. As soon as mama dies he took this woman in. It wasn't more than a week after mama I told him that he ought to be ashamed, and I said so much to him that he slapped me. He never had hit me before, and think, hit me about that hoar, I never would eat at the same table. After she came there to live I would leave for school at 6 o'clock in morning, and I wouldn't come home until late at night. I hated to go home. I promised to poison both of them and they believed me. They tried to get Miss R. to put me in the C. D. Home a long time before she sent me. Miss R. said she didn't blame me for not wanting to stay around them. They would throw up to me about my real mother, that she had had four children and never been married. I never heard anything about this till this woman came.[13]

In some cases the delinquent behavior of these girls has not only been taken over from their parents or other adults but represents their response to what is held up to them as their expected role in life. A woman who called the probation officer for aid in managing her thirteen-year-old niece described the latter as follows:

> But I know Mary. I ought to when I have had her every since she was five months old. I know and understand her. She is exactly like her mama. Her mama is my baby sister, but the truth is the truth. She had Mary when she was only 15 by an old nigger that didn't have a dime to his name. He run off and she never heard of him again after he got her in trouble. I kept her in my house until Mary was born and treated her good and helped her with the baby. Then when Mary was five months old this gal ups and runs off with another nigger and I ain't laid eyes on her from that day to this. Mary has never seen her mama, I understand alright.

This girl's aunt was reputed to have once been a prostitute and was known to be engaged at the time of the complaint in bootlegging. Her neighbors described her as "just another whore" and claimed that she forced her niece to "hustle" in order to get money for food and clothing.[14]

Occasionally, delinquency on the part of these girls is the result of the gradual breaking-down of standards that have been built up in the rural environment. This is shown in the following document, which was furnished by a seventeen-year-old girl.[15] Moreover, this document is of particular interest because it shows that, although the girl's immediate family was broken by desertion on the part of the father, in the rural community the children were integrated into the larger family group. However, when the girl came to live in the urban environment, the absence of a normal family life became the means by which she was led into delinquency.

> From the time that I can remember anything my mother and we children were living with our grandfather who had a farm out at ——— Tennessee. I was happy and so were my brothers I remember and sisters until grandpa would begin fussing. I remember how he used to fuss long before I remember what he would be saying. I would know that something made him mad. Soon my mother married again to a man who had pretty good money for a country farmer. Then mama moved away to a town about seven miles from us. All of us cried and begged her to take us but she wouldn't. She said grandpa and grandma had helped raise us up to where we was then and that we was just the size where we could be of help to them, and said that we could help pay grandma and grandpa for the expenses they had been at for us. She said our father had never done anything for us. That was the first time I had heard her say anything about our father to remember. I guess when grandpa would be fussing he would be saying something about him, but I didn't know it. Anyhow I wondered how he looked and asked grandma about him but she wouldn't say much. But before I was much larger I looked and asked grandma about him and found out that papa quit my mama about

four months before my youngest brother was born and came here with another woman. This woman use to come to the house when mama and papa was living together and tried to be so nice to mama. Mama really didn't know that papa and this woman was going together.

Grandma said when one of mama's friends told her about it she got mad at her. Not long after this papa pretended that his oldest brother was at the point of death in the city, and that he had to go at once. He didn't come back again until my baby brother had been born and was six years old. He didn't know papa and was scared of him like he would be of any other strange man. When my baby brother saw him he said "Oh there is Jimmy Holloman." He really didn't know papa. Then papa got mad about that. That night my brother had an earache and was crying. Papa got mad about this and said that he needed a whipping for keeping up all that racket. Grandpa told him if he laid his hand on the child he would kill him dead. Papa left next day and didn't come no more until grandpa had been dead a long time. Mama had married and we were all large children. He came to visit his sister and brother who lived at home. Folks use to say that I looked exactly like his sister, Aunt Molly. But Grandma didn't like that because she said that Aunt Molly was nothing but a slut. She was married but she had had ten children and wasn't but two of them her husband's. The other eight had stray daddies. We didn't know how to act toward him and none of us would call him papa. We would just begin talking and wouldn't call him anything. He stayed a month. He swore that he wasn't married but he got a lot of letters while he was there. He went fishing one day and me and my sister went into his things and found some things that almost made us faint. We found first two letters from two children of his that he had in ——— a little town not far from here. They were thanking him for sending them some stockings and other clothes. The oldest one of these children was a boy and we found out after we come here that this boy was almost as old as my youngest brother. The other was a girl. We couldn't speak for a while after we read these letters. There was a letter from their mama too. She said in that letter something I will never forget the longest day I have about people calling her a fool for still being crazy about him but that as long as she was satisfied they could go to hell. My grandma and grandpa had said so many times that papa was nothing but a nasty, stinking, low down nigger, who was too lazy to work and take care of a family. I don't know why we ought to have been surprised to find out more dirt but we were. I dreaded for him to come back from fishing and hoped that he would soon go home. There he was sending this woman and those bastards things when he hadn't send us hardly $20 worth the whole while that he had been away.

Later, the girl came to the city to live with her father and stepmother. Her story continues:

> I hated so bad to live in the place in which they were living. It was an apartment flat with three families living upstairs and three downstairs. Brother said that he had heard that not a one of the couples was married. He didn't believe that papa was married to this woman either. They played cards all day Sunday. This made me sick because grandma had never allowed us to go to dances let alone play cards. I had to sleep in the same room with papa and his wife. Brother slept in a cot in the kitchen. There wasn't but two rooms. Papa and this woman would often wake us up in the night doing their business. I wouldn't let on that they woke me up. The springs would squeak and this woman wouldn't let that noise do but I could hear easy enough. This made me sick again I never had heard such at grandma's house and I looked down on that kind of stuff. My sister came and we just lived through it. Sister and I dreaded for night to come. We hated papa more and more.

The two sisters and their brother continued to go church as they had done in the country. This caused their father to ridicule them about their "country" habits. Tension between the father and the children continued to

TABLE 2 Number of Delinquent and Neglected Negro Boys and Girls Arrested in the Harlem Area, 1930-34

		Year				
Sex	*Age*	*1930*	*1931*	*1932*	*1933*	*1934*
Delinquent						
Male	10-16	362	265	212	229	271
	Under 10	36	18	9	9	9
Female	10-16	27	15	20	28	36
	Under 10	0	1	0	1	1
Neglected						
Male	10-16	11	10	5	5	6
	Under 10	16	9	5	7	9
Female	10-16	10	3	1	3	1
	Under 10	6	6	11	6	7

become more acute until finally there was an open break in which the children engaged in a fist fight with their father. As the result, the girls were put out of the home and reported to the court as being incorrigible. Instead of sending them to the detention home as the father requested, the court put them on probation to their brother. When their brother married, they were without a home. The girl who was charged with sex delinquency because of her conduct, described below, and sent to the detention home, ends her story with the following comment:

> After I had seen so much out of my father, and my brother had changed so I just seemed to slip. When I began living on the place I would have one day off. I didn't have any place to go. My boy friend invited me to spend my off-time over his place. Everybody sows their wild oats at some time or other in their lives, I don't believe that I am guilty of any sin because I am going to marry this feller.

Let us turn our attention from this southern city to New York City, where, as we have seen, Negro juvenile delinquency rates suddenly jumped in 1928 to 342 per 10,000 boys as compared with 170 in 1927.[16] In 1930 there were for all the boroughs 839 Negro children, or 11.8 per cent of the total of 7,090 children, brought before the Children's Court. When delinquents from all agencies were considered, there were 1,065 Negro children, or 10.3 per cent of the total 10,374 children. However, the proportion of Negro delinquents among the delinquents in both groups varied in the different boroughs. The rate was highest in the Manhattan borough, where Negro delinquents before the Children's Court comprised 26 per cent of the total; whereas, in the borough of Brooklyn, Negro cases comprised only 5.4 per cent of all the delinquents before the court.[17]

For our purposes here, we shall consider Negro boys and girls arrested because of delinquency and neglect in the Harlem area during the years 1930-34.[18] On the whole, the number of Negro boys and girls arrested for delinquency has declined since 1930, although the figures for 1934 indicate that the number of delinquents was mounting again. This was especially noticeable in the case of the delinquent girls (see Table 2). The vast majority of the Negro delinquents were between ten and sixteen years of age; only about 3 per cent of the boys, except in 1930, being under ten years of age. However, if the chil-

TABLE 3* Number of Negro Boys and Girls Brought Into the Juvenile Court of Cook County During Each Fiscal Year, December 1, 1919—November 30, 1929

Year	*1920*	*1921*	*1922*	*1923*	*1924*	*1925*	*1926*	*1927*	*1928*	*1929*
Delinquent:										
Boys	182	194	177	161	310	326	320	342	427	435
Girls	128	100	116	108	107	98	117	154	166	132
Dependent:										
Boys	45	30	26	26	52	79	86	79	109	81
Girls	40	26	37	46	61	50	73	76	101	102

* Taken from the records of the Institute for Juvenile Research.

dren arrested because of neglect are considered separately, we find that the vast majority were under ten years of age.

When we analyze the offenses for which these boys and girls were arrested, we find that, as in Nashville, the chief offense of the boys was larceny and burglary; whereas 50 per cent of the girls were charged with incorrigibility. Thus, in 1934 about 30 per cent of the delinquent boys were charged with larceny and 10 per cent with burglary. Among the more serious offenses charged against the boys, assaults and holdups ranked third and fourth, respectively; whereas sex offenses held second place among the girls. Two boys were charged with homicide in 1931 and one with the same offense in 1932. Although there was no change in the rank of these various offenses among either girls or boys during the five years, the proportion of boys arrested for larceny and burglary increased appreciably, while the proportion for assaults and holdups declined slightly.[19] The majority of the less serious crimes were indicative of the lack of recreational facilities and programs for the children of the Harlem community. For example, in 1934 eleven of the boys were charged with hitching on trolleys and twenty-seven with stealing rides on subways. On the other hand, the comparatively few boys charged with selling on the streets or shining shoes most likely reflected the general poverty of the families in the area.

The relation of juvenile delinquency to the organization of the Harlem Negro community is not so apparent as in Chicago, where, as we shall see, it is definitely related to economic and cultural organization of the Negro community.[20] In Chicago the percentage of Negro delinquent cases among the cases brought before the juvenile court has steadily increased since 1900. In that year 4.7 per cent of all cases of boys before the court were Negro boys.

The percentage of Negro boys increased for each five-year period until it reached 21.7 in 1930.[21] In Table 3 we have the number of delinquent and dependent boys and girls brought into the juvenile court each year during the decade 1920-1929. Naturally, these figures do not include all cases of delinquency; in fact, they do not include all the cases of arrests for delinquency. For example, in 1927 there were 1,503 boys arrested for juvenile delinquency, although only 342 cases were taken into the court.[22]

The marked increase in the proportion of Negro cases has coincided with the increase in the Negro population during and since the war period. However, what is more important is that this increase has followed the settlement of the Negro migrant in areas characterized by a high delinquency rate.[23]

The Negro, like other groups marked off from the general population because of color and low economic and cultural status, has

TABLE 4 Number of Negro Boys Arrested for Juvenile Delinquency and Rate of Delinquency in Seven Zones of the South Side Negro Community, Chicago, 1926

	Zone I	*Zone II*	*Zone III*	*Zone IV*	*Zone V*	*Zone VI*	*Zone VII*
Boys arrested	33	208	373	364	223	59	5
Rate	42.8	31.4	30.0	28.8	15.7	9.6	1.4

found a dwelling-place in the deteriorated area just outside the Loop.[24] In the zone nearest the center of the city, the juvenile delinquency rate, based upon arrests, was over 40 per cent.[25]

From a physical standpoint this area showed extreme deterioration and gave evidence of the expansion of the central business district. On the one hand, there were dilapidated houses carrying signs of rooms for rent at fifteen and twenty cents a bed, junk shop markets with stale meat, and crowded Negro quarters with filthy bedding half-visible through sooty and broken window panes. On the other hand, new motorcar salesrooms furnished signs of the future role which the regenerated area would play in the organization of the city. In keeping with the general character of the area, all organized community life had disappeared, and inhabitants were, on the whole, remnants of broken families and foot-loose men and women. In 1921 the men in the county jail who claimed residence in this area comprised over 9 per cent of the adult males living in the area.

Although the delinquency rates in the next three zones were lower than in the first zone, they were still comparatively high. About three out of ten boys from ten to seventeen years of age were arrested for juvenile delinquency in these zones. The significant drop in the delinquency rate appeared in the fifth zone, where only 15 per cent of the boys of juvenile-court age were arrested for delinquency. In the sixth zone the delinquency rate continued to decline sharply, and in the seventh zone only 1.4 per cent of the boys were charged with delinquent behavior (see Table 4).

The decline in delinquency coincided with the decline in dependency, family desertion, and illegitimacy in the seventh zone indicating the expansion of the Negro population. The rates were high in those areas that were characterized by physical decay and the lack of organized community life. In these areas the customary forms of social control, as represented by the family and the simple folk culture of the migrants from southern communities, tended to break down or disappear altogether. Consequently, some of the fairly well-organized families lost control of their children who took over from boys or gangs patterns of delinquent behavior which were characteristic of these areas. The children from the numerous broken families, and whose mothers had to carry the entire burden of supporting their families, easily drifted into delinquency. In the third zone, where prostitution and other types of criminal behavior flourished, not only were the children subjected to the criminal influences in the neighborhood, but they were also influenced by the criminal behavior of their parents. The decline in the delinquency rate in the areas toward the periphery of the community coincided with the increasing stabilization of family life and the disappearance of various forms of social disorganization.

What we have observed in regard to juvenile delinquency in the Negro community in Chicago is characteristic of other cities, in the South as well as the North. Though the process of selection which is apparent in the economic and cultural organization of Negro communities is less pronounced and not so well defined in some cities, the incidence of juvenile delinquency is closely tied up with the organization of the community. Juvenile delinquency flourishes in those areas where the Negro, because of the numerous broken homes and the employment of the mother, the children lack parental control which is sometimes able to offset the influence of the vicious environment. Negro families with higher aspirations who are able to achieve some economic security are constantly escaping from the deteriorated slum areas. They move as far as they are able into the areas where the more stable families and substantial elements in the Negro population live and maintain ordered community life. This selective process is the outcome of the rigorous competition which Negro families must face in the modern urban environment, and their success or failure depends largely upon their cultural as well as economic sources.

Notes

1. U.S. Department of Labor, *Juvenile Court Statistics and Federal Juvenile Offenders* (Children's Bureau Pub. 232 [Washington, 1936]), p. 29. Only of the 255 courts reporting delinquency furnished information on color.

2. *Ibid.*, p. 81.

3. As defined in the report of the Committee on Socially Handicapped Delinquency, of the White House Conference on Child Health and Protection, "delinquency is any such juvenile misconduct as might be dealt with under law" (*The Delinquent Child* [New York], p. 23).

4. U.S. Department of Labor, *op. cit.*, p. 29.

5. *Ibid.*, p. 10; see also Sophia Robinson, *Can Delinquency Be Measured* (New York, 1936), pp. 62-64.

6. See T. J. Woofter, Jr., *Negro Problems in Cities* (New York, 1928).

7. U.S. Department of Labor, *op. cit.*, p. 10.

8. The information on Nashville is taken from a Master's thesis written under the direction of the author (see Mary LaVerta Huff, "Juvenile Delinquency in Nashville" [Fisk University thesis (Nashville, Tenn., 1934)]).

9. However, in 1932 the number of delinquent boys increased to 324 and the number of girls to 83. This increase might have been due to the apprehension of more delinquents when the Negro probation force was enlarged.

10. From court record.

11. From court record.

12. Huff, *op. cit.*, p. 56.

13. Quoted in *ibid.*, p. 61.

14. *Ibid.*, p. 74.

15. *Ibid.*, pp. 77-79.

16. See p. 350 above.

17. Robinson, *op. cit.*, p. 61.

18. This information was collected in 1935 from the records of the police precincts while the author was engaged in a study of Harlem for the Mayor's Commission on Conditions in Harlem (see Map V).

19. A study of delinquent and neglected Negro children in New York City twelve years ago showed a different distribution of offenses for the boys. According to that study, the most common charges against Negro boys were disorderly conduct and desertion of home; whereas approximately 85 per cent of the Negro girls were charged with desertion of home and ungovernable and wayward conduct. The most common charges against the whites were stealing and burglary. Thus, our figures indicate that the charges against Negro boys are at present similar to those against white boys (see Joint Committee on Negro Child Study, *A Study of Delinquent and Neglected Children before the New York City Children's Court in 1925* [New York, 1927], p. 6).

20. See the author's *The Negro Family in Chicago*, chap. ix, for a full discussion of the relation of delinquency rates to the economic and cultural organization of the Negro community.

21. *Ibid.*, p. 206. During this same period the percentage of Negro girls in the total cases increased from 11 to 20.9.

22. *Ibid.*, p. 205, n.1.

23. Shaw, who has shown in a number of well-known studies the relation between delinquency and community disorganization, makes the following statement: "It is interesting to note that the main high rate areas of the city—those near the Loop, around the Stock Yards and the South Chicago steel mills—have been characterized by high rates over a long period. Our data are based on records that go back thirty years, and the early and late juvenile court series show conclusively that many of the areas have been characterized by high rates throughout the entire period. It should be remembered that relatively high rates have persisted in certain areas notwithstanding the fact that the composition (racial) of population has changed markedly" (Clifford Shaw et al., *Delinquency Areas* [Chicago, 1929], p. 203).

24. Cf. Sophonisba P. Breckinridge and Edith Abbott, *The Delinquent Child and the Home* (New York, 1912), p. 153.

25. See Map IV, p. 303.

INTRODUCTION

Earl R. Moses, author of this article and the following one, received a master's degree in sociology from the University of Chicago in 1932 and a Ph.D. in sociology from the University of Pennsylvania in 1948, where he studied under Thorsten Sellin. Later, he taught at Morgan State University in Baltimore, Maryland.

This article uses the ecological approach and examines the concept of delinquency areas developed by Clifford R. Shaw and Henry D. McKay. Like Frazier, Moses focuses on the role of family and community factors. In this article, Moses summarizes findings of a study of Negro delinquents in Chicago in the 1930s. According to Moses, it is the second article based on materials of the study. The first appeared in 1933 in *Opportunity,* a publication of the National Urban League. The methodology for this study included analyses of 2,449 juvenile court cases from December 1928 to November 1929. The data are used to compare delinquency for both Black and White males and females in selected areas. White areas in close proximity and similar to Negro areas (disorganized, areas in transition, and organized) were included for comparative purposes. In this study, rates of Negro delinquency were higher than White rates. However, Negro and White delinquents were found to be similar in several ways. Moses identifies two patterns of delinquent behavior, indigenous and transplanted. He is also among the first to identify family mobility within the socially disorganized areas as a contributor to delinquency.

COMMUNITY FACTORS IN NEGRO DELINQUENCY

EARL R. MOSES

The basic pattern of geographic distribution of juvenile delinquents in urban communities has established what is currently recognized as "delinquency areas." This concept is primarily the outgrowth of a study entitled *Delinquency Areas,* Shaw, *et al,* in which the authors, through use of geographic distribution maps and rates of delinquency applied to several series of data, show how delinquency tends to concentrate in certain areas of the urban community in response to natural processes in urban development.[1] Other studies, although sometimes showing moderate variations, have substantiated the basic pattern presented in the study just cited. In a highly penetrating and elucidating study entitled, *The Negro Family in Chicago,* Dr. E. Franklin Frazier, the author, dealt with the disorganization and reorganization of Negro family life in response to natural processes involved in orientation to an urban community. The extent of juvenile delinquency was used by Dr. Frazier as one of the indices for measuring the character of Negro zones of settlement. The geographic distribution of juvenile delinquents and of rates of delinquency assume, therefore, considerable significance in showing differences in these zones of settlement.

This paper will deal with a study undertaken as a natural outgrowth of the two studies cited above. The three studies have in common the same urban community (Chicago) as a background for study; comparable elements in that the investigations and data involve concurrent or consecutive years;[2] and, moreover, there is a similarity in the point of view as related to juvenile delinquency. This study,[3] "Community Factors in Negro Delinquency," has a point of departure from the intensive consideration of juvenile delinquency among a specific racial group. The study, however, is not confined to the Negro but also draws on data dealing with juvenile delinquency among whites for points of comparison. It should be clearly understood that this paper will not attempt to present the data and detailed findings of the study. Rather an attempt will be made to summarize the character of the study, several points dealing with methodological procedure, and the major findings and tentative conclusions of the study.

From Moses, E. R. (1936). Community factors in negro delinquency. *Journal of Negro Education, 5*(2), 220-227. Reprinted with permission of the Journal of Negro Education.

Nature of the Study

The object of this study was to ascertain community factors that are conducive to juvenile delinquency among Negroes in Chicago. The following are representative questions around which the study evolved: What are Negro areas? What are the characteristics of such areas? Are there differences in Negro zones of settlement? If so, why? To what extent does a zonal approach to delinquency reveal differences in the character of Negro communities? To what extent does the distribution of Negro delinquents reflect differences in the character of Negro zones of settlement? How far is the Negro delinquent the product of the Negro community? The following are the major hypotheses, which the study tested:

The characteristics of Negro areas vary from community to community, depending upon such factors as delinquency and crime, when used as indices of community organization or disorganization. Negro delinquency is not evenly distributed over all Negro areas of settlement but varies by zones. The characteristics of these areas, using juvenile delinquency as the chief index of measurement, will show that there are not only differences but marked extremes in Negro zones of settlement.

The abnormally high increase of juvenile delinquency among Negroes in proportion to the total Negro population in Chicago is due largely to the settling of Negro migrant families in areas of deterioration and disorganization. The Negro delinquent, therefore, is to a great extent the product of settlement in disorganized areas where delinquent patterns of behavior prevail and where the *mores* and traditions of the community are conducive to the development of delinquent careers. Moreover, Negro delinquency shows similar rates of delinquency and patterns of delinquent behavior by communities as in non-Negro areas.

The parents of Negro delinquents are a mobile group, but they do not tend to move out of areas characterized by high rates of delinquency into areas which are characterized by low rates of delinquency. Lack of movement out of these disorganized areas is largely due to low occupational and income levels, which force Negro migrant families to live in areas of deterioration. These are areas characterized by high rates of delinquency.

Materials of the Study

The materials of the study involved two lines of approach: (1) life-history documents of case studies of delinquent Negro boys; and (2) statistical data. The life-history document materials were gathered on a basis of intensive contacts with delinquent Negro boys. For nearly two years the writer served as a volunteer worker (on a limited time basis), cooperating with a State of Illinois parole officer. Boys from the St. Charles School for Boys were paroled to the writer. Cooperating with a volunteer worker in the Boys Court, cases were also secured from that court. On the basis thus afforded for close contacts life-history documents were gathered. These documents are invariably presented in the first person and represent materials written by the patient or are translations of verbatim stenographic notes taken in the course of interviews. In addition a careful canvass was made of all official records and the records of cooperating agencies dealing with a given case. Moreover, whenever possible, the stories of family and non-family members, recorded in the first person, were secured to supplement the patient's "own story." Numerous such documents were gathered in connection with this study. Materials, designed to supplement and illustrate formal data, were culled from sixteen such documents and used in this study.

The statistical data involved a total of 2,449 juvenile court cases of delinquent boys and girls appearing before the Juvenile Court of Cook County, Illinois, during the calendar court year December 1, 1928 to November 30, 1929 inclusive. The total cases subdivided into 403 Negro male, 158 Negro female, 1,413 white male, and 475 white female cases. The official juvenile court record of each case was canvassed with reference to thirty-six items.[4] The analyses of the data formed the major statistical materials of the study. These data were finally summarized in the presentation of 16 tables, 12 supplementary tables, 3 figures, and 10 geographic distribution maps.

The Selection of Areas

Inasmuch as the materials of the study were largely analyzed in terms of small unit areas, the basis of the selection of these areas has especial significance in relation to the results obtained in this study. The selection of areas used in this study involve a two-fold aspect. First, there was the selection of the three types of areas set forth in the study; and, secondly, the selection of areas for the comparison of delinquency between Negroes and whites.

Negro communities were divided into three types of areas, namely, areas of disorganization, areas in transition, and organized communities. This classification of Negro areas is based on, (1) location, with reference to the general framework of the concentric circle theory of city growth set forth by Dr. E. W. Burgess; (2) Dr. Franklin Frazier's study of family and community organization and disorganization as presented in his study, *The Negro Family in Chicago*; and (3) the character of community institutions, and the physical and social character of the areas. The areas were arranged into square-mile units. These units were placed into order of zones by miles from the center of the city outward. High rates of delinquency were found to be concentrated in the areas nearest to the Loop, and low rates of delinquency on the periphery of Negro habitation in the city.

In order to get comparable areas for comparison with white delinquency, white areas contiguous to Negro areas were chosen. These areas resembled the physical and social character of the Negro areas. Moreover, the distribution of high and low rates of delinquency were similar to the distribution for Negroes, except on the periphery of the city around industrial property where high rates also prevail.

This paper has thus far dealt with the major questions and the hypotheses central to the study, the materials of the study, and a pertinent note on methodological procedure. Our interest now turns to summarizing the findings and tentative conclusions of the study. It was indicated above that no attempt will be made to present the data and findings of the study. However, the materials that follow will attempt to summarize the findings and tentative conclusions established by this study.[5]

Findings and Tentative Conclusions

The disproportionate share of delinquency and crime contributed by Negroes cannot be gainsaid. Statistical data on every hand can lead to no other conclusion. Various theories have been set forth in the literature to explain the prevalence of delinquency and crime among Negroes. Some writers explain Negro criminality as being the result of heredity; others explain it on a basis of environment; to many a combination of heredity and environment offers a satisfactory explanation; while to still others a satisfactory explanation is offered on a basis of defective mentality, feeble-mindedness, illiteracy, or racial degeneracy.

Turning to the implications of statistical data on delinquency and crime for Chicago, the generalization set forth above holds true for this urban community. In proportion to their relative percentage in the total population, Negroes contribute a disproportionate share of delinquency and crime in Chicago. In 1930 the Negro population formed 6.9 per cent of the total population in Chicago. Yet Negro delinquents composed 21.8 per cent of the total number of delinquents. Moreover, Negro Boys' Court age offenders and adult Negro males contribute approximately the same per cent of the total cases of crime as Negro juvenile delinquents contribute total delinquents.

The increase in Negro delinquents has been at a much faster rate than the growth of the Negro population. While the Negro population, over a period of three decades, slightly more than trebled, Negro delinquents increased seven-fold. The increase among adult Negro criminals has been at a much slower rate, increasing in the same span of years only three-fold. The rapid increase of Negro juvenile delinquents is not attributed to tendencies inherent in the race; nor is the increase attributed to the transplantation of migrant Negro boys who are inclined toward delinquent behavior. Rather, the problem of juvenile delinquency is more intimately bound up with community patterns of behavior and the deteriorated areas that Negroes occupy.

It is in community situations and factors within the community that are conducive to delinquency that the problem of delinquency among Negroes may with profit be studied. To a marked degree community situations in relation to delinquency offer the explanation of delinquency among Negroes. Negro areas of settlement are not homogeneous communities. Instead, three major types of areas may be differentiated in Chicago. These types of areas are, areas of disorganization, areas in transition, and organized Negro communities. There are marked contrasts in the character of these types of areas. Areas of disorganization are characterized by a more or less nondescript and unstable population, encroaching business, physical deterioration, high degree mobility, and pathological conditions generally. In such areas life is free. Organized Negro communities, on the other hand, are characterized by more or less common traditions, relatively stable population and high degree of organization. In these communities concerted action is possible on matters of vital interest to the members of the community. Areas in transition have characteristics that are marginal to the two types of areas just discussed. The area in transition is an area in flux, where changes are rapid. Life tends to become free; disorder and confusion compete with order and organization. More enterprising members of the area seek to escape encroaching vice, disorder and physical deterioration by moving into an organized community.

The foregoing types of areas form a frame of reference in which the problem of Negro delinquency may profitably be studied. The wide differences in the character of these types of areas have a degree of relationship to the distribution of Negro delinquents in Chicago. Moreover, delinquency in the Negro group shows a high degree of correspondence to the types of areas in which Negroes live. First, there is the problem of the segregation of Negroes into rather compact areas. Secondly, the only areas open to Negroes without contest have been areas characterized by marked physical deterioration or those in process of deterioration. Third, while Negro areas are adjacent to white areas they have limited social contacts with white communities.

Delinquency among Negroes is not evenly distributed over all Negro areas but varies by small unit areas or zones. Furthermore, delinquency varies to a marked extent in the three types of areas previously defined. Delinquency concentrates in areas of disorganization. The Negro delinquent is to a marked degree the product of conditions within these areas.

Rates of delinquency also vary by zones and types of areas. Negro percentages of delinquency in proportion to the total Negro juvenile population recede in general in movement outward from the central business district (the Loop) toward the periphery of the city. Percentages of delinquency likewise vary considerably between the types of Negro areas. The higher rates of delinquency prevai in areas of disorganization, and lower rates o delinquency are in organized Negro communities.

It was previously indicated that the increase in Negro delinquency is not attributed to the transplantation of migrant Negro boys who are inclined toward delinquent behavior. Instead, the Negro delinquent is primarily the product of migration and settlement in areas of deterioration. Of the total Negro delinquents appearing before the Juvenile Court in 1929, 77.2 per cent were born in the South. More than one-fourth of the Negro delinquents in that year were born in Mississippi. Negro boys, however, do not become delinquent immediately upon arrival in Chicago, but after they arrive, get settled, and take on patterns of behavior which characterize the community. In the series of 1929 the average Negro boy became delinquent after living in Chicago upwards of five years. The mean average of the length of residence in Chicago in 1929 for Negro delinquent boys was eight and nine months.

Mobility is an important factor in delinquency among Negroes. Negro families in which there are delinquents tend to move within the same area or same type of area. Movement is primarily of a highly localized and random character. It is essentially an intra-neighborhood movement. Moreover, this movement takes place primarily in areas of deterioration and disorganization. Thus the individual is constantly subjected to disorganized community influences. Furthermore, the character of movement among Negroes depends upon two important factors. First, Negroes are restricted in movement primarily to areas of predominantly Negro population. These are usually areas of deterioration or those in process of deterioration. Secondly, economic sufficiency is a potent factor in movement within the Negro community. Economic sufficiency in turn reflects occupational status. The majority of Negro migrants from the South are forced into areas of deterioration because of lack of economic resources, low occupational status, and low level incomes. Settlement in areas of deterioration is a means of gaining a foothold. But escape from these areas, even within the Negro community, is difficult.

The lack of adequate community facilities in Negro areas with which to deal with pre-delinquent, semi-delinquent, and delinquent Negro boys accentuates the problem of delinquency. There is virtually a complete lack of foster-homes for placement of pre-delinquent, semi-delinquent, and delinquent Negro boys. Moreover, a lack of non-state institutions to which semi-delinquent Negro boys may be referred sometimes necessitates institutional commitment. The limited provisions for organized recreational interests for leisure time activities is also conducive to delinquency in the Negro community. The limited park space and organized recreational facilities in Negro areas are indicative of the limited provisions for organized recreational interests. Finally, the high coefficients obtained in correlating delinquency, unemployment, charity cases, and illiteracy with one another indicate close relationships of these factors with one another. One cannot, of course, say that any one factor is the basic cause of another. All of these factors are probably an outgrowth from a common factor. One fact, however, is certain, namely, that these cases tend to concentrate in the same areas. And these areas are primarily areas of disorganization

The character of delinquency among Negroes is similar to delinquency among whites. Compared with other studies of delinquency the character of Negro delinquency is similar to whites in five ways: (1) There is a similarity in the pattern of geographical distribution of male delinquents. (2) Negro and white females likewise evidence a similarity in the pattern of geographical distribution. (3) There is a similarity in zonal rates of delinquency and in the receding of rates of delinquency in movement outward from the "Loop." (4) Group associates or the "gang" is an important factor in delinquency among both Negroes and whites. And, (5), nature of delinquencies varies by areas. Sometimes there is a particular type of delinquency which characterizes a definite area.

There are no extremely wide differences in delinquency between Negroes and whites. Whatever differences that are evident are variations within large patterns of delinquency. These patterns in turn are fundamentally similar. The variations between Negro and white delinquency are as follows: (1) Rates of delinquency in Negro areas are generally higher than in the white areas. This difference in rates arises out of the restriction of Negroes to compact and deteriorated areas that have only limited social contacts with white communities. (2) Recidivism among Negroes is higher than among whites, although the basic pattern of distribution of recidivism is similar. Negro recidivism is related to the deteriorated areas that they occupy. (3) Differences in race create special problems such as Negroes being primarily restricted to areas characterized by deterioration, and the lack of community facilities to deal with semi-delinquents and delinquents.

There are two major patterns of delinquent behavior. There are indigenous and transplanted patterns of delinquent behavior. Both patterns are found among Negro delinquents in Chicago. But the transplanted pattern is confined largely to the older group of juvenile age delinquents and the Boys' Court age offenders. The individuals among whom the transplanted pattern is found have usually become emancipated from family and formal controls. They frequently go from city to city, usually on random traveling escapades. The indigenous pattern of behavior is acquired into community situations. Virtually all delinquent behavior among Negroes in Chicago falls into the indigenous pattern. This pattern especially characterizes the areas of disorganization. In these areas rates of delinquency are highest.

With the rapid increase of the Negro population in Chicago, Negro areas of habitation have greatly expanded. With this expansion there has also been a decided concentration of Negroes into compact areas. Likewise have Negro areas of delinquency undergone the two-fold process of expansion of the areas characterized by delinquency and concentration of delinquents in the areas of disorganization. The rapidity of growth of Negro areas has made rapid orientation to the urban community difficult for many migrants. Consequently, the rapidity with which Negro areas have been settled has caused confusion and disorganization, and involved difficulties in adjustment to the new surroundings. Delinquency, then, has increased in startling proportions. But, as has been indicated in the materials above, the distribution of Negro delinquents is largely confined to the areas of disorganization and those areas in process of deterioration.

To summarize the study on which this paper is based, it seems safe to assume that the problem of delinquency among Negroes in Chicago is not a problem of race but is more intimately bound up with settlement in areas of deterioration where delinquent patterns of behavior prevail, and the deteriorated character of areas to which Negroes are primarily restricted.

Notes

1. For a detailed presentation of the specific point of view just indicated see, *Delinquency Areas,* Shaw et al., and *Social Factors in Juvenile Delinquency,* Clifford R. Shaw and Henry D. McKay. For studies showing the influence of patterns of behavior characteristic of disorganized communities see, *The Jack Roller,* Clifford R. Shaw, and the *Natural History of a Delinquent Career,* Clifford Shaw and Maurice Moore.

2. Dr. E. Franklin Frazier and Mr. Clifford R. Shaw carried on parts of the investigation during the same years. The present study was undertaken during the latter part of the period of their investigations. This study, moreover, used data involving the period of their investigations.

3. This study, "Community Factors in Negro Delinquency," is a part of a larger study, "The Negro Delinquent in Chicago." The larger study has four major divisions, namely, (1) community factors in Negro delinquency, (2) family backgrounds of Negro delinquency

(3) the problem of recidivism, and (4) personality adjustment and delinquent behavior. This paper will treat only community aspects of the problem.

4. All cases obviously, did not have complete information on all items.

5. A complete draft of the study, "Community Factors in Negro Delinquency," is available at the University of Chicago Library, the Chicago Urban League, and the Department of Research, Divisions X-XIII, Washington Public Schools. Some of the data embodied in the study are presented in a paper entitled, "Social and Economic Aspects of Housing Among Negroes in Chicago, with special reference to juvenile delinquency," Appendix 11, *Negro Housing*, a publication of the President's Conference on Home Building and Home Ownership. Moreover, an article based on materials of the study was published in *Opportunity*, October 1933.

INTRODUCTION

This article by Earl R. Moses provides an ecological analysis of crime in four areas in Baltimore, Maryland. It appeared 11 years after the last article and focuses more on adult felons than juvenile delinquents. Unlike the previous article, Moses addresses a problem common in criminology research—comparing Negroes and Whites without considering their differences. Although he attempted to compare similar areas in the earlier article, in this one he strives to correct this methodological deficiency even more by selecting two Negro and two White areas in the city that have equated (similar) physical and socioeconomic characteristics. All are low-income areas and physically disorganized. The primary objective of the study is to determine if differentials in crime rates exist for these equated areas. Even in equated areas, Negro crime rates continued to be higher than White crime rates. Moses, like most Black scholars, points to social and economic factors that contribute to this differential. However, unlike other Black scholars, he does not believe the differential is due to discriminatory policies. The article concludes with a discussion of the role of community characteristics in shaping behaviors conducive to crime.

Differentials in Crime Rates Between Negroes and Whites, Based on Comparisons of Four Socio-Economically Equated Areas

Earl R. Moses

Students of crime commonly agree that Negroes in urban centers contribute a disproportionate share of juvenile delinquency and crime when compared with their proportion of the total population. This does not mean, however, that Negroes are innately predisposed toward crime.

The Problem of Comparing Crime Rates Between Negroes and Whites

Comparisons generally made of criminality between Negroes and whites are not comparisons of similar things. Dr. Edwin H. Sutherland, for example, gives no credence to innate disposition toward criminality based on the biology of race.[1]

This study compares four socio-economically equated areas: two Negro and two white areas. These are geographically distributed so that there are contiguous white and Negro areas, yet each contiguous group is located in different parts of the city (Baltimore, Maryland).

Our primary equation pattern is the equation of communities, based on comparable socio-economic status. These four communities have striking resemblances as to physical characteristics, i.e., architectural pattern of housing, age of dwellings, size of lots, and streets lighted by gas. Physical deterioration

From Moses, E. R. (1947). Differentials in crime rates between negros and whites based on comparisons of four socio-economically equated areas. *American Sociological Review, 12*, 411-420.

is evident in all four areas. A secondary equation pattern is that of persons living in the areas based on occupations.

The Equation of Areas

We will describe the characteristics of the equated areas; show their geographic location and population characteristics; state the indices used in equating the areas; delineate the socio-economic characteristics of the areas; and, finally, note the socio-economic characteristics common to all areas.[2] For the area locations, see map on the next page. The white areas are designated as Area 1 and Area 2: the Negro areas as Area A and Area B, being respectively located contiguous to Area 1 and Area 2.

Population Characteristics

Population characteristics of the areas follow.

Area 1. White, principally of foreign-born extraction. Poland contributes the largest population of foreign birth; Russia, second, although numerically far smaller than those from Poland; a few Germans and Italians who have infiltrated from surrounding settlements. This area is near water-front industrial areas, and its white population is 31,997.[3]

Area A. Negro; popularly called "East Baltimore"; many migrants, as authenticated by governmental and school statistics; total Negro population 32,595; a predominance of unskilled workers.

Area 2. White, primarily of foreign-born extraction; white population 23,795. Lithuania dominates the foreign-born, Russia and Germany next, and a few are from Ireland, Italy, Poland, Greece, etc.

Area B. Negro; total Negro population 20,190; part of the popularly called "West Baltimore" Negro community; many migrants; mostly unskilled workers.

Indices of Equation

The indices used to equate the four areas follow: (1) Race: Predominance of either a white or Negro population; (2) similar sex distributions; (3) similar distributions by age groups; (4) own or rent place of dwelling; (5) comparable rentals; (6) comparable property valuations of owner groups; (7) major occupational patterns; (8) years of schooling completed; and, (9) number of persons in household.

Equating the Areas

The following comparative data for contiguous areas establish, in the writer's opinion, enough similarities to justify them as being equated areas, even though some variations appear.

Distribution by Race, Sex and Age Groups

The comparative data in Table 1 summarize the distribution of population by race,[4] sex and age groups, and generally show them to be similar. The fluctuations at several age group levels are to be expected since the white population represents a settlement of long residence, while many among the Negroes represent a relative recent migrant population, including parents and their children. Fewer persons in the upper age levels among Negroes than among the whites may be accounted for not only by high mortality rates among Negroes in congested areas, but also the non-migration of an elderly age group into the areas.

Home Ownership and Tenant Occupancy

Table 2 shows comparative data by areas on home ownership, tenant occupancy, rents, and valuations of owned homes. The median gross monthly rent appeared to be the best index available for these areas. It was not possible on this item to exclude data on Negroes in

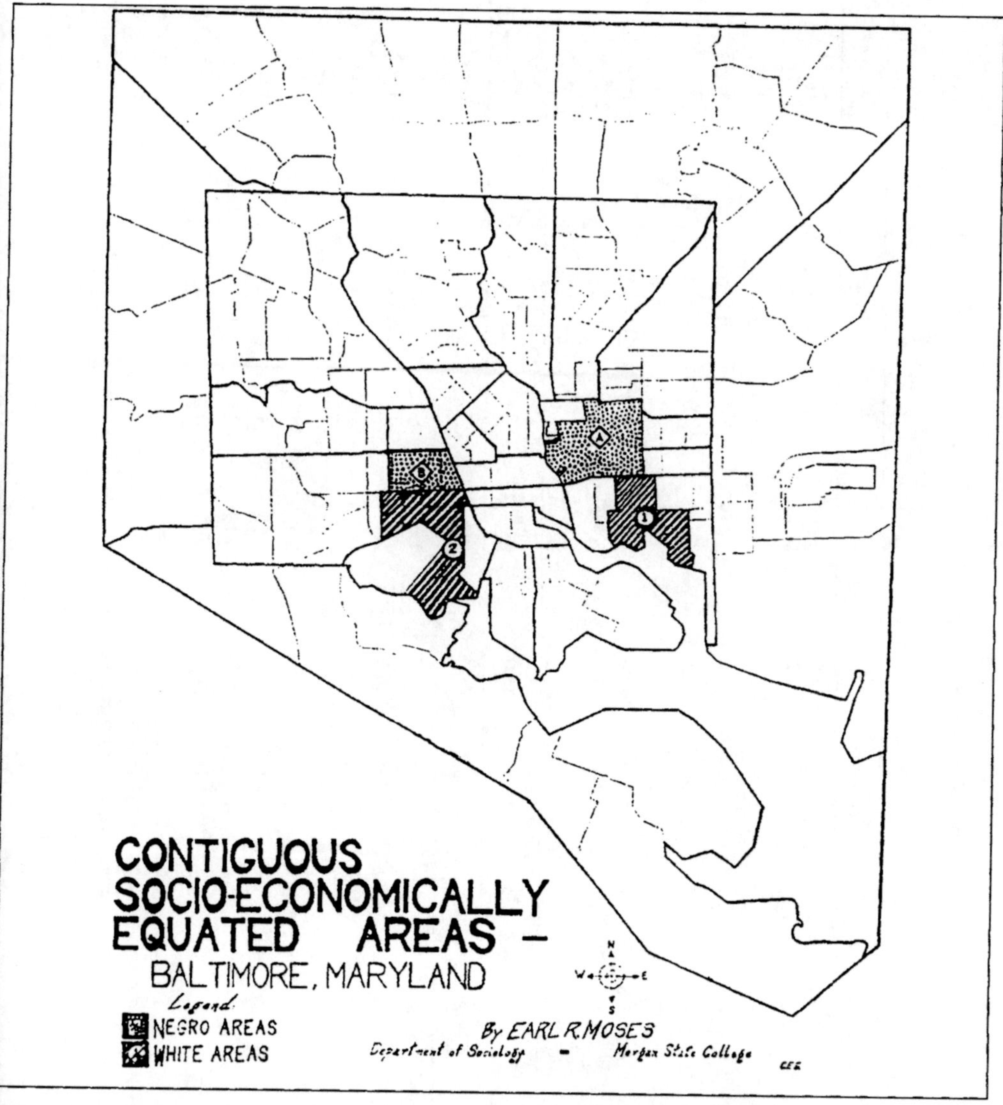

Figure 1 Contiguous Socio-Economically Equated Areas (Baltimore, Maryland)

white areas, but a check showed only a small number of Negroes in the census tracts composing each white area.

Valuation of homes occupied by owners are careful estimates. Some inadequacy as to availability of data, and the lack of completely homogeneous data by race probably influenced to some extent the average valuation figure given in the table.

Although the total occupied units are reasonably comparable, a wide variation in owner-occupied units is seen between Areas 1 and 2, compared with Areas A and B. The differences favor the white areas. This reflects the longer residence in their areas, plus, perhaps, larger accumulated savings, more freedom in buying as opposed to residence in restricted areas, and greater ease in financing home purchase. This is worth noting since all the areas in this study represent low socioeconomic indices compared with the city as a whole.

Comparison of median gross rents for the several areas shows Negroes paying higher rents than whites. These differentials con-

TABLE 1 Distribution of the Population in Equated White and Negro Areas, Classified by Race, Sex, and Age Groups

	Area 1						*Area A*[1]					
Age Groups	*Total*	*%*	*Male*	*%*	*Female*	*%*	*Total*	*%*	*Male*	*%*	*Female*	*%*
Under 5	2,412	7.5	1,234	7.4	1,178	7.7	3,118	9.5	1,572	9.7	1,546	9.5
5 to 14	5,455	17.0	2,751	16.4	2,704	17.7	6,168	18.9	3,032	18.6	3,136	19.2
15 to 24	7,107	22.2	3,585	21.4	3,522	23.1	5,791	17.8	2,619	16.1	3,172	19.4
25 to 44	9,852	30.8	5,446	32.6	4,406	28.8	12,055	37.0	6,112	37.6	5,943	36.4
45 to 64	5,620	17.6	2,969	17.8	2,561	17.3	4,517	13.9	2,458	15.1	2,059	12.6
65 and over	1,551	4.8	733	4.4	818	5.4	946	2.9	471	2.9	475	2.9
Totals: Age Groups	31,997	99.9	16,718	100.0	15,279	100.0	32,595	100.0	16,264	100.0	16,331	100.0
Totals: Race & Sex	31,997	100.0	16,718	52.2	15,279	47.8	32,595	100.0	16,264	49.9	16,331	50.1

	Area 2						*Area B*					
Age Groups	*Total*	*%*	*Male*	*%*	*Female*	*%*	*Total*	*%*	*Male*	*%*	*Female*	*%*
Under 5	1,772	7.4	882	7.4	890	7.5	1,693	8.4	847	8.7	846	8.1
5 to 14	3,976	16.7	2,013	16.8	1,963	16.6	3,710	18.4	1,862	19.2	1,848	17.6
15 to 24	4,595	19.3	2,271	19.0	2,324	19.6	3,345	16.6	1,476	15.2	1,869	17.8
25 to 44	7,041	29.6	3,686	30.8	3,355	28.3	7,517	37.2	3,585	36.9	3,932	37.5
45 to 64	4,970	20.9	2,492	20.8	2,478	20.9	3,175	15.7	1,610	16.6	1,565	14.9
65 and over	1,440	6.1	615	5.1	825	7.0	759	3.7	334	3.4	425	4.1
Totals: Age Groups	23,794	100.0	11,959	99.9	11,835	99.9	20,199	100.0	9,714	100.0	10,485	100.0
Totals: Race & Sex	23,794	100.0	11,959	50.3	11,835	49.7	20,199	100.0	9,714	48.1	10,485	51.9

1. There are 36 males and 10 females in the classification "Other non-white" who live in this area. These are not included in the total population of this area. However, U.S. Census data include these persons in the figures on school years completed, major occupations, home ownership, rentals, and persons per household. These additions are unimportant in relation to the total Negro population in the area. Similar minor additions are true likewise for Area B.

TABLE 2 Comparative Data by Areas on Home Ownership, Tenant Occupancy, Rentals, and Valuations of Owned Property

Areas	*Total Occupied Units*	*Owner Occupied Units*	*%*	*Tenant Occupied Units*	*Median Gross Monthly Rent (Dollars)*	*Average Monthly*	*Average Valuation of Home (Dollars)*
1	8,095	3,685	45.5	4,410	17.68		2,009
A	8,060	381	4.7	7,679	22.8		2,145[1]
2	6,228	2,191	35.2	4,037	22.8		1,864[2]
B	4,754	278	5.8	4,476	23.75		2,386[3]
City-wide						25.82	
White household						28.14[4]	
Non-white household						19.46	

1. Not available for Negroes only.
2. Estimated average.
3. Estimated average; also, not available for Negroes only.
4. *Redevelopment of Blighted Residential Areas in Baltimore,* Commission on City Plan, July 1, 1945, p. 21.

TABLE 3 Major Occupational Patterns in the Four Areas

	Professional Workers			*Craftsmen, Foremen and Kindred Workers*			*Domestic Service Laborers*			*Laborers*		
Areas	*Total*	*Male*	*Female*	*Total*	*Male*	*Female*	*Total*	*Male*	*Female*	*Total*	*Male*	*Female*
1	257	143	114	2,055	1,911	144	79	4	75	2,123	2,008	115
A	133	84	49	451	442	9	2,498	66	2,432	4,544	4,479	65
2	142	75	67	1,766	1,662	104	127	2	125	844	812	32
B	155	73	82	235	230	5	2,437	116	2,321	2,437	2,364	73

form to the alleged fact that Negroes pay higher rents than whites for comparable dwellings. This is not in conflict with the fact that the city-wide averages show Negroes pay much lower rents than whites. It must be remembered that the city-wide averages include wide extremes of economic sufficiency, and likewise, wide differences in rent. Thus the city-wide averages are not comparable to rents paid in these areas.

Major Occupational Patterns

Table 3 shows the occupations in which most of the gainful workers are employed. Employment is comparatively negligible in categories other than those listed. The figures show two patterns pertinent to this study: (1) persons engaged in professional work are decidedly in the minority in all four areas; and (2) although occupational dominance is at the lowest occupational levels, the white workers are one step up the occupational ladder above Negroes. White males predominate as craftsmen, foremen, and kindred workers; Negro males predominate as laborers. The large number of Negro females employed have a virtual monopoly as domestic service workers.

Years of Schooling Completed

The average adult has had a sixth-grade education or less. The median years of schooling completed for persons 25 years and over are:

TABLE 3A

	Median School Years Completed	
Areas	*Males*	*Females*
1	6.7	5.9
A	5.3	6.0
2	4.6	4.4
B	6.1	6.5

TABLE 3B

	Median Number of Persons in Household		
Areas	*All Occupied Units*	*Owner-Occupied Units*	*Tenant-Occupied Units*
1	3.39	4.08	2.94
A	3.92	Inadequate data	Inadequate data
2	3.32	3.46	3.27
B	3.45	3.71 (estimated)	3.10 (estimated)

Number of Persons in Household

The size of the household is comparable in all areas. Either no average is shown, or an estimated average is given for the subclassifications in the Negro areas. Census tract data were not available "where the base is less than 100."

Other Quasi-Equation Indices

Additional data were collected relative to the equating of areas as to the state of repair of dwellings, proportion of homes with a radio, pattern of refrigeration (ice or mechanical), and pattern of heating (central heating unit or not). In all areas, (1) a substantial number of houses needed repairs; (2) there was a preponderant use of ice for refrigeration; (3) radios were present in a substantial proportion of homes (83.6 per cent or more); and (4) a preponderant lack of a central heating unit. The disparity between the presence or absence of a central heating plant was far greater in Areas 1 and A than in Areas 2 and B.

The data in Table 4 show selected indices of health status in the four areas. These data cover a five year period. This span of time makes for relative stabilization of figures and rates, compared with fluctuations which may be evident in data compiled for any one year. Moreover, attention is called to the fact that the midpoint of the period is 1940, which is prior to the heavy migration of workers and their families into Baltimore during the war years. Thus the data show a relatively normal pattern of health conditions prior to the greater congestion of population incident to the war period. A careful examination of these data show more unfavorable health conditions in Areas A and B, but they also reveal a similar low health status in all areas.

Summary of Characteristics of the Areas

The characteristics which either are common to all areas, or are similar in contiguous areas are summarized below.

Similarities

1. Each area is relatively homogeneous as to racial population. Because of the segregated pattern of residence in Baltimore there is virtually no overlapping as to residence. Moreover, the numerical similarity in the total population in each of the contiguous areas is close enough to be used for comparative purposes.

2. In spite of some differences which were noted earlier, there is a similarity in the distributions by sex and age groups in contiguous areas.

3. Contiguous areas have a comparable number of total dwelling units occupied. This numerical similarity is markedly close in Areas 1 and A.

4. Occupational dominance in all areas is in the lower occupational levels.

TABLE 4 Indices of Health Status in the Four Areas[1]

Areas	*Live Births (1938-1942)*	*Infant Deaths (1938-1942)*	*Infant Death Rate per 1,000 Live Births (1938-1942)*	*New Cases of Tuberculosis Reported (1938-1942)*	*Tuberculosis Case Rate per 10,000 Population: 1938-1942*
1	2,965	137	46.2	306	19.1
A	3,999	257	64.3	736	45.1
2	2,333	128	54.9	195	16.3
B	2,333	164	70.3	462	45.7

1. Data compiled by the Bureau of Vital Statistics of the Baltimore City Health Department. Data shown are figures and rates compiled by white and non-white in each area.

5. All areas are characterized by a low educational status of adults, the educational status being below the 7th grade.

6. The size of household is comparable in all areas.

7. Data of quasi-equation indices show additional points of low socio-economic status comparable to data showing equation of areas. Similarly, low health status is evident in all these areas. It may be added, however, that although data reveal comparable low standards, conditions are somewhat less favorable in Negro areas than in the corresponding white areas.

Differences

Characteristic differences between the white and Negro areas are summarized below.

1. The white populations are predominantly of foreign-born extraction. They are a settled population of long residence in their areas. On the other hand, there is a large element of migrants in the two Negro populations.[5] The difference in settlement patterns make for some differences in age group distributions, though not wide enough to invalidate comparisons between contiguous areas.

2. Home ownership is greater among the whites than among the Negroes. Conversely, the Negroes are a larger tenant group.

3. Negroes pay somewhat higher rents than whites for comparable dwelling units.

4. The whites are one step up the occupational ladder above Negroes, although occupational dominance in all areas is at the lowest occupational levels.

The materials presented above show that the areas in this study have homogeneous populations, and also that they are socio-economically equated areas. These areas, moreover, are below the city-wide average as to socio-economic status. Furthermore, they are areas characterized by urban blight. Based on these equatings as to externalities, we thus assume equal planes of living in these areas. Having established the equation of areas, we turn now to an examination of crime rates in these equated areas.

Differentials in Crime Rates in Equated Areas

Do differentials in crime rates persist even in face of the equation of areas? Felonies committed during 1940 will be our chief index to the extent of crime in these equated areas. Felonies may be divided into two groups: (1) felonies reported to the police and where the victim is known, but the offender is unknown or not apprehended; and, (2) felonies reported to the police, where both the victim and the accused are known; where the accused has been brought to trial, either in 1940 or subse-

TABLE 5 Persons Accused of Felonies During 1940, Classified by Area (Race) and Sex, and Showing Area Rates of Felonious Crime

	Males		*Females*	
Areas	*Accused Persons*	*Area Rate*[1]	*Accused Persons*	*Area Rate*[1]
1	25	2.36	—	—
A	153	15.11	23	2.34
2	17	2.21	—	—
B	76	12.47	5	0.74

1. The area rate is a ratio, expressed in thousands, between the number of accused persons in relation to the area population 21 years of age and over, classified by race and sex. Although some under 21 years of age were charged with a felony, the proportion of such cases compared with those 21 and over was not unduly large. The maximum age in this series was 59. Since census data are not available for exact age groups of persons younger than 21 which correspond to those under 21 who had committed felonies, it was judged that a valid ratio would be obtained by including the cases under 21 since there were adults in the population figures who were over 59 years of age.

quently; and, where a definite judicial disposition has been made of the case. Cases within the second group are used herein.

Cases of felony for the year 1940 have been selected for several reasons. First, the 1940 U. S. Census data were used for the socio-economic equation of areas. Second, it was desirable to select a year prior to the heavy migration into Baltimore incident to the war period. This allowed for an assumed relative normal pattern of criminal behavior in Baltimore. Finally, felony cases were selected also because they are the more serious types of criminal behavior, requiring more careful investigations than misdemeanors. Thus it was felt that though fewer cases in number than for misdemeanors, felony cases would represent a fairly reliable index to the extent of criminality in a given year.

Crime Rates

Table 5 shows the extent of crime in the four areas during 1940. It will be noted that the crime rate for Area 1 is 2.36 compared with 15.11 for Area A. Similarly, the rate for Area 2 is 2.21 compared with 12.47 for Area B. There were no felonies committed by white females in Areas 1 and 2 to compare with those committed by Negro females in Areas A and B. Several striking differences are evident. In the first place, differences in crime rates persist even in equated areas. Secondly, there is a wide difference in these rates. Finally, the rates among the Negro females correspond more closely to the rates for the white males, than do the rates when comparing white males with Negro males.

Juvenile delinquency rates also are higher in the Negro areas than in the white areas. Juvenile delinquency rates per 1,000 of population, ages 6-17, for the years 1939-1942, inclusive, were computed for these areas. The rate for Area 1 was 14.4, for Area A, 26.7, for Area 2, 22.0, and for Area B, 28.4. Differentials in rates persist in juvenile delinquency even as felonies, although less markedly so.

Types of Offenses

Crimes committed by persons living in one of the fear areas, without regard to the place where the crime was committed, were canvassed, classified by areas and by sex. Space limitation necessitates a summary of these findings. A striking fact evident in the figures is that all murder and manslaughter offenses were committed by Negroes. Indeed, when the offenses are classified according to "crimes against persons" and "crimes involving property" more than 40.0 per cent of the crimes in Area A, and more than 50.0 per cent of those in Area B are crimes against persons, such as murder, manslaughter, rape, and aggravated assault. It is of value to note that, though fewer in number, the offenses in 13 categories other than murder and manslaughter in Areas 1 and 2 correspond roughly to a pattern similar to that in Areas A and B. But even with a general similarity one important difference may be noted, namely, that in Areas A and B some crimes against persons involved loss of life, whereas there was no such outcome in Areas 1 and 2.

Multiple Felonies

There were few cases of clear recidivism for 1940. Instead, there were cases where the same person committed more than one offense prior to arrest, and where trial and sentence covered the several different acts. It should be kept in mind that penalties inflicted for felonies often would insure incarceration for periods longer than one year. Persons involved in the 1940 cases thus either may have been or subsequently may have become recidivists. Our analysis concerns only the cases for one year. Hence we refer to multiple felonies rather than recidivism.

Multiple felonies occurred most frequently in Area A. The nature of the offenses, number of persons involved, and the time element in each case are summarized in the data which follow. Sample cases only are presented.

Area A. One act of burglary; one person; a second act of burglary, involving the same person and one other person; second act occurred 3 months later than the first act. Short sentence served for first act prior to commission of second act.

Area 2. Four separate acts, involving the same person. One act of assault, and 1 assault to rape act on the same day. Similarly, on the next day 1 act of assault, and 1 assault to rape act. Four separate victims; 2 separate acts each day.

Area B. Three separate acts of burglary; same 2 persons involved; two acts one day, third act on the succeeding day.

Convictions

The felony cases for 1940 were canvassed with reference to their disposition by the court. This was done to determine whether or not wide differences were evident in convictions in Areas 1 and 2 compared with convictions in Areas A and B. It was found that 17.0 per cent of the cases in Area A, and 17.3 per cent of the cases in Area B were found "Not Guilty." In Area 1 only 1 per cent was found "Not Guilty," while in Area 2, 17.6 per cent were so found.

Attention is called to the fact that percentages determined for Areas 1 and 2 are not to be regarded as equally valid as those for Areas A and B since there are far fewer cases in Areas 1 and 2 than in Areas A and B. But even in face of this limitation, based on an examination of the proportions convicted to the total cases in each area, there is no reason to even suspect that Negroes were more readily convicted than whites. This is important since it rules out an element of policy as influencing the higher crime rates in Areas A and B than in Areas 1 and 2.

Tentative Findings and Conclusions

The basic assumption with which we started in this study is that most comparisons of crime rates do not take into account differences in socio-economic status between the groups compared. Thus we equated contiguous areas to determine if differentials in crime rates persisted after equation. Felony cases during 1940 were used as an index to criminality. Crime rates in the 2 Negro areas continued to be higher than in the 2 white areas.

The primary equation pattern was the equating of communities, with reference to socio-economic status. There was also a relative equation of persons, based principally on the predominance of low status occupations. Thus, there was on the one hand, an equation based on externalities, viz., housing, and urban blight, and, on the other hand, an equating of population with the consequent assumption of equal planes of living.

That these areas are equated will hardly be seriously questioned. However, one recognizes that the equation is basically the equating of objective aspects of the areas. This fails to take into account subjective aspects, such as cultural meanings, which are basic to behavior patterns characteristic of a group. Even though holding to the validity of an equation of externalities, it is questionable whether or not a high degree of equation of subjective factors is obtainable.

Regarding criminal behavior in these areas we noted that there was no evidence of a policy whereby conviction rates were unfavorable to Negroes. Moreover, there was evidence of a general similarity in the patterns of offenses between Negroes and whites, although among the Negroes were concentrated the offenses involving loss of life. In light of these facts the validity of the determination of crime rates is judged equally valid as the equation of areas.

Although there was a basic similarity in the equation pattern, there were also some differences which were judged to be significant in their implications. Of these, the most significant variation was the fact that although both groups were predominantly in low occupational lines, the whites in Areas 1 and 2 were one step up the occupational ladder over the Negroes in Areas A and B. This fact raises the question as to whether or not the relatively fixed occupational status of the Negro does not reflect itself in a differential in the plane of living even though white and Negro areas are equated as to externalities and the relative equation of persons.

Homicides are more prevalent among Negroes. One alleged prevalent mode of behavior among Negroes is that of carrying knives and guns. If one accepts this as widespread, one accepts the accompanying alleged attitude of "security" borne of having a weapon. The presence of weapons often leads to their use, more than likely resulting in high homicide rates. Another stereotyped conception of behavior among Negroes is that of an enhanced prestige among the Negro criminal growing out of being considered a "bad" man. Fear of such a person often leads either to a bullying attitude, or the challenging of such behavior; aggravated assault or homicide frequently being the outcome.

While one cannot accept the foregoing stereotyped modes of behavior as the explanation of higher crime rates among Negroes, neither can one deny that in many cases these are factors conducive to criminal behavior. A more reasoned explanation is to be found in the poverty of life in the deteriorated areas inhabited by them. One recognizes this poverty on every hand and in a variety of its manifestations. Because of it, life in these areas has been reduced largely to organic survival; and the reflex of this is an organic plane of living. This poverty is more than economic; it is pervasive in character: bad housing, overcrowding, restricted areas of settlement, limited outlets of expression, as in recreation, restricted employment opportunities, etc. On every hand the Negro is hedged in by racial proscriptions.

The white areas have a population characterized by low economic status and a foreign-born extraction, but they are also a population of long residence in these areas, in contrast to a Negro population predominantly of relative recent migration. The Negroes with generally fewer resources have correspondingly heavier economic drains on their limited means than a comparable socioeconomic status white population, (e. g., Negroes generally pay higher rents than whites for comparable houses.) Based on longer residence, wider occupational opportunities, easier financing of purchasing house, etc., home ownership is far greater among the whites than Negroes.

Due to a low socio-economic status, accentuated by racial proscriptions, the Negroes in these areas, even as elsewhere, do not have a freedom of wholesome expression comparable to that of a similarly situated white group. Out of these and similar conditions arise elements conducive to greater criminality, as well as other forms of pathology, among the Negro population. It is out of community situations comparable to those just indicated that there develops a characteristic mode of behavior which is conducive to the emergence of the Negro criminal.

NOTES

1. For the delineation of other factors which may operate to make for criminality among Negroes see, Edwin H. Sutherland, *Principles of Criminology,* Lippincott, 1939, p. 122.

2. Acknowledgement herewith is given the following: Mr. Wallace Reidt, Assistant Managing Director, The Criminal Justice Commission, Baltimore, for use of the records of that organization dealing with felony cases during 1940; Dr. W. Thurber Fales, Director, Statistical Section, Baltimore City Health Department, for making valuable suggestions regarding the selection of areas used in this study, and for making available data on health conditions and juvenile delinquency; Mr. Isadore Seeman, Director, Bureau of Vital Records, for compiling these data; to four Morgan State College students, Misses Pauline Bates, Mildred McGlotten, Mildred Reynolds, and Mrs. Willodyne S. Gaston, for clerical assistance; and, to Dr. Thorsten Sellin, of the University of Pennsylvania, is due a special measure of thanks for his guidance throughout the period of the study.

3. All population data are based on the U. S. Census, 1940, unless otherwise specifically stated.

4. In Areas 1 and 2 the Negro population and all data pertaining to them have been excluded from the figures presented in this study. Similar exclusions for the white population have been made in Areas A and B. Thus the data presented correspond to the racial type composing the given area. Negroes and whites often may live in the same census tract, but in different sections of it. Because of the segregated pattern of residence in Baltimore there is virtually no overlapping as to residence in the four areas used in this study.

5. Dr. W. Thurber Fales writes: "Natural increase therefore accounted for 51.8 per cent of the increase in the white population and 14.9 per cent of the increase in the non-white population. The remainder of the increase between the 1930 and 1940 census is due to migration into the City. Since only 14.9 per cent of the net increase for colored population was accounted for by natural increase, it is obvious that the immigration to the City has been much more pronounced for the Negro than for the white population." *The Councillor,* June, 1941.

PART II

CONTEMPORARY CLASSICS

10

INTRODUCTION

A. Leon Higginbotham, Jr. (1928-1998) was a judge and advocate of and for civil rights. Appointed to the federal bench in 1964, Higginbotham was elevated to the Third U.S. Circuit Court of Appeals for Pennsylvania in 1977. He retired from the bench in 1993 and became Public Service Professor of Jurisprudence at Harvard University's Kennedy School of Government. Asked by South Africa's president Nelson Mandela to serve as a mediator during that country's first elections in which Blacks could vote, Judge Higginbotham helped draft South Africa's democratic constitution in 1994. One year later, he received the nation's highest civilian honor, the Presidential Medal of Freedom. Reportedly, the late Supreme Court Justice Thurgood Marshall called him "a great lawyer and a very great judge."

Judge Higginbotham's writings on the history of race in America have been critically acclaimed. *Shades of Freedom: Racial Politics and Presumptions of the Legal Process* (1996) was the second volume of his multivolume study of "Race and the American Legal Process." In this book, he examined the link between law and racism from colonial times to the present. Higginbotham used case law to document the role the law played in creating and embracing notions of racial inferiority. He noted that present-day racial discrimination was supported by both *Dred Scott v. Sandford,* in which the Supreme Court concluded that "blacks had no rights which the white man was bound to respect," and *Plessy v. Ferguson,* which approved the isolation of Blacks from Whites.

In this excerpt from *Shades of Freedom: Racial Politics and Presumptions of the Legal Process,* Higginbotham demonstrates how the state judicial system, which is instructed to provide equal treatment before the law, serves as a microcosm of the larger society by enforcing the inferior position of Blacks in its treatment of Black victims, offenders, and lawyers. This enforcement of the issue of racial inferiority begins at the entrance to the courthouse and continues through all courtroom and courthouse activities and interactions.

UNEQUAL JUSTICE IN THE STATE CRIMINAL JUSTICE SYSTEM

A. LEON HIGGINBOTHAM, JR.

[Can] American justice, American liberty, American civilization, American law, and American Christianity . . . be made to include and protect alike and forever all American citizens in the rights which have been guaranteed to them by the organic and fundamental laws of the land?—Frederick Douglass[1]

RACE MATTERS[2]

Chiseled in marble over the entrance to the United States Supreme Court is the ultimate American aspiration: "Equal Justice Under Law." Also written with careful thought, the Preamble of the United States Constitution reads:

> We the People of the United States, in Order to form a more perfect Union, *establish* Justice, insure domestic Tranquility, provide for the common defense, promote general Welfare, and secure the Blessings of Liberty to ourselves and our Posterity, do ordain and establish this Constitution for the United States of America.[3]

Thus, after formation of "a more perfect Union," the next national priority was to "*establish* Justice." But the American irony has been that, even after the Civil War, the judicial system has not been one of "*Equal* Justice Under Law." From a racial standpoint the system has been one dominated often by the *un*equal justice imposed upon African Americans.

To use Cornel West's felicitous phrase, "Race [m]atters."[4] In the criminal justice system the fact of one's race sometimes has been a critical factor in determining whether prosecutions are initiated or terminated, whether the jury returns a verdict of guilty or not guilty, whether certain judicial instructions are given to the jury, whether witnesses are or are not believed, and in determining the formulation of ultimate judicial rulings. I do not want to be misunderstood. I am not suggesting that factors of race have been decisive in *all* cases or in the *majority* of cases. I am submitting, however, that during the nineteenth and twentieth centuries, the issue of race has mattered in a substantial number of cases. As we approach the end of the twentieth century,

---

it is to be hoped that there indeed has been a diminution in the number of cases in which the issue of race has been significant. Unfortunately, I remain confident that even today there are many cases whose outcome can be explained only by way of racial considerations. I recognize these statements are serious indictments of the criminal justice system, but nevertheless, I submit that the cases that will be discussed hereafter corroborate my general thesis. In 1996, despite the innumerable words espoused by lawyers, lawyer-politicians, and law professors proclaiming the progress of American law, for many there still persists a nagging doubt as to whether the legacy of legally sanctioned racism will be eradicated in this decade or even in the next century.[5]

This chapter explores efforts to move from the legal order of the colonial and antebellum periods, with its patent racism and unequal justice, to a more neutral system that does not reinforce the values of slavery jurisprudence, including the precept of inferiority, in which African Americans are perceived and treated as inferior. As discussed below, the movement theoretically away from a judicial system marked by unequal justice has nevertheless shown a troubling pattern of racist actions and statements that have diverted the journey from slavery jurisprudence and the precept of black inferiority.

Racial segregation and other forms of discrimination have a long and tragic history in the criminal justice system of many state courts. When one race receives harsher treatment than another, the court is announcing to the world that one group is perceived as superior and the other inferior, the latter not being entitled to the quality of justice that is assured to the dominant group. The entire antebellum period was so infected with racism that it was the remote exception, rather than the rule, when witnesses, defendants, or litigants who were African American were treated just like everyone else.

Racism in the courts is reflective of significant symptoms, signals, and symbols of racism in the broader society. Many state court cases exemplify the unfair treatment of African American citizens by courts—both northern and southern—despite the abolition of slavery and the enactment of the Thirteenth, Fourteenth, and Fifteenth Amendments. These cases are an endorsement of the slavery jurisprudence embodied in the precept of inferiority. Post–Civil War history lends itself to the question whether in general the courts have been protectors of or impediments to African Americans' exercise of the right to equal justice.

Racism in the Courts as Symptoms, Signals, and Symbols of Racism in the Broader Society

From my experience as a United States District Court judge and later as a Court of Appeals judge, I have always been impressed with the divergence of views as to how widely the virus of racism infects the justice system. Many white judges share an underlying belief about the rarity of racist occurrences in the courtroom; they assume that instances of racism are infrequent, peripheral, tangential, and almost irrelevant episodes to the central function and experiences of adjudicating the cases before them. In contrast, I know of only one African American federal judge who minimizes the significance of the fact that societal racism, even unintentionally, often affects the adjudicatory and fact-finding process of courts.

My view is that those past and present instances of racism are more than mere aberrations or isolated blemishes that occasionally crop up and mar the normally effective dispensation of justice. Rather, they are symptoms, signals, and symbols of racism in the broader society. When racism occurs in the courts, it is symptomatic of racist attitudes, myths, and assumptions that constitute the ideology of societal racism. Such instances of courtroom racism also act as signals, triggering and mobilizing those racist attitudes and stereotypes in the minds of all the courtroom participants, and possibly affecting the judgment and actions of the judge, jury, and attorneys at this and other junctures in the case. Finally, racist occurrences in the courts are particularly powerful symbols, acting to reinforce, legitimate, and perpetuate racism in the broader society.

Reflecting on the American experience, Professor Charles Lawrence III has developed a theory of racism as the systemic imputation of stigma onto African Americans through the courts and through extralegal action.[6] As he explains, racism is part of the common cultural heritage of all Americans.[7] According to Lawrence, racism is a group of assumptions about the world and its inhabitants that are expressed, often unconsciously, in a "mutually reinforcing and pervasive pattern of stigmatizing actions that cumulate to compose an injurious whole that is greater than the sum of its parts."[8] These assumptions are based on notions, explicit or implicit, of African Americans as dirty, lazy, oversexed, in poor control of their kids, and otherwise less than fully human.[9] Indeed, such assumptions give rise to behavior, such as the establishment of race-segregated housing and bathrooms, that dramatize white stereotypes of African Americans as impure, contaminating, or untouchable.[10] Similarly, the use of devices that reduce the number of African American policemen or that challenge the competency of African American professors and managers, reinforces a cultural message that whites should be in positions of authority over African Americans.[11] While, as Lawrence's article demonstrates, these cultural messages can be decoded, they are often tacit, or even unconscious.[12]

Racism in the Courtroom as a Symptom of Societal Racism

Courts do not dispense justice in sterile isolation, unaffected by the prevailing political, social, and moral attitudes and currents of the broader society in which they operate.[13] Judges, prosecutors, and other lawyers are not immune to the unconscious influence of—indeed they may even consciously subscribe to—the group of negative stigmatizing assumptions that Lawrence describes as characteristic of the ideology of racism. Thus, the broader societal racism may, consciously or unconsciously, infect the attitudes and behavior of judges and lawyers in the courtroom.

Racism in the Courtroom as a Signal of Societal Racism

A second important effect of instances of racism in the courtroom is the indication that racial bias affects other courtroom participants besides the judge or lawyer who makes a racist declaration. Instances of racism in the courtroom tap into the ideology of societal racism and are symptomatic of the existence of societal racism. A racist remark or insinuation by a judge or prosecutor acts as a signal, triggering and mobilizing a host of attitudes and assumptions that may be consciously held, or unconsciously harbored, by the judge, jury, and lawyers in the courtroom. The effect of the racist act or statement can be felt beyond its immediate context: it acts to trip additional racist assumptions at other junctures in the proceeding.

In the United States, segregated courthouse restrooms, cafeterias, and spectator seating also acted as signals. In these cases all participants, particularly juries in criminal or civil trials involving an African American defendant or litigant, were constantly reminded that African Americans were to be accorded inferior status in this society. Every time jurors and spectators walked into a courtroom, they were presented with a ringing affirmation of the assumptions, myths, and attitudes that compose the ideology of racism in the United States.

When a prosecutor or judge appeals to fears of African American violence directed against whites, elaborate and detailed myths about African Americans are ushered into the conscious and unconscious minds of courtroom participants. Once these racist attitudes and assumptions have been tapped into, the judge, jury, and lawyers are more likely to stimulate and rely on their collective consciousness or unconsciousness, applying related racist myths and stereotypes that African Americans are untrustworthy, dishonest, and shiftless to other issues during the trial or hearing.

When a judge or prosecutor makes a racially disparaging remark during the course of a trial, the comment may affect the judgment and actions of the judge, jury, and attorneys for the duration of the case. Consequently, instances of racism in the courtroom cannot be viewed as isolated incidents, limited in effect to the immediate context in which they occurred, or as "harmless error."

As Professor Anthony Amsterdam has commented:

> [W]hen a prosecutor makes racist comments in closing arguments to a jury, more is going on in the trial than those specific comments. Courts that hold such comments as "harmless error" seem to view the situation as one in which the prosecutor tried, but failed to interject racial prejudice into a case that was otherwise free of racial prejudice. This view is exactly backwards. Unless a case has already been infected with racial prejudice, the prosecutor would never venture to make the racist comments in the first place. Prosecutors do not make arguments that they do not expect the jury to buy, and prosecutors particularly do not make arguments that they have any reason to fear that even one juror will actively resent. Before a prosecutor (even a personally bigoted prosecutor) would try to use the defendant's race (or a defense witness's race) against the defendant in a jury argument, the prosecutor would have to be pretty confident that the argument will fall on fertile ground. Thus, the very fact that a racist pitch is made in closing argument almost always means that the prosecutor has read the jury—on the basis of knowledge about the individual jurors or their backgrounds or the community or on the basis of a hundred signs that may be very subtle or very glaring in the atmosphere of the courtroom but are totally undetectable on the cold, written record preserved for appeal—and that the prosecutor has decided that, with *this* jury in *this* case, a racist pitch will work. Courts that ignore this reality are willfully blind.[14]

Racism in the Courtroom as Cultural Symbolism

In addition to acting as signals for those participants in the courtroom, instances of racism in the courts also send signals beyond the confines of any particular courtroom and affect society at large. The judicial system is charged with interpreting, upholding, and enforcing the law. Since most societies claim to offer their citizens equal justice under the law, the courts are the presumed repositories of equality and the solemn fora for the just adjudication of the law without regard to race, creed, color, appearance, or any other categorical distinction. Because of this role, instances of racism in the courtroom are particularly powerful symbols that act to legitimate, reinforce, and perpetuate the culture of racism operating in society as a whole.15 Similarly, when courthouses in the southern United States maintained segregated restrooms, cafeterias, and spectator sections in courtrooms—the solemn fora of equality before the law and equal protection by the law—they sent a symbolic message that legitimated, reinforced, and perpetuated the segregation that was a way of life in the post-Plessy South and helped to justify the ideology of racism underlying its existence and enforcement.

Likewise, when judges overruled defense objections to prosecutors' racist actions, the courts symbolically were affirming the racist myths and stereotypes of black untrustworthiness, dishonesty, lack of control, and proclivity to violence and rape, especially toward whites. By so doing, the courts helped to perpetuate the racist ideology of which these attitudes were a part.

Acts of racism in the courts are symptomatic of the society's cultural racism. They trigger other racist assumptions in the minds of courtroom participants and symbolize to society the legitimacy of the ideology of racism. Even murals in a courthouse can convey racist assumptions that African Americans instantly recognize and to which whites may be oblivious regarding their implications. Professor Jack Bass describes a Jackson, Mississippi, courthouse mural as follows:

> A heavy off-white drapery hangs from the ceiling and covers the wall that faces spectators in the fourth-floor federal courtroom above the old post office in Jackson, Mississippi. Although many façades in today's American South hide the harsh, historic reality of an unjust social order that crumbled in the civil rights revolution of the 1960s, the curtain in the Jackson courtroom is a literal mask.
>
> Behind it there is a brightly colored mural, 40 feet across and 20 feet high, painted by an artist of Czech extraction, commissioned in 1939 by the Works Progress Administration (WPA). The tableau begins at the left where a black mammy is picking cotton in a green field. It moves to a poorly dressed, graying black man sitting on stone steps, happily strumming a banjo. As the plantation master moves to dismount, another deferential black reaches up to help. A hoopskirted white woman stands in front of the columned plantation house with her daughter. A stern-faced judge, dressed in black suit and string tie, dominates the foreground. He has a law book under his arm.[16]

Apartheid in the Courthouse

Segregated Spectator Seating

In American courtrooms there has never been any formal segregation among the various white groups. Protestants have not been segregated from Catholics, or Jews from Gentiles. For those white persons whose ancestors were born, as an example, in England, France, Germany, Italy, Sweden, or from any other European nation where predominantly the citizens are white, there has never been any segregation in the courtroom on the basis of national origin. Thus one must identify the evolution of these racial segregation policies and how the courts justified this different treatment for African Americans.

In 1948—the same year the Nationalist Party came into power in South Africa to initiate apartheid—the Mississippi Supreme Court, in *Murray v. State,*[17] was asked to reverse the murder conviction of an African American man tried in a courtroom that segregated African American spectators, allowing them to sit only in the balcony. The court's language reveals the long tradition and implicit approval of courthouse racial segregation: "It is asserted that the seating arrangement, suggested pursuant to a custom whose immemorial usage and sanction has made routine, resulted in a concentration in the balcony of those of the same race as the defendant."[18] The court's language not only implicitly approved of that "routine" tradition, but its decision permitted its continuance:

> Assuming that this seating arrangement was insisted upon and deemed prejudicial to such as were piqued thereby—as to which there is no showing—such reactions may not be magnified into a fancied denial of constitutional rights and thereupon made assignable to the defendant.[19]

The court affirmed the conviction.

In 1963, fifteen years after the *Murray* case, when the success of the civil rights movement had sensitized the country to the derogatory meaning of segregation, the Supreme Court finally recognized, in *Johnson v. Virginia,*[20] that race-segregated seating in courts constituted a denial of equal protection.

Ford T. Johnson, Jr., an African American, was seated in a section of the Richmond Traffic Court reserved for whites, and when requested by the bailiff to move, refused to do so. The judge then summoned the petitioner to the bench and instructed him to be seated in the right-hand section of the courtroom, the section reserved for African Americans.

The petitioner moved back in front of the counsel table and remained standing with his arms folded, stating that he would not comply with the judge's order. Upon refusing to obey the judge's further direction to be seated, he was arrested for contempt. At no time did Johnson behave in a boisterous or abusive manner, and there was no disorder in the courtroom.[21]

The state, in its brief to the Supreme Court, conceded that seating space in the Richmond Traffic Court "is assigned on the basis of racial designation, the seats on one side of the aisle being for use of Negro citizens and the seats on the other side being for the use of white citizens."[22] The Supreme Court reversed the conviction, noting:

> It is clear from the totality of circumstances, and particularly the fact that the petitioner was peaceably seated in the section reserved for whites before being summoned to the bench, that the arrest and conviction rested entirely on the refusal to comply with the segregated seating requirements imposed in this particular courtroom. Such a conviction cannot stand, for it is no longer open to question that a State may not constitutionally require segregation of public facilities. State-compelled segregation in a court of justice is a manifest violation of the State's duty to deny no one the equal protection of its laws.[23]

The ultimate insight that race-segregated seating in courtrooms denied a spectator "equal" protection doubtless rested on what Professor Lawrence has characterized as the central insight of *Brown v. Board of Education*: that equal protection doctrine includes the right to be free from social ostracism and its stigmatizing effect on the "hearts and minds" of African American adult citizens as well as on African American children.[24]

The Barriers of Standing

Regrettably, *Johnson* was not the end of the matter. As in non–civil rights areas, some of the Court's contributions to social justice have been curtailed by rigid enforcement of standing requirements. Just after *Johnson,* an African American demonstrator was tried in a racially segregated Louisiana courtroom. The Louisiana Supreme Court, in considering appellant's claim that racial segregation in the courtroom had denied him a fair trial in violation of his due process and equal protection rights, acknowledged that the courtroom in question had been segregated for many years.[25] However, the court affirmed the conviction, distinguishing *Johnson* on the basis that the African American defendant did not have standing to challenge the segregation of those African American spectators who came to watch his trial:

> [I]n the *Johnson* case the objection to segregation was made by a Negro who had been arrested for contempt of court for sitting in seats assigned for white citizens, and the arrest and conviction was for that conduct. In the case before us, there is no charge against the defendant for having violated the court-imposed seating arrangement and none of the parties upon whom the segregation was imposed are before this court in this case. Hence the *Johnson* case is not authority for reversing this conviction. It has not been made to appear that the segregation resulted in a miscarriage of justice to the defendant. . . . If it were otherwise, it would result that every Negro convicted in that court in the past would be entitled to have his conviction set aside.[26]

Thus, the courtroom segregation would be allowed to continue at least until challenged by the proper party, an African American spectator.[27] The court refused to conclude that the racist setting of a courtroom could, in any possible manner, affect the administration of justice.

Whites-Only Courthouse Cafeterias: One Court's View of "Separate but Equal" as a Step Forward

Shortly after the decision in *Brown v. Board of Education,* African American residents of Harris County, Texas, challenged a policy which excluded them from the privately operated cafeteria in the new county courthouse.[28] The court entered a judgment declaring that the county could not constitutionally deny African Americans the right to patronize the only courthouse cafeteria. However, the court did not go beyond the mandate of "separate but equal" in its injunction. Thus, it required the county only to make "specific assurances that facilities will be made available for the use of colored persons under circumstances and conditions substantially equal to those afforded members of the white race," and enjoined the private operator from excluding African Americans "solely by reason of their race or color under the circumstances here prevailing."[29] Apparently, the court was declaring that the county could properly exclude African Americans from the cafeteria as long as it provided African Americans access to "substantially equal" eating facilities.[30] This requirement of "equality" rested on a white judiciary's failure to perceive the stigmatizing—and thus unconstitutional—effects of segregation, especially in official settings, which serve a legitimizing role.

Race-Segregated Restrooms

In 1958, a young African American lawyer by the name of E. A. Dawley, Jr., filed a suit in federal court against the city of Norfolk, Virginia, for a mandatory injunction to remove the word "colored" from doors to certain restrooms in courthouse buildings occupied and used exclusively by state courts and judges.[31] He alleged that the "presence of these signs conveys the thought that the [state] judges consider Negro attorneys inferior, which, in turn, adversely affects the prestige of Negro attorneys in the eyes of the public and thereby diminishes their earning capacity."[32] Dawley cited and relied on *Brown v. Board of Education* in arguing that such segregation generates a feeling of inferiority among African Americans because of African American lawyers' lower status in the community. The trial judge called counsel's theory "ingenious," but then belittled it, concluding that:

> there is no more reason to suggest that judges deemed Negro attorneys inferior than there is to say that a white attorney is inferior because he may use a restroom marked "White." . . . To say that there is a loss of earning power, or a denial of equal protection laws . . . would reduce the law to an absurdity.[33]

By insisting that a policy of courtroom segregation did not carry the stigmatizing message that contact with African Americans in intimate settings, such as restrooms (or swimming pools), is contaminating, the trial judge embraced the formalism of *Plessy v. Ferguson*,[34] which had recently been implicitly rejected by the recognition in *Brown* that segregation stigmatizes African American schoolchildren.[35] Professor Charles Black, however, in defending *Brown* in the face of formalist attacks, voiced perhaps the most eloquent description by a contemporary Southerner of the real meaning of segregation:

> I am sure it never occurred to anyone, white or colored, to question [segregation's] meaning. The fiction of "equality" is just about on a level with the fiction of "finding" in the action of trover. I think few candid southerners deny this.
>
> . . . Segregation in the South grew up and is kept going because and only because the white race has wanted it that way. . . .
>
> Segregation is historically and contemporaneously associated in a *functioning complex* with practices, which are indisputably and grossly discriminatory. . . . [Black discusses the exclusion of African Americans from voting and the poor quality of African American schools.] Then we are solemnly told that segregation is not intended to harm the segregated race, or to stamp it with the mark of inferiority. How long must we keep a straight face?
>
> The society that has just lost the Negro as a slave, that has just lost out in an attempt to put him under quasi-servile "Codes," the society

> that views his blood as a contamination and his name as an insult, the society that extralegally imposes on him every humiliating mark of low caste . . . this society, careless of his consent, moves by law . . . to cut him off from mixing in the general public life of the community. The Court that refused to see inequality in this cutting off would be making the only kind of law that can be warranted outrageous in advance—law based on self-induced blindness, on flagrant contradiction of known fact.[36]

It is because segregation was indeed part of "a functioning complex" of discriminatory practices that the marking of racially separate restroom facilities was an official public statement that those in power thought African Americans were inferior. And when, by the use of separate restroom facilities, the state announces in the courthouse that African Americans are inferior, it is not surprising that a potential African American client, who will be appealing to the discretion of the (white) courts, or seeking the leniency of the (white) sentencing judge, might be leery of having an African American lawyer as his counsel—one whom the state brands so "inferior" that he cannot even use the same toilets as whites. In finding Dawley's legal theory absurd, both the trial judge and the appellate court were oblivious to the symbolic power of this branding.

Overt Discrimination by Judges in the Courtroom

Failure to Accord Black Witnesses the Civilities Customarily Accorded to White Witnesses

In 1963, an African American woman was testifying on her own behalf in a habeas corpus proceeding arising out of a civil rights demonstration.[37] The state solicitor persisted in addressing the African American witnesses by their first names.[38] When the solicitor addressed the petitioner as "Mary," she refused to answer, insisting that the prosecutor address her as "Miss Hamilton."[39] The trial judge directed her to answer, but again she refused. The trial judge then cited her for contempt.[40] On appeal, the Alabama Supreme Court affirmed because, it said, the record showed that the witness's name was "Mary Hamilton," not "Miss Mary Hamilton."[41] Miss Mary Hamilton received a five-day sentence because of her insistence that she be treated with the same dignity accorded to white witnesses in the court.

To justify the contempt citation, the Alabama Supreme Court had to go through analytic contortions. It relied on *Ullmann v. United States,*[42] a McCarthy era case in which a United States Attorney was investigating matters of alleged espionage and membership in the Communist Party. Ullmann, who had been called to testify before a grand jury under a grant of immunity, nevertheless refused to testify on the grounds of his Fifth Amendment right against self-incrimination.[43] The Alabama Supreme Court wrenched the *Ullmann* court's comment that every man has a duty to testify and that wide latitude ought to be allowed in the cross-examination of witnesses, out of their factual context. The court upheld the contempt citation of Miss Mary Hamilton.[44] The court thus blithely ignored a crucial difference between the cases: Miss Hamilton was not refusing to testify—she merely wanted to be called "Miss," the way a white woman would have been addressed. In contrast, Ullmann presumably would not have testified even if he were called "Sir," "Dr.," "Your Honor," "My Lord," or "Reverend."

Fortunately, the Supreme Court of the United States granted certiorari and summarily reversed the contempt judgment.[45] Some might say that this case exemplifies an unjustifiable waste of legal talent and judicial effort to determine whether the appellation "Miss" should be used in cross-examination. I disagree. At the core of this case stood an individual insistent that a judicial system, which is supposed to dispense justice fairly, treat her with the dignity and sensitivity that Alabama courts automatically accorded to white middle-class men and women.[46]

The Denial of Standing to a Lawyer Seeking to Assert His Client's Right to Be Addressed With the Civilities Accorded to Whites

Again, constitutional victories at the Supreme Court level cannot provide a full solution to overt racial discrimination in the courtroom unless the lower courts are willing to give these decisions practical effect, rather than formalistically limiting them through the doctrine of standing. For example, the *Hamilton* decision did not provide a remedy for the defendants in *Farmer v. Strickland.*[47] *Farmer* involved resentencing hearings for an African American man convicted of murder in Georgia. Throughout the hearings, the prosecuting attorney continually addressed the defendant by his first name while addressing white witnesses by their titles. The defense attorney, Farmer, explained to the trial judge that the discrepancy was "demeaning. . . . He is not his friend."[48] The trial judge sharply overruled Farmer's objections. When the prosecutor persisted in calling the defendant by his first name and Farmer continued to object, the court held Farmer in contempt and sentenced him to a day in jail.

The Fifth Circuit affirmed the state court's denial of a writ of habeas corpus, rejecting Farmer's argument that *Hamilton* and *Johnson* were controlling and that his objections were "the only way to vindicate effectively and fairly [the defendant's] right to be free of racial discrimination in the courtroom."[49] The circuit court called Farmer's argument "vacuous," distinguishing *Hamilton* and *Johnson* because the decisions in those cases reverse contempt convictions which had been imposed because "*the contemnors* had refused to comply with racially discriminatory orders given to them in open court."[50] Here the trial judge's ruling that Farmer's client could be addressed by his first name, "even though clearly racially discriminatory to the client under the *Johnson* holding, certainly cannot be said to have infringed on any rights of Farmer to be free from racial animus."[51] One lesson, then, of the *Farmer* case is that Supreme Court decisions banning overt race discrimination in the courtroom cannot be relied upon to ensure consistent judicial neutrality. Instead, judges who are unsympathetic to the cause of equal justice will continue to use doctrine, such as standing, that enhances their ability to blunt the impact of the Court's rulings.[52]

Examples of Racially Discriminatory Courtroom Treatment Resting on Derogatory Myths About African Americans as a People

The cases canvassed above are not isolated or unique. Instead, they have grown from the same root that has spawned hundreds of cases and hundreds of thousands of actual instances of discriminatory treatment. To begin to grasp the manifold contours of racism in American courts, one must analyze some of these additional cases. The racist conduct in these cases has ranged from outrageously blatant appeals to racial hatred and fear to mere references to the race of a defendant or witness.[53] These cases reflect the ways in which courts have directly or indirectly contributed to the maintenance of black subjugation within an interlocking system of discriminatory practices and beliefs: enforcing the precept of inferiority.

Racially Based Statements by Counsel

In many American cases, counsel have attacked the credibility of African American defendants and witnesses by appealing to stereotypical notions of African Americans as either fools or liars.

One group of cases has seen such racially derogatory prosecutorial appeals reversed by appellate courts, which described them as clearly discriminatory. For instance, the Supreme Court of Mississippi, in *Moseley v.*

State,[54] reversed a conviction where the prosecutor had made numerous racist statements. The defendant was charged with violating prohibition laws. In his closing argument, the prosecutor told the jury that "[i]t is just a question of whether or not you believe this negro or [a white witness]."[55] Upon the defense counsel's objection to this statement, the prosecutor retorted: "she is a negro: look at her skin. If she is not a negro, I don't want you to convict her."[56] The trial judge did not rule on the defendant's objection, but merely asked [w]ell, what is she?"[57] In reversing, the court held that these statements "had nothing to do with the case, except as an appeal to race antipathy and prejudice."[58] The court also admonished the trial judge, who, "by ignoring the objection of appellant's counsel, seems to have approved the issue presented by the lawyer for the state."[59]

In a closing argument in another early southern case, a prosecutor told the jury: "You know the Negro race—how they stick up to [*sic*] each other when accused of a crime, and that they will always get up an alibi, prove it by perjured testimony of their own color, and get their accused companion clear if they can."[60] On appeal, the court held that these statements constituted an appeal to racial prejudice that required reversal.[61]

Another early Alabama case, one that preceded *Brown,* specified that racially derogatory comments in the courtroom constituted a violation of equal protection. The Alabama trial court had overruled a defense objection to a prosecutor's assertion that "[y]ou must deal with a Negro in the light of the fact that he is a Negro, and applying your experience and common sense."[62] The appellate court, reversing the conviction, said that the statement was "improper and calculated to prejudice the defendant before the jury. . . . The fact that the defendant was of the Negro race did not deprive him of the equal protection of the law, or necessarily discredit his testimony. . . ."[63]

Such cases are by no means limited to the early part of this century and before, nor to courts in the southern states. A prosecutor in a Texas trial court in the 1950s stated: "I am not criticizing the defendant for bringing a witness of the same race. I just want to let you know for the purpose of the record they try to help their own race."[64] The trial judge denied defendant's motion that the jury be instructed not to consider the prosecutor's statement.[65] The appellate court reversed the conviction, calling the prosecutor's argument "an appeal to racial prejudice. . . . *The implication was clear that state's counsel sought to condemn as a class all testimony coming from members of the colored race.*"[66]

In the 1970s, one Illinois prosecutor remarked in his closing argument:

> First of all, concerning the defendant's witness, you have to remember that they don't live in the same social structure that we do, that you and I do. The witnesses that the defendant brought are street people—simple as that. The society they live in do [*sic*] not consider the truth a great virtue. The society they live in, they lie every day. It is nothing to them to protect one of their own kind by lying.[67]

The defendant and his witnesses were African American; the prosecution's witness was white. The appellate court reversed the conviction, stating that "[t]he apparent attempt to depict defendant's witnesses as liars, not on the basis of the evidence, but on the basis that they would perjure themselves to help a member of the same race is clearly prejudicial."[68]

While one might take some comfort that each of these attempts by prosecutors to use racial antipathy to win their cases was reversed, it is worth pondering why similar cases from the same region, at the same time, were *not* reversed. In the following four early southern cases, prosecutors made equally crass appeals to negative stereotypes of African Americans in contests of credibility between African American and white witnesses, and appellate courts failed to reverse.

The Texas Court of Criminal Appeals in 1910 affirmed the conviction of an African American for carrying a gun, in *Johnson v. State.*[69] Among other disparaging remarks concerning the credibility of African Americans, the prosecutor at trial told the jury: "The negro race is all alike and about the same the world over—they are untruthful and unreliable—they are, as a rule, a set of reprobates and liars. . . ."[70] If anything, this comment is more overtly offensive than any of those in cases that led to a reversal. Yet, the appellate court affirmed the conviction, holding that "the matter is not of sufficient importance to require a reversal."[71]

Similarly, the Supreme Court of Louisiana in 1906 refused to reverse a murder conviction in a case where the prosecutor urged the jury to disregard the testimony of African American defense witnesses and then told the jury: "[y]ou must believe the testimony of these two white boys, two American citizens."[72] The Louisiana Supreme Court accepted the conclusion of the trial court that the prosecutor's statements were not intended to inject racial prejudice into the proceedings, but merely to distinguish the prosecution and defense witnesses. Without questioning the effect of the comments on the jury, the court refused to reverse the conviction.[73] Equally disturbing as this refusal to reverse is the implicit suggestion that the use of "citizens" could distinguish American-born whites and African Americans.

In *James v. State,*[74] the prosecutor asked the jury, "[a]re you gentlemen going to believe that nigger sitting over there [pointing at the defendant], with a face on him like that, in preference to the testimony of [a white] deput[y]?"[75] The Alabama Court of Appeals upheld the conviction, holding that the trial court did not err in refusing to uphold the defendant's objection to this comment.[76] Finally, in *Allen v. State,*[77] the court held that the trial judge did not err in refusing to exclude, upon defendant's objection, the prosecutor's statement that "[the defendant's lawyers] ask you to believe a couple of Negroes instead of the white girls."[78]

Just as these prosecutorial comments were effective because they appealed to then-common societal prejudices, the courts' curt refusals to reverse were a product of their members' conscious or unconscious internalization of those prejudices. Had these courts viewed African Americans as fully human, they would have seen how stigmatizing each prosecutor's comments were to the individual witnesses. Moreover, they might have reflected on how harmful they were, since failure to reverse legitimized the systemic discrediting of African Americans' testimony. In a society such as ours, where courts wield coercive power on behalf of the state in administering criminal law and in structuring social and individual relations in civil law, to disadvantage a group in the courtroom systematically by allowing them to lose all contests of credibility is to ensure their continued societal disadvantage. To privilege the testimony of whites is to allow the state to abuse its power. To have a southern prosecutor appeal to race hatred when one is on trial for one's life is as terrifying—and as dangerous—as facing the police beatings that we so easily deplore in the early American cases.79 The unequal protection from the state's use of force once contributed powerfully to the exploitation of African Americans by whites in the South and elsewhere. If we wish to preserve even our limited advances toward equality for African Americans in this century, courts must be vigilant to prevent any such infection of trials by race hatred.

Prosecutorial Appeals to Fear of Violence by African Americans

In numerous instances, prosecutors have tried to stimulate white jurors' fears that violent racial minorities would prey upon their families and communities if the defendant and others of his race were not convicted. As Charles Lawrence notes, such comments appeal to the general white stereotype of African Americans as less controlled, and so more violent or more prone to crime than whites, and are on par with a South African judge's comment that blacks kill from a "lust for stabbing."[80] In this manner, prosecutors have both perpetuated and capitalized on racist stereotypes by characterizing African Americans as particularly prone to violence.[81]

In several cases, the appellate courts have recognized these appeals as racist stereotypes and reversed defendants' convictions. For example, in California during the 1970s, a district attorney prosecuting an African American man for the rape of a black girl reminded the jury that "maybe the next time it won't be a little black girl from the other side of the tracks; maybe it will be somebody that you know; maybe it will be somebody that I know. And maybe next time he'll use the knife. . . ."[82] The United States Court of Appeals for the Ninth Circuit reversed the conviction, holding that the comments constituted a "highly inflammatory and wholly impermissible appeal to racial prejudice."[83]

In another more recent prosecution, also from the North, the prosecutor, as described by the reviewing court:

> talked of black crimes in general . . . and how crimes committed against blacks by blacks are a serious problem in our society. The prosecutor next designated Detroit as the murder capital of the United States. . . . The prosecutor then argued that the defendant and his accomplice wanted to make it in Joliet like it is in Detroit, a city of fear . . . he asked the jurors to think of their own death as the result of a crime, referred to lawlessness ravaging this [Joliet] community, and that an acquittal would be to invite an open season for shooting victims and would encourage "these people" to commit more crimes of violence.[84]

Defendant's counsel made repeated objections to the prosecutor's remarks during trial; the response of the trial judge to those objections is unclear. The appellate court, reversing on other grounds, called the remarks "not only intemperate but prejudicial."[85]

In a case against an African American man for robbery of another African American, the prosecution remarked that "[i]f you don't stop them now, they will next be robbing white people."[86] The trial judge overruled an objection to this statement, but the Mississippi Supreme Court reversed the conviction.[87]

Although some courts have had the sensitivity to recognize racism when they have seen it, it is equally important to recognize that some appellate courts have permitted prosecutorial appeals to stereotypes of African Americans as violent, by holding that such appeals constitute "harmless error." These only help to perpetuate injustice in the criminal justice system. They have effectively condoned the sheriffs and police that use the legal system as a tool for subjugating African Americans, by allowing African Americans to be convicted simply for being African American, rather than for the evidence linking them with a particular crime. Indeed, the threat of groundless conviction has always been relied upon as an effective way of enforcing deference in African American men toward whites. Thus, in a Mississippi rape case, the prosecutor, in closing remarks, stated: "[Y]ou can acquit the defendant on this charge and let him go free, and if you do he may kill another person, and the next time it may not be a colored person."[88] The trial judge sustained an objection to this remark but overruled a motion for a mistrial. The Mississippi Supreme Court found that, because the trial court had sustained the objection, no reversible error had occurred.[89]

In 1962, a California appellate court affirmed the conviction of an African American man, despite a prosecutor's remark that:

> We should not be forced to be in a position where we cannot enjoy ourselves, where our children—we have to be in fear that something might happen to our children.
>
> I am not saying this for the fact that there might be a number of Negroes there. I am saying this strictly from the fact that if this type of activity that you heard of exists, if it keeps going on, no one can be safe to go there, or to even enjoy the facilities that they have in Griffith Park.[90]

The appellate court deemed the remarks not prejudicial, since "any reasonably minded juror" would interpret the statement to mean that "defendants of every race or color should be treated equally under the law."[91]

In *Brown v. State,*[92] the prosecutor remarked in his closing argument that "prejudice against defendant and his race was brought upon themselves by the damnable heinous crimes, such as murder and rape, committed by them."[93] The trial court instructed the jury to disregard the statement, and the appellate court held that in view of the court's instruction, the statement did not constitute reversible error, despite the fact that it was an explicit appeal to racial prejudice.

Appeals to the Stereotype of African Americans as Prone to Rape White Women

While rape is a form of violence, it differs in the cultural imagination significantly from forms of violence that are not committed specifically against women.[94] Moreover, the myth that African American men are particularly prone to rape white women was an especially important part of the mythology that sustained the reign of Jim Crow.[95] It is no accident that the lynchings that were used to enforce white dominance were often based upon the allegation that the victim of the lynching had raped a white woman;[96] nor is it coincidence that many of the men on death row in the southern states at that time were African Americans convicted of raping white women.[97] I therefore treat rape cases separately.

The Supreme Court of Alabama affirmed the conviction of an African American who, in the company of eight other African Americans, was charged with raping a white girl on a train.[98] During the trial, the prosecutor asked the jury: "How would you like to have your daughter on that train with nine Negroes in a car?"[99] The Alabama Supreme Court held that the trial judge did not err in overruling the defendant's objection to the statement as inflammatory.[100]

In *Garner v. State,*[101] where an African American defendant was convicted of raping a white girl, the prosecuting attorney stated in his closing argument that it was "not uncommon to pick up a paper and see where some brute has committed this crime . . . where a brute of his race has committed this fiendish crime."[102] The trial court overruled defendant counsel's objection to this statement, but the appellate court reversed the conviction.[103]

In *Kindle v. State,*[104] the Arkansas Supreme Court upheld the rape conviction of an African American defendant in which the prosecutor told the jury in his closing argument: "Gentlemen, you don't know that he will rape the same color the next time."[105] The court, in affirming the rape conviction, described the remark as "highly improper," but noted that the prosecutor withdrew the remarks at the suggestion of the court and the defense did not object or raise an exception at the time.[106]

All these remarks both rely on and reinforce the common stereotype of African Americans as prone to rape, and particularly to raping white women.

Claims of African American Race Hatred Toward Whites

Prosecutors also appeal to the white fear that African Americans harbor a hatred for whites, which they will manifest violently. In a case in which an African American defendant was convicted of murder, the prosecutor stated: "I am well enough acquainted with this class of niggers to know that they have got it in for the race in their heart, and in their hearts call them all white sons of bitches."107 The trial judge refused defense counsel's request that he reprimand the prosecutor and admonish him against the use of such language. The appellate court reversed the conviction.[108]

In a prosecution of an African American for killing a white, in which the defendant was convicted of manslaughter, the prosecutor stated that "a member of this defendant's race is ordinarily a peaceful man, but when he does have trouble with a member of the white race, he gets murder in his heart."[109] The trial court sustained the defense counsel's objection, and instructed the jury to disregard the statement.[110] However, the prosecutor continued to remark on the respective races of the defendant and victim, prompting the appellate court to reverse the conviction.

In *Moulton v. State,*[111] the Alabama Supreme Court reversed a conviction in a case where the prosecutor told the jury: "Unless you hang this Negro, our white people living out in the country won't be safe; to let such crimes go unpunished will cause riots in our land."[112] This comment, coming only two generations after the Civil War, when there had in fact been some widely publicized riots by slaves anticipating freedom, appealed to the white fear that African Americans might rise up as a body and shake off their subjugation. As these appellate courts rightly perceived, an African American defendant cannot have a fair trial where the prosecutor appeals to the white fear that African Americans hate whites and will express that hatred violently.

Racist Characterizations of African Americans—From "Pickaninny" to "Nigger"

Because of the various derogatory myths about African Americans, partly canvassed in the cases discussed above, prosecutors could summon up hostile stereotypes of African Americans by simply referring to them by the derogatory names that were part of the system of Jim Crow. The early emphasis in the civil rights movement on exacting courtesy from courts and others—requiring the use of Negro instead of "nigger," last names instead of first names[113]—indicates the importance of such apparently semantic distinctions. Those who refer to African Americans as "niggers" see them as lazy, dirty, or oversexed, while "black man" and "African American" carry with them an image of competence and dignity.

Reported cases are replete with instances of counsel making racist statements, ranging from blatantly explicit exclamations to subtly pernicious comments and nearly benign remarks. In some instances, courts have held such comments to be sufficiently prejudicial to require reversal of a conviction. In others, appellate courts have upheld convictions where trial courts struck from the record offensive remarks or instructed the jury to disregard the comments. But in some cases, even egregious comments that neither have been stricken nor criticized by a trial judge were held not to constitute reversible error.

A number of courts have perceived the implicit appeal to racial prejudice in derogatory comments. During the prosecution of a mulatto man for murder in *Hampton v. State,*[114] the appellate court reversed the conviction where the prosecutor had made the following statements:

> Not a Negro in that great concourse of Negroes who threatened (*sic*) to be respectable has dared to come here and testify in behalf of this mulatto . . . mulattoes should be kicked out by the white race and spurned by the Negroes . . . they [mulattoes] were Negroes as long as one drop of the accursed blood was in their veins they had to bear it . . . these Negroes thought they were better than other Negroes, but in fact they were worse than Negroes; they were Negritoes, a race hated by the white race and despised by the Negroes, accursed by every white man who loves his race, and despised by every Negro who respects his race.[115]

A more blunt espousal of racial prejudice is difficult to imagine.

In *Jones v. State,*[116] the Court of Appeals of Alabama reviewed, among other issues, racist remarks by a prosecutor during the trial of an African American convicted of vehicular homicide. Referring to the defendant's negligent operation of an automobile, the prosecutor told the jury "[h]e was trying to save his own yellow head and that of his black mammy and pickaninny sitting on the back of the car."[117] While the trial court sustained the defendant's objection to this remark, the trial judge denied the defendant's motion that the jury be instructed to disregard it, stating "the court does not think it highly improper."[118] The Court of Appeals reversed and held that the remarks were improper and that the trial court erred in refusing to so instruct the jury.[119]

In *Funches v. State,*[120] the trial court did not rule on an objection by the defendant to the following statement by the prosecutor:

> The defendant in this case has got enough white man's blood in him to make him a man of judgment and sense, and he is a smart fellow indeed, and on the other hand, he has enough African in him to make him as mean as Hades itself.[121]

While the appellate court condemned this statement, it did not reach the issue of whether it constituted reversible error, but reversed the case on other grounds.[122]

In *Cooper v. State,*[123] the appellate court reversed a conviction where the prosecutor made the following comments at trial:

> But, gentlemen, while this is just another Negro killing . . . it is important to you as citizens of this County, because it is your tax dollars that are being spent to try to keep some semblance of law and order out here in our Negro section. And, gentlemen, it is a far more serious proposition than it may appear to you on its face. Ninety per cent of every tax dollar that is spent in law enforcement in this Country is because of the crimes that are committed by Negroes.[124]

In the case of an African American man charged with the crime of cohabitating with a white woman, the prosecutor remarked in his closing argument: "Since the days of the Carpetbagger colored people have thought, and still think, that they are as good as a white man."[125] The trial judge instructed the jury to disregard the statement, but declined to withdraw the case from the jury. Later in his closing argument, the prosecutor made the following comment: "Down here in the south there are few white people and a great number of colored people, and we should keep the colored man in his place."[126] The trial judge overruled the defendant's objection to that statement. The appellate court reversed the conviction, ruling that these and other remarks by the prosecutor constituted an appeal to racial prejudice.[127] They also make clear the fact that prejudice is explicitly aimed at subjugation of African Americans by whites.[128]

In *Manning v. State,*[129] the Supreme Court of Tennessee reversed a murder conviction where, at trial, the prosecutor condemned whites for appearing as character witnesses for the African American defendant. Among the statements made by the prosecutor were the following:

> How can any white man come in here and tell you that he knows the reputation of a colored man in this Community—it was a disgrace for [a white police officer] to come in here and say that man had a good character. I think that's a disgrace to any County.[130]

This was but another way of saying that, because whites dominate African Americans, and in part use the criminal justice system to do so, a white man, especially a white policeman, must never attempt to aid an African American defendant in the courtroom.

Even though it reversed the conviction, in its opinion the Tennessee Supreme Court displayed a racist, patronizing attitude: "Our judges, court officials, and jurors, are uniformly white men. The white race is dominant and the Negroes are, in a sense, our wards."[131]

In *United States ex. rel. Haynes v. McKendrick,*[132] the United States Court of Appeals for the Second Circuit reversed a 1966 conviction in a New York state case133 in which the prosecutor had made numerous racist statements at trial, including the following:

> There is something about it, if you have dealt with colored people and have been living with them and see them you begin to be able to dis-

> cern their mannerisms and appearances and to discern the different shades and so on. . . .
>
> [Defense attorney for petitioner Haynes] knows [blacks'] weaknesses and inability to do certain things that maybe are commonplace for the ordinary person to do or remember or know certain things. . . . It gets confusing when you talk to some of these black youngsters like that because they don't express themselves as clearly as you and I might possibly be able to do so. . . .[134]

The prosecutor also went on at length about how many African Americans were wearing "exotic" hairstyles and sideburns, and how different such hairstyles were ordinary (i.e., white) people's conceptions of normal hairstyles.[135] Because whites have negative stereotypes of African Americans, to focus on differences even between white and African American styles is a covert appeal to racial prejudice, as the appellate court correctly saw.

The preceding cases attest to the importance of the appellate process as the first line of defense against court-sanctioned racism. However, many appellate courts, captives of their own conscious or unconscious racism, have allowed racially derogatory comments in the courtroom to go unchecked. For example, in *Dodson v. State,*[136] the Court of Criminal Appeals of Texas upheld a conviction of an African American for assault with intent to murder. The defendant had been employed by the victim to cut cotton all day for sixty cents. The defendant threw a rock at his employer after the latter threatened the defendant with violence for daring to quit his job at mid-day and then demand part or all of his sixty cent wage.[137] At trial, the prosecutor told the jury that "[i]t is just such impudent and sassy negroes as the defendant is shown by the evidence to be causing trouble in this country."[138] In holding that this remark was not prejudicial, the court noted, among other things, that "we do not see how [the remark] could have injured the appellant."[139] The injury is obvious, however; the suggestion that the African American defendant be punished for having responded "impudently" to economically exploitive treatment, rather than for what he had actually done, was just the type of reasoning that kept the structures of economic exploitation in place. A legal system that allows such patterns of exploitation, rather than the relevant facts of an incident, to draw the lines between assault with intent to murder and ordinary assault cannot be other than substantively unjust.

The Supreme Court of Alabama, in *Davis v. State,*[140] overturned an appellate court's reversal of a conviction of an African American for assaulting a white who had intervened in a fight between the defendant and another African American. The reversal was based upon a statement by the prosecutor that "the jury should deal harshly with such cattle."[141] Although the trial judge denied a motion for a mistrial based upon this reference to the defendant, he did admonish the jury to ignore the prosecutor's remarks, and to "try this defendant just as you would a white man."[142] In overturning the appellate court's reversal, the Alabama Supreme Court held that "there [wa]s nothing to illustrate the probable effects of the solicitor as prejudicial, when considered in the light of the admonition of the judge."[143]

In many other cases, appellate courts have upheld convictions despite prosecutors' references to African American defendants and witnesses in such racist terms as "black rascal,"[144] "burr-headed nigger,"145 "mean negro,"[146] "big nigger,"[147] "picaninny,"[148] "mean nigger,"[149] "three nigger men,"[150] "nigger,"[151] and "nothing but just a common Negro, [a] black whore."[152] It is inconceivable to me that these same courts would have allowed a prosecutor to make equally repulsive comments directed at other minorities, such as referring to a Jewish witness or defendant as a "kike," or to an Italian as a "wop." Thus, these court rulings are as much a reflection of judicial insensitivity and racism as they are of the racism of the prosecutors who spoke these heinous epithets.

JUDICIAL CONDUCT

All the instances of prosecutorial misconduct explored above also contain elements of judicial misconduct insofar as the trial judges overruled defense objections, denied motions for mistrials based upon racist statements of the prosecutor, or failed to declare mistrials based on racist comments *sua sponte.* Likewise, we have seen instances where appellate judges have refused to reverse convictions despite egregious injections of racial prejudice, bias, or similar irrelevant, but damaging, considerations into a trial.

While few in number, acts of overt racism on the part of judges also have been reported. In an *en banc* opinion, the Supreme Court of California ordered the public censure of a Superior Court judge named Stevens, who was found by the state's Commission on Judicial Performance ("Commission") to have made repeated racist comments off the bench during his judicial tenure.[153]

In a concurring opinion, Justice Kaus noted the numerous contexts in which the judge had made racist remarks. Judge Stevens had referred to African Americans as "Jig," "dark boy," "colored boy," "nigger," "coon," and "jungle bunny."[154] In a probate case between African American litigants the judge stated, in the presence of court personnel only, "let's get on with this Amos and Andy show."[155] During an in-chambers discussion, the judge stated that "Filipinos can be good hard-working people" and "that they are clean, unlike some black animals who come into contact with the court."[156] Again in chambers, the judge stated that his court clerk was "lazier than a coon."[157] While none of these comments were made while court was in session, it is not difficult to imagine the dispiriting effect on the African American, Hispanic, and Asian communities of being forced to deal with this judge's racism during in-chambers conferences, and the encouragement that his open racism must have given to more subtly racist lawyers in the community to treat minority lawyers with less than full professional respect and courtesy.

Justice Mosk dissented from the court's order for public censure for Judge Stevens. Noting that the Commission was authorized by statute to discipline judicial conduct, not speech, Justice Mosk claimed that there was no finding of judicial misconduct by the Commission.[158] The Commission did find that, "according to most witnesses . . . Judge Stevens has at all times performed his judicial duties fairly and equitably, and free from actual bias against any person regardless of race."[159] Even in the face of such an outrageous and persistent display of racism, Justice Mosk was satisfied that Judge Stevens's comments bore no relation to the performance of his judicial duties, and could not agree with the Commission that such mere speech was "prejudicial to the administration of justice" or that it "brings the judicial office into disrepute."[160] One is tempted to respond to this artificial speech conduct distinction with Charles Black's rejoinder to the formalism of those who defended the doctrine of "separate but equal" on the grounds that it did not stigmatize African Americans: "How long must we keep a straight face?"[161]

In his charge to the jury in *State v. Belk,*[162] the trial judge referred to defendants in a robbery prosecution as "three black cats in a white Buick."[163] The Supreme Court of North Carolina affirmed the lower court's ruling that this reference "unduly influenced the jury" and was an improper expression of judicial opinion.[164] The court did not consider the racist nature of the statement, however, or comment on the fact that the judge specifically identified the defendants as African American. Instead, the court went into an almost comical analysis of the probability that, by calling the defendants "cats," the judge was not referring to felines, but to the slang term for a "worldly, wise, or hep" man who "dresses in the latest style and pursues women."[165]

Finally, lest one believe that demonstrations of racial bias by judges are reserved exclusively for disenfranchised, poor, African American criminal defendants, the case of *Berry v. United States*[166] is instructive. In that case, the rich and famous grandfather of rock 'n' roll, Mr. "Back in the U.S.A." Chuck Berry was denied a fair trial through the hostile and racially motivated conduct of a United States District Court trial judge. While the United States Court of Appeals for the Eighth Circuit failed to describe any of the racist conduct of the trial judge, the court noted that:

> It seems safe to say that . . . a trial judge who, in the presence of a jury, makes remarks reflecting upon a defendant's race or from which an implication can be drawn that racial considerations may have some bearing upon the issue of guilt or innocence, has rendered the trial unfair.[167]

One can take comfort in the appellate court's clear grasp of equal protection doctrine, but it is still discomforting to note that the doctrine had to be enforced by an appellate panel.

The examples above are primarily from reported appellate cases. Many of the criminal justice proceedings at the trial court level were not transcribed when no appeals were filed, and thus those cases are not available for review by scholars. In thousands of cases where racial slights and denigrations occurred, no objections were made and no appeals were taken on racial grounds. It is my hunch that, out of every thousand cases where racial denigration occurred, probably fewer than two were appealed. Nevertheless, among the appellate cases reported, the often openly hostile language and actions on the part of prosecutors, judges, and court officials reveal a jurisprudential culture in which there were much-displayed notions of black inferiority in the state criminal justice system.

NOTES

1. RAYFORD W. LOGAN, THE BETRAYAL OF THE NEGRO 9-10 (1965) (emphasis in original) (quoting Frederick Douglass).

The material in this chapter substantially based on A. Leon Higginbotham, Jr., *Racism in American and South African Courts: Similarities and Differences*, 65 N.Y.U. L. REV. 479 (1990). These notes include the state reporter citations along with the regional citations in order to help those who wish to research the individual states' criminal justice systems.

2. *See generally* CORNEL WEST, RACE MATTERS (1993).

3. U.S. CONST. pml. (emphasis added).

4. *See* West, *supra* note 2.

5. *See, e.g.*, DERRICK BELL, RACE, RACISM AND AMERICAN LAW 33 (2D ED. 1980).

6. CHARLES LAWRENCE III, *The Id, the Ego, and Equal Protection: Reckoning with Unconscious Racism*, 39 STAN. L. REV. 317, 329 (1987).

7. *Id.* at 363.

8. *Id.* at 330, 351.

9. *Id.* at 333-34, 341, 352.

10. *Id.* at 352, 357, 367.

11. *Id.* at 370, 372.

12. *Id.* at 322, 326.

13. CHARLES WARREN, THE SUPREME COURT IN UNITED STATES HISTORY 2 (1923):

> The Court is not an organism disassociated from the conditions and history of the times in which it exists. It does not formulate and deliver its opinions in a legal vacuum. Its Judges are not abstract and impersonal oracles, but are men whose views are necessarily, though by no conscious intent, affected by inheritance, education and environment and by the impact of history past and present.

Oliver Wendell Holmes shared this perception:

> The life of the law has not been logic: it has been experience. The felt necessities of the time, the prevalent moral and political theories, intuitions of public policy, avowed or unconscious, *even the prejudices which judges share with their fellow-men. . . .*

OLIVER W. HOLMES, THE COMMON LAW 1 (1881) (emphasis added).

14. Letter from Anthony Amsterdam, Professor, New York University School of Law, to A. Leon Higginbotham, Jr. 4 (Oct. 10, 1989).

15. For discussion of the American culture of racism and reflections on the significance of the trial and acquittal of the white officers who beat Rodney King, see A. Leon Higginbotham, Jr. & Aderson B. François, *Looking for God and Racism in All the Wrong Places*, 70 DENV. U. L. REV. 191 (1993).

16. JACK BASS, UNLIKELY HEROES: THE DRAMATIC STORY OF THE SOUTHERN JUDGES WHO TRANSLATED THE SUPREME COURT'S *BROWN* DECISION INTO A REVOLUTION FOR EQUALITY 13 (1981). It is purely coincidental that the mural appears in a federal rather than a state courthouse. It captures the essence of what I discuss in this chapter

regarding symptoms and symbols of racism in the state judicial process.

17. Murray v. State, 202 Miss. 849, 33 So. 2d 291 (1948).

18. *Id.* at 857, 33 So. 2d at 292.

19. *Id.*

20. 373 U.S. 61(1963).

21. *Id.* at 62.

22. *Id.*

23. *Id.* (citations omitted).

24. *See* Charles Lawrence, *supra* note 6, at 350 (1987).

25. *See* State v. Cox, 244 La. 1087, 1108, 156 So. 2d 448, 456 (1963), *rev'd,* 379 U.S. 536 (1965).

26. *Id.* (citations omitted).

27. The United States Supreme Court, in a landmark decision, reversed Cox's conviction on First Amendment grounds but did not discuss the question of segregation in the courtroom. *See* State v. Cox, 379 U.S. 536 (1965).

28. Plummer v. Casey, 148 F. Supp. 326 (S.D. Tex, 1955), *aff'd,* 240 F.2d 922 (5th Cir. 1956), *cert. denied,* 353 U.S. 924 (1957).

29. *Id.* at 329.

30. For an analysis of the application of the equal protection doctrine to facilities owned and operated by the state, but leased to private parties, see Burton v. Wilmington Parking Auth., 365 U.S. 715 (1961).

31. Dawley v. Norfolk, 159 F. Supp. 642 (E.D. Va, 1958), *aff'd,* 260 F.2d 647 (4th Cu. 1958), *cert. denied,* 359 U.S. 935 (1959).

32. *Id.* at 644.

33. *Id.* at 645. The judge thereafter declined to consider the claim as presented by the pleadings because it "is exclusively one cognizable by the state courts." *Id.*

34. 163 U.S. 537, 544 (1896) ("Laws permitting, and even requiring, . . . separation [of African Americans and whites] in places where they are liable to be brought into contact do not necessarily imply the inferiority of either race to the other. . . .").

35. Brown v. Board of Educ., 347 U.S. 483, 494 (1954).

36. Charles Black, *The Lawfulness of the Segregation Decisions,* 69 YALE L.J. 421, 424-26 (1960) (emphasis added).

37. *Ex parte* Mary Hamilton, 275 Ala. 574, 574, 156 So. 2d 926, 929 (1963), *rev'd,* 376 U.S. 650 (1964). For an acknowledgment that the use of first names for African Americans was part of the southern caste system, see Black, *supra* note 36, at 425.

38. *See* Petitioner's Brief at 2, Hamilton v. Alabama, 376 U.S. 650 (1964) (No. 793).

39. *Hamilton,* 275 Ala. at 574-75, 156 So. 2d at 926.

40. *Id.*

41. *Id.,* 156 So. 2d at 927.

42. 350 U.S. 422 (1956).

43. The Supreme Court ruled that, since he had been granted immunity, he had to testify because it was "every man's duty to give testimony before a duly constituted tribunal unless he invokes some valid legal exemption in withholding it." *Hamilton,* 175 Ala. at 575, 156 So. 2d at 927 (quoting *Ulllmann,* 350 U.S. at 439).

44. *Id.,* 156 So. 2d at 927.

45. Hamilton v. Alabama, 376 U.S. 650 (1964).

46. Constance Baker Motley, the distinguished civil rights lawyer and former Chief Judge of the United States District Court for the Southern District of New York, recalls being subjected to similar indignities. "Often a southern judge would refer to the men attorneys as Mister, but would make a point of calling me 'Connie,' since traditionally black women in the South were called only by their first name."

KAREN B. MORELLO, THE INVISIBLE BAR: THE WOMAN LAWYER IN AMERICA, 1683 TO THE PRESENT 161 (1986). (White women in the South are traditionally referred to as "Miz First Name," a practice that separates them out from the most respectful, white male appellation, "Mr. Last Name," and poor whites, referred to as "poor white trash" or "crackers," have also been denied dignity in public settings.)

47. 652 F.2d 427 (5th Cir. 1981), *cert. denied,* 455 U.S. 944 (1982). *See* Tom Wicker, *Worthy of Contempt,* N.Y. TIMES, Mar. 27, 1979, at A25 (an editorial describing the effects of the contempt citation on Farmer's ability to argue subsequent death penalty appeals).

48. *Farmer,* 652 F.2d at 430.

49. *Id.* at 435.

50. *Id.* (emphasis in original).

51. *Id.*

52. Likewise, judges who are sympathetic to the cause might use the standing doctrine liberally to enhance the ability of individuals to challenge discriminatory practices. *See* Steven L. Winter, *The Metaphor of Standing and the Problem of Self-Governance,* 40 STAN. L. REV. 1371, 1418-52 (1988).

53. The cases are replete with instances of prosecutors continually referring to the race of the witness or defendant. Although these references often have a clearly racist message, I have chosen, due to sheer volume, not to review those cases here.

54. 73 So. 791 (Miss. 1917).

55. *Id.* at 791.

56. *Id.*

57. *Id.*

58. *Id.* at 792.

59. *Id.* at 791.

60. Tannehill v. State, 159 Ala. 51, 52, 48 So. 662, 662 (1909).

61. *Id.* For a similar result, also from this time period in Alabama, see Perdue v. State, 17 Ala. App. 500, 86 So. 158 (1920). There, the Alabama Court of Appeals reversed a conviction in which the trial court overruled the defendant's objections to the following statement by the prosecutor: "Yes gentlemen of the jury, you know the

Negro, and you know that even when one gets into trouble the others all come in and swear lies to get him out." *Id.* at 501, 86 So. at 158.

62. Simmons v. State, 14 Ala. App. 103, 104, 71 So. 979, 979 (1916).

63. *Id.*

64. Allison v. State, 157 Tex. Crim. 200, 201, 248 S.W.2d 147, 147 (1952).

65. *Id.*, 248 S.W.2d at 148.

66. *Id.* (emphasis in original).

67. People v. Richardson, 49 Ill. App. 3d 170, 172-73, 363 N.E.2d 924, 926 (1977).

68. *Id.* at 173-74, 363 N.E.2d at 927.

69. Johnson v. State, 59 Tex. Crim. 11, 11, 127 S.W. 559, 559 (1910).

70. *Id.*

71. *Id.* at 12-13, 127 S.W. at 559-60.

72. State v. Lee, 116 La. 607, 615, 40 So. 914, 917 (1906).

73. *Id.*

74. 18 Ala. App. 618, 92 So. 909 (1922).

75. *Id.*

76. *Id.* at 617-18, 92 So. at 910.

77. 22 Ala. App. 74, 112 So. 177 (1927).

78. *Id.* at 74-75, 112 So. at 177.

79. *See, e.g.*, Brown v. Mississippi, 297 U.S. 278 (1935); Chambers v. Florida, 309 U.S. 227 (1939).

80. S. v. Augustine, 1980 (1) S.A. 503, 506 (A.D.) (quotation translated from Afrikaans).

81. While I cannot address it here, prosecutors have used similar stereotypes against other racial minorities as well. *See, e.g.*, People v. Reyes, 133 Cal. App. 574, 577, 24 P.2d 531, 532 (1933) (In murder trial with a Mexican American defendant, the prosecutor told the jury: "Mexicans are peculiar, they are a stoical race. They can face death unflinchingly, the average Mexican can, and perhaps that is why they can take other lives unflinchingly and quite calmly."). The appellate court affirmed the conviction, stating that the defendant was convicted after a "full, fair, and impartial trial." *Id.* at 578, 24 P.2d at 532.

82. Kelly v. Stone, 514 F.2d 18, 19 (9th Cir. 1975) (on appeal from district court's denial of a writ of habeas corpus on grounds of prosecutorial misconduct).

83. *Id.*

84. People v. Lurry, 77 Ill. App. 3d 108, 113-14, 395 N.E.2d 1234, 1237-38 (1979).

85. *Id.* at 114, 315 N.E.2d at 1238.

86. Reed v. State, 232 Miss. 432, 434, 99 So.2d 455, 456 (1958).

87. *Id.* (stating that "[t]he jury had the duty and right to evaluate [the principal witnesses's] testimony and other evidence independently of the emotional factor of racial prejudice being injected into the case by the State's attorney").

88. Herrin v. State, 201 Miss. 595, 602, 29 So. 2nd 452, 453 (1947).

89. *Id.*, 29 So. 2d at 454.

90. People v. Jones, 205 Cal. App 2d 460, 466, 23 Cal. Rptr. 418, 422 (1962).

91. *Id.*

92. Brown v. State, 50 Tex. Crim. 79, 95 S.W. 126 (1906).

93. *Id.* at 83, 95 S.W. at 128.

94. *See* SUSAN ESTRICH, REAL RAPE 20-26, 82-82 (1987) (distinguishing rape from other violent crimes).

95. *See* BELL, *supra* note 5, at 68; JOEL KOVEL, WHITE RACISM: A PSYCHOHISTORY 67-71 (1970).

96. GEORGE M. FREDRICKSON: THE BLACK IMAGE IN THE WHITE MIND: THE DEBATE ON AFRO-AMERICAN CHARACTER AND DESTINY, 1817-1914, at 67-71 (1970); N.A.A.C.P., THIRTY YEARS OF LYNCHING IN THE UNITED STATES, 1889-1918, at 8 (W.L. Katz ed., 1969); CLAUDE H. NOLAN, THE NEGRO'S IMAGE IN THE SOUTH 46-50 (1967); JOHN G. VAN DEUSEN, THE BLACK MAN IN WHITE AMERICA 154-58 (1944); IDA B. WELLS-BARNETT, ON LYNCHINGS: SOUTHERN HORRORS; A RED RECORD; MOB RULE IN NEW ORLEANS 1 (1969); WALTER F. WHITE, ROPE AND FAGGOT: A BIBLIOGRAPHY OF JUDGE LYNCH (1969); ROBERT L. ZANGRANDO, THE N.A.A.C.P. CRUSADE AGAINST LYNCHING, 1909-1950, at 3 (1980).

97. *See, e.g.*, McClesky v. Kemp, 481 U.S. 279, 328-35 (1987) (Brennan, J., dissenting); Furman v. Georgia, 408 U.S. 238, 250-251 (1972), *reh'g denied*, 409 U.S. 902 (1972). *See also* Marvin E. Wolfgang & Marc Riedel, *Rape, Race and the Death Penalty in Georgia*, 45 AM. J. OF ORTHOPSYCHIATRY 658 (1975); Rupert C. Koeninger, *Capital Punishment in Texas, 1924-1968*, 15 CRIME & DELINQ. 132, 141 (1969).

98. Weems v. State, 236 Ala. 261, 263, 182 So. 3, 4 (1938).

99. *Id.*

100. *Id.*, 182 So. at 4-5.

101. Garner v. State, 120 Miss. 744, 83 So. 83, 83 (1919).

102. *Id.* at 751, 83 So. at 83.

103. *Id.* at 751, 83 So. at 84.

104. 165 Ark. 284, 264 S.W. 856 (1924).

105. *Id.* at 289, 264 S.W. at 857.

106. *Id.*

107. Taylor v. State, 50 Tex. Crim. 560, 561, 100 S.W. 393, 393 (1907).

108. *Id.*, 100 S.W. at 394.

109. Roby v. State, 147 Miss. 575, 575, 113 So. 185, 185 (1927).

110. *Id.*, 113 So. at 186.

111. 199 Ala. 411, 74 So. 454 (1917).

112. *Id.* at 412, 74 So. at 454.

113. For a discussion of these early efforts by one of their participants, see Derrick Bell, *Foreword: The Civil Rights Chronicles*, 99 HARV. L. REV. 4, 13 & n.3[illegible] (1985). *See also* Mari J. Matsuda, *Looking to the Bottom*

Critical Legal Studies and Reparations, 22 HARV. C.R.-C.L. L. REV. 323, 357 n.140 (1987) (noting that initial demand in what became Montgomery bus boycott was for courteous treatment on buses).

114. 88 Miss. 257, 40 So. 545 (1906).

115. *Id.* at 259, 40 So. at 545-46.

116. 21 Ala. App. 234, 109 So. 189 (1926).

117. *Id.* at 236, 109 So. at 190.

118. *Id.*

119. *Id.* at 237, 109 So. at 190-91. Even white, purported scholars have referred to African Americans as pickaninnies. *See* W. CLEON SKOUSEN, THE MAKING OF AMERICA: THE SUBSTANCE AND MEANING OF THE CONSTITUTION 733 (1985). For a critique of these scholars, see A. Leon Higginbotham, Jr., *The Bicentennial of the Constitution: A Racial Perspective,* 22 STAN. L. REV. 8 (1987).

Former Arizona Governor Evan Meecham created a furor when he said that he did not believe that the term "pickaninny" was offensive, and that in his day black people referred to their own children as pickaninnies. E.J. Montini, *To Slur with Love: Meecham Must Know Something That Blacks Don't,* ARIZ. REPUBLIC, Mar. 26, 1987, at A2. Columnist E.J. Montini responded to the governor's comment:

> I spoke to a black man here and . . . never in his life have his parents referred to him as a pickaninny.
>
> Then it struck me. What about *my* family?
>
> I can't remember a single tender moment when my father or mother called me a "wop" or "dago." Not once.
>
> My parents say they're old fashioned people with old fashioned values—like the governor. But not once did they express their affection for me through one of the many quaint ethnic slurs available to them.
>
> Not once did I hear, "Hi Eddie, my little guinea."
>
> So I investigated further. Not one of the Mexican Americans I talked to was referred to by his parents as a "spic" or "wetback."
>
> None of the Jewish mothers called her offspring "kikes" or "hymies" or even "Jew-boys."
>
> None of the Polish parents I know referred to their children as "polacks." Including a family I know whose given name was Pollack.
>
> Based on this overwhelming evidence, it's obvious that family values in America have collapsed and why a person like Gov. Meecham wants to return us to the good old days, an era when white men were "men" and black men were "boys." It was less confusing then, a time when black boys were pickaninnies, and all the little spics and wops and kikes knew their place.

Id.

120. 125 Miss. 140, 87 So. 487 (1921).

121. *Id.* at 151-52, 87 So. at 488.

122. *Id.* at 150-51, 87 So. at 488.

123. 136 Fla. 23, 186 So. 230 (1939).

124. *Id.* at 25-26, 186 So. at 230-31.

125. William v. State, 25 Ala. App. 342, 343, 146 So. 422, 423 (1933).

126. *Id.* at 343-44, 146 So. at 423.

127. *Id.* at 344, 146 So. at 423-24.

128. For an equally overt appeal to prejudice, and an example of how prejudice was a direct attempt to dominate African Americans, see Blocker v. State, 112 Tex. Crim. 275, 16 S.W.2d 253 (1929). In that case, the prosecutor explained the victim's assault on defendant, an African American man, as "an effort on his part to keep this negro in his place, and Southern gentlemen will not condemn him for it." *Id.* at 278, 16 S.W.2d at 254. The prosecutor also stated: "I have lived in this country all my life and I do not have to tell twelve Southern men what to do in this case." *Id.* The trial judge instructed the jury to disregard the first comment. The appellate court reversed, stating that the prosecutor's argument "constituted a veiled and covert appeal to race prejudice." *Id.*

A Mississippi case from the same period also bluntly espoused notions based on the notion that the criminal law's purpose was to keep African Americans who fought their domination in their place. In Collins v. State, 100 Miss. 435, 56 So. 527 (1911), an African American defendant was convicted of murdering an African American man where the prosecutor made the following comments to the jury: "This bad nigger killed a good nigger. The dead nigger was a white man's nigger, and these bad niggers like to kill that kind. The only way you can break up this pistol toting among these niggers is to have a necktie party." *Id.* at 440. 56 So. at 528. The trial judge apparently did not instruct the jury to disregard this statement. The appellate court reversed the conviction, noting that "the appellant may be a bad negro, and a very undesirable member of society, yet he is entitled to go before the jury of the land untrammeled by voluntary epithets, the occasion for which is not shown justified by this record." *Id.* As in the cases discussed in the section above, without appellate supervision, the criminal law could be used to reinforce the power structure that supported the domination of African Americans.

129. 195 Tenn. 94, 257 S.W.2d 6 (1953).

130. *Id.* at 98, 257 S.W.2d at 8.

131. Even though it reversed the conviction, the Tennessee Supreme Court's opinion displayed a racist, patronizing attitude: "Our judges, court officials, and jurors, are uniformly white men. The white race is dominant and the Negroes are, in a sense, our wards." *Id.* at 99, 257 S.W.2d at 9 (quoting Roland v. State, 137 Tenn. 663, 665, 194 S.W. 1097, 1097 (1917)). The prosecutor rebuked whites for appearing as character witnesses for African American defendants.

132. 481 F.2d 152 (2d Cir. 1973).

133. *See* People v. Haynes, 33 A.D.2d 893, 308 N.Y.S.2d 316 (1969).

134. *McKendrick,* 481 F.2d at 155.

135. *See id.* at 154-55. The Second Circuit commented in detail on all of the prosecutor's racist remarks, noting that their cumulative effect was to admonish the all-white jury to think of African Americans as a group separate from and foreign to themselves. *See id.* at 155 n.3.

136. 45 Tex. Crim. 574, 78 S.W. 514 (1904).

137. *Id.* at 575, 78 S.W. at 516.

138. *Id.* at 577, 78 S.W. at 516.

139. *Id.*

140. 233 Ala. 202, 172 So. 344 (1936).

141. Id. at 203, 172 So. at 344.

142. *Id.*

143. *Id.,* 172 So. at 345.

144. State v. Miles, 199 Mo. 530, 533, 98 S.W. 25, 31 (1906).

145. Adams v. State, 86 Tex. Crim. 422, 423, 216 S.W. 863, 864 (1919).

146. Green v. State, 105 P.2d 795, 797 (Okla. Ct. App. 1940).

147. State v. Hubbard, 165 Kan. 406, 408, 195 P.2d 604, 605 (1948).

148. People v. Curry, 97 Cal. App. 2d 537, 551, 218 P.2d 153, 161 (1950).

149. Quarles v. Commonwealth, 245 S.W.2d 947, 949 (Ky. Ct. App. 1951).

150. Thornton v. State, 451 S.W.2d 898, 903 (Tex. Crim. App. 1970).

151. Thornton v. Beto, 470 F.2d. 657, 658 (5th Cir. 1972), *cert. denied,* 411 U.S. 920 (1973).

152. Hilson v. State, 96 Tex. Crim. 550, 551, 258 S.W. 826 (1924).

153. *In re* Stevens, 31 Cal. 3d 403, 645 P.2d 99, 183 Cal. Rptr. 48 (1982). *Cf.* Phillips v. Joint Legislative Comm., 637 F.2d 1014 (5th Cir. 1981) (holding that evidence of racist comments by a judge, from the bench and in published opinions, as well as statistics concerning high reversal rate in civil rights cases heard by the judge, were insufficient to require recusal in a case where there was no evidence of bias against any particular parties to the suit in question); John Leubsdorf, *Theories of Judging and Judge Disqualification,* 62 N.Y.U.L. REV. 237, 256, 258-60 (1987).

154. Stevens, 31 Cal. 3d at 404, 645 P.2d at 99, 183 Cal. Rptr. at 48 (Kaus, J., concurring).

155. *Id.*

156. *Id.,* 645 P.2d at 100, 183 Cal. Rptr. at 49.

157. *Id.,* 645 P.2d at 99, 183 Cal. Rptr. at 48. The judge's racist comments were by no means reserved for African Americans, however. During his tenure, the judge referred to Hispanics as "cute little tamales," "Taco Bell," "spic," and "bean." *Id.* at 405, 645 P.2d at 100, 183 Cal. Rptr. at 49. On one occasion, the judge said that a Hispanic attorney who changed his position on a settlement was "acting like a Mexican jumping bean." *Id.*

158. *Id.* at 405-06, 645 P.2d at 100-101, 183 Cal. Rptr. at 48.

159. *Id.* at 404, 645 P.2d at 99, 183 Cal. Rptr. at 48.

160. *Id.*

161. Black, *supra* note 36, at 425.

162. 268 N.C. 320, 150 S.E.2d 481 (1966).

163. *Id.* at 324, 150 S.E.2d at 484.

164. *Id.*

165. *Id.* at 325, 150 S.E.2d at 484-85.

166. 283 F.2d 465 (8th Cir. 1960).

167. *Id.* at 467.

11

INTRODUCTION

Robert Staples is Professor Emeritus in the Department of Social and Behavioral Sciences at the University of California, San Francisco. Staples has written numerous books and articles in the areas of family sociology, especially Black family patterns, and human sexual behavior. His work in the area of the Black family has focused on the impact of race and racism on the role of the Black family, the Black woman, and the Black man. These works exemplify Staples's efforts to challenge the concepts of mainstream sociology, which present numerous myths about the Black family and the sexuality of both Black men and women. The importance of applying the Black perspective to sociology was introduced by Staples in his earlier book, *The Introduction to Black Sociology* (1976). Staples has also examined changes in the configuration of family and relationships between Black men and women.

In this article originally published in *Phylon* in 1975, Staples uses Franz Fanon's colonial model to explain the relationship between race and crime in America. He argues that the Black community is dominated politically, economically, and socially by leaders of the racially dominant group. As a result, crime by Blacks in America is defined not only by the behavior of the Black offender but also by the vagaries of racism that determine the definition of serious crime and serious offenders and the nature of access to the criminal justice system and its intermediaries. Staples acknowledges the need for more research into the use of the colonial model to explain race and crime. He is also steadfast in his view that race, a political identity, provides a more encompassing explanation of the issue of crime for Blacks than for Whites because Blacks of all social classes are victimized, whereas the victimization of Whites depends on their specific social class.

WHITE RACISM, BLACK CRIME, AND AMERICAN JUSTICE

An Application of the Colonial Model to Explain Crime and Race

ROBERT STAPLES

In the past hundred years criminologists have shown great interest in the relationship between race and crime. Various theories have been put forth to explain the association between racial membership and criminal activity. These theories have ranged from Lombroso's[1] discredited assertion that certain groups possess inherent criminal tendencies to the more widely accepted theory that certain racial groups are more commonly exposed to conditions of poverty which lead them to commit crimes more often.[2] The purpose of this paper is to examine the relationship of race and crime in a new theoretical framework which will permit a systematic analysis of racial crime within the political-economic context of American society. One function of this model will be to delineate the nature of the solution required to reduce the magnitude of crime among certain racial groups.

The approach here used to explain race and crime is the colonial model. This framework has been formulated and used in the writings of Fanon, Blauner, Carmichael and Hamilton, Memmi, and others.[3] It is particularly attributed to Fanon, whose analysis of colonial relationships in Africa has been transferred to the American pattern of racial dominance and subjugation. While there are many criminologists who will summarily dismiss this model as lacking any relevance for understanding the relationship between race and crime, it merits a hearing since many blacks, especially those presently incarcerated, give it considerable credence. In fact, it is their self-definition as political prisoners that has motivated the many prison protests that have occurred in recent years.

Basically, the colonial analogy views the black community as an underdeveloped colony whose economics and politics are controlled by leaders of the racially dominant group. Using this framework, it is useful to view race as a political and cultural identity rather than to apply any genetic definitions. Race is a political identity because it defines the way in which an individual is to be treated

---

From Staples, R. (1975). White racism, black crime, and American justice: An application of the colonial model. *Phylon, 36,* 14-22. Reprinted with permission of *Phylon* and the author.

by the political state and the conditions of one's oppression. It is cultural in the sense that white cultural values always have ascendancy over black cultural values, thus what is "good" or "bad," "criminal" or "legitimate" behavior is always defined in terms favorable to the ruling class. The result is that crime by blacks in America is structured by their relationship to the colonial structure, which is based on racial inequality and perpetuated by the political state.

Obviously, there are some imperfections in the colonial analogy as a unitary heuristic model to explain race and crime. More theoretical and empirical research is necessary before the structural forms characteristic of classical colonialism may be mechanically applied to the complexities of crime in America. Yet, the essential features of colonialism are manifest in American society. Blacks have been, and remain, a group subjected to economic exploitation and political control; and they lack the ability to express their cultural values without incurring serious consequences. While other colonial factors such as the geographical relationship of the colonial masters to the colonized, the population ratio, and the duration of colonization may be missing, they do not profoundly affect the form or substance of black and white relations in America: white superordination and black subordination.

In using this model I am not dissuaded by the complications of class often interjected into the issue of crime and race. Domestic colonialism is as much cultural as economic. While members of the white working class are more victimized by their class location than other whites, they are not subjected to the dehumanized status of blacks of all social classes. The racist fabric of white America denies blacks a basic humanity and thus permits the violation of their right to equal justice under the law. In America the right to injustice is an inalienable right; but for blacks it is still a privilege to be granted at the caprice and goodwill of whites, who control the machinery of the legal system and the agents of social control.

Law and Order

One of the key elements in securing the citizenry's obedience to a nation's laws is the belief of the citizens that the laws are fair. A prevalent view of the law among blacks is summed up in Lester's statement that "the American Black man has never known law and order except as an instrument of oppression. The law has been written by white men, for the protection of white men and their property, to be enforced by white men against Blacks in particular and poor folks in general."[4] Historically, a good case can be made for the argument that the function of law was to establish and regulate the colonial relationship of blacks and whites in the United States. Initially, the colonial system was established by laws which legitimated the subordination of the black population.

The legalization of the colonial order is best represented in the Constitution itself. While the Constitution is regarded as the bulwark of human equality and freedom, it denied the right to vote to Afro-Americans and made the political franchise an exclusive right of white property owners. In fact, blacks were defined as a source of organic property for white slave holders in the notorious 3/5 clause. This clause allowed the slaveowner to claim 3/5 constituency for each slave that he possessed. Since non-citizens are beyond the pale of legal equality, the Dred Scott decision affirmed that slaves were not citizens and could not bring suit in the courts. As the ultimate blow to the aspirations of blacks, in 1896 the Supreme Court upheld racial segregation in its "separate but equal" decision in the Plessy *v.* Ferguson case.[5]

In a contemporary sense, blacks are not protected by American law because they have no power to enforce those laws. They have no law of their own and no defense against the laws of the colonizers. Thus, the power to define what constitutes a crime is in the hands of the dominant caste and is another mechanism of racial subordination. How crime is defined reflects the relationship of the colonized to the colonizers. The ruling caste defines those acts as crimes which fit its needs and purposes and characterizes as criminals individuals who commit certain kinds of illegal acts, while other such acts are exempted from prosecution and escape public disapprobation because they are not perceived as criminal or a threat to society.

As a result of the colonial administration's power to define the nature of criminality, the white-collar crimes[6] which involve millions of dollars go unpunished or lightly punished, while the crimes of the colonized involving nickels and dimes result in long jail sentences. The main executor of the colonial regime can wage a war that takes thousands of lives in direct violation of the Constitution, while the colonized are sent to the gas chambers for non-fatal crimes such as rape. It is no coincidence that the two criminal acts for which politicians wanted to preserve the death penalty were kidnapping and airline hijacking, the former a crime committed mainly against the wealthy while the latter is a political act against the state.

Internal Military Agents

In any colonial situation, there must be agents to enforce the status quo. A classical colonial world is dichotomized into two parts of society, and the policeman acts as the go-between. Fanon describes it in Colonial Africa:

> In the colonies it is the policeman and the soldier who are the official instituted go-betweens, the spokesman of the settler and his rule of oppression. . . . By their immediate presence and their frequent and direct action, they maintain contact with the native and advise him by means of rifle-butts and napalm not to budge. It is obvious here that the agents of government speak the language of pure force. The intermediary does not lighten the oppression, nor seek to hide the domination; he shows them up and puts them into practice with the clear conscience of an upholder of the peace, yet he is the bringer of violence into the home and into the mind of the native.[7]

One could hardly find a more perfect analogy on the role of the policeman than in the findings of the United States Commission on Civil Rights in the 1960s. Police brutality was discovered to be a fact of daily existence for Afro-Americans and a primary source of abuse by whites against any challenge by blacks to the status quo. In essence:

> Police misconduct often serves as the ultimate weapon for keeping the Negro in his place, for it is quite clear that when all else fails, policemen in some communities can be trusted to prevent the Negro from entering a "desegregated" school or housing project, a voting booth, or even a court of law. They may do it merely by turning their backs on private lawlessness, or by more direct involvement. Trumped up charges, dragnet roundups, illegal arrests, the "third degree" and brutal beatings are all part of the pattern of "white supremacy."[8]

In order to enforce this type of colonial rule, policemen must have certain traits. First and foremost, they must be members of the dominant racial group. Almost every major urban area has a police force that is predominantly white, although the cities themselves may contain mostly blacks. The highest ratio of black policemen to the black population is found in Philadelphia, where 29 percent of the city's population is black and 20 percent of the police force is black. The lowest is probably New Orleans, with the black population composing 41 percent of the total population and 4 percent of the police force.[9]

It is not only that the police force is composed mostly of members of the colonizers' group, but they also represent the more authoritarian and racist members of that sector. One survey disclosed that the majority of white police officers hold antiblack attitudes. In predominantly black precincts, over 75 percent of the white police expressed highly prejudiced feelings towards blacks, and only 1 percent showed sympathy toward the plight of blacks.[10] A series of public hearings on police brutality in Chicago revealed that candidates for the police department who do poorly on the psychological tests or who demonstrate personality problems while undergoing training in the police academy are assigned to "stress areas" in Chicago's black and brown ghettos.[11] The predominantly black city of Oakland, California, was recruiting its police officers among men recently returned from military service in Vietnam.

Considering the characteristics of policemen assigned to the black colony, it is no surprise to find that for the years 1920-1932, of 479 blacks killed by white persons in the South, 54 percent were slain by white police officers.[12] In more recent periods cities outside the South provide interesting statistics. Seventy-five percent of the civilians killed by Chicago police in 1971 were black.[13] The state of California reports that blacks, who make up 7 percent of its population, were 48 percent of the persons killed by policemen in 1971.[14]

Even less surprising are the studies which show blacks believe that policemen are disrespectful, that police brutality exists in their areas, and that blacks are treated worse than whites by the police.[15] Besides the abuse suffered at the hands of white police officers, two basic types of complaint are the basis for these beliefs. One is that the police in black communities are more tolerant of illegal activities such as drug addiction, prostitution, and street violence than they would be in white communities. The other is that the police see as much less urgent the calls for help and complaints from black areas than from white areas.[16]

Such complaints about the police force are due to ignorance of their functional role in colonial society. The police are not placed in black communities to protect the indigenous inhabitants, but to protect the property of the colonizers who live outside those communities and to restrain any black person from breaking out of the colonial wards in the event of violence. No amount of "proper" behavior on the part of the police, therefore, nullifies the fundamental colonial machinery which imposes law and order according to the definitions of the colonizers. The law itself constitutes the basis for colonial rule; and the ideology of white supremacy shapes the police force, the courts, and the prisons as instruments of continued colonial subjugation.

Crime by Blacks

The colonial character of American society tends to structure the racial pattern of crime. In the urban areas, where most blacks live, the majority of serious property crimes such as burglary, larceny (over $50), and auto thefts are committed by whites. More blacks than whites are arrested for serious crimes of violence such as murder, rape, and aggravated assaults. These crimes of violence by blacks are most often committed against other blacks.[17] The homicide rate for blacks is about ten times the rate for whites. Indeed, homicide is the second leading cause of death among black males aged 15-25, the third leading cause between 25-44.[18] In interracial crimes of violence, whites attack and assault blacks more often than blacks attack and assault whites.[19]

The above statistics follow the typical pattern in the colonial world. The violence with which the supremacy of the values of whites is affirmed and the aggressiveness which has infused the victory of these values into the ways of life and thought of the colonized mean that their challenge to the colonial world will be to claim that same violence as a means of breaking into the colonizers' forbidden quarters. According to Fanon, colonized men will initially express against their own people this aggressiveness which they have internalized. This is the period when the colonized terrorize and beat each other, while the colonizers or policemen have the right to assault the natives with impunity. This is a pattern of avoidance that allows the colonized to negate their powerlessness, to pretend that colonialism does not exist. Ultimately, this behavior leads to armed resistance against colonialism.[20]

The cultural values of white supremacy place little premium on the lives of blacks in the United States. A native's death is of little importance to the continuation of colonial rule, except that it may deprive a particular colonizer of the labor of a skilled worker. Hence, while blacks are generally given longer prison terms than whites for the same crime, they get shorter sentences for murder.[21] According to Bullock,

> These judicial responses possibly represent indulgent and non-indulgent patterns that characterize local attitudes concerning property and intra-racial morals. Since the victims of most of the Negroes committed for . . . [murder] were also Negroes, local norms tolerate a less rigorous enforcement of the law; the disorder is mainly located within the Negro society. Local norms are less tolerant (in Black crimes against white property), for the motivation to protect white property and to protect "white" society against disorder is stronger than the motivation to protect "Negro" society.[22]

The Colonial Machinery

Colonial practices are not confined to the police. Rather, the political state, which is also dominated by whites, controls the dispensation of justice from police apprehension to prison; and these all serve the interests of the colonizers. In the courts, most judges in the state, federal, circuit, superior and supreme courts are appointed by the political state, and not elected. No black person in the United States has the power to appoint a judge to the bench. Consequently, there are almost no black judges in the South, and few in the North and West.[23] Moreover, any blacks appointed to the bench are likely to possess the values of the colonizers.

A trial by jury guarantees no more equal justice to the accused black offenders. Blacks are still systematically excluded from juries in some parts of the South, and are often underrepresented on juries in which they are allowed to serve. Sometimes they are excluded by more subtle and indirect means such as preemptory challenges by the prosecution, requirements of voter registration, property ownership, or literacy tests.[24] Despite the American creed of equal justice before the law, few black offenders before the courts will receive a neutral hearing before a jury of normal white Americans. As Fanon states, in a racist society the normal person is racist.[25]

Blacks are further victimized by the lack of adequate legal representation. Since colonial administrations allow few natives to attain professional skills and become members of the native bourgeoisie, there is a scarcity of black lawyers to represent black alleged offenders before the courts. Another feature of colonialism is the creation of dependency in the natives upon the members of the ruling group to achieve ordinary rights of citizenship. Thus, black defendants often choose white lawyers over black ones because they feel they can neutralize the impact of racism in decisions rendered by a white judge and jury. Many black defendants, of course, cannot afford an attorney and must accept a court-appointed lawyer. In federal larceny cases, 52 percent of the blacks did not have their own lawyers, as compared to 25 percent of the whites.[26]

Another disadvantage faced by black defendants is the illegitimacy of their cultural values. There are several examples of words and phrases used by blacks which have a totally different meaning in the white community. These cultural differences are particularly crucial in certain types of crimes such as assault and battery and public obscenity. But the colonial order insists that the natives' society is lacking in values, and that differences in cultural symbols, *i.e.,* language, are not recognized in a court of law. There are other linguistic barriers in the courtroom that affect black defendants. Often, they may not comprehend the legal jargon of the attorneys and give answers based on their mistaken interpretation of the language used in the courtroom.[27]

Given all these factors, black defendants are often shortchanged in the decisions of the courts and the length of their prison sentences. Most of the available data reveal that blacks usually receive longer prison terms than whites for the same criminal offenses. They are particularly discriminated against when one considers their chances of receiving probation or a suspended sentence. In larceny cases, for example, 74 percent of guilty blacks were imprisoned in state larceny cases compared to only 49 percent of guilty whites. The racial gap in larceny cases is greater than in assault convictions because larcenies by blacks are more often committed against whites, while assaults occur more frequently against other blacks. Hence, racial disparities in prison sentencing are not only related to the skin color of the alleged offender, but to that of his victim, too.[28]

It is in the area of capital punishment that the racial, and thus colonial, factors stand out. The statistics on capital punishment in the United States reveal most glaringly the double standard of justice that exists there: One for the wealthy and another for blacks and poor people. Even the former Warden of Sing Sing prison once remarked, "Only the poor, the friendless, and the foreign born are sentenced to death and executed."[29] But it is particularly the colonial wards of America, *i.e.,* blacks, who have received the heaviest brunt of this dual standard of American justice.

For blacks in America, capital punishment is only a transfer of the functions of lynch mobs to the state authority. Under the auspices of the political state, blacks have been executed for less serious crimes and crimes less often receiving the death penalty, particularly rape, than whites. They were of a younger age than whites at the time of execution and were more often executed without appeals, regardless of their offense or age at execution. Of the 3,827 men and 32 women executed since 1930, 53 percent were black. The proportion of blacks on death row in 1972 was 52 percent. It is in the South that discrimination in capital punishment is most evident. Practically all executions for rape took place in the South. In that region, 90 percent of those executed for rape were black.[30]

Again, the colonial pattern emerges. The two things the colonizers fear most are the stealing of their possessions and the rape of their women, and they punish with special fury the crime of sexual violation of upper-caste women. About 85 percent of the black rape offenders executed had white victims,[31] although the overwhelming majority of the black males' rape victims are black women.

Political Prisoners

The combination of the colonial administration of justice and the oppression of blacks has resulted in the internment of a disproportionate number of blacks in the nation's prisons. The number of blacks in prison is three times their representation in the society at large.[32] There are actually more blacks in prison than in college. Yet, as Angela Davis has observed:

> Along with the army and the police, prisons are the most essential instruments of state power. The prospect of long prison terms is meant to preserve order; it is supposed to serve as a threat to anyone who dares disturb existing social relations, whether by failing to observe the sacred rules of property, or by consciously challenging the right of an unjust system of racism and domination to function smoothly.[33]

In recent years the number of prison protests by black prisoners have risen. Part of the reason is the prisoners' self-definition as political prisoners. Two basic types of political prisoners may be defined. One kind is the person arrested under the guise of criminal charges, but only because of the state's wish to remove the political activist as a threat to the prevailing racial conditions. Examples of this type are Angela Davis, Bobby Seale, and H. Rap Brown. The second type is more numerous and consists of those blacks who are arbitrarily arrested and then "railroaded" through the courts, where they face white politically appointed judges, all-white juries, without a lawyer, or with an appointed lawyer who suggests a guilty plea in exchange for a reduced sentence.

Since most crimes by blacks have black victims, not all black prisoners are *ipso facto* political prisoners. The incarceration of these blacks stems from the subjugated condition of black people in the United States. As Chrisman asserts, "a Black prisoner's crime may or may not have been a political action against the state, but the state's action against him is always political."[34] The basis for this judgment is that black criminals are not tried and judged by the black community itself, but that their crimes are defined and they are convicted and sentenced by the machinery of the ruling colonial order, whose interests are served by the systematic subjugation of all black people. As long as crime by blacks occurs within the context of racial subjugation and exploitation, blacks will continue to believe that their criminal acts will not be objectively and fairly treated, but rather that the treatment will be affected by the racial inequality which constitutes the essence of American colonialism. In this paper the colonial model has been applied to explain the relationship between crime and race. While the fit between theory and empirical data is not perfect, it does point the way to reducing some of the racial inequities in American criminal justice. Among the remedies suggested by this model is community control of the police. Community control would respond to the charge that the police in black neighborhoods constitute an occupation army in their midst. Policemen would be chosen by the people in the community and required to live in their precinct. In this way, blacks would have greater assurance that the police are there to protect their interests rather than the property of whites who live outside the community.[35]

Another remedy to be considered is a trial by jury of one's peers. This means a jury whose experiences, needs, and interests are similar to those of the defendant. When this is not feasible, proportional representation of blacks on juries, in the legal staff, and on the bench might be considered. While these suggestions will not radically affect the socioeconomic conditions that generate crime, they will at least reduce the impact of domestic racism on the administration of justice to the black population.

NOTES

1. Gina Lombroso, "Ferrero," in *Criminal Man According to the Classifications of Cesare Lombroso* (New York, 1911).

2. C. F. Marvin Wolfgang and Bernard Cohen, *Crime and Race: Conceptions and Misconceptions* (New York, 1970).

3. Frantz Fanon, *The Wretched of the Earth* (New York, 1966); Robert Blauner, "Internal Colonialism and Ghetto Revolt," *Social Problems* XVI (Spring, 1969), 393-408; Stokely Carmichael and Charles Hamilton, *Black Power* (New York, 1967); Albert Memmi, *The Colonizer and the Colonized* (Boston, 1967).

4. Julius Lester, *Look Out, Whitey: Black Power's Gon' Get Your Mama* (New York, 1968), p. 23.

5. Cf. Mary Berry, *Black Resistance—White Law: A History of Constitutional Racism in America* (New York, 1971).

6. Edwin H. Sutherland, *White Collar Crime* (New York, 1949).

7. Fanon, *op. cit.*, p. 31.

8. Wallace Mendelson, *Discrimination* (Englewood Cliffs, New Jersey, 1968), pp. 143-44.

9. *Report of the National Advisory Commission on Civil Disorders* (New York, 1968), p. 321.

10. Albert J. Reiss, Jr., "Police Brutality—Answers to Key Questions," *Transaction*, V (July-August, 1968), 10-19.

11. Testimony of Dr. Evrum Mendelsohn of the Elmhurst Psychological Center before Congressman Ralph Metcalfe's Public Hearing on Police Brutality in Chicago, September 1, 1972.

12. Gunnar Myrdal, *An American Dilemma* (New York, 1944).

13. Testimony of a team of law students from Northwestern University at the Metcalfe hearing, August 30, 1972.

14. Report by Evelle Younger, Attorney General of the State of California, cited in *The Los Angeles Sentinel,* August 10, 1972, p. A2.

15. Report of the National Advisory Commission on Civil Disorders, *op. cit.,* p. 302.

16. *Ibid.,* p. 268.

17. United States Department of Justice, Federal Bureau of Investigation, "Crime in the United States," *Uniform Crime Reports,* 1969.

18. Lee N. Robins, "Negro Homicide Victims—Who Will They Be?" *Transaction,* V (June, 1968), p. 16.

19. Marvin Wolfgang, *Patterns in Criminal Homicide* (Philadelphia, 1958).

20. Fanon, *op. cit.,* p. 43.

21. Wolfgang, *Crime and Race, op. cit.,* p. 82.

22. Henry A. Bullock, "Significance of the Racial Factor in the Length of Prison Sentences," *The Journal of Criminal Law, Criminology and Police Science,* VII (November, 1961), 411-17.

23. United States Commission on Civil Rights Report, 1963, p. 124.

24. United States Commission on Civil Rights Report, *Justice* (Washington, D.C., 1961), p. 92.

25. Frantz Fanon, "Racism and Culture," in *Toward the African Revolution* (New York, 1967).

26. Stuart Nagel, *The Legal Process From a Behavioral Perspective* (Homewood, Illinois, 1969).

27. Daniel H. Swett, *Cross Cultural Communications in the Courtroom: Applied Linguistics in a Murder Trial,* a paper presented at the Conference of Racism and the Law (San Francisco, December 1967), pp. 2-5.

28. Nagel, *op. cit.*

29. Cited in Hugo Bedau, *The Death Penalty in America* (New York, 1967), p. 411.

30. William Bowers, *Racial Discrimination in Capital Punishment: Characteristics of the Condemned* (Lexington, Massachusetts, 1972).

31. *Ibid.*

32. National Prisoner Statistics, 1971.

33. Angela Davis, "The Soledad Brothers," *The Black Scholar,* II (April-May 1971), 2-3.

34. Robert Chrisman, "Black Prisoners, White Law," *The Black Scholar,* II (April-May 1971), 45-46.

35. Cf. Arthur Waskow, "Community Control of the Police," *Transaction,* VI (December 1969), 4-5.

12

INTRODUCTION

Vernetta D. Young's work has focused on race, gender, and crime. She has examined the role of race in the patterns of criminal behavior (including drug use), incarceration, and victimization of women. Young uses the social constructionist tradition to examine the influence of race and gender on the history of juvenile institutions and on the patterns of incarceration of women in the state of Maryland. Her research interests also extend to the inclusion of works by African Americans in the field of criminology/criminal justice.

In this article, Young challenges the liberation hypothesis, an explanation of criminal behavior that was based on stereotypical presentations of Black females, Black males, and Black families. She concludes that the explanations for racial differences advanced by Adler have little value since the empirical differences they purport to explain are not supported by the data. Young suggests that we need to develop explanations of behavior that are grounded in fact as opposed to suppositions and racial stereotypes to explain the interrelationships between women, race, and crime.

WOMEN, RACE, AND CRIME

VERNETTA D. YOUNG

This article examines the interrelationships among women, race, and crime as they are purported to occur in the comprehensive discussion of female crime provided by Freda Adler in 1975. Adler's thesis was that patterns of female criminality differ because of differential opportunities historically available to offenders. The empirical assertions concerning the pattern of crime for black and white males and females are examined using victim survey data. It was concluded that the explanations for racial differences in female crime and delinquency advanced by Adler have little value since the empirical differences they purport to explain are not supported by the data.

The purpose of this chapter is to examine the interrelationships among women, race, and crime as they are purported to occur in the comprehensive discussion of female crime provided by Adler (1975). A central hypothesis advanced by Adler is that patterns of female criminality differ by race because of differential opportunities historically available to offenders.

Adler (1975) speculates that the current pattern of black female crime is indicative of the future pattern for white female criminals. She proposes that, since slavery, "sex-role convergence" has occurred among black males and black females to a far greater degree than among white males and white females. This has led, according to Adler, to a similarity, not only in the criminal behavior patterns of black males and black females but also in the patterns for black females and white males. Furthermore, with the emergence of the women's liberation movement, Adler suggests that there will be the same sex-role convergence among white males and white females resulting in similar patterns of criminal behavior.

In addition to Adler's general thesis, a number of more specific propositions relevant to the relations among sex, race, and crime were also advanced and merit empirical scrutiny:

(1) The pattern of criminal involvement for females differs by race with black female

offenders concentrated in crimes against persons and property and white female offenders involved in both "blue-collar" crimes (vice, assault, robbery, and so on) and white-collar crime.

(2) The pattern of criminal behavior of black females is closer to the pattern of white males than it is to that of white females.

(3) Black female criminality parallels the criminality of black males more closely than the criminality of white females does that of white males.

(4) The ratio of black to white female criminal involvement is much larger than the black to white male ratio.

This chapter will address the tenability of Adler's predicted relationships. Victim survey data will be used to address Adler's assertions concerning the pattern of crime for blacks and whites with a central focus on female criminality. Ideally, a test of Adler's theory would rely on longitudinal data, relating changes in patterns of female criminality to changes in sex-role convergence. However, at a minimum, the theory also demands that the postulated relationships among sex, race, and crime are empirically tested. The victim surveys, based on representative samples of households and commercial establishments, provide new data that permit an examination of characteristics of offenders and incidents that are independent of official statistics. Thus, for example, they provide information about the offenders in victimizations regardless of whether the event was reported to the police.

The Data

Under the auspices of the Law Enforcement Assistance Administration, the Bureau of the Census conducts the National Crime Survey. This series of victimization surveys, initiated in 1972, is composed of both a national panel survey and a number of city surveys. The data to be used in this article are derived from the city surveys. Between 1972 and 1975, 26 of the nation's largest cities were surveyed.[1] In each of the cities surveyed, a stratified probability sample of households was drawn and residents were asked to report personal and household victimizations suffered by household members age 12 or older during the 12 months preceding the interview. Only personal victimizations (i.e., rape, robbery, assault, and larceny from the person) will be studied here, as it is only in these face-to-face confrontations that the victim can report on the characteristics of the offender. Demographic information about the household and the respondent (age, race, sex, education, family income), a series of individual screen questions designed to discover whether any of the survey crimes had occurred during the preceding 12 months, and (when the preceding was answered affirmatively) a detailed incident report were the three major portions of the survey instrument for personal and household respondents.[2]

Offender Characteristics and Crime Patterns

Studies in the area of female crime and delinquency generally report consistent findings with respect to race and age. Black and other minority women and young women have been found to be disproportionately involved in crime and delinquency (Hendrix, 1972; Katzenelson, 1975). Similarly, the victim survey data indicate that female offenders were perceived to be black in 64% of the victimizations, white in 29%, other racial groups in 5%, and from more than one racial group in 2%.[3]

With regard to the age of the offender(s), however, in victimizations committed by only one offender (lone offender), persons 21 and over account for 67% of white female crime and 56% of black female crime. By contrast, for multiple female offenders[4] the 12-14- and the 15-17-year-old groups account for 69%

(33% and 36%, respectively) of black female crime.

Finally, lone criminal offenders made up a larger proportion of white female criminality (79%) than they did of either black (61%) or other racial groups (64%). Conversely, black females (39%) and females from other racial groups (36%) were more likely to be involved in group offenses than were white females (21%).

Pattern of Crime by Race of Offender(s)

One empirical finding Adler relied upon heavily in support of her etiological statements was:

> The figures nation-wide illustrate unequivocally that the black female's criminality exceeds that of the white female *by a much greater margin* than black males over white males [Adler, 1975: 139; italics added].

In the victim survey data, however, the ratio between the volume of crime for black males and white males was about 2 to 1 and this ratio held for black females and white females (69% to 31%).[5]

With respect to the pattern[6] of female crime by race, a number of studies indicate that the pattern differs for black and white females (Van Der Hyde, 1970; Katzenelson, 1975). Furthermore, it has been reported that the pattern of crime for black females and black males is more alike than the pattern for white females and white males (Wolfgang, 1958; Adler, 1975). These hypotheses are testable with the victimization data. The data indicate that, contrary to the Adler's hypothesis, overall the patterns of criminal involvement in personal victimizations reported for lone female offenders by race were very similar across offense categories. Assault, simple and aggravated, comprised the bulk of offenses reported for both white and black female offenders.

The pattern for multiple female offenders is somewhat different. Black female offender groups differed substantially from white female offender groups in some specific offense categories. Assault (simple and aggravated) made up 72% of total victimizations by white offenders but only 44% of the total by black offenders. Theft (robbery and larceny with contact) accounted for 56% of the victimizations by black female offender groups but only about 28% of those by white female offender groups.

Briefly, these data indicate that the patterns of crime for lone black and white female offenders are very similar whereas those for multiple female offenders differ considerably by race. White female offender groups were more than two and one-half times more likely to be involved in assaultive offenses than in theft offenses, whereas black female offender groups were about as likely to be involved in assaultive as in theft offenses.

Adler's second hypothesis, that the pattern for black males and females is more alike than that for white males and females, is also testable. Simple and aggravated assault account for 75% of victimizations by lone white females and 71% of those by lone white males but 66% of victimizations by lone black females and only 40% of those by lone black males. Theft offenses (robbery and larceny with contact) accounted for 25% of all victimizations committed by lone white females, 24% of those by lone white males, 34% of those by lone black females, and 55% of those by lone black males. In multiple-offender victimizations, there is a difference of 21 percentage points in the contributions of assaultive offenses to total victimizations by black females (44%) and the contribution to total victimization by black males (23%). For white offenders, there is only a 13 percentage point difference by sex of the offender group. This same level of difference is apparent when looking at theft offenses. Thus, the pattern of crime is more similar for white males and females than for black males and females, thereby questioning (or failing to support) Adler's hypothesis.

Adler's final hypothesis is that the pattern of crime for black females is closer to the pattern of white males than it is to that of white females. The data indicate that the pattern for lone black females is very similar to that of both lone white female and lone white male offenders. In the case of multiple offenders, the pattern for multiple black female offenders is more similar to that of multiple white male offenders than it is to that of multiple white female offenders. Although the difference is very small, the pattern for multiple black female offenders is more similar to that of multiple black males than it is to multiple white males. Therefore, it seems more reasonable to conclude that the pattern of crime for black females is close to the pattern of crime for white male offenders in both lone and multiple victimizations and close to that of white female offenders in lone but not in multiple victimizations.

Summary and Implications

These data indicate that there is no simplistic answer to the question of whether female offenders differ by race. Adler (1975), in examining the relationship between race, sex, and involvement in crime, based her explanations of assumed differences in female criminality by race on assumptions about the historical impact of slavery on black women, on black men, and, generally, on the black family.

In this article, offender characteristics and crime patterns were examined using a previously unexplored data source—victimization surveys. Because these surveys are not dependent on official sources and include crimes not reported to the police, they are useful in assessing the empirical validity of some of Adler's hypotheses. First, Adler hypothesized that the ratio between the volume of crime for black females and white females would be greater than that for black males and white males. This hypothesis was not supported by the victim survey data. Second, Adler hypothesized that the patterns of criminal behavior for black males and black females were more alike than the patterns for white males and white females. The victim survey data indicated that the patterns of crime for black males and black females were less similar than those for white males and white females.

Finally, Adler hypothesized that the pattern of crime for black females was closer to the pattern of white males than it was to that of white females. This hypothesis was partially supported by the victim survey data. In multiple-offender victimizations, the pattern for crime for black females was closer to that of white males than to that of white females; however, in lone-offender victimizations, there was very little difference in the patterns of crime for the three groups.

Briefly, black and white female offenders were found to be similar in their pattern of involvement in personal victimizations. They differed mostly, however, in the group context of their victimizations which in turn accounted for differences in the age of the offender. Differences by race of the offender were apparently related to the type of offense and other offender characteristics.

There are two limitations of this study that should be noted. First, the offender characteristics reported here are based on victims' reports of perceived characteristics. The validity of these perceptions has not been carefully studied to date. Second, the range of offense behavior studied here is limited to interpersonal crimes of theft and violence. Excluded are organizational and white-collar crimes and crimes against commercial establishments. Thus, these results cannot be seen as indicative of the validity of Adler's hypothesis with respect to these offenses. With these limitations in mind, overall Adler's hypothesis concerning the relationship between race, sex, and crime was not supported. Briefly, Adler's explanation of black female criminality rests heavily on her assumptions about the historical impact of slavery on the black family. According to Adler, as a consequence of the slave era there exists sex-role reversal among black males and black females. These circumstances are meant to explain why the pattern of black female criminality differs from that of the white female and why the pattern for black females is closer to the pattern of white males than it is to the pattern for white females. In addition, they are meant to explain why the pattern of criminal behavior for blacks by sex is more parallel than is the pattern for whites by sex. The implication from this study is that the explanations for racial differences in female crime and delinquency advanced by Adler (1975) have little value since the differences they purport to explain are not supported by the data.

This study indicates that the phenomenon of female crime and race is one of considerable complexity. Although a general description of the female offender and her victimization is relatively easy to deduce, there are, as this report has demonstrated, important relationships by race between offender characteristics that affect differences in the victimization interaction involving black and white female offenders.

Notes

1. The following cities were surveyed: Atlanta, Baltimore, Cleveland, Dallas, Denver, Newark, Portland, St. Louis, Chicago, Detroit, Los Angeles, New York, Philadelphia, Boston, Buffalo, Cincinnati, Houston, Miami, Milwaukee, Minneapolis, New Orleans, Oakland, Pittsburgh, San Diego, San Francisco, and Washington, D.C.

2. For a more comprehensive discussion of the data source, see Garofalo and Hindelang (1978).

3. The 26 cities had a total female population of 9 million persons: 68% white, 29% black, and 2% other (figures do not equal 100% due to rounding).

4. Multiple-offender victimizations included only those same-sex and same-race offender groups.

5. Lone- and multiple-offender victimizations were combined to determine the ratios.

6. Pattern of crime in this context refers to the type of crime.

References

Adler, F. Sisters in Crime: The Rise of the New Female Criminal. New York: McGraw-Hill, 1975.

Garofalo, J. and M. J. Hindelang. An Introduction to the National Crime Survey. Analytic Report SD-VAD-4. Law Enforcement Assistance Administration, National Criminal Justice Information and Statistics Service. Washington, DC: Government Printing Office, 1978.

Hendrix, O. A Study in Neglect: A Report on Women Prisoners. Report submitted by Omar Hendrix, Ford Foundation Travel-Study Grants, 1972.

Katzenelson, S. "The female offender in Washington, D.C." Washington, DC: Institute of Law and Social Research, 1975.

Van Der Hyde, V. Study of Female Offenders. Olympia, WA. Office of Research, Division of Institutions, Department of Social and Health Services, 1970.

Wolfgang, M. E. Patterns in Criminal Homicide. Philadelphia: University of Pennsylvania Press, 1958.

13

INTRODUCTION

Darnell F. Hawkins has written numerous books and articles on African Americans and the criminal justice system. In his works, he has challenged both theoretical and methodological approaches to examining the relationship between race and crime. Hawkins argues that a number of the theoretical explanations purporting to explain race and crime have assumed a "one-size-fits-all" perspective that in effect ignores key structural, situational, and institutional factors relevant to the lives of Blacks in America. For example, in his critique of the subculture of violence theory as an explanation for why Blacks commit a disproportionate share of homicides, Hawkins argues for the inclusion of factors related to the historical behavior of law, the presence of racial discrimination and bias in the operation of the criminal justice system, and the cultural values of Blacks.

In the following article, first published in *Social Forces* in 1987, Hawkins argues that the inconsistent findings in the literature on race and punishment are attributable to a lack of theoretical clarity and methodological problems. He indicates that most of the work in this area was grounded in the original formulation of conflict theory. He contends that because that model focuses on class with a very limited discussion of race, it fails to adequately explain racial differentials in criminal punishment. Hawkins proposes to revise the conflict model by incorporating race and regional differences, as well as group threat concerns.

BEYOND ANOMALIES

Rethinking the Conflict Perspective on Race and Criminal Punishment

 DARNELL F. HAWKINS
University of Illinois at Chicago

Research on race and punishment for crime has produced inconsistent findings. Most previous reviews of the literature have been focused primarily on the numerous methodological flaws that may give rise to such inconsistencies. In this paper I suggest that inconsistent or anomalous findings in this area of research may also result from problems of conceptualization and theory. More specifically, it is argued that the conflict perspective must be substantially revised to begin to account for various anomalies observed by empirical researchers. Such a need for revision is the consequence of both problems in the original formulation of the perspective and its oversimplification within the empirical literature.

One of the most widely debated issues in the criminological literature is whether there is racial bias in the administration of justice. In addition to numerous empirical investigations, there have been efforts in recent years to review previous studies and to determine where the weight of the evidence lies (Green 1971; Hagan 1974; Hagan and Bumiller 1983; Hardy 1983; Kleck 1981; Spohn et al. 1981-82). As in other areas of social research, most studies of racial bias in the administration of justice involve black-white comparisons. Reviews of empirical investigations have shown a large number of these studies to report significantly greater rates and levels of punishment for blacks than for whites.[1] Others report no significant differences between the races. Still others find that

Reprinted from *Social Forces, 65*(3), 719-745. Hawkins, D. (1987). Beyond anomalies: Rethinking the conflict perspective on race and criminal punishment. Released time to prepare this paper was provided by the R. J. Reynolds Foundation and by the National Science Foundation, Grant No. RII-8421196. I thank John Hagan, Michael Radelet, and anonymous referees for their helpful comments on earlier drafts. Address correspondence to the author, Black Studies Program and Department of Sociology, University of Illinois, Chicago, IL 60680.

in certain instances, whites receive significantly more punishment for crime than do blacks (e.g., Bernstein et al. 1977; Bullock 1961; Gibson 1978; Levin 1972). This latter finding is often described as an anomaly or inconsistency given the theoretical model that has guided research on this topic.

Another anomalous finding that has become a part of the literature on race and criminal punishment derives from post hoc regional comparisons. Beginning with researchers such as Sellin (1928), the finding of less punishment for blacks than whites in the South in some instances has been said to be the product of leniency toward black offenders. Other studies have reported substantial punitiveness toward blacks as compared to whites in areas outside the South. Thus, the notion of anomalies has also been linked to unexpected regional differences in criminal punishment, that is, leniency in the South (at least during the 1920-40s) and harshness in the non-South (Kleck 1981).

Although the recent state-of-the-art reviews cited above often treat both theoretical and empirical studies, there has been little effort to probe fully the theoretical and conceptual limitations of previous research. Rather, most have been purely methodological critiques (e.g., Gibson 1978). In this paper I examine the theoretical underpinnings of previous research on race and punishment for crime and suggest direction for future investigation. I propose that the lack of consensus regarding the impact of race on criminal justice outcomes stems as much from a lack of theoretical clarity as it does from the methodological problems noted in earlier reviews of the literature. The need for an examination of theoretical issues is evident when one considers the conclusions reached in recent reviews.

A major source of criticism of the research on racial bias and a reason cited for the inconsistencies across studies has been the failure of researchers to control for relevant legal variables. This criticism has been targeted particularly at studies done during the 1940s and 1950s (Hagan 1974). Yet Hagan and Bumiller (1983) report that of the pre-1968 studies that controlled for offense and record, two of the most relevant legal variables, 3 studies found discrimination while 8 found no discrimination. On the other hand, of the 20 post-1968 studies that controlled for these variables one-half found discrimination while the other half reported none. These and other reviews suggest that apart from methodological flaws there are major problems of conceptualization and theory that underlie the inconsistencies observed across studies of racial discrimination in the administration of justice.

A number of investigators (Kleck 1981; Liska et al. 1985; Peterson and Hagan 1984) have recently raised significant questions regarding the adequacy of existing theory for explaining black-white punishment differentials. But most of these critiques have been done within the context of primarily empirical analyses and there has been little effort devoted to a systematic rethinking of the theoretical frameworks that have guided research on race and criminal punishment. I attempt such a systematic rethinking through an examination of anomalous findings reported in previous research. The major arguments advanced in this discussion are:

1. Researchers have perhaps used the term "anomalies" too hastily to describe findings which, examined in more detail, are not deserving of the label. Some of these seeming anomalies stem from methodological flaws in the empirical investigations; others result from inappropriate conceptualization and theory.
2. Many of what are perceived to be anomalies or inconsistencies in research on racial bias in the criminal justice system result from oversimplification of the conflict perspective, the principal investigatory model used in past studies.
3. This oversimplification stems from two sources. First, there is a lack of specificity within the conflict perspective itself regarding the relationship between race and criminal punishment. Second, researchers have

failed to fully acknowledge the existence of what are now termed anomalies or inconsistencies in the body of research that was relied on to devise the conflict perspective. The work of the major conflict theorists and the studies they rely on report rather systematic departures from those patterns predicted by the oversimplified model. Hence various anomalies and inconsistencies could be said to be an integral part of a fully elaborated conflict perspective.

4. Apart from oversimplification, the reported anomalous findings may point to more substantial flaws in the conflict perspective as it has been used in research on social control. Even in its fully elaborated form the conflict perspective fails to account for a wide range of factors that may be relevant for understanding racial differentials in criminal punishment. Thus, despite the complexity of the theoretical and empirical base from which the conflict perspective was derived, it requires substantial rethinking and revision. Among other things, a revised model must begin to explain and predict those findings now considered to be anomalous.

I propose that the conflict perspective must be revised to address more specifically the question of the role played by various contingencies or mediating factors identified in past studies. Such factors as victim characteristics and region have been linked to various anomalous findings. Recent research has also identified other contingencies. The perspective must also be reduced to readily testable hypotheses that will help researchers avoid the errors of interpretation seen in previous empirical work. Below, I discuss several sets of concerns that must be incorporated into a more comprehensive conflict theory. Although I make an effort to reduce these concerns to testable hypotheses, such efforts are more successful in some instances than in others. I do propose that future researchers must proceed to revise more fully the conflict perspective in light of the findings and issues discussed below.

Race and the Conflict Perspective: An Oversimplification

Most of the empirical investigations and reviews of the literature noted above trace the topic of racial discrimination in the criminal justice system to the work of Chambliss and Seidman (1971), Quinney (1970), Sellin (1928), Turk (1969), and a few other researchers described as conflict theorists.[2] As noted above, the conflict perspective in its original formulation was much more complex than those restatements of it found in most empirical studies and recent reviews. Even more complex were the empirical and theoretical bases from which the conflict perspective was derived. What are the forms this oversimplification has taken and how do we explain its persistence in the literature? There are several potential explanations.

As in other areas of social research, the oversimplification of the conflict model is due partly to the fact that it is a perspective rather than a well-formulated theory with testable hypotheses. Neither the work of Quinney nor that of Chambliss and Seidman, the principal architects of the perspective, represents a theory per se. Their propositions (Chambliss and Seidman 1971, pp. 473-75; Quinney 1970, pp. 15-25) are stated in forms similar to testable hypotheses but they have many limitations. In addition, there are other problems with the original formulations of the perspective by these two groups of analysts that bear more directly on the issues raised in this paper. A major area of concern is their limited discussion of race. The various propositions outlined in the two studies generally refer to social class rather than racial differences in the administration of justice.

Social Class and Race

Both Quinney's (1970) and Chambliss and Seidman's (1971) theoretical discussions contain references to the treatment of blacks by the criminal justice system. Yet in both instances the attention paid to black crime and discrimination against blacks is minimal when one considers the disproportionate presence of blacks within the American system of criminal justice for more than a century.[3] This relative inattention to issues of race stems partly from the class-based theoretical framework proposed by both sets of theorists. Within this framework, predicted discrimination against blacks by agencies of criminal justice is said to result from their generally low socioeconomic status in American society. That is, race effects are said to be less important for determining rates and levels of criminal punishment than the effects of social class (Liska et al. 1985). This model predicts similar treatment for blacks, American Indians, Asian Americans, Hispanics, lower-class whites, and other low-status groups. Thus, it may be argued that the underpinnings of the conflict perspective derive from classical Marxist conceptions of the significance of social class. Although the work of most conflict theorists, including Quinney or Chambliss and Seidman, does not represent an orthodox Marxist interpretation, the ideas of Marx are evident within the perspective.[4]

Regardless of its precise origins, the result of such an orientation has been a lack of debate among advocates of the conflict perspective over one of the most widely discussed issues in American race relations, that is, to what extent is the treatment of blacks in the United States a function of their racial as opposed to their purely social class status?5 Another result is that most of the statements of Quinney and of Chambliss and Seidman that have been used as examples of the conflict perspective in tests of racial discrimination do not specifically refer to race bias at all. For example, the following propositions of Chambliss and Seidman, taken from their concluding discussion of poverty and the criminal process, are used in several empirical studies as a statement of the conflict perspective.

> Where laws are so stated that people of all classes are equally likely to violate them, the lower the societal position of an offender, the greater is the likelihood that sanctions will be imposed on him.[6]
>
> When sanctions are imposed, the most severe sanctions will be imposed on persons in the lowest social class (1971, p. 475).

Examples of racial differentials in the criminal justice system are cast within this social class analytic framework.

Although Quinney (1970) does refer to specific problems of blacks within the criminal justice system, his approach is similar to that of Chambliss and Seidman. In discussing the application of criminal definitions, Quinney says, "The probability that criminal definitions will be applied varies according to the extent to which the behaviors of the powerless conflict with the interests of the power segments" (1970, p. 18). He discusses racial differentials in the same context as other power-related differentials, for example, those based on social class or age. Neither Quinney nor Chambliss and Seidman raise the question of whether discrimination against blacks may be greater than that against powerless or subordinate segments of the population who are white. Thus, to the extent that racial differences in criminal punishment result from extra-class-based influences, the conflict model as derived from these researchers may not be adequate for explaining the racial patterns observed in many empirical investigations. For example, Liska et al. (1985) report race to be much more significant than social class for explaining rates of arrest across major American cities during recent years.

Perhaps more importantly, the failure of conflict theorists to discuss race has left subsequent researchers without theoretical referents for their empirical research designs and findings. As a result of these limitations, researchers who propose to empirically evaluate the propositions of Quinney and Chambliss and Seidman often use race as a proxy for social class status and proceed to test what is then labeled the "conflict perspective." This perspective is generally credited with proposing that *blacks or other non-whites will receive more severe punishment than whites for all crimes, under all conditions, and at similar levels of disproportion over time.* This expectation is sometimes qualified with suggestions that (1) given the legacy of racism in the South, black-white differences may be greater there; and (2) as American race relations improve over time, there may be a gradual change in the black-white punishment differential. Yet since most empirical investigations are not longitudinal or comparative, these caveats generally are not applicable. It is ironic that despite the social class orientation of the original conflict perspective, most empirical tests of the model have involved racial comparisons. This may be largely due to the unavailability of SES data for persons charged with crime.

Race and Punishment: Mediating Factors and Contingencies

How well-grounded are the expectations noted above in the work of the original conflict theorists? While it is true that Chambliss and Seidman and Quinney failed to specify possible extra-social-class effects of race on criminal punishment, their work does not support a simplistic expectation of greater punishment for blacks than whites under all circumstances. Their investigations and the various studies they cite note at least two major factors found to be associated with the racial patterning of punishment for crime: victim racial characteristics and region. In most early empirical investigations the former was not controlled for and may have been the source of some seemingly anomalous findings.

Victim Characteristics

In a brief discussion of the racial context of arrest, Quinney (1970) cites the earlier work of Johnson (1941) and Banton (1964) which reported that policemen were much less likely to arrest blacks charged with the murder of other blacks than those accused of the murder of whites.[7] In a discussion of differential sentencing by race Quinney (1970) notes similar race-of-victim effects as reported in investigations by Garfinkel (1949), Johnson (1941), and Sellin (1935). At least in regards to homicide it is accurate to say that researchers in the conflict tradition have long been aware of a hierarchy of seriousness based on the race of the victim and offender (e.g., Hawkins 1983). The existence of such a hierarchy suggests that not all black offenders will receive harsher punishment than all white offenders who are convicted of murder and that the race of the victim must be seen as a factor that mediates the level of punishment. In fact, a rapidly growing body of literature reports that the race of the victim is an important factor affecting criminal punishment for a variety of offenses. Victim effects have been reported for cases of rape (LaFree 1980) and robbery (Thomson and Zingraff 1981). Other studies that have reported the race of the victim to be an important factor include Myers (1979), Wolfgang and Riedel (1973), and Zimring et al. (1976). In considering these studies Kleck observed, "There appears to be a general pattern of less severe punishment of crimes with black victims than those with white victims, especially in connection with imposition of the death penalty. In connection with non-capital sentences, the evidence is too sparse to draw any firm conclusions" (1981, p. 799).

The conclusion regarding the imposition of the death penalty has also been supported by several more recent investigations (Baldus et al. 1983; Bowers and Pierce 1980; Gross and Mauro 1984; Paternoster 1983, 1984; Radelet 1981).[8] In fact, Radelet and Paternoster found that in the absence of consideration of the race of the victim there was not a significant difference between the punishments assigned to black and white murderers in Florida and South Carolina. Such findings suggest that earlier reports of more lenient treatment for black murderers (Bullock 1961) must be reexamined to consider the impact of victims' race on black-white punishment differences. Thomson and Zingraff (1981) argued that the failure to consider victim racial characteristics constitutes a major flaw in previous studies of sentencing disparity. Although race-of-victim effects have recently become a firmly established finding in the empirical literature, such effects have not been incorporated fully into the conflict perspective or any alternative model. That is, researchers have seldom asked why the observed patterns exist. What conditions within the larger society and/or the criminal justice system produce these victim-based punishment differentials? Do such effects suggest that conflict theorists should have targeted victim characteristics rather than offender characteristics as the major determinant of differential punishment across racial and social class groupings?

The earlier studies (Garfinkel 1949; Johnson 1941) explicitly reported that punishment varied on the basis of both victim and offender characteristics. For example, the most punishment was observed for those offenses involving black offenders and white victims. From most to least serious Johnson lists the homicide dyads as "(1) Negro versus White, (2) White versus White, (3) Negro versus Negro, and (4) White versus Negro" (1941, p. 98). Johnson specifically argued against a view that the race of the offender was the only variable of significance. He says:

> Our hypothesis is simply that differentials in the treatment of the Negro offenders in southern courts do exist but are obscured by the fact that conventional criminal statistics take into account only the race of the *offender.* If caste values and attitudes mean anything at all, they mean that offenses by or against Negroes will be defined not so much in terms of their intrinsic seriousness as in terms of their importance in the eyes of the dominant group (p. 98).

But apart from generalized conceptions of dominant and subordinate roles within a racial caste system, Johnson fails to explain fully why he expected and observed the patterns of punishment noted. For example, why are black-on-black offenses more serious than white-on-black? What societal values are reinforced by such a system of punishment? Two interrelated explanations were implicit in Johnson's analysis and have been made somewhat explicit in later research. One explanation focuses on the victim-offender dyad; the other on the victim qua victim.

The first explanation proposes that black offender/white victim crimes are the most harshly punished because such acts represent the greatest threat to the white structure of authority. A black who murders a white is said to offend against not only an individual whom the state has an obligation to represent in the criminal process, but also against the system of state authority itself. Thus, this victim-offender dyad is unique in comparison to the other three, none of which represents an attack (symbolic or otherwise) on the system of racially stratified state authority. In this respect black-on-white homicide within the racial caste system of the South is similar to the killing of a policeman or an official of the government. Only whites who kill public officials or law enforcement agents would be expected to receive levels of punishment similar to those generally given to black killers of ordinary white citizens. On the other hand, the lesser punishment for the killing of blacks by whites is in conformity with a value system which often allows whites to aggress against blacks with impunity. Like many aspects of southern life this pattern of punishment had its origin in slavery (Hindus 1980). Johnson proposes that it was still operative in the South of the 1930s. But he notes that patterns in northern states may have differed.

The second explanation was also suggested by Johnson and further developed by Garfinkel (1949). It places the greatest emphasis on the racial characteristics of the homicide victim. This explanation centers around the devalued status of the black victim and black life, in general, in the United

States. This has been a recurrent theme in studies of black crime and punishment (Hawkins 1983; Kleck 1981; LaFree 1980; Myrdal 1944; Peterson and Hagan 1984; Thomson and Zingraff 1981; Wolfgang and Riedel 1973). This view holds that the lives and persons of whites are more valued than those of blacks in American society. Offenses against whites are said to be more severely punished than those against blacks regardless of the race of the offender. Empirical support for this position has come from recent studies of indictments and sentences for murder in Florida and South Carolina (Paternoster 1983, 1984; Radelet 1981).

Up to this point there have been too few methodologically sophisticated studies of homicide sentencing that have considered the race of victims to determine whether racial punishment patterns are affected by interacting victim-offender traits or are dependent on the victim's race alone. It is likely that both effects are operative in some cases. The Johnson ranking is also not substantially different from that expected if race of the victim were the pivotal concern. The crucial question is whether there are essentially two dyads instead of four as Johnson suggested, that is, any race offender versus white victim and any race offender versus black victim. There are also too few studies that compare the South and non-South to determine whether either of these effects is observable in the processing and punishment of offenders outside the South. Most studies have been done in southern states. Further, although race-of-victim effects have been noted for a variety of nonhomicide offenses involving interpersonal violence (assault, rape, robbery), these studies are also too few to reach definitive conclusions. Johnson noted that studies of offenses less serious than murder would probably show more clear-cut extremes of leniency toward black in-group offenses. Peterson and Hagan (1984) suggested that even the sentencing of drug offenders may be affected by race-of-victim concerns.

Despite the lack of large numbers of follow-up studies, it is clear that proponents of the conflict perspective and those who attempt to test it must begin to consider race-of-victim effects. It is also clear that it represents something more than simply another extralegal variable to be added to a multivariate model. The limited body of previous research on this issue raises a number of fundamental questions regarding the conceptual and theoretical bases of the conflict perspective—questions which are considered in more detail toward the end of the paper. I propose that victims' race is a significant factor affecting punishment not only for those crimes against the person considered in previous investigations but also for a variety of property-related offenses. For example, one should expect such effects for offenses such as larceny, burglary, fraud, and various other forms of theft and conversion. Of course, many property crimes have no individual victim in some instances. Nevertheless, some of the institutions that are victims of such crimes may be more likely to be perceived as "white" than others. I am proposing that careful study of racial patterns in sentencing for these crimes will reveal harsher punishment when the victimized individual *or* institution is perceived as white than where the victimized entity is nonwhite. That differential may be the result of another factor—racially defined perceptions of appropriate and inappropriate criminal behavior that are partly derived from victim-offender considerations. This is discussed below.

Crime Type, Race, and Appropriateness

Criminologists have consistently shown the influence of crime type on the official response to criminal activity, but this knowledge has seldom been incorporated into models of racial discrimination. This lack of a substantive consideration of crime or offense type occurs despite the fact that crime type is often statistically "controlled" for in many empirical studies (e.g., Hagan 1974; Kleck 1981). Most researchers who attempt to test the conflict model appear to begin with a presumption that nonwhites will receive harsher punishment than whites regardless of the type of crime (offense category) committed. The perspective, unlike various alternative social-threat-oriented explanations (see the power-threat discussion below), does not propose that the level of social control used against blacks and against whites will differ more for some offenses than for others. On the other hand, previous research and theory suggest that the following proposition-like conclusion is warranted:

> *Certain types of crime in multiracial societies are perceived by the public at large and by agencies of social control as race-specific or race-appropriate. A member of a given racial group will receive the harshest punishment for committing those crimes perceived to be racially inappropriate.*

In order to move such a statement beyond the level of tautology we must more clearly delineate what is meant by "inappropriate" in this context. First, appropriateness or propriety is not merely a measure of the extent of a given criminal activity among one racial group as compared with another. For example, several researchers have noted that law enforcement and judicial officials may "crack down" on those offenses that are at high levels or are increasing at disproportionate rates. The level or rate of increase for a given crime may also vary by race. Blumstein (1982) argued that to some extent racial differentials in imprisonment may result from an effort by the judicial system to punish more severely those black offenders who commit the types of crimes that have the greatest racial imbalance, for example, robbery. Since blacks are more disproportionately involved in robbery than in many other types of crime, the result is an overall pattern of greater punishment for blacks than whites. In addition to this phenomenon, I propose that there are racial status-related notions of propriety and impropriety that adhere to various types of crimes. These notions may be affected by racial differentials in crime type involvement but are also derived from other sources.[9] Some related research may help illustrate the phenomenon.

Because of the system of racial and socioeconomic stratification in the U.S., white-collar offenses are seen primarily as "white crime" whereas most street crimes against property are seen as "nonwhite crime." Within the street crime category, there may be further divisions along racial lines. Mayas (1977) found that violent street crime was generally associated with blacks. There is also evidence that rape is perceived to be a black offense (Abbott and Calonico 1974). Such race-crime typing has also been observed in other societies. O'Connor (1984) observed that a sample of respondents to a social survey in Australia tended to describe the typical violent criminal as a lower-class white male or an aborigine male. On the other hand, the typical swindler was described as a middle-class, white professional. Such crime typing in both the United States and Australia may reflect certain social realities, that is, differential offending by various racial-social groups. Or it may be essentially a status-related stereotype. Such stereotypes may be grounded in notions of the causes of crime. Regardless of its basis such typing may affect the official response to criminal activity.

For instance, Bernstein et al. (1977) analyzed a sample of all males arraigned in a city in New York State from December 1974 to March 1975. An unexpected finding was that white defendants as well as defendants who had been employed for longer periods of time were most severely sentenced. In attempting to explain this finding they used information obtained from interviews suggesting that some judges and prosecutors assume that nonwhites commit crimes because the nonwhite subculture accepts such behavior. These subcultural differences were said to be considered by the judges and prosecutors thereby making the offenses of nonwhites seem less pernicious. Expectations were said to be higher for white defendants, hence they received greater punishment. Of course, the effects of race and social-class-related notions of "normal crimes" on public defense and prosecutorial decision-making have been documented by Sudnow (1965) and Swigert and Farrell (1977). None of these researchers made comparative studies of the sentencing of white and nonwhite offenders across several crime types. But they do propose that certain types of crimes are perceived as more normal or appropriate for some racial and social class groups than for others.

It may also be the case that what is considered race-inappropriate crime varies over time and across various social contexts (Hagan and Bernstein 1979; Peterson and Hagan 1984). For example, Peterson and Hagan observed that between 1963 and 1976 there was a trend away from harsher punishment and toward more leniency for black drug offenders. They related this change to changes in the social significance of race in the locality studied. But they also provided evidence of the continued operation of race-inappropriate differentials. It was observed that lenient treatment of nonwhite drug offenders peaked between 1969 and 1973. This leniency, however, was restricted to *ordinary* nonwhite drug offenders, not big dealers. Nonwhite *big dealers* were said to have received the harshest punishment of all. Small drug sales had perhaps come to be seen as appropriate for black offenders (indeed, expected behavior) while large drug sales were seen as more appropriate for whites.

In another study, Hagan and Bernstein (1979) studied the sentencing of draft resisters during a 14-year period between 1963 and 1976. They found that during the early period black resisters were more likely than white resisters to be imprisoned. During the latter period white resisters were more likely to be imprisoned. They argued that when political dissent becomes widespread, majority group members can present an even greater threat than minority group members to governing authority. In this instance the level of racial inappropriateness appeared to vary with the level of lawbreaking within each group. But their explanation was largely devised to account for this one unexpected finding and leaves many questions unanswered.

I propose that these assorted studies all point to the existence of a race/crime-specific perception of the appropriateness of criminal behavior that affects racial differentials in criminal sentencing and other criminal justice decision-making. On the basis of the operation of such a perception there is reason to predict that:

1. Blacks will be more severely punished than whites for white-collar offenses.[10]
2. The black-white punishment differential will be greater for white-collar offenses than for street crimes against property.
3. After controlling for relevant legal variables and race of victim, smaller black-white differentials will be observed for homicide than for any other type of crime.[11]

This last proposal is based on the idea that elasticity of the race-inappropriateness concept is less for the most serious of offenses. For example, homicide is generally considered to be among the most inappropriate and abnormal of crimes. Yet even for the most morally reprehensible acts, there will likely be racial differences in punishment based on the idea that racial groups adhere to different moral standards (Bernstein et al. 1977; Swigert and Farrell 1977). Homicide may also be seen as normal (Swigert and Farrell 1977) among blacks and the poor simply because of its disproportionate incidence among those groups.

There is also a likely interaction between victim-offender traits and what is deemed to be racially inappropriate crime. Crimes involving white victims will be seen as more inappropriate for nonwhite offenders than the same criminal acts involving nonwhite victims. Thus, in addition to the factors discussed earlier that may lead to harsher punishment for nonwhite offender–white victim offenses, such offenses may be seen as more inappropriate. Similarly, offenses by nonwhites against "white" institutions will likely be seen as less appropriate than similar offenses against "nonwhite" institutions. Support for the significance of both victim characteristics and crime appropriateness considerations can be found in a statement by Myrdal:

> In criminal cases the discrimination does not always run against a Negro defendant. It is part of the southern tradition to assume that Negroes are disorderly and lack elementary morals, and to show great indulgence toward Negro violence and disorderliness 'when they are among themselves.' . . . As long as only Negroes are concerned and no whites are disturbed, great leniency will be shown in most cases. . . . The sentences for even major crimes are ordinarily reduced when the victim is another Negro. Attorneys are heard to plead in the juries: 'Their code of ethics is a different one from ours.' . . . Leniency toward Negro defendants in cases involving crimes against other Negroes is thus actually a form of discrimination. . . . For offenses which involve any actual or potential danger to whites, however, Negroes are punished more severely than whites (1944, p. 551).

Race and Region

The significance of region for determining patterns of punishment for crime has also been duly noted by conflict theorists within criminology as well as by some race relations theorists. Chambliss and Seidman say, "Regional differences are rather striking. A higher proportion of blacks are convicted and executed in the South than any other section of the country, and they are convicted there for a greater variety of crimes. . . . Execution for rape is an almost exclusively southern phenomenon" (1971, p. 466). In the study of American race relations and of criminal justice system outcomes, black-white differences across regions have been largely attributed to cultural factors, for example, northern tolerance versus southern bigotry *or* southern paternalism versus northern racial egalitarianism. Such cultural values are said to explain both the finding of harsher punishment for black than for white offenders in the South and the sometimes-observed leniency granted black criminal offenders in the South as compared with those in the North (see Kleck 1981).

Despite the historically based perception of greater racial bias in the South than outside of it and the observations of early researchers such as Johnson (1941) and Sellin (1935), Welch et al. (1985) note that very few studies make simultaneous regional comparisons when evaluating the impact of race on criminal sentencing. In addition, when regional differences are observed a rather simplistic, culture-based northern-southern dichotomy may be too hastily accepted when other factors may be more significant. For example, researchers may not have controlled for race-of-victim effects, rural-urban differences, crime type, etc. A brief summary of some recent findings on regional variations in the sentencing of blacks and whites illustrates the theoretical and methodological issues involved in such research.

Kleck (1981) reported that the death penalty for murder has not generally been imposed in a fashion discriminatory toward blacks except in the South. In a recent study of punishment of burglary and robbery offenders, Welch et al. (1985) found that southwestern and southeastern jurisdictions were more likely to engage in discrimination. Conversely, studies by Spohn et al. (1981-82) and Levin (1977) have found significant discrimination against blacks in incarceration rates in several northern urban jurisdictions. In fact, recent incarceration statistics show a larger gap between black and white rates of imprisonment outside the South than within it (Christianson 1981; Dunbaugh 1979; Hawkins 1985).[12]

These findings suggest that a revised conflict perspective must predict the direction of regional differences in black-white punishment differences and provide plausible explanations for them. As Kleck (1981) observes current regional differences in black and white punishment for crime are not easily explained. This is due both to the simplistic northern-southern bias assumptions embodied in past research and to seemingly anomalous findings—evidence of both leniency and harshness in the South and discrimination in nonsouthern areas. Below I discuss the theoretical significance of past studies of regional variation in criminal punishment differences by race by considering a recurring theme in the literature—southern leniency.

Kleck (1981; citing Kuhn 1962) correctly notes that past researchers have failed to recognize the significance of anomalies and have thus not been alert to the need to alter their fundamental assumptions. Yet one must first interpret the significance of such anomalies before they can be effectively used to modify existing assumptions. For example, we must determine to what extent the term "leniency" is the appropriate label for the racial-regional differences in punishment for crime reported in previous investigations. A review of the concept of leniency as it has been used in the literature on race and criminal punishment reveals: (1) it is a concept that was based originally on primarily anecdotal data about southern criminal justice practices;[13] (2) the term has been used indiscriminately to refer to any pattern of punishment for blacks that is lower than that observed for whites. Often statistically insignificant differences are so labeled; (3) the term has also been used to explain seemingly anomalous patterns across regions. It is generally predicted that the overall level of punishment for blacks will be higher in the South than in the non-South. However, it is also said that leniency (the underpunishment of blacks in comparison to whites) occurs mainly in the more paternalistic South; (4) recent investigations, especially, have used the term without regard for the contingent factors that originally underlay the concept. For example, they have not considered type-of-offense differences or victim-offender effects. Much of this pattern of usage of the term can be seen in the recent work of Kleck (1981).

Kleck concludes that one of the most important subsidiary findings of his literature review is the identification of studies which report that black defendants are sometimes treated more leniently than whites. He also reaches this conclusion on the basis of his own empirical analysis of the death penalty. He notes that for the nation as a whole, in the remote and recent past, blacks have been less likely than whites to receive the death sentence for homicide (p. 799). He further concludes that this has been especially true outside the South. Thus, for Kleck the anomaly lies in a reversal of predicted outcomes: a pattern of seemingly more lenient punishment for blacks in the non-South than in the South. In attempting to make sense of this pattern, he refers to earlier studies that reported leniency toward blacks in the South. He concludes that there was a southern pattern of leniency toward blacks in an earlier era and that there is a present-day pattern of leniency toward blacks outside the South.

After listing four studies conducted in various regions between 1961 and 1978 which reported less punishment for blacks than whites, Kleck goes on to discuss a pattern of lenient treatment of black defendants in the South during the 1940s and before. Such treatment is attributed to a southern brand of paternalism that viewed blacks as "child-like creatures who were not as responsible for their actions as whites were, and who therefore could not be held accountable to the law to the extent that whites were" (p. 800). Mention of such a view is attributed to Dollard (1937), Garfinkel (1949), and Myrdal (1944). Apart from a question of the accuracy of this description of southern race relations in general (which I discuss below), Kleck fails to reconcile such a conclusion with: (1) the extremely high rates of imprisonment and execution of blacks in the South during the late nineteenth and early twentieth centuries for homicide, rape, robbery, larceny, and numerous minor offenses (e.g., Adamson 1983, 1984); and (2) the extent to which presumed leniency may be due to race-of-victim effects. That is, were white officials lenient only for those offenses involving black victims? Unlike the earlier investigations, the studies conducted between 1961 and 1978 generally do not control for the race of the victim.

I propose that: (1) to the extent that there was statistical "underpunishment" of blacks in comparison with whites in the South, it varied with the race of the victim, crime type, and other concerns discussed in the present paper; (2) to the extent that blacks have been treated more leniently than whites in the non-South during more recent years, these patterns, too, are affected by such contingencies; and (3) since black crime in the aggregate is primarily intraracial, is usually within socially "appropriate" categories, and is seldom directed at white structures of authority (Silberman 1978), an aggregate-level finding of lesser punishment for black offenders is to be expected in many instances. It is the variation within that overall pattern of supposed leniency that Kleck fails to fully acknowledge and, that, a revised conflict perspective must explain.

Power Threat Versus Subordination

The existence of regional differences in black-white punishment is related to another significant set of issues that must be confronted by a revised conflict model. To what extent are racial differentials in social control due to individual attributes of the victim and/or offender, and to what extent to the attributes of the group from which these persons come? Is the treatment of blacks by the criminal justice system primarily a response to the threat they pose to white authority structures or is it primarily a response to their subordinate status? Since all subordinate groups represent potential threats, how variable is the ability of such groups (e.g., blacks in the U.S.) to pose a substantial challenge to those in power?

Built into the conflict model is the notion that the treatment of individuals by the criminal justice system is largely a function of their *group status.* However, in attempting to explain differential punishment for crime, conflict theorists place greater emphasis on group subordination and powerlessness than on threat. Lower-class individuals are said to have fewer resources with which to resist the imposition of criminal sanctions. This is one of the basic tenets of the conflict model. This distinguishes it from more recent Marxist interpretations of historical patterns of black punishment. For instance, Adamson (1983, 1984) has argued that immediate post–Civil War social control of blacks by criminal justice systems in the South reflected the fact that black criminals were both potential threats to white control and potential assets (prison labor).

In a similar vein, Blalock (1956, 1957, 1967) has proposed that the level of power resources available to minority groups is more variable than that assumed in the conflict perspective. He also proposes that dominant majority groups often must mobilize to maintain their power advantage over subordinate minority groups. Subordinate groups' advantage is a function of their population size and also the socioeconomic resources available to them. Blalock (1967) notes that only under conditions of slavery would minority resources be zero. For several decades, researchers have utilized this hypothesis to examine the relationship between the relative size of the black population and the extent of various forms of inequality between blacks and whites across regions. They have examined such diverse measures of inequality as political participation (Heer 1959; Key 1949), income (Blalock 1956, 1957; Frisbie and Neidert 1977), occupational status (Glenn 1963, 1964), school desegregation (Pettigrew 1957), and lynchings (Corzine et al. 1983).

Blalock (1967) does not specifically discuss criminal justice outcomes as a measure of discrimination. He does argue that the three major areas of discrimination which have characterized American race relations patterns are directly linked to what he calls the "power-threat factor." The percent nonwhite within a given geographical area is said to have an impact on whites' fear of competition and of the threat posed by nonwhites to white authority. Power threat is generally described as the actual or perceived potential of a minority group to pose a realistic challenge to white political or economic control. He proposes that the three types of discrimination or prejudice in which the power-threat factor should predominate are: (1) restriction of a minority's political rights, (2) symbolic forms of segregation, and (3) a threat-oriented ideological system. Some criminological research suggests that the disproportionate processing of blacks within the criminal justice system likely reflects elements of each of these areas of discrimination.

A series of recent studies has probed the links between the size of the nonwhite population, race relations, and police strength. Jacobs (1979) reports that metropolitan areas with larger numbers of blacks had stronger law enforcement agencies than areas with fewer blacks in 1970 but not in 1960. In a follow-up Jackson and Carroll (1981) use the racial composition of the city, the level of black mobilization activity, and the frequency of riots in the 1960s as predictors of police strength in a sampling of 90 nonsouthern cities during 1971. They also derive their hypotheses from the work of Blalock (1967). They conclude that police expenditures are a resource that is mobilized or expanded when a minority group appears threatening to the dominant group.

Liska et al. (1981) look at police department strength in 109 U.S. municipal areas between 1950 and 1972. They report that the effect of racial composition depends on geographical region and year (before or after civil disorders). The greatest effects are noted for the South and after the civil disorders of the 1960s. The dramatic increases noted in police size during the late 1960s and early 1970s cannot be accounted for in terms of reported crime rates alone. Instead they suggest that such increases were influenced by the relative size of racially dissimilar groups associated with street crime and in the South by the extent to which such groups were segregated. The latter conclusion is based on the observation that population composition effects were strongest in the South after the desegregation efforts of the 1960s.

A recent study by Liska et al. (1985) provides additional support for the significance of power-threat factors in the social control of blacks. Using data on arrests for 77 U.S. cities over 100,000 population, they find no support for the traditional conflict perspective which holds that class composition has a greater effect on arrest rates than does racial composition.

Although percent nonwhite and percent poor are related, percent poor shows no effect on the certainty of arrests. On the other hand, two race-related variables show significant effects. The percent nonwhite and a measure of segregation significantly increase the number of arrests per 100,000 known crimes. However, they do not find that the certainty of arrest is greater for blacks than for whites. Rather, they suggest that their findings support the hypothesis that a high percentage of nonwhites and a low level of segregation increase the perceived threat of crime. These perceptions increase pressure on police to control crime, which in turn increases the certainty of arrests for both whites and nonwhites. Since their study does not examine the post-arrest processing of persons across these cities, most of the questions regarding the effects of these variables on differential punishment remain unanswered.

These criminal justice-related findings suggest that Blalock's theory may be relevant for predicting geographical and temporal patterns of black-white social control. Power-threat considerations may also be useful for explaining black-white punishment differences across crime types. Some crimes may be seen as more threatening to white authority than others. To the extent that race-related societal forces exert an influence on police strength, such social control sentiments may also be expected to influence the entire criminal justice system. This is likely to be a result of the facts that the police initiate the criminal justice process and that the police and nonpolice criminal justice personnel and institutions are affected by the same social conditions. A racial power threat can be hypothesized to influence the behavior of not only the police themselves but also various other government officials. Hence prosecutors, judges, correctional officials, and others should be similarly affected and likely to produce similar race-related outcomes. More importantly, these findings suggest that the failure of the conflict perspective to consider power-threat considerations constitutes a major obstacle to effectively using it to explain black-white punishment differences, both within and across geographical areas.

Offenders, Victims, and the State

In the introduction to this paper I suggested that the debate over anomalous findings may point to more substantial flaws in the conflict perspective than the problem of oversimplification. Some of those flaws can be noted in the preceding discussion of power threat. In this final section I discuss other, somewhat more global flaws and relate them to the discussion of anomalous findings. A growing body of literature has provided significant critiques of the conflict perspective on social control. Numerous critics have raised questions similar to those in the present discussion but few have specifically considered the issue of race and punishment. There are two major areas of criticism that have been directed at the conflict perspective which are relevant for the present discussion. One line of critique involves a symbolic interactionist-like evaluation of the processes within the criminal justice system that produce racially different outcomes. The second centers on the failure of the conflict perspective to fully consider the political economy of racial differentials in punishment.

The conflict perspective in both its original and oversimplified form is flawed both from an interactionist perspective and from the view of the larger structural theory from which it was derived. This has led to a failure of conflict theorists to fully incorporate a concern for victim characteristics into their model despite acknowledging race-of-victim effects. The perspective as used in most empirical research presumes that there are only two significant, racially identifiable actors or entities in the administration of justice—a nonwhite offender and a white system of justice (or other subordinate group offender versus dominant group justice). Thus, the perspective has at its core a model of the modern criminal justice system which according to McDonald (1976a, 1976b) has forgotten the victim. McDonald argues that as a result of developments over the last century and more, the victim has come to play a more limited role in the administration of justice than in colonial America or pre-modern England. He further says that often today the victim is twice victimized, first by the offender and then by the criminal justice system itself.

The increased interest in victims by both scholars and politicians over the last 10-15 years suggests that McDonald may be correct. On the other hand, the limiting of the role of the victim in the administration of justice and a neglect of the victim's welfare—e.g., lack of monetary compensation—does not necessarily mean that victims have not continued to be actors in the justice system. Victim characteristics have remained as both legal and extralegal influences on decision-making within the criminal justice system. Consideration of certain victim characteristics—age and sex—is built into the criminal law explicitly and implicitly. It is also well documented that prosecutors, judges, jurors, and other decision-makers take into account a variety of victim characteristics even when these are not specified by law. For example, the person who victimizes an old person is likely to receive a more severe punishment than an offender of similar characteristics who commits the same crime against a younger person. In this respect the victim has never left the criminal justice system, and has remained an actor of sorts within that system. In fact, it may be argued that in the absence of victims as active participants, their characteristics may influence decision-making to a greater extent than in the past. And, of course, in a racially stratified society a victim's race will be a significant concern (e.g., see the mock jury studies of Miller and Hewitt [1978], and Ugwuegbu [1976]).

The conflict perspective's failure to fully consider the influence of victim characteristics thus results from a failure to appreciate fully the complexities of the decision-making processes within the criminal justice system, including its diversity of potential actors. Consequently extralegal variables in the conflict model have been seen only as attributes of the offender or official representative of the state. A fuller model must "bring the victim back in" in much the same way as McDonald (1976a) advocates bringing the victim back into the modern system of criminal justice. But the oversimplified decision-making apparatus portrayed in the conflict model's criminal justice system stems from more than just the absence of the victim. Much of it can be attributed to a related but more global weakness of the conflict model—the portrayal of the state as a hegemonic authority. Like the failure to consider victims, such a view of the criminal justice system leads to a tendency to view racial patterns in punishment as more anomalous than they actually are.

Spitzer notes that while there has been a tendency towards rationalization of social control in modern societies, this has not been accomplished without significant countereffects. Among these countereffects are various conflicts of interest that derive from the creation of "pockets of resistance" to the rationalization process (1983, pp. 327-29). He includes professionals, civil servants, bureaucratic functionaries, unionized workers, and other interest groups among such resistors. These groups themselves are said to have been formed as mechanisms to destroy structures of privilege and to facilitate rationalized people-processing in an earlier age. Ignatieff (1983) also notes that one of the flaws of recent research on social control is the idea that the state has a monopoly over legitimate means of violence, including punishment as social control. The observations of Spitzer and Ignatieff together may suggest that no one entity *within* the system of state authority has a monopoly over criminal punishment. In the U.S. there has been a historical pattern of institutionalization and rationalization of racial dominance. The criminal justice system has been one mechanism for achieving this end. Yet to understand the treatment of black criminal defendants within that system, a more complex decision-making process than that described within the conflict perspective must be considered. A brief discussion of the seemingly anomalous finding of leniency toward some black criminal defendants in the South illustrates both the operation of Spitzer's and Ignatieff's countervailing influences and the complexity of the structural and interactional processes that shape criminal justice decision-making.[14]

The Myth of Leniency?

As earlier noted, many observers of sentencing patterns in the South during the 1930s and 1940s reported finding leniency in the treatment of black defendants. On the basis of a simplified conflict perspective such departures from rational social control aimed at racial dominance should not have occurred and therefore must, it seemed, be explained by the influence of irrational paternalism or unexamined victim traits. Yet a more detailed examination of the social context and political economy within which the reported leniency occurred suggests other possible factors and raises questions about the validity of labeling such findings anomalous or even as leniency.

The South of the early 1900s was characterized by an elaborate system of sharecropping. This system of quasi-serfdom depended less on the criminal justice system as a means of social control than did the political economies of the North. This system of labor use also provided actors for the criminal justice decision-making process in addition to the professionals assigned to such tasks. Landowners frequently saw no benefit in sending black laborers to prison for crime when their labor was needed for sharecropping. In the South of the 1930s and 1940s a decision to send a landowner's sharecropper to prison merely meant that the sharecropper would be assigned as a chain gang laborer on a state project, or more likely to a work project that would benefit other private business proprietors, including other landowners. What developed was a more or less formal system of brokerage in which various landowners used their political influence to divert accused black offenders out of the criminal justice system.[15]

Johnson's (1941) speculation that the least serious offenses would show the greatest leniency was likely accurate. Such diversion probably worked more effectively for minor offenses and perhaps most effectively of all for minor offenses against blacks. The fact that such leniency was not an "intrinsic" characteristic of the southern criminal justice system is illustrated by the fact that extremely large numbers of blacks continued to be sentenced to chain gangs for minor offenses from the 1920s through the 1950s. Many of these came from the urban areas or towns where no organized system of diversion occurred. Given the financial benefit to be derived from the labor of these urban prisoners who were not part of the sharecropping system, leniency was most likely not widely practiced. In fact, there is sufficient evidence to suggest that blacks most often received harsher sentences than whites (Adamson 1983, 1984; Myrdal 1944; Sellin 1935; Zimmerman 1947).

This suggests that a detailed examination of the social processes and actors involved in generating the supposed pattern of leniency in the South may reveal that the term is inaccurately used. The notion of leniency used in previous research generally is seen as an attribute of a prosecutor or judge who assigns less punishment to black than to white offenders without any rational basis for doing so. That is, the rational response (to perpetuate racial dominance) would be to assign greater punishment. If such leniency did exist in the system described above, one must ask to what extent criminal justice system officials alone made the decisions or to what extent they benefited from such leniency.[16] Many criminal justice officials in the South during the 1930s and 1940s likely benefited politically and/or economically from what are perceived as acts of leniency. These forces within the political economy, in addition to effects of race of the victim, crime type, and other considerations, must be included in a revised conflict perspective designed to explain racial differentials in criminal punishment.

Beyond Anomalies

I have argued that what have been labeled anomalies in past reviews of research on race and criminal punishment instead represent patterns that in some instances have long been recognized by researchers. These patterns are anomalous only if one adopts an oversimplified version of the conflict perspective as it has been developed within criminology. Such an oversimplification stems partly from the lack of specificity in the conflict perspective regarding the relationship between race and criminal punishment and a concomitant lack of testable hypotheses. On the other hand, other reported anomalies may point to major flaws in many of the presumptions inherent in the original conflict perspective.

Further research must incorporate a theoretical perspective that includes at least four major departures from the now-traditional conflict model. First, criminal punishment must be seen as contingent not only on the race of the criminal offender but also on the race of the victim. Second, researchers must begin to recognize the theoretical as opposed to the purely methodological significance of grouping crime into categories and using such groupings to assess levels of racial difference in punishment. The use of such categorizations is important for improving our understanding of the dynamics of assigned punishment for crime across racial groups. Third, power-threat considerations must be considered when assessing temporal or regional variations in black and white punishment. Finally, researchers should follow the lead of Peterson and Hagan (1984) in examining the historical and contextual dimensions of the relationship between race and criminal punishment. That is, variations in levels of punishment by race must be more fully analyzed and explained within the context of the larger structural forces from which they emanate and in their proper temporal perspective. Such a historical-contextual analysis would allow for more attention to the political economy of criminal punishment. Indeed, such modifications as those above would produce a conflict perspective that is closer to the Marxist tradition from which the perspective is largely derived.

While I have argued for a systematic rethinking of the conflict perspective, it must also be recognized that much of the discussion above supports Greenberg's (1981; citing Marx) contention that it may not be possible to construct *universal* laws that are not historically contingent. Many of the economic and social conditions that shaped black-white punishment differentials during the early part of this century have undergone significant change over the last quarter-century. Those societal forces that shape the current levels of disproportionate punishment of blacks in the United States may, therefore, differ from those that were operant in the past. On the other hand, the inability of researchers to develop non-historically contingent propositions must not obscure the fact that black-white criminal punishment differentials have remained at similar levels for more than one hundred years.

Notes

1. I use the word punishment in a generic sense throughout this paper. It refers to all decisions or outcomes within the system of criminal justice. This includes not only sentencing, but also decisions to prosecute and indict, to release on bail or parole, etc. This term also refers both to the likelihood that a criminal sanction will be imposed and to the severity of the sanction. I am largely excluding studies of police decision-making.

2. Although the term has been widely used, there is still substantial disagreement over exactly what constitutes the conflict perspective and which researchers are its major proponents. I have selected the works of Chambliss and Seidman and of Quinney as representative of the perspective largely because they are most often cited in the empirical literature. They are cited largely because in comparison with Sellin or Turk they provide a wider range of proposition-like statements that have proved useful in empirical tests.

3. For example, the index for the Quinney study shows that only 15 of more than 300 pages specifically treat issues of race, minority status, ethnicity, etc. Chambliss and Seidman limit their discussion of such issues to about 20 of 500 pages.

4. Of course, orthodox Marxists have paid relatively little attention to the study of criminal justice, per se. An exception is Bonger (1943, 1969), who also made a valuable contribution to the study of race and crime. In his later work Quinney approaches crime and crime control from an explicitly Marxian stance.

5. The most recent revival of this debate has centered around Wilson's (1978) notion of the declining significance of race. During the early to middle 1900s the debate involved black intellectuals and civil rights leaders who challenged ideas of American communists and socialists regarding the causes of the race problem. See Liska et al. (1985) for an important recent empirical investigation of the comparative effects of race and social class on crime control.

6. This proposition also illustrates other problems (or lack of clarity) within the conflict perspective. There are very few offenses that people of all social classes and races in the U.S. are *equally* likely to violate. Even if one could perfect some measure of "real" crime, the system of socioeconomic and racial stratification is such that it would be expected to differentially "generate" crime across racial and social class groupings. National arrest statistics have consistently shown that blacks are not arrested at rates equal to their share of the general population for most major offense categories. They are consistently overrepresented. For example, the Uniform Crime Reports over the last few years show blacks to be arrested at rates equal to their share of the population for only two offenses—liquor law violations and driving under the influence. Thus, when speaking of black-white

comparisons, the "all things being equal" stipulation places an unrealistic constraint on the empirical researcher. On the other hand, the proposition does highlight the fact that the conflict perspective seeks to explain both the probability that sanctions will be imposed and the severity of sanctions.

7. Banton provides a quote from a southern police detective's captain as illustrative of southern views of black and white homicide. The captain was quoted as saying, "In the town there are three classes of homicide. If a nigger kills a white man, that's murder. If a white kills a nigger, that's justifiable homicide. If a nigger kills a nigger, that's one less nigger" (1964, p. 173). Unfortunately, researchers have not investigated the impact of such racial bias on police decisions to arrest or gather evidence.

8. Most recent work on race-of-victim effects in the administration of punishment for homicide has a decidedly legal slant and shows little concern for the development of theory. Much of it may be described as applied social-legal research whose purpose is to encourage the federal courts to consider *proportionality* questions when adjudging the constitutionality of the death penalty. This is an important objective, but such a goal means that researchers pay little attention to explaining the patterns observed. The focus is also exclusively on race-of-offender effects in homicide cases (as opposed to other crime types).

9. It is possible that crimes that are disproportionately committed by one racial group will come to be associated with that group over time. On the other hand, the linking of some categories of crime to certain racial groups may not be dependent on comparative levels of criminal activity. For example, although for the nation at large and for most local areas the black burglary rate is considerably lower than the black robbery rate, it is likely that both will be seen by the public as "typical" black crimes. Further, on the basis of arrest statistics, embezzlement is nearly as typical for blacks (as compared to whites) as is burglary.

10. There is no agreement as to what is meant by white-collar offenses. I am using the term in its traditional sense to refer to crime committed by persons of high socioeconomic status, usually in the course of their occupation. I am excluding most organizational crime, for example, corporate malfeasance or nonfeasance. I include FBI crime categories such as embezzlement and fraud. I also include the numerous offenses not included in official crime statistics.

11. It is important to control for legally relevant variables when ascertaining the effects of crime type. For example, Jankovic (1978) found that nonwhites convicted of driving under the influence were more likely than whites to receive a prison term. Some evidence suggests that this is largely a result of an interaction among race, social class, and the availability of paid counsel. Affluent whites are more likely to be convicted of this offense than of other offenses. These individuals are also more likely than poorer blacks to afford paid counsel who can help them avoid prison terms. A result is that the white DUI offender will have a greater advantage over black DUI offenders than white burglars will have over black burglars.

12. Rural-urban differences have also been found to be a possible factor affecting racial punishment patterns. For example, Pope (1975) reported that discrimination against blacks was greater in rural than in urban areas of California.

13. The notion of leniency is generally attributed to Myrdal (1944), who bases his conclusion on the work of Johnson (1941) and others. It is anecdotal in the sense that such conclusions are not based on extensive empirical research but instead are based on statements by some observers of southern judicial practices.

14. One of the more promising areas of investigation along these lines involves analyses of prosecutorial discretion. Researchers must determine how prosecutors take victim characteristics into account in indicting or plea bargaining with black and white offenders. For example, Radelet and Pierce (1985) reported that prosecutors for 1,017 homicide defendants in Florida were most likely to "upgrade" police homicide classifications where blacks were accused of killing whites. Concomitantly, these offenses were least likely to be "downgraded." Such effects were found after controlling for various legally relevant sentencing-related criteria.

15. See Myrdal (1944) for a discussion of southern sentencing practices. Of particular interest also is Myrdal's discussion of the sentencing of black petty offenders (drunkards and vagrants) and the benefits derived from the intercession of whites.

16. Many of the criminal justice officials, such as policemen, prosecutors, and judges, in the rural South during the period likely had vested interests in diverting some black offenders from the formal system of punishment. Many were landowners or operators of businesses that depended on the availability of cheap labor. Others were likely to have been "controlled" by persons with such interests.

References

Abbott, D., and J. Calonico. 1974. "Black Man, White Women—The Maintenance of a Myth: Rape and the Press in New Orleans." Pp. 141-53 in *Crime and Delinquency: Dimensions of Deviance,* edited by Marc Riedel and Terence Thornberry. Praeger.

Adamson, Christopher R. 1983. "Punishment After Slavery: Southern State Penal Systems, 1865-1890." *Social Problems* 30:555-69.

———. 1984. "Toward a Marxian Penology: Captive Criminal Populations as Economic Threats and Resources," *Social Problems* 31:435-38.

Baldus, David C., Charles Pulaski, and George Woodworth. 1983. "Comparative Review of Death Sentences." *Journal of Criminal Law and Criminology* 74:661-753.

Banton, Michael, 1964. *The Policeman in the Community.* Tavistock.

Bernstein, Ilene Nagel, William R. Kelly, and Patricia A. Doyle. 1977. "Societal Reaction to Deviants: The Case of Criminal Defendants." *American Sociological Review* 42:743-55.

Blalock, Hubert M. 1956. "Economic Discrimination and Negro Increase." *American Sociological Review* 21:584-88.

———. 1957. "Percent Non-White and Discrimination in the South." *American Sociological Review* 22: 677-82.

———. 1967. *Toward a Theory of Minority Group Relations.* Wiley.

Blumstein, Alfred. 1982. "On the Racial Disproportionality of the United States' Prison Populations." *Journal of Criminal Law and Criminology* 73:1259-81.

Bonger, Wilhelm. 1943. *Race and Crime.* Columbia University Press.

———. 1969. *Criminality and Economic Conditions.* Indiana University Press.

Bowers, William J., and Glenn L. Pierce. 1980. "Arbitrariness and Discrimination Under Post-Furman Capital Statutes." *Crime and Delinquency* 26:563-635.

Bullock, H. A. 1961. "Significance of the Racial Factor in the Length of Prison Sentences." *Journal of Criminal Law, Criminology and Police Science* 52:411-17.

Chambliss, William J., and Robert B. Seidman. 1971. *Law, Order, and Power.* Addison-Wesley.

Christianson, Scott. 1981. "Our Black Prisons." *Crime and Delinquency* 27:364-75.

Corzine, Jay, James Creech, and Lin Corzine. 1983. "Black Concentration and Lynchings in the South: Testing Blalock's Power-Threat Hypothesis." *Social Forces* 61:774-96.

Dollard, John. 1937. *Caste and Class in a Southern Town.* Yale University Press.

Dunbaugh, Frank M. 1979. "Racially Disproportionate Rates of Incarceration in the United States." *Prison Law Monitor* 1:205, 219-22.

Frisbie, W. Parker, and Lisa Neidert. 1977. "Inequality and the Relative Size of Minority Populations: A Comparative Analysis." *American Journal of Sociology* 82:1007-30.

Garfinkel, Harold. 1949. "Research Note on Inter- and Intra-Racial Homicides." *Social Forces* 27:369-81.

Gibson, James L. 1978. "Race as a Determinant of Criminal Sentences: A Methodological Critique and a Case Study." *Law and Society Review* 12:455-78.

Glenn, Norval D. 1963. "Occupational Benefits to Whites from the Subordination of Negroes." *American Sociological Review* 28:443-48.

———. 1964. "The Relative Size of the Negro Population and Negro Occupational Status." *Social Forces* 43:42-49.

Green, Edward. 1971. "Research on Disparities." Pp. 529-39 in *Crime and Justice: The Criminal in the Arms of the Law.* Vol. II, edited by Leon Radzinowicz and Marvin Wolfgang. Basic Books.

Greenberg, David F. 1981. *Crime and Capitalism.* Mayfield.

Gross, Samuel R., and Robert Mauro. 1984. "Patterns of Death: An Analysis of Racial Disparities in Capital Sentencing and Homicide Victimization." *Stanford Law Review* 37:27-153.

Hagan, John. 1974. "Extra-legal Attributes and Criminal Sentencing." *Law and Society Review* 8:357-83.

Hagan, John, and Ilene Bernstein. 1979. "Conflict in Context: The Sanctioning of Draft Resisters, 1963-76." *Social Problems* 27:109-22.

Hagan, John, and Kristin Bumiller. 1983. "Making Sense of Sentencing: A Review and Critique of Sentencing Research." Pp. 1-54 in *Research on Sentencing: The Search for Reform.* Vol. II, edited by Alfred Blumstein et al. National Academy Press.

Hardy, Kenneth A. 1983. "Equity in Court Dispositions." Pp. 183-207 in *Evaluating Performance of Criminal Justice Agencies,* edited by Gordon P. Whitaker and Charles D. Phillips. Sage.

Hawkins, Darnell F. 1983. "Black-White Homicide Differentials: Alternatives to an Inadequate Theory." *Criminal Justice and Behavior* 10:407-40.

———. 1985. "Black-White Imprisonment Rates: A State-by-State Ecological Analysis." Paper presented at annual meeting of the Academy of Criminal Justice Sciences.

Heer, David M. 1959. "The Sentiment of White Supremacy: An Ecological Study." *American Journal of Sociology* 64:592-98.

Hindus, Michael S. 1980. *Prison and Plantations: Crime, Justice and Authority in Massachusetts and South Carolina, 1767-1878.* University of North Carolina Press.

Ignatieff, Michel. 1983. "State, Civil Society and Total Institutions: A Critique of Recent Social Histories of Punishment." Pp. 75-105 in *Social Control and the State,* edited by Stanley Cohen and Andrew Scull. St. Martin's.

Jackson, Pamela I., and Leo Carroll. 1981. "Race and the War on Crime: The Sociopolitical Determinants of Municipal Police Expenditures in 90 Non-Southern U.S. Cities." *American Sociological Review* 46:290-305.

Jacobs, David. 1979. "Inequality and Police Strength: Conflict Theory and Coercive Control in Metropolitan Areas." *American Sociological Review* 44:913-25.

Jankovic, Ivan. 1978. "Social Class and Criminal Sentencing." *Crime and Social Justice* 10:9-16.

Johnson, Guy B. 1941. "The Negro and Crime." *The Annals of the American Academy of Political and Social Science* 217:93-104.

Key, Vladimir Orlando, Jr. 1949. *Southern Politics.* Knopf.

Kleck, Gary. 1981. "Racial Discrimination in Criminal Sentencing: A Critical Evaluation of the Evidence with Additional Evidence on the Death Penalty." *American Sociological Review* 46:783-805.

Kuhn, Thomas S. 1962. *The Structure of Scientific Revolutions*. University of Chicago Press.

LaFree, Gary. 1980. "The Effect of Sexual Stratification by Race on Official Reactions to Rape." *American Sociological Review* 45:842-54.

Levin, Marlin A. 1972. "Urban Politics and Judicial Behavior." *Journal of Legal Studies* 1:220-21.

———. 1977. *Urban Politics and Criminal Courts*. University of Chicago Press.

Liska, Allen E., Mitchell B. Chamlin, and Mark D. Reed. 1985. "Testing the Economic Production and Conflict Models of Crime Control." *Social Forces* 64:119-38.

Liska, Allen E., Joseph J. Lawrence, and Michael Benson. 1981. "Perspectives on the Legal Order: The Capacity for Social Control." *American Journal of Sociology* 87:413-26.

McDonald, William F. 1976a. "Towards a Bicentennial Revolution in Criminal Justice: The Return of the Victim." *American Criminal Law Review* 13:649-73.

———. 1976b. *Criminal Justice and the Victim*. Sage.

Mayas, Jean-Marie. 1977. "Perceived Criminality: The Attribution of Criminal Race from News-Reported Crime." Unpublished Ph.D. dissertation, University of Michigan.

Miller, M., and J. Hewitt. 1978. "Conviction of a Defendant as a Function of Juror-Victim Racial Similarity." *Journal of Social Psychology* 105:159-60.

Myers, Martha A. 1979. "Offended Parties and Official Reactions: Victims and the Sentencing of Criminal Defendants." *Sociological Quarterly* 20:529-40.

Myrdal, Gunnar. 1944/1972. *An American Dilemma*. Pantheon.

O'Connor, Michael E. 1984. "The Perception of Crime and Criminality: The Violent Criminal and Swindler as Social Types." *Deviant Behavior* 5:255-74.

Paternoster, Raymond. 1983. "Race of Victim and Location of Crime: The Decision to Seek the Death Penalty in South Carolina." *Journal of Criminal Law and Criminology* 74:754-85.

———. 1984. "Prosecutorial Discretion in Requesting the Death Penalty: A Case of Victim-Based Racial Discrimination." *Law and Society Review* 18:437-78.

Peterson, Ruth D., and John Hagan. 1984. "Changing Conceptions of Race and Sentencing Outcomes." *American Sociological Review* 49:56-70.

Pettigrew, Thomas F. 1957. "Demographic Correlates of Border-State Desegregation." *American Sociological Review* 22:683-89.

Pope, Carl E. 1975. *The Judicial Processing of Assault and Burglary Offenders in Selected California Counties*. National Criminal Justice Information Statistics Service. U.S. Department of Justice.

Quinney, Richard. 1970. *The Social Reality of Crime*. Little, Brown.

Radelet, Michael L. 1981. "Racial Characteristics and the Imposition of the Death Penalty." *American Sociological Review* 46:918-27.

Radelet, Michael L., and Glenn L. Pierce. 1985. "Race and Prosecutorial Discretion in Homicide Cases." *Law and Society Review* 19:587-621.

Sellin, Thorsten. 1928. "The Negro Criminal: A Statistical Note." *The Annals of the American Academy of Political and Social Science* 140:52-64.

———. 1935. "Race Prejudice in the Administration of Justice." *American Journal of Sociology* 41:212-17.

Silberman, Charles. 1978. *Criminal Violence-Criminal Justice: Criminals, Police, Courts, and Prisons in America*. Random House.

Spitzer, Steven. 1983. "The Rationalization of Crime Control in Capitalist Society." Pp. 312-33 in *Social Control and the State*, edited by Stanley Cohen and Andrew Scull. St. Martin's.

Spohn, Cassia, John Gruhi, and Susan Welch. 1981-82. "The Effect of Race on Sentencing: A Reexamination of an Unsettled Question." *Law and Society Review* 16:71-80.

Sudnow, David. 1965. "Normal Crimes: Sociological Features of the Penal Code in a Public Defender's Office." *Social Problems* 12:255-76.

Swigert, Victoria, and Ronald A. Farrell. 1977. "Normal Homicides and the Law." *American Sociological Review* 42:16-32.

Thomson, Randall J., and Matthew T. Zingraff. 1981. "Detecting Sentence Disparity: Some Problems and Evidence." *American Journal of Sociology* 86:869-80.

Turk, Austin T. 1969. *Criminality and Legal Order*. Rand McNally.

Ugwuegbu, Dennis Chiniaeze E. 1976. "Black Jurors' Personality Trial Attribution to a Rape Case Defendant." *Social Behavior and Personality* 4:193-201.

Welch, Susan, Cassia Spohn, and John Gruhl. 1985. "Convicting and Sentencing Differences Among Black, Hispanic and White Males in Six Localities." *Justice Quarterly* 2:67-77.

Wilson, William J. 1978. *The Declining Significance of Race*. University of Chicago Press.

Wolfgang, Marvin E., and Marc Riedel. 1973. "Race, Judicial Discretion, and the Death Penalty." *The Annals of the American Academy of Political and Social Science* 407:119-33.

Zimring, Franklin E., Joel Eigen, and Sheila O'Malley. 1976. "Punishing Homicide in Philadelphia: Perspectives on the Death Penalty." *University of Chicago Law Review* 43:227-52.

14

Introduction

In his work, Darnell Hawkins (see Chapter 13) has asserted that research on Black Americans has suffered from two major flaws. First, as noted earlier, factors relevant to the lives of Black Americans have been ignored. As a result, information based on somebody else's story has been used to explain the behavior of Black Americans. Second, stereotypical views of Black Americans that cater to the prejudices of members of the majority have been used to explain both action and inaction on the part of actors in the criminal justice system.

This article focuses on the barriers to the prevention of family violence in the Black community. Hawkins argues that the historical devaluation of Black life is based in part on the high rate of Black homicide, which is one barrier to the prevention of Black family violence. He argues further that the undervaluing of Black life over White life is evident in the criminal justice system when punishments of Black offenders are harsher than those for White offenders and crimes against White victims are punished more severely than those against Black victims. Hawkins also contends that the stereotypical view, held by law enforcement and members of the judiciary, that violence is normal in the Black community results in an unwillingness to intervene in family violence and a failure to prevent further violence.

Devalued Lives and Racial Stereotypes

Ideological Barriers to the Prevention of Family Violence Among Blacks

Darnell F. Hawkins

Because a large proportion of all interpersonal violence among blacks, as among other groups, occurs within the family context, the black family is a likely target for an emphasis on violence intervention. Black family violence can be reduced. Social researchers and policymakers have so far largely concentrated on the more or less technical aspects of violence prevention: the perfection of methodologies for identifying high-risk groups and individuals, assessing the effectiveness of intervention strategies, and similar concerns. In this chapter, I examine one of the least explored problems: the constraining influence of certain ideological currents on the perceived feasibility or possibility of successful prevention. Only if these ideological barriers are seriously confronted and discarded will rates of family violence among blacks be lowered.

Ideological Barriers

Efforts to intervene in domestic violence among blacks must confront three major ideologically based barriers. The first derives from the noninterventionist sentiments historically associated with family violence in the United States. Such sentiments, despite some diminution in recent years, still persist. Further, despite increasing public concern and legislation sometimes requiring intervention in domestic disputes, the prevention of family violence among blacks faces still other race-specific ideological barriers. One such barrier derives from the historical devaluation of black life in the United States. The other is a product of stereotypical views of the normality of violence among blacks. Both are interrelated and emanate from historical patterns of racism and oppression in American society. In this chapter I discuss these race-specific ideological currents and their significance for past and present efforts to intervene in black family violence. Much of the attention is focused on the impact of these beliefs and values on the actions of public officials who are likely to be in a position to devise and implement strategies for the prevention of family violence, among them, law enforcement and judicial authorities, medical doctors, psychologists-counselors, public health officials, social workers, and similar professionals.

Five arguments are important to this discussion:

1. In comparison to whites, the persons and lives of blacks are less valued in American society.
2. The devaluation of black life is evidenced in many ways but is perhaps most apparent in the sentencing of criminal defendants.
3. Linked to the devalued status of blacks is a stereotyped view of violence as more normal among blacks than among whites.
4. This view of the normality of black violence has also been associated with a more limited law enforcement and judicial response to acts of violence in the black community than that found in the white community.
5. Both the devalued status of the black victim and the acceptance of violence as normal among blacks pose significant barriers to the intervention into and prevention of family violence within the black community.

These observations are not new, of course. Similar themes have been proposed by various analysts of black-white relations throughout much of U.S. history. But these beliefs have particular relevance given increased governmental efforts at violence prevention.

It may be argued that the devalued status of blacks in American society is not unique. That is, other nonwhite minority groups and perhaps the entire lower class itself (whites and nonwhites) can be described as devalued in comparison to whites and persons of higher social class status. Marxist and other class-based theoretical approaches suggest that the devalued status of blacks derives from their position in the class structure. It is beyond my scope here to debate the merits of such an argument. I do not argue for the uniqueness of the social status of blacks in American society, although an argument could certainly be made for such. Similarly, much of the evidence of the devalued status of blacks I provide could well be applicable to other subgroups in the United States.[1]

Like other social phenomena, the devalued status of blacks and the perception of violence as normal among them are both ideological constructs and also potentially empirically assessable social facts. To understand fully the impact of these phenomena on the prevention of family violence among blacks, we must take a sociology of knowledge approach. Social scientists have described the operation of these phenomena within the larger American society. But social science itself has been greatly affected by the same racial bias that it seeks to analyze. Social scientists have also been involved in efforts to overcome the racial bias that produces the results from the devaluing of black life and views of the normality of violence among blacks. The major emphasis in this chapter is on social science as both an analyst and embodiment of these phenomena. I believe that the ideological barriers I describe are evident in both social scientific thought and in opinions held by the American public. I also believe that a truly critical and reflexive social science may be one step toward the solution of the problems posed by these barriers to the prevention of family violence within the black community.

The Cheapness of Black Life: Proof and Causes

Predictably, much of the proof or evidence offered by observers to show the cheapness of black life in the United States involves the crime of homicide. Two major observations or conclusions have been widely reported. First, it has been suggested that the fact that the rate of homicide and other interpersonal violence is considerably higher among blacks than among whites is itself an indication of an undervaluing of life within the black community. That is, blacks themselves do not value their own lives or the lives of others of their race. One result is frequent acts of interpersonal aggression. Over the last fifty years, considerable debate has ensued over the question of whether this social-cultural condition is the result of slavery and racial oppression or a carry-over from the African heritage of black Americans. An early analyst of homicide, Brearly (1932), argued that the disproportionate incidence of black homicide may stem from both racial oppression and African cultural traditions. He says,

> His historical background may also help to explain the Negro's attitude toward the taking of human life. In central Africa, his ancestral home, both birth and death rates were high, and violent death was frequent and often unpunished, especially if the victim were a slave. A lack of regard for the person and personality of others seems to have been almost characteristic of central African culture. When the Negro was brought to America as a slave, his owners did little to encourage high esteem for the sanctity of life. On the contrary, they often treated the Negro as if he were only a relatively valuable domestic animal, disciplining him by corporal punishment, using his wives and daughters as concubines, and increasing the instability of his family by the sale or exchange of its members. This background may influence the traditions and attitudes of the Negro of today and decrease his regard for the sacredness of human life. (pp. 113-114)

This view of causes of black homicide has been frequently restated by subsequent researchers even in more recent years (see Curtis 1975). Silberman (1978), on the other hand, argues that the propensity to violence among blacks is not part of the cultural heritage American blacks brought from Africa. Instead he concludes that "violence is something black Americans learned in this country" (p. 123). Despite the disagreement over the exact origins of high rates of black violence, such violence is frequently used to argue for the existence of a value system among blacks that is characterized by a lack of regard for the sacredness of life. Further, this belief underlies subculture of violence theory (Wolfgang and Ferracuti 1967) and is also a basis for a view of the normality of violence among blacks. In this instance (as proof of devalued lives) researchers appear to follow the line of argument depicted in the diagram:

The second source of proof offered by social scientists for the cheapness of black life is similar. Emphasis, however, is placed not on the values and behavior of blacks themselves but rather on the actions of whites toward blacks. Further, much less emphasis is placed on historical antecedents. This view holds that the devaluation of black life stems mainly from white oppression and is best

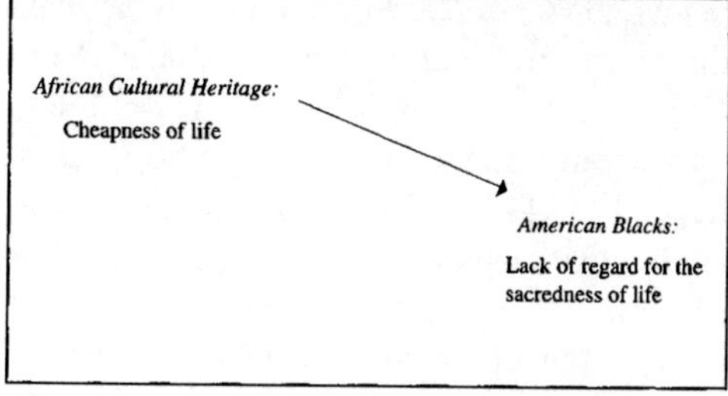

Figure 14.1a African Cultural Heritage

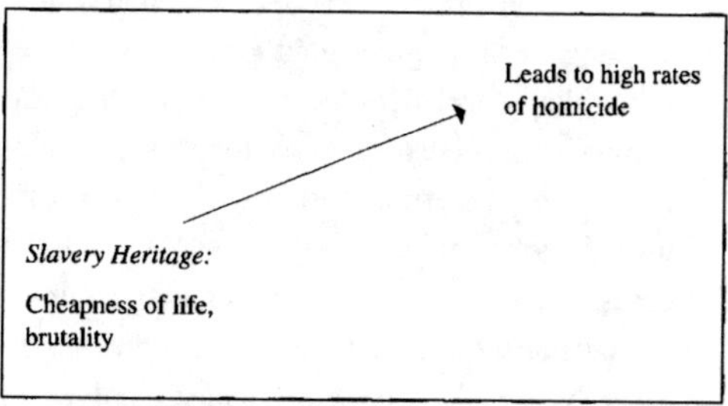

Figure 14.1b Slavery Heritage

observed in the actions of public officials, especially those within the system of criminal justice. Proponents of this view generally document the culpability of whites in fostering a system of justice that values the lives of whites more than those of blacks even in recent years.

Some of the first observations regarding this kind of devaluing of black life within an official bureaucratic context come from studies of the sentencing of black and white murderers.[2] In attempting to probe the question of whether black criminal defendants are more harshly punished than white defendants, researchers have noted a significant race-of-the-victim effect. One of the earliest empirical investigations was done by Johnson (1941). He proposed that the four black-white homicide offender-victim dyads could be ranked in seriousness from most to least serious as follows: (1) Negro versus white, (2) white versus white, (3) Negro versus Negro, (4) white versus Negro. He reported that data on court prosecutions in Virginia, North Carolina, and Georgia between 1930 and 1940 confirmed this ordering of offenses. Myrdal (1944, p. 551) used this and similar studies to conclude:

> In criminal cases the discrimination does not always run against a Negro defendant. It is part of the Southern tradition to assume that Negroes are disorderly and lack elementary morals, and to show great indulgence toward Negro violence and disorderliness "when they are among themselves." . . . As long as only Negroes are concerned and no whites are disturbed, great leniency will be shown in most cases. . . . The sentences for even major crimes are ordinarily reduced when the victim is another Negro. Attorneys are heard to plead in the juries: "Their code of ethics is a different one from ours." . . . Leniency toward Negro defendants in cases involving crimes against other Negroes is thus actually a form of discrimination. . . . For offenses which involve any actual or potential danger to whites, however, Negroes are punished more severely than whites.

Myrdal's and Johnson's conclusions were based on observations in the South during the 1930s and before. Thus it is reasonable to ask how generalizable their conclusions are—to the non-South and to the present time.

Empirical studies of criminal justice outcomes report that these findings and conclusions are applicable to other areas of the United States and are descriptive of decision-making patterns even in recent years. Wolfgang and Riedel (1973) and LaFree (1980) reported that rape sentencing during the 1970s showed an offender-victim pattern similar to that described by Johnson (1941). In addition a long list of studies have shown a comparable racial pattern for not only homicide and rape but also assault and robbery (Garfinkel 1949; Zimring, Eigen, and O'Malley 1976; Myers 1979; Radelet 1981; Baldus, Pulaski, and Woodworth 1983; Paternoster 1983). Radelet, Baldus et al., and Paternoster report that even during the 1970s and 1980s, the killer of a white (regardless of race) is much more likely to be sentenced to death than the killer of a black. In summarizing these findings, Kleck (1981, p. 799) says, "There appears to be a general pattern of less severe punishment of crimes with black victims, especially in connection with the imposition of the death penalty."

The differential punishment of crimes involving black and white victims likely begins with the actions of law enforcement officials. Although there have not been many empirical studies of this aspect of law enforcement, several researchers have suggested that the race of the victim and offender is a factor affecting police decision making. Banton (1964, p. 173) quotes the captain of police detectives in a southern town during World War I: "In this town there are three classes of homicide. If a nigger kills a white man, that's murder. If a white man kills a nigger, that's justifiable homicide. If a nigger kills a nigger, that's one less nigger." Johnson (1941), and Myrdal (1944) noted that this kind of racial bigotry was characteristic of the police response to black crime during the 1920s, 1930s, and 1940s. Investigations conducted after the urban riots of the 1960s suggest that similar bias has existed during more recent years.

The kinds of empirical findings reported in the research on sentencing have led a number of researchers to speak of black victims of homicide and other crimes as devalued victims (Kleck 1981; Hawkins 1983; Peterson and Hagen 1984). Thus, racist perceptions by public officials of the value of black life have led to differential treatment of black and white offenders and victims.

Hawkins (1983) suggests that the devalued status of the black victim affects the actions of a wide range of officials who respond to violent behavior or other crime: police, health care workers, prosecutors, judges, juries, and others. The devalued status of the black victim also has relevance for understanding the attitudes of public officials toward family violence among blacks. Crime statistics document the fact that a large proportion of all assaults and homicide among blacks, as among nonblacks, occurs within the context of the family. Lundsgaarde (1977) noted that homicide offenders who murdered members of their family received less punishment than those who killed nonfamily. The literature on the devalued status of the black victim suggests that among black and white domestic murderers, blacks will receive less punishment than whites.[3]

The underpunishment of blacks who offend against other blacks is not just a finding from social science research. It is an often-discussed problem within the black community itself.[4] Many analysts have noted that the seeming vigilantism among blacks that often leads to assault or homicide results partly from their inability to rely upon the criminal justice system to settle disputes and dispense justice fairly. If homicide is a means of dispute resolution in the absence of more appropriate and less violent means (Levi 1980), then the high rate of criminal violence among blacks is a direct result of the devaluing of black life by officials within the American system of criminal justice.

These observations highlight the mixture of social fact and racial stereotype that has shaped public attitudes and policy toward blacks in the United States. On the one hand, blacks have historically been depicted as adhering to lesser moral standards than whites. The high rate of black homicide is used as proof of such moral bankruptcy. On the other hand, the acceptance of this viewpoint by public officials leads to patterns of intervention and law enforcement that in many instances may exacerbate already high levels of violence among blacks. Thus, the undervaluing of black life may represent a formidable barrier to current efforts to reduce violence, including family violence, within the black community. So may concomitant perceptions of the normality of violence among blacks, a common theme in American social thought and social science theory. This theme too is reflected in statements and behaviors of public officials in response to homicide in the black community and has been documented in social science research.

The Normality of Violence Among Blacks

David Sudnow published in 1965 a particularly significant study of some of the sociological features of the criminal code in a public defender's office. The study represented a pioneering effort designed to look at the actual practice of criminal case processing by public defenders at such practices as plea bargaining and other forms of sentence determination. An equally significant result of the investigation was his finding that public defenders tended to use a system of social typing for crimes and criminal offenders. They justified such typing on the basis of their on-the-job experiences, which taught them that some kinds of offenders were likely to repeat the same offense while others were not repeat violators. If the latter were repeat violators, they were said to do so less frequently. Sudnow used the term *normal crimes* to describe "those occurrences whose typical features, e.g., the way they usually occur and the characteristics of persons who commit them (as well as the typical victims and typical scenes), are known and attended by the P.D." He goes on to say that for any of a series of these offense types, the public defender "can provide some form of proverbial characterization" (1965, p. 260).

Sudnow provides several examples of such proverbial characterizations. Most involved typing of the social class and/or race of the offender and victim. Such typings may have served the purpose of expediting the public defender's and prosecutor's processing of large numbers of cases, but the potential for bias and discrimination in such characterizations is obvious. Swigert and Farrell (1977), who explored this aspect of criminal typing in their study of homicide processing, concluded that a stereotype of the homicide offender as a "normal primitive" existed among court-appointed diagnosticians of homicide in a large urban jurisdiction in the northeastern United States. This classification represented a conception of criminality that combined both race and class characteristics. They cite the following description, developed by the diagnostic clinic they studied, as the basis for the homicide criminal typing:

> While treated as a diagnostic category, the designation "normal primitive" constitutes a *social* description of a group of people whose behavior, *within their own social setting,* is best described as normal. The "normal primitive" comes largely from the foreign-born and black populations. Their lives are characterized by impoverished economic conditions which, as with their behavior, may be described as "primitive." Occupational achievements center around unskilled, menial labor, and these careers are often sporadic. *Educational levels are minimal and testing indicates borderline to low-average intelligence. While the children of the foreign-born do acclimate to a less "primitive" existence, the offspring of the black population seem unaffected by improved educational and social opportunities.*
>
> The personality characteristics of the "normal primitive" are childlike or juvenile, the behavior and attitude of being similar to that of an eight- to twelve-year-old boy. At the same time, acceptance as a man by this group is very important. In this regard, the "normal primitive" is sensitive and takes offense to any question of his masculinity.
>
> Interaction among such individuals often occurs in bars where arguments readily result in aggressive encounters. Compelled to fight any challenger of his masculinity or courage, the "normal primitive" protects himself by carrying a lethal weapon.
>
> In summary:
>
> The primitive man is comfortable and without mental illness. He has little, if any, education and is of dull intelligence. His goals are sensual and immediate—satisfying his physical and sexual needs without inhibition, postponement or planning. There is little regard for the future extending hardly beyond the filling of his stomach and the next payday or relief check. His loyalties and identifications are with a group that has little purpose in life, except surviving with a minimum of sweat and a maximum of pleasure. He has the ten-year-old boy's preoccupation with prowess and "being a man." Unfortunately, he lacks the boy's external restraint and supervision so that he is more or less an intermittent community problem and responsibility. (Cited by Swigert and Farrell 1977, p. 19; emphasis in original)

Swigert and Farrell found that this conception of the normal primitive had significant consequences for the assignment of public counsel, denial of bail, and a plea of guilt before the judge. The lack of legal resources resulted in more severe sanctions awarded by the court. Swigert and Farrell, however, did not control for race of the victim as a factor in the punishment.[5] I propose that the conception they describe is characteristic of the beliefs of many public officials, including police, public defenders, prosecutors, judges, and others in the criminal justice system. It is also evident among the larger public. Variants of this theme are found in social scientific theory. I suggest further that this conception of the etiology of criminal violence and the characteristics of typical offenders and victims represents a substantial, but often unacknowledged, barrier for assaultive violence and homicide prevention efforts, especially among blacks.

Swigert and Farrell's study (1977) and my own earlier work (1983) have suggested that the normal primitive criminal conception is quite similar to and may have some of the same flaws and consequences as the popular social scientific description of members of the subculture of violence. Such descriptions can be found in the earlier work of Pittman and Handy (1964) and Wolfgang and Ferracuti (1967). Such descriptions undoubtedly reflect a sincere effort on the part of social researchers to provide some explanation, albeit largely based on description, for the extremely high rates of violence among certain segments of the population. But there are problems caused by this form of explanation. One is a conclusion by researchers that to the extent that violence results from social values, it is predictable and more or less normal among persons within certain subcultural groupings, such as blacks and lower-class whites. Swigert and Farrell (1977) argue that such subcultural explanations may be largely a function of the effectiveness with which the stereotype of the violent criminal has been applied by the legal system. But in most instances, the view of violence as normal among blacks leads to the same pattern of official response that has been linked to the devalued status of blacks: less intervention and punishment.

Bernstein, Kelly, and Doyle (1977) reported an unexpected finding in their study of felony sentencing in New York State. White defendants, as well as defendants who had been employed for longer periods of time, were more severely sentenced than nonwhites and persons who were unemployed or employed for shorter periods. In interviews, Bernstein, Kelly, and Doyle found that the judges and prosecutors who handled the cases assumed that nonwhites commit crimes because their subculture accepts such behavior; hence offenses of nonwhites seemed less pernicious to them. Their expectations for white defendants, on the other hand, were higher and failure to meet such expectations appeared more noxious—thus, the more severe sanction (1977, p. 753).

In a similar vein, I have suggested (1983, pp. 426-427) that the official view of violent behavior as normal among blacks, especially among lower-class blacks, also affects the etiology of black homicide. Violent behavior of all types is considered normal among such persons and therefore ultimately unpreventable; hence the police, who are repeatedly called upon to investigate incidences of violent behavior within the black community, make few efforts at prevention. The view of the normality of violence among blacks affects both punishment and intervention and prevention efforts. As in the instance of devalued lives, this view is perhaps best illustrated by looking at the attitudes and behavior of the police.

Police and other law enforcement agents often are able to pinpoint high-crime blocks and neighborhoods. They may also believe that they are able to identify individuals or types of individuals who commit or are perceived to commit acts of criminal violence. In fact, since police perceptions of crime often greatly influence defense and prosecutorial decision making, Swigert and Farrell's clinic description of the normal primitive may be largely a restatement of police views of the homicidal criminal. Police views of the typical assault and homicide offender are remarkably similar to the clinical description. Police perceptions may be accurate descriptions of reality in some cases, but in others, they may merely reflect biases found in the larger society.[6] In addition, their views often reflect more directly a kind of "those people will always do that sort of thing" sentiment that is only implicit in Swigert and Farrell's clinical description and in the ideas of subculture of violence theorists. Such a remedying of these larger societal problems is seen as necessary before criminal violence can be successfully prevented or reduced. They often question the effectiveness of remedial approaches to violence prevention that do not address these larger societal causal factors. There is much validity to such an approach, but the result is sometimes a conclusion that little, if anything, can be done to prevent violence among deprived groups in American society as it is currently structured. Another result is that whites and the middle class are considered more likely targets of intervention than blacks and the lower class.

I believe that to a large extent, the ideological currents I have described characterize the thinking and actions of many of the government officials, practitioners, and social researchers who are attempting to address the problem of assaultive violence and homicide among the poor and blacks in the United States. Thus a view of the inevitability and unpreventability of violence among certain population groups is part of the ideological baggage many people bring to discussions of violence prevention. That set of values is as much a part of American society as is the excessive violence among certain subgroups in the population at which current prevention efforts are directed. Indeed the view that violence among blacks is unpreventable has been a common theme in public discourse and social scientific writings for more than a century.[7]

New Themes, Old Conclusions

It may be argued that many would-be intervenors in family violence among blacks today have disavowed racist perceptions of the devalued black victim and the normality of black violence. Rather than blame the victim, they highlight the social structural conditions under which blacks live in the United States: poverty, inequality, racism, deprivation, and similar factors in the genesis of criminal violence among blacks.[8] The problem with such extreme emphasis on these factors is that adherents believe that these larger societal problems must be remedied before criminal violence can be successfully prevented or reduced. There is much validity to such an approach, but the result is sometimes a conclusion that little, if anything, can be done to prevent violence among deprived groups in American society as it is currently structured. Another result is that whites and the middle class are seen as more likely targets of intervention than blacks and the lower class.

In summary the prevention and reduction of family violence within the black community may be impeded by the following kinds of ideologically based barriers:

1. The devalued status of the black victim and the view that violence is normal among blacks are reflected in a pattern of unequal legal response to black and white victims of violence.
2. This unequal treatment by police, judicial officials, and others is not only evidence of the devalued status of the black victim of violence; it may also contribute to further violence. To the extent that commonly occurring acts of minor violence are not investigated and major acts of intraracial violence go unpunished, patterns of vigilantism may emerge among blacks. Some evidence suggests that this may be a factor contributing to the high rates of violence in the black community.
3. The idea that violence is more or less normal, and hence inevitable, within the black community may affect the behavior of many potential intervenors outside the legal arena. If social service personnel, public health officials, counselors, and others share this view of black criminality, they may believe that their intervention efforts are futile and instead aim their work at the middle class and whites rather than lower-class blacks.
4. The belief that a high rate of violence among blacks is inevitable and normal is partly grounded in racial stereotype. It is also

a product of observations made by social scientists who have sought to explain disproportionate levels of violence within the black community. These social scientific conceptions, as well as racial bias, often are used to support conclusions that the prevention of violence among blacks will be largely unsuccessful absent major changes in the political economy or black subcultural values.

Preventing Black Family Violence

The devalued status of blacks in the United States is well documented, as are continuing perceptions of the normality of violence within the black community. Both ideological currents have relevance for the protection afforded black victims of violence and also for the successful reduction of rates of violence among blacks. Since a disproportionate amount of such violence occurs with the home, these ideological barriers have particular relevance for efforts to prevent family violence.

Historically black women and children have been afforded less protection from abuse within the family than any other groups within American society. White women and children have also been underprotected but much less so than blacks. Unless persisting ideological constraints are confronted and challenged, increasing official intervention in domestic violence will merely result in an unequal race-of-victim-based pattern of intervention similar to that found in the handling of nonfamily criminal violence. That is, black and poor victims of family violence may be ignored and most prevention efforts targeted at the white middle class. The avoidance of this kind of pattern may rest on careful consideration of the following kinds of concerns.

First, the greater frequency of homicide within the black community or among the poor in general does not itself suggest that such behavior is more normative or accepted. Homicide is still relatively infrequent even among poor blacks and represents an unacceptable form of behavior, as it does in other groupings within U.S. society or in other societies.

Second, homicide and other forms of violent behavior are preventable to a large extent, as a number of researchers have suggested (Wolfgang and Ferracuti 1967; Allen 1980; Hawkins 1983, 1984). Since a large proportion of homicides among blacks occurs among family members, the prevention and reduction of black family violence must be a top priority given present concern for the reduction of black homicide.

Finally, a promising form of prevention may focus on research and policies that consider situational aspects of the genesis of crime. These largely involve the design, management, or manipulation of the immediate environment in order to reduce opportunities for crime and to increase risks of detection (see Clarke 1983). These strategies of intervention place less emphasis on individual motives and malevolence or social structural factors and more emphasis on more manipulatable aspects of the social environment.

Notes

1. Explanations for the devalued status of blacks that emphasize the political economy may be extremely useful for providing a historical perspective. For instance, during slavery, blacks were valuable property. Landowners frequently intervened to stop the execution for capital crimes of slaves whom they owned. It was only after state legislatures passed laws providing for the reimbursement of owners for executed slaves that such intervention subsided (Higginbotham 1978). Under these circumstances, the lives of slaves were valuable. Nevertheless, there is considerable evidence that black-on-black offenses were more leniently treated than black-on-white offenses during slavery. After slavery ended, blacks became a surplus population to a large extent, and their lives became much less valuable to white authorities.

2. Most of the discussion in this chapter addresses the problem of the devaluation of black life as it is evidenced in official decision making within formal organizations. Of course, the cheapening of black life in American society is a product of the larger system of value. Evidence can be found in a variety of social settings and

throughout much of the history of the United States. A major contributor to (or reflection of) the devalued status of blacks has been the criminal law itself. Although the race-of-victim effects described in this chapter are due to extralegal sources of bias, during slavery the criminal law itself provided for differential punishment based on the race of the offender and victim. For instance, Magnum (1940) and Higginbotham (1978) note that in the antebellum South and North, statutes provided harsher penalties for certain crimes when committed by blacks than when committed by whites. Other laws made certain acts crimes only if they were perpetrated by blacks. Thus, it may be argued that the findings of Johnson (1941) and subsequent investigations merely reflect a continuation of historical patterns.

3. Researchers have not generally made such racial comparisons. That is, they have not categorized homicides as domestic versus nondomestic to ascertain levels of punishment by race. This has been partly due to small sample sizes in some studies. Nevertheless, the findings of Johnson (1941) and others would support an expectation of racial differences in the punishment of domestic homicides, as well as homicides committed against nonfamily.

4. That is, blacks are acutely aware of the double standard for the punishment of crime based on the race of the victim. A similar concern for this phenomenon is shown in black folklore. Charles Owens (1977, p. 3) cites a black folktale, "A Fine for Killing Two Negroes," from the work of Dorson (1967), as representative of black views of the low value of black life in the United States.

5. While Swigert and Farrell (1977) found that the conception of the normal primitive led to a more punitive response, they failed to distinguish between intraracial and interracial offenders. As the studies of racial disparities in sentencing show, blacks are likely to be treated more leniently when they kill other blacks.

6. Kephart (1957, pp. 88-93) reported that in a survey of police officers in Philadelphia, 75 percent overestimated the actual percentage of arrests involving blacks made in the districts to which they were assigned.

7. Immediately after the Civil War and well into the twentieth century, high rates of black crime, including homicide, were cited by some writers as proof of the genetic and/or social depravity of the black race; see Otken (1894).

8. For example, there have appeared several radical critiques of subcultural theorizing in recent years. Foremost among those providing such critiques have been researchers labeled as conflict theorists. In addition, some researchers have begun to explain high rates of black homicide and other violence by using models that describe the "internal colonialism" that characterizes the conditions under which blacks in the United States live. These more social structure-oriented explanations are important advances but still leave unresolved some of the problems of homicide prevention.

References

Allen, Nancy H. 1980. *Homicide: Perspectives on Prevention.* New York: Human Sciences Press.

Attorney General's Task Force on Family Violence. 1984. Washington, D.C.: Department of Justice.

Baldus, David C., Charles Pulaski, and George Woodworth. 1983. "Comparative Review of Death Sentences: An Empirical Study of the Georgia Experience." *Journal of Criminal Law and Criminology* 74(Fall):661-753.

Banton, Michael. 1964. *The Policeman in the Community.* London: Tavistock.

Bard, Morton. 1969. "Family Intervention Police Teams as a Community Mental Health Resource." *Journal of Criminal Law, Criminology and Police Sentence* 60, no. 2:247-250.

Berk, Sarah F., and Donileen R. Loseke. 1981. " 'Handling' Family Violence: Situational Determinants of Police Arrest in Domestic Disturbances." *Law and Society Review* 15, no. 2:315-346.

Bernstein, Ilene Nagel, William R. Kelly, and Patricia A. Doyle. 1977. "Societal Reaction to Deviants: The Case of Criminal Defendants." *American Sociological Review* 42(October):743-755.

Brearly, H.C. 1932. *Homicide in the United States.* Chapel Hill: University of North Carolina Press.

Calvert, R. 1974. "Criminal and Civil Liability in Husband-Wife Assaults." In *Violence in the Family,* pp. 88-90. Edited by S. Steinmetz and M. Straus. New York: Harper & Row.

Centers for Disease Control. 1983. *Homicide Surveillance Summary: 1970-78.* Atlanta, Ga.: Violence Epidemiology Branch, Center for Health Promotion and Education, Public Health Service, U.S. Department of Health and Human Services.

Clarke, Ronald V. 1983. "Situational Crime Prevention: Its Theoretical Basis and Practical Scope." In *Crime and Justice: An Annual Review of Research,* 4:225-256. Edited by Michale Tonry and Norval Morris. Chicago: University of Chicago Press.

Curtis, Lynn A. 1975. *Violence, Race and Culture.* Lexington, Mass.: Lexington Books.

Davison, T. 1978. *Conjugal Crime: Understanding and Changing the Wifebeating Pattern.* New York: Hawthorne Books.

Dennis, Ruth E. 1979. "The Role of Homicide in Decreasing Life Expectancy." In *Lethal Aspects of Urban Violence.* Edited by Harold M. Rose. Lexington, Mass.: Lexington Books.

Dexter, Lewis Anthony. 1958. "A Note on Selective Inattention in Social Science." *Social Problems* 61 (Fall):176-182.

Dobash, R.E., and R. Dobash. 1979. *Violence against Wives.* New York: Free Press.

Dorson, Richard. 1967. *American Negro Folktales.* Greenwich, Conn.: Fawcett Publications.

Dunn, Christopher S. 1976. *The Patterns and Distributions of Assault Incidence Characteristics Among Social Areas.* Analytic Report 14, Law Enforcement Assistant Administration, National Criminal Justice Information and Statistics Service. Washington, D.C.: Government Printing Office.

Farley, Reynolds. 1980. "Homicide Trends in the United States." *Demography* 17(May):177-88.

Field, Martha H., and Henry F. Field. 1973. "Marital Violence and the Criminal Process: Neither Justice nor Peace." *Social Science Review* 47(June):221-240.

Garfinkel, Harold. 1949. "Research Note on Inter- and Intra-racial Homicides." *Social Forces* 27:369-381.

Gelles, R. 1980. "Violence in the Family: A Review of Research in the Seventies." *Journal of Marriage and the Family* 42(December):873-885.

———. 1982. "Domestic Criminal Violence." In *Criminal Violence,* pp. 201-235. Edited by Marvin E. Wolfgang and Neil Alan Weiner. Beverly Hills: Sage.

Hawkins, Darnell F. 1983. "Black and White Homicide Differentials: Alternatives to an Inadequate Theory." *Criminal Justice and Behavior* 10(December):407-440.

———. 1984. "Sociological Research and the Prevention of Homicide Among Blacks." Paper prepared for the Black Homicide/Mental Health Workshop, Washington, D.C., June 14-16.

———. 1985. "Black Homicide: The Adequacy of Existing Research for Devising Prevention Strategies." *Crime and Delinquency* 31(January):83-103.

Higginbotham, A. Leon. 1978. *In the Matter of Color-Race and the American Legal Process: The Colonial Period.* New York: Oxford University Press.

Johnson, Guy B. 1941. "The Negro and Crime." *Annals of the American Academy of Political Science* 217: 93-104.

Kephart, William M. 1957. *Racial Factors and Urban Law Enforcement.* Philadelphia: University of Pennsylvania Press.

Kleck, Gary. 1981. "Racial Discrimination in Criminal Sentencing: A Critical Evaluation of the Evidence with Additional Evidence on the Death Penalty." *American Sociological Review* 46(December):783-805.

LaFree, Gary. 1980. "The Effect of Sexual Stratification by Race on Official Reactions to Rape." *American Sociological Review* 45:842-854.

Langley, R., and R.C. Levy. 1977. *Wife Beating: The Silent Crisis.* New York: E.P. Dutton.

Levi, Ken. 1980. "Homicide as Conflict Resolution." *Deviant Behavior* 1(April-September):281-307.

Lundsgaarde, Henry P. 1977. *Murder in Space City: A Cultural Analysis of Houston Homicide Patterns.* New York: Oxford University Press.

Magnum, Charles. 1940. *The Legal Status of the Negro.* Chapel Hill: University of North Carolina Press.

Myers, Martha A. 1979. "Offended Parties and Official Reactions: Victims and the Sentencing of Criminal Defendants." *Sociological Quarterly* 20:529-540.

Myrdal, Gunnar. 1944. *An American Dilemma.* New York: Pantheon.

Otken, Charles H. 1894. *The Ills of the South.* New York: G.P. Putnam's Sons.

Owens, Charles E. 1977. "What Price Justice." Introduction to *Blacks and Criminal Justice.* Edited by Charles E. Owens and Jimmy Bell. Lexington, Mass.: Lexington Books.

Parnas, R. 1967. "The Police Response to Domestic Disturbance." *Wisconsin Law Review* 1967:914-960.

Paternoster, Raymond. 1983. "Race of Victim and Location of Crime: The Decision to Seek the Death Penalty in South Carolina." *Journal of Criminal Law and Criminology* 74:754-785.

Peterson, Ruth D., and John Hagan. 1984. "Changing Conceptions of Race and Sentencing Outcomes." *American Sociological Review* 49(February):56-70.

Pittman, D.J., and W. Hardy. 1964. "Patterns in Criminal Aggravated Assault." *Journal of Criminal Law, Criminology, and Police Science* 56(December): 488-497.

Radbill, S. 1980. "Children in a World of Violence: A History of Child Abuse." In *The Battered Child,* pp. 3-20. 2d ed. Edited by R. Helfer and C. Kempe. Chicago: University of Chicago Press.

Radelet, Michael L. 1981. "Racial Characteristics and the Imposition of the Death Penalty." *American Sociological Review* 46(December):918-927.

Rose, Harold M. 1978. "The Geography of Despair." *Annals of the Association of American Geographers* 68:453-464.

———. 1981. *Black Homicide and the Urban Environment.* U.S. Department of Health and Human Services, National Institute of Mental Health. Washington, D.C.: Government Printing Office.

Roy, M., ed. 1977. *Battered Women.* New York: Van Nostrand Reinhold.

Ryan, William. 1971. *Blaming the Victim.* New York: Pantheon.

Shin, Yongsock, Davor Jedlicka, and Everett S. Lee. 1977. "Homicide among Blacks." *Phylon* 38(December):398-407.

Silberman, Charles E. 1978. *Criminal Violence-Criminal Justice: Criminals Police, Courts, and Prisons in America.* New York: Random House.

Star, B. 1980. "Patterns of Family Violence." *Social Casework* 61(June):339-346.

Stark, R., and J. McEvoy. 1970. "Middle Class Violence." *Psychology Today* 4(November):52-65.

Straus, Murray A. 1974. Foreword to *The Violent Home: A Study of Physical Aggression between Husbands and Wives* by R.J. Gelles. Beverly Hills: Sage.

Straus, Murray A., R.J. Gelles, and S.K. Steinmetz. 1980. *Behind Closed Doors: Violence in the American Family.* Garden City, N.Y.: Doubleday, Anchor Books.

Sudnow, David. 1965. "Normal Crimes: Sociological Features of the Penal Code in a Public Defender Office." *Social Problems* 12(Winter):255-276.

Swigert, Victoria, and Ronald A. Farrell. 1977. "Normal Homicides and the Law." *American Sociological Review* 42(February):16-32.

U.S. Department of Health and Human Services. 1980. Public Health Service. Office of Health Research, Statistics and Technology. National Center for Health Statistics. National Center for Health Services Research. *Health United States: 1980.* 1981. DHHS Publication (PHS)81-1232. Washington, D.C.: Government Printing Office.

———. 1981. *Public Health Reports.* Washington, D.C.: U.S. Government Printing Office.

Wolfgang, Marvin, and Franco Ferracuti. 1967. *The Subculture of Violence: Towards an Integrated Theory in Criminology.* London: Tavistock.

Wolfgang, Marvin, Franco Ferracuti, and Marc Riedel. 1973. "Race, Judicial Discretion, and the Death Penalty." *Annals of the American Academy of Political and Social Science* 407:119-133.

Zimring, Franklin E., Joel Eigen, and Sheila O'Malley. 1976. "Punishing Homicide in Philadelphia: Perspectives on the Death Penalty." *University of Chicago Law Review* 43:227-252.

15

INTRODUCTION

The Honorable Lee P. Brown was elected mayor of Houston, Texas, in 1997. Prior to that, Mayor Brown had served as chief of the city's police department between 1982 and 1990. In the interim, he served as police commissioner in New York City and as director of the White House Office of National Drug Control Policy during President Clinton's administration. Mayor Brown is one of the first African Americans to earn a doctorate in criminology. Both his master's degree and his dissertation were on police-community relations. He received his doctorate degree in 1970 from the University of California at Berkeley, where he studied under Joseph Lohman and Gordon Misner. Mayor Brown also has had an interesting and influential career in law enforcement that began in the San Jose, California, police department in 1960. In 1966, he developed the agency's police-community relations unit. During the next three decades, Brown served as the chief/director of several police departments, president of the International Association of Chiefs of Police, and the National Organization of Black Police Executives and is still nationally and internationally recognized for his expertise and contributions to policing.

As chief of police in Houston, Texas, Brown was instrumental in establishing community policing often referred to as neighborhood-oriented policing. This article describes the development and evolution of community policing in Houston from a few programs to a department-wide philosophy. The article also provides an overview of traditional policing, as well as research during the 1970s and 1980s that challenged traditional policing, and distinguishes community policing from it. More important, Brown defines community policing, identifies its major components, and describes its benefits. The article concludes with several questions about community policing that are still relevant today.

COMMUNITY POLICING
A Practical Guide for Police Officials

LEE P. BROWN
Houston Police Department, Texas

Like many other social institutions, American police departments are responding to rapid social change and emerging problems by rethinking their basic strategies. In response to problems such as crime, drugs, fear and urban decay, the police have begun experimenting with new approaches to their tasks.

Among the most prominent new approaches is the concept of community policing. Viewed from one perspective, it is not a new concept; indeed, the principles can be traced back to some of policing's oldest traditions.

What is new is the idea that community policing is not a particular program within a department, but instead should become the dominant philosophy throughout the department. Exactly what it means for community policing to become a department-wide philosophy and how a police executive can shift an organization from a more traditional philosophy to a community-policing philosophy has been unclear.

Our experience in Houston is beginning to clarify these issues. We are developing a concrete picture of what it means to operate a police department committed to a philosophy of community policing. We have also learned how to manage the process of evolution towards a philosophy of community policing. And we are learning how the basic administrative and managerial systems of the department must be changed to accommodate and encourage community policing. The purpose of this article is to make this experience available to the field, and to give concrete, operational content to what are otherwise mere abstractions and possibilities.

THE ORIGINS OF COMMUNITY POLICING

Houston's interest in community policing as an overall philosophy of policing did not

Brown, L.P. (1989). Community policing: A practical guide for police officials. Reprinted from *The Police Chief, 56*(8).

spring full-blown from any one person's mind. Instead, it has emerged from the evolution of police thought. That police leaders are challenging the assumptions they have held for several decades should not be construed as an attempt to debunk all that has worked well for many years. Rather, the rethinking should be seen as a sign of police leaders' commitment to ensuring that the strategies they adopt will be viable not only now but in the future as well. Only by refining what works well and scrapping or reshaping what no longer meets the community's needs can police departments confront the problems and deliver the services that citizens deserve and expect.

The evolution to community policing is not complete. What is commonly called traditional policing remains this country's dominant policing style. From its introduction in the 1930s through the 1970s, when it reached its peak of popularity, traditional policing has developed a number of identifying characteristics, such as the following:

- The police are reactive to incidents. The organization is driven by calls for police service.
- Information from and about the community is limited. Planning efforts focus on internally generated police data.
- Planning is narrow in focus, centering on internal operations—policies, procedures, rules and regulations.
- Recruitment focuses on the spirit of adventure rather than the spirit of service.
- Patrol officers are restrained in their role. They are not encouraged or expected to be creative in addressing problems and are not rewarded for undertaking innovative approaches.
- Training is geared toward the law enforcement role of the police, even though officers spend only 15 to 20 percent of their time on such activities.
- Management uses an authoritative style and adheres to the military model of command and control.
- Supervision is control-oriented, as it reflects and reinforces the organization's management style.
- Rewards are associated with participating in daring events rather than conducting service activities.
- Performance evaluations are based not on outcomes but on activities. The number of arrests made and the number of citations issued are of paramount importance.
- Agency effectiveness is based on data—particularly crime and clearance rates—from the FBI's Uniform Crime Reports.
- Police departments operate as entities unto themselves, with few collaborative links to the community.

For 40 years, traditional policing ostensibly served the public well, primarily because it was seen as a marked improvement over the policing style it had replaced—one that was characterized by negative political control and widespread corruption. Traditional policing gave citizens a false sense of security about police officers' ability to ensure the safety of the community.

The realization that it might not be as effective as it seemed came into sharp focus by the middle 1960s and early 70s, when riots and protests exploded across America and probing questions were raised about the apparent inability of the police to prevent—or at least control—such outbreaks.

It became increasingly clear that neither elected officials nor the public knew much about the police and their operations. The situation called for decisive action and led to the formation of a number of commissions to examine the events surrounding the riots and offer recommendations for improving police operations. The commissions' discussions included topics ranging from violence in cities and on college campuses to criminal justice standards and goals.

The attempts to remedy what was seen as an intolerable situation, however, were not confined to meeting room discussions. Massive amounts of money for police operations and research were funneled through the federal Law Enforcement Assistance Administration as part of the government's response to the concern.

Fortunately for the police profession, the 1970s fostered a full-scale attempt to analyze a host of policing issues. The extensive research effort, which continued into the 1980s, produced findings that prompted many thoughtful police professionals to rethink how best to use police resources. Some of the more significant findings are described below:[1]

1. Increasing the number of police officers does not necessarily reduce the incidence of crime nor increase the proportion of crimes that are solved. The relationship that does exist is between crime and adverse social conditions, such as poverty, illiteracy, illegal drugs, unemployment, population density and social heterogeneity.

2. Random patrol produces inconsistent results. It does not necessarily reduce crime nor enhance an officer's chances of apprehending a criminal suspect. Neither does it bring the police closer to the public or reduce citizens' fear of crime. The use of foot patrols (a popular tactic of community policing), on the other hand, has been shown to reduce the fear of crime, though not necessarily the actual *number* of crimes that are committed.

3. The assignment of one officer per patrol car is just as effective and just as safe as the assignment of two officers per car. The number of crimes committed does not rise, and the number of criminals apprehended does not fall when officers patrol solo. Nor do officers face a greater risk of injury or death when they travel alone.

4. Saturation patrol reduces crime by temporarily suppressing the illegal activities or displacing them to other areas.

5. Seldom do patrol officers encounter a serious crime in progress.

6. Rapid response is not as important as previously believed because there generally is an extended delay before citizens call the police. A rapid police response is important only in the small percentage of cases where a life is being threatened or apprehension of the suspect is possible. Citizens are satisfied instead with a predetermined response time upon which they can depend. For incidents that are minor and do not require an officer's presence at the scene, citizens are satisfied with alternative methods, such as having the incident report taken over the telephone.

7. Criminal investigations are not as successful as previously believed. Because crimes are more likely to be resolved if the suspect is apprehended immediately or a witness can either supply the person's name, address or license-plate number or recognize him in a photograph, successful investigations occur when the suspect is known and when corroborating evidence can be obtained for arrest and prosecution. A key source of information about crimes and criminal suspects is the public.

Additional proof—beyond the reams of data generated by researchers—that time-honored policing strategies were ineffective came in the form of a widespread fear of crime among citizens, record-high crime rates and record-high prison populations, despite the availability of more officers and more funds for law enforcement efforts. As a result, progressive police administrators soon began to question the efficacy of traditional policing strategies. Their review of the situation heralded the beginning of an incremental transition to community-oriented programs and thus the beginning of Phase I of community policing.

From Programs to Style

The growing awareness of the limitations of the traditional model of policing stimulated police departments across America to experiment with new approaches to reducing crime, stilling fears, improving police-community relations and restoring community confidence in the police. For the most part, these experiments were conceived and executed as discrete programs within traditional departments. That is, the programs were typically initiated as a response to a particular problem and involved only a small fraction of the organization. They were time-limited, explicitly identified as experiments and subject to particularly close scrutiny by researchers. Often the programs had their own champions and command structures within the departments.

Examples of these programs include the foot patrol experiments in Newark, New Jersey, and Flint, Michigan; the problem-solving project in Newport News, Virginia; the fear reduction programs in Houston, Texas, and Newark; the Community Patrol Officer Program in New York City; the Directed Area Responsibility Team experiment in Houston; the community-policing experiment in Santa Ana, California; the Basic Car Plan and Senior Lead-Officer programs in Los Angeles; and the Citizen-Oriented Police Enforcement program in Baltimore County, Maryland.

Often these programs had a curious fate. They were begun with great fanfare, they produced important results and then they faded within the departments that had initiated them. These programs—and their fates—constituted Phase I of the field's experience with community policing. They taught two important lessons.

First, taken together, the programs pointed toward some new frontiers for policing. They taught the field that if it viewed incidents as emerging from problems, this opened up new avenues for contributing to the solutions of the underlying problems. They taught that fear was an important problem in its own right, and there were things that police departments could do to reduce fear quite apart from reducing actual criminal victimization. Finally, they taught that the community could be an important partner in dealing with the problems of crime fear and drugs, and that to build that partnership with the community, the police had to find more effective ways of interacting and responding to their needs. These basic ideas provided the intellectual foundations for the emerging new conceptions of community policing.

Second, the ultimate demise of many of the programs showed the difficulty of trying to operate programs that embodied some of the important principles of community policing in the context of organizations whose administrative systems and managerial styles were designed for more traditional models of policing. It seemed clear that if the field as a whole or any police department within the field were to succeed in implementing community policing, it would have to be as an overall philosophy of the department.

The Development of Community Policing in Houston

Houston took these lessons to heart. Though tempted by the potential of community policing, the department worried about the tendency of individual programs to collapse after they had been operating for a while. It was also hard to see how one could move from a department committed to traditional policing to a department that had adopted community policing as a philosophy. Our solution to these problems was to follow the experience of the field and to understand that the implementation of community policing in Houston would also have to have two phases.

Phase I of community policing is the implementation of programs designed to provide the public with meaningful ways to participate in policing efforts. The initial phase *does not* require a complete change in the organization's operating style. Phase II, on the other hand, *does* require the organization to make such a change.

Because Phase I involves only the implementation of individual programs, the systems that support the organization's policing style—such as recruitment, training, performance evaluation, rewards and discipline—do not change. In other words, the individual programs are separate entities that do not involve the entire department or affect the entire community.

Phase II, however, involves more sweeping changes. It is not merely programs that are being implemented—it is the department's *style* that is being revamped. Unlike individual programs, style affects the entire department and the entire community.

The Houston Police Department evolved from Phase I to Phase II over a five-year period starting in 1982. The department operated under a set of values that emphasized problem solving and collaboration with the community. It also redesigned its patrol beats to reflect natural neighborhood boundaries. Most important, though, were its experiments with a variety of community-oriented programs that resulted in greater community involvement with the department.

At the end of the five-year evolutionary period, the department made an organizational commitment to adopt community policing as its dominant operating style. The department's experiences during Phase I were invaluable and made the transition to Phase II much easier, for the individual programs enabled the department to accomplish the following:[2]

- break down barriers to change;
- educate its leaders and rank-and-file members on the merits of community policing;
- reassure the rank-and-file that the community policing concepts being adopted had not been imported from outside the department but instead were an outgrowth of programs already in place;
- address problems on a small scale before making the full transition to community policing;
- reduce the likelihood that members of the department would reject the concepts of community policing as "foreign" or not appropriate for the department and the community;
- demonstrate to the public and elected officials the benefits of community policing;
- provide a training ground for community policing concepts and strategies;
- create advocates among those persons who would become community-policing trainers; and
- demonstrate its willingness to experiment with new ideas.

Based on Houston's experience, it is clear that organizations that have not operated Phase I community-policing programs will have to begin Phase II with a clear understanding of what community policing is and how it differs from traditional policing.

Although it is an operating style, community policing is also a philosophy of policing that contains several interrelated components. All are essential to the community-policing concept and help distinguish it from traditional policing.

Results vs. process. The first component of the community-policing philosophy is an orientation toward problem solving. Embracing the pioneering work of Herman Goldstein,[3] community policing focuses on results as well as process. Incorporated into routine operations are the techniques of problem identification, problem analysis, and problem resolution.

Values. Community policing also relies heavily on the articulation of policing values that incorporate citizen involvement in matters that directly affect the safety and quality of neighborhood life. The culture of the police department therefore becomes one that not only recognizes the merits of community involvement but also seeks to organize and manage departmental affairs in ways that are consistent with such beliefs.

Accountability. Because different neighborhoods have different concerns, desires and priorities, it is necessary to have an adequate understanding of what is important to a particular neighborhood. To acquire such an understanding, officers must interact routinely with residents and keep them informed of police efforts to fight and prevent neighborhood crime. As the communication continues, a cooperative and mutually beneficial relationship develops between the police and the community. Inherent in this relationship is the requirement that officers keep residents abreast of their activities. This ensures accountability to the community, as well as the department.

Decentralization. The decentralization of authority and structure is another component of community policing. Roles are changed as the authority to participate in the decision-making process expands significantly. The expansion of such authority in turn makes it necessary to alter organizational functions throughout the department.

Power sharing. Responsibility for making decisions is shared by the police and the community after the establishment of a legitimate partnership—one that not only enables but also encourages active citizen involvement in policing efforts. Passive citizen involvement will not suffice. Active participation is essential because citizens possess a vast amount of information that the police can use to solve and prevent neighborhood crime. Power sharing means that the community is allowed to participate in the decision-making process unless the law specifically grants the authority to the police alone.

Beat redesign. Beat boundaries are drawn to coincide with natural neighborhood boundaries, rather than in an arbitrary fashion that meets the needs of the police department. Individual neighborhoods are not placed in multiple beats. If questions arise about the neighborhood to which a citizen belongs, that person is asked to help the police determine the neighborhood with which he identifies.

Permanent assignments. Under community policing, shift and beat assignments are issued on a permanent, rather than a rotating, basis. This allows the beat officer to become an integral part of the community he has been assigned to protect. When a beat officer is reassigned to another area, his replacement is required to participate in an orientation period with the outgoing officer. During this time, the outgoing officer briefs his replacement on the contacts he has made and the knowledge he has gained over the past several months or years, thus providing a continuity of service to the community's citizens.

Empowerment of the beat officers. Rather than simply patrolling the streets, beat officers are encouraged to initiate creative responses to neighborhood problems. To do so, beat officers must become actively involved in the affairs of the community. In addition, they must be given the authority to make decisions as they see fit, based on the circumstances of the situation. This empowerment reflects the trust that police leaders have in their officers' ability to make appropriate decisions and to perform their duties in a professional, productive and efficient manner.

Investigations. The premise that neighborhood crime is best solved with information provided by residents is an aspect of community policing that makes it necessary to decentralize the investigative function and focus on neighborhood—or area-specific—investigations. Centralized investigations, however, cannot be eliminated entirely as these are needed to conduct pattern- or suspect-specific citywide investigations. Both levels, despite their different focus, are responsible for developing a knowledge base about crime in their area and for developing and carrying out strategies designed to resolve crime problems. Investigations under community policing, however, are viewed from a problem-solving perspective.[4]

Supervision and management. Under community policing, the role of persons at all levels within the organization changes. For example, the patrol officer becomes the "manager" of his beat, while the first-line supervisor assumes responsibility for facilitating the problem-solving process by training, coaching, coordinating and evaluating the officers under him. Management's role is to support the process by mobilizing the resources needed to address citizen concerns and problems. In carrying out this role, management needs to be both flexible and willing to allow officers to take necessary and reasonable risks in their efforts to resolve neighborhood problems and concerns.

Training. Also changed under community policing are all aspects of officer training. At the recruit level, cadets are given information about the complexities and dynamics of the community and how the police fit into the big picture. Cadet training also helps the future officer develop community-organizing skills, leadership abilities and a problem-solving perspective based on the understanding that such efforts will be more effective if departmental and community resources are used in concert.

Supervisory training, on the other hand, is designed to provide the skills needed to facilitate the problem-solving process. This is accomplished by training officers to solve problems, coordinating officers' activities, planning community-organizing activities and mapping out criminal investigations.

Because they must be the leaders of the changed roles that characterize community policing, management personnel's training includes the further development of leadership skills, including the ability to excite people about the concept of community policing.

Performance evaluation. With the changed roles for all personnel comes the need for a revised system for evaluating officer performance. Rather than simply counting numbers (e.g., number of citations issued, number of arrests made, number of calls handled), determinations of performance quality are based on the officer's demonstrated ability to solve problems and involve the community in the department's crime-fighting efforts. The criterion then becomes the *absence* of incidents such as criminal offenses, traffic accidents and repeat calls-for-service.

Managing calls-for-service. Inherent in the community-policing philosophy is the understanding that all police resources will be managed, organized and directed in a manner that facilitates problem solving. For example, rather than directing a patrol car to each request for police service, alternative response methods are used whenever possible and appropriate. Such alternative techniques include the taking of incident reports over the telephone, by mail, or in person at police facilities; holding lower-priority calls; and having officers make appointments with an individual or a group. The result is more time available for officers to engage in problem-solving and community-organizing activities that lead to improvements in quality of neighborhood life. Equally important, officers will be able to remain in their beats and handle those calls that require an on-scene response.

The Houston Police Department is committed to community policing and is in the process of implementing it under the name "neighborhood-oriented policing." It is a policing style progress that is responsive to the needs of the community and involves the redesigning of roles and functions for all departmental personnel.

One significant role change is that of the beat officer. No longer is his job structured solely around random patrols and rapid response to routine calls-for-service. Officers now are expected to develop innovative ways of solving neighborhood problems. Inherent in this expanded role is the need for increased communication and interaction with the people who live or work in the officer's beat.

For more than a year, the department has been engaged in its version of community policing, resulting in a wealth of experience and insights that can be used to construct a definition of community policing: *an interactive process between the police and the community to mutually identify and resolve community problems.*

Inherent in this definition is a rather dramatic change in the traditional orientation of the police toward the public. The formal separation of the police from the public no longer suffices. What is called for under community policing is the formation of a union between officers and citizens mutually committed to improving the quality of neighborhood life. The formation of such a partnership requires the police to use available resources more effectively and work with the community to resolve problems and prevent and control crime.

When considered in light of the necessary reorientation of management attitudes toward the public, community policing also can be thought of as a *management philosophy.* As such, community policing provides a conceptual framework for directing an array of departmental functions and requires management personnel to do the following:

- ensure cooperative interaction among various departmental functions;
- ensure collaborative interaction between officers and citizens so that a consensus can be reached on what needs to be done to improve the quality neighborhood life;
- integrate the desires and expectations of citizens with the actions taken by the police to identify and address conditions that have a negative effect on the quality of neighborhood life;
- ensure that all actions are designed to produce planned results; and
- begin addressing a number of organizational issues, such as determining the exact nature of management's responsibilities, deciding which activities best enable management to carry out its responsibilities and establishing an accountability system for monitoring progress and documenting results.

The Houston experience has shown that community policing is a better, smarter and more cost-effective means of using police resources, and that a new culture in which officers, supervisors and managers strive to become a part of—and not apart from—the community is needed as well. These findings serve to illustrate the dual nature of community policing. That is, it embodies both an operational philosophy and a management philosophy, and each benefits not only the police but also the community. The benefits to the *community* are as follows:[5]

- *A commitment to crime prevention.* Unlike traditional policing, which focuses on the development of efficient means of reacting to incidents, community policing strives to reaffirm Sir Robert Peel's premise that the basic mission of the police is to prevent crime and disorder.
- *Public scrutiny of police operations.* Because citizens will be involved with the police, they will be exposed to the "what," "why" and "how" of police work. Such involvement is almost certain to prompt critical examinations and discussions about the responsiveness and efficiency of police operations in addressing the community's problems.
- *Accountability to the public.* Until the advent of community policing, officers were accountable for their actions only to police management. Now officers also will be accountable to the public, with whom they have formed a cooperative partnership. Because citizens will be involved in activities such as strategic planning, tactic implementation and policy development, police personnel will need to become more aware of and concerned about the consequences of their actions.
- *Customized police service.* Because police services will be localized, officers will be required to increase their responsiveness to neighborhood problems and citizens' concerns. As police-citizen partnerships are formed and nurtured, the two groups will be better equipped to work together to identify and address problems that affect the quality of neighborhood life. For their part, police officers will develop a sense of obligation

or commitment to resolving neighborhood problems. The philosophy underlying traditional policing does not provide for such a commitment.

- *Community organization.* The degree to which the community is involved in police efforts to address neighborhood problems has a significant bearing on the effectiveness of those efforts. In other words, the success of any crime-prevention strategy or tactic depends on the police and citizens working in concert—not on one or the other carrying the entire load. Citizens therefore must learn what they can do to help themselves and their neighbors. The police, in turn, should take an active role in helping citizens achieve that objective.

The police also realize a number of benefits from community policing, including the following:[6]

- *Greater citizen support.* As citizens spend more time working with the police, they learn more about the police function. Experience has shown that as their knowledge increases, their respect for the police increases as well. This leads, in turn, to greater support for the police. Such support is important not only because it helps officers address issues of community safety, but also because it cultivates the belief that the police honestly care about the people they serve and are willing to work with all citizens in an attempt to address their concerns.
- *Shared responsibility.* Historically, the police have accepted the responsibility for resolving the problem of crime in the community. Under community policing, however, citizens develop a sense of shared responsibility. They come to understand that the police alone cannot eradicate crime from the community—that they too must play an active role in the crime-fighting effort.
- *Greater job satisfaction.* Because officers are able to resolve issues and problems within a reasonable amount of time, they see the results of their efforts fairly quickly. The net result for the officer is enhanced job satisfaction.
- *Better internal relationships.* Communication problems among units and shifts have been a long-standing problem in police agencies. Because community policing focuses on problem solving and accountability, it also enhances communication and cooperation among the various segments of the department that are mutually responsible for addressing neighborhood problems. This shared responsibility facilitates interaction and cooperative relationships among the different groups.
- *Support for organizational change.* The implementation of community policing necessitates a change in traditional policing roles and, in turn, a change in functional responsibilities. Both modifications require a restructuring of the department's organizational structure to ensure the efficient integration of various functions, such as patrol and investigations. The necessary changes include new management systems, new training curricula and delivery mechanisms, a new performance-evaluation system, a new disciplinary process, a new reward system and new ways of managing calls-for-service.

Questions Asked and Answered

In their book, *Community Policing: Issues and Practices Around the World,* David Bayley and Jerome Skolnick urge police leaders to be cautious about the success of community policing. It is advice well taken. The transition from a traditional style of policing to community-oriented style is not easy. It is therefore essential to identify, acknowledge and address any obstacles or legitimate concerns that might impede the transition. Some of the questions most often raised about community policing are discussed below.[7]

Is community policing social work?

Community policing calls for an expansion of the role of the police in that it focuses on problems from the citizens' points of view. Experience has shown that the concerns of citizens often are different from what the police would say they are. For example, before listening to citizens' concerns became routine, officers assumed that the public worried most about major crimes such as rape, robbery and burglary. After talking with the people who live and work in their beat, officers found that the community's main concerns were quality-of-life issues such as abandoned cars and houses, loud noises and rowdy youngsters.

It is for this reason—the need to address citizen concerns—that the role of the police has been expanded. This is not meant to imply, however, that the police are expected to solve the problems by themselves. On the contrary, it means that the police should be able to do at least one of two things: mobilize the community to solve the problem (e.g., organize a neighborhood clean-up program) or enlist the services of the appropriate agency to address the problem (e.g., the city Public Works Department to clear away debris).

Concerns that such activities are akin to social work are ill-founded. The police officer's expanded role does not even come close to meeting the definition of social work. As a profession, social work is an ongoing and often long-term relationship between the social worker and the client. This is in contrast to the short-term, problem-focused relationship that typically develops under community policing.

- *Will community policing result in less safe neighborhoods?*

By any standard, the police working alone have been unable to control crime effectively. Experience has shown that increased citizen involvement results in more efficient crime-control efforts. The success of Neighborhood Watch groups is but one example of the effectiveness of making crime fighting a joint effort. Other programs, such as Crime Stoppers, have led to the solution of many serious offenses. Because community policing includes the public as a full partner in the provision of crime-prevention and crime-fighting services, it stands to reason that public safety will increase rather than decrease.

- *Will officers be reluctant to enforce the law under community policing?*

Among the tenets of community policing is the need to develop a close relationship between beat officers and the people who live and work in that area. In most neighborhoods, only a small percentage of the population commits illegal acts. The goal of community policing is to become a part of the law-abiding majority and thereby develop a partnership to effectively deal with the law-violating minority.

Experience has shown that working closely with the "good" citizens will either displace the "bad" ones or drive them out of the area. It therefore is incorrect to suggest that as the police develop close relationships with the citizens on their beat, law violators will not be arrested.

- *Is community policing soft on crime?*

The police will always have as one of their primary roles the enforcement of laws. Under community policing, police officers not only will have an expanded skills base at their disposal, but also will have access to a previously untapped resource—input from members of the community. The two resources together provide officers with a most effective means of enforcing the laws and should eliminate any concerns that community policing will weaken officers' ability to perform this task. Rather than being soft on crime, community policing is a more effective method for fighting crime.

- *Will community policing result in unequal services to minority communities?*

Because community policing calls for the tailoring of police services to meet the unique needs of each neighborhood, minority communities can expect to receive better, rather than unequal, services. This is not to imply that one community will receive preferential treatment at the expense of another. Rather, it means that each community will receive services that are appropriate to its particular problems, concerns and priorities.

- *Will community policing result in police corruption?*

Experience has not shown or even suggested that community policing leads to corruption. For corruption to arise, there must be a culture ripe for its development, and such certainly is not the case with community policing, with its emphasis on police officer professionalism, expanded discretionary decision-making authority, trust in officers' sound judgment and good intentions, and officers' accountability to law-abiding citizens. This does not mean, however, that the police can ignore their responsibility to detect and respond to corruptive influences and incidents should they occur.

- *Will access to community policing be distributed fairly?*

This question would be appropriate only if community policing were no more than a program; however, it is an overall operating style and philosophy of policing. Nowhere among the tenets of community policing is there anything that would, in and of itself, result in the unequal distribution of services between the poor and the affluent. By its very nature, community policing calls for the appropriate delivery of services to all neighborhoods.

- *Will community policing require more resources?*

Because community policing is an operating style and not a new program, no additional officers are needed. More pertinent is the issue of how the agency's resources will be used. Experience has shown that community policing is a more cost-effective means of using available resources than is traditional policing for two reasons: Community participation in the crime-control function expands the amount of available resources, and the solving of problems (rather than responding again and again to the same ones) makes for a more efficient deployment of combined police and community resources.

- *Is community policing anti-technology?*

The use of "high-tech" equipment and applications is essential to the efficient practice of community policing. Without this technology, officers would find it difficult to provide the level and quality of services the community deserves. Computer-aided dispatching, computers in patrol cars, automated fingerprint systems and on-line offense reporting systems are but a few examples of the pervasiveness of technology in agencies that practice community policing.

- *Will older officers resist community policing?*

Experience with both community-oriented programs and community policing as an operating style has shown that older officers are more likely to accept community policing than are younger officers. The maturation that comes with age plays a significant role in older officers' greater willingness to adopt the new policing style. Research has shown that younger officers tend to become police officers because they are looking for adventure. As officers grow older, they become less interested in action and more interested in providing services.

CONCLUSION

As an operating style, community policing evolves and exists in two phases. Phase I involves the implementation of community-oriented programs designed to improve the ability of the police to address problems such as crime, drugs, fear and urban decay. These programs, however, are not intended to involve all members of the department or all members of the community. Phase I is also marked by a continuity in the organization's operating style and the systems that support it.

Phase II involves significant changes in the police mission and the organization's operational and management philosophies. Because community policing becomes the dominant service-delivery style, the corresponding support systems must change as well.

The transition, however, is not instantaneous; rather, it is evolutionary. An institution that traditionally has delivered services on the basis of time-honored conventional wisdom cannot be expected to easily or quickly adopt a new method of operating.

The phase of community policing in which an agency finds itself should not be used as a criterion for evaluating the agency. Experience has shown, however, that implementing Phase II is easier if the agency has had experience with individual community-oriented programs.

Because community policing is relatively new as a style of policing, questions have been raised about its effectiveness. Any doubts, however, should be put to rest. Experience has shown that community policing as a dominant policing style is a better, more efficient and more cost-effective means of using police resources. In the final analysis, community policing is emerging as the most appropriate means of using police resources to improve the quality of life in neighborhoods throughout the country.

Notes

1. Jerome H. Skolnick and David H. Bayley, *The New Blue Line: Police Innovations in Six American Cities* (New York: The Free Press, 1986), pp. 4-5.
2. See, for example, Lee P. Brown *et al., Developing Neighborhood Oriental Policing in the Houston Police Department* (Arlington, Virginia: International Association of Chiefs of Police, 1988), and Timothy N. Oettmeier and William H. Bieck, *Developing a Policing Style for Neighborhood Oriented Policing: Executive Session #1,* The Houston Police Department, February 1987.
3. Herman Goldstein, "Improving Policing: A Problem-Oriented Approach," *Journal of Crime and Delinquency,* 25 (April 1979), pp. 236-258.
4. Timothy N. Oettmeier and William H. Bieck, *Integrating Investigative Operations Through Neighborhood Oriented Policing: Executive Session #2,* The Houston Police Department, January 1989.
5. Jerome H. Skolnick and David H. Bayley, *Community Policing: Issues and Practices Around the World* (Washington, D.C.: National Institute of Justice, May 1988), pp. 67-70.
6. *Ibid.,* pp. 70-73.
7. *Ibid.,* pp. 81-87.

16

INTRODUCTION

Since 1992, Daniel Georges-Abeyie has been a faculty member at Arizona State University West. He is also very active in Amnesty International USA and serves as the State of Arizona Coordinator for Amnesty International's Program to Abolish the Death Penalty. During the late 1980s, Georges-Abeyie was one of several scholars who challenged the nondiscrimination thesis popularized by William Wilbanks. At the time this article was written, he taught in the School of Criminology at Florida State University. Later, he served as Associate Dean of the School of Criminology. In 1989, Georges-Abeyie served as a consultant to the State of Florida Supreme Court's Racial and Ethnic Bias Study Commission. His writings include a wide range of topics, including arson, Blacks and criminal justice, bombings, terrorism, victimization, and, most recently, capital punishment.

Rarely does an author present concepts that challenge the theoretical approaches in criminology as Georges-Abeyie does in this article. Here he calls attention to the importance of Black ethnic diversity, social distance, the spatial reality of crime, and petit-apartheid. Although all these concepts are not new, they often have been overlooked in contemporary research. Most important, Georges-Abeyie challenges the Black ethnic monolith paradigm, which assumes that one's racial identity equates his or her ethnic identity. He sensitizes the reader to ethnic, religious, and class differences of Blacks that must be taken into consideration when trying to understand and explain crime. He introduces the concept of Black ethnic heterogeneity that is reminiscent of earlier writings (see Work and Moses) that reported the ethnicity (nationality) of White immigrant Americans. Another important concept introduced in this article is *petit-apartheid.* Georges-Abeyie uses this term to describe the informal practices of criminal justice practitioners that Blacks often face, including intimidation, insults, and rude behavior. Recently, petit-apartheid has become the focus of studies of racial profiling, most notably the problem of driving while Black.

Race, Ethnicity, and the Spatial Dynamic

Toward a Realistic Study of Black Crime, Crime Victimization, and Criminal Justice Processing of Blacks

Daniel E. Georges-Abeyie

Data on the disproportionality of minority criminality in general, and Black criminality in particular, are readily available. Federal, state, and local crime reports document the apparent "tendency" for Blacks to be involved in crime and their preponderance in criminal victimization, arrest, and conviction statistics. Jurists such as New York State Supreme Court Justice Bruce Wright, former Detroit Records Court Justice (now Congressman) George W. Crockett, and former Maryland Justice Joseph C. Howard contend that while Blacks are disproportionately included among the ranks of crime perpetrators and victims, justice is not colorblind (see Georges-Abeyie, 1984a; Ware, 1976; Howard, 1967, 1975). That thesis is also shared by Harvard Law Professor Derrick Bell (1973a, 1973b) and scores of other academicians (e.g., Long, Long, Leon, and Weston [1975]; Christianson [1984]; McNeely and Pope [1981], Baldus, Pulaski, and Woodworth [1983], Georges-Abeyie [1984b], and the criminal justice "brain trust" of the United States House of Representatives). However, the thesis of a racially conscious criminal justice system has been challenged, in part by the claims of Rand Corporation social scientist Joan Petersilia (1984, 1985, 1988) and in total by Florida International University's William Wilbanks (1987). Petersilia's 1983 study asserts the following:

1. Minority suspects were more likely than whites to be released after arrest; however, after a felony conviction, minority offenders were more likely than whites to be given longer sentences and to be put in prison instead of jail;
2. In certain states, racial differences in post-sentencing treatment existed in the form of length of sentence served;
3. High post-arrest release rates for minorities do not indicate that police overarrest minorities in proportion to the kind and amount of crime they actually commit;

From George-Abeyie, D. (1989). Race, ethnicity, and the spatial dynamic. *Social Justice*. Reprinted with permission.

4. There are some evident racial differences in criminal motivation, weapons use, and prison behavior, but most are not statistically significant;

5. Controlling for the other major factors that might influence sentencing and time served, we found that minorities receive harsher sentences and serve longer in prison, all other things being equal. However, racial differences in plea bargaining and jury trials may explain some of the differences in length and type of sentence (Georges-Abeyie, 1984b: 27-29).

In a later study on sentencing and parole reform based on certain guidelines, Petersilia (1988) challenges claims that such guidelines discriminate against Blacks. She found that key predictors associated with crime, upon which the guidelines are based, are more prevalent among Blacks than among whites. She concludes that racial disparity, not discrimination is the result. Her study of racial equity in sentencing showed that for certain crimes a higher percentage of Black and Latino offenders were sentenced to prison than were other offenders. It also showed that certain factors could predict whether a person would be placed on probation or sent to prison, as well as the length of term imposed for those offenders who were imprisoned. In California, however, race did not appear to affect sentencing once other legal "cognizable factors" were controlled for.

Wilbanks argues that the U.S. criminal justice system is essentially "race blind" in its "official" processing of Blacks, and that if, or when, race is a factor, the system often operates in a racially biased manner that is less punitive toward the Black offender than toward his/her white counterpart. Thus, Wilbanks rejects what he has labeled the "discrimination thesis," that is, the reality of a systematic, systemic racially discriminatory criminal justice system. The Wilbanks thesis, which is a variant of an earlier thesis put forth by Hindelang (1984), correctly notes disproportionate Black involvement in Federal Bureau of Investigation Part One offenses. Petersilia rightly notes (as does Wilbanks) that "official" criminal justice agency data on the official, formal processing of Blacks might not document discrimination in a "systematic," "systemic" racially conscious manner. The underlying question is: Do the Hindelang/Petersilia/Wilbanks findings further society's comprehension of the dynamic of Black crime perpetration, criminal victimization, and criminal justice agency processing of Black suspects and convicted felons and misdemeanants? Further, does the Hindelang/Petersilia/Wilbanks thesis further comprehension of Black fear of the police, courts, and corrections—especially among low-income Blacks? I think not. In fact, the current array of popular criminological and criminal justice theories fail, for the most part, to offer insight into the dynamic of Black criminality, victimization, and criminal justice processing because they:

1. Lack a social ecological perspective;
2. Too often focus on the formal decision in the processing of Blacks; and
3. Analyze Blacks as an ethnic monolith who are often caught up in a criminal justice system which is really a morass of disjointed, interconnected agencies involving both an informal and formal decision-making process.

Current Criminological/Criminal Justice Theories

A cursory review of popular criminology and criminal justice texts[1] and journals[2] reveals the following as the most popular criminology/criminal justice orientations:

1. Psychological and biological explanations that center on personality traits and inner controls developed through the process of socialization during early childhood (Hirschi, 1969), or criminogenic factors associated with temperament, IQ, and hormonal abnormalities (Wilson and Herrnstein, 1985);

2. Sociological explanations that focus on anomie (Merton, 1968), subculture (including the incongruence of being lower class with middle-class values and aspirations [Cohen, 1955]), techniques of neutralization (Sykes and Matza, 1970), differential opportunity (Cloward and Ohlin, 1960), lower-class valuation (Miller, 1970), economic political power deprivation (Sellin, 1938; Turk, 1971, 1982), differential association (Sutherland and Cressey, 1978), and labeling (Becker, 1963).

What each of these contemporary approaches lacks is:

1. A social-ecological sensitivity cognizant of diverse Black ethnicity, which might result in research that identifies Black ethnic specific rates of offending behavior as well as differentials in the processing of ethnic-specific Black individuals;
2. Differentials in site and situational realities associated with the rates of crime commission within and outside the spatial domain of the black ghetto and the slum-ghetto;
3. Possible differentiation in how the criminal justice system processes Black subjects who reside within (or outside) the varied spatial domain of the Black ghetto and the slum-ghetto.

Race Does Not Equal Ethnicity: Rejection of the Black Ethnic Monolith Paradigm

Wilbanks, Petersilia, Hindelang and others have characterized Black criminality, criminal victimization, and criminal justice processing as if Negroid (i.e., Black) racial identity equates to ethnic homogeneity. Blacks, however, manifest varied ethnic identities, and these varied Black ethnic groups might manifest different rates of criminality and criminal victimization, as well as what Emory Bogardus refers to as "social distance."

In 1926, Bogardus noted the reality and importance of social distance when discussing desired interaction between different ethnic and racial groups. Social distance may be defined as "the degree of closeness or remoteness one desires in interaction with members of a particular group" (Parrillo, 1985: 491). Many factors are involved in the construct of "social distance." They include:

1. The extent of physiognomic, phrenologic, and anatomic difference (skeletal difference), some of which may be viewed as atavisms by the culturally dominant group;
2. Perceived extent of "contributions" to the national development;
3. Perceived extent of cultural and social network differences between minority/out-groups versus majority/in-groups;
4. Perceived threat to the social order;
5. Perceived criminality; and
6. Perceived "intrinsic worth."

Ethnicity and perceived social distance are interconnected; ethnicity affects social distance and social distance may impact perceived "ethnicity." Ethnicity was defined by Gordon (1964) as the intersection of race, nation of origin, and religion (a cultural variable). Thus, a traditional application of Black ethnic identity would be cognizant of Blacks of Caribbean, African, Central and South American origin (e.g., Puerto Rican, Virgin Islands, African American, Dutch Antilles and so on). The parameters of these cultural-social-spatial identities define more than the contours of national origins; they are the nexus of profound cultural variables such as religion.

Thus, one can, and should, be cognizant of Black Puerto Ricans, Cubans, Virgin Islanders, Jamaicans, Africans, African Americans, and others with very different religious traditions (e.g., Protestant, Catholic, Muslim, Baha'i, and Jewish). However, Black ethnic identities are further subdivided by color and hue realities that affect social networking which ranges from informal social clubs and cliques to formal legal arrangements such as marriage. These color and hue realities engender such social classifications as *more no, mulatto, blanco sucio, negro,* and *pardo.* The ethnic divisions in the Cuban American community, such as *Marielitos* and Castro-era refugees, mirror social-cultural-spatial realities which include race, color, and hue. Linguistic production of the terms Continentals (U.S.-born persons of a West Indian and/or Puerto Rican heritage) and Islanders (native-born persons) within these Caribbean cultures amply demonstrates these social realities along the axes of color and ethnicity. These terms have different meanings in the context of West Indian society, in contrast to their use in Puerto Rico. For a West Indian, these terms refer to intraracial, ethnic identities. For a Puerto Rican, these terms are used to distinguish both inter- and intraracial ethnic identities. The Puerto Rican manifestation of this is reflected in underground Puerto Rican organizations such as the U.S.-spawned Armed Forces for National Liberation (FALN) and the *Macheteros,* which originated in Puerto Rico.

African American ethnic identifiers often modify as they elaborate upon the classic tripartite ethnic definition bounded by religion, nation of origin, and race. These identifiers encompass not only color and hue; they also often distinguish individuals along regional and class lines, as well as on a multitude of indigenous factors. Predominately geographic "tags" distinguish, for example, between suburban versus urban origin and rearing; East Coast versus West Coast; Southern versus Northern or Midwestern origin, and even ghetto versus slum-ghetto, or non-ghetto origin and rearing. The ghetto versus slum-ghetto, and/or ghetto versus non-ghetto delineators have undergone further development, which can be described as containing an ethclass dimension. This is an economic dimension, characterized by intergenerational poverty, which might be best described in terms of ethcaste parameters.

Thus, should social distance be significant within and between Black ethnic groups, then is it not possible that social distance between Blacks and whites might impact every phase of the processing of Black ethnics? Is it not also conceivable that different Black ethnic groups are more involved in extralegal and illegal activity than are others, and that certain Black ethnics dominate certain criminal activities (or are believed to) and are thus viewed as more threatening than are other Black ethnics (e.g., Jamaican versus Hispanic, African American versus British West Indian, "dark-skinned" Negroids versus what some Blacks have derisively labeled "high yellas" and "brights")? In fact, social distance may influence perceived ethnicity to the extent that Black law violators are automatically assumed to be of a specific ethnic origin, that is, labeled Jamaican versus Virgin Islander (when an accent is noted), *Marieliro* versus Castro-era Cubano, Afro American versus West Indian, slum-ghetto versus Black suburbanite.

If one can speak of varied white ethnic traditions that include criminal and extralegal behaviors—for example, the criminally violent "Olde" traditions of California's San Joaquin Valley, the "hillbilly" tradition of "moonshining," the "swampbilly" and "swamp rat" traditions of the South Carolina and Georgia lowlands, as well as of the Florida Everglades—then is it not conceivable that certain Black ethnics (including the allegedly "crime-prone" Carolina Geechee-Gullah Maroons and Louisiana Creoles) might also be the victims of negative out-group labeling dynamics which lead to invidious processing by the criminal justice system?

The Spatial Factor and Its Significance in Criminal Justice Processing of Black Defendants

Racial segregation has been the spatial reality of American cities from the nation's earliest urbanization (Taeuber and Taeuber, 1965; Weaver, 1967; Wade, 1964; Hawley and

Rock, 1973; Johnson, 1972; Spear, 1967; Osofsky, 1968). De jure realities established and enforced racial segregation (Bell, 1973b; Long, Long, Leon, and Weston, 1975) until the tumultuous 1960s and early 1970s. Contemporary social distance realities (i.e., de facto customary practices) maintain a U.S. urbanscape marked by ghettoization and slum-ghettos. However, ghettos (zones of minority-group residential dominance with adequate housing and related characteristics) and slum-ghettos (zones of minority-group residential dominance denoted by inadequate housing, high morbidity and infant mortality rates, and related social pathologies) vary in the extent of minority-group residential dominance (Forman, 1971). Black ghetto and slum-ghetto morphologies (Rose, 1971; Grodzins, 1958; Taeuber and Taeuber, 1965; Georges-Abeyie, 1981) are characterized by:

1. A Zone of Transition, that is, those spatial units in which 30% to 49% of the resident population is Black. This is not a true ghetto or slum-ghetto manifestation. This is the territory rapidly being incorporated into the ghetto or slum-ghetto fringe.
2. A ghetto/slum-ghetto fringe, that is, those spatial units in which the population is 50% to 74% Black; and
3. A ghetto/slum-ghetto core, that is, those spatial units in which the population is 75% to 100% Black.

The concept of ghetto/slum-ghetto morphology is important because of the site and situational advantages (or disadvantages) associated with such residential zones. Site is the exact physical location of an event, and situation means the accessibility between two or more sites. Thus, when Black crime is discussed, one might note:

1. The site of the crime's occurrence;
2. The site of the offender's residence;
3. The site of the victim's residence;
4. The site of the initial, or subsequent, encounters between the victim and the assailant;
5. The degree of difficulty in movement, or extent of distance between the site of victimization and the site of the offender's residence;
6. The site of the jurors' or jurists' residence;
7. The situational factors associated with any of the previously noted sites.

The site of the criminal event, arrest, or of the offender's residence might affect the degree of threat jurors or jurists perceive when reviewing the particulars of a given case. The severity of the threat, anxiety, or danger perceived by the juror or jurist may, in part, be influenced by the zone in which the juror or jurist resides. For example, the juror or jurist may perceive more threat, anxiety, or fear if s/he resides within the same morphological zone of the same ghetto or slum-ghetto, or the same morphological zone of a different ghetto or slum-ghetto as the victim or alleged offender. The more dissimilar the juror's or jurist's zone of residence is from the site of the criminal event (or site of the alleged criminal's arrest), or the greater the physical distance the juror's or jurist's residence is from the site of the criminal event (or site of the alleged offender's arrest), the less threat the juror or jurist might perceive (i.e., the "distance decay" factor). The more threat, anxiety, and fear experienced by the juror (or perhaps the jurist), the less rigorous the evidence need be to convict a defendant regarded as socially distant from the juror or jurist. Also, the less social distance felt by the juror or jurist toward the victim, perhaps the less rigorous need be the evidence for conviction—especially if the juror or jurist perceives great social distance toward the defendant. These site and situational factors compounded by social distance determinants might influence the criminal justice system at all levels of formal and informal decision-making—from the initial police response to a call for help, to an issuance of work assignments in the correctional setting, to the decision to parole or not parole a convicted felon.

The varied Black ethnic groups may manifest different degrees of social distance toward other Black ethnics. In fact, it is conceivable that the ethclass identification of a given member of a Black ethnic group may result in that individual feeling considerable social distance toward other members of one's own ethnic group, that is, one might "out-reference" and thus manifest extreme punitive behavior when involved in discretionary situations which involve members of one's own ethnic group. Georges-Abeyie (1981: 101) noted that:

> . . . neither the anthropologist, the geographer, nor the social ecologist has examined the relationship of crime to the various zones of black racial ethnic residential dominance . . .

The urban anthropologist Valentine (1970) noted that Black ethnic diversity leads to differing mechanisms of internal community control. The inference is that crime rates may vary with different Black ethnic groups, as well as with the extent of Black ethnic heterogeneity within the various social-ecological zones of Black residential dominance. Thus, the following has been studied with regard to Black criminality, criminal justice processing, and criminal victimization:

1. Patterns of white-Black (victim-offender) victimization (Davis, 1976; Curtis, 1974, 1975; Georges and Kirksey, 1978);
2. Perceptions of crime in ghetto communities (Knowles and Brewer, 1973);
3. [Rudimentary] acknowledgment of differential nonwhite ethnic group crime rates within nonwhite communities (Kleinman and David, 1973);
4. The issue of race, status and criminal arrest (Green, 1970);
5. Racism and discrimination manifested within the [official decision-making process] of the U.S. criminal justice [system] in such areas as the law, the courts, and sentencing (Crockett, 1969, 1971; Staples, 1975; Somerville, 1968; Lundsgaarde, 1973; Burns, 1973; Bell, 1973a; Thornberry, 1973; Howard, 1975; Carroll and Mondrick, 1976; Jordan, 1974; Long et al., 1975);
6. Minorities as victims of police brutality and other police irregularities (Goldkamp, 1976; Hahn, 1971);
7. Minority attitudes and perceptions of the criminal justice process and the law (Martin and McConnell, 1972; Davis, 1974; Jacob, 1971; Thomas, Cage, and Foster, 1976; Hindelang, Gottfredson, Dunn, and Parisi, 1973, 1974, 1975, 1976; Furstenberg and Wellford, 1973; Kuykendall, 1970; Hahn, 1971; Knowles and Brewer, 1973; Block, 1974; Smith and Hawkins, 1973); and
8. Studies of Black police self-images (Bannon and Witt, 1973; Sax, 1968; Alex, 1982).

However, the research modalities utilized by contemporary social scientists, including Wilbanks (1987) and Petersilia (1984, 1985, 1988), assume ghetto, slum-ghetto, and Black ethnic uniformity. They ignore the interface of social distance and the complexity of Black ethnic diversity and social ecological morphology. They do not examine the dysfunctional impact of Black ethnic heterogeneity within the given morphological ones of a ghetto or ghetto-slum, nor do they examine the site and situational factors within these specific morphological zones. They do not examine the importance of the impact of the site and situational factors upon criminal justice practitioners charged with social control activities within the spatial domains of the ghetto and slum-ghetto. They do not examine the interface or site, situation, social morphology, and juror/jurist behavior when different Black ethnics are involved as defendants.

Significance of Black Ethnic Diversity—Role of Extralegal Social Controls

If Black ethnic diversity is real within the social-ecological zones of a given Black ghetto or slum-ghetto, then various extralegal and informal social controls—including ridicule, ostracism, corporal punishment, and praise—might be more deficient in some Black ghettos and slum-ghettos than others. Extralegal and informal social controls are important mechanisms utilized by the socialization process, which in turn influences the formulation of personality. Black ethnic diversity might also affect the rigor of formal and informal Neighborhood Watch activities, as well as the decision to come (or not to come) to the assistance of a neighbor involved in a criminal incident.

Systematic, Systemic, and Capricious Discrimination: The Role of Petit Apartheid Practices and the "Why" of Black Alienation from the U.S. Criminal Justice System

The Hindelang/Petersilia/Wilbanks thesis rejects the existence of systematic or systemic racially discriminatory practices within the U.S. criminal justice system. Petersilia is especially careful to confine her findings and conclusions to specific states—Texas, Michigan, and California. Yet, together, they limit their criminal justice analyses to discriminatory practices that are easily defined and observed in the formal decision-making process. The first issue is: What is systematic and/or systemic bias? Current U.S. law and jurisprudence cannot be technically considered "apartheid," since there is only one set of laws and formal legal practices are applicable to whites as well as to Blacks and other nonwhites. However, the criminal justice documents *Capital Punishment* (see Schlesinger, 1982) and *Sourcebook of Criminal Justice Statistics* (see Flannagan and Jamieson, 1988) note that certain legal sanctions, such as capital punishment for forcible rape of adult white females, have been almost exclusively reserved for Black and other nonwhite offenders. Once sentenced to die, a Black is much less likely to have a sentence commuted than is a comparable white person.

Studies that purport to examine racial equity in sentencing note that certain objective non-racial factors appear to be highly correlated with the length of term imposed for those offenders who are imprisoned. These variables include:

1. Having multiple current convictions count;
2. Having prior prison terms and juvenile incarcerations;
3. Being on adult and/or juvenile probation at the time of arrest;
4. Having been released from prison within 12 months of arrest;
5. Using a weapon;
6. Having a history of drug and/or alcohol addiction;
7. Being over 21 years old;
8. Going to trial and not being released prior to trial; and
9. Having been represented by a public defender.

Perhaps none of these factors could be legitimately used to validate a "discrimination thesis" couched in the rhetoric of systematic and/or systemic bias in the formal decision-making practices of the U.S. criminal justice system. The *Webster's New Twentieth Century Dictionary, Unabridged* (1983: 1853) defines "systematic" as:

1. Forming or constituting a system;
2. Based on or involving a system;
3. Made or arranged according to a system, method, or plan; regular or orderly;
4. Characterized by the use of method or orderly planning, methodical;
5. Of or having to do with classification. . . .

"Systemic" is defined by *Webster's (Ibid.)* as "pertaining to a system."

The essence of the concepts "systematic" and "systemic" is regularity and predictability, that is, if this, then that. Certainly, the

U.S. criminal justice system is more a process of interrelated but distinct legal entities than a "true" system. Racist decisions, especially formalized, legally sanctioned decisions involving Blacks and other nonwhites, are not predictable. This lack of predictability, however, should not be interpreted as an absence of prejudice or racism. American prejudice (an attitude) is not always made manifest via racism (a behavior). Westie (1965) notes that prejudice can be masked by "general valuations" (i.e., generally verbalized beliefs such as the belief in "equality," "universal brotherhood," and "fair play"); yet, it can be contradicted, in part or in total, via "specific valuations" which express social distance toward certain low-status ethnic groups (e.g., opposition to interracial marriage between Blacks and whites or a belief in the greater intrinsic worth or intelligence of whites versus Blacks). Westie's acknowledgement of incongruence between general and specific valuations can be taken one step further by noting the actualization of the "specific valuation," that is, by noting behavior. The failure of a jury or judge to convict a Black person who victimizes another Black, or of a non-Black who victimizes a Black, may not represent an absence of racism but rather the expression of the actualization of a specific valuation, of a social distance which values Black life less than white life.

A decision to parole or pardon a Black convicted felon, or to sentence such a felon to fewer years than one would a white counterpart with a comparable record, might again be an *actualization* of a negative specific valuation, tempered by social distance, and the juror's (or jurist's) realization that most Part One Index offenses are bound by racial segregation and income realities. Most Index offenses are intraracial and within the same socioeconomic class (robbery and arson may be two exceptions). The absence of predictability in the expression of the "specific valuation" (i.e., in the actualization of the specific valuation) obliges social scientists to question the attribute of "objectivity" associated with "objective" social science methodologies and modalities—such as the "objective" guidelines that eliminate or limit discretion in sentencing. Social scientists must be cognizant of the reality that some acts of law violation are viewed as lesser offending behaviors, as lesser contracultural modalities punished under criminal law statutes, or even treated as tort violations with relatively limited penalties.

Other criminal "modalities"—those disproportionately "perpetrated" by the poor and thus the nonwhite—are considered so dangerous and so injurious that they, in theory, offend the state and are punished as felonies. No objective guideline can be truly racially and ethnically blind if certain racial or ethnic groups, because of their intergenerational socioeconomic status and culture, are compelled or enticed into the very behaviors indexed by objective sentencing or arrest guidelines. Such guidelines are merely indices of race, ethnicity, and class, if not color-caste.

Thus, the "real" factors that disproportionately predispose various Black ethnic youth to the formal processing of a nondiscriminatory criminal justice system are the labeling of certain behaviors as contracultural (Curtis, 1975), deviant, and/or criminal, and the reality of poverty and other slum-ghetto social "pathologies." The poor disproportionately commit criminal violence (which gets reported) and certain property offenses, resulting in their early, youthful immersion into the criminal justice system. *They are processed early and often.* Discretionary decisions by law enforcement officers define their youthful transgressions as "motor vehicle theft" (a felony) rather than "unlawful use of a motor vehicle" (a misdemeanor), "assault" (a felony) rather than "disorderly conduct" (a misdemeanor), and the like. The court funnels these youth under *parens patriae* authority into juvenile services and criminal court rather than into diversion programs. Understaffed public defender agencies too often short-shrift their clients into plea bargains that assure early criminal records. Health care providers (doctors, nurses, psychiatric social workers) note bruised and battered Black flesh at public and private hospitals, and report questionable causations for such wounds to law enforcement authorities—an action that might result in frequent or early arrests of minority adults and youths. Public school teachers and administrators often act in similar ways.

The answer to why many low-income Blacks are alienated from the agencies of formal social control (i.e., the police, the courts, etc.) lies in an examination of the racial and ethnic composition of the agents who make up these agencies, as well as in the many petit apartheid realities low-status Blacks face on a daily basis. Social control institutions tend to select the most middle-class (or middle-class oriented) Eurocentric Blacks available in the minority applicant pool. This selection is assured by a battery of "objective" testing procedures followed by face-to-face interviews. Should progressively oriented departments be cognizant of the need for bilingual or multilingual agents, their selection procedures often remain monocultural and ethnocentric. Are Euro-centric, "objective" test procedures cognizant of the predominantly single-sex orientation of low-status Caribbean recreational institutions, which validate the playing of cards and dominoes, and the consumption of alcohol on the stoop, or the act of just "hanging out" on street corners, rather than bringing males into the home? What is "respectful" in one culture may be considered contracultural in another. Do social control agencies make a concerted effort to select agents who are cognizant of the simple fact that slum-ghetto dwellings lack usable recreation space such as basements and family rooms? Thus, young men are forced outdoors. Are social control agencies cognizant of (much less respectful of) the various informal social controls utilized by different Black ethnic groups? Do these agencies realize that virtually every slum-ghetto Black youth experiences multidimensional "value-space" (Curtis, 1975)—that is, they embrace the value-space of the dominant WASP middle-aged, male-dominate culture, their own lower-class "subculture," and the contracultural values of toughness, suspicion of the motives of others, pride in physical prowess, and fatalism, all of which are instrumental for survival in slum-ghetto environs? Do these agencies realize that Blacks of specific ethnic origin often know pals only by their first name or nickname and have no idea of the exact street address of their "homeboy's" residence? That some suspects are not "running a game" when they say they need bail in order to "secure" (i.e., locate) their alibi?

What of the almost omnipresent reality, or threat, of petit apartheid, that is, the informal practices of criminal justice agents and agencies, which include selectively inhumane and demeaning behavior by law enforcement, court, and corrections officials directed at nonwhite suspects and arrestees? These acts of intimidation and cruelty are seldom mandated as official agency policy. They may be in the form of insults, rude or indifferent behavior, posturing, or spoken communication. Petit apartheid may also take the form of the decision to stop and question or to stop and frisk. A case in point is the 1988 City of Philadelphia American Civil Liberties Union (ACLU) agreement to halt the Philadelphia Police Department's practice of stopping and questioning Black males between the ages of 20 to 40 years of age, ranging in height from five-feet-four-inches to five-feet-ten-inches, and weighing from 120 to 160 pounds, who happened to be in Philadelphia's Center City. The practice became more pervasive when the police were investigating the Center City "stalker incidents." The unofficial search-and-question technique was initiated in an attempt to apprehend a slender Black male who was suspected of raping eight females, one Hispanic and seven white.[3] Petit apartheid appears to have also been the reality in suburban Pittsburgh during 1987, when the Homestead Police Department officers made late-night, door-to-door requests of all Black males in the township to voluntarily submit to fingerprinting and blood tests. The initiative was in response to a series of rapes of elderly white females (and one elderly Black female) by a man wearing a ski mask who had a "Black-sounding voice."[4] Petit apartheid may have also been the reality of the Lower Providence Township (Montgomery County, Pennsylvania) Police Department's alleged practice of stopping automobiles with "black interiors," that is, with Black motorists.[5]

The very wording of the jury's charge may be expressed in terms of considerable social distance toward the defendant, and thus "closeness" toward the defenders of the social order. All of these formal or informal wordings and behaviors may manifest petit apartheid realities. The defendant's opportunity, or lack thereof, to dress appropriately or to not be shackled when first presented to the jury (i.e., the moment a person may "shuffle" or walk into court from the "waiting pen") may be a manifestation of petit apartheid realities that subliminally affect the determinations of both jurors and jurists.

Conclusion

A realistic study of Black crime, the criminal victimization of Blacks, or the criminal justice system processing of Black suspects and defendants must be cognizant of the following:

1. Black ethnic diversity, meaning race does not equate ethnicity;
2. Social distance realities among diverse Black ethnic groups, as well as between Blacks and whites;
3. The multidimensional "value-space" which afflicts slum-ghetto Black ethnics, a value-space that results in anomie and some contracultural behaviors which may be "criminalizable";
4. Formal and informal petit apartheid decisions that alienate, anger, and often inflame seemingly minor Black-white encounters into more serious conflict situations;
5. Ethnocentric behaviors and beliefs by white agents (or Eurocentric nonwhite agents) of social control who devalue Black ethnic cultural expressions and even view some of these subcultural and contracultural traditions as criminally deviant;
6. The difference between "general valuations," "specific valuations," and the *actualization* of negative "specific valuations," tempered by majority race feelings of considerable social distance toward Blacks as well as white expressions of ethnocentrism;
7. The social-ecological morphology of the ghetto and slum-ghetto, a morphology that results in the establishment of a ghetto transition zone, fringe, and core, as well as in differential rates of offending behaviors within each of these zones;
8. A social-ecological ghetto and slum-ghetto morphology that results in a differential site and situational advantages;
9. Possible differentials in rates of offending behavior by different Black ethnic groups;
10. The false premise of sentencing guidelines and other "objective" criminal justice modalities which are really indices of socioeconomic and racial/ethnic stratification that have taken on color-caste dimensions;
11. The reality that "objective" guidelines and modalities are not color, race, ethnic, caste, or class-blind if they directly relate to when and how certain racial, ethnic, or color-caste out-groups become tracked within the criminal justice system;
12. The importance of the difficult-to-measure, informal criminal justice system decisions which affect Black ethnic suspects and offenders from the initial law enforcement response to a call to the decision to grant (or not to grant) parole; and
13. The need to restructure the concept of ethnicity so that it applies to the African American experience, and thus does not merely rely upon the traditional tripartite construct of race, nation of origin, and religion.

If advertising agencies are cognizant of the conscious as well as the subliminal impact of social distance, race-ethnicity, and general physical appearance in the decision-making habits of the American public; if the jury selection process (including preemptory eliminations) is based on skin color, specific religious or political affiliation, or social affinity; if popular mass media magazines, television programming, cinema, and audio recordings are cognizant of the power of imagery, which includes the presentation of Eurocentric values, beliefs, and appearances; if "television influences attitudes toward racial or ethnic groups by the status of the parts assigned to their members, the kind of behavior they display within these parts, or even the type of products they promote" (Parrillo, 1985: 65-57); and if phenotype-based ethnic differences have been utilized, such as was employed in the classification of Arizona prisoners [as Knepper shows elsewhere in this issue], then is it not conceivable that Black racial and ethnic indicators may consciously or subliminally influence the decision-makers within the U.S. criminal justice system during all or some of its formal and informal processes—even those "objective" processes that focus on formal, easily observed, and recorded "empiricisms"? Racially and ethnically impacted empirical procedures that are directly related to when and how often Blacks are processed by social control agencies are indices of racial and ethnic discrimination, not just of racial and ethnic disproportionality. Institutional racism is concerned with impact, with result, not intent. Institutions that subordinate individuals because of their race or factors directly related to race (Downs, 1976) are institutionally racist. Thus "objective" sentencing procedures or petit apartheid law enforcement practices are institutionally racist in impact, if not always in intent.

NOTES

1. For this manuscript, the author conducted a survey of over 40 criminology and criminal justice texts published by leading U.S. publishers.

2. The following journals were reviewed: *Criminology; Journal of Police Studies; Social Justice; Crime and Delinquency; Journal of Research in Crime and Delinquency; Journal of Criminal Law and Criminology; Justice Quarterly News Magazine; Corrections; Police Chief;* and *Federal Probation.*

3. The so-called Center City "stalker incidents" were covered extensively by *The Philadelphia Inquirer* and *The Philadelphia Tribune* (see, e.g., *The Philadelphia Tribune,* [1988:1A]). The Center City "stalker incidents," according to Mr. Stefan Presser, who is the Pennsylvania ACLU Legal Director and Chief Attorney on these cases, involved the questioning of 269 Black "suspects" not taken into custody, and the taking into custody of 113 additional suspects. The Center City "stalker incidents" involved the wholesale suspension of the Fourth Amendment rights of Black males. The City and the ACLU are currently in negotiation for an out-of-court financial settlement for the abuse of numerous Black "suspects." Two other petit apartheid incidents involving the City of Philadelphia are noteworthy. "Operation Cold Turkey" (a police label), according to Mr. Presser, involved the round-up of more than 100 Hispanic youth because of the murder of a white police officer in the predominately Hispanic neighborhood of Spring Garden. The race and ethnicity of the original suspect or suspects were unknown by the Philadelphia Police Department. This case resulted in an out-of-court settlement of over $50,000 by the City of Philadelphia to Hispanic litigants ("suspects"). The City is also involved in a $500,000 settlement for its unlawful stopping of over 1,400 nonwhites (primarily Blacks) at 48 intersections within Philadelphia during the police search for the Center City "stalker incidents." All three of the aforementioned incidents involved the abridgement of Fourth Amendment rights of Black males and are examples of the petit apartheid realities too often faced by Blacks in the U.S.

4. This policy was instituted during the stewardship of Homestead Police Chief Christopher Kelly, currently with the Baldwin Borough Police Department.

5. In November of 1987, the Pennsylvania Human Relations Commission was scheduled to open hearings on the allegations of the aforementioned petit apartheid practices of the Lower Providence Township Police Department. Two federal lawsuits have been filed in U.S. District Court, in Philadelphia, alleging racial bias in the ticketing of Black motorists in Lower Providence Township of Montgomery County. One lawsuit was brought by a group of Black motorists; the other by six white former Lower Providence police officers.

REFERENCES

Alex, N.
1982 Black in Blue. Englewood Cliffs, NJ: Prentice-Hall.

Baldus, D.C., C. Pulaski, and G. Woodworth
1983 "Comparative Review of Death Sentences: An Empirical Study of the Georgia Experience." Journal of Criminal Law and Criminology 74: 661-725.

Bannon, J.D. and G.M. Witt
1973 "Black Policeman: A Study of Self-Images." Journal of Police Science and Administration 1: 21-29.

Becker, H.D.
1963 Outsiders: Studies in the Sociology of Deviance. New York: Free Press.

Bell, D.A.
1973a Race, Racism, and American Law. Boston: Little, Brown and Company.
1973b "Racism in American Courts: Cause for Black Disruption or Despair?" California Law Review 65: 165-203.

Block, R.
1974 "Why Notify the Police: The Victim's Decision to Notify the Police of an Assault." Criminology 11: 555-569.

Burns, H.
1973 "Black People and the Tyranny of American Law." Annals of the American Academy of Political and Social Science 401: 156-160.

Carroll, L. and M.E. Mondrick
1976 "Racial Bias in the Decision to Grant Parole." Law and Society Review 11,1: 93-107.

Christianson, S.
1984 "Our Black Prisons." D. Georges-Abeyie (ed.), The Criminal Justice System and Blacks. New York: Clark Boardman.

Cloward, R.A. and L.E. Ohlin
1960 Delinquency and Opportunity: A Theory of Delinquent Gangs. New York: Free Press.

Cohen, A.K.
1955 Delinquent Boys: The Culture of the Gang. New York: Free Press.

Crokett, G.W.
1971 "Racism in the Courts." Journal of Public Law 20,2: 385.
1969 "Racism in the Law." Science and Society 33: 223-230.

Crockett, O.
1984 "The Role of the Black Judge." D. George-Abeyie (ed.), The Criminal Justice System and Blacks. New York: Clark Boardman.

Curtis, L.A.
1975 Violence, Race, and Culture. Lexington, MA: Lexington Books.
1974 Criminal Violence. Lexington, MA: Lexington Books.

Davis, J.A.
1976 "Black Crime and American Culture." Annals of the American Academy of Political and Social Science 4: 89-98.
1974 "Justification for No Obligation: Views of Black Males Toward Crime and the Criminal Law." Issues in Criminology 9: 69-84.

Downs, A.
1976 Urban Problems and Prospects (2nd Edition). Chicago: Rand McNally.

Flanagan, Timothy J. and Katherine M. Jamieson
1988 Sourcebook of Criminal Justice Statistics. Washington, D.C.: U.S. Department of Justice.

Forman, R.E.
1971 Black Ghettos. White Ghettos, and Slums. Englewood Cliffs, NJ: Prentice-Hall.

Furstenberg, F.F. and C.F. Wellford
1973 "Calling the Police: The Evaluation of Police Service." Law and Society Review 7,3: 393-406.

Georges-Abeyie, D.
1984a "Interview with Judge Bruce McM. Wright." D. Georges-Abeyie (ed.), The Criminal Justice System and Blacks. New York: Clark Boardman.
1984b The Criminal Justice System and Blacks. New York: Clark Boardman.
1981 "Studying Black Crime: A Realistic Approach." P.J. Brantinghamn and P.L. Brantingham (eds.), Environmental Criminology. Beverly Hills, CA: Sage.

Georges, D. and K. Kirksey
1978 "Violent Crime Perpetrated against the Elderly in the City of Dallas, October 1974-September 1975." Journal of Environmental Systems 7,2: 149-197.

Goldcamp, J.S.
1976 "Minorities as Victims of Police Shootings: Interpretation of Racial Disproportionality and Police Use of Deadly Force." Justice System Journal 2: 269-183.

Gordon, Milton Myron
1964 Assimilation in American Life: The Role of Race, Religion, and National Origins. New York: Oxford University Press.

Green, E.
1970 "Race, Status, and Criminal Arrest." American Sociological Review 35: 476-490.

Grodzins, M.
1958 The Metropolitan Areas as a Racial Problem. Pittsburgh: University of Pittsburgh.

Hahn, H.
1971 "Ghetto Assessments of Police Protection and Authority." Law and Society Review 183: 183-193.

Hawley, A.H. and V.P. Rock
1973 Segregation in Residential Areas. Washington, D.C.: National Academy of Sciences.

Hindelang, M.J.
1984 "Variations in Sex-Race-Age Specific Incidence Rates of Offending." D. Georges-Abeyie (ed.), The Criminal Justice System and Blacks. New York: Clark Boardman.

Hindelang, M., R. Gottfredson, D.S. Dunn, and N. Parisi
1976 Sourcebook of Criminal Justice Statistics. Washington, D.C.: Government Printing Office.
1975 Sourcebook of Criminal Justice Statistics. Washington, D.C.: Government Printing Office.
1974 Sourcebook of Criminal Justice Statistics. Washington, D.C.: Government Printing Office.
1973 Sourcebook of Criminal Justice Statistics. Washington, D.C.: Government Printing Office.

Hirschi, T.
1969 Causes of Delinquency. Los Angeles: University of California Press.

Howard, J.C.
1975 "Racial Discrimination in Sentencing." Judicature 59,3: 120-125.
1967 The Administration of Rape Cases in the City of Baltimore and the State of Maryland. Baltimore: Monumental Bar Association.

Jacob, H.
1971 "Black and White Perceptions of Justice in the City." Law and Society Review 6,1: 69-89.

Johnson, J.W.
1972 Black Mountain. New York: Atheneum.

Jordon, V.E.
1974 "The Systems Propagates Crimes." Crime and Delinquency 20,3: 233-240.

Kleinman, P.H. and D.S. David
1973 "Victimization and Perception of Crime in a Ghetto Community." Criminology 11: 307-343.

Knowles, L. and J. Brewer
1973 "The Black Community: Attitudes toward Community Problems, Crime, and the Police." Police Chief 40: 48-51.

Kuykendall, J.L.
1970 "Police and Minority Groups: Toward a Theory of Negative Contacts." Police (September-October): 47-55.

Long, E., J. Long, W. Leon, and P. Weston
1975 American Minorities: The Justice Issue. Englewood Cliffs, NJ: Prentice-Hall.

Lundsgaarde, H.P.
1973 "Racial and Ethnic Classifications: An Appraisal of the Role of Anthropology in the Lawmaking Process." Houston Law Review (March).

Martin, J. and J. McConnell
1972 "Black Militant Ideology and the Law." Criminology 10: 111-116.

McNeely, R.L. and C.E. Pope (eds.)
1981 Race, Crime and Criminal Justice. Beverly Hills, CA: Sage.

Merton, R.
1968 Social Theory and Social Structure. New York: Free Press.

Miller, W.B.
1970 "Lower Class Culture as a Generating Milieu of Gang Delinquency." M.E. Wolfgang et al. (eds.), The Sociology of Crime and Delinquency (2nd ed.). New York: John Wiley.

Osofsky, G.
1968 Harlem: The Making of a Ghetto. New York: Harper Torchbooks.

Parrillo, V.N.
1985 Strangers to These Shores (2nd Edition). New York: John Wiley & Sons.

Petersilia, J.
1984 "Racial Disparities in the Criminal Justice System: Executive Summary of Rand Institute Study, 1983." D. Georges-Abeyie (ed.), The Criminal Justice System and Blacks. New York: Clark Boardman.

Petersilia, I., S. Klein, and S. Turner
1988 Racial Equity in Sentencing. Santa Monica, CA: Rand Corporation.

Petersilia, J. and S. Turner
1985 Guideline-Based Justice: The Implications for Racial Minorities. Santa Monica, CA: Rand Corporation.

Rist, R.C.
1970 "Student Social Class and Teacher Expectations: The Self-Fulfilling Prophecy in Ghetto Education." Harvard Education Review 49,3 (August): 411-451.

Rose, H.M.
1971 The Black Ghetto. New York: McGraw-Hill.

Sax, R.M.
1968 ". . . It Hurts to Be Black in Blue." Issues in Criminology 4: 1-11.

Schlesinger, Steven R.
1982 Capital Punishment: A National Prison Statistics Report. Washington, D.C.: U.S. Department of Justice.

Sellin, Thorsten
1938 "Culture, Conflict, and Crime." Social Science Research Council, Bulletin (No. 41). New York.

Smith, P.W. and R.O. Hawkins
1973 "Victimization, Types of Citizen-Police Contacts, and Attitudes toward the Police." Law and Society Review 8,1: 134-152.

Somerville, B.
1968 "Double Standards in Law Enforcement with Regard to Minority Status." Issues in Criminology 4: 35-48.

Spear, A.H.
1967 Black Chicago. Chicago: University of Chicago.

Staples, R.
1975 "White Racism, Black Crime, and American Justice: An Application of the Colonial Model to Explain Crime and Race." Phylon 36: 14-22.

Sutherland, E. and D. Cressey
1978 Criminology (10th Edition). Philadelphia: Lippincott.

Sykes, G.M. and D. Matza
1970 "Techniques of Neutralization. A Theory of Delinquency." M.E. Wolfgang et al. (eds.), The Sociology of Crime and Delinquency (2nd edition). New York: John Wiley.

Taeuber, K.E., and A.P. Taeuber
1965 Negroes in Cities. Chicago: Aldine.

The Philadelphia Tribune
1988 "City Agrees to Stop the Random Arrest of Blacks."

Thomas, C.W., R.I. Cage, and S.C. Foster
1976 "Public Opinion on Criminal Law and Legal Sanctions: An Examination of Two Conceptual Models." Journal of Criminal Law and Criminology 67: 110-116.

Thornberry, T.P.
1973 "Race, Socio-Economic Status and Sentencing in the Juvenile Justice System." Journal of Criminal Law and Criminology 64: 90-98.

Turk, A.
1982 Political Criminality. Beverly Hills, CA: Sage Publications.
1971 Criminality and the Legal Order. Chicago: Rand McNally.

Valentine, C.
1970 Culture and Poverty Critique and Counter Proposals. Chicago: University of Chicago.

Wade, R.C.
1964 Slavery in the Cities. London: Oxford University.

Ware, G. (ed.)
1976 From the Black Bar. New York: G.P. Putnam's Sons.

Weaver, R.C.
1967 The Negro Ghetto. New York: Russel & Russel.

Webster's New Unabridged Dictionary
1983 Second Edition. New York: Dorset and Baber.

Westie, F.R.
1965 "The American Dilemma: An Empirical Test." American Sociological Review 30 (August): 531-532.

Wilbanks, William
1987 The Myth of a Racist Criminal Justice System. Monterey, CA: Brooks Cole.

Wilson, James Q. and Richard Herrnstein
1985 Crime and Human Nature. New York: Simon and Schuster.

17

INTRODUCTION

William Oliver is a member of the steering committee of the Institute on Domestic Violence in the African American Community. The organization was founded in 1993, in response to a "one-size-fits-all" perspective that suggests that domestic violence means the same thing to all people. It provides the backdrop for Oliver's specific focus on the causes of interpersonal violence among African Americans and strategies to address the problem of domestic violence. His book, *The Violent Social World of Black Men,* originally published in 1994, examined the causes, effects, and circumstances involved in Black-on-Black violence. This book was reprinted in 1999.

The following article is one of Oliver's earlier publications. In it he rejects the genetic inferiority, culture of poverty, and racial oppression perspectives as explanations of social problems and presents in their stead the structural-cultural perspective. This perspective examines the interconnection of racism, racial discrimination, and the responses of African Americans to these conditions as necessary components of an explanation of high rates of social problems among Blacks. Oliver advocates the development of an Afrocentric cultural ideology that, among other values, emphasizes love of self, an awareness of African cultural heritage, and a commitment to economic and political development. He argues that this prevention strategy requires the involvement of the family, the educational system, the mass media, the church, and all other major institutions.

Black Males and Social Problems

Prevention Through Afrocentric Socialization

William Oliver

Most Americans are aware of the high rates of social problems among Black Americans. For example, Blacks are disproportionately represented among Americans experiencing academic failure, teenage pregnancy, female-headed families, chronic un employment, poverty, alcoholism, drug addiction, and criminal victimization (Poussaint, 1983; *U.S. News & World Report,* 1986). Consequently, there is a great deal of debate among politicians, journalists, academics, and ordinary citizens concerning the etiology of these problems. Those who attempt to explain the prevalence of these conditions among Blacks tend to argue one of three positions: genetic inferiority, culture of poverty, or racial oppression.

Advocates of the genetic inferiority perspective argue that the high rates of social problems among Blacks is a product or expression of Black peoples' innate inferiority to Caucasians and other racial groups. Moreover, advocates of this perspective argue that Blacks possess genetic traits and characteristics that predispose them to engage in problematic behavior at higher rates than White (Garrett, 1961; Jensen, 1973).

A major problem with genetic inferiority theories is that advocates of this perspective tend to differentially apply it in explaining the causes of social problems among various racial and ethnic groups. For example, White Americans have higher rates of academic failure, teenage pregnancy, female-headed families, drug addiction, and criminal involvement than do Europeans (Archer and Gartner, 1983; *Time Magazine,* 1985). However, the rate differences between White Americans and Europeans are almost always explained, in terms of differences in environmental and cultural conditions.

The genetic inferiority perspective is also criticized for failing to provide evidence of a specific genetic trait that causes crime or any

---

From Oliver, W. (1989, September). Black males and social problems: Prevention through Afrocentric socialization. *Journal of Black Studies, 20,* 15-39. Reprinted with permission of Sage Publications.

other major social problem (Montagu, 1941). For example, the genetic inferiority of Blacks is often based on the results of culturally biased intelligence tests (Clark, 1975; Hilliard, 1981). Advocates of the genetic inferiority perspective also tend to disregard the role of systematic racial discrimination in generating social problems among Blacks.

The culture of poverty perspective is another body of assumptions designed and often used to explain the etiology of social problems among Blacks. Advocates of this perspective argue that poverty, social disorganization (i.e., the breakdown of basic community institutions, including the family, church, and school), and inadequate socialization of children are the primary causes of the high rates of social problems among Blacks (Banfield, 1970; Moynihan, 1965). Moreover, advocates of this perspective have suggested that lower-class Blacks adhere to a distinctive set of cultural values and traditions that lead to or directly condone involvement in problematic behavior (Miller, 1958; Banfield, 1970).

A major criticism of the culture of poverty perspective as an explanation of the high rates of social problems among Blacks is that this perspective fails to explain why only a small percentage of Blacks who experience poverty and exposure to community social disorganization engage in behavioral patterns that suggest the internalization of values and norms in conflict with mainstream values and norms (Hill, 1972).

The third and probably the most popular explanation of social problems among Blacks is the racial oppression theory. Advocates of this perspective argue that the majority of Blacks, like the majority of other Americans, support mainstream values and goals (Cloward and Ohlin, 1960). However, historical patterns of political disenfranchisement and systematic deprivation of equal access to educational and employment opportunities have induced a disproportionate number of Blacks to engage in illegitimate means (e.g., robbery, drug dealing, and prostitution) to attain mainstream values and goals (Cloward and Ohlin, 1960).

In a more recent formulation of the racial oppression theory Wilson (1987) argues that historical patterns of racial discrimination and the technological transformation of the economy have produced disproportionately high rates of joblessness, female-headed families, poverty, drug abuse, and crime among Blacks.

A major criticism of racial oppression theories is that they tend to overpredict the number of Blacks who are likely to become involved in problematic behavior. For example, all Blacks are directly or indirectly affected by American racism; however, only a minority actively participate in activities that cause social problems.

A Structural-Cultural Perspective

Given the inadequacies of the genetic inferiority, culture of poverty, and racial oppression perspectives of Blacks and social problems, I would like to offer an alternative theoretical perspective based on the interrelationship between structural pressures and cultural adaptations.

The most fundamental assumption of the structural-cultural perspective is that the high rate of social problems among Blacks is the result of structural pressures and dysfunctional cultural adaptations to those pressures. The term structural pressures is used to refer to patterns of American political, economic, social, and cultural organization designed to perpetuate White superiority and Black inferiority. Thus, I argue that White racism and various patterns of racial discrimination are the predominant environmental pressures adversely impacting on the survival and progress of Black people.

Another major assumption of the structural-cultural perspective is that Blacks have failed to adequately respond to White racism.

The term dysfunctional cultural adaptation refers to specific styles of group adjustment that Blacks have adopted in response to structurally induced social pressures. The most problematic of these dysfunctional cultural adaptations include:

1. The failure of Blacks to develop an Afrocentric cultural ideology;
2. The tendency of Blacks, especially lower-class Blacks, to tolerate the "tough guy" and the "player of women" images as acceptable alternatives to traditional definitions of manhood.

Failure to Develop an Afrocentric Ideology

Throughout the world, all societies have established sets of ideas by which life is made understandable by their members (Vander Zanden, 1986: 136). Ideas such as these are generally referred to as an ideology. A society's ideology "tells people about the nature of their society and about its place in the world" (Vander Zanden, 1986: 136). In this sense, a society's ideology gives structure to how group members define themselves and their experiences and also provides impetus for group action. Thus the most important function of a society's ideology is that it forms the spiritual and intellectual foundation of group solidarity (Vander Zanden, 1986: 136).

A major aspect of the Euroamerican cultural ideology is that people of European descent are inherently more intelligent, beautiful, industrious, and just than are non-White people (Jordan, 1969; Froman, 1972). All Americans (Black, White, Hispanic, Asian, and others) are exposed to pro-White socialization messages disseminated by the school system, mass media, and religious institutions (Baldwin, 1980; Cogdell and Wilson, 1980).

In America, pro-White socialization is primarily anti-Black. Ideas of White superiority are embedded in every aspect of American society. For example, educational, religious, and mass media institutions all play a major role in the projection and dissemination of ideas and images that convey the innate superiority of Whites and the innate inferiority of Blacks (Boggle, 1974; Cogdell and Wilson, 1980; Staples and Jones, 1985).

The American educational system has played a major role in perpetuating negative images of Blacks by portraying them as descendants of savages and people who have failed to make a significant contribution to America or world civilization (Woodson, 1933; Baldwin, 1979; Perkins, 1986).

The superiority of Whites over Blacks has also been perpetuated by American religious philosophy and symbolism through the projection of White images of Christ and God (Welsing, 1980; Cogdell and Wilson, 1980; Akbar, 1983). This has had a devastating impact on the psychological development of Blacks. For example, "to embrace a White God is to reject the Black self" (Cogdell and Wilson, 1980: 115). Moreover, being socialized to perceive God as White creates the idea in the Black mind that people who look like the White image of God are superior and people who are non-White are inferior (Akbar, 1984: 54). The most significant problem emerging from the projection of God as White is summarized best in the comments of Welsing (1980: 28): "Therefore it can be said that all Blacks and other non-White Christians worship the White man as God—not as God but as the God. So the White man is perfect, good, supreme, and the only source of blessing." Hence, as a result of their religious socialization in America, "in the Black religious mind, a White man is their creator, protector, and salvationist" (Cogdell and Wilson, 1980: 117).

America's cultural ideology has been deliberately designed to glorify whiteness and to denigrate blackness. Consequently, this process has led to the cultural annihilation of

Black Americans (Mahubuti, 1978: 41, 118; Karenga, 1986). Unlike other American racial and ethnic groups, Blacks have failed to develop a distinct cultural tradition that contributes to the psychological, spiritual, cultural, and economic development of most Blacks. The Americanization of Africans in America has resulted in Blacks being locked into the role of America's permanent outsiders.

The failure of Blacks to develop an Afrocentric cultural ideology is a major source of psychological, social, political, and economic dysfunction among Black Americans (Williams, 1974; Mahubuti, 1978). Afrocentricity as defined by Asante is the centering of one's analysis and perceptions from the groundedness of the African person (Asante, 1987). For example, American cultural ideology promotes a specific set of values and images that define what is and what is not beautiful. Constant exposure to beauty standards that are antithetical to their racial characteristics causes generation after generation of Blacks to experience low self-esteem and self-hatred (Clark and Clark, 1947, 1980; Cogdell and Wilson, 1980: 1-16). Consequently, Black self-hatred has been a major factor that has historically contributed to the lack of unity among Blacks as well as a pervasive low evaluation of Blacks by Blacks. Hence, the failure of Blacks to develop an Afrocentric cultural ideology has prevented Blacks from developing the sort of collective philosophy, definitions, cultural traditions, and institutions that other American racial and ethnic groups have established in order to facilitate their survival and progress in American society.

Dysfunctional Definitions of Manhood

The tendency of lower-class Blacks to tolerate the "tough guy" and the "player of women" images as acceptable alternatives to traditional definitions of manhood is another major dysfunctional cultural adaptation to White racism.

In all societies men and women have distinctive sex roles that encompass a specific set of expectations and responsibilities (Perruci and Knudsen, 1983). Within American society the traditional masculine role prescribes that men be tough, emotionally unexpressive, self-reliant, economically successful, and oriented toward protecting and providing for a family (Brenton, 1966; Fasteau, 1975). Successful enactment of the traditional male role is generally dependent on a male's access to educational and employment opportunities. However, due to their membership in a racial group that has been systematically denied equal access to political and economic power, as well as educational and employment opportunities, a substantial number of Black males lack the skills and resources that are necessary to successfully enact the traditional male role (Welsing, 1974; Stewart and Scott, 1978; Staples, 1982).

Although all Blacks are subject to systematic attacks designed to have an adverse affect on their ability to survive and progress, Black males are its primary target because it is they that most Whites fear and who also represent the greatest threat to the continued political and economic subjugation of Blacks (Welsing, 1974; Kunjufu, 1983). The high rates of academic failure, unemployment, and imprisonment among Black males are dramatic examples of what Welsing (1974, 1978) has described as the "inferiorization process," that is, a systematic stress attack (involving the entire complex of political, legal, educational, economic, religious, military, and mass media institutions controlled by Whites) designed to produce dysfunctional patterns of behavior among Blacks in all areas of life. Through the inferiorization process, Blacks are conditioned to play the role of functional inferiors. That is, Blacks are socialized to be incapable of solving or helping to produce solutions to problems posed by the environment. However, for Whites, the inferiorization process is designed to facilitate their development as functional superiors. Thus, under the system of White supremacy, Whites are conditioned to solve or help to provide solutions to problems posed by the environment.

There is a great deal of evidence that indicates the adverse impact of the inferiorization process on Black males (Stewart and Scott, 1978; McGhee, 1984). For example, 44% of Black males are estimated to be functional illiterates (Kozol, 1985). Much of the responsibility for these high rates may be attributed to the public school system which promotes these students without their having obtained reading and writing skills (Staples, 1982: 3). Moreover, in some of the nation's largest cities, high school drop-out rates among Black males are 60 to 70% (Poussaint, 1983: 50). Consequently, as a result of their lack of marketable skills and discriminatory hiring practices, almost half (46%) of the 8.8 million working-age Black men are unemployed (*U.S. News & World Report,* 1986).

Black males are also disproportionately represented among persons incarcerated. For example, in 1985, Black males represented 47% of the U.S. prison population. Between 1978 and 1982, Black males were eight times more likely to be in prison than White males (Bureau of Justice Statistics, 1985b). As a result of their exposure to institutional racism and the inferiorization process, a substantial number of Black males have opted to re-define manhood in terms of toughness, sexual conquest, and thrill-seeking (Perkins, 1975; Staples, 1982). Adherence to these norms has given rise to two culturally distinct masculinity role orientations among Black males: the "tough guy" and the "player of women."

Toughness and Problematic Behavior

Black males' adherence to the "tough guy" image is a major factor contributing to the high rates of interpersonal violence among Blacks. Hence, the leading cause of death for Black males 15 to 34 years of age is homicide (Centers for Disease Control, 1985). The tough guy image is also a major factor contributing to the high rates of wife-beating among Blacks. For example, Strauss and his colleagues (1980) found that wife-beating was 400% more common among Black families than White families.

Another problem that has emerged from Black males' adherence to the tough guy image is the fear of Blacks by Blacks (Mahubuti, 1978: 233; Oliver, 1984). In many Black communities throughout the nation, Black people are becoming increasingly polarized as a result of the fear caused by Black males who terrorize the Black community. Their disproportionate involvement in lifestyles centered around idleness, alcohol and drug abuse, drug trafficking, and other acts of criminality is a major source of this fear.

Sexual Conquest and Problematic Behavior

Black males' adherence to the "player of women" image is another major factor precipitating social problems among Blacks. In his classic ethnographic study of Black males residing in a Washington, DC, ghetto, Liebow (1967: 142-143) observed that many lower-class Black males see themselves "as users of women" and are overtly concerned with presenting themselves as exploiters of women and expect other men to do the same. Hence, attempts to enact the "player of women" role is a major factor contributing to the fact that 25% of all Black babies are born to teenage mothers, 55% of Black babies are born out of wedlock and nearly 50% of Black families are headed by unmarried females (U.S. Bureau of the Census, 1983; *Ebony,* 1986). Moreover, Black males' adherence to the "player of women" image is responsible for the high rates of divorce among Blacks. According to the U.S. Bureau of the Census

(1983), in 1982 Blacks had a divorce rate (220 per 100,000) that was two times that of Whites (107 per 100,000).

Wilson (1987) has argued that these conditions are primarily products of structural pressures, that is, historical patterns of racial discrimination and social dislocation due to technological transformations in the economy. I acknowledge the power of structural pressures to impose constraints on the lives of uneducated, low-income Blacks. However, I also believe that these problems are products of a cultural context in which the Black community has allowed too many of its males to make the passage from boyhood to manhood by internalizing and acting out definitions of themselves "as users of women."

The remaining sections of this article are devoted to describing an alternative model for reducing the occurrence of social problems among Blacks. Although the model is applicable to Black males and females, I have limited discussion of its application to Black males, primarily because I believe that the most critical factor contributing to the high rates of social problems among Blacks is the dysfunctional cultural adaptation of Black males to White racism.

The Afrocentric World View

In recent years, an increasing number of Black scholars have begun to promote Afrocentricity as an intervention paradigm to facilitate the transformation of Blacks from a state of dependence to a state of independence and self-reliance (Asante, 1980, 1987; Karenga, 1980, 1987, 1988). The Afrocentric cultural ideology is a world view based on the values of classical African civilizations. Advocates of Afrocentricity argue that the high rates of social problems among Blacks are a direct result of the imposition of a Eurocentric world view on African Americans (Asante, 1980; Akbar, 1983; R. Karenga, 1986). According to Karenga (1988: 407), Eurocentric socialization has had an adverse impact on Blacks, including: (1) the internalization of a Euroamerican mode of assessing the self, other Blacks, American society, and the world; (2) the loss of historical memory of their African cultural heritage; and (3) self-hatred and depreciation of their people and culture. Thus, the failure of Blacks to develop an Afrocentric cultural ideology and world view has made Blacks vulnerable to structural pressures that promote definitions of Blacks as being innately inferior to Whites, ignorant, lazy, dependent, promiscuous, and violent.

An Afrocentric cultural ideology would encourage Black Americans to transcend cultural crisis and confusion by reclaiming traditional African values that emphasize "mankind's oneness with nature," "spirituality," and "collectivism." The cultural emphasis of Afrocentricity is in contrast to the Eurocentric world view which encourages "controlling nature," "materialism," and "individualism" (Mbiti, 1969). The Afrocentric world view is not anti-White. Rather, its primary objective is to facilitate "a critical reconstruction that dares to restore missing and hidden parts of our [Black peoples'] self-formation and pose the African experience as a significant paradigm for human liberation and a higher level of human life" (Karenga, 1988: 404).

In addition to the collective oriented values that formed the foundation of classical African civilizations, the resurrection of the African world view in America must also incorporate definitions and meanings that reflect the historical and contemporary experiences of African Americans in an alien context. Hence, there are two specific American definitional realities that must be incorporated in an African world view resurrected out of the American experience of displaced Africans.

First:

> The Afrocentric cultural ideology must acknowledge the omnipresence of White racism

> throughout American society and the adverse impact it has had on the psychological, cultural, political, and economic development of Black people.

Incorporating these facts in a collective Afrocentric cultural ideology will facilitate among Blacks a world view that offers a realistic interpretation of African Americans in terms of their unique cultural heritage and role in American society.

Second:

> The Afrocentric cultural ideology must recognize that terms such as colored, Negro, and Black do not define the essence or depth of Black American history, cultural heritage, or identity. Hence, it is critical that Black Americans re-define themselves as African Americans.

Every racial and ethnic subgroup in America, except for Blacks, describes themselves in terms of the lands of their origin. By re-defining themselves as African Americans, Blacks can begin to repair the psychic damage that has been inflicted upon them as a result of their exposure to Eurocentric values. Moreover, by redefining themselves as African Americans, Blacks will initiate the development of a cultural context in which Black youth will be guided toward identification with the Blacks of the classical African civilizations of Egypt, Ethiopia, and Nubia. It is critically important that Black children know that there is a great deal of archaeological, anthropological, and historical evidence that indicates that their native-born African ancestors were the first human beings to populate the earth, domesticate animals, engage in agriculture, develop a system of writing, establish universities, and practice monotheistic religion (James, 1954; Davidson, 1959; Jackson, 1970; Ben-Jochannan, 1970; Diop, 1974; Williams, 1974; Van Sertima, 1983, 1984).

In order to incorporate the African world view in the lives of African Americans, African American adults must begin to engage in Afrocentric socialization.

Afrocentric Socialization

The transmission of ideas, values, culture, and the development of the self are the primary functions of socialization. Hence, "socialization is the interactive process by which individuals acquire some of the values, attitudes, skills, and knowledge of the society in which they belong" (Coser et al., 1983: 106). Institutions such as the family, the educational system, mass media, and the church play a major role in the dissemination of a group's or society's values and cultural ideology. Thus, in order to facilitate the internalization of an Afrocentric cultural ideology or world view among young Black males, Blacks must restructure their primary institutions to insure that Black males will internalize Afrocentric values. The establishment of Afrocentric institutions is absolutely essential to the creation of an Afrocentric world view among Black males (Mahubuti, 1978: 127; Perkins, 1986). According to Mahubuti (1978: 20), "A people without life-giving and life-saving independent institutions are a weak and dependent people. They are a people without a proper and rational understanding of the world and the factors that keep a people strong, together, and in command of their own destiny."

Thus, Afrocentric socialization refers to an interactive process by which Black parents and adults structure their behavior and primary institutions to promote among Black youth the internalization of values that emphasize love of self, awareness of their traditional African cultural heritage, and personal commitment to the economic political development of African Americans and other people of African descent. In the remaining section of this article, a list of institution-specific recommendations that African Americans should adopt in order to facilitate

Afrocentric socialization of young Black males is provided.

The Family

1. Black parents must instill an Afrocentric value system in their children.

Families are the foundation of all cultural groups and societies due to the major role that they play in socializing children to internalize the values of their cultural group or society (Coser et al., 1983). In the last two decades, an increasing number of Black scholars have urged African Americans to adopt an Afrocentric value system in order to facilitate the transformation of Blacks from a state of dependence and cultural confusion to a state of independence, self-reliance, and cultural sanity (Karenga, 1977, 1986; Mahubuti, 1978; Kunjufu, 1983; Perkins, 1986).

Socialization of Black youth that is guided by the Afrocentric perspective would encourage young Blacks to know themselves through the study of African and African American history, to be proud of being Black, and to internalize definitions of adulthood that associate maturity with one's contribution to the mental and political liberation of Black people (Perkins, 1986). Moreover, Afrocentric socialization should be designed to encourage Blacks to define self- and group-destructive behavior (e.g., drug abuse, drug dealing, exploitation of other Blacks, and violence) as being anti-Black and in opposition to the interests of the African American community (Asante, 1980).

According to Karenga (1980, 1986), the premier advocate of Afrocentric cultural transformation, the high rates of social problems among Blacks could be substantially reduced if Black parents and other adults would teach their children to adopt the Afrocentric value system that he refers to as Nguzo Saba. Moreover, Karenga (1977) argues that the seven values that comprise the Nguzo Saba represent "the necessary core and moral minimum of any value system constructed to rescue or reconstruct Black lives in their own image and interest."

I agree with Karenga (1973, 1977, 1986). Any effort designed to facilitate the Afrocentric socialization of Black youth, especially Black boys, must include a collective oriented value system such as the Nguzo Saba. Listed below is a brief description of the seven core values that comprise the Nguzo Saba, followed by an explanation of how the internalization of these values by Black boys will benefit African Americans.

Umoja (Unity)

- To strive for and maintain unity in the family, community, nation, and race.

Socialization that emphasizes Umoja (Unity) communicates to young Black males that commitment to family, community, nation, and Black unity is a primary objective of African Americans. The internalization of Umoja would contribute to the emergence of cultural values and psychic restraints that would substantially reduce Black males' participation in behavior that is self- and group destructive.

Kujichagulia (Self-Determination)

- To define ourselves, name ourselves, create for ourselves, and speak for ourselves instead of being defined, named for, and spoken for by others.

The history of America clearly indicates that White Americans have used their familial, educational, political, mass media, and other cultural institutions to promote negative images of African Americans and other non-White people (Mahubuti, 1978; Baldwin, 1980; Cogdell and Wilson, 1980). The Afrocentric value Kujichagulia (Self-Determination) prescribes that Black parents socialize their children to define themselves as African Americans as opposed to niggers, coloreds, or Negroes. Socializing Black youth to define themselves as African Americans cannot and should not be regarded as complete simply by training them to replace one label for another. Socializing Black youth to define themselves as African Americans must also include making them aware of the cultural and political circumstances that have contributed to the emergence and evolution of terms such as niggers, coloreds, Negroes, and African Americans.

Socializing Blacks to define themselves as African Americans will reduce the high rates of low self-esteem and self-hate that Blacks have internalized as a result of their exposure to negative images and anti-Black propaganda disseminated by the educational system and the mass media. Defining themselves as African Americans will lead Blacks toward identifying with those Africans who were responsible for the classic ancient African civilizations and their many contributions to the modern world.

Ujima (Collective Work and Responsibility)

- To build and maintain our community together and make our sisters' and brothers' problems our problems and to solve them together.

American society places a great deal of emphasis on individualism. In its ideal form, America's emphasis on individualism asserts that a citizen should have freedom in his economic pursuits and should succeed by his own initiative. However, in practice, American individualism induces individuals to perceive their interests as being more important than the interests of their social group or society. Consequently, individualism is a major source of apathy, alienation, and conflict in American society.

The Afrocentric value of Ujima (Collective Work and Responsibility) is the most fundamental aspect of the traditional African world view. Ujima emphasizes elevating the interests of the community above those of the individual. According to Mbiti (1969: 108-109), native-born Africans have historically been socialized to define themselves by their relationship and social obligations to others in their community. Thus, the African world view socializes the child to perceive himself in terms of "I am because we are; and since we are, therefore, I am."

The commitment of Blacks to individualism has not rendered them rewards commensurate with those achieved by Whites. Moreover, as a result of the harsh economic conditions that Blacks experience, individualism is greatly exaggerated, "which causes values associated with unity, cooperation, and mutual respect to be systematically sacrificed" (Cogdell and Wilson, 1980: 221). Thus, Black males' commitment to individualism is a salient feature of the "tough guy" and "player of women" images.

Socializing Blacks to value Ujima would substantially reduce their participation in self- and group-destructive behavior. Ujima encourages Black parents and adults to define maturity and manhood in terms of actions that contribute to the progress and development of Black people. And by definition, individualistic behavior is defined as a sign of immaturity and boyhood. Thus, incorporating Ujima in the socialization of Blacks introduces a positive communal dynamic in which they are taught that achieving manhood is inseparable from actions that contribute to the progress and development of the African American community.

Ujamaa (Cooperative Economics)

- To build and maintain our own stores, shops, and other businesses and to profit from them together.

Structurally induced economic underdevelopment is a major factor precipitating the high rates of social problems in the Black community. According to Wilson (1987), the high rates of joblessness among Black men are directly related to the formation of female-headed families, welfare dependency, and criminality among Blacks. In order to overcome economic underdevelopment and the social problems associated with it, African American parents and adults must teach their boys to value Ujamaa.

The boy socialized to value Ujamaa will become a man who understands that it is important to the survival and progress of the African American community to support Black businesses. African Americans will never achieve social and political parity with other American racial and ethnic groups without establishing a solid economic base.

Emphasizing Ujamaa will cause Black businesses to prosper. Subsequently, the growth of Black businesses will increase the ability of African Americans to create jobs for themselves and discontinue the intergenerational tendency to depend on the federal government and non-Blacks to provide for their economic survival and progress. Hence, incorporating Ujamaa in the socialization of Black boys is absolutely critical to the transformation of Blacks from a state of dependency to a state of independence and self-reliance.

Nia (Purpose)

- To make our collective vocation the building and developing of our community in order to restore our people to their traditional greatness.

Systematic racial discrimination and oppression have been the most salient features of the African American experience in America (Franklin, 1947; Knowles and Prewitt, 1969). Nia is a critical element of Afrocentric socialization because of the emphasis this value places on making Black youth aware of the oppression that Africans and African Americans have experienced. Moreover, the Nia value encourages African American parents to instill in Black youth a commitment to devote their lives to eradicating those structural pressures and cultural conditions that prevent African Americans from achieving economic and political parity with White Americans.

Kuumba (Creativity)

- To do always as much as we can, in the way we can, in order to leave our community more beautiful and beneficial than we inherited it.

Throughout the United States, areas inhabited by lower- and working-class Blacks tend to be substantially more deteriorated than residential areas inhabited by comparable groups of White Americans. Although some of the responsibility for the deterioration in Black residential areas can be attributed to older housing stock and the lack of city services, apathy and lack of concern on the part of a large segment of the Black community also contribute to racial disparities in community deterioration.

Socializing Black youth to value Kuumba (Creativity) would contribute immensely to the aesthetic quality of African American communities as a result of the emphasis that this value places on community beautification. Socializing Black boys to value Kuumba would reduce the tendency of many of these boys, especially those prone to hanging out on street corners, from throwing trash anywhere and not showing respect for the property of others. Kuumba also emphasizes exposing children to creative arts such as drawing, painting, poetry, music, and other arts that promote spiritual awareness and harmony with nature and others. Hence, Black boys socialized to value Kuumba are more likely to evolve into men who are sensitive to the needs and concerns of others, and are therefore more likely to become good husbands, fathers, and neighbors.

Imani (Faith)

- To believe with all our hearts in our people, our parents, our teachers, our leaders, and the righteousness and victory of our struggle.

Afrocentric socialization of Black youth will be impossible if Black parents and adults do not strive to present themselves as living examples of Afrocentric consciousness. Hence, in order to facilitate the Afrocentric socialization of Black youth, Black parents and adults must undergo Afrocentric resocialization. That is, they must internalize new values and assume new roles that are consistent with an Afrocentric world view.

Adopting Welsing's (1974) "codes for Black behavioral conduct" is one way in which parents and adults could demonstrate to Black youth how to live an Afrocentric life. Welsing includes the following standards in her "codes for Black behavioral conduct":

- Stop name-calling one another
- Stop cursing one another
- Stop squabbling with one another
- Stop gossiping about one another
- Stop being discourteous toward one another
- Stop robbing one another
- Stop stealing from one another
- Stop fighting one another
- Stop killing one another
- Stop using and selling drugs to one another
- Stop throwing trash and dirt on the streets and in places where Black people live, work, and learn

Black youth exposed to adults who are structuring their behavior in accordance with Welsing's "codes of Black behavioral conduct" will be less likely to reject the basic teachings and requirements of Afrocentric socialization as idle talk. Through their interactions with parents and other adults, they will see the dignity and power that emanates from living an Afrocentric lifestyle. Moreover, Black men who adhere to the Welsing "codes" will function as positive examples of Black manhood and potent alternative role models to those men who define manhood in terms of toughness, sexual conquest, thrill-seeking and exploitation of others.

2. *Black parents and representatives of various community organizations must establish formal rite of passage ceremonies that will provide structure to the process by which Black boys make the passage into manhood.*

A major assumption of the Afrocentric perspective of the high rates of social problems among Blacks is that too many Black males adhere to definitions of manhood that promote self- and group-destructive behavior (Perkins, 1975; Staples, 1982; Oliver, 1984). Consequently, the 1980s has witnessed the emergence of a movement led by Black scholars and a small segment of the African American community in which Black parents are incorporating African styled rite of passage ceremonies in the socialization of Black boys (Fair, 1977; Kunjufu, 1983, 1986; Hare and Hare, 1985; Perkins, 1986). In their treatise, *Bringing the Black Boy to Manhood: The Passage,* the Hares (1985) argue that African Americans need to develop rite of passage ceremonies because "The socialization of Black boys in today's fractured family life is left too often to the peer groups and the streets. Street education is maladaptive, even antithetical, to school performance and parental teaching."

Although the various rite of passage ceremonies that have been proposed differ with respect to the required age range of the initiates and the specific content of manhood training, all have as their primary objective the promotion of Afrocentric values and a sense of collective commitment among Black youth. At the very minimum, a rite of passage ceremony for Black boys should include the following program components:

1. A group of committed adult males who will lead Black boys through the passage from boyhood to manhood (Fair, 1977; Kunjufu, 1983; Hare and Hare, 1985; Perkins, 1986).

2. Manhood Training—to help Black boys understand and appreciate the responsibilities of manhood. A major portion of this training should emphasize the Nguzo Saba, Welsing's "codes of Black behavioral con-

duct" and the importance of self-discipline in successfully enacting the roles of son, husband, father, and brother to one's relatives and neighbors (Hare and Hare, 1985; Perkins, 1986).

3. Sex Education—To help Black boys understand their sexuality and how to formulate responsible attitudes about the opposite sex and sexual relations (Perkins, 1986).

4. Cultural Enrichment—To help Black boys appreciate and value the significance of African and African American history and culture (Fair, 1977; Kunjufu, 1983; Perkins, 1986).

5. Political Awareness and Community Service—To help Black boys understand those factors that have contributed to the pathological social conditions that are prevalent throughout the national African American community. And, how to distinguish between actions that are in the interest of African Americans and those which are not. Also, to help Black boys develop an Afrocentric consciousness that leads to behavior that contributes to the needs of African Americans and other people of African descent (Fair, 1977; Hare and Hare, 1985; Perkins, 1986).

6. Educational Reinforcement—To help Black boys develop a realistic understanding about how educational achievement is an important aspect of their passage from boyhood to manhood (Hare and Hare, 1985).

7. Life Management—To teach Black boys how to integrate manhood, sex education, cultural enrichment, and political awareness training as a foundation for organizing and regulating their lives to achieve maximum effectiveness. Life management training should also include physical fitness, self-defense, survival, and family budgeting, as well as guided exploration of educational and career opportunities (Fair, 1977; Hare and Hare, 1985; Perkins, 1986).

The overall purpose of the manhood training that has been proposed has been cogently summarized by the Hares (1985: 1-9): "For the Black boy, we must find ways to punctuate his psyche with commitment for family and race, community and nation, and with motivation for responsibility, along with personal mastery."

The Educational System

The American educational system has played a major role in the socialization of Black youth. However, the overall impact of American education of African Americans has been more detrimental than beneficial (Woodson, 1933: xiii; Hale, 1982; Kunjufu, 1983, 1986). In his classic work, *The Mis-education of the Negro,* Carter Woodson (1933: xiii) argues that:

> The same educational process which inspires and stimulates the oppressor with the thought that he is everything and has accomplished everything worthwhile, depresses and crushes at the same time the spark of genius in the Negro by making him feel that his race does not amount to much and never will measure up to the standards of other peoples. The Negro thus educated is a hopeless liability of the race.

In order to facilitate the Afrocentric socialization of Black youth, the following recommendations should be implemented:

1. Black parents and concerned adults must become more involved in the administration of local educational systems. This can be achieved by regularly attending PTA meetings, establishing curriculum monitoring committees, running candidates for school board offices, and lobbying educational policy makers and administrators to incorporate African American history and culture in the educational curriculum.

2. To insure that African American children will be taught about the accomplishments of classic ancient African civilizations, African American parents must establish "independent Black schools." These schools should supplement or function as alternatives to traditional schools (Mahubuti, 1978; Perkins, 1986).

The Church

Christianity has been a major tool in the psychic and economic exploitation of African Americans (Blassingame, 1972; Buswell, 1964). In order to facilitate Afrocentric socialization of Black youth, the African American church should adopt the following recommendations:

1. The members of African American churches must establish policies that call for an immediate ban on exposing Black children to religious materials and religious doctrine that portray God, Jesus, and many of the other Biblical heroes as White people.
2. Sunday school and Bible study classes must be structured to not only make Black youth aware of Christ and his message, but where appropriate, as indicated by specific Biblical references and the works of scholars such as G. M. James's (1954) *The Greeks Were Not the Authors of Greek Philosophy, but the People of North Africa, Commonly Called the Egyptians,* and Yosef Ben-Jochannan's (1970) *African Origins of the Major Western Religions,* be made aware that Judaism, Christianity, and Islam were founded on the continent of Africa and that ancient Africans played a major role in their creation and evolution.
3. Members of African American churches must encourage their ministers and church leaders to allow their facilities and resources to be used to promote the Afrocentric socialization of Black youth.

The Media

Over the course of American history, all forms of media have been used to disseminate anti-Black propaganda and negative images of African Americans (Boggle, 1973; Staples and Jones, 1985). In order to promote the Afrocentric socialization of Black youth, the following recommendations should be implemented to counter the adverse impact the media has had on the psychic development of African Americans:

1. Black parents and adults should encourage Black youth to pursue careers in all sectors of the mass media industry in order to insure that African Americans will have positive input into the development of media products.
2. Black organizations must vigilantly monitor the major media institutions and be prepared to protest media products that portray African Americans in a racist manner.
3. In order to insure the dissemination of "the facts about Blacks" and realistic portrayals of Black people and their culture, African Americans must pool their resources and establish their own newspapers, magazines, book publishing companies, film production companies, theaters, and radio and television stations.

Conclusion

African Americans have spent too much time blaming White America for the high rate of social problems among Blacks. According to Elijah Muhammad (1965: 62), "Before we can be justified in accusing the other man, let us examine ourselves first."

Reducing social problems among African Americans through Afrocentric socialization of Black males is based on two primary assumptions. First, that White racism and historical patterns of racial discrimination are the most salient environmental pressures adversely affecting the ability of African Americans to survive and progress in America. And second, that African Americans have failed to establish an Afrocentric cultural ideology or world view that could be used to promote unity and to mitigate the adverse affects of racially motivated social pressures.

Afrocentric socialization is not a magic potion; it will not rid Black America of all of its social problems. However, it is certainly a much better option than continuing to allow substantial numbers of lower- and working-class Black boys to make the passage from boyhood to manhood under the tutelage of men who define manhood in terms of toughness, sexual conquest, and thrill-seeking.

References

AKBAR, N. (1983) Chains and Images of Psychological Slavery. Jersey City, NJ: New Mind Productions.

ARCHER, D. and R. GARTNER (1983) Violence and Crime in Cross National Perspective. New Haven, CT: Yale University Press.

ASANTE, M. (1980) Afrocentricity: The Theory of Social Change. Buffalo, NY: Amulefi Publishing Company.

ASANTE, M. (1987) The Afrocentric Idea. Philadelphia: Temple University Press.

BALDWIN, J. A. (1979) "Education and oppression in the American context." Journal of Inner City Studies 1: 62-83.

BALDWIN, J. A. (1980) "The psychology of oppression," pp. 95-110 in M. Asante and V. Abdular (eds.) Contemporary Black Thought. Beverly Hills, CA: Sage Publications.

BENJAMIN, L. (1983) "The dog theory: Black male-female conflict." Western Journal of Black Studies 7: 49-55.

BEN-JOCHANNAN, Y. (1970) African Origins of the Major Western Religions. New York: Alkebu-Ian Books.

BLAUNER, R. (1972) Racial Oppression in America. New York: Harper & Row.

BOGGLE, D. (1973) Toms, Coons, Mulattoes, Mammies, and Bucks: An Interpretive History of Blacks in American Films. New York: Viking Press.

BRENTON, M. (1966) The American Male. New York: Fawcett.

BUSWELL, J. O. (1964) Slavery, Segregation and Scripture. Grand Rapids, MI: William B. Eardmans Publishing Company.

CAZENAVE, N. (1981) "Black men in America—The quest for manhood," pp. 176-185 in H. P. McAdoo (ed.) Black Families. Beverly Hills, CA: Sage Publications.

Centers for Disease Control (1985) "Homicide among young Black males—United States, 1970-1982." Morbidity and Mortality Weekly Report 34: 629-633.

CLARK, C. (1975) "The Shockley-Jensen Thesis: A contexual appraisal." The Black Scholar 6 (10): 2-11.

CLARK, K. B. (1965) Dark Ghetto. New York: Harper & Row.

CLARK, K. B. and M. P. CLARK (1947) "Racial identification and preference in Negro children," pp. 169-178 in T. M. Newcomb and E. L. Hartley (eds.) Readings in Social Psychology. New York: Holt, Rinehart & Winston.

CLARK, K. B. and M. P. CLARK (1980) "What do Blacks think of themselves?" Ebony 16 (November): 176-183.

COGDELL, R. and S. WILSON (1980) Black Communication in White Society. Sarasota, CA: Century Twenty-One Publishing.

COSER, I., B. RHEA, P. A. STEFFAN, and S. L. KNOCK (1983) Introduction to Sociology. New York: Harcourt, Brace, Jovanovich.

DAVIDSON, B. (1959, revised edition 1970) The Lost Cities of Africa. Boston: Little, Brown and Company.

DIOP, C. A. (1974) The African Origin of Civilization—Myth or Reality. New York: Lawrence Hill & Company.

Ebony (1986) "The Black family." 42 (August): 4-162.

FAIR, F. (1977) Orita for Black Youth: An Invitation into Christian Adulthood. Valley Forge, PA: Judson Press.

FASTEAU, M. (1975) The Male Machine. New York: Macmillan.

FRANKLIN, J. H. (1947) From Slavery to Freedom. New York: Knopf.

GARRETT, H. (1961) "One psychologist's view of equality of the races." U.S. News and World Report 51 (August 14): 72-74.

HALE, J. (1982) Black Children, Their Roots, Culture, and Learning Styles. Provo, UT: Brigham Young University Press.

HANNERZ, U. (1969) Sculside: Inquiries into Ghetto Culture and Community. New York: Columbia University Press.

HARE, N. and J. HARE (1985) Bringing the Black Boy to Manhood: The Passage. San Francisco: The Black Think Tank.

HILLIARD, A. (1981) "IQ thinking as catechism: ethnic and cultural bias or invalid science?" Black Books Bulletin 7 (1): 2-7.

JACKSON, J. G. (1970) Introduction to African Civilizations. New York: University Books.

JAMES, C. M. (1954) Stolen Legacy. New York: Philosophical Library.

JENSEN, A. (1973) "The differences are real." Psychology Today 7 (December): 80-86.

KARENGA, M. (1988) "Black studies and the problematic of paradigm—The philosophical dimension." Journal of Black Studies 18: 395-414.

KARENGA, R. (1977) Kwanzaa: Origin, Concepts, Practice. Los Angeles: Kawaida Publications.

KARENGA, R. (1986) "Social ethics and the Black family." The Black Scholar 17 (5): 41-54.

KNOWLES, L. L. and K. PREWITT [eds.] (1969) Institutional Racism in America. Englewood Cliffs, NJ: Prentice-Hall.

KUNJUFU, J. (1983) Countering the Conspiracy to Destroy Black Boys—Volume I. Chicago: African American Images.

KUNJUFU, J. (1986) Countering the Conspiracy to Destroy Black Boys—Volume II. Chicago: African American Images.

LIEBOW, E. (1967) Tally's Corner. Boston: Little, Brown.

MAHUBUTI, H. (1978) Enemies: The Clash of Races. Chicago: Third World Press.

MBITI, J. S. (1969) African Religions and Philosophy. New York: Fredrick A. Praeger, Publishers.

MCGHEE, J. D. (1984) Running the Gauntlet: Black Men in America. New York: National Urban League.

MONTAGU, A. (1941) "The biologist looks at crime." Annals of the American Academy of Political and Social Science 217: 46-57.

MUHAMMAD, E. (1965) Message to the Black Man in America. Chicago: Muhammad Mosque of Islam No. 2.

OLIVER, W. (1984) "Black males and the tough guy image: a dysfunctional compensatory adaptation." Western Journal of Black Studies 8: 199-203.

PERKINS, U. E. (1975) Home Is a Dirty Street: The Social Oppression of Black Children. Chicago: Third World Press.

PERKINS, U. E. (1986) Harvesting New Generations: The Positive Development of Black Youth. Chicago: Third World Press.

POUSSAINT, A. F. (1983) "The mental health status of Blacks—1983," pp. 187-238 in J. D. Williams (ed.) The State of Black America—1983. New York: National Urban League.

STAPLES, R. (1982) Black Masculinity: The Black Male's Role in American Society. San Francisco: The Black Scholar Press.

STAPLES, R. and T. JONES (1985) "Culture, ideology and Black television images." The Black Scholar 16 (3): 10-20.

Time Magazine (1985) "Children having children." December 19: 78-84, 87-90.

U.S. Bureau of the Census (1983) America's Black Population—1978-1982. Washington, DC: Government Printing Office.

U.S. News & World Report (1986) "A nation apart." March 17: 18-28.

VAN SERTIMA, I. [ed.] (1983) Blacks in Science: Ancient and Modern. New Brunswick, NJ: Transaction Books.

VANDER ZANDEN, J. W. (1986) American Minority Relations. New York: Ronald Press.

WELSING, F. (1972) "The Cress theory of color confrontation." Washington, DC: Author.

WELSING, F. (1974) "The conspiracy to make Black males inferior." Ebony 29: 84-93.

WELSING, F. (1978) "Mental health: etiology and process," pp. 48-72 in L. Gary (ed.) Mental Health: A Challenge in the Black Community. Philadelphia: Dorrance.

WELSING, F. (1980) "The concept and the color of God and Black mental health." Black Books Bulletin 7 (1): 27-29, 35.

WILLIAMS, C. (1974) The Destruction of Black Civilization. Chicago: Third World Press.

WILSON, W. J. (1987) The Truly Disadvantaged: The Inner City, the Underclass, and Public Policy. Chicago: University of Chicago Press.

WOODSON, C. (1933) The Mis-education of the Negro. Washington, DC: Associated Publishers.

18

INTRODUCTION

Coramae Richey Mann was presented with the Distinguished Scholar Award of the American Society of Criminology Division of Women and Crime in 1995. This award recognized Mann's research on women, racial and ethnic minorities, and crime. More than that, it acknowledged her contributions to the field of criminology. Along with Daniel Georges-Abeyie and others, Mann challenged the nondiscrimination thesis presented by William Wilbanks in 1987. This debate led to the publication of her book *Unequal Justice: A Question of Color,* which presented a comprehensive review, critique, and analysis of the research on racial minorities in the United States. Furthermore, Mann expanded the concept of minority to include Hispanic Americans, Asian Americans, and American Indians in addition to African Americans.

In the following article, Mann notes that although minority women, especially Black women, make up the largest proportion of women in the criminal justice system, research has largely ignored this group of offenders. She examines the relationship between gender, race, and the criminal justice system by looking at arrests, the courts, and corrections. Mann argues that minority women are doubly discriminated against, first, because of the prejudicial treatment afforded women and second, because racial minorities are discriminated against in the criminal justice system. She contends that institutional racism operates to increase the severity of sanctions that the police, the courts, and other criminal justice actors impose on Black women offenders.

Minority and Female

A Criminal Justice Double Bind

Coramae Richey Mann

This article addresses the status of minority (Black, Hispanic, Native American) women offenders from arrest to incarceration. As such, it examines and synthesizes the scattered information on a group that is doubly discriminated against because of their gender and race/ethnicity status.[1] For many decades the study of women's deviance was rare and the reports available were limited to examinations of prostitution and other sexual deviance thought to be "typical" female offenses. It was gradually recognized that all women offenders did not fit this stereotype and that women were involved in a wide variety of activities that are labeled "criminal." In the 1970s, and more so in the 1980s, criminological inquiry and research turned to women as offenders, but there is still a dearth of studies of the processing of women at each level of the criminal justice system. This neglect is exacerbated in the case of minority or nonwhite women, especially Black women, who comprise the largest proportion of women caught in the criminal justice double bind. The scarcity of documented sources necessarily circumscribes the discussion presented here.

The Criminal Justice Processing of Minority Women: Arrest, Prosecution, and Sentencing

The Crimes

The Uniform Crime Reports (UCR) compiled by the Federal Bureau of Investigation are the most frequently utilized sources of arrest information in the United States today.[2] Unfortunately, the UCRs are not crosstabulated by gender and race, which makes it impossible to isolate the offenses for which minority women are arrested. Nonetheless, the parameters of the incidence of female crime

---

From Mann, R.C. Minority and female. *Social Justice.* Reprinted with permission.

can be estimated from aggregated data on race and gender when combined with a number of studies specifically addressing minority female offenders.

The latest available data reveal that in 1987, 31.3% of the total arrests were of minority persons, 29.7% of whom were Black (U.S. Department of Justice, 1988: 183). Blacks also made up 47.3% of persons arrested for Index violent crimes in 1987, yet comprised only 13% of the U.S. population.[3] Women, on the other hand, accounted for 17.7% of total 1987 arrests and 11.1% of Index violent crime arrestees (UCR, 1988: 181). Clearly, women make up a small proportion of arrests, especially for serious offenses, a pattern that has persisted since 1960 when female arrests were first recorded in a separate category (Rans, 1978). Of course, these statistics tell us little about the crimes of minority women, but a number of research efforts suggest that when each subgroup is compared with their white counterparts, the Black woman is as likely to be involved with the law as is the Black man.[4] Homicide and drug offenses are serious crimes of contemporary public concern and, excluding prostitution, are probably the offenses involving women that are most frequently examined. Early studies of criminal homicides by gender and race reveal that Black females are second to Black males in frequency of arrests (Wolfgang, 1958; Pokorny, 1965) and their conviction rates have been reported as 14 times greater than those of white females (Sutherland and Cressey, 1978: 30). More recent efforts tend to corroborate the previous studies by Wolfgang and Pokorny in showing extremely high proportions of Black females as both victims and offenders. As homicide offenders, Black females have been found to predominate in every major study where women offenders were included (e.g., Suval and Brisson, 1974; Biggers, 1979; Riedel and Lockhart-Riedel, 1984; Weisheit, 1984; Block, 1985; Formby, 1986; Goetting, 1987; Mann, 1987). Black men are their principal victims, since homicide is not only an intraracial but also an intergender event. Homicide has been reported as the leading cause of death among young Black males from 15 to 24 years of age (Mercy, Smith, and Rosenberg, 1983). Since the average age of the Black male homicide victim is older in cases of domestic homicide (about 38 years old) and in instances of nondomestic killing by a Black female assailant (about 29 years old, see Mann, 1988a), it is clear that Black men are at a high risk of death throughout their lifetimes. Thus, it is not surprising that homicide has been designated by the U.S. Public Health Service as the primary public health risk for Black men in the U.S.

In 1970, Williams and Bates reported an overrepresentation of Black females in female admissions to the Public Health Service Hospital in Lexington, Kentucky, for narcotic addiction. Most of these women (63.8%) were urban residents from New York, Chicago, and Washington, D.C., compared to only 22.8% of the white female addicts. More recently, Pettiway (1987: 746) found female heroin and other opiate users to be ethnically split: Blacks were 35%, whites 33.8%, and Hispanics 31.2% (Puerto Rican 16.4% and Cuban 14.8%). Both studies found a strong correlation between women's drug usage and crime. Mann (1988b) compared random samples of female homicide offenders in six major U.S. urban areas on the basis of drug and nondrug use. Few differences were found between the two groups; the majority of whom were Black (77.7%). This led to the conclusion that women who kill are similar to each other on a number of important characteristics, regardless of their substance abuses (alcohol or narcotics). While there were proportionately fewer Blacks in the homicide user group, Mann found there were almost twice the proportion of Hispanic assailants in the abuser group, compared to the nonabuser Hispanic group.

Arrests

Black women are seven times more likely to be arrested for prostitution than women of other ethnic groups (Haft, 1976: 212). Yet, it cannot be empirically established that Black prostitutes are more prevalent than prostitutes in other female racial/ethnic groups. One possible explanation for the disproportionate number of arrests is that Black prostitutes are forced to practice their profession on the streets instead of under the benevolent protection of a hotel manager or in luxury apartments, as predominantly white call girls are able to do. "Street walking" increases the likelihood of police contact and harassment as well as possible law enforcement racial bias:

> As might be expected, the largest proportion of arrests of Black prostitutes takes place in the inner cities where living standards are low, the level of desperation high, and police prejudice endemic *(Ibid.)*.

Are harassment and readiness to arrest indicative of police reactions to Black women offenders? A study of incarcerated female offenders reveals that Black women are more likely than white women to perceive police officers as excessively brutal, harassing, and unlikely to give them a break through nonarrest (Kratcoski and Scheuerman, 1974). The researchers conclude that the police discretionary power not to arrest was used more liberally with white women than with Black women.

Moyer and White (1981) hypothesized that police officers would apply more severe sanctions to a Black woman than to a white woman, especially if the Black woman was "loud, boisterous, aggressive, vulgar, and disrespectful"—characteristics seen by some whites as typical of Black people. In the second instance, the researchers reasoned, demeanor could also potentially predict law enforcement bias. While neither hypothesis was supported, type of crime in association with demeanor strongly influenced decisions of police officers where women were concerned, more so than with male offenders.

Pre-Trial, Prosecution, and Sentencing

In minority communities it is generally believed that in addition to the racial prejudice exhibited by the police toward minorities, the white-dominated judicial system also treats them more stringently (Deming, 1977). The few studies of the criminal justice processing of men and women appear to indicate differential treatment of nonwhite women offenders at every stage of the process.

According to earlier studies, at the pretrial stage minority women are frequently unable to make bail and are held in jail until their court hearing, or they are excessively detained relative to the type of offense committed (see, e.g., Barrus and Slavin, 1971; Nagel and Weitzman, 1971). Many judges deny bail or insist upon higher and higher bail for each prostitution arrest, and since 53% of arrested prostitutes are Black women, the impact upon this minority group is obvious (DeCrow, 1974). An analysis of grand larceny and felonious assault cases sampled from criminal cases in all 50 states isolated a *disadvantaged pattern* of discrimination which resulted in adverse treatment of Black women at virtually all stages of the criminal justice process, including the likelihood of being jailed before and after conviction more so than white women (Nagel and Weitzman, 1971).

Recent research suggests that, in some jurisdictions, the detention status of women offenders may not be related to race/ethnicity. Mann (1984: 168) reports that in the Fulton County (Georgia) criminal courts,

> no overall relationship was found between race and whether a defendant was held in detention before the court hearing, since 66.7% of the Black women and 63.6% of the white women were in jail at the time of their court hearing.

Mann did find that not a single Black female was released on her own recognizance compared to 9% of non-Blacks and that there was a slight tendency for higher bails set for Black women.

A court study by Daly (1987) compared Seattle and New York City jurisdictions and found that in both jurisdictions the Black and Hispanic female detention rates were lower than those of white women. And apparently being married was found to mitigate more strongly against detention for Black women than Hispanic women in New York City, where 62.6% of the female defendants were Black (a higher proportion than for Black men) and 28.8% were Puerto Rican (*Ibid.*: 161).

The poverty of most minority women offenders may contribute to either a lack of legal counsel or the necessity to rely upon public defenders instead of private attorneys for the defense of their cases. There are as many excellent public defenders as there are inept private attorneys, but it is generally acknowledged that the overwhelming case loads of public defenders permit little attention to individual defendants.[5]

Bias on the part of judges may also affect the appointment of free legal counsel. In one Alabama study, 42% of the white female defendants were afforded court-appointed counsel compared to only 26% of the Black females (Alabama Section, 1975). The reverse should have been indicated, since at that time the median income of Black families in Alabama was one-half that of white families.

A Washington, D.C., study noted the "Black-shift phenomenon," that is, 63% of the adult female population of the District of Columbia was Black. Yet the proportion of first bookings into detention was 73% Black, with Black women comprising 83% of those returned to jail from the initial court hearing, 92% of them receiving 30 days or more. For those given prison sentences, 97% were sentenced for three months or more (McArthur, 1974). For the District's white females, the comparable proportions were in descending order: 37% of adult female population, 27% of first detention bookings, 17% of returns to jail, eight percent 30 days or longer sentence, and only three percent sentenced to three months or longer (Adams, 1975: 185). In a re-analysis of these data, Adams did not find that the type of offense adequately explained the racial differences, but rather that "compared with whites, black women seem underdefended and oversentenced." Further, "they may have been overarrested and overindicted as well" (*Ibid.*: 193).

Foley and Rasche (1979: 104) found that "differential treatment is definitely accorded to female offenders by race." Over a 16-year period, they had studied 1,163 women sentenced to the Missouri State Correctional Center for Women. Their comparison of sentence lengths for all offenses, combined, showed no significant differences between Black and white female sentence lengths, but Black women did receive longer sentences (55.1 months) than white women (52.5 months). An examination of individual crimes revealed that Blacks received significantly longer sentences (32.8 months) than whites (29.9 months) for crimes against property, and served longer periods in prison. Although white women were accorded lengthier sentences for crimes against the person (182.3 months) at almost double the length for Black women (98.5 months), the actual time served was longer for Black women (26.7 months versus 23 months). In fact, the white women imprisoned for murder served one-third less time than did Black women who committed the same offense. The same held true for the analysis of drug offenses between the two groups. There was no significant difference in mean sentence length between them, yet Black women served significantly more time in prison (20.4 months) when compared with white female drug law violators (13.2 months).

Sentencing outcomes based on the race of the victim and offender are a source of much controversy where men are concerned,[6] but little attention has been devoted to the interracial homicides of women and the sentences received. Two recent studies suggest that the race of the victim influences sentencing of women homicide offenders. In a study of female homicide offenders in six U.S. cities for

1979 and 1983, Mann (1987) found modest (although not statistically significant) support for a devaluation hypothesis.[7] When Black women killed other Blacks, 40% of them received prison sentences, but if the victim was non-Black, 66.7% were imprisoned. Conversely, if both the victim and offender were non-Black, 45.3% of the female offenders were incarcerated, while 50% of non-Black women who killed Blacks went to prison. The other study, conducted by Shields (1987), examined female homicide in Alabama from 1930 to 1986. He found that in the few cases which crossed racial lines, the offenders—who were all Black—received severe sentences. In fact, the majority of convicted Black females received life sentences.

The Punishments

Another method of investigating the relationship between gender, race, and the criminal justice system is through examining the crimes for which women are imprisoned.

According to a national survey by the U.S. General Accounting Office (1979), of the women offenders released from prison in 1979, almost two-thirds (64.3%) were minorities, and more than one-half (50.2%) were Black. As seen in Table 1 (found at the end of the article along with all subsequent tables), each minority group is disproportionately represented in the inmate population according to its proportion in the general female population. On the other hand, as an incarcerated group, white females are substantially less populous.

Data excerpted from a national survey of incarcerated women reported by Glick and Neto (1977), shown in Table 2, reveal that Black women were more likely to be imprisoned for drug offenses (20.2%) and murder (18.6%). Drug offenses and forgery/fraud made up almost one-half (44.8%) of the crimes for which Native American women were in prison. Even more startling was the 40.3% of Hispanic women who were incarcerated for drug offenses—twice as frequently as Blacks.

An examination of the prison statistics from states with large numbers of minority women offers a more detailed picture of the offenses of these women. California, for example, incarcerates more women than any other state in the nation. In 1979, 19% of the women cited and arrested were Black, 17.3% were Mexican American, 0.96% were Native American, and 0.44% were Asian American (Hegner, 1981). Similar to the national results reported above, excluding the UCR catch-all "all other offenses," Table 3 shows that in California, Hispanic women (in this case, Mexican American) were more frequently arrested for drug offenses (24.2%), with burglary second (21.8%), and theft third (16.5%). Black women's arrests were primarily for theft (19.6%), assault (17.8%), and drugs (17.8%). Assault was the first-ranked offense of Native American women (30.5%), followed by drugs (11.8%) and theft (11.2%).

Kruttschnitt (1981) examined the sentencing outcomes of a sample of 1,034 female defendants processed in a northern California county between 1972 and 1976. She found that:

> . . . in three of the five offense categories either the defendant's race or her income significantly affects the sentence she receives. Specifically, black women convicted of either disturbing the peace or drug law violations are sentenced more severely than their white counterparts; lower-income women convicted of forgery receive the more severe sentences. . . . [T]he status of welfare is generally given the greatest weight and appears to have a more consistent impact than either race or income alone on the sentences accorded these women (*Ibid.*, 256).

In a separate analysis to determine if the relatively severe sentences were due to race, low-income, or welfare status, Kruttschnitt (*Ibid:* 258) found that most of the effect of race on sentencing was direct and not indirect through welfare, or that "the impact of race on sentencing appears to have little to do with the fact that blacks are more likely to be welfare recipients than whites."

In terms of incarceration in the California prison system, Table 4 compares the three major offenses of each minority group with that of white females and gives the proportions of those receiving prison sentences. Although there may be mitigating circumstances involved in the dispositions of individual cases, Table 4 reveals some curious race/ethnic differences between the women felons in California. Whereas 50% of the Mexican American women arrested for homicide end up in prison, only 30.2% of whites, 24.8% of Blacks, and 20% of Native American women convicted of this offense were sentenced to prison, despite comprising higher proportions of those originally arrested for this crime. Similarly, although Black women accounted for 21.2% of women arrested for drug law violations, only 25.8% of those offenders were sent to prison. Mexican American women were more likely than Black women to receive a prison sentence for drugs (33.3%) compared to their arrest proportion (13.4%). In contrast, white women drug violators, who represent the primary group arrested for this offense (65.1%), were far less likely to be imprisoned (39.4%) than any minority female group. It seems that in terms of homicide and drug violations, minority women, and particularly Mexican Americans, are treated differentially by the California criminal justice system. As seen in Table 4, the offenses of robbery, assault, and burglary also show disproportionate prison sentences for Mexican Americans, when compared to white and other minority females.

It has been demonstrated that the Black female offender is more likely to be arrested and imprisoned than any other female minority group, but the California statistics just cited indicate that the number of arrests of Hispanic women are slowly gaining on those of Black women. The similarities of the crimes of California and New York Hispanic women, who are culturally different and from opposite shores of the country, are provocative. The most frequent offense for which a Puerto Rican woman offender in New York State was sentenced in 1976 was also dangerous drugs (53.8%), with robbery second (17.9%) and homicide third (10.3%) (Wright, 1981). New commitments to the facilities of the New York State Department of Correctional Services in that year reveal that Puerto Rican female commitments comprised 22.1% of all New York State female commitments for drugs compared to 51.5% Black and 25.3% white. Puerto Rican women were also 8% of the women imprisoned for homicide, while comprising only a portion of the 5% of the national Hispanic female population. Black women were 80% of the women sent to prison for homicide in New York that year; whites were 12%.

One might wonder why it is that in California white women are less likely to be imprisoned for drug law violations than Mexican American women when this crime is the primary arrest offense for both groups. Are white women referred to drug treatment programs while minority women are sent to prison? Why are white California women more likely to go to prison for robbery than Black women? Could it be because they rob from business establishments and Blacks rob from individual Blacks? Currently there are no hard-and-fast answers to such questions, but scattered evidence seems to indicate that minority women are not treated equitably by the criminal justice system.

Incarcerated Minority Women

Jails, particularly rural Southern jails, are "targets for the sexual abuse" of the women who occupy them, especially Black inmates, according to Sims (1976: 139). Sexual harassment is typical, but cases such as that of Black inmate Joan Little, who killed the white jailer in Beaufort County, North Carolina, who had sexually molested her, are atypical. Few women in jails kill the jailers and male inmates who sexually humiliate and molest them.

Many jails housing women are dirty and unsanitary. Health care is rare; so are recreational programs. There is no way to separately house women who would participate in work release programs, and, thus, such programs are rare for jailed women. Because of their small numbers in comparison to men, training and education programs for women in jails are generally impossible. Yet a great number of the women in the nation's jails, most of whom are Black, are misdemeanants (43.5%) or unsentenced (46.7%), and have committed victimless crimes (Glick and Neto, 1977: 70). Female offenders of all ages—the sentenced as well as the unsentenced, the mentally ill, the potentially dangerous psychotics, from prostitutes to accused murderers—are confined together in jail because of a lack of housing for female offenders (U.S. General Accounting Office, 1979).

Prisons for women have their own psychologically devastating effects on women, especially for the over 50% minority population occupying them (Goetting and Howsen, 1983). The appalling lack of interest in women's prisons is typically attributed to their small numbers when compared to male felons. Thus, the majority of correctional funds are directed towards men's prisons to the neglect of female prison facilities. As a result, medical and health services—particularly those peculiar to women's special gynecological and obstetrical needs—are poor or lacking. The federal General Accounting Office found that women in prisons have fewer vocational programs at their disposal compared to men, or an average of three compared to the 10 in men's facilities (U.S. General Accounting Office, 1979). The existing programs follow the sex stereotype of the traditional female role—clerical skills, cosmetology, and food services (Glick and Neto, 1977: 77)—and are geared toward lower-paying jobs. Prison industries in women's facilities rarely provide training beyond that leading to employment as a hotel maid, cook, waitress, laundry worker, or garment factory worker (Simon, 1975).

The frequent location of women's prisons in rural areas introduces special problems for a woman offender. To be physically distant from one's children, family, friends, and legal counsel results in a deprivation of communication that reinforces the female inmate's feeling of isolation and powerlessness (Gibson, 1976). Those women who are mothers (variously estimated at 56% to 70% [Glick and Neto, 1977])—and most minority women in prison are mothers—experience special problems related to custody, support, and other legal matters pertaining to their children (McGowan and Blumenthal, 1976). Because of these distances, an imprisoned woman has greater difficulty obtaining legal counsel or conferring with her attorney.

In an atmosphere that is tense and oppressive, minority women face additional problems related to the rural locations of women's prisons. Most of the staff are whites recruited from the farm and rural areas surrounding the prisons, while the majority of the inmates are nonwhites from urban areas, a mixture that contributes to ever-present friction. A majority of both white and nonwhite (Black and American Indian) female inmates in Kruttschnitt's study (1983) of the Minnesota Correctional Institution for Women felt that race/ethnicity influenced correctional officers' treatment of the female inmates. Over two-thirds of the minority women perceived racial discrimination in the institution and 29.4% felt that job assignments were influenced by race (35.3% had no opinion). Nonwhite women, who comprised 42% of the Minnesota prison population (where 93% of the staff and administration were white), cited "race relations" as the most frequent response for infra-inmate assaults (Kruttschnitt, 1983: 585).

In many institutions for women felons, Hispanic women are not permitted to speak Spanish, to read or write letters in their native language, to subscribe to Spanish-language magazines or newspapers, or to converse with their visitors in Spanish (Burkhart, 1973:

153). Since many Hispanic inmates do not speak English, these customary procedures tend to isolate these women even more than other minorities.

Alejandrina Tomes, a Puerto Rican nationalist, who has never been convicted of an act of violence, was arrested in 1983 on charges of possessing weapons and explosives and seditious conspiracy against the government (Reuben and Norman, 1987: 882). Upon conviction in 1985, Ms. Tomes received a sentence of 35 years in prison. She and a white self-proclaimed revolutionary, Susan Rosenberg, who has been associated with the Weather Underground group (McMullian, 1988: C1), were put in a new "high security" facility in Lexington, Kentucky, on October 29, 1986. Below is a graphic description of the conditions under which they were housed:

> The two women . . . are confined to subterranean cells twenty-three hours a day. They are permitted one hour of exercise in a yard measuring fifty feet square; upon their return they are strip-searched. That daily outing is the only time they see sunlight, except when they leave the facility for medical or dental treatment. On those occasions they are handcuffed and manacled by chains around their waists. In their cells they are kept under constant surveillance by guards or television cameras. . . . They say they are exposed to various forms of sensory deprivation designed to alter their personalities. The lights in their cells glare down on them continuously, and they are forbidden to cover them in any way (Reuben and Norman, 1987: 881).

Distance also denies a woman access to her parole board (Arditi et al., 1973). In the criminal justice system parole is not a right, but a privilege. One earns parole by demonstrating the ability to function in society in an "acceptable way." The criteria parole boards use to grant parole are vague, and both institutional and noninstitutional criteria are used in decisions. In addition to the institutional behavior of a woman, industrial time, meritorious "good time" earned, as well as original and prior offense records may be a part of the release decision. Women convicted of property crimes, drug offenses, or alcohol-related offenses are those who experience less successful parole outcomes (Simon, 1975), yet these are the crimes that usually result in the incarceration of minority women. Parole boards expect higher standards of proper conduct from women than they do from men. A double sex standard which holds that "extramarital sex is normal for men but depraved for women" might more readily lead to denial or revocation of parole for women (Haft, 1974). Minority women, particularly unwed minority mothers, are frequently viewed by society as being more carefree sexually and of looser moral fiber.

Whatever thoughts occupy the minds of parole board members concerning minority women inmates, there is some evidence that their release from prison differs significantly because of race/ethnicity. Foley and Rasche (1979: 103) found that white women in Missouri more frequently received parole than did Black women (41.3% versus 33.3%), while Black women were more likely to be released from prison through commutation of their sentences. As a result, Blacks served a highly significant 30% more actual time (19.4 months) than whites (14.9%).

Excluding the lynchings of untold numbers of Black females in the early years of this nation, a preliminary inventory of confirmed lawful executions of female offenders from 1625 to 1984, reported by Strieb (1988), reveals that for the 346 female offenders for whom race is known, 229, or 66%, were Black women, and 108 were white women (31%). Apparently these proportions have reversed in recent years. In their compilation of a list of the women executed since 1900, Gillispie and Lopez (1986) found that of the 37 women killed, 32% were Black and 68% white. Nonetheless, relative to their numbers in the general population, Black women are disproportionately represented on the death rows of this country. As of August 1, 1988, to the time of this writing, seven of the 22 female death-row inmates are Black (31.8%), and one of the two female inmates under the age of 18 awaiting death is Black.

Conclusions and Recommendations

The most cogent conclusion one can draw from an examination of the minority woman offender in the United States criminal justice system is that despite awakening interest in female criminality, little attention is devoted to the Black, Hispanic, or Native American female offender. Vernetta Young incisively describes the dilemma that confronts Black women in American society, a depiction which is equally applicable to all minority women:

> Black women in American society have been victimized by their double status as blacks and as women. Discussions of blacks have focused on the black man; whereas discussions of females have focused on the white female. Information about black females has been based on their position relative to black males and white females. Consequently, black women have not been perceived as a group worthy of study. Knowledge about these women is based on images that are distorted and falsified. In turn, these images have influenced the way in which black female victims and offenders have been treated by the criminal justice system (Young, 1986: 322).

The other obvious conclusion is that the few available studies of the minority woman offender tend to document differential treatment due to her racial/ethnic status. Discrimination and a lack of concern for her needs and those of her family are witnessed on every level of the system—arrest, pre-trial, judicial, and corrections.

Since the number of incarcerated women is not large, comprising only a little over 4% of the inmate population in the United States, a comprehensive national survey of all female offenders in the District of Columbia, and all 50 states and territories, would provide a sound, empirical basis for policy changes that could ameliorate the status and condition of arrested, incarcerated, probationed, and paroled minority female offenders in this nation.

Law enforcement personnel, on the streets and in the station houses, should be sensitized to the special situations faced by the minority mothers whom they arrest. Further, they should be intensively trained in race and community relations as a part of their academy curriculum, as well as in continuing training sessions throughout their careers. Emphasis in such training should be on the cultural nuances of the various racial/ethnic groups in the nation, human relations training, and cross-cultural interactions. Since the majority of police officers are men, special training should be available in the psychology of women and intergender relations.

Efforts should be made to release arrested minority women on their own recognizance, since they are often of low income and cannot make bail. If bail is felt to be required, it should be within the realm of possibility for the specific female offender. Since a majority of minority woman offenders are heads of households, any alternatives to outright release of a minority female offender should minimize the disruption of family ties.

Many changes are needed in the laws and the administration of justice by the criminal courts in regard to all women offenders. The following items should be considered:

1. Indeterminate sentencing exclusively applied to women should be eliminated;
2. Prostitution should be decriminalized, particularly since such laws have a discriminatory effect against minority women, while ignoring the male customer who is usually white;
3. Other victimless crimes, such as drug and alcohol abuse, should be viewed as the diseases they are and decriminalized;
4. Educational programs should be initiated to orient both Native Americans and

criminal justice personnel to the rights of Native Americans and the discretion and powers of tribal laws and courts; translators should be provided at every level of the criminal justice system for those minorities who are not English speaking; and

5. More women and minority judges and other administrators should be installed at every level of the judicial system.

The corrections system is probably the area most in need of change, yet it is the most entrenched and resistant of all the elements of the criminal justice system, despite its potential for administrative policy change due to its strong state control. In their plea for treatment intervention for female offenders, Iglehart and Stein (1985: 152) note that "historically, the female offender has been forgotten, ignored, or merely footnoted when the treatment and rehabilitation of offenders are discussed." Every effort should be made to maintain and strengthen the fragile family ties of minority woman offenders incarcerated in jails and prisons through widened avenues of communication, more home furloughs, conjugal visits, and family life and childcare educational programs. Pregnant inmates should be permitted to keep their newborn infants while in prison to enhance the bonding process. Legal services, law libraries, and access to courts should be afforded to all women in prison to assist them in preparing defenses and appeals and to properly deal with legal problems concerning their children.

All language restrictions should be eliminated and translators should be available for those minority women not proficient in the English language. Corrections officers should be bilingual in those areas with large numbers of Spanish-speaking inmates. More and better medical, vocational, and educational programs should be provided in women's correctional facilities to maintain sound health and prepare women for nontraditional jobs to gainfully support themselves and their families upon release. Finally, minority women offenders should be released from prison under the same conditions and with the same considerations as nonminority women through timely determination by parole boards and commissions containing minority women in equal proportions to those in the prison system of each state.

For over 15 years I have labored over the etiology of crime and thought that understanding female crime would offer the key to a general theory of crime causation based on the political, economic, and social realities of an inequitable society such as ours. The notion of generating theory diminishes in importance with the realization of the injustices perpetrated against all racial/ethnic minorities in the U.S. criminal justice system through institutional racism. Particularly distressing is the double discrimination experienced by minority women offenders simply because they are nonwhite and happen also to be female; they are the most powerless of the powerless.

Perhaps in another 15 years, the real meaning of a criminal justice system dominated by white males will be sufficiently documented that the "grand" theory will fall into place. But somehow I doubt it. According to Sophocles, "knowledge must come through action," to which Disraeli would add, "justice is truth in action." The path is clearly demarcated.

Notes

1. Two groups of female offenders are excluded from this discussion—Asian American women offenders and adolescent female offenders. In the first instance, the small numbers preclude an examination of this offender group, since Asian American women comprise less than 1% of arrested women. Girls present peculiar problems because of their age and the uniqueness of their processing through the juvenile justice system.

2. Reporting problems from the various jurisdictions introduce multiple potential errors, but more importantly, these statistics are based upon the U.S. Census which consistently undercounts minorities, especially Blacks and Hispanics.

TABLE 1 Proportions of Incarcerated Women in Federal and State Prisons, 1978, Compared to Proportions in the General Female Population, by Race/Ethnicity

	% in Prison	*% in Female Population*
White	35.7	82.0
Black	50.2	11.0
Hispanic	9.1	5.0
Native American	3.2	.04
All Others	1.8	1.6
TOTALS	100.0	100.0

SOURCE: U.S. Government Accounting Office, Washington, D.C., 1979, p. 8.

TABLE 2 Offense Data on U.S. Incarcerated Women by Race/Ethnicity, 1979,* in Percentages

Offense	*White*	*Black*	*Hispanic*	*Native American*	*Total*
Murder	12.9	18.6[2]	8.6	13.4[3]	15.3[3]
Other Violent	2.2	2.3	.09	3.0	2.1
Robbery	9.2	13.8	8.7[3]	6.6	11.3
Assault	3.2	7.5	1.6	5.8	5.5
Burglary	6.2	4.2	12.7[2]	6.0	5.7
Forgery/Fraud	22.3[1]**	11.3	8.2	23.8[1]	15.6[2]
Larceny	8.1	14.1[3]	8.6	7.2	11.2
Drugs	20.4[2]	20.2[1]	40.3[1]	21.0[2]	22.1[1]
Prostitution	1.3	3.1	2.4	0.7	2.4
Other Nonviolent	14.1[3]	5.0	8.0	12.5	8.7
TOTALS***	100.0	100.0	100.0	100.0	100.0

* Compiled from Glick and Neto (1977), Table 4.10.14.
** Numbers indicate rank order.
*** Rounded to 100.0.

3. Beginning in 1987, the UCR program ceased collection of "ethnic origin" data; however, in 1986 Hispanics were listed separately and were 12.7% of total arrests and 14.7% of arrests for Index violent crimes.

4. As the female minority group most studied and most involved in the U.S. criminal justice system, the focus throughout this article is on Black women. However, it is contended that other minority women share the same type of experiences in the system.

5. Observations of women's criminal court cases indicated that the public defenders observed in the 11 courts were sorely pressed for time. Many had only minutes to talk to their clients, most of whom were assigned at the arraignment. As a result, over 95% of the cases were plea bargained.

6. The most cogent example is capital punishment. According to the NAACP Legal Defense Fund, since the 1976 reinstitution of capital punishment, 30.69% of those executed were minority defendants with white victims, but not a single white defendant with a minority victim had been executed as of August 1988.

7. The idea here is that the criminal justice system "values" white lives and "devalues" Black and other minority lives in the imposition of *harsher sentences* if the victim is white rather than Black. This devaluation is particularly appropriate in an interracial crime.

TABLE 3 Arrest Offenses of Woman Felons in California, 1979, by Race/Ethnicity

	White		*Black*		*Mexican American*		*Native American*	
Arrest Offense	*N*	*%*	*N*	*%*	*N*	*%*	*N*	*%*
Homicide								
N=228	86	(0.7)	113	(1.5)	24	(0.7)	5	(2.7)
%=100.0	37.7		49.6		10.5		2.2	
Rape								
N=17	9	(0.07)	4	(0.05)	4	(0.01)	0	—
%=100.0	52.9		23.5		23.5		—	
Robbery								
N=919	355	(3.0)	403	(5.5)	143	(4.2)	18	(9.6)
%=100.0	38.6		43.9		15.6		1.9	
Assault								
N=3,082	1,232	(10.3)	1,310	(17.8)[2]	483	(14.2)	57	(30.5)[1]
%=100.0	39.9		42.5		15.7		1.9	
Burglary								
N=3,320[3]	1,649	(13.7)[3]	908	(12.4)	744	(21.8)[2]	19	(10.2)
%=100.0	49.7		27.4		22.3		0.6	
Theft								
N=3,793[2]	1,771	(14.7)[2]	1,437	(19.6)[1]	564	(16.5)[3]	21	(11.2)[3]
%=100.0	46.7		37.9		14.9		0.5	
Auto Theft								
N=845	402	(3.3)	283	(3.9)	147	(4.3)	13	(7.0)
%=100.0	47.6		33.5		17.4		1.5	
Drugs								
N=6,172[1]	4,017	(33.4)[1]	1,309	(17.8)[3]	824	(24.2)[1]	22	(11.8)[2]
%=100.0	65.1		21.2		13.4		.36	
All Other								
N=4,590	2,502	(20.8)	1,577	(21.5)	479	(14.0)	32	(17.1)
%=100.0	54.5		34.4		10.4		0.7	
Totals								
N=22,966	12,023	(100.0)	7,344	(100.0)	3,412	(100.0)	187	(100.0)
%=100.0	52.4		32.0		14.9		0.8	

SOURCE: California Bureau of Criminal Statistics and Special Services, 1980.
Notes 1-3: Rankings excluding "all other" offense category.

TABLE 4 Proportions of California Women Felons Arrested and Imprisoned in 1979, by Race/Ethnicity

Race/ Ethnicity:	*White*		*Black*		*Mexican American*		*Native American*		*Totals*
Offense	*N*	*%*	*N*	*%*	*N*	*%*	*N*	*%*	*%*
Homicide									
Arrest	86	(37.7)	113	(49.6)	24	(10.5)	5	(22)	228
Prison	26	(38.8)	28	(41.8)	12	(17.9)	1	(1.5)	67
% Arrest/ Prison	—	30.2	—	24.8	—	50.0	—	20.0	—
Rape									
Arrest	9	52.9	4	23.5	4	(23.5)	—	—	—
Prison	1	(100.0)	—	—	—	—	—	—	1
% Arrest/ Prison	—	11.6	—	—	—	—	—	—	—
Robbery									
Arrest	335	(38.6)	403	(43.9)	143	(15.6)	18	(1.9)	919
Prison	41	(51.2)	23	(28.8)	16	(20.0)	—	—	80
% Arrest/ Prison	—	11.6	—	5.7	—	11.2	—	—	—
Assault									
Arrest	1,232	(39.9)	1,310	(42.5)[2]	483	(15.7)	57	(1.9)[1]	3,082
Prison	14	(37.8)	21	(56.8)	2	(5.5)	—	—	—
% Arrest/ Prison	—	1.1	—	1.6	—	2.3	—	—	—
Burglary									
Arrest	1,649	(49.7)[3]	908	(27.4)	744	(22.3)[2]	19	(0.6)[2]	3,320[3]
Prison	30	(53.9)	12	(36.5)	17	(28.3)	—	—	59
% Arrest/ Prison	—	1.8	—	1.3	—	2.3	—	—	—
Theft									
Arrest	1,771	(47.6)2	1,437	(37.9)[1]	564	(14.9)[3]	21	(.05)[3]	3,793[2]
Prison	28	(53.9)	19	(36.5)	4	(7.7)	1	(1.9)	52
% Arrest/ Prison	—	1.6	—	1.3	—	0.7	—	4.8	—
Auto Theft									
Arrest	402	(47.6)	283	(33.5)	147	(17.4)	13	(1.5)	845
Prison	4	(57.1)	3	(42.9)	—	—	—	—	7
% Arrest/ Prison	—	0.9	—	1.1	—	—	—	—	—
Drugs									
Arrest	4,017	(65.1)[1]	1,309	(21.2)[3]	824	(13.4)[1]	22	(0.36)	6,172[1]
Prison	26	(39.4)	17	(25.8)	22	(33.3)	1	(1.5)	66
% Arrest/ Prison	—	.06	—	1.3	—	2.7	—	4.5	—
All Other									
Arrest	2,502	(54.5)	1,577	(34.4)	479	(10.4)	32	(0.7)	4,459
Prison	74	(55.6)	42	(31.6)	15	(11.3)	2	(1.5)	133
% Arrest/ Prison	—	2.9	—	2.7	—	6.7	—	6.3	—
Totals									
Arrests	12,023	(52.4)	7,344	(32.0)	3,412	(14.9)	187	(0.8)	22,966
Prison	244	(48.6)	165	(32.9)	88	(17.5)	5	(1.0)	502
% Arrest/ Prison	—	2.0	—	2.3	—	2.6	—	2.7	—

SOURCE: California Bureau of Criminal Statistics and Special Services, 1980.
Notes 1-3: rankings excluding "all other" category.

References

Adams, Stuart N.
1975 "The 'Black-Shift' Phenomenon in Criminal Justice." The Justice System Journal: 185-194.

Alabama Section
1975 "Alabama Law Review Summer Project 1975: A Study of Differential Treatment Accorded Female Defendants in Alabama Criminal Courts." Alabama Law Review 27: 676-746.

Arditi, Ralph R., Frederick Goldberg, M. Martha Hanle, John H. Peters, and William R. Phelps
1973 "The Sexual Segregation of American Prisons." Yale Law Journal 82,6: 1229-1273.

Barrus, C. and A. Slavin
1971 Movement and Characteristics of Women's Detention Center Admissions, 1969. Washington, D.C.: District of Columbia Department of Corrections.

Biggers, Trisha A.
1979 "Death by Murder: A Study of Women Murders." Death Education 3: 1-9.

Block, Carolyn Rebecca
1985 Lethal Violence in Chicago Over Seventeen Years: Homicides Known to the Police, 1965-1981. Chicago: Illinois Criminal Justice Information Authority.

Burkhart, Kathryn
1973 Women in Prison. Garden City, NJ: Doubleday.

Daly, Kathleen
1987 "Discrimination in the Criminal Courts: Family, Gender, and the Problem of Equal Treatment." Social Forces 66,1: 152-175.

DeCrow, Karen
1974 Sexist Justice. New York: Vintage.

Deming, Richard
1977 Women: The New Criminals. New York: Thomas Nelson.

Foley, Linda A. and Christine E. Rasche
1979 "The Effect of Race on Sentence, Actual Time Served and Final Disposition of Female Offenders." John A. Conley (ed.), Theory and Research in Criminal Justice. Cincinnati: Anderson.

Formby, William A.
1986 "Homicides in a Semi-Rural Southern Environment." Journal of Criminal Justice 9: 138-151.

Gibson, Helen E.
1976 "Women's Prisons: Laboratories for Penal Reform." L. Crites (ed.), The Female Offender. Lexington, MA: D.C. Heath.

Gillispie, L. Kay and Barbara Lopez
1986 "What Must a Woman Do to Be Executed?" Paper presented at annual meetings of the American Society of Criminology.

Glick, Ruth M. and Virginia T. Neto
1977 National Study of Women's Correctional Programs. Washington, D.C.: Government Printing Office.

Goetting, Ann
1987 "Homicidal Wives: A Profile." Journal of Family Issues 8,3: 332-341.

Goetting, Ann and Roy Michael Howsen
1983 "Women in Prison: A Profile." The Prison Journal (Fall/Winter): 27-46.

Haft, Marilyn G.
1976 "Hustling for Rights." L. Crites (ed.), The Female Offender. Lexington, MA: D.C. Heath.
1974 "Women in Prison: Discriminatory Practices and Some Legal Solutions." Clearinghouse Review 8: 1-6.

Hegner, Quinton
1981 California Bureau of Criminal Statistics and Special Services.

Iglehart, Alfreda P. and Martha P. Stein
1985 "The Female Offender: A Forgotten Client?" Social Casework: The Journal of Contemporary Social Work 66,3: 152-159.

Kratcoski, Peter C. and Kirk Scheuerman
1974 "Incarcerated Male and Female Offenders' Perceptions of Their Experiences in the Criminal Justice System." Journal of Criminal Justice 2: 73-78.

Kruttschnitt, Candace
1983 "Race Relations and the Female Inmate." Crime and Delinquency (October): 577-591.
1981 "Social Status and Sentences of Female Offenders." Law and Society Review 15,2: 247-265.

Mann, Coramae Richey
1988a "Getting Even? Women Who Kill in Domestic Encounters." Justice Quarterly 5,1: 33-51.
1988b "Female Homicide and Substance Use: Is There a Connection?" Paper presented at the annual meeting of the American Society of Criminology.
1987 "Black Female Homicide in the United States." Paper presented at the National Conference on Black Homicide and Public Health.
1984 "Race and Sentencing of Female Felons: A Field Study." International Journal of Women's Studies 7,2: 160-172.

McArthur, Virginia A.
1974 From Convict to Citizen: Programs for the Woman Offender. Mimeo.

McGowan, Brenda G. and Karen L. Blumenthal
1976 "Children of Women Prisoners: A Forgotten Minority." L. Crites (ed.), The Female Offender. Lexington, MA: D.C. Heath.

McMullian, Bo
1988 "Women's Wing Part of Prison." The Tallahassee Democrat (February 26): Cl-C2.

Mercy, James A., Jack C. Smith, and Mark L. Rosenberg
1983 "Homicide among Young Black Males: A Descriptive Assessment." Presented at the annual meeting of the American Society of Criminology.

Moyer, Imogener L. and Garland F. White
1981 "Police Processing of Female Offenders." L. Bowker (ed.), Crime in America. New York: Macmillan.

Nagel, Swart and Lenore Weitzman
1971 "Women as Litigants." The Hastings Law Journal 23,1: 171-198.

Pettiway, Leon E.
1987 "Participation in Crime Partnerships by Female Drug Users: The Effects of Domestic Arrangements, Drug Use, and Criminal Involvement." Criminology 25,3: 741-765.

Pokorny, Alex D.
1965 "A Comparison of Homicide in Two Cities." Journal of Criminal Law, Criminology and Police Science 56,4: 479-487.

Rans, Laurel L.
1978 "Women's Crime: Much Ado About. . . ?" Federal Probation (March).

Reuben, William A. and Carlos Norman
1987 "The Women of Lexington Prison." The Nation (June 27): 881-883.

Riedel, Mare and Lillie Lockhart-Riedel
1984 "Issues in the Study of Black Homicide." Paper presented at the annual meeting of the American Society of Criminology.

Shields, Alan J.
1987 "Female Homicide: Alabama 1930-1986." Paper presented at the annual meetings of the American Society of Criminology.

Simon, Rita
1975 The Contemporary Woman and Crime. Washington, D.C.: Government Printing Office.

Sims, Patsy
1976 "Women in Southern Jails." L. Crites (ed.), The Female Offender. Lexington, MA: D.C. Heath.

Strieb, Victor L.
1988 American Executions of Female Offenders: A Preliminary Inventory of Names, Dates, and Other Information (3rd Edition). Xerox, prepared for distribution to research colleagues.

Sutherland, Edwin H. and Donald R. Cressey
1978 Criminology. Philadelphia: J.D. Lippincott.

Suval, Elizabeth M. and R.C. Brisson
1974 "Neither Beauty nor Beast: Female Homicide Offenders." International Journal of Crime and Penology 2,1: 23-24.

U.S. Department of Justice
1988 Crime in the United States 1987. Washington, D.C.: Government Printing Office.

U.S. General Accounting Office
1979 Female Offenders: Who Are They and What Are the Problems Confronting Them? Washington, D.C.: Government Printing Office.

Weisheit, Ralph A.
1984 "Female Homicide Offenders: Trends Over Time in an Institutionalized Population." Justice Quarterly 1,4: 471-489.

Williams, Joyce and William M. Bates
1970 "Some Characteristics of Female Narcotic Addicts." International Journal of the Addictions 5,2: 245-256.

Wolfgang, Marvin E.
1958 Patterns in Criminal Homicide. Philadelphia: University of Pennsylvania Press.

Wright, Emilie D.
1981 Statistical Analysis Center, Division of Criminal Justice Services, State of New York.

Young, Vernetta D.
1986 "Gender Expectations and Their Impact on Black Female Offenders and Victims." Justice Quarterly 3,3: 305-327.

19

INTRODUCTION

Katheryn Russell's work has focused on criminal law, the sociology of law, and race and crime. She submits that much of what we know about race and crime is based on preconceptions, myths, and stereotypes. She challenges the viability of research based on this misinformation and identifies a number of approaches to address these biases. Russell also looks for new and insightful approaches to examine the role of race in the criminal justice system.

In the following article, Russell argues that the development of a Black criminology is needed to ensure the fair and unbiased representation of Blacks in criminological research. She suggests that Black criminology include both the assessment of applying mainstream theories to Blacks and the development of new theories to explain the involvement of Blacks in crime. Russell also argues that there must be an increase in the number of Black criminologists for the development of Black criminology.

Development of a Black Criminology and the Role of the Black Criminologist

Katheryn K. Russell

In its study of black criminality, the discipline of criminology has failed to cultivate a cohesive, continuous and recognized body of research—what is termed a "black criminology." Inasmuch as the theoretical framework of the discipline is limited by its failure to develop this subfield, policy recommendations proposed to and adopted by the criminal justice system are limited. It is argued that the development of a black criminology is necessary to fill this gap—in much the same way that feminist criminology filled a void. The components and scope of this subfield are outlined and the role of the black criminologist in the development of a black criminology is evaluated. It is argued that although black criminologists are needed to chart a black criminology, their participation alone is insufficient for the full development and vitality of this subfield.

Two crises face the discipline of criminology. First is the discipline's failure to provide a well-developed, vibrant, and cohesive subfield that seeks to explain crime committed by blacks—what is termed a "black criminology." Second, and related to the first, is the paucity of blacks in the field. Although there is a body of literature examining black criminality, it is neither comprehensive nor cohesive. The empirical findings in this area have consistently shown the race variable to be a significant predictor of criminal conduct. The discipline, however, has not systematically cultivated or recognized a subfield that addresses reasons why the race variable is such a significant predictor. Much of the existing

From Russell, K. K. (1992). Development of a black criminology and the role of the black criminologist. *Justice Quarterly, 9*(4), 667-683. Reprinted with permission of the Academy of Criminal Justice Sciences.

empirical research provides a test of well-established criminological theories. A void has been created by the discipline's failure to develop new theoretical analyses.

The manifest reason for the development of a black criminology is that it will enable the discipline to go beyond the simple observation of a phenomenon—that blacks are disproportionately involved in crime[1]—and will encourage the testing of new paradigms to explain the race-crime relationship. This subfield could increase the policy options available to address the problem.

This paper is divided into two sections. The first section includes an overview of the existing literature that addresses race and crime, a discussion of the historical context of race and crime research, why a black criminology is necessary, and an outline of its breadth and scope. The second section looks at the number of blacks in the discipline and examines whether an increase in this number would cultivate the study of the race-crime relationship. It is concluded that an increase in the number of black criminologists appears to be necessary to establish a black criminology. This increase, however, is alone insufficient to secure its long-term place in the discipline.

Development of a Black Criminology

Existing Research

In response to the call for a black criminology, one might suggest that a great deal of research on blacks and crime already exists. In the last few years, there has been a surge in the attention given to black crime, in both academic and media circles. A close look at this work, however, reveals that much of the literature on blacks and crime could be classified as criminal justice research, not as criminology. The few edited volumes that examine race and crime are revealing: They primarily address the impact of the criminal justice system on blacks (see for example, Georges-Abeyie 1985; Lynch and Patterson 1991; Owens and Bell 1980; Reasons and Kuykendall 1972).[2] None of the edited volumes is devoted exclusively to the development of theory that seeks to explain black criminality.[3] The call for a black criminology is a call for developing and expanding *theoretical* research on crime committed by blacks.

The Race Variable[4]

Empirical studies have consistently shown that blacks have disproportionate rates of arrest, conviction, and incarceration (see Blumstein et al. 1986). The discipline has not undertaken holistic analyses of these findings. Study after study has established the significance of the race variable. However, these studies have consistently failed to develop a broad-based analytical and theoretical framework for explaining the phenomenon of disproportionality. Just how to handle the race variable is the Achilles' heel of the discipline. Rather than examining this variable more thoroughly, the discipline continues to avoid involvement. This reaction is particularly ironic, in view of the number of black offenders in the criminal justice system.

Given the history of race and crime research,[5] the discipline's reluctance to fully explore the race issue is not surprising. The long-standing criminological taboo against discussing any relationship between race and crime (Karmen 1980) can be traced back to early research, which asserted a link between criminal tendencies and genetic factors (e.g., Lombroso 1972). Recent failures to address the issue may be explained, in part, by the adverse reaction to Moynihan's (1965) report on the black family.

The Moynihan report, which attributed the high rates of poverty in the black community to the disproportionate number of female-headed households, was severely criticized as racist by liberals and black leaders alike. According to the report, black "pathology" results in "poverty, failure and isolation among black children and predictably high levels of crime and delinquency" (Moynihan 1965:38).[6]

The hackles raised by this report were as much a response to its findings as they were to the group making the findings. Research purporting to study and resolve race-crime issues are commonly viewed with suspicion, particularly by blacks. A case in point is the recent controversy erupted by the proposed conference, "Genetic Factors in Criminal Behavior," cosponsored by the National Institutes of Health and the Institute for Philosophy and Public Policy at the University of Maryland. Many people expressed alarm at the title of the conference as well as with its apparent goal of building on the long-ago discredited myth of a genes-race-crime link. The conference, scheduled originally for October 1992, has been placed on indefinite hold. During the same period, the existence of the federal "Violence Initiative" at the National Institute of Mental Health (NIMH) was made public. The Initiative would target for evaluation and treatment grade-school-age, inner-city youth who are predicted to become violent.[7]

Given both the history of research on blacks and crime, as well as the fact that laws protecting the rights of blacks and other minorities have been slow in coming, it is not surprising that many blacks question any attempt to link crime with race.[8] Although this suspicion is understandable and necessary as a check on potential racial stereotyping in sociological study, it has a downside: A much-needed discussion of crime committed by blacks has been largely neglected. LaFree, Drass, and O'Day (1992) note that although race and crime research has the potential to stigmatize, "the consequences of ignoring possible differences between blacks and whites are potentially even more damaging" (1992: 158, note 1).[9]

The discipline as a whole has shied away not only from analyses of race and crime, but also from exploring and developing new theoretical paradigms. Much of the criminological research on race and crime has tested established theories rather than developing new theories that explore the link between these two variables. Further, this attention has been sporadic. At the turn of the century, a number of articles examining black criminality were written (see for example, Myers and Simms 1988). This research was followed by a great deal of attention during the 1950s and 1960s, particularly following the civil rights movement. Today, however, there is no core group of criminologists devoted to exploring the race and crime relationship. It appears that those criminologists who have studied race and crime may have other primary research interests.

Is a Black Criminology Really Necessary?

The value of a black criminology can be said to parallel the value of a feminist criminology. Naffine states that the goal of feminist criminology is "to have women fairly represented in the criminological literature [and] to have their experiences rendered faithfully through rigorous scholarship" (1987:2). This goal also holds true for a black criminology. What follows is a discussion of whether Naffine's admonition, as applied to the examination of blacks and crime, has been heeded.

Georges-Abeyie (1989, 1990) finds deficiencies in current theoretical approaches which seek to explain crime committed by blacks. Two of the areas he cites are 1) the lack of social-ecological sensitivity that takes into account the diversity of black ethnicity and 2) the dearth of approaches that examine the possible difference in how the criminal justice system treats blacks who live inside and outside a ghetto. Georges-Abeyie further notes that recent studies examining black rates of arrest, conviction, and incarceration have mistakenly equated racial identity with ethnic homogeneity. He argues that there is no monolithic black ethnic paradigm. It should be apparent that the rates of offending may differ for different black groups—for example, American-born blacks, Puerto Ricans,

Cubans, Virgin Islanders, Jamaicans, and Africans.

Related to the concerns raised by Georges-Abeyie is the issue of racial definitions. In *Who Is Black?* Davis (1991) discusses the historical "one drop rule." According to this rule, a person with one drop of black blood is considered to be black. The 1918 U.S. Census Bureau estimated that at least three-quarters of all black persons were racially mixed (1991:57). Further, Wolfgang (1964) observes that although black criminality is discussed frequently, there is no clear, logical definition of who is and is not black. Specifically, Wolfgang points out, a black person may be "anyone with one-fourth, one-eighth or one-sixteenth [black] ancestry" (1964:14). Scientists have used and continue to use social and cultural definitions of race (Davis 1991:165).[10]

The above discussion supports the argument that a host of undeveloped paradigms may emerge that help explain black crime. Rather than concluding that current theories fail, it might be more accurate to say the existing ones present an incomplete picture. It is plausible that one's ethnicity, inasmuch as it relates to one's life experiences, could have some relationship to criminal involvement and criminal processing (Bailey 1991).

One of the issues raised by a call for a black criminology is whether its goals would be more effectively met by a call for a subfield that examines *racial difference.*[11] This subfield would be valuable because it would provide analyses of race and crime without regard to the degree (disproportionate or otherwise) of a particular group's involvement in the criminal justice system. Therefore, it could broaden our understanding of the relationship between race and crime (see Bailey 1991). Specifically, this subfield would provide for the examination of the criminality of racial/ethnic minority groups as a unit (or as subgroups). Such a subfield could examine why some white ethnic groups have been disproportionately involved in crime, could make comparisons across ethnic groups, and could address Native American criminality (see T. Young 1990).

Another issue raised by the development of a black criminology is whether it is encompassed by an existing subfield of the discipline. Feminist criminology, which encompasses the criminality of black females, has given only secondary attention to the race-crime relationship. This fact can be attributed to the politically sensitive nature of the race-crime discussion (Simpson 1989, 1991). Simpson cautions that because of the importance of this relationship, such "reticence" in addressing it "leaves the interpretive door open to less critical perspectives" (1989:618).

There should be discipline-wide recognition that how particular racial/ethnic groups are treated in American society and how they internalize this treatment have some bearing on those groups' involvement in crime. A proposal for a subfield that examines racial difference does not conflict with a call for a black criminology. In fact, the development of a black criminology would be a first step toward the development of this subfield. Further, these issues are not addressed by an existing subfield.

What Does a Black Criminology Entail?[12]

If the development of feminist criminology is any indication, the growth of a black criminology will create its own subdivisions. Further, a black criminology would encompass the application of existing theories to blacks, as well as the development of new theories to explain or refute (Young and Sulton 1991:104) the disproportionate rate of crime committed by blacks and the nature and scope of that crime.

Although black criminologists and sociologists have produced a sizable body of literature (see Greene 1979; Young and Sulton 1991), this should not be confused with the existence of a black criminology. The existing work has not solidified into either a recognized or recognizable subfield which could be called a black criminology. This situation may exist in part because many of the contributions to this literature have been made by noncriminologists (see for example, Myers and Simms 1989). It also may reflect the fact that these writings as a whole do not constitute a cohesive body of work. The dearth of theoretical research in the race-crime area, combined with the waxing and waning of interest in the topic, explain why the existing literature fails to constitute a subfield.

Scope of a Black Criminology

As Young and Sulton note, "Whether there is a distinct theoretical paradigm that can be classified as the 'African American' perspective is subject to debate" (1991:102). Consequently the development of a black criminology cannot be limited to any one perspective. A black criminology would include the full panorama of theoretical analyses—e.g., from radical to conservative; from micro to macro. Hopefully the development of a black criminology would move beyond the testing of widely used variables (e.g., age, race, gender, socioeconomic status and employment status) to develop and test the effects of new and unexplored variables. One example of theory development would be an extension of labeling theory to include an analysis of the perceived impact of "petit-apartheid" (Georges-Abeyie 1990). Developing, operationalizing, and testing a "racism" variable is another example.[13] This variable could be measured as both a perceived and an actual event.[14]

Further, those empirical tests already done, which seek to test the race-crime nexus, would be considered part of a black criminology. One example would be a test of the impact of racial inequality on homicide rates among blacks and among whites. Messner and Golden (1992) used four indicators of racial inequality to consider interracial differentials in education, employment, income opportunities and residential patterns. The findings from the authors' sample of 154 cities provide support for the hypothesis that racial inequality has a positive effect on the black offending rate.

Some criminologists (e.g., Young and Sulton 1991) have asserted that racism is one of the antecedent causes of criminal behavior for some blacks. In keeping with this assertion, Staples (1975) offers a "colonial" model to explain the race-crime relationship. According to this model, the black community is viewed as an "underdeveloped colony whose economics and politics are controlled by leaders of the racially dominant group" (1975:14). Crime by blacks is "structured by their relationship to the colonial structure which is based on racial inequality and perpetuated by the political state" (1975:15). This paradigm allows race to be viewed as a cultural and political identity rather than as a genetic category. This model, however, has not been empirically tested.[15]

The above discussion makes clear that there is no shortage of research questions for which a black criminology subfield would provide an umbrella. Further, it is clear that much of the existing race-crime research could be considered part of a black criminology.

Is a Black Criminology Part of Mainstream Criminology?

In the preliminary stages of development, a black criminology is likely to be considered a subfield, separate from mainstream criminology. This segregation is particularly likely because in its nascent stages, to ensure its vitality and integrity, it must be the province of black criminologists. Once a foundation is established, however, there is every reason to believe that a black criminology will be considered part of the mainstream especially given the discipline's emphasis on street crime and the disproportionate number of blacks in the criminal justice system.

Additional Benefits of a Black Criminology

Beyond the main effect of enhancing theory development for the discipline, the development of a black criminology would

TABLE 1 Number of Criminology Doctoral Degrees Awarded to Black and White Students, 1980-1990 (U.S. Citizens Only)

	Black		*White*		
	Men/Women	*(Total)*	*Men/Women*	*(Total)*	*Total*
1980	0	0	21/5	(26)	26
1981	0	0	22/8	(31)	31
1982	2/2	(4)	16/14	(30)	34
1983	1/1	(2)	30/6	(36)	38
1984	2/0	(2)	19/10	(29)	31
1985	1/1	(2)	20/6	(26)	28
1986	0/1	(2)	16/5	(21)	23
1987	1/0	(1)	13/5	(18)	19
1988	4/4	(8)	15/7	(22)	30
1989	0/4	(4)	17/6	(23)	27
1990	1/1	(2)	20/15	(35)	37
Totals	12/15	(27)	210/84	(297)	324

SOURCE: National Science Foundation, et al. (1991).

yield tertiary benefits, including curriculum diversification. Just as an increase in the number of minority undergraduate students has led to nationwide attempts to expand undergraduate curricula (see, for example, Duffee and Bailey 1991; Spence and Phillips 1990; Weiner 1990), an increase in the number of black criminologists in academia would encourage the growth of a diversified curriculum. In addition to furnishing a broader base for undergraduate courses, a black criminology could provide the grist for new graduate courses. Further, it would by definition contribute to the literature on multicultural criminology (see Barak 1991).

What Will Happen If a Black Criminology Is Not Developed?

Short of heeding the call to develop a black criminology, the discipline will continue with business as usual. The absence of a black criminology places the discipline in a theoretical time warp. The void created by this absence holds new theories, paradigms, and analyses which would advance our understanding of the race-crime relationship. A continued failure to encourage the development of this subfield will signal an unwillingness to address a currently taboo area. In the long term, this failure will call into question the integrity of the discipline's policy recommendations related to race and crime. Failure to develop and cultivate a black criminology will not cause the problems associated with race and crime to go away. Rather, it will limit the discipline's ability to help explain this relationship and to guide policy accordingly.[16]

THE BLACK CRIMINOLOGIST

A Look at the Numbers

By all accounts, fewer than 50 blacks in the nation have received doctorates in criminology or criminal justice (see Garrett and Darlington-Hope 1988; Heard and Bing 1992; V. Young 1989). Data from the National Science Foundation, et al., show that in

1990, 42 persons received graduate degrees in criminology. Thirty-seven of these persons were white (88%) and two were black (4.7%).[17] The Foundation's data also show that between 1980 and 1990, 399 U.S. citizens were awarded doctorates in criminology[18] (see Table 1). Of this number, 27 (8%) were black.

Lack of aggressive recruiting strategies, limited availability of financial aid, and the small number of black role models in the field have been suggested as factors contributing to the small proportion of blacks in the discipline (see Berg and Bing 1990; Flanagan 1990; Russell 1990). The small percentage of black criminology doctorates reflects a broader phenomenon. In the social sciences as a whole,[19] black doctoral recipients in 1989 accounted for only 3.9 percent of the total number. Further, the Foundation reports that the number of black doctoral recipients decreased from 4.4 percent in 1979 to 3.6 percent in 1989. This decline is largely attributable to the steady decrease in the number of black men earning doctoral degrees, which fell by 23 percent over the past decade. According to the figures, blacks were the only racial/ethnic minority group whose representation declined over that 10-year period (Thurgood and Weinman 1990:11).[20]

Even if a broad definition of criminologist is employed—that is, a member of one of the discipline's societies or academies—the number of blacks is still minimal. According to recent figures, blacks comprise approximately 3.8 percent of the 1,066 members of the Academy of Criminal Justice Sciences (ACJS) (Berg and Bing 1990).[21]

This colorful absence has not gone unnoticed by the discipline. Measures have been taken to address the dearth of minority group members in the field. Examples include 1) the American Society of Criminology (ASC) scholarship for racial and ethnic minorities[22] and its creation of a task force to study how to attract minorities to the field; 2) this journal's decision to devote an issue to the work of racial and ethnic minority scholars,[23] and; 3) the ACJS Initiative which commits the Academy to find ways to increase the participation of minorities and women (Flanagan 1991).[24]

Recent studies, however, show that a promising number of blacks currently are enrolled in criminology and criminal justice doctoral programs (Flanagan 1990; Record 1990; Russell 1990). A 1990 survey of the 17 existing criminology and criminal justice doctoral programs (ACJS 1990) revealed that 583 students are enrolled in these programs, of whom 448 (77%) are white and 59 (10.1%) are black (Russell 1990).

Flanagan, in his examination of the number of female and minority faculty members and doctoral students in 13 criminal justice programs, concluded that recent figures give cause for optimism regarding true diversification of the discipline (1990:204). He found that in the fall semester of 1989, minority group members accounted for more than 16 percent of the incoming doctoral students.[25] Flanagan further noted that the percentage of minority students who have enrolled recently in graduate programs is higher than the percentage who have received degrees in recent years.[26]

The Unique Offering of the Black Criminologist

The dearth of black representation in any of the sciences deserves comment. The small number of blacks in criminology, the behavioral science that focuses predominantly on street crime, is particularly noteworthy in view of blacks' disproportionate rates of arrest, conviction, and incarceration.

The black criminologist is necessary to the development of a black criminology. The argument here is that the development of a black criminology necessitates the involvement of black criminologists. In order to establish that the representation of blacks in the field is related to developing a black criminology, it must first be established that black criminologists have something unique to offer this subfield. In no way is it suggested that the proportion of blacks in the discipline should proportionately mirror the number of blacks who fall within the jurisdiction of the criminal justice system. Rather, it is argued that the experiences and interests of black criminologists as applied to theory development may help to advance our understanding of the relationship between the black experience and black involvement in crime.

What about the black criminologist is important to the development of a black criminology? Does she make a unique offering to the field? Young and Sulton (1991) argue that black criminologists, as a group, can offer a unique perspective to the discipline. They also argue that the work of black criminologists, which largely favors a holistic approach to explaining crime committed by blacks, has been ignored systematically by the discipline.[27] Further, Young and Sulton suggest that many explanations of black crime are based on myths and misconceptions about the black community. Although black criminologists have something unique to offer the discipline, just what that offering is cannot be universally labelled. As the 1991 confirmation hearings for Justice Clarence Thomas made clear, there is no monolithic black perspective. Similarly, it is unlikely that there is a single black criminological perspective.[28] Without question, however, a black criminologist is likely to be more familiar than a white criminologist with "black life" and the black community.

Berg and Bing (1990) note that many educated blacks are particularly concerned about the plight of blacks less fortunate than themselves; in fact, they feel obligated to improve the quality of life for those individuals. The difference in perspective and focus of black criminologists is evident by their push to publish their work in "ethnically relevant media" (1990:157). Inasmuch as black criminologists have shown a particular concern for examining the role of blacks in the criminal justice system, their entry into the discipline should be encouraged because it would aid in the development of a black criminology.

In addition, an increase in the number of black academic criminologists is likely to increase the possibility that minority graduate and undergraduate students will be mentored. Berg and Bing (1990) suggest that the small number of minority faculty members in the field, combined with an increasing number of minority undergraduate students, has had consequences for the discipline in general and for minority faculty and students in particular. The lack of minority role models has inhibited minority undergraduates from entering academia. As a result, many minority faculty members feel they constitute an invisible, fringe group. This makes it less likely they will encourage undergraduate minority students to enter the field.

As per developing a black criminology, there is no downside to an increase in the number of black criminologists. An increase in the number of black criminologists can only aid in the development of this subfield. An analogy is provided by the increase in the number of women in the discipline and the development of a feminist criminology. The recent increase in the number of women has brought forth more than an increase in the representation of women. The numerical increase has been accompanied by an increase in the number of critiques and analyses of the discipline's historical treatment of women (Millman 1985), in the development of theories designed specifically to explain female criminality, in examination of the adequacy of existing theories in explaining female crime (Naffine 1987), and in studies of the treatment of women throughout the various stages of the criminal justice system (see Spohn, Gruhl, and Welch 1987).

The small number of black criminologists may be partially responsible for the inability of current theoretical applications and approaches to provide a wide range of explanations for the causes of crime committed by blacks, both as a group and as a multitude of subgroups. In the comparable context of examining female criminality, Naffine (1987) addresses the importance of women taking an active role in this area:

> The demand is that *women be allowed to give their own account of themselves,* so that their criminal and conforming actions are invested with a greater sense of the sort of instrumentality and intelligence which criminologists have been willing to recogni[z]e in the male (1987: 3) (emphasis not in original).

As is the case with the female criminologist, the black criminologist brings something different to the table than her nonblack counterpart. The resulting gap, based on a difference in the interests and experiences of the black criminologist, could be filled by a black criminology.

Taking a cue from the development of feminist criminology, from Naffine's admonition, and from overall concerns of legitimacy, the seeds for developing a black criminology need to be planted by black criminologists.[29] Once this subfield is established, however, all criminologists should be encouraged to contribute to its growth.

This suggestion raises the question of potential self-study bias. Can blacks study blacks objectively? The answer is an unequivocal yes. Just as white criminologists can and do study white offenders, black criminologists can study black offenders. Further, one of the express purposes of the peer review process is to provide a check on the structural and substantive validity of reported research findings.

Possible Outcomes

Two types of diversity could result from an increase in the number of blacks in the discipline. First and most likely is "diversity of theory." I propose this term to describe the breadth of theory likely to emerge as more groups are represented adequately within the discipline. This diversity would include expansions and refinements of existing theories and the development and testing of new theories that initially may fall outside mainstream criminology.[30] The development of a black criminology is one possible example. "Diversity in ethnicity" is a second possible result of an increase in the number of black criminologists. This would occur if such an increase had no effect on the discipline beyond, the increase in the number of blacks—e.g., if a number of blacks entered the field who had no interest in studying blacks and criminology/criminal justice.

CONCLUSION

From its birth, the discipline of criminology has sought to provide a theoretical framework through which crime can be analyzed. Over time, criminologists have offered a broad array of paradigms. The discipline, however, has yet to create, develop, and sustain a subfield that addresses black criminality—what is termed a black criminology. This void reflects the de facto creation of an "untouchable" area. It has been argued that the development of a black criminology would serve a function comparable to the development of feminist criminology: It would provide a framework for developing and testing new theories. The call for a black criminology is a call for criminologists to expand their theorizing and testing of the causes of crime committed by blacks. The role of the black criminologist is critical in this respect. In the short term, a black criminology may risk "ghettoization" within the discipline—it may not be considered mainstream[31] because in its early stages it would be the province of a small number of persons in the discipline. Although the role of the black criminologist is critical to the development of a black criminology, alone it is insufficient to sustain this subfield. In the long term, the contributions of all criminologists are required. The overall contribution of a black criminology to the discipline cannot be overstated. Our failure thus far to develop a black criminology limits the policy recommendations we can offer to address race and crime issues.

REFERENCES

Academy of Criminal Justice Sciences (1990) *Guide to Graduate Programs in Criminal Justice and Criminology, 1990-1991.* Cincinnati: Anderson.

Bailey, F. (1991) "Law, Justice, and 'Americans': An Historical Overview." In M. Lynch and B. Patterson (eds.), *Rare and Criminal Justice,* pp. 10-21. New York: Harrow and Heston.

Barak, G. (1991) "Cultural Literacy and a Multicultural Inquiry Into the Study of Crime and Justice." *Journal of Criminal Justice Education* 2(2): 173-92.

Bell, D. (1992) *Faces at the Bottom of the Well: The Permanence of Racism.* New York: Basic Books.

Berg, B. and R. Bing III (1990) "Mentoring Members of Minorities: Sponsorship and 'The Gift.' " *Journal of Criminal Justice Education* 1(2):153-65.

Biafora, F., Jr., G. Warheit, R. Zimmerman, A. Gil, E. Apospori, W. Vega, and D. Taylor (1992) "Cultural Mistrust and Deviant Behaviors among Ethnically Diverse Black Adolescent Boys." Paper presented at annual meeting of the American Society of Criminology, in New Orleans.

Blumstein, A., J. Cohen, J. Roth, and C. Visher, eds. (1986) *Criminal Careers and "Career Criminals."* Washington, DC: National Academy Press.

Cashmore, E. and B. Troyna, eds. (1982) *Black Youth in Crisis.* London: George Allen & Unwin.

Davis, F.J. (1991) *Who Is Black?* University Park: Pennsylvania State University Press.

Duffee, D. and F. Bailey (1991) "A Criminal Justice Contribution to a General Education Diversity Requirement." *Journal of Criminal Justice Education* 1:141-57.

Flanagan, T. (1990) "Criminal Justice Doctoral Programs in the United States and Canada: Findings from a National Survey." *Journal of Criminal Justice Education* 1:195-213.

——— (1991) "Editor's Note." *Journal of Criminal Justice Education* 2(1):1-2.

Garrett, G. and M. Darlington-Hope (1988) "Report of the Affirmative Action Survey Subcommittee." Submitted to the Academy of Criminal Justice Sciences Executive Board, San Francisco.

Georges-Abeyie, D., ed. (1985) *The Criminal Justice System and Blacks.* New York: Clark Boardman.

——— (1989) "Race, Ethnicity, and the Spatial Dynamic: Toward a Realistic Study of Black Crime, Crime Victimization, and Criminal Justice Processing." *Social Justice* 16:35-54.

——— (1990) "The Myth of a Racist Criminal Justice System?" In B. MacLean and D. Milovanovic (eds.), *Racism, Empiricism and Criminal Justice,* pp. 11-14. Vancouver: Collective Press.

Greene, H.T. (1979) *A Comprehensive Bibliography of Criminology and Criminal Justice Literature by Black Authors from 1895 to 1978.* College Park, MD: H.T. Greene.

Hacker, A. (1992) *Two Nations: Black and White, Separate, Hostile, Unequal.* New York: Scribner.

Heard, C. and R. Bing III (1992) "African American Faculty and Students on Predominately White University Campuses: Issues and Viewpoints." Paper presented at the annual meeting of the American Society of Criminology, New Orleans.

Hooks, B. (1989) *Talking Back.* Boston: South End Press.

Karmen, A. (1980) "Race Inferiority, Crime and Research Taboos." In E. Sagarin (ed.), *Taboos in Criminology,* pp. 81-114. Beverly Hills: Sage.

Kennedy, R. (1989) "Racial Critiques of Legal Academia." *Harvard Law Review* 102:1745-1819.

LaFree, G., K. Drass, and P. O'Day (1992) "Race and Crime in Postwar America: Determinants of African American and White Rates, 1957-1988." *Criminology* 30(2):157-85.

Lombroso, G. (1972) *Criminal Man According to the Classification of Cesare Lombroso.* Montclair, NJ: Patterson Smith.

Lyman, S. (1970) *The Black American in Sociological Thought.* New York: Putnam.

Lynch, M. and B. Patterson, eds. (1991) *Race and Criminal Justice.* New York: Harrow and Heston.

Mann, C.R. (1993) *Unequal Justice.* Bloomington, Indiana University Press.

Messner, S. and R. Golden (1992) "Racial Inequality and Racially Disaggregated Homicide Rates: An Assessment of Alternative Theoretical Explanations." *Criminology* 30(3):421-47.

Millman, M. (1985) " 'She Did It All for Love': A Feminist View of the Sociology of Deviance." In M. Millman and R. Moss Kanter (eds.), *Another Voice,* p. 251. New York: Anchor Books.

Moynihan, D.P. (1965) *The Negro Family: The Case for National Action.* Washington, DC: Office of Planning and Research, U.S. Department of Labor.

Myers, S. and M. Simms, eds. (1988) *The Economics of Race and Crime.* New Brunswick, NJ: Transaction Press.

Naffine, N. (1987) *Female Crime.* Boston: Allen & Unwin.

National Science Foundation, National Institutes of Health, U.S. Department of Education, U.S. Department of Agriculture and National Research Council (1991) *Survey of Earned Doctorates.*

Owens, C. and J. Bell, eds. (1980) *Blacks and Criminal Justice.* Lexington, MA: Lexington Books.

Reasons, C. (1974) "Race, Crime and the Criminologist." In C. Reasons (ed.), *Crime and the Criminal,* pp. 89-97. Pacific Palisades, CA: Goodyear.

Reasons, C. and J. Kuykendall, eds. (1972) *Race, Crime and Justice.* Pacific Palisades, CA: Goodyear.

Record, A. (1990) "Enrollment in Criminal Justice Graduate Programs, Fall 1988." *Journal of Criminal Justice Education* 1(1):117-18.

Rice, M. (1990) "Challenging Orthodoxies in Feminist Theory: A Black Feminist Critique." In L. Gelsthorpe and A. Morris (eds.), *Feminist Perspectives in Criminology,* pp. 57-69. Philadelphia: Open University Press.

Russell, K.K. (1990) "A Nationwide Survey of Affirmative Action Programs in Criminology/Criminal Justice Programs." Paper presented at the annual meeting of the American Society of Criminology, Baltimore.

Simpson, S. (1989) "Feminist Theory, Crime, and Justice." *Criminology* 27:605-31.

——— (1991) "Caste, Class, and Violent Crime: Explaining Difference in Female Offending." *Criminology* 29:115-35.

Spence, C. and M. Phillips (1990) "Women, Values and the Law: Women Teaching and Learning about Gender, Ideology, and Law." *Social Justice* 17(3): 189-94.

Spohn, C., J. Gruhl, and S. Welch (1987) "The Impact of the Ethnicity and Gender of Defendants on the Decision to Reject or Dismiss Felony Charges." *Criminology* 25(1):175-91.

Staples, R. (1973) "What Is Black Sociology? Toward a Sociology of Black Liberation." In J. Ladner (ed.), *Death of White Sociology,* pp. 161-72. New York: Random House.

——— (1975) "White Racism, Black Crime and American Justice: An Application of the Colonial Model to Explain Crime and Race." *Phylon* 36 (March):14-22.

Thurgood, D.H. and J.M. Weinman (1990) *Summary Report, 1989: Doctorate Recipients from United States Universities.* Washington, DC: National Academy Press.

Weiner, S. (1990) "Accrediting Bodies Must Require a Commitment to Diversity When Measuring a College's Quality." *Chronicle of Higher Education* 37, October 10, pp. B1-B3.

Wilbanks, W. (1987) *Myth of a Racist Criminal Justice System.* Monterey, CA: Brooks/Cole.

Wilson, J.Q. and R. Herrnstein (1985) *Crime and Human Nature.* New York: Simon and Schuster.

Wilson, W.J. (1984) "The Urban Underclass." In L.W. Dunbar (ed.), *Minority Report.* New York: Pantheon.

Wolfgang, M. (1964) *Crime and Race.* New York: Institute of Human Relations, American Jewish Committee.

Young, T. (1990) "Native American Crime and Criminal Justice Requires Criminologists' Attention." *Journal of Criminal Justice Education* 1(1):111-16.

Young, V. (1989) "The Role of African American Scholars in Criminal Justice and Criminology." Paper presented at the annual meeting of the Academy of Criminal Justice Sciences, in Washington, DC.

Young, V. and A.T. Sulton (1991) "Excluded: The Current Status of African American Scholars in the Field of Criminology and Criminal Justice." *Journal of Research in Crime and Delinquency* 28(1):101-16.

Notes

1. Criminologists continue to debate whether black involvement in crime reflects disparity or discrimination in the criminal justice system. Some observers have labeled the system skewed in its emphasis on "street" crime—which urban blacks in particular are more likely to be charged with—as opposed to "suite" crime—which whites are more likely to be charged with. Few persons, however, would deny the objective existence of a black offender crime problem.

2. Also see, Myers and Simms (1988).

3. See Mann's (1993) *Unequal Justice,* which offers explanations for minority crime.

4. Some commentators refer to this as the "racial variable" (Reasons 1974:89).

5. See Lyman's (1970) discussion of the sociological treatment of black Americans.

6. Some of the word choices used in this report (e.g., "pathology") still would raise eyebrows today. It is questionable whether the reported findings would cause such a political stir today. In fact, the report outlines the historical factors that affect the status of the black family, including slavery. The findings are based in part on the conclusions of black sociologists and community leaders (Moynihan 1965:34).

7. In spring 1992, NIMH researcher Frederick Goodwin, the spokesman for this initiative, compared the inner city to a jungle and inner-city black youths to rhesus monkeys who are predatory and excessively focused on sex.

8. Most recently, concerns have been raised about the work of Wilson and Herrnstein (1985) and Wilbanks (1987).

9. LaFree et al. also note support for Wilson (1984): "[B]ecause there has been so little recent systematic research on black-white differences and so few cogent explanations of black social dislocations, racial stereotypes of life and behavior have not been sufficiently rebutted" (1992:158-59, note 1).

10. Wolfgang (1964) notes that a study on the frequency distributions of crimes committed by "pure" and by "mixed" blacks would be worth examining. One might argue that such a study would allow researchers to test whether the criminal justice system treats persons of pure black ancestry differently from persons of mixed ancestry. The larger question of how to determine who is

of pure or mixed African ancestry likely deals a fatal blow to testing this hypothesis.

11. I thank one of the anonymous deputy editors for raising this important point, which is also discussed by Lyman (1970:122).

12. The term black criminology has been used by Staples: "A Black criminology will reveal how crime is defined along racial and class lines. So called white-collar crimes committed by the wealthy against the working-class citizenry are either ignored or lightly punished and are a negligible part of crime statistics" (1973:171). Insofar as Staples uses the term to describe the development of theory, my use of the term matches his.

Rice (1990) suggests that a black criminology exists. This term, however, has been limited to describing research in Britain, which focuses primarily on black males (Cashmore and Troyna 1982). So far as young blacks in Britain faces some of the same social conditions as young blacks in the United States, this research could provide some guidance.

13. Research examining "cultural mistrust" is an example of this (Biafora et al., 1992).

14. To operationalize this variable, it must be first determined whether it will be measured as a micro or a macro phenomenon (see Bell 1992; Hacker 1992). Further, it must be determined whether it will be measured as an actual or perceived event.

15. In addition to an empirical test of this model in an American context, this paradigm could also be used for cross-cultural analyses.

16. Simpson (1989) observes that the failure to fully explore the interplay between race and crime makes our analysis incomplete in other areas as well.

17. Of the remaining graduates, two were Asian and the other was "unknown."

18. The National Science Foundation compiles information based on classifications by the graduate student. It reports data from those students who have selected criminology (from a list) as their major field of study. It is possible, though not likely, that a student might select "other social sciences."

19. "Social sciences" includes psychology, anthropology, economics, political science and international relations, sociology, and all other social sciences.

20. The percentage of American Indians who received doctorates increased from .3 percent in 1979 to 4 percent in 1989; for Hispanics, the figure increased from 1.9 percent to 2.5 percent; and for Asians it increased from 1.8 percent to 3.7 percent.

21. The American Society of Criminology (ASC) does not collect race/ethnicity data from its membership.

22. One fellowship of $12,000 is awarded annually.

23. Although this is not an effort to recruit minority group members into the field, it reflects an attempt to bring the work of minority scholars to the fore.

24. In response to concerns raised by the Rodney King beating, verdict, and aftermath, *Law and Human Behavior* issued a call for papers for a special issue titled "Race, Ethnicity and the Law" (*Criminologist* 17: 5, September-October 1992).

25. Flanagan defines "minority" as black, Hispanic, American Indian, or Asian. Information on specific ethnic groups is not provided.

26. Flanagan attributes this surge in the number of minority students to the increased availability of financial support and to greater recruitment efforts (1990:204, 212).

27. The issue raised by Young and Sulton's article—whether the works of black criminologists have been systematically ignored by the discipline—is important, though separate from the issue this paper seeks to address.

28. For a thought-provoking discussion and analysis of the importance of contributions by black legal academicians on racial critiques of the law, see Kennedy (1989).

29. Hooks states, "Until the work of black writers and scholars is given respect and serious consideration, this overvaluation of work done by whites, which usually exists in a context wherein work done by blacks is devalued, helps maintain racism and white-supremacist attitudes" (1989:43-44).

30. Examples of such diversity include the development of white-collar, radical/critical, and feminist criminology.

31. This segregation has occurred with feminist and radical-critical criminology.

20

INTRODUCTION

Elijah Anderson, a sociologist and an ethnographer, has chronicled the behavior of inner-city African Americans in Philadelphia in a number of books and articles. Anderson received the Robert E. Park Association Award of the American Sociological Association for his book *Streetwise: Race, Class and Change in an Urban Community* (1990). He also wrote the "Introduction" to the republication of W. E. B. Du Bois's landmark study, *The Philadelphia Negro.* Anderson is a member of the W. E. B. Du Bois Collective Research Institute established at the University of Pennsylvania in 1998. The institute aims to encourage and support interdisciplinary research and to continue the focus on urban issues raised by Du Bois. As a result of his writings and his involvement as director of the Philadelphia Ethnography Project and associate editor of *Qualitative Sociology,* Anderson has been viewed by some as being in the forefront of continuing in the tradition of Du Bois.

The following article, "The Code of the Streets," was originally published in 1994 in *The Atlantic Monthly.* This article has given birth to a recent book, *Code of the Street: Decency, Violence, and the Moral Life of the Inner City* (1999). In the article, Anderson argues that racism, unemployment, and the inability to gain a positive self-image through traditional channels have spawned an urban environment of hopelessness and alienation. It is these factors that "cause" the interpersonal violence and aggression attributed to young people. Anderson contends that "decent" people and "street" people live side by side in an urban environment that is governed by the "code of the streets." This code, which is geared toward receiving respect through alternative measures, is one that street people live by and decent people must abide by for their own survival.

The Code of the Streets

Elijah Anderson

Of all the problems besetting the poor inner-city black community, none is more pressing than that of interpersonal violence and aggression. It wreaks havoc daily with the lives of community residents and increasingly over into downtown and residential middle areas. Muggings, burglaries, carjackings, and drug-related shootings, all of which may leave their victims or innocent bystanders dead, are now common enough to concern all urban and many suburban residents. The inclination to violence springs from the circumstances of life among the ghetto poor—the lack of jobs that pay a living wage, the stigma of race, the fallout from rampant drug use and drug trafficking, and the resulting alienation and lack of hope for the future.

Simply living in such an environment places young people at special risk of falling victim to aggressive behavior. Although there are often forces in the community which can counteract the negative influences, by far the most powerful being a strong, loving, "decent" (as inner-city residents put it) family committed to middle-class values, the despair is pervasive enough to have spawned an oppositional culture, that of "the streets," whose norms are often consciously opposed to those of mainstream society. These two orientations—decent and street—socially organize the community, and their coexistence has important consequences for residents, particularly children growing up in the inner city. Above all, this environment means that even youngsters whose home lives reflect mainstream values—and the majority of homes in the community do—must be able to handle themselves in a street-oriented environment.

This is because the street culture has evolved what may be called a code of the streets, which amounts to a set of informal rules governing interpersonal public behavior, including violence. The rules prescribe both a proper comportment and a proper way to respond if challenged. They regulate the use of violence and so allow those who are inclined to aggression to precipitate violent encounters in an approved way. The rules have been established and are enforced mainly by the street-oriented, but on the streets the distinction between street and decent is often irrelevant; everybody knows that if the rules are violated, there are penalties. Knowledge of the code is thus largely defensive; it is literally necessary for operating in public. Therefore, even though families with a decency

---

From Anderson, E. (1994, May). The code of the streets. *The Atlantic Monthly*, pp.80-94. Reprinted with permission.

orientation are usually opposed to the values of the code, they often reluctantly encourage their children's familiarity with it to enable them to negotiate the inner-city environment.

At the heart of the code is the issue of respect—loosely defined as being treated "right," or granted the deference one deserves. However, in the troublesome public environment of the inner city, as people increasingly feel buffeted by forces beyond their control, what one deserves in the way of respect becomes more and more problematic and uncertain. This in turn further opens the issue of respect to sometimes intense interpersonal negotiation. In the street culture, especially among young people, respect is viewed as almost an external entity that is hard-won but easily lost, and so must constantly be guarded. The rules of the code in fact provide a framework for negotiating respect. The person whose very appearance—including his clothing, demeanor, and way of moving—deters transgressions feels that he possesses, and may be considered by others to possess, a measure of respect. With the right amount of respect, for instance, he can avoid "being bothered" in public. If he is bothered, not only may he be in physical danger but he has been disgraced or "dissed" (disrespected). Many of the forms that dissing can take might seem petty to middle-class people (maintaining eye contact for too long, for example), but to those invested in the street code, these actions become serious indications of the other person's intentions. Consequently, such people become very sensitive to advances and slights, which could well serve as warnings of imminent physical confrontation.

This hard reality can be traced to the profound sense of alienation from mainstream society and its institutions by many poor inner-city black people, particularly the young. The code of the streets is actually a cultural adaptation to a profound lack of faith in the police and the judicial system. The police are most often seen as representing dominant white society and not caring to protect inner-city residents. When called, they may not respond, which is one reason many residents feel they must be prepared to take extraordinary measures to defend themselves and their loved ones against those who are inclined to aggression. Lack of police accountability has in fact been incorporated into the status system: the person who is believed capable of "taking care of himself" is accorded a certain deference, which translates into a sense of physical and psychological control. Thus the street code emerges where the influence of the police ends and personal responsibility for one's safety is felt to begin. Exacerbated by the proliferation of drugs and easy access to guns, this volatile situation results in the ability of the street-oriented minority (or those who effectively "go for bad") to dominate the public spaces.

Decent and Street Families

Although almost everyone in poor inner-city neighborhoods is struggling financially and therefore is a certain distance from the rest of America, the decent and the street family in a real sense represent two poles of value orientation, two contrasting conceptual categories. The labels "decent" and "street," which the residents themselves use, amount to evaluative judgments that confer status on local residents. The labeling is often the result of a social contest among individuals and families of the neighborhood. Individuals of the two orientations often coexist in the same extended family. Decent residents judge themselves to be so while judging others to be of the street, and street individuals often present themselves as decent, drawing distinctions between themselves and other people. In addition, there is quite a bit of circumstantial behavior—that is, one person may at different times exhibit both decent and street orientations, depending on the circumstances. Although these designations result from so much social jockeying, there do exist concrete features that define each conceptual category.

Generally, so-called decent families tend to accept mainstream values more fully and attempt to instill them in their children. Whether married couples with children or single-parent (usually female) households, they are generally "working poor" and so tend to be better off financially than their street-oriented neighbors. They value hard work and self-reliance and are willing to sacrifice for their children. Because they have a certain amount of faith in mainstream society, they harbor hopes for a better future for their children, if not for themselves. Many of them go to church and take a strong interest in their children's schooling. Rather than dwelling on the real hardships and inequities facing them, many such decent people, particularly the increasing number of grandmothers raising grandchildren, see their difficult situation as a test from God and derive great support from faith and from the church community.

Extremely aware of the problematic and often dangerous environment in which they reside, decent parents tend to be strict in their child-rearing practices, encouraging children to respect authority and walk a straight moral line. They have an almost obsessive concern about trouble of any kind and remind their children to be on the lookout for people and situations that might lead to it. At the same time, they are themselves polite and considerate of others, and teach their children to be the same way. At home, at work, and in church, they strive hard to maintain a positive mental attitude and a spirit of cooperation.

So-called street parents, in contrast, often show a lack of consideration for other people and have a rather superficial sense of family and community. Though they may love their children, many of them are unable to cope with the physical and emotional demands of parenthood, and find it difficult to reconcile their needs with those of their children. These families, who are more fully invested in the code of the streets than the decent people are, may aggressively socialize their children into it in a normative way. They believe in the code and judge themselves and others according to its values.

In fact, the overwhelming majority of families in the inner-city community try to approximate the decent-family model, but there are many others who clearly represent the worst fears of the decent family. Not only are their financial resources extremely limited, but what little they have may easily be misused. The lives of the street-oriented are often marked by disorganization. In the most desperate circumstances people frequently have a limited understanding of priorities and consequences, and so frustrations mount over bills, food, and, at times, drink, cigarettes, and drugs. Some tend toward self-destructive behavior; many street-oriented women are crack-addicted ("on the pipe"), alcoholic, or involved in complicated relationships with men who abuse them. In addition, the seeming intractability of their situation, caused in large part by the lack of well-paying jobs and the persistence of racial discrimination, has engendered deep-seated bitterness and anger in many of the most desperate and poorest blacks, especially young people. The need both to exercise a measure of control and to lash out at somebody is often reflected in the adults' relations with their children. At the least, the frustrations of persistent poverty shorten the fuse in such people—contributing to a lack of patience with anyone, child or adult, who irritates them.

In these circumstances a woman—or a man, although men are less consistently present in children's lives—can be quite aggressive with children, yelling at and striking them for the least little infraction of the rules she has set down. Often little if any serious explanation follows the verbal and physical punishment. This response teaches children a particular lesson. They learn that to solve any kind of interpersonal problem one must quickly resort to hitting or other violent behavior. Actual peace and quiet, and also the appearance of calm, respectful children conveyed to her neighbors and friends, are often what the young mother most desires, but at times she will be very aggressive in trying to get them. Thus she may be quick to beat her children, especially if they defy her law, not because she hates them but because this is the way she knows to control them. In fact, many street-oriented women love their children dearly. Many mothers in the community subscribe to the notion that there is a "devil in the boy" that must be beaten out of him or that socially "fast girls need to be whupped." Thus much of what borders on child abuse in the view of social authorities is acceptable parental punishment in the view of these mothers.

Many street-oriented women are sporadic mothers whose children learn to fend for themselves when necessary, foraging for food and money any way they can get it. The children are sometimes employed by drug dealers or become addicted themselves. These children of the street, growing up with little supervision, are said to "come up hard." They often learn to fight at an early age, sometimes using short-tempered adults around them as role models. The street-oriented home may be fraught with anger, verbal disputes, physical aggression, and even mayhem. The children observe these goings-on, learning the lesson that might makes right. They quickly learn to hit those who cross them, and the dog-eat-dog mentality prevails. In order to survive, to protect oneself, it is necessary to marshal inner resources and be ready to deal with adversity in a hands-on way. In these circumstances physical prowess takes on great significance.

In some of the most desperate cases, a street-oriented mother may simply leave her young children alone and unattended while she goes out. The most irresponsible women can be found at local bars and crack houses, getting high and socializing with other adults. Sometimes a troubled woman will leave very young children alone for days at a time. Reports of crack addicts abandoning their children have become common in drug-infested inner-city communities. Neighbors or relatives discover the abandoned children, often hungry and distraught over the absence of their mother. After repeated absences, a friend or relative, particularly a grandmother, will often step in to care for the young children, sometimes petitioning the authorities to send her, as guardian of the children, the mother's welfare check, if the mother gets one. By this time, however, the children may well have learned the first lesson of the streets: survival itself, let alone respect, cannot be taken for granted; you have to fight for your place in the world.

Campaigning for Respect

These realities of inner-city life are largely absorbed on the streets. At an early age, often even before they start school, children from street-oriented homes gravitate to the streets, where they "hang"—socialize with their peers. Children from these generally permissive homes have a great deal of latitude and are allowed to "rip and run" up and down the street. They often come home from school, put their books down, and go right back out the door. On school nights eight- and nine-year-olds remain out until nine or ten o'clock (and teenagers typically come in whenever they want to). On the streets they play in groups that often become the source of their primary social bonds. Children from decent homes tend to be more carefully supervised and are thus likely to have curfews and to be taught how to stay out of trouble.

When decent and street kids come together, a kind of social shuffle occurs in which children have a chance to go either way. Tension builds as a child comes to realize that he must choose an orientation. The kind of home he comes from influences but does not determine the way he will ultimately turn out—although it is unlikely that a child from a thoroughly street-oriented family will easily absorb decent values on the streets. Youths who emerge from street-oriented families but develop a decency orientation almost always learn those values in another setting—in school, in a youth group, in church. Often it is the result of their involvement with a caring "old head" (adult role model).

In the street, through their play, children pour their individual life experiences into a common knowledge pool, affirming, confirming, and elaborating on what they have observed in the home and matching their skills against those of others. And they learn to fight. Even small children test one another, pushing and shoving, and are ready to hit other children over circumstances not to their liking. In turn, they are readily hit by other children, and the child who is toughest prevails. Thus the violent resolution of disputes, the hitting and cursing, gains social reinforcement. The child in effect is initiated into a system that is really a way of campaigning for respect.

In addition, younger children witness the disputes of older children, which are often resolved through cursing and abusive talk, if not aggression or outright violence. They see that one child succumbs to the greater physical and mental abilities of the other. They are also alert and attentive witnesses to the verbal and physical fights of adults, after which they compare notes and share their interpretation of the event. In almost every case the victor is the person who physically won the altercation, and this person often enjoys the esteem and respect of onlookers. These experiences reinforce the lessons the children have learned at home: might makes right, and toughness is a virtue, while humility is not. In effect they learn the social meaning of fighting. When it is left virtually unchallenged, this understanding becomes an ever more important part of the child's working conception of the world. Over time the code of the streets becomes refined.

Those street-oriented adults with whom children come in contact—including mothers, fathers, brothers, sisters, boyfriends, cousins, neighbors, and friends—help them along in forming this understanding by verbalizing the messages they are getting through experience: "Watch your back." "Protect yourself." "Don't punk out." "If somebody messes with you, you got to pay them back." "If someone disses you, you got to straighten them out." Many parents actually impose sanctions if a child is not sufficiently aggressive. For example, if a child loses a fight and comes home upset, the parent might respond, "Don't you come in here crying that somebody beat you up; you better get back out there and whup his ass. I didn't raise no punks! Get back out there and whup his ass. If you don't whup his ass, I'll whup your ass when you come home." Thus the child obtains reinforcement for being tough and showing nerve.

While fighting, some children cry as though they are doing something they are ambivalent about. The fight may be against their wishes, yet they may feel constrained to fight or face the consequences—not just from peers but also from caretakers or parents, who may administer another beating if they back down. Some adults recall receiving such lessons from their own parents and justify repeating them to their children as a way to toughen them up. Looking capable of taking care of oneself as a form of self-defense is a dominant theme among both street-oriented and decent adults who worry about the safety of their children. There is thus at times a convergence in their child-rearing practices, although the rationales behind them may differ.

Self-Image Based on "Juice"

By the time they are teenagers, most youths have either internalized the code of the streets or at least learned the need to comport themselves in accordance with its rules, which chiefly have to do with interpersonal communication. The code revolves around the presentation of self. Its basic requirement is the display of a certain predisposition to violence. Accordingly, one's bearing must send the unmistakable if sometimes subtle message to "the next person" in public that one is capable of violence and mayhem when the situation requires it, that one can take care of oneself. The nature of this communication is largely determined by the demands of the circumstances but can include facial expressions, gait, and verbal expressions—all of which are geared mainly to deterring aggression. Physical appearance, including clothes, jewelry, and grooming, also plays an important part in how a person is viewed; to be respected, it is important to have the right look.

Even so, there are no guarantees against challenges, because there are always people around looking for a fight to increase their share of respect—or "juice," as it is sometimes called on the street. Moreover, if a person is assaulted, it is important, not only in the eyes of his opponent but also in the eyes of his "running buddies," for him to avenge himself. Otherwise he risks being "tried" (challenged) or "moved on" by any number of others. To maintain his honor he must show he is not someone to be "messed with" or "dissed." In general, the person must "keep himself straight" by managing his position of respect among others; this involves in part his self-image, which is shaped by what he thinks others are thinking of him in relation to his peers.

Objects play an important and complicated role in establishing self-image. Jackets, sneakers, and gold jewelry reflect not just a person's taste, which tends to be tightly regulated among adolescents of all social classes, but also a willingness to possess things that may require defending. A boy wearing a fashionable, expensive jacket, for example, is vulnerable to attack by another who covets the jacket and either cannot afford to buy one or wants the added satisfaction of depriving someone else of his. However, if the boy forgoes the desirable jacket and wears one that isn't "hip," he runs the risk of being teased and possibly even assaulted as an unworthy person. To be allowed to hang with certain prestigious crowds, a boy must wear a different set of expensive clothes—sneakers and athletic suit—every day. Not to be able to do so might make him appear socially deficient. The youth comes to covet such items—especially when he sees easy prey wearing them.

In acquiring valued things, therefore, a person shores up his identity—but since it is an identity based on having things, it is highly precarious. This very precariousness gives a heightened sense of urgency to staying even with peers, with whom the person is actually competing. Young men and women who are able to command respect through their presentation of self—by allowing their possessions and their body language to speak for them—may not have to campaign for regard but may, rather, gain it by the force of their manner. Those who are unable to command respect in this way must actively campaign for it—and are thus particularly alive to slights.

One way of campaigning for status is by taking the possessions of others. In this context, seemingly ordinary objects can become trophies imbued with symbolic value that far exceeds their monetary worth. Possession of the trophy can symbolize the ability to violate somebody—to "get in his face," to take something of value from him, to "dis" him, and thus to enhance one's own worth by stealing someone else's. The trophy does not have to be something material. It can be another person's sense of honor, snatched away with a derogatory remark. It can be the outcome of a fight. It can be the imposition of a certain standard, such as a girl's getting herself recognized as the most beautiful. Material things, however, fit easily into the pattern. Sneakers, a pistol, even somebody else's girlfriend, can become a trophy. When a person can take something from another and then flaunt it, he gains a certain regard by being the owner, or the controller, of that thing. But this display of ownership can then provoke other people to challenge him. This game of who controls what is thus constantly being played out on inner-city streets, and the trophy—extrinsic or intrinsic, tangible or intangible—identifies the current winner.

An important aspect of this often violent give-and-take is its zero-sum quality. That is, the extent to which one person can raise himself up depends on his ability to put another person down. This underscores the alienation that permeates the inner-city ghetto community. There is a generalized sense that very little respect is to be had, and therefore everyone competes to get what affirmation he can of the little that is available. The craving for respect that results gives people thin skins. Shows of deference by others can be highly soothing, contributing to a sense of security, comfort, self-confidence, and self-respect. Transgressions by others which go unanswered diminish these feelings and are believed to encourage further transgressions. Hence one must be ever vigilant against the transgressions of others or even *appearing* as if transgressions will be tolerated. Among young people, whose sense of self-esteem is particularly vulnerable, there is an especially heightened concern with being disrespected. Many inner-city young men in particular crave respect to such a degree that they will risk their lives to attain and maintain it.

The issue of respect is thus closely tied to whether a person has an inclination to be violent, even as a victim. In the wider society people may not feel required to retaliate physically after an attack, even though they are aware that they have been degraded or taken advantage of. They may feel a great need to defend themselves *during* an attack, or to behave in such a way as to deter aggression (middle-class people certainly can and do become victims of street-oriented youths), but they are much more likely than street-oriented people to feel that they can walk away from a possible altercation with their self-esteem intact. Some people may even have the strength of character to flee, without any thought that their self-respect or esteem will be diminished.

In impoverished inner-city black communities, however, particularly among young males and perhaps increasingly among females, such flight would be extremely difficult. To run away would likely leave one's self-esteem in tatters. Hence people often feel constrained not only to stand up and at least attempt to resist during an assault but also to "pay back"—to seek revenge—after a successful assault on their person. This may include going to get a weapon or even getting relatives involved. Their very identity and self-respect, their honor, is often intricately tied up with the way they perform on the streets during and after such encounters. This outlook reflects the circumscribed opportunities of the inner-city poor. Generally people outside the ghetto have other ways of gaining status and regard, and thus do not feel so dependent on such physical displays.

By Trial of Manhood

On the street, among males these concerns about things and identity have come to be expressed in the concept of "manhood." Manhood in the inner city means taking the prerogatives of men with respect to strangers, other men, and women—being distinguished as a man. It implies physicality and a certain ruthlessness. Regard and respect are associated with this concept in large part because of its practical application: if others have little or no regard for a person's manhood, his very life and those of his loved ones could be in jeopardy. But there is a chicken-and-egg aspect to this situation: one's physical safety is more likely to be jeopardized in public *because* manhood is associated with respect. In other words, an existential link has been created between the idea of manhood and one's self-esteem, so that it has become hard to say which is primary. For many inner-city youths, manhood and respect are flip sides of the same coin; physical and psychological well-being are inseparable, and both require a sense of control, of being in charge.

The operating assumption is that a man, especially a real man, knows what other men know—the code of the streets. And if one is not a real man, one is somehow diminished as a person, and there are certain valued things one simply does not deserve. There is thus believed to be a certain justice to the code, since it is considered that everyone has the opportunity to know it. Implicit in this is that everybody is held responsible for being familiar with the code. If the victim of a mugging, for example, does not know the code and so responds "wrong," the perpetrator may feel justified even in killing him and may feel no remorse. He may think, "Too bad, but it's his fault. He should have known better."

So when a person ventures outside, he must adopt the code—a kind of shield, really—to prevent others from "messing with" him. In these circumstances it is easy for people to think they are being tried or tested by others even when this is not the case. For it is sensed that something extremely valuable is at stake in every interaction, and people are encouraged to rise to the occasion, particularly with strangers. For people who are unfamiliar with the code—generally people who live outside the inner city—the concern with respect in the most ordinary interactions can be frightening and incomprehensible. But for those who are invested in the code, the clear object of their demeanor is to discourage strangers from even thinking about testing their manhood. And the sense of power that attends the ability to deter others can be alluring even to those who know the code without being heavily invested in it—the decent inner-city youths. Thus a boy who has been leading a basically decent life can, in trying circumstances, suddenly resort to deadly force.

Central to the issue of manhood is the widespread belief that one of the most effective ways of gaining respect is to manifest "nerve." Nerve is shown when one takes another person's possessions (the more valuable the better), "messes with" someone's woman, throws the first punch, "gets in someone's face," or pulls a trigger. Its proper display helps on the spot to check others who would violate one's person and also helps to build a reputation that works to prevent future challenges. But since such a show of nerve is a forceful expression of disrespect toward the person on the receiving end, the victim may be greatly offended and seek to retaliate with equal or greater force. A display of nerve, therefore, can easily provoke a life-threatening response, and the background knowledge of that possibility has often been incorporated into the concept of nerve.

True nerve exposes a lack of fear of dying. Many feel that it is acceptable to risk dying over the principle of respect. In fact, among the hard-core street-oriented, the clear risk of violent death may be preferable to being "dissed" by another. The youths who have internalized this attitude and convincingly display it in their public bearing are among the most threatening people of all, for it is commonly assumed that they fear no man. As the people of the community say, "They are the baddest dudes on the street." They often lead an existential life that may acquire meaning only when they are faced with the possibility of imminent death. Not to be afraid to die is by implication to have few compunctions about taking another's life. Not to be afraid to die is the quid pro quo of being able to take somebody else's life—for the right reasons, if the situation demands it. When others believe this is one's position, it gives one a real sense of power on the streets. Such credibility is what many inner-city youths strive to achieve, whether they are decent or street-oriented, both because of its practical defensive value and because of the positive way it makes them feel about themselves. The difference between the decent and the street-oriented youth is often that the decent youth makes a conscious decision to appear tough and manly; in another setting—with teachers, say, or at his part-time job—he can be polite and deferential. The street-oriented youth, on the other hand, has made the concept of manhood a part of his very identity; he has difficulty manipulating it—it often controls him.

Girls and Boys

Increasingly, teenage girls are mimicking the boys and trying to have their own version of "manhood." Their goal is the same—to get respect, to be recognized as capable of setting or maintaining a certain standard. They try to achieve this end in the ways that have been established by the boys, including posturing, abusive language, and the use of violence to resolve disputes, but the issues for the girls are different. Although conflicts over turf and status exist among the girls, the majority of disputes seem rooted in assessments of beauty (which girl in a group is "the cutest"), competition over boyfriends, and attempts to regulate other people's knowledge of and opinions about a girl's behavior or that of someone close to her, especially her mother.

A major cause of conflicts among girls is "he say, she say." This practice begins in the early school years and continues through high school. It occurs when "people," particularly girls, talk about others, thus putting their "business in the streets." Usually one girl will say something negative about another in the group, most often behind the person's back. The remark will then get back to the person talked about. She may retaliate or her friends may feel required to "take up for" her. In essence this is a form of group gossiping in which individuals are negatively assessed and evaluated. As with much gossip, the things said may or may not be true, but the point is that such imputations can cast aspersions on a person's good name. The accused is required to defend herself against the slander, which can result in arguments and fights, often over little of real substance. Here again is the problem of low self-esteem, which encourages youngsters to be highly sensitive to slights and to be vulnerable to feeling easily "dissed." To avenge the dissing, a fight is usually necessary.

Because boys are believed to control violence, girls tend to defer to them in situations of conflict. Often if a girl is attacked or feels slighted, she will get a brother, uncle, or cousin to do her fighting for her. Increasingly, however, girls are doing their own fighting and are even asking their male relatives to teach them how to fight. Some girls form groups that attack other girls or take things from them. A hard-core segment of inner-city girls inclined toward violence seems to be developing. As one thirteen-year-old girl in a detention center for youths who have committed violent acts told me, "To get people to leave you alone, you gotta fight. Talking don't get you out of stuff." One major difference between girls and boys: girls rarely use guns. Their fights are therefore not life-or-death struggles. Girls are not often willing to put their lives on the line for "manhood." The ultimate form of respect on the male dominated inner-city street is thus reserved for men.

"Going for Bad"

In the most fearsome youths such a cavalier attitude towards death grows out of a very limited view of life. Many are uncertain about how long they are going to live and believe they could die violently at any time. They accept this fate; they live on the edge. Their manner conveys the message that nothing intimidates them; whatever turn the encounter takes, they maintain their attack—rather like a pit bull, whose spirit many such boys admire. The demonstration of such tenacity "shows heart" and earns their respect.

This fearlessness has implications for law enforcement. Many street-oriented boys are much more concerned about the threat of "justice" at the hands of a peer than at the hands of the police. Moreover, many feel not only that they have little to lose by going to prison but that they have something to gain. The toughening up one experiences in prison can actually enhance one's reputation on the streets. Hence the system loses influence over the hard core who are without jobs, with little perceptible stake in the system. If mainstream society has done nothing *for* them, they counter by making sure it can do nothing *to* them.

At the same time, however, a competing view maintains that true nerve consists in backing down, walking away from a fight, and going on with one's business. One fights only in self-defense. This view emerges from the decent philosophy that life is precious, and it is an important part of the socialization process common in decent homes. It discourages violence as the primary means of resolving disputes and encourages youngsters to accept nonviolence and talk as confrontational strategies. But "if the deal goes down," self-defense is greatly encouraged. When there is enough positive support for this orientation, either in the home or among one's peers, then nonviolence has a chance to prevail. But it prevails at the cost of relinquishing a claim to being bad and tough, and therefore sets a young person up as at the very least alienated from street-oriented peers and quite possibly a target of derision or even violence.

Although the nonviolent orientation rarely overcomes the impulse to strike back in an encounter, it does introduce a certain confusion and so can prompt a measure of soul-searching, or even profound ambivalence. Did the person back down with his respect intact or did he back down only to be judged a "punk"—a person lacking manhood? Should he or she have acted? Should he or she have hit the other person in the mouth? These questions beset many young men and women during public confrontations. What is the "right" thing to do? In the quest for honor, respect, and local status—which few young people are uninterested in—common sense most often prevails, which leads many to opt for the tough approach, enacting their own particular versions of the display of nerve. The presentation of oneself as rough and tough is very often quite acceptable until one is tested. And then that presentation may help the person pass the test, because it will cause fewer questions to be asked about what he did and why. It is hard for a person to explain why he lost the fight or why he backed down. Hence many will strive to appear to "go for bad," while hoping they will never be tested. But when they are tested, the outcome of the situation may quickly be out of their hands, as they become wrapped up in the circumstances of the moment.

An Oppositional Culture

The attitudes of the wider society are deeply implicated in the code of the streets. Most people in inner-city communities are not totally invested in the code, but the significant minority of hard-core street youths who are have to maintain the code in order to establish reputations because they have—or feel they have—few other ways to assert themselves. For these young people the standards of the street code are the only game in town. The extent which some children—particularly those who through upbringing have become most alienated and those lacking strong and conventional social support—experience, feel, and internalize racist rejection and contempt from mainstream society may strongly encourage them to express contempt for the more conventional society in turn. In dealing with this contempt and rejection, some youngsters will consciously invest themselves and their considerable mental resources in what amounts to an oppositional culture to preserve themselves and their self-respect. Once they do, any respect they might be able to garner in the wider system pales in comparison with the respect available in the local system; thus they often lose interest in even attempting to negotiate the mainstream system.

At the same time, many less alienated young blacks have assumed a street-oriented demeanor as a way of expressing their blackness while really embracing a much more moderate way of life; they, too, want a nonviolent setting in which to live and raise a family. These decent people are trying hard to be part of the mainstream culture, but the racism, real and perceived, that they encounter helps to legitimate opppositional culture. And so on occasion they adopt street behavior. In fact, depending on the demands of the situation, many people in the community slip back and forth between decent and street behavior.

A vicious cycle has thus been formed. The hopelessness and alienation many young inner-city black men feel, largely as a result of endemic joblessness racism, fuels the violence they engage in. This violence serves to confirm the negative feelings many whites and some middle-class blacks harbor toward the ghetto poor, further legitimating the oppositional culture and the code of the streets in the eyes of many poor young backs. Unless the cycle is broken, attitudes on both sides will become increasingly entrenched, and the violence, which claims both black and white, poor and affluent, will only escalate.

21

INTRODUCTION

Becky Tatum is the first recipient of the W. E. B. DuBois Fellowship sponsored by the U.S. Department of Justice, National Institute of Justice. Tatum recently authored *Crime, Violence and Minority Youth* (2000). Noting that mainstream theoretical perspectives often ignore race, racism, and structural relations, she focuses on alternative perspectives on crime and examines the interconnections between race, gender, and crime in her research.

Like Staples, Tatum examines how the colonial model contributes to our understanding of crime and delinquency behavioral responses of blacks. Tatum provides the reader with an overview of the colonial theory developed by Frantz Fanon that includes a summary of the four phases of colonization, the psychological consequences of colonialism, and internal colonialism. The internal colonialism model is used to explain the exploitation and subordination of African Americans in the United States. The article concludes with a discussion of whether internal colonialism adequately explains crime and delinquency.

The Colonial Model as a Theoretical Explanation of Crime and Delinquency

Becky Tatum

Introduction

Empirical research on the relationship between race and crime spans many decades. Historically, the findings of this research reveal a disproportionate involvement in criminal activity by people of color in comparison to their representation in the population. Most of the crime statistics point to young African American males as being the major perpetrators of crime.

National arrest statistics in 1991 suggest that African Americans under 18 years of age account for 29 percent of the Part One Index crimes which include murder, forcible rape, robbery, aggravated assault, larceny-theft, arson, burglary and motor vehicle theft (FBI 1992). However, in 1991, these youths comprised only 4% of the total U.S. population (U.S. Bureau of the Census 1992).

The overrepresentation of African Americans in crime and delinquency is reaffirmed by victimization and self-report data. Victimization data in 1991 show that African Americans account for 28 percent of single-offender victimizations and 38 percent of multiple-offender victimizations, which include rape, robbery and assault (U.S. Department of Justice 1992). Self-report data (National Youth Survey) stress the importance of distinguishing between prevalence and incidence rates of delinquency. While prevalence comparisons in delinquent behavior show few differences between African American and White youth from lower, working and middle class backgrounds, the incidence of delinquent behavior appears to be greater among

From Tatum, B. (1994). The colonial model as a theoretical explanation of crime and delinquency. In A. T. Sulton (Ed.), *African American Perspectives on: Crime, Causation, Criminal Justice Administration, and Crime Prevention* (pp. 33-52). Woburn, MA: Butterworth-Heinemann.

low-income and African American youths (Elliott and Ageton 1980).

Numerous theoretical models have attempted to explain the association between race, crime and delinquency. Traditional theoretical models range from anomie, social disorganization and relative deprivation to differential involvement in crime, biological determinism and a subculture of violence. One theoretical model that has not been fully examined and is absent from mainstream criminology is the theory of internal colonialism.

The colonial model is a socio-psychological perspective. It assesses the impact of the social context which an individual experiences on the psychological factor of alienation. In particular, the theory examines the relationship between structural oppression, alienation and three adaptive forms of behavior—assimilation, crime or deviance, and protest.

According to this model, individuals who are the victims of social, economic and political oppression are likely to perceive that oppression, and as a result develop feelings of alienation in which the commission of crime is an adaptive response. In the colonial model, race or color is the ascriptive criterion for differences in subjection to situations of oppression.

The purpose of this paper is to review the original version of the colonial model and the application of the model (internal colonialism) to the United States. Second, this paper will address the adequacy of internal colonialism in explaining the association between race and crime.

The Colonial Model

Colonialism is a social system traditionally characterized by a state's establishment of political control over a foreign territory and the settlement of those foreigners in the territory for purposes of exploitation and political hegemony (Staples 1989). Colonialism has existed for centuries and has involved territories originally inhabited by White and non-White people.

The colony theory, as developed by Frantz Fanon (1963 and 1967a), is concerned with the colonization of non-Western or non-White people by European nations. A psychiatrist and activist from Martinique, Fanon writes about the racial relations that exist between Blacks and Whites in the third world countries of Asia and Africa.

Colonization is a process which has four distinct phases. The clearest delineation of the four phases of colonization is discussed by Blauner (1969). The first phase involves a forced, involuntary entry of a foreign racial group into the geographical territory of the society being colonized. Specifically, a small minority of outsiders enters a country and establishes control over its majority population. The primary objective of the outsiders is to obtain valuable economic resources. First contact between the two groups usually involves a system of trade where the outsiders trade relatively worthless items for more expensive and valuable items. Observing that the native inhabitants are unaware of the value of their goods, the outsiders move to subjugate and exploit them for their own economic gain (Davidson 1976).

The second phase of colonialization involves the establishment of a colonial society. This society can be characterized by three interrelated processes of cultural imposition, cultural disintegration and cultural recreation. In a colonial society, actors from two different social worlds come together in a situation where one set of actors are citizens of a powerful technologically superior European state. These Europeans possess social and economic privileges that are not shared by the native people. The unequal distribution of power and special privileges of Europeans result in the creation of two distinct social actors—the colonizers (immigrants) and the colonized (native).

Cultural disintegration occurs when the colonists alter the cultural and social organizations of the colonized people. This alteration is more than a result of the natural processes of contact and acculturation. The colonizing power institutes a policy which constrains, transforms or destroys indigenous values, orientations, and ways of life (Fanon 1963). Due to economic and political power, the colonizers are able to carry out a process of cultural imposition in which their culture and values have ascendancy over native culture and values. In the colonial society, it is necessary to re-create or redefine the culture of the native. The colonizer paints the native as the quintessence of evil (Fanon 1963). Native society is described as lacking values and as being insensible to ethics. The customs of the native people, their traditions, and their myths are defined as signs of the poverty of spirit and constitutional depravity. Zoological terms are used to describe the native. The colonizer speaks of the native's reptilian motions, the stink of the native quarters, those children that seem to belong to no one, and that laziness stretched out in the sun (Fanon 1963).

The colonizing power also remakes history by referring to the history of the mother country. Schools teach colonized children to negatively view their culture. These children are taught the colonizer's history, language, values and life styles. They are told that this life style is superior to that of the children's parents or elders. In essence, native children are taught to reject their own culture and to accept those images of themselves and their social world which the colonizer has created and maintained.

The third phase of colonization involves a relationship by which members of the colonized group tend to be governed by representatives of the colonizer's power. A colonial society is divided into two separate groups—the colonized and the colonizer—who are pitted against each other. In the colonies, the police and the soldiers are the official maintainers of the colonizers and their rule of oppression. The police and the soldiers maintain frequent and direct contact with the native. Their role in the colonial social system is to put oppression and domination into practice, with the clear conscience that they are the "upholder of the peace" (Fanon 1963). Yet, they are the messengers of violence which disrupts the home and the mind of the native (Fanon 1963).

The development of a caste system based on racism is the fourth phase of colonization. Racism is a principle of social domination by which a group seen as inferior or different in terms of alleged biological characteristics is exploited, controlled and oppressed socially and psychologically by a superordinate group (Blauner 1969). Racism occurs within the political, social and economic institutions. The government and its laws protect the interests of the colonizers. The prosecution of injustices against the native receives little governmental support and the native learns that he should expect nothing from the colonizer's justice system.

For the colonizer, the colony is a place where jobs are guaranteed, wages are high, advancement is rapid and businesses are profitable (Memmi 1968). In this society, the cause is the consequence. As Davidson (1976) explains:

> If the living conditions of the colonizer are high, it is because those of the colonized are low; if he can benefit from plentiful and undemanding labor servants, it is because the colonized man who can be exploited will not be protected by the laws of the colony; if he can easily obtain administrative positions, it is because they are reserved for him and the colonized are excluded from them; the more freely he breathes, the more the colonized are choked.

Despite the fact that colonial privileges are unequally distributed among the colonizers, those at the bottom of that ladder retain their allegiance to the colonial administration for their position in the colony is superior to their previous position in the mother country. Although they also may be victimized, those colonizers who occupy the bottom rung enjoy privileges superior to the colonized people. In order to reserve their limited advantages, they must identify with the very same economically powerful interests whose victims they are themselves (Zahar 1974).

In his theory, Fanon does not directly address the issue of perceived oppression. However, from examining his works, it is evident that the colonized are likely to perceive themselves as being oppressed and are also likely to be cognitive of this oppression. According to Fanon (1967a), the oppressive conditions that the colonized experience constantly remind them that they are "different" and emphatically show them their "place."

Although race is the major emphasis of the colonial model, Fanon does recognize a social class hierarchy among the colonized. All colonized individuals do not suffer from the oppressive conditions of the social order to the same extent. In fact, the bourgeois fraction of the colonized people represent the part of the colonized nation that is necessary and irreplaceable if the colonial machine is to run smoothly (Fanon 1963). Although their position in society is lower than the colonizers of any status, in regards to the natives, they enjoy more privileges. As a result, there is an antagonism which exists between the native who is excluded from the advantages of colonialism and his counterpart who manages to turn colonial exploitation to his account (Fanon 1963). The colonialists make use of this antagonism by pitting one against the other.

To summarize, the colonial process is initiated when members of one racial group forcefully enter the territory of another for the purpose of economic exploitation. The political and economic dominance of the immigrants enable them to create a society in which their culture and values are more salient than those of the native people. The native culture is systematically destroyed and is redefined in negative terms. The relationship between the two groups—the colonizers (immigrants) and the colonized (natives)—is maintained by representatives of the colonizers. The colonizers establish a caste system based upon racism in which political power and social and economic privileges are reserved for members of the dominant power structure. As a result of their structural exclusion, the colonized are likely to perceive that they are oppressed and be cognitive of their oppression. A social class hierarchy exists among the colonized in regards to colonial privileges.

Psychological Consequences of Colonialism

The colonization process produces a state of alienation within the colonized people. Although Fanon's work *Black Skin, White Masks* is a study of alienation, Fanon never defines the concept. It is clear from Fanon's work, however, that when he speaks of alienation, he is describing the separation of a person from his individuality, his existential condition, his culture or community or his essential self.

Robert Staples provides a definition of alienation using the colonial model. According to Staples (1989), alienation is a feeling of psychological deprivation arising from the belief that one is not a part of society and that the values of a nation are not congruent with the individual's own orientation. Alienation, as utilized by Staples and Fanon, differs from the Marxists' concept of alienation in that the alienated state of mind is the result of social and political exploitation as well as economic exploitation. Colonized individuals are deprived of an investment or stake in economic, social and political institutions. Moreover, Fanon and Staples argue that this exploitation is a result of race, not class.

Fanon describes five types of alienating experiences that colonized people undergo: self-alienation, alienation against significant others (or one's racial group), alienation against general others, cultural alienation, and alienation against the creative social praxis. Self-alienation involves alienation from one's corporeality and personal identity. It is also a condition of separation or attempted separation of the individual from himself. The example of "separation" that Fanon (1967a) provides is a Senegalese who learns Creole in order to pass as an Antilles native. Being "Senegalese" is part of the existential self of a native of Senegal, and to run away from this is to manifest alienation.

Alienation against significant others involves estrangement from one's family and social or racial group. Here, the individual hates in others those characteristics he hates most in himself. His expressed contempt for and attacks against his family, social or racial group are the means by which he refrains from recognizing and expressing his self-contempt (Wilson 1990).

Estrangement between different racial groups characterizes alienation against general others. This aspect of alienation involves the notion of superordination and subordination in which all relations between the colonized and the colonizer are determined. Violence, paranoia and distrust are characteristic of this type of alienation. Violence and distrust can be displayed by both the colonizer and the colonized; however, the victims of the violence of the colonized are usually not members of the dominant group. The victims of the violence of the colonized are usually other colonized individuals.

Cultural alienation involves estrangement from one's language and history. Fanon argues that language and education are two of the most potent instruments that are utilized in the systematic alienation of the colonized. Language is more than a medium of communication. Language is viewed as a system of symbols and as a conserver of intergenerational experience which has great potential for influencing thought and action. Diversity of languages in the world has led to a diversity of cultures—namely the totality of such institutions as religion, kinship, social stratification and ideology (Jinadu 1986). To adopt the language of the dominant group is to assume the dominant group's cultural forms and thought patterns.

According to Fanon (1967a), the fact that the culture is different from the group into which one is born is evidence of separation from oneself. This separation is enhanced through the system of formal education. The colonized are taught the history of the dominant group. The symbols of "good guys" are the dominant group; the symbols of "bad guys" are the colonized. As a result, the colonized views his culture negatively and embraces the language, culture and history of the dominant group. Fanon (1967a) recognizes, however, that the adoption of the dominant culture by the colonized is often the key that can open doors (politically, socially or economically) which previously have been closed to him.

Last, alienation against the creative social praxis is concerned with the denial or abdication of self-determining socialized and organized activity which is the very foundation of the realization of human potential (Bulhan 1985). The colonized believes that he does not have a measure of choice, influence or control in what happens to him or in what he can make happen. The colonized is full of self-doubt and has a readiness to compromise.

Fanon (1967a) notes the colonizer is also alienated. The alienation of the colonizer is the result of the kinds of social relations that are present in the colonial society. Characterizing and treating the colonized as inhuman results in the colonizer assuming inhuman features (Zahar 1974). Other than denoting the dual alienation of the colonizer and the colonized, Fanon unfortunately does not fully address the alienation of the colonizer in his theory.

Colonized people react to their alienation in one of three ways. First, colonized individuals may choose to imitate the oppressor and assimilate into his culture. What Fanon discusses is behavioral assimilation or acculturation in that the values, attitudes and behavior of the dominant group are adopted. This process is called "identification with the aggressor." According to Fanon (1963):

> The "inferior race" denies itself as a different race. It shares with the "superior race" the convictions, doctrines, and other attitudes concerning it. Having judged, condemned and abandoned his cultural form, his language, his food habits, his sexual behavior, his way of sitting down, or resting, of laughing, of enjoying himself, the oppressed flings himself upon the imposed culture with the desperation of a drowning man.

The ideal of identifying with the colonizer can also be manifested in the relationship of the colonized to each other, especially if one enjoys a higher status. The colonized individual with higher status dislikes colonized individuals of lower status and he may express some of the most racist stereotypes about the colonized.

Second, the colonized individual may defend assaults on his personality by turning his anger and frustration against himself or his people. This is displaced aggression which results in a higher incidence of alcoholism, psychiatric disorders, hypertension and crime—particularly homicide—among the oppressed. As Fanon (1963) explains:

> The colonized man will manifest this aggressiveness which has been deposited in his bones against his own people. This is the period when the niggers beat each other up, and the police do not know which way to turn when faced with astonishing waves of crime.

Since the colonized cannot defend his personality in the larger social arena, the last resort is to defend his personality via other colonized individuals. In the eyes of the colonizer, this type of auto-destruction is evidence of the inherent inferiority of the colonized individual.

Third, the colonized may defend assaults on his personality by openly resisting the colonial order. These "radical" individuals seek to restore traditions, self- and group confidence among the oppressed. Horizontal violence turns into vertical counterviolence. Destructive behaviors give way to proactive revolutionary praxis and anger and tensions find appropriate targets and constructive avenues of discharge (Bulhan 1989).

It may be argued that individuals who engage in protest are no longer alienated. They have regained their identity and they have reclaimed their history and culture. They work to restore self and group confidence and they promote group cohesion among the oppressed. These individuals, however, still feel that they are not a part of society and that the values of the nation are not congruent with their own orientation. Thus, they are still alienated. Rather than internalizing the alienation, the alienation is externalized and redirected in the service of personal and collective liberation (Bulhan 1985).

Fanon (1963a) advocates violence as being indispensable in the decolonization process. He maintains that colonialism is inherently violent and will only yield when it is confronted with greater violence. He further argues that colonialism creates in the native a perpetual tendency toward violence. The advocation of violence as a tool for liberation is where Fanon's sociological argument loses much of its support among critics who view Fanon's recommendation as an advocation for barbarism and terrorism. Others argue that Fanon is seeking "whatever means necessary" to end the exploitation of man by man (Smith 1973).

Internal Colonialism

Internal colonialism occurs when foreign control of a state or territory is eliminated and the control and exploitation of subordinate groups passes to the dominant group within the newly created society. Although there is no forceful entry by a foreign group, internal colonialism has the other identifying characteristics of classical colonialism (e.g. caste system based upon racism, cultural imposition, cultural disintegration and re-creation, and members of the colonized being governed by representatives of the dominant power). Moreover, internal colonialism is a social system which is deeply grounded in the sharp differentiation of White and non-White labor (Feagin 1978). Groups are brought into a society of internal colonialism by force which includes enslavement, incarceration and annexation (Feagin 1978).

Internal colonialism in North America predates the Revolutionary War of 1773-1777. The process of systematic subordination of non-Europeans in North America begins with the genocidal attempts of colonizing settlers to uproot native populations and force them off desirable lands (Feagin 1978). Unlike other racial minorities, the analogy between classical and domestic colonialism for Native Americans involves the forced entry of a foreign force.

Other examples of internal colonialism include Pacific and Asian people who were imported as indentured servants or annexed in the expansionist period of United States development; slave labor from Africa which was utilized as a dominant source of labor in the agricultural South; the utilization of cheap Mexican labor in the Southwest; and groups such as the Filipinos and Hawaiians who were brought in as contract labor due to the fact that their homelands are United States possessions. Although each group entered the society of internal colonialism differently, the common underlying factor is that the start of their subordination is linked to economic exploitation and incorporation, which is a major factor in classical colonialism.

The model of internal colonialism has often been used to explain the African American experience in the United States (See Frazier 1957; Blauner 1969, 1972; Carmichael and Hamilton 1967; Staples 1975, 1989). Internal colonialism analysts examine how the subordination or colonized status of African Americans is linked to economic, political and social incorporation. Specifically, they are concerned with the establishment and persistence of a racial stratification system and the social processes which maintain subordination (Feagin 1978). A summary of the historical, economic, political and social exploitation and subordination of African Americans is presented below.

Economic Subordination

Unlike other racial and ethnic groups entering the United States, the economic (as well as social and political) subordination of African Americans began with the institution of slavery. Some of the first Africans who were brought to the American colonies in 1619 were treated as indentured servants. However, by the mid-1600s, the slave status of Africans had been fully institutionalized into the laws of several colonies and was even reflected in the U.S. Constitution. For the next two and one-half centuries, virtually all African immigrants were brought by force to serve in involuntary servitude. In the agricultural South, slaves formed an important source of forced labor. Slaves were classified as being "property" and could be sold or passed as a tract of land, horse or ox. With the average maintenance cost of $19 per year, the slave represented the lowest and the worst of the modern laborers (Du Bois 1962).

The economic exploitation of African Americans continued after the institution of slavery was abolished. Emancipation did not change the economic structure. The lack of land reform and the absence of economic changes resulted in most freed slaves being forced to sell their labor to the same agricultural system that had prospered when it enslaved them. What emerged was actually a form of semi-slavery. Tied to one farm and economically exploited by the system of sharecropping tenant farming, it was virtually impossible for African American laborers to gain any type of independence.

To ensure a cheap and controlled labor supply for plantations, vagrancy laws (Black

Codes) allowed police officers to pick up itinerant African American laborers to provide forced labor on local farms under threat of imprisonment on chain gangs (Feagin 1978; Wilson 1973). Black Codes further relegated "persons of color" to the occupation of farmer or servants unless they secured a special license and paid an annual tax (Frazier 1957).

Outside the agricultural system, African Americans were segregated into "unskilled Negro jobs," and were prohibited from participating in the expanding industrial sectors in the South. African Americans in northern cities, both prior to and after the Civil War of 1861-1865, faced similar situations, with African American laborers often being displaced by European immigrant workers or forced into lower-level unskilled occupations. In short, the African American worker was denied access to money, jobs and technology that would assure economic advancement within the dominant social structure.

European immigrants suffered from similar forms of economic exploitation. European immigrants also were relegated to unskilled, lower-paying occupations and were paid less than their Anglo-Saxon White counterparts. For the Irish, there was evidence of wage slavery in which Irish coal miners worked for groceries and rent (commonly called "bobtail checks"), equaling their wages (Feagin 1978). However, a major difference between the economic exploitation of European immigrants and the "Negro freedman" can be seen in regards to economic displacement based upon race and the intensity of the economic exclusion.

African Americans provided a serious form of labor competition for poor and working class Whites. African Americans worked cheaply, partly from custom and partly as their own defense against competition (Du Bois 1962). To eliminate this competition, both the North and South enacted legislation to create a color-caste labor system. This type of legislation was not created for European immigrants, although there were laws passed in the American colonies to discourage Irish immigration. In essence, the racial stratification system that was developed in this country placed European laborers above African American laborers and afforded them greater opportunities in which to move up the economic ladder.

The decline of the significance of cotton and the industrial growth in northern cities led to the migration of African Americans northward after World War I in 1914-1918. The drastic curtailment of European immigrants during World War I resulted in an acute labor shortage in the northern factories. In need of unskilled and semi-skilled labor, northern industrialists began a campaign to attract African American labor from the South. African American laborers were offered free transportation and high wages if they agreed to migrate North (Wilson 1973).

African American migrants represented the younger and better-educated segment of the southern African American population (Feagin 1978; Jaynes and Williams 1989). These individuals saw northern cities as an economic "promised land." Instead of economic promise, what many African Americans found was an urban economy which exhibited oppressive economic conditions similar to those experienced in the South. The better-paying or foreman jobs were frequently reserved for White workers. Thus, there was a slow shift from tenant farming and sharecropping to unskilled and semi-skilled jobs in the industrial sectors.

A relatively small number of professional African Americans were present, having primarily been educated at one of the 117 predominantly African American colleges. Reconstruction had increased the educational opportunities for African Americans. Although their schools were grossly inferior to those of Whites, African Americans became teachers, lawyers, physicians, inventors and ministers. The services of these professionals, however, were confined to the African American community because of racism or the reluctance of Whites to use their services. *De facto* and *de jure* segregation also restricted these individuals to residences in predominantly African American neighborhoods.

This pattern of occupational subordination of African Americans into the secondary and lower-skilled job market continues with the effects of these long-standing discriminatory practices still seen today. Data show that African Americans are disproportionately employed in low-wage jobs that are unprotected by tenure and seniority, and in manufacturing and goods-producing industries that are particularly sensitive to upward and downward business cycles which affect layoffs and unemployment (Blackwell 1985; Jaynes and Williams 1989).

Although some of the disparity may be explained by differences in levels of education, part of the disparity can be explained by continuing patterns of discrimination in hiring practices and salaries (Blackwell 1985; Hacker 1992). African Americans are perceived to lack basic skills or work experience, or to be less reliable than White workers. Because of these perceptions, some employers recruit through high schools and newspapers that only reach White middle-class neighborhoods (Kirschenman and Neckerman 1990) or relocate to areas where few African Americans live (Blauner 1992). Even when African Americans and Whites are matched with similar resumes and trained to behave comparably, Whites receive about 50 percent more job offers (Turner, Fix and Struyk 1991).

Using 1990 census data, Hacker (1992) shows that African Americans who finish college have a jobless rate 2.24 times that of Whites with high school diplomas. The data also show substantial differences in income for college graduates for African American and White men. African American college men earn only slightly more than White men with high school diplomas and African American men who finish graduate school earn $771 compared to $1,000 for their White counterparts (Hacker 1992). Although African American women come closer to economic parity with White women (5+ years of college—$973 for every $1,000 earned by White women), the greater economic parity between African American and White women results largely from the fact that few women of either race rise far in the occupational hierarchy (Hacker 1992).

Political Subordination

The political power and participation of African Americans has varied over the last two centuries. Although slaves were nonparticipants in the political system, a few free African American male property owners in the New England states were able to vote in the early decades of political development (Walton 1972). Their impact upon the political process, however, was at best minuscule. At the end of the Civil War, legislation such as the Civil Rights Act of 1866, as well as the 13th, 14th and 15th amendments, increased African American participation in the electoral process.

The Reconstruction period brought about remarkable changes. Not only did African American men have the right to vote, but southern state constitutional conventions often included African American delegates. African Americans served in the U.S. House of Representatives, in the United States Senate, and were lieutenant governors and governor of southern states. Although African Americans enjoyed political participation, and, as a result, were able to promote a number of educational and political reforms, they never presented a challenge to the dominant White economic and political power structure.

The movement of African Americans from a limited to somewhat moderate political participation was short-lived. The end of Reconstruction brought a gradual, although definite, change in the political participation of African Americans and retarded their integration into the American political system. Once again, African American political participation was reduced to a limited status. In the

South, African American voters were disenfranchised through such tactics as the poll tax, literacy tests, and the grandfather clause. Unlike southern African Americans, African Americans in the North were enfranchised but their political capabilities were truncated by the white-controlled political machines and gerrymandering. The first decade of the twentieth century was a low point for African Americans politically in that the political exclusion of African Americans was directly institutionalized.

The political experience of recent European immigrants during the nineteenth century, and the first decades of the twentieth century, differed from that of African Americans. For the most part, recent European immigrants were able to benefit from urban political machines which played an important role in penetrating discrimination barriers, providing jobs and in facilitating upward mobility (Feagin 1978; Vander Zanden 1983). By the time African Americans had migrated in large numbers to northern urban centers, the urban political machines were being dismantled. As a result African Americans were not able to fully benefit from the sociopolitical influence that had been provided to other groups.

Furthermore, no other immigrant group faced the degree of systematic exclusion from urban political machines as did African Americans (Wilson 1980). African Americans were excluded from meaningful participation in the White-controlled political machines by practices of gerrymandering and by assignment to positions within the political machine where the flow of power was unidirectional—from the party headquarters to the segregated African American institutions. Consequently, African Americans were deprived of the kind of political development enjoyed by European immigrants whose political success on the local level enabled them to integrate their interests into the wider politics of the state and nation (Wilson 1980).

However, the second part of the twentieth century reveals an encouraging trend in African American political participation and political power. There has been a dramatic increase in the number of African Americans being elected to local, state and federal offices. Although this is evidence of increased African American political power, in comparison to Whites, African Americans have not achieved full participation within the political process (Jaynes and Williams 1989). And, African American priorities are not fully appreciated nor are they recognized by either major political party.

Part of this inability to affect public policy decisions is due to the fact that African American political success has come primarily in cities where significant numbers of African American voters reside. These cities have declining employment and tax revenue bases. They are characterized by overburdened schools, housing and health care systems. Large numbers of these urban populations receive public assistance, which limits African American influence in the policy process (Jaynes and Williams 1989).

African American voting and political power in urban centers has been further diluted by pressures for regional and metropolitan governments as well as by the privatization of previously provided public services. These governments have moved many of the patronage positions—planning, health, fire, sanitation, water—formerly run by the city to suburban areas. In the suburbs, they are more likely to be dominated by White suburbanites (Turner, Singleton and Musick 1990).

Social Subordination

The historical, economic and political subordination of African Americans is supplemented by a social system that serves to relegate them to a lower caste. American society labeled African slaves, as well as the emancipated freedmen, as "inferior beings." This perception proceeded into the first part of the twentieth century with African Americans being characterized as mentally, biologically and morally inferior.

Moreover, African Americans have suffered from the intentional destruction of their original African culture. To maximize domination and control, Whites involved in the slave trade separated slaves from the same tribes, kingdoms and linguistic groups. This practice destroyed much of the integral culture of the diverse African people.

As a result, most present-day African Americans have little knowledge of their cultural heritage, languages, or religions. When one speaks of the African American culture, he refers to the traditional forms of behavior, beliefs, values and styles that have grown out of the African American sense of mental and social isolation (Frazier 1957). While White ethnic groups often have given up their traditional ways in order to assimilate into dominant society, there is no intentional action to destroy their cultural heritage, languages, religions or traits.

While Jim Crow laws have been abolished and racist ideologies are not openly proclaimed by community leaders, the social status of African Americans for the most part remains lower than the social status of Whites. And the social system reserves certain statuses and privileges for Whites.

The dual stratification system to which African Americans are subjected enables them to obtain status and privileges within the hierarchy of their caste; however, they are not able to alter their group or racial status. Race relegates African Americans to a subordinate status within the larger society.

This is not to argue that the social status of African Americans has not changed for the better for many African Americans. Whether one uses pre–World War II or the mid 1960s as a baseline, African American social status has dramatically improved (Jaynes and Williams 1989). African Americans have experienced gains in incomes, levels of education, and skilled and white-collar occupations. However, increased social status has not eliminated the racial separation that still exists. There is still the tendency for African Americans to be stereotyped as being inferior based upon racial group membership (Hacker 1992; Jaynes and Williams 1989) and to be excluded from various spheres of social participation (Jaynes and Williams 1989). Research shows that within desegregated settings throughout American society, African Americans do not share equal authority and representation throughout an organization or institution and are noticeably absent from decision-making positions (Jaynes and Williams 1989). NORC data from 1958 to 1982 show that in practice many Whites refuse or are reluctant to participate in social settings (e.g., neighborhoods and schools) in which significant numbers of African Americans are present (Jaynes and Williams 1989).

Behavioral Adaptations to Structural Conditions

The internal colonialism theory argues that African Americans have suffered greater social, political and economic oppression than their White counterparts. This has been the case historically, and as a consequence of this history, racial inequality between African Americans and White Americans is evident today. Structural oppression, however, has behavioral consequences. People live within a social context and react to their social environment. African Americans are likely to perceive that they are racially oppressed and as a result of these perceptions develop feelings of alienation.

Alienation, in turn, leads to assimilation, crime and delinquency, or protest. If crime is the outcome of alienation, the victims of the violence are primarily other African Americans. As in the colonial world, it is not uncommon for African Americans to turn their frustration and aggression against themselves or against other African Americans as exhibited in the form of high suicide rates, high rates of drug abuse and high rates of homicide.

▒ Adequacy in Explaining Crime and Delinquency

Internal colonialism offers a different perspective of the relationship between race and crime in the United States. Internal colonialism shifts the focus of the study of crime from the victims of oppression to exploitative structural systems (Staples 1989). Crime and delinquency are the behavioral responses of African American adults and adolescents to a social environment that subjects them to limited opportunities for subsistence and social rewards, and limited access to social power because of race.

Internal colonialism is also valuable in explaining the relationship between race and crime because it examines the historical process of structural oppression, which provides a fuller understanding of the current conditions and perceptions of African Americans. Thus, it illuminates the relationship between structural oppression, alienation, crime and delinquency. The historical aspect of the internal colonialism theory as well as the model's conceptualization of alienation separates it from other structural models.

The model of internal colonialism, however, suffers from theoretical and empirical limitations. Presently, the model is not well-defined. The theory fails to clearly identify factors that may lead individuals to a behavioral response. Two individuals can be subjected to similar oppressive conditions, yet respond differently to their social environment. What factors cause some individuals to assimilate while others choose crime, delinquency or protest?

Second, the theory fails to address the relevancy of experiencing one or more aspects of alienation. Are individuals who experience only one type of alienation more alienated than individuals who experience several types of alienation? Furthermore, does more than one type of alienation affect the selection of a behavioral response?

A third theoretical shortcoming of the model involves the issue of race and class. Class differences among the colonized are not adequately addressed by the model. While internal colonialism stresses the importance of race, it is clear that structural oppression, as well as alienation, is likely to vary among the African American population according to social class position. In particular, how do structural oppression and alienation vary by race and social class, and what effect do these variations have upon behavioral responses?

Fourth, the internal colonial model fails to address the issue of alienation or class differences among Whites. The model implies that the alienation of African Americans and Whites differs but fails to delineate this difference. Furthermore, the model does not indicate how the alienation of Whites varies by social class or how African American and White alienation differs by race and class.

Fifth, the model fails to account for variations in historical structural oppression of different racial minorities (e.g., African Americans, Hispanics, Native Americans). The relationships of various racial groups to the White power structure bear similarities, but are not identical. Moreover, the model fails to account for variations in structural oppression and alienation that are the result of racial gradation (or differences in skin color) within the same racial group.

And sixth, other behavioral responses to a colonial environment are possible. African Americans (and other racial minorities) may protest a colonial society without engaging in the type of revolutionary activity that is discussed by Fanon. Rather, African Americans may seek to promote racial pride and to avoid racism by only participating in African American social and economic institutions. This voluntary separation is an acknowledgment that they have given up on the American dream of inclusion and assimilation (Cohen 1993).

The theoretical limitations of the model have made it difficult to test its propositions. Most studies using the model have been analytical essays or qualitative pieces describing the existence of one or more of the model's propositions. Other than Austin's (1983) examination of the impact of decolonization upon intragroup violence in the Caribbean, no other study has utilized the model to empirically assess the relationship between colonization and crime.

Part of the difficulty in empirically testing the model is the transformation of variables that identify a colonial society into measures (Chalout and Chalout 1979). Some of the components of the internal colonialism framework (e.g., alienation and institutional racism) are difficult to operationalize and empirically test.

In order to improve the model of internal colonialism, the theoretical and empirical limitations that are discussed above must be resolved. Some of the problems of the model are now being addressed by internal colonialism analysts. Only through further research can these limitations be corrected and the model fully tested.

Summary

According to Ohlin (1983), "many competing biological, psychological, social and cultural theories of criminality have emerged. Yet none are sufficient to account for the rates and forms of crime today." The vacuum that is created by the insufficiency of current mainstream theoretical explanations warrants the examination of theoretical models that to a large extent fall outside the paradigm of traditional criminological thought.

The model of internal colonialism explains the association between race and crime by examining the relationship between structural oppression and alienation. The model, however, needs to be subjected to rigorous examination. The full explanatory power of the model cannot be assessed until this is accomplished.

References

Austin, R. 1983. "The Colonial Model, Subcultural Theory and Intragroup Violence." *Journal of Criminal Justice* 11:93-104.

Blackwell, J. 1991. *The Black Community: Diversity and Unity* (3rd ed.). New York: Harper and Row Publishers.

———. 1985. *The Black Community: Diversity and Unity* (2nd ed.). New York: Harper and Row Publishers.

Blauner, R. 1992. "The Ambiguities of Racial Change." In *Race, Class, and Gender: An Anthology*, edited by M. L. Andersen and P. H. Collins. Belmont, CA: Wadsworth Publishing Company.

———. 1972. *Racial Oppression in America*. New York: Harper and Row.

———. 1969. "Internal Colonialism and Ghetto Revolt." *Social Problems* 16:393-408.

Bulhan, H. A. 1985. *Frantz Fanon and the Psychology of Oppression*. New York: Plenum Publishing Corporation.

Carmichael, S. and C. V. Hamilton. 1967. *Black Power.* New York: Oxford University Press.

Chalout, N. and Y. Chalout. 1979. "The Internal Colonialism Concept: Methodological Considerations." *Social and Economic Studies* 28:85-99.

Cohen, S. July 25, 1993. "Blacks Reject Integrated Lifestyles By Choice." *The Herald Sun*, p. Al.

Davidson, D. V. 1976. "The Sociology of Oppressed Cultures: An Analysis of the Socio-Cultural Dynamics of Colonialism." *The Review of the Black Political Economy* 6:421-437.

Dessous, N. 1987. "Fanon and the Problem of Alienation." *The Western Journal of Black Studies* 11:80-91.

Du Bois, W. E. B. 1962. *Black Reconstruction in America: 1860-1880*. New York: Maxwell McMillian International.

Elliott, K. S. and S. Ageton. 1980. "Reconciling Race and Class Differences in Self-Reported and Official Estimates of Delinquency." *American Sociological Review* 45:95-110.

Fanon, F. 1967a. *Black Skin, White Masks*. New York: Grove Weidenfeld.

———. 1967b. *A Dying Colonialism*. New York: Grove Press.

———. 1963. *The Wretched of the Earth*. New York: Grove Press.

Feagin, J. R. 1978. *Racial and Ethnic Relations.* New York: Prentice-Hall.

Federal Bureau of Investigation. 1992. *Crime in the United States.* Washington, D.C.: U.S. Government Printing Office.

Frazier, E. F. 1957. *Race and Culture Contacts in the Modern World.* Boston: Beacon Press.

Hacker, A. 1992. *Two Nations: Black and White, Separate, Hostile, Unequal.* New York: Charles Scribner and Sons.

Hansen, E. 1977. *Frantz Fanon: Social and Political Thought.* Columbus: Ohio State University Press.

Jinadu, L. A. 1986. *Fanon: In Search of the African Revolution.* London: KPI.

Jaynes, C. D. and R. M. Williams, eds. 1989. *A Common Destiny: Blacks and American Society.* Washington, D.C.: National Academy Press.

Kirschenman, J. and K. Neckerman. 1990. *Hiring Strategies, Racial Bias, and Inner-City Workers.* Mimeo. University of Chicago.

Memmi, A. 1968. *Dominated Man.* New York: Orion Press.

Ohlin, L. 1983. "The Future of Juvenile Justice Policy and Research." *Crime and Delinquency* 29:463-472.

Sigmon, S. B. 1987. "An Existential Psychohistory of Frantz Fanon." *The Western Journal of Black Studies* 11:76-79.

Staples, R. 1989. *The Urban Plantation.* Oakland: The Black Scholar Press.

———. 1975. "White Racism, Black Crime and American Justice: An Application of the Colonial Model to Explain Race and Crime." *Phylon* 36:14-22.

———. 1974. "Internal Colonialism and Black Violence." *Black World* 23:16-34.

Turner, J. H., R. Singleton and D. Musick. 1990. *Oppression: A Socio-History of Black-White Relations in America.* Chicago: Nelson-Hall.

Turner, M. A., M. Fix and R. J. Struyk. 1991. *Opportunities Denied, Opportunities Diminished: Discrimination in Hiring.* Washington, D.C.: Urban Institute.

U.S. Bureau of the Census. 1992. *The Black Population in the United States: March 1991.* Washington, D.C.: U.S. Government Printing Office.

U.S. Department of Justice. 1992. *Criminal Victimizations in the United States, 1991.* Washington, D.C.: Bureau of Justice Statistics.

Vander Zanden, J. W. 1983. *American Minority Relations* (4th ed.). New York: McGraw-Hill, Inc.

Walton, H. Jr. 1972. *Black Politics.* Philadelphia: J. P. Lippincott Press.

Wilson, A. 1990. *Black on Black Violence: The Psychodynamics of Black Self-Annihilation in Service of White Domination.* New York: Afrikan World Infosystems.

Wilson, W. J. 1987. *The Truly Disadvantaged: The Inner City, the Underclass, and Public Policy.* Chicago: University of Chicago Press.

———. 1980. *The Declining Significance of Race: Blacks and Changing American Institutions.* Chicago: University of Chicago Press.

———. 1973. *Power, Racism and Privilege: Race Relations in Theoretical and Sociohistorical Perspectives.* Chicago: University of Chicago Press.

Zahar, R. 1974. *Frantz Fanon: Colonialism and Alienation.* New York: Monthly Review Press.

22

INTRODUCTION

Paul D. Butler is an attorney who has seen the law in operation from both sides of the legal aisle. He has been involved in the prosecution of both white-collar occupational crimes and street crimes. On the other side, he defended white-collar criminals and practiced civil litigation. After joining the faculty of the George Washington University Law School in 1993, Butler's published work has been in the area of race and crime. He argues that affirmative action should be extended to criminal law. He suggests that the criminal law already sanctions through a number of its policies and procedures (e.g., segregation in prison and the hiring of minority law enforcement officers). He argues that we could employ a similar approach in the criminal justice system by not using capital punishment in cases involving a Black offender and a White victim and by ensuring that the prison population of the United States be topped at 13% African American, thereby taking into account the discriminatory treatment of Black offenders.

However, it was Butler's work in the area of race-based jury nullification that has received national attention and is presented here. He confronts the unwillingness of Americans—but, more important, actors in the criminal justice system—to acknowledge that race plays a role in the decisions of members of the criminal justice system. He argues that race plays a role when a Black person commits a crime and when a Black juror deliberates on the fate of the Black defendant. Moreover, Butler contends that race should play a role in the decisions of Black jurors to acquit Black defendants in criminal cases. As an advocate for jury nullification, he asserts that Black jurors have a moral right to practice jury nullification because, historically, they have not been afforded the benefits of either the rule of law or the practice of democracy that would negate the need for such a practice.

RACIALLY BASED JURY NULLIFICATION

Black Power in the Criminal Justice System

PAUL BUTLER

Wonders do not confuse. We call them that
And close the matter there. But common things
surprise us. They accept the names we give
with calm, and keep them. Easy-breathing then
We brave our next small business. Well, behind
Our backs they alter. How were we to know.

—Gwendolyn Brooks

[T]he time that we're living in now . . . is not an era where one who is oppressed is looking toward the oppressor to give him some system or form of logic or reason. What is logical to the oppressor isn't logical to the oppressed. And what is reason to the oppressor isn't reason to the oppressed. The black people in this country are beginning to realize that what sounds reasonable to those who exploit us doesn't sound reasonable to us. There just has to be a new system of reason and logic devised by us who are at the bottom, if we want to get some results in the struggle that is called "the Negro revolution."

—Malcolm X

INTRODUCTION

I was a Special Assistant United States Attorney in the District of Columbia in 1990. I prosecuted people accused of misdemeanor crimes, mainly the drug and gun cases that overwhelm the local courts of most American cities. As a federal prosecutor, I represented the United States of America and used that

From Butler, P. Racially based jury nullification: Black power in the criminal justice system. Reprinted by permission of the Yale Journal Company and William S. Hein Company. From *The Yale Law Journal, 105*, 677-725.

power to put people, mainly African American men, in prison. I am also an African American man. While at the U.S. Attorney's office, I made two discoveries that profoundly changed the way I viewed my work as a prosecutor and my responsibilities as a black person.

The first discovery occurred during a training session for new Assistants conducted by experienced prosecutors. We rookies were informed that we would lose many of our cases, despite having persuaded a jury beyond a reasonable doubt that the defendant was guilty. We would lose because some black jurors would refuse to convict black defendants who they knew were guilty.

The second discovery was related to the first, but was even more unsettling. It occurred during the trial of Marion Barry, then the second-term mayor of the District of Columbia. Barry was being prosecuted by my office for drug possession and perjury. I learned, to my surprise, that some of my fellow African American prosecutors hoped that the mayor would be acquitted, despite the fact that he was obviously guilty of at least one of the charges—he had smoked cocaine on FBI videotape. These black prosecutors wanted their office to lose its case because they believed that the prosecution of Barry was racist.

Federal prosecutors in the nation's capital hear many rumors about prominent officials engaging in illegal conduct, including drug use. Some African American prosecutors wondered why, of all those people, the government chose to "set up" the most famous black politician in Washington, D.C. They also asked themselves why, if crack is so dangerous, the FBI had allowed the mayor to smoke it. Some members of the predominantly black jury must have had similar concerns: They convicted the mayor of only one count of a fourteen-count indictment, despite the trial judge's assessment that he had "never seen a stronger government case." Some African American prosecutors thought that the jury, in rendering its verdict, jabbed its black thumb in the face of a racist prosecution, and that idea made those prosecutors glad.

As such reactions suggest, lawyers and judges increasingly perceive that some African American jurors vote to acquit black defendants for racial reasons, a decision sometimes expressed as the juror's desire not to send yet another black man to jail. This Chapter examines the question of what role race should play in black jurors' decisions to acquit defendants in criminal cases. Specifically, I consider trials that include both African American defendants and African American jurors. I argue that the race of a black defendant is sometimes a legally and morally appropriate factor for jurors to consider in reaching a verdict of not guilty or for an individual juror to consider in refusing to vote for conviction.

My thesis is that, for pragmatic and political reasons, the black community is better off when some nonviolent lawbreakers remain in the community rather than go to prison. The decision as to what kind of conduct by African Americans ought to be punished is better made by African Americans themselves, based on the costs and benefits to their community, than by the traditional criminal justice process, which is controlled by white lawmakers and white law enforcers. Legally, the doctrine of jury nullification gives the power to make this decision to African American jurors who sit in judgment of African American defendants. Considering the costs of law enforcement to the black community and the failure of white lawmakers to devise significant nonincarcerative responses to black antisocial conduct, it is the moral responsibility of black jurors to emancipate some guilty black outlaws.

Part I of this Chapter describes two criminal cases in the District of Columbia in which judges feared that defendants or their lawyers were sending race-conscious, "forbidden" messages to black jurors and attempted to regulate those messages. I suggest that the judicial and public responses to those cases signal a dangerous reluctance among many Americans to engage in meaningful discourse about the relationship between race and crime. In Part II, I describe racial critiques of the criminal justice system. I then examine the evolution of the doctrine of jury nullification and suggest, in light of this doctrine, that racial considerations by African American jurors are legally and morally right. Part III proposes a framework for analysis of the kind of criminal cases involving black defendants in which jury nullification is appropriate, and considers some of the concerns that implementation of the proposal raises.

My goal is the subversion of American criminal justice, at least as it now exists. Through jury nullification, I want to dismantle the master's house with the master's tools. My intent, however, is not purely destructive; this project is also constructive, because I hope that the destruction of the status quo will not lead to anarchy, but rather to the implementation of certain noncriminal ways of addressing antisocial conduct. Criminal conduct among African Americans is often a predictable reaction to oppression. Sometimes black crime is a symptom of internalized white supremacy; other times it is a reasonable response to the racial and economic subordination every African American faces every day. Punishing black people for the fruits of racism is wrong if that punishment is premised on the idea that it is the black criminal's "just desserts." Hence, the new paradigm of justice that I suggest in Part III rejects punishment for the sake of retribution and endorses it, with qualifications, for the ends of deterrence and incapacitation.

In a sense, this Chapter simply may argue for the return of rehabilitation as the purpose of American criminal justice, but a rehabilitation that begins with the white-supremacist beliefs that poison the minds of us all—you, me, and the black criminal. I wish that black people had the power to end racial oppression right now. African Americans can prevent the application of one particularly destructive instrument of white supremacy—American criminal justice—to some African American people, and this they can do immediately. I hope that this Essay makes the case for why and how they should.

I. Secret Messages Everyone Hears

Americans seem reluctant to have an open conversation about the relationship between race and crime. Lawmakers ignore the issue, judges run from it, and crafty defense lawyers exploit it. It is not surprising, then, that some African American jurors are forced to sneak through the back door what is not allowed to come in through the front: the idea that "race matters" in criminal justice. In this part, I tell two stories about attempts by defense attorneys to encourage black jurors' sympathy for their clients, and then I examine how these attempts provoked many people to act as though the idea of racial identification with black defendants was ridiculous or insulting to black people. In fact, the defense attorneys may well have been attempting to encourage black jurors' sympathy as part of their trial strategies. The lesson of the stories is that the failure of the law to address openly the relationship between race and crime fosters a willful and unhelpful blindness in many who really ought to see and allows jury nullification to go on without a principled framework. This Chapter offers such a framework and encourages nullification for the purpose of black self-help.

A. *United States v. Marion Barry*

The time is January 1990. The mayor of the District of Columbia is an African American man named Marion Barry. African Americans make up approximately 66% of the population of the city. The mayor is so popular in the black community that one local newspaper columnist has dubbed him "Mayor for Life." Barry is hounded, however, by rumors of his using drugs and "chasing women." Barry denies the rumors and claims that they are racist.

On January 18, 1990, the mayor is contacted by an old friend, Rasheeda Moore, who tells him that she is visiting for a short time, and staying at a local hotel. The mayor stops by later that afternoon and telephones Ms. Moore's room from the lobby of the hotel. He wants her to come downstairs to the lobby for a drink, but she requests that he come up to her room. The mayor assents, joins Ms. Moore in the room, and the two converse. At some point, Ms. Moore produces crack cocaine and a pipe, and invites the mayor to smoke it. He first demurs, then consents, and after he inhales smoke from the pipe, agents of the FBI and the Metropolitan Police Department storm the room. It turns out that Ms. Moore is a government informant, and the police have observed and videotaped the entire proceeding in the hotel room. The mayor is arrested and subsequently charged with one count of conspiracy to possess cocaine, ten counts of possession of cocaine, and three counts of perjury for allegedly lying to the grand jury that had investigated him. The mayor publicly asserts that he is the victim of a racist prosecution.

It is the last week in June 1990. The mayor is on trial in federal court. The judge is white. Of the twelve jurors, ten are African American. Rasheeda Moore, the government's star witness, is expected to testify. The mayor has four passes to give to guests he would like to attend his trial. On this day, he has given one pass to Minister Louis Farrakhan, the controversial leader of the Nation of Islam. Farrakhan has publicly supported Barry since his arrest, in part by suggesting that the sting operation and the prosecution were racist. When Farrakhan attempts to walk into the courtroom, a U.S. deputy marshal bars his entry. When Barry's attorney protests, the judge states, outside of the jury's hearing, that Farrakhan's "presence would be potentially disruptive, very likely intimidating, and he is a persona non grata for the [rest] of this case." Rasheeda Moore then takes the stand.

The next day, the Reverend George Stallings appears at the trial with one of Barry's guest passes in hand. Stallings is a black Roman Catholic priest who, the previous year, received extensive publicity when he accused the Catholic Church of being hopelessly racist, left it, and founded his own church. When Stallings reaches the courtroom, the deputy marshal, following the instructions of the judge, does not let him enter. The judge explains, again outside of the jury's hearing, that Stallings is "in my judgment, not an ordinary member of the public and his presence would very likely have the same effect as Mr. Farrakhan's." The judge also indicates that there are "others who fit the same category." Barry's attorney asks for a list of those persons. The judge replies, "I think you will know them when you see them."

In the wake of these two episodes, the American Civil Liberties Union, representing Barry, Farrakhan, and Stallings, files an emergency appeal of the trial judge's decision. It argues that the judge's refusal to allow Barry's guests to attend the trial violated Barry's Sixth Amendment right to a fair trial and the First Amendment rights of the guests. In response, the judge's attorneys state that the judge excluded Farrakhan and Stallings because their presence in the courtroom would send an "impermissible message" of "intimidation" and "racial animosity" to jurors and witnesses. The judge's attorneys argue that the excluded persons' views of the prosecution had been highly publicized and that their appearance at the trial was consistent with Barry's "publicly avowed strategies of seeking a hung jury and jury nullification." The judge's attorneys argue that Farrakhan and Stallings attended the trial "not to view the proceedings or to show generalized concern, but instead to send a forbidden message to the jury and witness."

The U.S. Court of Appeals for the District of Columbia Circuit rules that Farrakhan and Stallings should have presented their constitutional claims to the trial judge prior to seeking relief in the appellate court. Accordingly, it remands the case back to the trial judge. Because the trial has been halted pending appeal, however, the D.C. Circuit, in light of the "exigent circumstances," lists several "pertinent considerations" for the trial judge on remand. The considerations mainly concern the judge's power to regulate the attendance of those who threaten physically to disrupt a courtroom. The court does note, though, that:

> No individual can be wholly excluded from the courtroom merely because he advocates a particular political, legal, or religious point of view—even a point of view that the district court or we may regard as antithetical to the fair administration of justice. Nor can an individual be wholly excluded from the courtroom because his presence is thought to send an undesirable message to the jurors except that of physical intimidation.

The trial judge hears the message of the court of appeals. In lieu of resolving Farrakhan's and Stallings's constitutional claims, he instead seeks assurances from their attorneys that their clients know how to conduct themselves in a courtroom. Indeed, the judge provides the attorneys with his own "special rules" of decorum regarding the trial, stating that "any attempt to communicate with a juror may be punished as criminal contempt of court." Farrakhan's and Stallings's attorneys assure the court that their clients will act with decorum in the courtroom. The trial continues. The mayor is eventually convicted of one of the indictment's fourteen counts (for perjury), but not of the count in which he smoked the cocaine on videotape.

B. The Attorney Who Wore Kente *Cloth*

It is now June 11, 1992. John T. Harvey, III, is an African American criminal defense attorney who practices in the District of Columbia. Harvey represents a black man who is charged with assault with intent to murder. The case is scheduled for arraignment before a white judge. At the arraignment, Harvey wears a business suit and tie, and his jacket is accessorized by a colorful stole made of *kente* cloth. *Kente* cloth is a mutltihued woven fabric originally worn by ancient African royalty, and many African Americans have adopted it as a fashion statement and a symbol of racial pride.

In pretrial proceedings, the judge had warned Harvey that he would not be permitted to wear *kente* cloth before a jury. According to Harvey, the judge told him that wearing the fabric during a jury trial "was sending a hidden message to jurors." The judge had informed Harvey that he had three options: He could refrain from wearing the *kente* cloth; he could withdraw from the case; or he could agree to try the case before the judge, without a jury. Harvey's client decided to plead guilty. At the June 11 hearing, however, Harvey refuses to enter his client's plea before the judge because he doubts that the judge will be impartial. The judge then removes Harvey from the case, "not on the basis of [the] Kente cloth, but on the basis that [Harvey] will not enter a plea which [his] client wishes to enter."

The same day, another client of Harvey's is scheduled to go to trial, also for assault with intent to kill, before another white judge. During the voir dire, the judge asks if any of the jurors are familiar with Harvey, whose battle with the other judge was well publicized. Four of the potential jurors know of the controversy. "[T]he concern we think we have here," the judge says, is "that we won't influence a juror improperly." He also informs them of case law in another jurisdiction suggesting that a court may prevent a Catholic priest from wearing a clerical collar in court. When Harvey asks the judge to inform the potential jurors of contrary cases, the judge refuses. The judge subsequently states:

> "For the record, Mr. Harvey is black. Aside from the courtroom clerk, he is the only black person who is participating in this trial. . . . He is wearing a so-called Kente cloth around his neck, and he has recently received wide publicity, which I am sure he loves.
>
> "I have wondered with my own conscience whether for me to simply wait for the government or someone else to object is the proper approach to avoid a war with Mr. Harvey, which I am not anxious for—either personally or on behalf of the Superior Court. . . . I also note that this is costing us all a lot of time . . . and I don't appreciate it."

Ultimately, the judge allows Harvey to wear the cloth, but he suggests that when Harvey submits an attorney fee voucher to him for approval, he might not allow Harvey to be paid for the time the *kente* cloth issue has consumed. Harvey's client is tried before an all-black jury and is acquitted.

C. The Judicial and Popular Response: Willful Blindness

As described above, the trial judge's attempt to exclude Farrakhan and Stallings from Barry's trial met with disapproval from the D.C. Circuit. In the case of John Harvey, no higher court had occasion to review the judge's prohibition against the *kente* cloth, but, as discussed below, much of the public reaction to the judge's prohibition was critical. These responses scorned the trial judge's fears that black jurors might acquit on the basis of racial identification rather than the "evidence." The D.C. Circuit and many observers, however, failed to acknowledge the significance of the "forbidden" message. I believe that this failure was deliberate. It reflected an intention to avoid serious consideration of the issue of black jurors acquitting black defendants on the basis of racial identification. Simply put, the D.C. Circuit and some of the public did not want to face the reality that race matters, in general and in jury adjudications of guilt and innocence.

1. The D.C. Circuit: We Hate Fights

The D.C. Circuit's per curiam opinion discussed the issue before it as though the judge's concern was that Barry's invitees would cause some type of physical disruption. The court listed a series of five "pertinent considerations," four of which actually were not pertinent because they involved the physical disruption of courtrooms or physical threats to witnesses.

The only *relevant* consideration was so vague that it was nearly useless: The trial judge must exercise his discretion to exclude people from attending criminal matters "consistently with the First and Fifth Amendment rights of individuals to attend criminal trials." The court's discussion of this consideration is even more ambivalent: No one can be *"wholly"* excluded from a trial, even if he advocates a point of view that "we *may* regard as antithetical to the fair administration of justice" or if his presence sends an "undesirable message" to jurors. Because the appellate court did not suggest a procedure for *partial* exclusion of courtroom spectators, the trial judge's response was to pretend as though he had been concerned all along about physical disruption and subsequently to insist that Farrakhan and Stallings act in accordance with his rules of decorum. In the view of the D.C. Circuit, trial guests should keep their hands and their feet to themselves, but their messages may run amuck. In reality, Farrakhan's and Stallings's manners in the courtroom were an issue created by the appellate court. Ironically, the trial judge's response—the patronizing insistence that Farrakhan and Stallings agree to behave themselves—smacks of racism more than does his initial decision to exclude them from the courtroom.

United States v. Barry suggests that no trial spectator can be barred from a courtroom unless she threatens physically to disrupt the trial. In this respect, the court established a severe restriction on the discretion of judges to control public access to trials. Not all courts have taken this position, however. Two of the few other federal appellate courts that have considered symbolic communication by trial spectators have found it appropriate to regulate this type of communication. In one case, the Ninth Circuit stated that "when fair trial rights are at significant risk . . . the First Amendment rights of trial attendees can and must be curtailed at the courthouse door." In another case, the Eleventh Circuit ordered the retrial of a man convicted of the murder of a prison guard, partly because of the presence, at the first trial, of numerous uniformed prison guards. The court was concerned that the guards' presence posed an unacceptable risk of prejudicing the jurors.

Significantly, the decisions from the Ninth and Eleventh Circuits involved cases in which the presence of the spectators was not thought to implicate race. The D.C. Circuit is the first appellate court to consider a "forbidden" racial message. My intention in noting this distinction is not to criticize the restrictive standard the D.C. Circuit established; indeed, there are potentially troubling implications of standards that allow trial judges more discretion in terms of which "secret" messages to regulate. I suggest, however, that the D.C. Circuit's holding was not mandated by clear constitutional dictates and was not supported by precedent from other federal jurisdictions. Indeed, other appellate courts have considered and regulated the contents of the messages that trial spectators were thought to be sending. Those cases suggest that the D.C. Circuit could have talked about race, and yet it did not.

2. The Skeptics: What's Race Got to Do With It?

The response of a number of commentators to the controversy over John Harvey's *kente* cloth was disdainful of the trial judge's apprehension about race-based appeals to black jurors. For example, the *Washington Times* characterized one of the judge's concerns as "[s]heer, unadulterated goofiness." The editorial continued:

> [The judge] apparently believes that the [kente] cloth is no innocent fabric but rather possesses hypnotic powers of seduction, powers that will turn the judicial system on its head and hold jurors in its sway. . . .
>
> . . . [W]hile most of us common folk are puzzled by this kind of judicial behavior, lawyers are widely inured to the fact that judges are free to act like fools with impunity—even when it is an abuse of discretion, an abuse of power, a waste of time and an injustice to someone who has come before the court seeking justice.

The *Washington Post* opined:

> There is absolutely no reason in logic or law for Judge Scott to tell Mr. Harvey that he cannot wear a kente cloth before a jury—regardless of the jurors' race. The very suggestion is offensive to black jurors, that they somehow lose their judgment and objectivity at the sight of a kente cloth.

The National Bar Association, an African American lawyers' group, expressed a similar concern, and one black attorney called the judge's actions "almost unbelievable" and wondered why the judge "injected race" into the trial proceedings by making an issue of the *kente* cloth. Even the prosecutors in the *kente* cloth case "remained conspicuously silent" and refrained from endorsing the judge's concerns about the cloth.

D. The Forbidden Message Revealed

I am fascinated by the refusal of these actors to take seriously the possibility and legal implications of black jurors' sympathy with black defendants. The criminal justice system would be better served if there were less reluctance to consider the significance of race in black jurors' adjudications of guilt or innocence. The remainder of this Chapter argues that race matters when a black person violates American criminal law and when a black juror decides how she should exercise her power to put another black man in prison.

The idea that race matters in criminal justice is hardly shocking; it surely does not surprise most African Americans. In the Barry and Harvey stories, I believe that it was known by all of the key players: judges, jurors, attorneys, defendants, and spectators. The trial judges in those cases were correct: Somebody—the controversial black demagogue, the radical black priest, the *kente*-cloth-wearing lawyer—was trying to send the black jurors a message. The message, in my view, was that the black jurors should consider the evidence presented at trial in light of the idea that the American criminal justice system discriminates against blacks. The message was that the jurors should not send another black man to prison.

There is no way to "prove" what Farrakhan's and Stallings's purposes were in attending Barry's trial—nor can I "prove" the intent of the *kente*-cloth-wearing lawyer. I believe that my theory that they were encouraging black jurors' sympathy is reasonable, based on the relevant players' statements, the trial judge's observations, and common sense and experience. Even if one is unwilling to ascribe to those players the same racially based motivations that I do, acknowledgement and concern that some black jurors acquit black defendants on the basis of race are increasing, as my experience at the U.S. Attorney's Office showed. For the remainder of this Chapter, I focus on the legal and social implications of this conduct by black jurors.

II. "Justice Outside the Formal Rules of Law"

Why would a black juror vote to let a guilty person go free? Assuming that the juror is a rational actor, she must believe that she and her community are, in some way, better off with the defendant out of prison than in prison. But how could any rational person believe that about a criminal? The following section describes racial critiques of the American criminal justice system. I then examine the evolution of the doctrine of jury nullification and argue that its practice by African Americans is, in many cases, consistent with the Anglo American tradition and, moreover, is legally and morally right.

A. The Criminal Law and African Americans: Justice or "Just Us"?

Imagine a country in which more than half of the young male citizens are under the supervision of the criminal justice system, either awaiting trial, in prison, or on probation or parole. Imagine a country in which two-thirds of the men can anticipate being arrested before they reach age thirty. Imagine a country in which there are more young men in prison than in college. Now give the citizens of the country the key to the prison. Should they use it?

Such a country bears some resemblance to a police state. When we criticize a police state, we think that the problem lies not with the citizens of the state, but rather with the form of government or law, or with the powerful elites and petty bureaucrats whose interests the state serves. Similarly, racial critics of American criminal justice locate the problem not so much with the black prisoners as with the state and its actors and beneficiaries. As evidence, they cite their own experiences and other people's stories, African American history, understanding gained from social science research on the power and pervasiveness of white supremacy, and ugly statistics like those in the preceding paragraph.

For analytical purposes, I will create a false dichotomy among racial critics by dividing them into two camps: liberal critics and radical critics. Those are not names that the critics have given themselves or that they would necessarily accept, and there would undoubtedly be disagreement within each camp and theoretical overlap between the camps. Nonetheless, for the purposes of a brief explication of racial critiques, my oversimplification may be useful.

1. The Liberal Critique

According to this critique, American criminal justice is racist because it is controlled primarily by white people, who are unable to escape the culture's dominant message of white supremacy, and who are therefore inevitably, even if unintentionally, prejudiced. These white actors include legislators, police, prosecutors, judges, and jurors. They exercise their discretion to make and enforce the criminal law in a discriminatory fashion. Sometimes the discrimination is overt, as in the case of Mark Fuhrman, the police officer in the O.J. Simpson case who, in interviews, used racist language and boasted of his own brutality, and sometimes it is unintentional, as with a hypothetical white juror who invariably credits the testimony of a white witness over that of a black witness.

The problem with the liberal critique is that it does not adequately explain the extent of the difference between the incidence of black and white crime, especially violent crime. For example, in 1991, blacks constituted about 55% of the 18,096 people arrested for murder and non-negligent manslaughter in the United States (9924 people). One explanation the liberal critique offers for this unfortunate statistic is that the police pursue black murder suspects more aggressively than they do white murder suspects. In other words, but for discrimination, the percentage of blacks arrested for murder would be closer to their percentage of the population, roughly twelve percent. The liberal critique would attribute some portion of the additional 43% of non-negligent homicide arrestees (in 1991, approximately 7781 people) to race prejudice. Ultimately, however, those assumptions strain credulity, not because many police officers are not racist, but because there is no evidence that there is a crisis of that magnitude in criminal justice.

In fact, for all the faults of American law enforcement, catching the bad guys seems to be something it does rather well. The liberal critique fails to account convincingly for the incidence of black crime.

2. *The Radical Critique*

The radical critique does not discount the role of discrimination in accounting for some of the racial disparity in crime rates, but it also does not, in contrast to the liberal critique, attribute all or even most of the differential to police and prosecutor prejudice. The radical critique offers a more fundamental, structural explanation.

It suggests that criminal law is racist because, like other American law, it is an instrument of white supremacy. Law is made by white elites to protect their interests and, especially, to preserve the economic status quo, which benefits those elites at the expense of blacks, among others. Due to discrimination and segregation, the majority of African Americans receive few meaningful educational and employment opportunities and, accordingly, are unable to succeed, at least in the terms of the capitalist ideal. Some property crimes committed by blacks may be understood as an inevitable result of the tension between the dominant societal message equating possession of material resources with success and happiness and the power of white supremacy to prevent most African Americans from acquiring "enough" of those resources in a legal manner. "Black-on-black" violent crime, and even "victimless" crime like drug offenses, can be attributed to internalized racism, which causes some African Americans to devalue black lives—either those of others or their own. The political process does not allow for the creation or implementation of effective "legal" solutions to this plight, and the criminal law punishes predictable reactions to it.

I am persuaded by the radical critique when I wonder about the roots of the ugly truth that blacks commit many crimes at substantially higher rates than whites. Most white Americans, especially liberals, would publicly offer an environmental, as opposed to genetic, explanation for this fact. They would probably concede that racism, historical and current, plays a major role in creating an environment that breeds criminal conduct. From this premise, the radical critic deduces that but for the (racist) environment, the African American criminal would not be a criminal. In other words, racism creates and sustains the criminal breeding ground, which produces the black criminal. Thus, when many African Americans are locked up, it is because of a situation that white supremacy created.

Obviously, most blacks are not criminals, even if every black is exposed to racism. To the radical critics, however, the law-abiding conduct of the majority of African Americans does not mean that racism does not create black criminals. Not everyone exposed to a virus will become sick, but that does not mean that the virus does not cause the illness of the people who do.

The radical racial critique of criminal justice is premised as much on the criminal law's *effect* as on its intent. The system is discriminatory, in part, because of the disparate impact law enforcement has on the black community. This unjust effect is measured in terms of the costs to the black community of having so many African Americans, particularly males, incarcerated or otherwise involved in the criminal justice system. These costs are social and economic, and include the perceived dearth of men "eligible" for marriage, the large percentage of black children who live in female-headed households, the lack of male "role models" for black children, especially boys, the absence of wealth in the black community, and the large unemployment rate among black men.

3. Examples of Racism in Criminal Justice

Examples commonly cited by both liberal and radical critics as evidence of racism in criminal justice include: the Scottsboro case; the history of the criminalization of drug use; past and contemporary administration of the death penalty; the use of imagery linking crime to race in the 1988 presidential campaign and other political campaigns; the beating of Rodney King and the acquittal of his police assailants; disparities between punishments for white-collar crimes and punishments for other crimes; more severe penalties for crack cocaine users than for powder cocaine users; the Charles Murray and Susan Smith cases; police corruption scandals in minority neighborhoods in New York and Philadelphia; the O.J. Simpson case, including the extraordinary public and media fascination with it, the racist police officer who was the prosecution's star witness, and the response of many white people to the jury's verdict of acquittal; and, cited most frequently, the extraordinary rate of incarceration of African American men.

4. Law Enforcement Enthusiasts

Of course, the idea that the criminal justice system is racist and oppressive is not without dissent, and among the dissenters are some African Americans. Randall Kennedy succinctly poses the counterargument:

> Although the administration of criminal justice has, at times, been used as an instrument of racial oppression, the principal problem facing African Americans in the context of criminal justice today is not over-enforcement but under-enforcement of the laws. The most lethal danger facing African Americans in their day-to-day lives is not white, racist officials of the state, but private, violent criminals (typically black) who attack those most vulnerable to them without regard to racial identity.

According to these theorists, whom I will call law enforcement enthusiasts, the criminal law may have a disproportionate impact on the black community, but this is not a moral or racial issue because the disproportionate impact is the law's effect, not its intent. For law enforcement enthusiasts, intent is the most appropriate barometer of governmental racism. Because law enforcement is a public good, it is in the best interest of the black community to have more, rather than less, of it. Allowing criminals to live unfettered in the community would harm, in particular, the black poor, who are disproportionately the victims of violent crime. Indeed, the logical conclusion of the enthusiasts' argument is that African Americans would be better off with more, not fewer, black criminals behind bars.

To my mind, the enthusiasts embrace law enforcement too uncritically: They are blind to its opportunity costs. I agree that criminal law enforcement constitutes a public good for African Americans when it serves the social protection goals that Professor Kennedy highlights. In other words, when locking up black men means that "violent criminals . .

who attack those most vulnerable" are off the streets, most people—including most law enforcement critics—would endorse the incarceration. But what about when locking up a black man has no or little net effect on public safety, when, for example, the crime with which he was charged is victimless? Putting aside for a moment the legal implications, couldn't an analysis of the costs and benefits to the African American community present an argument against incarceration? I argue "yes," in light of the substantial costs to the community of law enforcement. I accept that other reasonable people may disagree. But the law enforcement enthusiasts seldom acknowledge that racial critics even weigh the costs and benefits; their assumption seems to be that the racial critics are foolish or blinded by history or motivated by their own ethnocentrism.

5. The Body Politic and the Racial Critiques

I suspect that many white people would agree with the racial critics' analysis, even if most whites would not support a solution involving the emancipation of black criminals. I write this Chapter, however, out of concern for African Americans and how they can use the power they have now to create change. The important practicability question is how many African Americans embrace racial critiques of the criminal justice system and how many are law enforcement enthusiasts?

According to a recent *USA Today/CNN/Gallup* poll, 66% of blacks believe that the criminal justice system is racist and only 32% believe it is not racist. Interestingly, other polls suggest that blacks also tend to be more worried about crime than whites; this seems logical when one considers that blacks are more likely to be the victims of crime. This enhanced concern, however, does not appear to translate into endorsement of tougher enforcement of traditional criminal law. For example, substantially fewer blacks than whites support the death penalty, and many more blacks than whites were concerned with the potential racial consequences of the strict provisions of the Crime Bill of 1994. While polls are not, perhaps, the most reliable means of measuring sentiment in the African American community, the polls, along with significant evidence from popular culture, suggest that a substantial portion of the African American community sympathizes with racial critiques of the criminal justice system.

African American jurors who endorse these critiques are in a unique position to act on their beliefs when they sit in judgment of a black defendant. As jurors, they have the power to convict the defendant or to set him free. May the responsible exercise of that power include voting to free a black defendant who the juror believes is guilty? The next section suggests that, based on legal doctrine concerning the role of juries in general, and the role of black jurors in particular, the answer to this question is "yes."

B. Jury Nullification

When a jury disregards evidence presented at trial and acquits an otherwise guilty defendant, because the jury objects to the law that the defendant violated or to the application of the law to that defendant, it has practiced jury nullification. In this section, I describe the evolution of this doctrine and consider its applicability to African Americans. I then examine Supreme Court cases that discuss the role of black people on juries. In light of judicial rulings in these areas, I argue that it is both lawful and morally right that black jurors consider race in reaching verdicts in criminal cases.

1. What Is Jury Nullification?

Jury nullification occurs when a jury acquits a defendant who it believes is guilty of the crime with which he is charged. In finding the defendant not guilty, the jury refuses to be bound by the facts of the case or the judge's instructions regarding the law. Instead, the jury votes its conscience.

In the United States, the doctrine of jury nullification originally was based on the common law idea that the function of a jury was, broadly, to decide justice, which included judging the law as well as the facts. If jurors believed that applying a law would lead to an unjust conviction, they were not compelled to convict someone who had broken that law. Although most American courts now disapprove of a jury's deciding anything other than the "facts," the Double Jeopardy Clause of the Fifth Amendment prohibits appellate reversal of a jury's decision to acquit, regardless of the reason for the acquittal. Thus, even when a trial judge thinks that a jury's acquittal directly contradicts the evidence, the jury's verdict must be accepted as final. The jurors, in judging the law, function as an important and necessary check on government power.

2. *A Brief History*

The prerogative of juries to nullify has been part of English and American law for centuries. In 1670, the landmark decision in *Bushell's Case* established the right of juries under English common law to nullify on the basis of an objection to the law the defendant had violated. Two members of an unpopular minority group—the Quakers—were prosecuted for unlawful assembly and disturbance of the peace. At trial, the defendants, William Penn and William Mead, admitted that they had assembled a large crowd on the streets of London. Upon that admission, the judge asked the men if they wished to plead guilty. Penn replied that the issue was not "whether I am guilty of this Indictment but whether this Indictment be legal," and argued that the jurors should go "behind" the law and use their consciences to decide whether he was guilty. The judge disagreed, and he instructed the jurors that the defendants' admissions compelled a guilty verdict. After extended deliberation, however, the jurors found both defendants not guilty. The judge then fined the jurors for rendering a decision contrary to the evidence and to his instructions. When one juror, Bushell, refused to pay his fine, the issue reached the Court of Common Pleas, which held that jurors in criminal cases could not be punished for voting to acquit, even when the trial judge believed that the verdict contradicted the evidence. The reason was stated by the Chief Justice of the Court of Common Pleas:

> A man cannot see by anothers eye, nor hear by anothers ear, no more can a man conclude or inferr the thing to be resolv'd by anothers understanding or reasoning; and though the verdict be right the jury give, yet they being not assur'd it is so from their own understanding, are forsworn, at least in foro conscientiae.

This decision "changed the course of jury history." It is unclear why the jurors acquitted Penn and Mead, but their act has been viewed in near mythological terms. Bushell and his fellow jurors have come to be seen as representing the best ideals of democracy because they "rebuffed the tyranny of the judiciary and vindicated their own true historical and moral purpose."

American colonial law incorporated the common law prerogative of jurors to vote according to their consciences after the British government began prosecuting American revolutionaries for political crimes. The best known of these cases involved John Peter Zenger, who was accused of seditious libel for publishing statements critical of British colonial rule in North America. In seditious libel cases, English law required that the judge determine whether the statements made by the defendant were libelous: the jury was not supposed to question the judge's finding on this issue. At trial, Zenger's attorney told the jury that it should ignore the judge's instructions that Zenger's remarks were libelous because the jury "had the right beyond all dispute to determine both the law and the facts." The lawyer then echoed the language of *Bushell's Case,* arguing that the jurors had "to see with their eyes, to hear with their own ears, and to make use of their own consciences and understandings, in judging of the lives, liberties or estates of their fellow subjects." Famously, the jury acquitted Zenger, and another case entered the canon as a shining example of the benefits of the jury system.

After Zenger's trial, the notion that juries should decide "justice," as opposed to simply applying the law to the facts, became relatively settled in American jurisprudence. In addition to pointing to political prosecution of white American revolutionaries like Zenger, modern courts and legal historians often cite with approval nullification in trials of defendants "guilty" of helping to free black slaves. In these cases, Northern jurors with abolitionist sentiments used their power as jurors to subvert federal law that supported slavery. In *United Slates v. Morris,* for example, three defendants were accused of aiding and abetting a runaway slave's escape to Canada. The defense attorney told the jury that, because it was hearing a criminal case, it had the right to judge the law, and if it believed that the Fugitive Slave Act was unconstitutional, it was bound to disregard any contrary instructions given by the judge. The defendants were acquitted and the government dropped the charges against five other people accused of the same crime. Another success story entered the canon.

3. Sparf *and Other Critiques*

In the mid-nineteenth century, as memories of the tyranny of British rule faded, some American courts began to criticize the idea of jurors deciding justice. A number of the state decisions that allowed this practice were overruled, and in the 1895 case of *Sparf v. United States,* the Supreme Court spoke regarding jury nullification in federal courts.

In *Sparf,* two men on trial for murder requested that the judge instruct the jury that it had the option of convicting them of manslaughter, a lesser-included offense. The trial court refused this request and instead instructed the jurors that if they convicted the defendants of any crime less than murder, or if they acquitted them, the jurors would be in violation of their legal oath and duties. The Supreme Court held that this instruction was not contrary to law and affirmed the defendants' murder convictions. The Court acknowledged that juries have the "physical power" to disregard the law, but stated that they have no "moral right" to do so. Indeed, the Court observed, "If the jury were at liberty to settle the law for themselves, the effect would be . . . that the law itself would be most uncertain, from the different views, which different juries might take of it." Despite this criticism, *Sparf* conceded that, as a matter of law, a judge could not prevent jury nullification, because in criminal cases "[a] verdict of acquittal cannot be set aside." An anomaly was thus created, and has been a feature of American criminal law ever since: Jurors have the power to nullify, but, in most jurisdictions, they have no right to be informed of this power.

Since *Sparf,* most of the appellate courts that have considered jury nullification have addressed that anomaly and have endorsed it. Some of these courts, however, have not been as critical of the concept of jury nullification as the *Sparf* Court. The D.C. Circuit's opinion in *United States v. Dougherty* is illustrative. In *Dougherty,* the court noted that the ability of juries to nullify was widely recognized and even approved "as a necessary counter to case-hardened judges and arbitrary prosecutors." This necessity, however, did not establish "as an imperative" that a jury be informed by the judge of its power to nullify. The D.C. Circuit was concerned that "what makes for health as an occasional medicine would be disastrous as a daily diet." Specifically:

> Rules of law or justice involve choice of values and ordering of objectives for which unanimity is unlikely in any society, or group representing the society, especially a society as diverse in cultures and interests as ours. To seek unity out of diversity, under the national motto, there must be a procedure for decision by vote of a majority or prescribed plurality—in accordance with democratic philosophy. To assign

> the role of mini-legislature to the various petit juries, who must hang if not unanimous, exposes criminal law and administration to paralysis, and to a deadlock that betrays rather than furthers the assumptions of viable democracy.

The idea that jury nullification undermines the rule of law is the most common criticism of the doctrine. The concern is that the meaning of self-government is threatened when twelve individuals on a jury in essence remake the criminal law after it has already been made in accordance with traditional democratic principles. Another critique of African American jurors engaging in racially based jury nullification is that the practice by black jurors is distinct from the historically approved cases because the black jurors are not so much "judging" the law as preventing its application to members of their own race. The reader should recognize that these are moral, not legal, critiques because, as discussed above, the legal prerogative of any juror to acquit is well established. In the next section, I respond to these moral critiques.

C. The Moral Case for Jury Nullification by African Americans

Any juror legally may vote for nullification in any case, but, certainly, jurors should not do so without some principled basis. The reason that some historical examples of nullification are viewed approvingly is that most of us now believe that the jurors in those cases did the morally right thing; it would have been unconscionable, for example, to punish those slaves who committed the crime of escaping to the North for their freedom. It is true that nullification later would be used as a means of racial subordination by some Southern jurors, but that does not mean that nullification in the approved cases was wrong. It only means that those Southern jurors erred in their calculus of justice. I distinguish racially based nullification by African Americans from recent right-wing proposals for jury nullification on the ground that the former is sometimes morally right and the latter is not.

The question of how to assign the power of moral choice is a difficult one. Yet we should not allow that difficulty to obscure the fact that legal resolutions involve moral decisions, judgments of right and wrong. The fullness of time permits us to judge the fugitive slave case differently than the Southern pro-white-violence case. One day we will be able to distinguish between racially based nullification and that proposed by certain right-wing activist groups. We should remember that the morality of the historically approved cases was not so clear when those brave jurors acted. After all, the fugitive slave law was enacted through the democratic process, and those jurors who disregarded it subverted the rule of law. Presumably, they were harshly criticized by those whose interests the slave law protected. Then, as now, it is difficult to see the picture when you are inside the frame.

In this section, I explain why African Americans have the moral right to practice nullification in particular cases. I do so by responding to the traditional moral critiques of jury nullification.

1. African Americans and the "Betrayal" of Democracy

There is no question that jury nullification is subversive of the rule of law. It appears to be the antithesis of the view that courts apply settled, standing laws and do not "dispense justice in some ad hoc, case-by-case basis." To borrow a phrase from the D.C. Circuit, jury nullification "betrays rather than furthers the assumptions of viable democracy." Because the Double Jeopardy Clause makes this power part-and-parcel of the jury system, the issue becomes whether black jurors have any moral right to "betray democracy" in this sense. I believe that they do for two reasons that I borrow from the jurisprudence of legal realism and critical race theory: First, the idea of "the rule of law" is more mythological than real, and second, "democracy," as practiced in the United States, has betrayed African

Americans far more than they could ever betray it. Explication of these theories has consumed legal scholars for years, and is well beyond the scope of this Essay. I describe the theories below not to persuade the reader of their rightness, but rather to make the case that a reasonable juror might hold such beliefs, and thus be morally justified in subverting democracy through nullification.

2. *The Rule of Law as Myth*

The idea that "any result can be derived from the preexisting legal doctrine" either in every case or many cases, is a fundamental principle of legal realism (and, now, critical legal theory). The argument, in brief, is that law is indeterminate and incapable of neutral interpretation. When judges "decide" cases, they "choose" legal principles to determine particular outcomes. Even if a judge wants to be neutral, she cannot, because, ultimately, she is vulnerable to an array of personal and cultural biases and influences; she is only human. In an implicit endorsement of the doctrine of jury nullification, legal realists also suggest that, even if neutrality were possible, it would not be desirable, because no general principle of law can lead to justice in every case.

It is difficult for an African American knowledgeable of the history of her people in the United States not to profess, at minimum, sympathy for legal realism. Most blacks are aware of countless historical examples in which African Americans were not afforded the benefit of the rule of law: Think, for example, of the existence of slavery in a republic purportedly dedicated to the proposition that all men are created equal, or the law's support of state-sponsored segregation even after the Fourteenth Amendment guaranteed blacks equal protection. That the rule of law ultimately corrected some of the large holes in the American fabric is evidence more of its malleability than of its virtue; the rule of law had, in the first instance, justified the holes.

The Supreme Court's decisions in the major "race" cases of the last term underscore the continuing failure of the rule of law to protect African Americans through consistent application. Dissenting in a school desegregation case, four Justices stated that "the Court's process of orderly adjudication has broken down in this case." The dissent noted that the majority opinion "effectively . . . overrule[d] a unanimous constitutional precedent of 20 years standing, which was not even addressed in argument, was mentioned merely in passing by one of the parties, and discussed by another of them only in a misleading way." Similarly, in a voting rights case, Justice Stevens, in dissent, described the majority opinion as a "law-changing decision." And in an affirmative action case, Justice Stevens began his dissent by declaring that, "[i]nstead of deciding this case in accordance with controlling precedent, the Court today delivers a disconcerting lecture about the evils of governmental racial classifications." At the end of his dissent, Stevens argued that "the majority's concept of *stare decisis* ignores the force of binding precedent."

If the rule of law is a myth, or at least is not applicable to African Americans, the criticism that jury nullification undermines it loses force. The black juror is simply another actor in the system, using her power to fashion a particular outcome; the juror's act of nullification—like the act of the citizen who dials 911 to report Ricky but not Bob, or the police officer who arrests Lisa but not Mary, or the prosecutor who charges Kwame but not Brad, or the judge who finds that Nancy was illegally entrapped but Verna was not—exposes the indeterminacy of law, but does not create it.

3. *The Moral Obligation to Disobey Unjust Laws*

For the reader who is unwilling to concede the mythology of the rule of law, I offer another response to the concern about violating it. Assuming, for the purposes of argument, that the rule of law exists, there still is no moral obligation to follow an unjust law. This principle is familiar to many African Americans who practiced civil disobedience during the civil rights protests of the 1950s and 1960s. Indeed, Martin Luther King suggested that morality requires that unjust laws not be obeyed. As I state above, the difficulty of determining which laws are unjust should not obscure the need to make that determination.

Radical critics believe that the criminal law is unjust when applied to some antisocial conduct by African Americans: The law uses punishment to treat social problems that are the result of racism and that should be addressed by other means such as medical care or the redistribution of wealth. Later, I suggest a utilitarian justification for why African Americans should obey most criminal law: It protects them. I concede, however, that this limitation is not *morally* required if one accepts the radical critique, which applies to all criminal law.

4. Democratic Domination

Related to the "undermining the law" critique is the charge that jury nullification is antidemocratic. The trial judge in the *Barry* case, for example, in remarks made after the conclusion of the trial, expressed this criticism of the jury's verdict: "The jury is not a mini-democracy, or a mini-legislature. They are not to go back and do right as they see fit. That's anarchy. They are supposed to follow the law." A jury that nullifies "betrays rather than furthers the assumptions of viable democracy." In a sense, the argument suggests that the jurors are not playing fair: The citizenry made the rules, so the jurors, as citizens, ought to follow them.

What does "viable democracy" assume about the power of an unpopular minority group to make the laws that affect them? It assumes that the group has the power to influence legislation. The American majority-rule electoral system is premised on the hope that the majority will not tyrannize the minority, but rather represent the minority's interests. Indeed, in creating the Constitution, the Framers attempted to guard against the oppression of the minority by the majority. Unfortunately, these attempts were expressed more in theory than in actual constitutional guarantees, a point made by some legal scholars, particularly critical race theorists.

The implication of the failure to protect blacks from the tyrannical majority is that the majority rule of whites over African Americans is, morally speaking, illegitimate. Lani Guinier suggests that the moral legitimacy of majority rule hinges on two assumptions: 1) that majorities are not fixed; and 2) that minorities will be able to become members of some majorities. Racial prejudice "to such a degree that the majority consistently excludes the minority, or refuses to inform itself about the relative merit of the minority's preferences," defeats both assumptions. Similarly, Owen Fiss has given three reasons for the failure of blacks to prosper through American democracy: They are a numerical minority, they have low economic status, and, "as a 'discrete and insular' minority, they are the object of 'prejudice'—that is, the subject of fear, hatred, and distaste that make it particularly difficult for them to form coalitions with others (such as the white poor)."

According to both theories, blacks are unable to achieve substantial progress through regular electoral politics. Their only "democratic" route to success—coalition building with similarly situated groups—is blocked because other groups resist the stigma of the association. The stigma is powerful enough to prevent alignment with African Americans even when a group—like low-income whites—has similar interests.

In addition to individual white citizens, legislative bodies experience the Negrophobia described above. Professor Guinier defines such legislative racism as

> a pattern of actions [that] persistently disadvantag[es] a fixed legislative minority and encompasses conscious exclusion as well as marginalization that results from "a lack of interracial empathy." It means that where a prejudiced majority rules, its representatives are not

> compelled to identify its interests with those of the African American minority.

Such racism excludes blacks from the governing legislative coalitions. A permanent, homogeneous majority emerges, which effectively marginalizes minority interests and "transform[s] majority rule into majority tyranny." Derrick Bell calls this condition "democratic domination."

Democratic domination undermines the basis of political stability, which depends on the inducement of "losers to continue to play the political game, to continue to work within the system rather than to try to overthrow it." Resistance by minorities to the operation of majority rule may take several forms, including "overt compliance and secret rejection of the legitimacy of the political order." I suggest that another form of this resistance is racially based jury nullification.

If African Americans believe that democratic domination exists (and the 1994 congressional elections seem to provide compelling recent support for such a belief), they should not back away from lawful self-help measures, like jury nullification, on the ground that the self-help is antidemocratic. African Americans are not a numerical majority in any of the fifty states, which are the primary sources of criminal law. In addition, they are not even proportionally represented in the U.S. House of Representatives or in the Senate. As a result, African Americans wield little influence over criminal law, state or federal. African Americans should embrace the antidemocratic nature of jury nullification because it provides them with the power to determine justice in a way that majority rule does not.

D. *"[J]ustice must satisfy the appearance of justice": The Symbolic Function of Black Jurors*

A second distinction one might draw between the traditionally approved examples of jury nullification and its practice by contemporary African Americans is that, in the case of the former, jurors refused to apply a particular law, e.g., a fugitive slave law, on the grounds that it was unfair, while in the case of the latter, jurors are not so much judging discrete statutes as they are refusing to apply those statutes to members of their own race. This application of race consciousness by jurors may appear to be antithetical to the American ideal of equality under the law.

This critique, however, like the "betraying democracy" critique, begs the question of whether the ideal actually applies to African Americans. As stated above, racial critics answer this question in the negative. They, especially the liberal critics, argue that the criminal law is applied in a discriminatory fashion. Furthermore, on several occasions, the Supreme Court has referred to the usefulness of black jurors to the rule of law in the United States. In essence, black jurors symbolize the fairness and impartiality of the law. Here I examine this rhetoric and suggest that, if the presence of black jurors sends a political message, it is right that these jurors use their power to control or negate the meaning of that message.

As a result of the ugly history of discrimination against African Americans in the criminal justice system, the Supreme Court has had numerous opportunities to consider the significance of black jurors. In so doing, the Court has suggested that these jurors perform a symbolic function, especially when they sit on cases involving African American defendants, and the Court has typically made these suggestions in the form of rhetoric about the social harm caused by the exclusion of blacks from jury service. I will refer to this role of black jurors as the "legitimization function."

The legitimization function stems from every jury's political function of providing American citizens with "the security . . . that they, as jurors actual or possible, being part of the judicial system of the country can prevent its arbitrary use or abuse." In addition to, and perhaps more important than, seeking the truth, the purpose of the jury system is "to impress upon the criminal defendant and the community as a whole that a verdict of conviction or acquittal is given in accordance with the law by persons who are fair." This purpose is consistent with the original purpose of the constitutional right to a jury trial, which was "to prevent oppression by the Government."

When blacks are excluded from juries, beyond any harm done to the juror who suffers the discrimination or to the defendant, the social injury of the exclusion is that it "undermine[s] . . . public confidence—as well [it] should." Because the United States is both a democracy and a pluralist society, it is important that diverse groups appear to have a voice in the laws that govern them. Allowing black people to serve on juries strengthens "public respect for our criminal justice system and the rule of law."

The Supreme Court has found that the legitimization function is particularly valuable in cases involving "race-related" crimes. According to the Court, in these cases, "emotions in the affected community [are] inevitably . . . heated and volatile." The potential presence of black people on the jury in a "race-related" case calms the natives, which is especially important in this type of case because "[p]ublic confidence in the integrity of the criminal justice system is essential for preserving community peace." The very fact that a black person can be on a jury is evidence that the criminal justice system is one in which black people should have confidence, and one that they should respect.

But what of the black juror who endorses racial critiques of American criminal justice? Such a person holds no "confidence in the integrity of the criminal justice system." If she is cognizant of the implicit message that the Supreme Court believes her presence sends, she might not want her presence to be the vehicle for that message. Let us assume that there is a black defendant who, the evidence suggests, is guilty of the crime with which he has been charged and a black juror who thinks that there are too many black men in prison. The black juror has two choices: She can vote for conviction, thus sending another black man to prison and implicitly allowing her presence to support public confidence in the system that puts him there, or she can vote "not guilty," thereby acquitting the defendant, or at least causing a mistrial. In choosing the latter, the juror makes a decision not to be a passive symbol of support for a system for which she has no respect. Rather than signaling her displeasure with the system by breaching "community peace," the black juror invokes the political nature of her role in the criminal justice system and votes "no." In a sense, the black juror engages in an act of civil disobedience, except that her choice is better than civil disobedience because it is lawful. Is the black juror's race-conscious act moral? Absolutely. It would be farcical for her to be the sole color-blind actor in the criminal process, especially when it is her blackness that advertises the system's fairness.

At this point, every African American should ask herself whether the operation of the criminal law in the United States advances the interests of black people. If it does not, the doctrine of jury nullification affords African American jurors the opportunity to control the authority of the law over some African American criminal defendants. In essence, black people can "opt out" of American criminal law.

How far should they go? Completely to anarchy? Or is there some place between here and there, safer than both? The next part describes such a place, and how to get there.

III. A Proposal for Racially Based Jury Nullification

To allow African American jurors to exercise their responsibility in a principled way, I make the following proposal: African American jurors should approach their work cognizant of its political nature and their prerogative to exercise their power in the best interests of the black community. In every case, the juror should be guided by her view of what is "just." For the reasons stated in the preceding parts of this Chapter, I have more faith in the average black juror's idea of justice than I do in the idea that is embodied in the "rule of law."

A. A Framework for Criminal Justice in the Black Community

In cases involving violent *malum in se* crimes like murder, rape, and assault, jurors should consider the case strictly on the evidence presented, and, if they have no reasonable doubt that the defendant is guilty, they should convict. For nonviolent *malum in se* crimes such as theft or perjury, nullification is an option that the juror should consider, although there should be no presumption in favor of it. A juror might vote for acquittal, for example, when a poor woman steals from Tiffany's, but not when the same woman steals from her next-door neighbor. Finally, in cases involving nonviolent, *malum prohibitum* offenses, including "victimless" crimes like narcotics offenses, there should be a presumption in favor of nullification.

This approach seeks to incorporate the most persuasive arguments of both the racial critics and the law enforcement enthusiasts. If my model is faithfully executed, the result would be that fewer black people would go to prison; to that extent, the proposal ameliorates one of the most severe consequences of law enforcement in the African American community. At the same time, the proposal, by punishing violent offenses and certain others, preserves any protection against harmful conduct that the law may offer potential victims. If the experienced prosecutors at the U.S. Attorney's Office are correct, some violent offenders currently receive the benefit of jury nullification, doubtless from a misguided, if well-intentioned, attempt by racial critics to make a political point. Under my proposal, violent lawbreakers would go to prison.

In the language of criminal law, the proposal adopts utilitarian justifications for punishment: deterrence and isolation. To that extent, it accepts the law enforcement enthusiasts' faith in the possibility that law can prevent crime. The proposal does not, however, judge the lawbreakers as harshly as the enthusiasts would judge them. Rather, the proposal assumes that, regardless of the reasons for their antisocial conduct, people who are violent should be separated from the community, for the sake of the nonviolent. The proposal's justifications for the separation are that the community is protected from the offender for the duration of the sentence and that the threat of punishment may discourage future offenses and offenders. I am confident that balancing the social costs and benefits of incarceration would not lead black jurors to release violent criminals simply because of race. While I confess agnosticism about whether the law can deter antisocial conduct, I am unwilling to experiment by abandoning any punishment premised on deterrence.

Of the remaining traditional justifications for punishment, the proposal eschews the retributive or "just desserts" theory for two reasons. First, I am persuaded by racial and other critiques of the unfairness of punishing people for "negative" reactions to racist, oppressive conditions. In fact, I sympathize with people who react "negatively" to the countless manifestations of white supremacy that black people experience daily. While my proposal does not "excuse" all antisocial conduct, it will not punish such conduct on the premise that the intent to engage in it is "evil." The antisocial conduct is no more evil than the conditions that cause it, and, accordingly, the "just desserts" of a black offender are impossible to know. And even if just desserts were susceptible to accurate measure, I would reject the idea of punishment for retribution's sake.

My argument here is that the consequences are too severe: African Americans cannot afford to lock up other African Americans simply on account of anger. There is too little bang for the buck. Black people have a community that needs building, and children who need rescuing, and as long as a person will not hurt anyone, the community needs him there to help.

Assuming that he actually will help is a gamble, but not a reckless one, for the "just" African American community will not leave the lawbreaker be: It will, for example, encourage his education and provide his health care (including narcotics dependency treatment) and, if necessary, sue him for child support. In other words, the proposal demands of African Americans responsible self-help outside of the criminal courtroom as well as inside it. When the community is richer, perhaps then it can afford anger.

The final traditional justification for punishment, rehabilitation, can be dealt with summarily. If rehabilitation were a meaningful option in American criminal justice, I would not endorse nullification in any case. It would be counterproductive, for utilitarian reasons: The community is better off with the antisocial person cured than sick. Unfortunately, however, rehabilitation is no longer an objective of criminal law in the United States, and prison appears to have an antirehabilitative effect. For this reason, unless a juror is provided with a specific, compelling reason to believe that a conviction would result in some useful treatment for an offender, she should not use her vote to achieve this end, because almost certainly it will not occur.

B. Hypothetical Cases

How would a juror decide individual cases under my proposal? For the purposes of the following hypothesis, let us assume criminal prosecutions in state or federal court and technically guilty African American defendants. Easy cases under my proposal include a defendant who possessed crack cocaine, and a defendant who killed another person. The former should be acquitted, and the latter should go to prison.

The crack cocaine case is simple: Because the crime is victimless, the proposal presumes nullification. According to racial critiques, acquittal is just, due in part to the longer sentences given for crack offenses than for powder cocaine offenses. This case should be particularly compelling to the liberal racial critic, given the extreme disparity between crack and powder in both enforcement of the law and in actual sentencing. According to a recent study, African Americans make up 13% of the nation's regular drug users, but they account for 35% of narcotics arrests, 55% of drug convictions, and 74% of those receiving prison sentences. Most of the people who are arrested for crack cocaine offenses are black; most arrested for powder cocaine are white. Under federal law, if someone possesses fifty grams of crack cocaine, the mandatory-minimum sentence is ten years: in order to receive the same sentence for powder cocaine, the defendant must possess 5000 grams. Given the racial consequences of this disparity, I hope that many racial critics will nullify without hesitation in these cases.

The case of the murderer is "easy" solely for the utilitarian reasons I discussed above. Although I do not believe that prison will serve any rehabilitative function for the murderer, there is a possibility that a guilty verdict will prevent another person from becoming a victim, and the juror should err on the side of that possibility. In effect, I "write off" the black person who takes a life, not for retributive reasons, but because the black community cannot afford the risks of leaving this person in its midst. Accordingly, for the sake of potential victims (given the possibility that the criminal law deters homicide), nullification is not morally justifiable here.

Difficult hypothetical cases include the ghetto drug dealer and the thief who burglarizes the home of a rich family. Under the proposal, nullification is presumed in the first case because drug distribution is a nonviolent, *malum prohibitum* offense. Is nullification morally justifiable here? It depends. There is no question that encouraging people to engage in self-destructive behavior is evil; the question the juror should ask herself is whether the remedy is less evil. I suspect that the usual answer would be "yes," premised on deterrence and isolation theories of punishment. Accordingly, the drug dealer would be convicted. The answer might change, however, depending on the particular facts of the case: the type of narcotic sold, the ages of the buyers, whether the dealer "marketed" the drugs to customers or whether they sought him out, whether it is a first offense, whether there is reason to believe that the drug dealer would cease this conduct if given another chance, and whether, as in the crack case, there are racial disparities in sentencing for this kind of crime. I recognize that, in this hypothetical, nullification carries some societal risk. The risk, however, is less consequential than with violent crimes. Furthermore, the cost to the community of imprisoning all drug dealers is great. I would allow the juror in this case more discretion.

The juror should also remember that many ghetto "drug" dealers are not African American and that the state does not punish these dealers—instead, it licenses them. Liquor stores are ubiquitous on the ghetto streets of America. By almost every measure, alcoholism causes great injury to society, and yet the state does not use the criminal law to address this severe social problem. When the government tried to treat the problem of alcohol use with criminal law, during Prohibition, a violent "black" market formed. Even if the juror does not believe that drug dealing is a "victimless" crime, she might question why it is that of all drug dealers, many of the black capitalists are imprisoned, and many of the non-black capitalists are legally enriched. When the juror remembers that the cost to the community of having so many young men in jail means that law enforcement also is not "victimless," the juror's calculus of justice might lead her to vote for acquittal.

As for the burglar who steals from the rich family, the case is troubling, first of all, because the conduct is so clearly "wrong." As a nonviolent *malum in se* crime, there is no presumption in favor of nullification, though it remains an option. Here, again, the facts of the case are relevant to the juror's decision of what outcome is fair. For example, if the offense was committed to support a drug habit, I think there is a moral case to be made for nullification, at least until drug rehabilitation services are available to all.

If the burglary victim is a rich white person, the hypothetical is troubling for the additional reason that it demonstrates how a black juror's sense of justice might, in some cases, lead her to treat defendants differently based on the class and race of their victims. I expect that this distinction would occur most often in property offenses because, under the proposal, no violent offenders would be excused. In an ideal world, whether the victim is rich or poor or black or white would be irrelevant to adjudication of the defendant's culpability. In the United States, my sense is that some black jurors will believe that these factors are relevant to the calculus of justice. The rationale is implicitly premised on a critique of the legitimacy of property rights in a society marked by gross economic inequities. While I endorse this critique, I would encourage nullification here only in extreme cases (i.e., nonviolent theft from the very wealthy) and mainly for political reasons: If the rich cannot rely on criminal law for the protection of their property and the law prevents more direct self-help measures, perhaps they will focus on correcting the conditions that make others want to steal from them. This view may be naive, but arguably no more so than that of the black people who thought that if they refused to ride the bus, they could end legally enforced segregation in the South.

C. Some Political and Procedural Concerns

1. What If White People Start Nullifying Too?

One concern is that whites will nullify in cases of white-on-black crime. The best response to this concern is that often white people do nullify in those cases. The white jurors who acquitted the police officers who beat up Rodney King are a good example. There is no reason why my proposal should cause white jurors to acquit white defendants who are guilty of violence against blacks any more frequently. My model assumes that black violence against whites would be punished by black jurors; I hope that white jurors would do the same in cases involving white defendants.

If white jurors were to begin applying my proposal to cases with white defendants, then they, like the black jurors, would be choosing to opt out of the criminal justice system. For pragmatic political purposes, that would be excellent. Attention would then be focused on alternative methods of correcting antisocial conduct much sooner than it would if only African Americans raised the issue.

2. How Do You Control Anarchy?

Why would a juror who is willing to ignore a law created through the democratic process be inclined to follow my proposal? There is no guarantee that she would. But when we consider that black jurors are already nullifying on the basis of race because they do not want to send another black man to prison, we recognize that these jurors are willing to use their power in a politically conscious manner. Many black people have concerns about their participation in the criminal justice system as jurors and might be willing to engage in some organized political conduct, not unlike the civil disobedience that African Americans practiced in the South in the 1950s and 1960s. It appears that some black jurors now excuse some conduct—like murder—that they should not excuse. My proposal, however, provides a principled structure for the exercise of the black juror's vote. I am not encouraging anarchy. Instead, I am reminding black jurors of their privilege to serve a higher calling than law: justice. I am suggesting a framework for what justice means in the African American community.

3. How Do You Implement the Proposal?

Because *Sparf*, as well as the law of many states, prohibits jurors from being instructed about jury nullification in criminal cases, information about this privilege would have to be communicated to black jurors before they heard such cases. In addition, jurors would need to be familiar with my proposal as framework for analyzing whether nullification is appropriate in a particular case. Disseminating this information should not be difficult. African American culture—through mediums such as church, music (particularly rap songs), black newspapers and magazines, literature, storytelling, film (including music videos), soapbox speeches, and convention gatherings—facilitates intraracial communication. At African American cultural events, such as concerts or theatrical productions, the audience could be instructed on the proposal, either verbally or through the dissemination of written material; this type of political expression at a cultural event would hardly be unique—voter registration campaigns are often conducted at such events. The proposal could be the subject of rap songs, which are already popular vehicles for racial critiques, or of ministers' sermons.

One can also imagine more direct approaches. For example, advocates of this proposal might stand outside a courthouse and distribute flyers explaining the proposal to prospective jurors. During deliberations, those jurors could then explain to other jurors their prerogative—their power—to decide justice rather than simply the facts. *Sparf* is one Supreme Court decision whose holding is rather easy to circumvent: If the defense attorneys cannot inform the people of their power, the people can inform themselves. And once informed, the people would have a formula for what justice means in the African American community, rather than having to decide it on an ad hoc basis.

I hope that all African American jurors will follow my proposal, and I am encouraged by the success of other grass-roots campaigns, like the famous Montgomery bus boycott, aimed at eliminating racial oppression. I note, however, that even with limited participation by African Americans, my proposal could have a significant impact. In most

American jurisdictions, jury verdicts in criminal cases must be unanimous. One juror could prevent the conviction of a defendant. The prosecution would then have to retry the case, and risk facing another African American juror with emancipation tendencies. I hope that there are enough of us out there, fed up with prison as the answer to black desperation and white supremacy, to cause retrial after retrial, until, finally, the United States "retries" its idea of justice.

CONCLUSION

This Chapter's proposal raises other concerns, such as the problem of providing jurors with information relevant to their decision within the restrictive evidentiary confines of a trial. Some of these issues can be resolved through creative lawyering. Other policy questions are not as easily answered, including the issue of how long (years, decades, centuries?) black jurors would need to pursue racially based jury nullification. I think this concern is related to the issue of the appropriate time span of other race-conscious remedies, including affirmative action. Perhaps, when policymakers acknowledge that race matters in criminal justice, the criminal law can benefit from the successes and failures of race consciousness in other areas of the law. I fear, however, that this day of acknowledgement will be long in coming. Until then, I expect that many black jurors will perceive the necessity of employing the self-help measures prescribed here.

I concede that the justice my proposal achieves is rough because it is as susceptible to human foibles as the jury system. I am sufficiently optimistic to hope that my proposal will be only an intermediate plan, a stopping point between the status quo and real justice. I hope that this Chapter will encourage African Americans to use responsibly the power they already have. To get criminal justice past the middle point, I hope that the Essay will facilitate a dialogue among all Americans in which the significance of race will not be dismissed or feared, but addressed. The most dangerous "forbidden" message is that it is better to ignore the truth than to face it.

23

INTRODUCTION

Russell's latest work, *The Color of Crime: Racial Hoaxes, White Fear, Black Protectionism, Police Harassment, and Other Macroaggressions,* has received critical acclaim. In the book, she looks at racial bias in the criminal justice system, the role of race in the media, and other informal interactions between Blacks and members of the criminal justice system that contribute to minority distrust of the justice system. Russell examines the protective response of Blacks to O.J. Simpson and the illusiveness of White crime. A number of other issues, such as racial hoaxes, are also addressed in this book.

In this article, Russell examines both White-on-Black and Black-on-White racial hoaxes. In both instances, false allegations of involvement in criminal behavior are based on race. Russell contends that the White-on-Black racial hoaxes are more detrimental in part because they are based on stereotypes and the demonization of Black men. These stereotypes center on a view of the Black man as dangerous and perpetuate what Russell defines as the criminal Black man myth. She advocates that those who take advantage of this mythology to hide their own crime be punished. She suggests these racial hoaxes be treated as crime and that penalties be enhanced. Russell sees these affirmative race-based sanctions as the appropriate instruments to prevent this behavior and to reduce the "disconnect" that Blacks feel with respect to the justice system.

The Racial Hoax as Crime

The Law as Affirmation

Katheryn K. Russell

Introduction

In recent years, the issue of racism in the criminal justice system has reemerged. The result has been a panoply of attacks and counterattacks about the effectiveness of the justice system. The critique of the criminal justice system has centered primarily upon the application of existing law[1] and the system's treatment of minorities in general[2] and Blacks in particular.[3] The fractured debate often pits ideology and methodology against one another: some argue that the formal stages of the criminal justice system reflect little or no bias,[4] while others argue that informal stages are significant as well, and must be evaluated for a determination of bias.[5] Within this controversy one fact remains constant: the deep divide between Blacks and Whites regarding the presence and persistence of racism in the criminal justice system.

Study after study has shown that Blacks and Whites hold contrary views on the fairness of the criminal justice system's operation.[6] Blacks tend to be more cautious in their praise and frequently view the system as unfair and racially biased.[7] By contrasts, Whites have a favorable impression of the justice

From Russell, K.K. (1996). The racial hoax as crime: The law of affirmation. *Indiana Law Journal, 71*,593.

system.[8] Two common expressions exemplify these opposing viewpoints: "the system works" (Whites) and "justice means just us" (Blacks). The point is not that Whites are completely satisfied with the justice system, but rather that, relative to Blacks, they have faith in the system. A substantial portion of the American public is indeed dissatisfied. This dissatisfaction is reflected in calls for criminal sanctions which are more swift (reduce criminal appeals process), more certain (truth-in-sentencing legislation), and more severe (three-strikes legislation).[9]

A variety of rationales have been offered to explain the gap in Black racial "connectedness" to the criminal justice system. Foremost is the differential group experience Blacks and Whites have with the justice system's operation. For example, Blacks are more likely to be victims of police harassment/brutality or know someone who has been a victim.[10] Further, they are more likely to perceive that the criminal justice system treats members of their group unfairly because of their race.[11] It is maintained herein that the disconnect Blacks experience is as much a reflection of affirmative acts of racial discrimination within the criminal justice system as it is a reflection of the need for more affirmative race-based sanctions within the justice system.[12] The latter is the focus of this Article.

Specifically, this Article argues for the increased use of the law as racial affirmation. This use of the law would recognize and punish ongoing racial discrimination, with the goal of bringing balance to the use of the term "race" as it relates to crime. As it now stands, the phrase "race and crime" is almost always a negative referent for "Blacks and crime." This Article focuses on one way in which law can be created and used as a means of racial affirmation, and the Article questions whether it should be a crime falsely to accuse someone Black of a crime knowing that the offender is not Black.[13] In doing so, it examines some of the reasons for America's existing racial polarization, reflected in large part by the divide on the issue of racial discrimination and disparity in the criminal justice system. The Article concludes that those who play on the negative racial caricature of Blacks should face an enhanced penalty—over and above that for misleading or providing false information to the police.

There is a manifest need to focus more upon how the law, existing and potential, can at a minimum reduce and at a maximum halt the perpetuation of the *criminalblackman* myth. This Article, consisting of four Parts, addresses this need. Part I provides an examination of seven recent, well-known racial hoaxes[14] and provides a sociological analysis of the phenomena of racism and the racial hoax, and how these phenomena affect Black and White individuals and groups. Part II outlines a paradigm for analyzing whether the racial hoax should be made criminal. Part III examines the relationships between perceptions of injustice, the absence of affirmative race law, and violence. Additionally, Part III considers the economics of the racial hoax law. Finally, Part IV reviews the law of hate crimes and assesses whether a racial hoax law would logically fit within its parameters. Part IV also outlines the requisite components of such a law.

I. The Phenomenon of the Racial Hoax

A. Cases in Point

In January 1996, Robert Harris claimed that he and his fiancée, Teresa McLeod, had been shot and robbed on a quiet Baltimore, Maryland, street. Harris said the assailant was an armed Black man wearing a camouflage jacket and black and white pants. Harris was shot once and McLeod was shot several times. McLeod died at the scene. Within two days of the murder, Harris confessed to his involvement: He had hired a hit man to rob and kill his fiancée. The alleged motive was Harris' mistaken belief that he was the beneficiary of McLeod's $250,000 life insurance policy.[15]

On October 25, 1994, Susan Smith, a White South Carolina mother, told police that she had been carjacked by a young Black male. According to Smith, the man drove off with her two young sons, Michael, age three, and Alex, age fourteen months. In the following week, Smith publicly pled for their lives, telling them "your Momma loves you. . . . Be strong."[16] The case attracted international attention and garnered the services of both federal and state law enforcement officials. Nine days after her initial 911 call, Smith confessed to the killings.[17]

In April 1992, Jesse Anderson, a White man, told the police that while leaving a suburban Milwaukee restaurant he and his wife were attacked by two Black men. According to Anderson, the men stabbed him and his wife. His wife was stabbed multiple times in the face, head, and upper body. She died following the attack. After a five-day search for the fictional Black criminals, Anderson was arrested and charged with his wife's murder. Two factors led the police to focus their investigation on Anderson: lab results from blood samples, and information that Anderson had called his wife's insurance company one month prior to her murder to determine whether her $250,000 policy was in effect. Anderson was subsequently convicted of first-degree intentional homicide.[18]

In 1990, a female student at George Washington University in Washington, D.C. falsely stated that a White woman had been raped at knifepoint by two young Black men with "particularly bad body odor."[19] The story exploded across campus and was a call to action for school officials, campus activists, and the school's rape crisis center. The day following the school newspaper's publication of her account, the press was informed that the story was a fabrication. Miriam Kashani, the student who was the newspaper's main source for the "rape" story, held a press conference and stated that she "had hoped the story, as reported, would highlight the problems of safety for women . . . [and] never meant to hurt anyone or racially offend anyone."[20] One has to wonder why, given Kashani's stated goals, her perpetrators were depicted as Black. Kashani's tale served to reinforce the myth of interracial (Black-on-White) rape—in fact, three-quarters of all rapes are intraracial (*e.g.*, White-on-White or Black-on-Black).[21]

The Charles Stuart case involved a White man who claimed that a Black man had shot him and his pregnant wife. His wife and unborn child died after the attack. Mission Hill, a largely Black neighborhood in Boston, was combed in search of the killers.[22] Charles Stuart picked a Black man named Willie Bennett in a lineup as the person who "most resembled" the attacker.[23] Based upon inconsistencies in his story and information obtained from his brother, Matthew Stuart, the police focused their investigation upon Charles Stuart.[24] Shortly thereafter, Charles Stuart committed suicide.[25]

There are several common features in the Smith, Anderson, and Stuart cases. First, with each of these, the heinousness of the actual offense—a husband killing his wife, a mother killing her two children—quickly eclipsed the racial hoax.[26] Also, in each of these cases, there were calls for an apology to the Black community[27]—clearly indicating that some "communal" or group injury had occurred. While Susan Smith's brother offered an apology to the Black community,[28] Ray Flynn, the mayor of Boston, refused to apologize. Beyond the similarity in community[29] response, the White-on-Black hoaxes feature White women front and center. In fact, the Smith, Anderson, and Stuart cases involved White mothers—the symbol of American virtue—as victims of Black male deviance.

Only one of the four racial hoaxes discussed above, the Kashani case, involved rape. Historically, rape was the most common criminal hoax played on Black men. The case of the Scottsboro Boys is perhaps the best-known example of the use of Black men as scapegoats for crime. In 1931, Victoria Price and Ruby Bates, two young White women, alleged that they had been assaulted and raped by nine "Negro boys.[30] After swift pretrial procedures, eight of the Black boys were sentenced to death. The ninth case resulted in a hung jury. During the trial and in press reports, Bates and Price were portrayed as symbols of Southern White womanhood. Eventually, Bates recanted her story; Bates' admission, however, did not result in freedom for the eight young Black men.[31] The hoax was successful, making this case perhaps the most notorious racial hoax case in our history.

Instances of other White-on-Black hoaxes abound.[32] It is impossible, though, to know how many times racial hoaxes have been used to cover criminal tracks. There are no state or national statistics on the incidence and prevalence of racial hoaxes.

The case involving Tawana Brawley provides an interesting counterpoint to the above hoaxes. In November 1987, Brawley, a fifteen-year-old Black girl from Wappingers Falls, New York, told police she had been abducted and raped by six White men. Brawley said that the men were police officers. She said she was smeared with feces, placed in a plastic bag, and left in a gutter. The story drew widespread attention. After convening for seven months, the grand jury declined to issue any indictments. Although Brawley stands by her original account, the incident has been widely discounted as a hoax.[33]

In a second Black-on-White hoax, in 1990, Sabrina Collins, a Black student at Emory University, said that she had received hate mail and death threats and that racial epithets had been scrawled on her dormitory wall.[34] According to Collins, the attack so traumatized her that she fell mute.[35] Separate investigations by the District Attorney and the County Solicitor concluded that the incident was a hoax.[36]

Attempts to catalogue the Brawley and Collins cases along with the hoaxes discussed earlier miss the point. Such a comparison ignores the vast power differential between the hoax perpetrators in these two groups.[37] It is noteworthy that both of the Black-on-White racial hoaxes were framed as "hate crimes" by the perpetrators.[38] Collins and Brawley stated that they had been attacked because they were Black. By contrast, the White-on-Black racial hoaxes were framed as random acts of Black violence. It is as if neither Brawley nor Collins could envision a random White-on-Black crime.[39] This is a significant observation because it reflects the public's prevailing view of crime—that Blacks run amok committing depraved, unprovoked acts of violence against Whites, while only those Whites who are known racists—Ku Klux Klan types—commit crimes against Blacks. Further, in neither case was there a call for an apology to the "White community." This underscores the absence of an aggrieved community—a clear distinction between Black-on-White and White-on-Black hoaxes. Using these distinctions as a starting point, the next Section considers the sociological ramifications of the racial hoax.

B. The Sociology of the Racial Hoax

Assessing the impact and weight of the racial hoax requires a look at the "body" of crime, in terms of both race and gender. By all indicators, the young Black man is the symbol of American criminality.[40] The Black male has always been perceived as a physical threat; however, until recently, that threat was portrayed in sexual terms. Historically, he was viewed as a threat to the purity of the White female.[41] In the past twenty years, the image of the Black male as rapist has evolved into the image of the Black male as the symbolic pillager of all that is good and pure. The *criminalblackman* stereotype persists, even though it is contradicted by official data.[42] The common perception of the Black male influences how the racial hoax affects Blacks and Whites, as individuals and as group members.

On an individual level, the impact of the hoax is race-specific. Not only does the hoax perpetuate the existing lore regarding the Black male as criminal, it also helps to create it. We may assume that for many young children of all races, the Charles Stuart story was their first experience with "race and crime." For them, hearing about the horrible Black man who shot an innocent White man and killed his pregnant wife and unborn baby made the *criminalblackman* imprint indelible—the myth was created.[43] The stamp of this image upon a new generation occurs every time a hoax is perpetrated. The hoax and its fallout place both shame and blame upon Blacks. Particularly disturbing is the fact that even after the hoax is uncovered, Blacks are still perceived as being at fault.[44]

For Blacks as a group, racial hoaxes underscore unfairness and the racism of Whites. For instance, many Blacks were initially skeptical of Susan Smith's story and troubled that so many Whites believed it so quickly.[45] For Whites as a group, the hoax supports the prevailing myth that Blacks pose the greatest crime threat to Whites. For both groups the racial hoax fosters an "us-versus-them" sentiment. Blacks and Whites divide further by race as the hoax takes its expected course. Law enforcement is called into action to protect an innocent White person from further harm and to apprehend a widely perceived threat—a menacing Black man. The incident arouses sympathy and leads to calls for swift, harsh, and certain punishment. The collective racial consciousness of each group gains more strength and permanence with each hoax.

Among the most damaging effects the hoax has upon Blacks is that it enhances the appeal of conspiracy theories. Studies show that Blacks are more likely to believe race-related government conspiracy theories.[46] Black susceptibility to such theories is borne of government-sanctioned atrocities, such as chattel slavery and the Tuskegee syphilis experiment.[47] Whites are less suspicious of government operations. These differing perceptions create great tension between Blacks and Whites. Blacks are increasingly perceived as paranoid, and this further marginalizes them from the mainstream.

II. Racism[48] as Crime

A. Views of Commentators

Why should the racial hoax be punished? Consideration of this question requires an examination and analysis of racist acts and their impact upon Blacks in particular and society as a whole.[49] This discussion relies upon three articles to provide a context for assessing whether the racial hoax should be criminalized. The first is an article by Professor Patricia Williams on "spirit-murder."[50] In the article, Williams argues that although racism is difficult to see in its more subtle forms, it should nevertheless be made criminal. The second article, by Professor Peggy Davis, examines how the everyday slights that Blacks experience shape their perceptions of justice.[51] Finally, Professor Wendy Brown-Scott's analysis of the impact of "state lawlessness" upon Blacks provides a framework for considering the racial hoax a crime.[52] Together, these three articles provide a paradigm for analyzing the sociology of racism—of which the racial hoax is a part—and a structure for discussing whether the racial hoax should be made criminal.

According to Williams, racism is "an offense so deeply painful and assaultive as to constitute something [called] 'spirit-murder.' "[53] For Blacks, spirit-murder is constant. There is a daily onslaught of Black crime stories played out in the media, which unfailingly portray Blacks as ignorant and criminal. Williams examines the ways in which incidents with obvious racial aspects are neutralized as private, nonracial incidents. She details several high-profile criminal cases (*e.g.*, Howard Beach, Bernhard Goetz) involving assaults by Whites upon Blacks.[54] In each instance, the public and political response was to both excuse the offenders' behavior and to deny there was a larger racial context in which to consider the incident.[55] Williams refers to this as "privatization"—segregating individual incidents, thereby making it impossible to group cases together and discuss their broader implications; the result is "socialized blindness."[56] Williams is concerned less with fault than with the grave harm of inaction:

> We need to elevate . . . spirit-murder to the conceptual, if not punitive level of a capital moral offense. We need to see it as a cultural cancer; we need to open our eyes to the spiritual genocide it is wreaking on blacks, whites, and the abandoned and abused of all races and ages. We need to eradicate its numbing pathology before it wipes out what precious little humanity we have left.[57]

Whereas Williams provides a macrolevel analysis of individual incidents of racism, Davis concentrates upon one-on-one Black/White encounters as the unit of analysis. Davis refers to these encounters as "microaggressions." Microaggressions are defined as "subtle, stunning often automatic and nonverbal exchanges which are put downs" of blacks by [Whites].[58] Davis asserts that microaggressions are a fact of life for Blacks.[59] Subjection to microaggressions erodes self-confidence, as Blacks internalize negative images. The criminal justice system, in particular, is fraught with microaggressions. The experience that Blacks have within the system, as victims, offenders, or as jurors, often reinforces any negative perceptions they may have had prior to their experience.[60] The negative stereotypes of Blacks that Whites learn at an early age causes the onslaught of microaggressions. These images are developed, reinforced, assimilated, and over time accepted as "truth rather than opinion."[61]

Microaggressions—individually directed, incessant, and cumulative assaults—do not operate in a vacuum. In addition to one-on-one aggressions, Blacks are confronted with assaults upon their group. Group assaults are termed "*macro*aggressions." Macroaggressions are attacks, insults, and/or pejorative statements made against Blacks by Whites. Unlike microaggressions, however, they are neither directed at nor designed to offend a specific Black person. Further, they are primarily characterized by the effect they have of rendering Blacks invisible and portraying them in a stereotypically negative light. Finally, macroaggressions are played out through the press at the national level, and as a result become part of our collective racial consciousness.[62]

For a one-month period during February 1995, newspaper articles were culled for examples of macroaggressions.[63] During this period, several macroaggressions garnered national attention: (1) Ann Arbor, Michigan, police officials required 100 Black men to submit to DNA testing to "clear" themselves of rape and murder charges;[64] (2) merchants in a Georgia town posted a criminal "offenders" sheet, which only listed the names of Black patrons;[65] (3) Rutgers University President Francis Lawrence made derogatory comments about Blacks;[66] and (4) in St. Louis, Missouri, more than fifty blacks were sprayed with Kool-Aid from a fire extinguisher on Martin Luther King, Jr.'s birthday in 1991 and 1992.[67] The month-long search yielded a total of nine macroaggressions.[68]

Like Williams and Davis, Brown-Scott considers the way that racism harms Blacks. Unlike Williams and Davis, however, Brown-Scott examines the state's role in promoting racism. Her analysis seeks the source of the harm inflicted by individual and group racism. Specifically, Brown-Scott identifies state lawlessness as the cause. State lawlessness includes both the abuse of legal power and the withholding of laws to protect Blacks.[69] As examples of state lawlessness. Brown-Scott cites slavery and the "contemporary second-class citizenship experienced by many African Americans."[70] The allocation of state resources having a disproportionately negative impact on Blacks and the levels of economic and psychological subordination reflect this second-class citizenship. According to Brown-Scott, instances of state lawlessness are typically invisible and are therefore difficult legally to redress.[71]

Brown-Scott focuses primarily upon the macrostructural harm resulting from state lawlessness. In particular, she notes the growth of racial enclaves which could spiral into an "apartheid state"[72] as well as the continued and justified mistrust Blacks have of the state.[73] Although she does not detail the impact of state lawlessness upon individual Blacks, she would likely agree with Professor Mari Matsuda that

> [t]he aloneness comes not only from the hate message itself, but also from the government response of tolerance. When hundreds of police officers are called out to protect racist marchers, when the courts refuse redress for racial insult, when racist attacks are officially dismissed as pranks, the victim becomes a stateless person.[74]

The paradigm created by Williams, Davis, and Brown-Scott has three major premises. The first is the invisibility of the harm to Blacks caused by White racism. This is coupled with the invisibility of the harm to Whites caused by White racism. The harm to Blacks is exacerbated by the fact that the harm is largely unacknowledged. The second component is that the unfair treatment Blacks have received, which is the source of their perceptions of injustice, prevents them from full individual and group participation in mainstream American life.[75] The third part concerns the subsequent impact of reduced Black participation and what it bodes for the future of race relations and justice. The result could be alienation, criminal offending, or greater tension between the races. At the core, Williams, Davis, and Brown-Scott make it clear that the legal system does not adequately respond to spirit-murder, microaggressions, and state lawlessness. As a result, these social phenomena cause continuous and cumulative harm.

B. The Paradigm and the Racial Hoax

The paradigm which emerges from the three articles permits an argument to be made that the racial hoax should be a crime. Specifically, Williams argues that spirit-murder is the outcome of a system of "formalized distortions of thought [which] . . . produces social structures centered around fear and hate."[76] In both its individual and group dimensions, the racial hoax typifies spirit-murder. Davis notes that the law has to include the voices of those who face discrimination. Without such voices the law will never be perceived as legitimate: "So long as legal decision making excludes black voices, and hierarchical judgments predicated upon race are allowed insidiously to infect decisions of fact and *formulations of law,* minorities will perceive, with cause, that the courts are fully capable—and regularly guilty—of bias."[77] What is needed, then, are laws which do not, by their definition or application, reflect bias. A racial hoax law meets this test. Such a law would be a liberating "formulation of law," which would affirm the reality of racial discrimination. Likewise, Brown-Scott describes state lawlessness as omissions made by the state which are "invisible to society because they fall outside the scope of conventional civil rights claims or because they are not easily verifiable independent of the testimonies of the victims."[78] Brown-Scott concludes that in a society concerned with racial equality, Whiteness must be "deprivileged" and Whites "must bear a greater burden of correcting the wages of privilege."[79] A racial hoax law would benefit both Blacks and Whites. As Whites would become more understanding and cognizant of the existing discrimination against Blacks, the groundwork would be laid for smoother interracial relations.

We miss the point if we examine each racial hoax case separately. We cannot conclude that what Susan Smith did was an isolated event *and* what Jesse Anderson did was an isolated event *and* what Charles Stuart did was an isolated event. Nor can we simply dismiss Smith, Anderson, and Stuart as "crazy."[80] These cases beg for holistic analysis. Nonrecognition of the racial hoax by the criminal law exemplifies the very "privatization" that Williams decries. The following section considers the paucity of affirmative race law and how it affects crime.

III. The Law as Affirmation and Its Relationship to Criminal Offending

A. Affirmative Race Law

The goal of a color-blind society is not the same thing as the attainment of a color-blind society. As the Williams, Davis, and Brown-Scott articles establish, Blacks face social discrimination. This discrimination has an impact on how Blacks are treated, how Blacks perceive Whites, how Blacks perceive themselves, how Whites perceive Blacks, and how Whites perceive themselves. Racial inequality, both actual and perceptual, is a social fact.[81] Failure to acknowledge inequality not only ensures that it will continue, but also further exacerbates the pain experienced by its victims.

The legal system needs more laws which acknowledge American racial history and operate as a bulwark against existing racial subordination and discrimination.[82] This kind of law can be characterized as the *law as affirmation.* Developing law as affirmation[83] is necessary to build Black trust in police, courts, and corrections. The distrust Blacks currently have of the criminal justice system has several ramifications. One concern is strained police-community relations in Black neighborhoods. Under these conditions, Blacks are less likely to assist police in crime solving, which is particularly troubling considering that Blacks are disproportionately to be crime victims.[84]

A law proscribing racial hoaxes would exemplify the law as affirmation. Specifically, it would serve as a symbol of intolerance for the fiscal harm (wasted law enforcement resources) and the psychic harm (reinforcing criminal stereotypes)[85] of such actions.[86] Some might question the legitimacy of affirmative race law. For instance, an opponent might argue that Blacks, who offend at a disproportionately high rate, are responsible for the existing criminal stereotype. According to this argument perception is reality. While Blacks are overrepresented in arrest data given their percentage in the total U.S. population, they do not comprise the majority of those arrested in any given year.[87]

A component of this argument is that Blacks' lack of faith in the criminal justice system is the result of their overinvolvement in criminal activity. Criminologist James Q. Wilson offers perhaps the most concise articulation of this view. He opines that there is a positive, causal relationship between Black crime and White racism.[88] If Blacks would cease to offend disproportionately, Wilson contends White racism would simply wither away. Beyond being both ahistorical and counterintuitive, this argument lacks any empirical grounding.[89] Further, such reasoning excuses prejudice and racial discrimination against all Blacks because of the criminal actions of a relative few.[90] The *criminalblackman* stereotype, which labels all Black males as criminal, is proof. This *criminalblackman* depiction permeates public and social institutions. Unfortunately, Blacks, no matter what their level of social status, can rise no higher than the prevailing deviant image.[91] Finally, the criminal stereotype has been used to justify more punitive sanctions that will disproportionately affect Blacks, as the federal sentencing guidelines illustrate. For instance, the guidelines mandate harsher penalties for possessing crack cocaine than for possessing powder cocaine.[92]

In sum, the *criminalblackman* stereotype makes manifest the need for affirmative race law. As this section has argued, the failure to develop a greater body of affirmative race law has a number of costs, including psychological, sociological, and economic harm.

The next section shows that there is an additional harm in rejecting affirmative race law: its impact upon criminal offending.

B. Absence of Affirmative Race Law and Criminal Offending

Equally important in assessing the legitimacy of affirmative race law is determining what impact the disconnection between Blacks and the criminal justice system has upon law-abiding behavior. It is argued herein that the failure to acknowledge this dissonance combined with the absence of affirmative race law may promote a range of antisocial reactions, from alienation to criminal violence. Defiance theory has been offered to explain when the perception of unfair legal sanctions may increase criminal offending.[93] Defiance theory is based upon Professor John Braithwaite's theory of shaming,[94] which posits that how society responds to criminal behavior either increases or decreases the probability of criminal offending. Society may either respond by "reiterative shaming," which expresses community disapproval followed by community reacceptance,[95] or with "stigmatization," which places blame upon the offender.[96]

Defiance theory predicts that a person's perception that he has been punished unfairly, or that members of his group have been punished unfairly, increases the probability that he will engage in criminal behavior. The perception of unfair treatment may come from formal contacts with the criminal justice system (*e.g.*, court proceedings) or informal contacts (*e.g.*, vehicle stops, street stops). With regard to Blacks, inequity and perceived bias in the justice system at the very least create a psychic and emotional environment in which criminal behavior can be committed and rationalized.[97]

For young Black men, criminal justice shaming is stigmatizing rather than reintegrative. They are labeled deviant *before* any formal contact with the justice system. In a discussion on police disrespect in citizen-police encounters, Professor Lawrence Sherman notes that "young males, especially the poor and minorities, are much more exposed than lower crime groups to police disrespect and brutality, both vicariously and in person, *prior* to their peak years of first arrest and initial involvements in crime."[98]

Given the *criminalblackman* label, police interactions with Black men are likely to reinforce existing stereotypes. Police come away from encounters with Black men believing that Black men are hostile and disrespectful; Black men come away from encounters with police believing that the police are hostile and disrespectful. This cycle creates further outcast status for Black men and increases the probability of an antisocial response.[99]

Sociology Professor Anthony Lemelle, in a thorough discussion of the "forced criminality" of Black males, provides support.[100] He states, "Black males are primarily concerned with avoiding shame and guilt in situations with the police. . . . To avoid embarrassment, shame and guilt—in short, emasculation—the males seek to neutralize the militarylike systems that occupy their communities."[101] It is shame and emasculation that many Blacks experience in their encounters with agents of the criminal justice system, leading to stigmatization, not reintegration. Lemelle continues, "[T]he police techniques of interrogation often implicate them in the assumption that Black males are *guilty until they are proven innocent.*"[102] Lemelle concludes that the end result is the rejection of the legitimacy of the criminal justice system. "[B]lack males form a position of opposition that results directly from their social experiences, which undermine the normal methods of institutional control."[103] The tension Lemelle describes pits Blacks directly against the criminal justice system. The standoff leaves Blacks on one side believing that they have been prejudged, unable to get equitable treatment, and therefore, justified in rejecting the law's legitimacy. On the other side is the criminal justice system, with preconceptions that Blacks are defiant and deviant based solely upon the criminal actions of a few.[104] There can be no victors, Pyhrric or otherwise, in a match where battle lines are constantly redrawn with ever-growing distance between Blacks and Whites.

Defiance theory, coupled with Lemelle's discussion of "forced criminality," provides support for the argument that there is an additional link in the shaming-defiance causal chain.[105] It is posited that for Blacks the perceived existence of unfair sanctions, combined with the absence or lack of adequate sanctions for race-based harms, cause a diminished faith in the justice system, which in turn sets the stage for criminal offending. At least for now, two of these variables—the presence and absence of race-based legal sanctions—are linked. This causal process is illustrated below:

presence of unfair legal sanctions on the basis of faith +
absence of/inadequate legal sanctions for race-based harms
→ lack of faith in the system
→ dissonance
→ violence

This model, which unites defiance theory and affirmative race law, does not purport to explain all criminal offending. If the proffered relationships are accurate, then the development of more laws which acknowledge the continuing inequality between Blacks and Whites is necessary to show that the legal system can work for everyone. More importantly, such laws may lead to a decrease in criminal activity. Indeed, the existing shame-stigmatization cycle demonstrates the need for affirmative race law, such as a racial hoax sanction.

An example provided by Professor Williams illuminates the nexus between racism and crime. Williams, a Black woman, begins her spirit-murder article by recounting a racial incident in which she was denied entrance to a clothing store by a White clerk.[106] Williams details her rage,[107] which she was ultimately able to channel into a public complaint.[108] Referring to her store encounter, Williams confides, "My rage was admittedly diffuse, even self-destructive, but it was *symmetrical*."[109] Williams, a well-known and well-respected law professor, had a legal, productive medium through which to express her anger. The majority of young Black men, embarrassed and angered by the sting of racism, have no such outlet. Thus, Williams argues that there is a causal relationship between racism and crime.

Several recent incidents provide examples of how spirit-murder, micro/macroaggressions, and state lawlessness can escalate into violence. In January 1995, four Black teens in Kentucky were accused of killing a White man, purportedly because he hung a Confederate flag in the back of his truck.[110] In February 1995, a White rookie police officer shot and killed an unarmed Black youth in a Paterson, New Jersey, drug bust. In response to the New Jersey shooting, one young Black man stated, "The youth of Paterson, we don't want to be violent, but we want justice served[,] . . . if justice is not served, then there will be *repercussions*."[111] This statement is consistent with Brown-Scott's observation that the uprisings in poor communities are examples of the potential of repressive state action to cause unrest.[112] The young Black man in Paterson felt that the state had acted beyond its legal authority and that he had no legal way to voice his discontent and be heard. The attempted murder of Stacey Koon, one of the police officers convicted of violating Rodney King's civil rights, is an example of these "repercussions." On the eve of Koon's release from a halfway house, a lone Black gunman went searching for him. Randall Tolbert, the gunman, took three hostages when he was unable to find Koon. He killed one hostage and then was killed by police. According to Tolbert's brother, Randall "wanted to protest that Stacey Koon was [housed in a Black community]" and felt that Koon "should still be in prison." His brother also observed, "It was like they were trying to slap us in the face by putting him here."[113]

Within a one-year period (September 1994 to September 1995), police departments in three major cities—New York, Los Angeles, and Philadelphia—faced allegations of department-wide, long-standing police corruption.[114] Each set of allegations resulted in internal investigations and commission reports. Common to each scandal was that the primary targets of the police lawlessness were minority communities. In Philadelphia, for instance, five police officers pleaded guilty to making false arrests, planting drugs, filing false police reports, and robbing victims during a three-year period.[115] Cases involving some 1400 officers were reviewed.[116] Such official brutality and harassment serve to create further disillusionment within minority communities. For some, particularly Black men who are the primary target of police brutality, disillusionment may become anger, then rage. The concern is whether this rage will cause retaliation, either in the form of intraracial[117] or interracial violence. The latter could take the form of Blacks committing crimes in White communities and the targeting of White law enforcement officials.[118] The criminal actions of police officers and the potential response of minority communities attest to the need for affirmative race law.

As the above instructs, we cannot afford to overlook the link between racism and crime. Poll data show that the void between Black and White views on the legitimacy of the justice system continues to widen.[119] There is every indication that this trend will continue, but the need for racial restoration is not apparent to all. People continue to call for the eradication of "race-conscious" remedies that benefit minorities.[120] In particular, affirmative action programs have been under attack[121] and heightened barriers have been erected to reduce the number of persons who have access to the American mainstream.[122] Concurrently, there has been the steady barrage of legislation, which is increasingly retributive and will have a disproportionate impact upon Blacks because they are disproportionately involved in the criminal justice system.[123] In fact, the recent trend more closely resembles retrenchment than reform. In perhaps the most glaring example, the House of Representatives, in a debate about adopting a "good faith" exception for warrantless federal searches, voted down an amendment that was a verbatim recital of the Fourth Amendment.[124]

C. *Economics of the Racial Hoax*

Beyond causing sociological injury, the racial hoax also exacts a financial toll. Consequently, economic factors are relevant to an analysis of whether racial hoaxes should be criminalized. Untold resources have been wasted on efforts to locate a fictional *criminalblackman.* In Trenton, New Jersey, which has seen its share of racial hoaxes,[125] a city official commented, "This kind of accusation [racial hoax]. . . affects us all. It terrorizes a community and discriminates against a race of people. And it is the kind of crime that costs taxpayers thousands of dollars to launch massive, futile investigations."[126]

Indeed, a consideration of the economic consequences of the Susan Smith, Jesse Anderson, and Charles Stuart investigations underscores this point.[127] These cases involved countless days of manhunts, police investigations, and court proceedings. In the Smith case, several agencies were involved in the nine-day search. A precise accounting of the costs is not available, but is estimated in the thousands of dollars.[128] The F.B.I. and the South Carolina State Law Enforcement Division provided both manpower (*e.g.*, air and ground searches) and technical services (*e.g.*, computer equipment).[129] The Union County Sheriff's Office and City of Union employees also provided assistance.[130] Beyond their cost to taxpayers, hoaxes frequently spawn their own cottage industry—for example, civil suits, countersuits, tax investigations, book deals, and paraphernalia. National data collection on the economic impact of racial hoaxes at state and federal levels would buttress the argument for criminalizing the hoax.

IV. A Legal Response: The Law and the Logistics

A. *False Reporting Statutes*

Most jurisdictions have statutes that penalize the filing of a false police report.[131] However, these laws are rarely applied to punish a racial hoax perpetrator. None of the racial hoax offenders in the cases discussed above were charged with filing a false police report. At a minimum, it would be expected that in those cases where the hoax was a total fabrication, for example, the Kashani rape case,[132] false reporting charges would be filed. Notably, of the six cases discussed earlier, only Brawley faced civil sanctions through the legal system.[133] The failure to impose any legal sanctions for these hoaxes suggests that the existing penalties are ineffective; the fact that most false report violations constitute misdemeanors may explain their ineffectiveness. On the one hand, adding a false report charge to a case like Susan Smith's might look like an overzealous prosecution. Conversely, pursuing such a charge against Miriam Kashani might look like a waste of the prosecutor's time, energy, and resources. The fact that existing false report laws were not applied in any of the highly publicized racial hoax cases underscores the need for putting more teeth into the law. The following sections examine the law on hate crimes and assess the components of a racial hoax law.

B. The Law on Hate Crimes

Hate crime[134] statutes are typically divided into two types.[135] First, there are those which treat hate crimes as independent criminal offenses. These are referred to as "pure bias" statutes. The Minnesota statute at issue in *R.A.V. v. St. Paul*[136] is an example of this type.[137] The *R.A.V.* Court held that the state's bias crime law had content-based provisions, which rendered it facially invalid, in violation of the First Amendment.[138]

A second type of hate crime statute is one that provides for the "penalty enhancement" of bias-motivated crimes. Under this type of statute, one who commits a criminal offense as a result of bias (*e.g.*, against race, sex, religion, sexual orientation) faces additional penalties. A number of states have adopted the model bias crime provision drafted by the Anti-Defamation League.[139] The federal government has also enacted penalty enhancement legislation.[140]

Penalty enhancement statutes have been upheld by the U.S. Supreme Court. In *Wisconsin v. Mitchell,*[141] a Black defendant challenged the state's penalty enhancement statute. Mitchell, who had been convicted of beating a White boy, faced an increased penalty because his crime was motivated by bias. Under state law, he faced an additional five years for his bias crime.[142] Finding the provision content-neutral, the Court noted that "bias-inspired conduct" is an appropriate arena for penalty enhancement, because it is "thought to inflict greater individual and societal harm."[143] Further, the Court observed, such conduct is likely to provoke "retaliatory crimes, inflict distinct emotional harm on their victims, and incite community unrest."[144] A racial hoax law could be framed as either a pure bias crime or as a penalty enhancement. Given that the Supreme Court has upheld bias crime enhancement, this seems to be the safer constitutional route. However, a content-neutral bias statute would also likely withstand constitutional scrutiny.

C. The Racial Hoax as Crime

1. Constitutional Concerns

The road to making the racial hoax a crime is, constitutionally speaking, a much smoother road than the one which earlier hate crime legislation had to travel. This is primarily because the First Amendment is a nonissue in the racial hoax context.[145] It is a long-standing principle of constitutional law that where speech entails imminent, lawless action, it is not accorded First Amendment protection.[146] Thus, one does not have the right to yell "fire" in a crowded video store.[147]

Where one uses a racial hoax to mislead law enforcement, certain, immediate responses can reasonably be expected by both law enforcement and the community. The speech element of the racial hoax triggers numerous actions, including deployment of police officers to particular neighborhoods to locate potential suspects, creation of "wanted" posters, notification of the media, announcement of all-points bulletins, and meetings by the police and/or community groups to discuss strategy on how to proceed. The person uttering the words of a racial hoax has done more than simply speak. He has pointed his finger at a community of people in an attempt to thwart justice. By design, the speech of the racial hoax is lawless conduct, unprotected by the Constitution.

2. *Logistics of a Racial Hoax Law*

The individual, group, and societal harms caused by the racial hoax were discussed in Parts II and III. These concerns outline the parameters of a racial hoax law. Next this Article looks at one state's proposal for criminalizing the hoax.

a. *New Jersey Legislation*

New Jersey is the only state which has considered legislation specifically designed to target racial hoax perpetrators. The legislation, proposed in January 1995, was drafted in direct response to two White-on-Black racial hoaxes.[148] The proposed New Jersey statutory amendment to "False Reports to Law Enforcement Authorities" reads:

> a. Falsely incriminating another. . . . (2) A person who knowingly gives or causes to be given false information or a description of a fictitious person to any law enforcement officer with purpose to implicate another because of race, color, religion, sexual orientation or ethnicity commits a crime of the third degree. . . .
>
> c. A person who violates subsection b. [fictitious reports] is guilty of a crime of the fourth degree if the person acted with purpose to implicate another because of race, color, religion, sexual orientation or ethnicity.
>
> d. Restitution. In addition to any other fine, fee or assessment imposed, any person convicted of an offense under this section shall be ordered to reimburse the governing body of the municipality for the costs incurred in investigating the false information or the fictitious report.[149]

Because New Jersey is the only jurisdiction that has considered racial hoax legislation, it will serve as a referent for the following discussion on the elements of a racial hoax law. There are, broadly speaking, four perpetrator/victim racial hoax combinations:

White perpetrator/Black victim (A) (e.g., Harris, Smith, Anderson, Kashani, and Stuart)	Black perpetrator/Black victim (C)
Black perpetrator/White victim (B) (e.g., Brawley and Collins	White perpetrator/White victim (D)

The White-on-Black and Black-on-White hoaxes (Cells A & B) should be the emphasis of a racial hoax law.[150]

b. *The Offender*

A racial hoax law should be written such that anyone, regardless of race, who perpetrates a hoax will be subject to sanction. The earlier discussion and analysis supports this approach. The nature of and damage done by the hoax is so great that nobody should be excluded from those who can be charged. Theoretically, there is harm done irrespective of whether the hoax perpetrator is White or Black. Practically, however, there is no empirical evidence of Black-on-Black hoaxes.[151] All of the hoaxes discussed have involved "cross-racial fabrication" (Cells A & C).[152]

There might be a different community response and injury depending upon the race of the offender. Where a White offender points the finger at a Black person, it acts to further polarize Black and White communities. As a result, Blacks feel more vulnerable to indiscriminate police practices and Whites feel more vulnerable to crime by Blacks. Conversely, where the hoax perpetrator is Black and the victim is Black, it is probable that the hoax "crime" will not be taken as seriously.

The police are not likely to treat as seriously the claim of victimization of someone Black as they would a similar claim by someone White.[153]

White-on-Black hoaxes, like the Charles Stuart and Susan Smith cases, receive a great deal of media attention, as predicted by this model. It is also less probable that a Black-on-Black hoax would be uncovered because such a fabrication would appear to reflect the status quo—the erroneous belief that the majority of crime is Black-on-Black. In fact, Whites comprise the majority of those arrested in any given year.[154] Furthermore, more than eighty percent of all crime is intraracial; that is, with most crimes, the offender and victim are of the same race.[155] Given that there were no Black-on-Black hoaxes found, the argument for extending a racial hoax law to include them is theoretical only. The Black-on-Black and the White-on-Black hoax should be sanctioned because they both perpetuate the existing *criminalblackman* stereotype.

Professor Mari Matsuda, in a compelling argument for making race-based hate speech a crime, contends that only Whites can be offenders.[156] She states that the harm of racist speech is greatest where the speech reinforces an "historically vertical relationship."[157] Likewise, Professor Marc Fleischauer, in his discussion of hate crime, argues that penalty enhancement should only attach when there is a White offender.[158] Without this "Whites only" rule, "minorities will be subjected to enhanced penalties at a disproportionate rate compared to Whites because it is the nature of society for the majorities to prosecute minorities more frequently and with more vigor than vice versa."[159] The fact that *Wisconsin v. Mitchell*[160]—the only hate crime sentencing enhancement case decided by the U.S. Supreme Court—involved a Black defendant, supports Fleischauer's observations.

While Fleischauer and Matsuda make strong arguments, the line that they draw between the race of the perpetrator and race of the victim should not be applied to the racial hoax. First, unlike the victim of racist hate speech, the victim of a racial hoax is not directly assaulted by the offender. Second, it is not just one person who is harmed by a racial hoax, but an entire community. The harm of a Black-on-Black hoax is different in degree from the harm of a White-on-Black hoax; both, though, cause harm because the racial hoax operates as a macroaggression.[161] Given the harm done by pointing a false finger at a Black person, anyone of any race who perpetrates a criminal hoax should be penalized. Notably, the New Jersey legislation does not make a distinction based upon race of the perpetrator.

c. *Targets and Victims*

With regard to who classifies as a victim for the racial hoax, two key questions arise. First, should a racial hoax law mandate an identifiable, named victim—a "Willie Bennett requirement"?[162] Under existing false report statutes, it is not required that there be an identifiable victim. Therefore, no such requirement should be part of a racial hoax law. The goal of false reporting statutes is to punish intentional efforts to thwart law enforcement. Whether there is an identifiable victim or not, the racial hoax causes harm which justifies a sanction.

Professor Frederick Lawrence, discussing the breadth of harm caused by hate crimes, points out that "[t]he victim suffers for being singled out on the basis of her race, and the general community of the target racial group is harmed as well."[163] As applied to the racial hoax, once a "victim" says "a Black guy did it," she has hurled a racial epithet which is actionable. Given the predictable response of law enforcement to such statements, the hoax is akin to physical harassment solely on the basis of race. It is as if Susan Smith, Jesse Anderson, Miriam Kashani, and Charles Stuart called every Black man a "low life," "hoodlum," or "criminal" because of his race. It is Blacks as a group, and Black men in particular, who are directly harmed. The New Jersey legislation recognizes the need to penalize someone who uses a racial hoax to target a specific person because of his race ("False Incrimination"), as well as the need to penalize someone who uses the hoax to create a nonexistent villain ("Fictitious Reports").[164]

Assuming there is a legally cognizable victim, a second important question regarding victim status is which racial groups should receive protection under a racial hoax law. A strong argument can be made for requiring a Black victim.[165] Ideally, a racial hoax law would only be actionable where the finger has been pointed at someone Black. This is based upon the enduring *criminalblackman* image.[166] Fleischauer, in his discussion of Florida's hate crime statute, argues that it would be constitutional to make minorities the only protected group.[167] Fleischauer observes that one of the express goals of hate crime legislation is to curb racism and empower minorities.[168] To allow a racial hoax law to encompass both White-on-Black hoaxes and Black-on-White hoaxes unfairly accords the two equal weight. As the above discussion on the sociology of the racial hoax makes clear,[169] beyond the individual harm a racial hoax may cause to a targeted Black person, it brings harm to Blacks as a group and creates more tension between Blacks and Whites. There is no indication that the harm of a White-on-Black hoax or Black-on-Black hoax is comparable to the harm of either a White-on-White or Black-on-White hoax. The New Jersey amendment is silent with regard to victim's race—the inference being that a victim can be of any race.

The Equal Protection Clause presents the biggest roadblock to the proposed restriction on who qualifies as a victim for the racial hoax law. Such a distinction is legally justified because the harms of the hoax (White-on-Black and Black-on-Black versus Black-on White and White-on-White) differ. Further, Black-on-White and White-on-White hoaxes are not without legal sanction; existing false reporting statutes provide a penalty for these hoaxes. While Black-on-White hoaxes do occur (as in the Tawana Brawley case), they are so infrequent that their inclusion in racial hoax laws is unnecessary. Likewise, White-on-White hoaxes, while they do occur, do not pose the same societal problems as those where the victim is Black. Considering the U.S. Supreme Court's "colorblind" leanings,[170] however, the safest route would be to draft racial hoax legislation so as to protect a victim of any race.

d. Intent

A racial hoax law could be written to require that the perpetrator act either "purposefully" or "knowingly." If "knowledge" were required, the prosecution would only have to show that the hoax perpetrator was "practically certain" that law enforcement forces would respond and that some harm would occur as a result of the race labeling. A "purposeful" intent requirement, on the other hand, would require prosecutors to prove the hoax perpetrator had as his or her "conscious object" the bringing about of the particular result—triggering law enforcement and causing harm to a specific Black person or Blacks as a group.[171]

The New Jersey legislation appears to impose a general intent requirement. Under the proposal, one could be charged with false incrimination on the basis of race, where one "knowingly provides false information to a law enforcement officer with purpose to implicate another because of race."[172] To avoid the problem of attempting to determine whether the hoax perpetrator intended to cause harm to Blacks as a group or to any particular Black person, specific intent should not be an element of a racial hoax offense. The very fact that a racial hoax has been employed means that existing stereotypes have been reinforced and racial dissension furthered. Therefore, society has been harmed. Professor Charles Lawrence offers support:

> Traditional notions of intent do not reflect the fact that decisions about racial matters are in-

> fluenced in large part by factors that can be characterized as neither intentional—in the sense that certain outcomes are self-consciously sought—nor unintentional—in the sense that the outcomes are random, fortuitous, and uninfluenced by the decisionmaker's beliefs, desires, and wishes.[173]

Furthermore, given the insidious, amoeba-like qualities of racism, a specific intent requirement (*e.g.*, intent to harm on the basis of race of alleged suspect) would render it virtually impossible to hold someone accountable. The prosecution should not be required to establish intent to mislead law enforcement, and they should not be required to prove that the hoax perpetrator is a racist. As set forth in the New Jersey law, it is sufficient that the perpetrator has blamed someone because of his race. The reasons behind the fingerpointing should be irrelevant.

Each of the facial hoaxes discussed above involved a crime index offense.[174] There is no reason, however, to limit a racial hoax law to these eight offenses. For example, a racial hoax might be perpetrated for the non-index crimes of assault and fraud. The New Jersey proposal does not limit its application to specific crimes.[175]

e. Penalties and Remedies

Perpetrating a racial hoax should subject one to a felony charge. The hoax is a serious crime and has ramifications beyond any one specific case. Further, a penalty must be imposed which would deter others from devising hoaxes. A state could decide to impose a criminal fine and/or prison term. Given that two of the five White-on-Black hoaxes were perpetrated by a person considered to be middle class (Charles Stuart and David Anderson), a fine would have had to have been substantial to deter them. Interestingly, both Anderson and Stuart created a hoax as a scheme to get money. Prison time for the hoax may be a more effective deterrent than a fine.

Beyond a prison term and/or a criminal fine, a hoax perpetrator should be required to pay restitution. The New Jersey provision requires restitution in the amount of law reinforcement costs for deployed resources.[176] Additionally, payment of court costs and restitution to any identifiable victims should be imposed.

In addition to imposing criminal penalties and restitution, an apology requirement ought to be considered. The hoax offender should be required to apologize to the public in general, and the Black community in particular, for playing on racial stereotypes.[177] Also, the apology would be one step toward healing a racially divided community. Without question, with White-on-Black hoaxes the most aggrieved group will be the Black community. Following Susan Smith's confession, there were numerous calls for an apology to the Black community. One journalist commented, "This may be difficult for non-minorities to accept, but black people do feel [e]specially violated by Susan Smith's lie."[178] Demands were also made for an apology in the Anderson, Kashani, and Stuart cases.[179] At the same time the Black community is injured, so is the White community. An apology, therefore, is due the entire community.[180]

f. Reporting Requirement

In the same way that there are reporting requirements for bias crimes,[181] there should be reporting requirements for racial hoaxes. It is impossible to estimate the annual frequency of racial hoaxes, as there exists no data bank for this information. More importantly, it is difficult to piece together this information because it is not part of the recorded case information upon closing a case file. A national database should be created which tracks information on racial hoaxes, including the race, sex, and age of the offender and victim; the underlying hoax offense; the number of days of the hoax; and an estimate of the economic cost attributable to the hoax. These data could be compiled as a part of the information collected for the Hate Crime Statistics Act.[182]

Conclusion

As the above analysis makes clear, there is a manifest need to continue developing race-affirming legislation. The empirical literature shows that Whites and Blacks perceive two separate justice systems in operation, one which works and one which does not. The negative perception Blacks have—based in part on a long history of legalized racial subordination—should not be ignored. One way this perception gap can be addressed is by changing the reality of existing law and making the law more responsive to existing racial realities. This can be done by creating affirmative race law. Discussing the import of bias crime legislation, Professor Frederick Lawrence correctly states that it "represent[s] the highest expression of a social commitment to racial, religious, and ethnic harmony."[183]

A racial hoax law is offered as one way to fill this legal void. With the exception of the New Jersey legislation, there has been a deafening legal silence to the ravages of the racial hoax. Williams, Davis, and Brown-Scott, in their tripartite discussions of spirit-murder, microaggression, and state lawlessness, provide a paradigm for assessing the value of a racial hoax law.

Beyond theoretical support for making the racial hoax a crime, there is criminological support as well. The *criminalblackman* stereotype, which is continually reinforced by the shame-stigmatization cycle, makes the nexus between perceptions of criminal injustice and criminal activity more than a theoretical proposition.

Further, as the legal analysis makes clear, such a law is constitutionally permissible. Not only is a racial hoax law constitutionally acceptable, it is arguably legally mandated. It provides a legal route for addressing this country's racial past, as it is played out today in perceptions of crime. Just as important, given that hate crime statutes are similar to antidiscrimination laws,[184] a racial hoax law is a natural and necessary extension of legally cognizable racial harm.

In sum, a racial hoax law acknowledges American racial history, the power of negative stereotypes based upon this history, and the need for legal redress. Absent a specific legal intervention, like a racial hoax law, people will continue to use hoaxes to play the race card and avoid criminal liability. In fact, without substantive legal consequence, we are encouraging people to employ racial hoaxes. A racial hoax law would deter such incidents. Further enactment would send a message, both real and symbolic, that we will not tolerate the wide-ranging and deleterious impact of racial hoaxes.

Notes

1. United States v. Clary, 846 F. Supp. 768 (E.D. Mo.), *rev'd*, 34 F.3d 709 (8th Cir. 1994). The court of appeals held that federal sentencing guidelines which provide a harsher penalty for crack cocaine possession than for the same amount of powder cocaine are without legal justification and are the result of "unconscious racism." *Id* at 791-93.

2. *See, e.g.*, RONALD B. FLOWERS, MINORITIES AND CRIMINALITY (1990).

3. *See generally* DANIEL GEORGES-ABEYIE ET AL., THE CRIMINAL JUSTICE SYSTEM AND BLACKS (1987).

4. *See* STEPHEN P. KLEIN ET AL., RACIAL EQUITY IN SENTENCING 11 (1988) (finding that in California the race of the defendant is not related to the sentence imposed); William Wilbanks, *The Myth of a Racist Criminal Justice System*, in RACISM, EMPIRICISM AND CRIMINAL JUSTICE 5 (Brian D. MacLean & Dragan Milovanovic eds., 1990) (concluding there is no systemic bias against Blacks in the criminal justice system). Wilbanks finds that there is a "canceling-out effect." While some decision makers favor Whites, "there appears to be an equal tendency for other individual decision makers to favor blacks over whites." *Id* at 6 (emphasis in original). This research is in contrast to earlier findings that race does have an impact on sentence.

JOAN PETERSILIA, RACIAL DISPARITIES IN THE CRIMINAL JUSTICE SYSTEM (1983).

5. *See* GEORGES-ABEYIE ET AL., *supra* note 3, at 11, 12 (arguing that the focus upon formal stages of the justice system obscures "petit apartheid" which is the "most significant contemporary form of racism . . . e.g., the everyday insults, rough or brutal treatment, and unnecessary stops, questions, and searches of blacks; the lack of civility faced by black suspects/arrestees").

6. *See, e.g.,* PEGGY C. DAVIS, *Law as Microaggression,* 98 YALE L.J. 1559 (1989) (citing NATIONAL CENTER FOR STATE COURTS, THE PUBLIC IMAGE OF COURTS (1977)).

7. *See, e.g.,* ROBERT L. YOUNG, *Race, Conceptions of Crime and Justice, and Support for the Death Penalty,* 54 SOC. PSYCHOL. Q. 67, 72-73 (1991) (finding that the differing views of the justice system are in part rooted in levels of trust in law enforcement). Racially divided public opinion in the O.J. Simpson case attests to this. In July, 1995, a USA Today/CNN/Gallup poll reported that 87% of the Black respondents believe Simpson was a victim of a racist criminal justice system. Only six percent of the Whites polled held the same opinion. Richard Price, *Racial Split Widens,* USA TODAY, July 25, 1995, at 3A. A number of Blacks within the legal system also negatively perceive the criminal justice system, including judges, *see generally* LINN WASHINGTON, BLACK JUDGES ON JUSTICE (1994), and students, *see, e.g.,* Melissa H. Barlow & David E. Barlow, *Confronting Ideologies of Race and Crime in the Classroom: The Power of History,* 6 J. CRIM. JUST. EDUC. 105, 110-11 (1995).

Blacks are more likely to be distrustful of the criminal justice system, yet they hold punitive attitudes on crime comparable to those of Whites. This is in part explained by greater fear of criminal victimization. Steven F. Cohn et al., *Punitive Attitudes Toward Criminals: Racial Consensus or Racial Conflict,* 38 SOC. PROBS. 287, 288 (1991).

8. *See, e.g.,* GEORGE GALLUP, JR., THE GALLUP POLL: PUBLIC OPINION 1993, at 231 (1994) (reporting that 74% of Whites polled rated local police to be "excellent" or "good," while only 48% of Blacks share this belief).

9. *See, e.g.,* NEWT GINGRICH ET AL., CONTRACT WITH AMERICA 37-64 (Ed Gillespie & Bob Schellhas eds., 1995); Rick Bragg, *Chain Gangs to Return to Roads of Alabama,* N.Y. TIMES, Mar. 26, 1995, at A16.

10. *See, e.g.,* ANDREW HACKER, TWO NATIONS: BLACK AND WHITE, SEPARATE, HOSTILE, UNEQUAL 189 (1992); *Developments in the Law—Race and the Criminal Process,* 101 HARV. L. REV. 1472, 1494-98 (1988); Tracey Marlin, *"Black and Blue Encounters"—Some Preliminary Thoughts About Fourth Amendment Seizures: Should Race Matter?* 26 VAL. U. L. REV. 243 (1991). See TOM R. TYLER, WHY PEOPLE OBEY THE LAW 94-112 (1990), for a discussion of the effect of experience on the perceived legitimacy of justice operations.

11. *See* Davis, *supra* note 6, at 68-71. Some have argued for the construction of a variable which would examine race-specific "group experiences." *See, e.g.,* Katheryn K. Russell, *The Racial Inequality Hypothesis,* 18 L. & HUM. BEHAV. 305 (1994). The racial divide between Blacks and Whites with regard to the O.J. Simpson case supports the "group experience" concept. See Richard C. Dieter, *Secondary Smoke Surrounds Capital Punishment Debate,* CRIM. JUST. ETHICS, Winter-Spring 1994, at 2; Kenneth B. Noble, *The Simpson Defense: Source of Black Pride,* N.Y. TIMES, Mar. 6, 1995, at A10.

12. Examples of the former include police brutality and judicial bias. Examples of the latter include Title VII of the Civil Rights Act of 1964, 42 U.S.C. §§ 2000e-2000e-17 (1988 & Supp. V 1993) (prohibiting discrimination on the basis of race and sex, among other things); Hate Crimes Statistics Act, 28 U.S.C. § 534 (1990) (authorizing the Attorney General to gather hate crime data); 42 U.S.C. § 1983 (1988) (prohibiting racial discrimination by one acting under the color of law).

13. New Jersey has proposed legislation which would subject racial hoaxes to criminal sanction. N.J. Assembly Bill 2553, 206th Leg., 2d Sen. (1995), *available in* WESTLAW, NJ-Bills Database. For further discussion, see *infra* part IV.C.

14. A racial hoax occurs when (1) someone fabricates a crime then blames it on, for example, a Black person; or (2) an actual crime has been committed and someone falsely blames, for example, a Black person. The Miriam Kashani "rape" case and Susan Smith "kidnapping" case, respectively, are examples.

15. Amy Argetsinger, Insurance May Be Motive in Fiancée's Slaying, WASH. POST, Feb. 1, 1996, at DI; *Police Say Md. Man Had Fiancée Killed, Blamed Black Robber,* WASH. POST Jan. 30, 1996, at B6.

16. Richard Grant, *Mother of All Crimes,* INDEPENDENT (London), Feb. 25, 1995, at 16.

17. Smith was charged with two counts of capital murder. Notably, she was not charged with filing a false police report. *See* Henry Eichel, *Mother May Face Death Penalty: Confessed to Drowning Sons,* RECORD (Bergen, N.J.), Jan. 16, 1995, at A1. In August 1995, Smith was sentenced to life in prison. Under South Carolina law, Smith will serve a minimum of 30 years in prison. S.C. CODE ANN. § 16-3-20 (Law. Co-op. 1993). It is a misdemeanor, under South Carolina law, to give false information to a law enforcement official. Upon conviction, one may be fined $200 or imprisoned for up to 30 days. *Id.* § 16-17-725.

18. *See, e.g.,* Rogers Worthington, *Once a Victim, Now a Suspect, Husband Held as Cops Question Account of Wife's Slaying,* CHI. TRIB., Apr. 28, 1992, at 1; *Milwaukee Media Criticized on Murders* (National Public Radio broadcast, Apr. 30, 1992), available in LEXIS, News Library, Script File. In an odd twist, Anderson was

murdered in prison along with serial murderer Jeffrey Dahmer. Don Terry, *Suspect in Dahmer Killing Said, "I'm the Chosen One,"* N.Y. TIMES, Nov. 30, 1994, at A18. It has been speculated that Anderson was targeted along with Dahmer because of the racial upheaval his hoax caused. *See, e.g.*, Rupert Cornwell, *Race Theory Emerges in Dahmer Jail Murder,* INDEPENDENT (London), Nov. 30, 1994, at 31.

19. Felicity Barringer, *False Rape Report Upsetting Campus,* N.Y. TIMES, Dec. 12, 1990, at A21.

20. Jonetta R. Barras, *Blacks See Racism in Rape Hoax at GWU,* WASH. TIMES, Dec. 12, 1990, at B4.

21. *Id*; see BUREAU OF JUSTICE STATISTICS, U.S. DEP'T OF JUSTICE, CRIMINAL VICTIMIZATION IN THE UNITED STATES 1992, at 61 (1994).

22. JOE R. FEAGIN & HERNAN VERA, WHITE RACISM 64 (1995).

23. Michael Grunwald, *For Boston, Harsh Reminder; Five Years Ago, Stuart's Racist Hoax Was Hatched—and Believed,* BOSTON GLOBE, Nov. 4, 1994, at 17.

24. Stuart had talked to his brother about killing Carol Stuart for her insurance money and asked him to dispose of her purse after the shooting incident. FEAGIN & VERA, *supra* note 22, at 64.

25. *Id.* at 63-67.

26. Commenting on how the racial angle is often overlooked, Pulitzer Prize–winning journalist William Raspberry notes, "[H]ere is a woman [Susan Smith] suspected of killing her own children, and we want to chastise her for racial insensitivity?" William Raspberry, *Automatically Suspect,* WASH. POST, Nov. 5, 1994, at A19. One commentator, referring to the media's treatment of the Stuart case stated, "[The press is] covering everything in detail except the most important story—the color story." Christopher Edley, Jr., *Racist Media, Politicians Sustained Boston Hoax,* MANHATTAN LAW., Mar. 1990, at 18.

27. See Edley, Jr., *supra* note 26, at 18.

28. Michele Parente, *Black Community Is Given an Apology: Drowned Boys' Uncle Speaks for the Family,* NEWSDAY, Nov. 9, 1994, at A66.

29. Edley, *supra* note 26, at 18.

30. DAN T. CARTER, SCOTTSBORO: A TRAGEDY OF THE AMERICAN SOUTH 5-6 (1969). The Scottsboro injustices were addressed in *Powell v. Alabama,* 287 U.S. 45 (1932), which fleshed out the parameters of the Sixth Amendment right to a fair trial.

31. *See generally* CARTER, *supra* note 30.

32. In January 1995, a White man in the Trenton, New Jersey, area told authorities that he saw a Black man abducting a White girl whose mouth had been bound with duct tape. Five hours later it was determined that the story was a hoax. Steve Adubato, *Toughen Penalties for False Accusation Based Upon Race,* RECORD (Bergen, N.J.), Jan. 24, 1995, at B7. A Camden, New Jersey, case in 1990 involved prosecutor Sam Asbell, who claimed that he had been chased by two Black gunmen as part of an assassination plot. He later admitted to making the story up and pled guilty to filing a false police report. *Id.* In 1989, Tanya Dacri, a White Philadelphia mother of an infant boy, said that while in a shopping mall parking lot, her child was abducted by two Black men. She subsequently pled guilty to murdering and dismembering her son. She was found guilty of first degree murder. Don Williamson, *We Have to Stop Creating Bogeymen,* SEATTLE TIMES, Jan. 9, 1990, at A6.

33. *See* ROBERT D. MCFADDEN ET AL., OUTRAGE: THE STORY BEHIND THE TAWANA BRAWLEY HOAX (1990).

34. Peter Applebome, *Woman's Claim of Racial Crime Is Called a Hoax,* N.Y. TIMES, June 1, 1990, at A14.

35. *Id.*

36. *Id.*

37. Andrew Kopkind observed that while the Stuart hoax triggered police invasions of Black communities, illegal searches and seizures, and racial slurs by law enforcement officials against Blacks, there was "[n]o comparable repression of the white community in New York State follow[ing] Brawley's charge." Andrew Kopkind, *The Stuart Case: Race, Class, and Murder in Boston,* 250 NATION 149, 149, 153 (1990).

38. "Hate crimes" have been defined as "crime[s] in which the defendant's conduct was motivated by hatred, bias, or prejudice, based on the actual or perceived race, color, religion, national origin, ethnicity, gender, or sexual orientation of another individual or group of individuals." H.R. 4797, 102d Cong., 2d Sess. (1992).

39. White-on-Black homicide is less prevalent than Black-on-White homicide. For 1993, White-on-Black murders make up 5% of the total murders with Black victims, while Black-on-White murders make up 15% of all murders with White victims. *See* FEDERAL BUREAU OF INVESTIGATION, U.S. DEP'T OF JUSTICE, CRIME IN THE U.S. 1993, at 17 (1994). In general, there is more Black-on-White crime than White-on-Black crime because "there are more whites for blacks to interact with, and therefore potentially more black [on] white crime." CORAMAE RICHEY MANN, UNEQUAL JUSTICE 33 (1993).

40. *See, e.g.*, Jandrucko v. Colorcraft/Fuqua Corp., No. 163-20-6245 (Fla. Dept. of Labor and Employment Sec. Apr. 26, 1990). *Jandrucko* involved an elderly White woman who told authorities she was mugged by a Black man and said the incident left her afraid of all Blacks. She sought and was granted workers' compensation. Jandrucko admitted that she did not see the face of her attacker. She only saw his dark-colored arms. This means the offender could have been a Black person, a dark-skinned Latino, or a tanned White person. The Florida Senate has since passed legislation precluding workers' compensation awards for phobias based upon race. Karen Branch, *Bill Bans Fear of Co-Workers as a Workers' Comp Claim,* MIAMI HERALD, Mar. 3, 1993, at B8; see also Walter L. Updegrave, *Crime: Who's Safe,*

Who's Not, MONEY, June 1994, at 114, 119-21. For a provocative discussion of "negrophobia" and the criminal law, see Jody Armour, *Race Ipsa Loquitur: Of Reasonable Racists, Intelligent Bayesians and Involuntary Negrophobes,* 46 STAN. L. REV. 781 (1994). While the focus of this negative stereotype falls squarely on the head of the Black male, its impact upon the Black female should not be overlooked. As the mother and mate of the Black male, she is intrinsically linked to and implicated by this stereotype.

41. *See, e.g.,* DERRICK A. BELL, RACE, RACISM AND AMERICAN LAW §§ 2.1-2.3 (1980); GUNNAR MYRDAL, AN AMERICAN DILEMMA 60 (1964) (discussing the "white man's . . . order of discriminations") (emphasis omitted). This threat was codified into law. Historically, the rape of a White woman by a Black man (slave, free, or otherwise) was punishable by death. *See, e.g.,* A. LEON HIGGINBOTHAM, JR., IN THE MATTER OF COLOR 263 (1978).

42. Official data for the last 10 years show that Whites consistently comprise between two-thirds and three-quarters of all arrests in any given year. *See* FEDERAL BUREAU OF INVESTIGATION, U.S. DEP'T OF JUSTICE, CRIME IN THE U.S. 1984-1993 (1994). *See generally* Katheryn K. Russell, White Crime (1994) (unpublished manuscript on file with author) (arguing that the discipline of criminology is overly focused upon Black crime and does not offer comparable attention to White crime).

43. Speculating about the impact of the Susan Smith hoax, one commentator asks, "What message is being sent to our young Black boys trying to find their place in a world that limits their importance to about 100 entertainers and 200 athletes?" Kevin Ross, *The Bogeyman Still Haunts Many White Minds,* EMERGE, Feb. 1995, at 84. Another notes, "Some blacks wonder how they can raise a younger generation of African Americans with enough self-esteem and lack of bitterness in the face of lingering racism." Deepti Hajela, *Blacks Wonder Why Hoax So Easily Believed; Crime Revives Questions of Prejudice,* SUN-SENTINEL (Fort Lauderdale), Nov. 5, 1994, at 16A; *see also* ROBYN HOLMES, HOW YOUNG CHILDREN PERCEIVE RACE (1995); Davis, *supra* note 6, at 1562 (stating that children assimilate negative racial stereotypes before they reach the age of judgment).

44. *See, e.g.,* Kopkind, *supra* note 37, at 154.

45. Hajela, *supra* note 43, at 16A.

46. *See, e.g.,* Lydia Saad & Leslie McAneny, *Black Americans See Little Justice for Themselves,* GALLUP POLL MONTHLY, Mar. 1995, at 32. There was a large gap between Black and White attitudes on O.J. Simpson's guilt. At one time, 75% of White but only 25% of Black respondents believed the murder charges were at least probably true. Price, *supra* note 7, at 3A. In 1995, there was discussion in the Black community that the criminal allegations made against three major Black entertainment figures, Mike Tyson, Michael Jackson, and O.J. Simpson, were part of a plot to destroy successful Black men. *Conversation with Mike Tyson* (Black Entertainment Television broadcast, Aug. 16, 1995). *See generally* PATRICIA A. TURNER, I HEARD IT THROUGH THE GRAPEVINE: RUMOR IN AFRICAN AMERICAN CULTURE (1993) (discussing prevalence of conspiracy theories in the Black community).

47. *See, e.g.,* JAMES H. JONES, BAD BLOOD: THE TUSKEGEE SYPHILIS EXPERIMENT (1993).

48. The use of the term "racialism" may be preferable to the use of the term "racism." By eliminating the hysteria associated with racism, perhaps a more objective sociological and legal assessment can be made of acts which cause race-based harm. *See* Stephen Carter, *When Victims Happen to Be Black,* 97 YALE L.J. 420, 443 (1988); Davis, *supra* note 6, at 1570. For purposes of this paper, the Author uses "racist" to connote conduct which causes race-based harm, without reference to the actor's intent.

49. See Richard Delgado, *Words That Wound: A Tort Action for Racial Insults, Epithets, and Name Calling,* in WORDS THAT WOUND 89, 90-96 (Mari Matsuda et al. eds., 1993), for an excellent discussion of the impact of racist speech upon Blacks and Whites.

50. Patricia Williams, *Spirit-Murdering the Messenger: The Discourse of Fingerpointing as the Law's Response to Racism,* 42 U. MIAMI L. REV. 127 (1987).

51. *See generally* Davis, *supra* note 6.

52. Wendy Brawn-Scott, *The Communitarian State: Lawlessness or Law Reform for African Americans?* 107 HARV. L. REV. 1209 (1994).

53. Williams, *supra* note 50, at 129.

54. *Id.* at 136-39, 144-48, 152-54.

55. *Id.*

56. *Id.* at 152.

57. *Id.* at 155 (citation omitted). This phenomenon was also evident in the O.J. Simpson case after the "Mark Fuhrman tapes" were made public in August 1995. On tape, Fuhrman, now a retired L.A.P.D. detective, discussed beating and framing citizens, bragged of lies he told the police department, used slurs to describe minorities and women, and boasted about his membership in a police group named "Men Against Women." *See, e.g.,* David Margolick, *What the Tapes in the Simpson Case Say,* N.Y. TIMES, Aug. 23, 1995, at A14. The reaction to the tapes was mixed. Some commentators believed Fuhrman was puffing, others suggested he was an aberrant rogue cop, and still others argued that his racism bore no relevance to Simpson's guilt or innocence. For many Blacks, however, the Fuhrman tapes validated their long-standing complaints of police brutality. William Claiborne and Kathryn Wexler, *Tapes Hit Home for L.A. Blacks,* WASH. POST, Aug. 31, 1995, at Al.

58. Davis, *supra* note 6, at 1565 (quoting Chester M. Pierce et al., *An Experiment in Racism: TV Commer-*

cials, in TELEVISION AND EDUCATION 62, 66 (Chester M. Pierce ed., 1978)).

59. *Id.* at 1569. *See generally* PHILOMENA ESSED, UNDERSTANDING EVERYDAY RACISM (1991).

60. Davis, *supra* note 6, at 1570.

61. *Id.* at 1562.

62. Davis notes that macroaggressions could be characterized as microaggressions vis-à-vis each individual who heard them. E-mail message from Professor Peggy S. Davis to Professor Katheryn K. Russell (Apr. 14, 1995) (on file with *Indiana Law Journal*).

63. *The New York Times* and *The Washington Post* were the primary sources for the one-month search.

64. *World News Saturday: Bitter Dispute over DNA Testing of Blacks in Ann Arbor* (ABC television broadcast, Feb. 4, 1995). There were earlier regional reports of this case. *See, e.g.,* Maryanne George, *Women Living in Fear,* CHI. TRIB., Dec. 27, 1994, at 7.

65. *See* Ronald Smothers, *Pilloried on a List That's Guilt by Name,* N.Y. TIMES, Feb. 5, 1995, at 18. Smothers describes how Union Point, Georgia, merchants, with the support of their mayor, imposed a ban upon 21 Blacks. The ban, implemented in December 1994, prohibited those listed from entering the town's commercial establishments and threatened criminal trespass charges for violations. The list was devised as an anticrime measure. Though suspected of criminal activity, none of the 21 had ever been convicted of any crime. In late February 1995, the merchants lifted the ban. The U.S. District Court judge who negotiated the settlement stated, "[The store owners'] efforts to prevent crime were not motivated by any racial motivation." *Georgia Shops Lift Ban on 21 Blacks,* WASH. POST, Feb. 23, 1995, at A5.

66. On November 11, 1994, Rutgers President Francis Lawrence made the following statement: "The average SAT for African Americans is 750. . . . Do we set standards in the future so that we don't admit anybody with the national test? Or do we deal with a disadvantaged population that doesn't have that genetic hereditary background to have a higher average?" *Rutgers Game Halted by Protesting Students,* WASH. POST, Feb. 8, 1995, at A3.

67. *Around the Nation,* WASH. POST, Feb. 11, 1995, at A2 (stating that David Walden and Shawn Daniels of Missouri pled guilty to federal civil rights violations for these offenses—driving around St. Louis on the 1991 and 1992 Martin Luther King holidays "spraying more than 50 blacks with water and koolaid from a fire extinguisher").

68. In addition to the four instances cited above, *see, e.g., Campus Protest Against Slurs,* N.Y. TIMES, Feb. 16, 1995, at A22 (reporting racist hate mail left in the mail boxes of University of California, Boalt Hall, minority law students—"Rejoice you crybaby niggers. It's affirmative action month. . . . When I see you in class it bugs the hell out of me because you're taking the seat of someone qualified"); *Confederate Flag Stays,* WASH. POST, Feb. 19, 1995, at A12 (reporting that the South Carolina attorney general, reversing previous opinion, determined that the confederate flag should be allowed to fly despite long-standing protests against it as an inappropriate reminder of slavery); *News in Brief,* WASH POST, Feb. 17, 1995, at A2 (reporting that the Mississippi state senate in 1995, 100 years after federal adoption, ratified the Thirteenth Amendment to the U.S. Constitution which outlaws slavery); *TV Column,* WASH. POST, Feb. 1. 1995, at D10 (reporting White Detroit weather reporter fired after likening a Black man to a gorilla); *2 Charged in Anne Arundel Church Break-In,* WASH. POST, Feb. 23. 1995, at Md. 3 (reporting that two youths were charged with burglary for breaking into a church and spraying the letters "KKK" on a carpet with a fire extinguisher).

Other instances of macroaggressions have occurred since February 1995. Three are particularly noteworthy: the incident involving five White Greenwich, Connecticut, high school students who placed a coded message in their yearbook that spelled out "Kill All Niggers," Jacques Steinberg, *Racist Message Reveals Rift,* N.Y. TIMES, June 21, 1995, at 84; the videotaped Whites-only picnic attended by Alcohol, Tobacco, and Firearms agents that featured racist slogans and a sign that read, "Nigger Check Point," Tim Weiner, *F.B.I. Says at Least 7 Agents Attended Gathering Displaying Racist Paraphernalia,* N.Y. TIMES, July 19, 1995, at A12; and the computer game "Freedom!" in which the players take on the role of Black slaves. Players begin the game as illiterate slaves, referred to as "boy." The game, sold by the Minnesota Educational Computing Corporation, was one of the computer games available for students to play in the Tempe, Arizona, Elementary School District. *School's Computer Game on Slavery Prompts Suit,* N.Y. TIMES, Aug. 28, 1995, at A10.

69. Brown-Scott, *supra* note 52, at 1209.

70. *Id.*

71. *Id.* at 1213.

72. *Id.* at 1209.

73. *Id.* at 1212.

74. Mari Matsuda, *Public Response to Racist Speech,* in WORDS THAT WOUND, *supra* note 49, at 25 (discussing the impact of race-based hate speech upon its victims) (emphasis added).

75. Noted historian John Henrik Clarke states (referring to the Bernhard Goetz case): "The lack of citizenship for black America has reached a point where we can't lie about it anymore. . . . We cannot tell the world anymore about our great democracy and melting pot theory when there is an African nation existing within the United States that is still lacking full citizenship." Susan Taylor Martin, *A Case of Hate: Attack on N.Y. Girl, and Reaction to It, Stirs Racial Tensions,* ST. PETERSBURG TIMES, Mar. 20, 1988, at 1A.

76. Williams, *supra* note 50, at 151.

77. Davis, *supra* note 6, at 1577 (emphasis added).

78. Brown-Scott, *supra* note 52, at 1213-14.

79. *Id.* at 1224. For an interesting discussion of White privilege, see Peggy McIntosh, *White Privilege and Male Privilege: A Personal Account of Coming to See Correspondences Through Work to Women's Studies,* in RACE, CLASS, AND GENDER 76-87 (Margaret L. Anderson & Patricia H. Collins eds., 1995); *see also* Cheryl I. Harris, *Whiteness as Property,* 106 HARV. L. REV. 1707 (1994).

80. Referring to the Tanya Dacri racial hoax, one commentator states, "[P]eople excused [her] story, because she was crazy. She may have been crazy, but she understood the state of U.S. race relations. She understood that a White woman raising the specter of crazed, violent Black men would strike a responsive chord in the press and with the general public." Williamson, *supra* note 32, at A6.

81. Émile Durkheim defined a social fact as one which is external to the individual and is coercive in nature. ÉMILE DURKHEIM, THE RULES OF SOCIOLOGICAL METHOD 50-59 (1982).

82. See *supra* note 12 and accompanying text. Courts have been loathe to accord legal relevance to past racial discrimination. *See, e.g.,* McCleskey v. Kemp, 481 U.S. 279 (1987) (holding that statistical proof of racial discrimination in capital sentencing is insufficient to establish a violation of the Equal Protection Clause); Cato v. United States, No. 94-17102 (9th Cir. Dec. 4, 1995) (holding that African Americans are not entitled to reparations under the U.S. Constitution). Further, there has been a shift from race-conscious remedies to race-neutral ones. See Gary Pellet, *Criminal Law, Race, and the Ideology of Bias: Transcending the Critical Tools of the Sixties,* 67 TUL. L. REV. 2231 (1993), for a detailed discussion of color-conscious versus color-blind approaches to criminal law.

83. This must be part of a larger effort to present an accurate picture of race and crime. *See, e.g.,* Richard Delgado, *Rodrigo's Eighth Chronicle: Black Crime, White Fears—On the Social Construction of Threat,* 80 VA. L. REV. 503 (1994) (providing an in-depth analysis of the costs of "White crime"—compared with the costs of "Black crime"—as well as White crime's causes and its relationship to white-collar crime); *see also* Russell, *supra* note 42. In addition to the enactment of new laws, affirmative race law encompasses the vigorous enforcement of existing laws which promote racial justice. For instance, sanctioning law enforcement officials who have violated the rights of Black citizens would constitute affirmative race law.

84. In 1992, Black households had the highest rate of victimization—199 per 1000 households. This contrasts with 147 per 1000 households for Whites. BUREAU OF JUSTICE STATISTICS, *supra* note 21, at 20. The level of victimization for young Black males is particularly stark. They "experience[] violent crime at a rate significantly higher than the rates for other age or racial groups. . . . Males age 16 to 19 were particularly at risk; their violent victimization rate was almost double the rate for white males. . . ." LISA D. BASTIAN & BRUCE M. TAYLOR, BUREAU OF JUSTICE STATISTICS, U.S. DEP'T OF JUSTICE, YOUNG BLACK MALE VICTIMS (1994).

85. *See, e.g.,* Jan Glidewell, *Racial Hoax Shows Our Inner Bias,* ST. PETERSBURG TIMES, Nov. 20, 1994, at 1 (stating that "even [Union, South Carolina, police chief] Wells' masterful handling of the situation could not help but leave black people everywhere angry and hurt").

86. *See, e.g.,* Les Payne, *A Rape Hoax Stirs up Hate,* NEWSDAY, Dec. 16, 1990, at 6 (concluding that "crying wolf should be severely punished").

87. Figures for 1993 show that Whites comprised 67% of total arrests. FEDERAL BUREAU OF INVESTIGATION, *supra* note 38, at 235.

88. James Q. Wilson, *To Prevent Riots, Reduce Black Crime,* WALL ST. J., May 6, 1992, at A16; *see also* BYRON ROTH, PRESCRIPTION FOR FAILURE (1994).

89. For a thoughtful discussion of the relationship between White racism and Black crime, see DERRICK BELL, AND WE ARE NOT SAVED: THE ELUSIVE QUEST FOR RACIAL JUSTICE 245-48 (1988).

90. *See, e.g.,* ELLIS COSE, THE RAGE OF A PRIVILEGED CLASS 93-95 (1993).

91. *Id.*

92. United States v. Clary, 846 F. Stipp, 768 (E.D. Mo.), *rev'd,* 34 F.3d 709 (8th Cir. 1994) (holding that federal sentencing guidelines which provide a harsher penalty for crack cocaine possession than for the same amount of powder cocaine are without legal justification, and noting that the law has grossly disproportionate impact upon minorities).

93. Lawrence W. Sherman, *Defiance, Deterrence, and Irrelevance: A Theory of the Criminal Sanction,* 30 J. RES. CRIME & DELINQ. 445 (1993).

94. JOHN BRAITHWAITE, CRIME, SHAME AND REINTEGRATION (1989).

95. *Id.* at 100-01.

96. *Id.* at 101.

97. *See, e.g.,* Thomas J. Bernard, *Angry Aggression Among the "Truly Disadvantaged,"* 28 CRIMINOLOGY 73, 80 (1990) ("Racial and ethnic discrimination involves intentionally harming, threatening, or insulting people and intentionally blocking their goal-directed activities[.]" (citations omitted)); Gresham M. Sykes & David Mate, *Techniques of Neutralism: A Theory of Delinquency,* 22 AM. SOC. REV. 664 (1957) (stating that techniques include "denial of injury" and "condemnation of the condemners").

98. Sherman, *supra* note 93, at 464.

99. This process essentially turns labeling theory on its head. Labeling theory predicts that once an individual has had a formal contact with the criminal justice system and is thereby labelled deviant, he is likely to act in con-

formity with the label. Therefore, labelling theorists argue, the deviant label should be avoided. Today, because Black males are presumed deviant, they are treated as deviant and may subsequently act in ways which conform to the label. *See, e.g.,* GEORGE B. VOLD & THOMAS J. BERNARD, THEORETICAL CRIMINOLOGY 252-57 (3d ed. 1986).

100. ANTHONY J. LEMELLE, JR., BLACK MALE DEVIANCE (1995).

101. *Id.* at 40.

102. *Id.* at 41 (emphasis added).

103. *Id.* at 42.

104. English researcher John Pitts refers to this practice as the difference between "epic" versus "lyric" criminology. Epic criminology, which describes much of U.S. criminology, focuses upon cultural characteristics, such as childrearing patterns, to explain crime. Conversely, lyric criminology emphasizes the characteristics of criminals (*e.g.,* socioeconomic status, education level) to explain crime. John Pitts, *Thereotyping Anti-racism, Criminology, and Black Young People,* in RACISM AND CRIMINOLOGY 108 (Dee Cook & Barbara Hudson eds., 1993).

105. For a supporting political theory, see Thomas Simon, *A Theory of Social Injustice,* in THE RADICAL PHILOSOPHY OF LAW 54-72 (David S. Caudill & Steven J. Gold eds., 1995). Simon sketches the outline of a theory of social injustice. His theory seeks to "catalogu[e] and compar[e] the various forms of injustice." *Id.* at 56. Simon notes that it is critical to the success of such a theory "for people to first get straight on what is wrong." *Id.* at 57. Once harm is acknowledged, compensation and restitution can be made available. Simon also discusses the various reactions to powerlessness, including rage, which can take the form of harming an innocent victim. Simon's central theoretical focus is upon the entrenched powerlessness of certain groups (*e.g.,* minorities). He concludes that "[w]hen group powerlessness cuts across generations, when it becomes a . . . defining feature of the group, it should receive top priority on the democratic agenda." *Id.* at 71.

106. Williams, *supra* note 50, at 127-29.

107. "I was enraged. At that moment I literally wanted to break all of the windows in the store and take lots of sweaters. . . ." *Id.* at 128.

108. PATRICIA J. WILLIAMS, THE ALCHEMY OF RACE AND RIGHTS 46 (1991) (recounting how she typed up a detailed account of the incident, made it into a poster, and attached it to the United Colors of Benneton store window).

109. *Id.* (emphasis added).

110. Carol Castenada, *In Kentucky, Confederate Flag is Fatal,* USA TODAY, Jan. 30, 1995, at 4A. Two men have been convicted of murder and sentenced to life in prison. *2 Convicted in Killing over Confederate Flag,* N.Y. TIMES, Jan. 13, 1996, at 7.

111. Neil MacFarquhar, *Angry Calm at the Services for Teen-Ager Slain by Police,* N.Y. TIMES, Feb. 27, 1995, at B5 (emphasis added).

112. Brown-Scott, *supra* note 52, at 1216-17.

113. Tom Gorman & Bettina Boxall, *Family Tells of Slain Gunman's Anger at Koon,* L.A. TIMES, Nov. 25, 1995, at Al.

114. *See, e.g.,* INDEPENDENT COMM'N ON THE LOS ANGELES POLICE DEP'T, REPORT OF THE INDEPENDENT COMMISSION ON THE LOS ANGELES POLICE DEPARTMENT (1995) (commission report stemming from the March 1991 beating of Rodney King); Joe Domanick, *Fuhrman Is Not an Exception,* WASH. POST, Sept. 1, 1995, at A25.

115. *See, e.g.,* Debbie Goldberg, *Police Scandal Creates Storm in Philadelphia,* WASH. POST, Aug. 17, 1995, at A3. Don Terry, *Philadelphia Shaken by Criminal Police Officers,* N.Y. TIMES, Aug. 28, 1995, at Al.

116. Goldberg, *supra* note 115, at A3.

117. *See, e.g.,* James Bennet, *A Woman's Plunge to Death Transfixes Detroit,* N.Y. TIMES, Aug. 23, 1995, at Al. Bennett writes about a Black woman who was involved in two minor traffic accidents. The car she hit was driven by a Black man who gave chase. She was forced to stop and was dragged out of her car by the driver and his two passengers. Her clothes were ripped off and she was beaten. To avoid further assault, the woman jumped off a bridge to her death.

118. Some counties have experienced an increase of assaults against police officers. *See, e.g.,* Jon Jeter, *Officer Slaying Not Tied to a Fight, P. G. Police Say,* WASH. POST, May 4, 1995, at C1.

119. The Gallup Poll data for 1993 reported that in response to the question, "Do you think that the American justice system is biased against Black people or not?" thirty-three percent of Whites responded yes while more than twice as many Blacks (68%) did so. Gallup Poll data for the last decade show a burgeoning gulf between how Blacks and Whites view the police. Respondents were asked, "How would you rate the honesty and ethical standards of (the police)?" In 1985, 48% of the Whites stated "very high/high," while only 35% of Blacks said "very high/high." BUREAU OF JUSTICE STATISTICS, U.S. DEP'T OF JUSTICE, SOURCEBOOK OF CRIMINAL JUSTICE STATISTICS—1985, at 159 (Timothy J. Flanagan & Edmund F. McGarrell eds., 1986). By 1993, the gap between Whites and Blacks had doubled: 53% of Whites said "very high/high" and 28% of Blacks said "very high/high." BUREAU OF JUSTICE STATISTICS, U.S. DEP'T OF JUSTICE, SOURCEBOOK OF CRIMINAL JUSTICE STASTISTICS—1993, at 165 (Kathleen Maguire & Ann L. Pastore eds., 1994).

The jubilant reaction to the Simpson verdict, by some sectors of the Black community, makes manifest how little faith many Blacks have in the criminal justice system. Professor Paul Butler offers "racially based jury nullification" as one way to empower Black jurors and bridge the racial gap in perception of fairness in the justice system. Paul Butler, *Racially Based Jury Nullification: Black Power in the Criminal Justice System,* 105 YALE L.J. 677 (1995).

120. *See, e.g., U-Md Combines Black Scholarships with 2nd Program,* WASH. POST, Feb. 6, 1995, at B3 (highlighting actions taken since a federal appeals court in Podberesky v. Kirwan, 38 F.3d 147 (4th Cir. 1995), held that the University of Maryland's Benjamin Banneker scholarship program for incoming Black freshman violated the Equal Protection Clause).

121. *See, e.g.,* B. Drummond Ayres, Jr., *Conservatives Forge New Strategy to Challenge Affirmative Action,* N.Y. TIMES, Feb. 16, 1995, at A1 (referring to the California ballot initiative against state affirmative action programs). Such political maneuvers are examples of what Professor Derrick Bell calls "the principle of involuntary sacrifice." He uses this term to describe how subordinated racial groups are used as political tools to benefit those racial groups in power. The sacrifice takes place so that "identifiably different groups of Whites" can establish or reestablish a relationship. BELL, *supra* note 41, § 1.9, at 29-30. Specifically, in the affirmative action debate, Blacks are being used by politicians to show that they support color-blind laws at the expense of Black progress. It looks as though this is also being done at the expense of White women—the primary benefactors of affirmative action. *Id.*

122. *See, e.g.,* Dan Stein & Herman Schwartz, *Entitlements for Undocumented Aliens,* A.B.A. J., Feb. 1995, at 42 (discussing California's Proposition 187).

123. *See, e.g.,* MARC MAUER & TRACY HOLING, THE SENTENCING PROJECT, YOUNG BLACK AMERICANS AND THE CRIMINAL JUSTICE SYSTEM: FIVE YEARS LATER 1-2 (1995).

124. Katharine Q. Seelye, *House Backs Bill to Require Restitution from Criminals,* N.Y. TIMES, Feb. 8, 1995, at 16A ("[T]he Republicans defeated a Democratic amendment that simply reiterated the words of the Fourth Amendment to the Constitution. The vote was 303 to 121.").

125. See Adubato, *supra* note 32.

126. Douglas H. Palmer, mayor of Trenton, N.J., Press Release, Jan. 12, 1995.

127. The police handling of the Harris case, *supra* note 15, stands in marked contrast. In the Harris case, the police "didn't go on a witch-hunt for an African American male." *Police Say Md. Man Had Fiancée Killed, Blamed Black Robber, supra* note 15, at B6.

128. Telephone interview with Hugh Munn, South Carolina State Law Enforcement Division (Aug. 15, 1995); *see also* Jo-Ann Clegg, *Susan Smith Should Pay Dearly: Unfit Parents Should Take Heed,* NORFOLK VIRGINIAN-PILOT, Nov. 11, 1994, at 7 ("For more than a week she lied to the authorities, thus triggering an investigation that cost tax payers millions of dollars and had thousands of people searching. . . .").

129. Telephone Interview with Hugh Munn, *supra* note 128.

130. Telephone Interview with Linda Jenkins, Deputy Clerk Advisor, Union, S.C., Sheriff's Office (Aug. 15, 1995).

131. *See, e.g.,* CAL. PENAL CODE § 148.5 (West Supp. 1995); MD. ANN. CODE art. 27, § 150 (1994); MASS. ANN. LAWS ch. 269, § 13A (Law. Co-op. 1992).

132. *See supra* notes 19-21 and accompanying text.

133. The assistant county prosecutor filed a $530 million defamation suit against Tawana Brawley and her advisors. The prosecutor won a default judgment. *See Browley Case Ruling Favors Ex-Prosecutor,* N.Y. TIMES, May 10, 1991, at B3. Further, steps were taken to sanction her attorneys for obstruction of justice. *See, e.g.,* John Bonomi, *About Justice: Odd Bedfellows Before the Bar,* NEWSDAY, July 10, 1990, at 48.

134. Professor Frederick Lawrence prefers the term "bias crime" rather than "hate crime," to describe more accurately the perpetrators' actions. Frederick M. Lawrence, *Resolving the Hate Crimes/Hate Speech Paradox: Punishing Bias Crimes and Protecting Racist Speech,* 68 NOTRE DAME L. REV. 673, 673-74 n.1 (1993).

135. *Id.* at 682.

136. 505 U.S. 377 (1992).

137. The statute provided:

> Whoever places on public or private property a symbol, object, appellation, characterization or graffiti, including, but not limited to, a burning cross or Nazi swastika, which one knows or has reasonable grounds to know arouses anger, alarm or resentment in others on the basis of race, color, creed, religion or gender commits disorderly conduct and shall be guilty of a misdemeanor.

Id. at 380.

138. *Id.* at 396.

139. The ADL model statute provides:

> A. A person commits the crime of intimidation if, by reason of the actual or perceived race, color, religion, national origin or sexual orientation of another individual or group of individuals, he violates section [] of the Penal Code (insert Code provision for criminal trespass, criminal mischief, harassment, menacing, assault and/or any other appropriate statutorily proscribed criminal conduct).
>
> B. Intimidation is a misdemeanor/felony (the degree of criminal liability should be made at least one degree more serious than that imposed for commission of the offense).

ANTI-DEFAMATION LEAGUE, HATE CRIMES STATUTES: A STATUS REPORT (1991).

140. Hate Crimes Sentencing Enhancement Act of 1993, Pub. L. No. 103-322, 108 Stat. 2096 (1994).

141. 113 S. Ct. 2194 (1993). In October 1989, Mitchell and some of his friends discussed a scene from the movie "Mississippi Burning." In the scene, a White man beat a young Black boy who was praying. After their conversation, Mitchell and his friends decided to "move on some white people," and severely beat a White boy who was passing by. *Id.* at 2196.

142. WIS. STAT. § 939.645 (1994). Notably, the five-year penalty enhancement provision exceeds the two-year maximum sentence for the crime of aggravated battery.

143. *Mitchell,* 113 S. Ct. at 2201.

144. *Id.*

145. Professor Lawrence refers to the free-speech-versus-bias-crime debate as a "false paradox." He states:

> The apparent paradox of seeking to punish the perpetrators of racially motivated violence while being committed to protecting the bigot's right to express racism is a false paradox. Put simply, we are making this problem harder than it needs to be. We must focus on the basic distinction between bias crimes—such as racially motivated assaults or vandalism—and racist speech.

Lawrence, *supra* note 134, at 676.

146. *See, e.g.,* Brandenburg v. Ohio, 395 U.S. 444 (1969).

147. This is an updated version of Justice Oliver Wendell Holmes' pronouncement that one does not have the right to "shout fire in a theatre." Schenck v. United States, 249 U.S. 47, 52 (1919).

148. Adubato, *supra* note 32, at B7.

149. N.J. Assembly Bill 2553, 206th Leg., 2d Sess. (1995), available in WESTLAW, NJ-Bills Database. False incrimination absent bias is a fourth-degree offense, N.J. STAT. ANN. § 2C:28-4(a) (West 1995), punishable by imprisonment for a maximum of eight months, *id.* § 2C:d3-6(ax4), and/or a $7500 fine. *Id.* § 2C:43-3(b). The penalty for a third-degree offense is imprisonment for three to five years, *id.* § 2C:43-6(a)(3), and/or a fine of $7500. *Id.* § 2C:43-3(b). Absent bias, the filing of a fictitious police report would be a disorderly persons charge, *id.* § 2C:2B-d(b), which is not considered a crime in New Jersey. *Id.* § 2C:1 4(b). No official action was taken on the bill during the 1994-1995 legislative session. The bill, renumbered A5 61-1996, is now in the Assembly Judiciary Committee. Telephone Interview with Dominick DeMarco, Legislative Aide to Congresswoman and bill sponsor Shirley Turner (February 2, 1996).

150. There are a number of other possible racial combinations, such as White-on-Latino and Latino-on-Black. As argued throughout this Article, the perception and stereotype of Blacks as criminal is so deeply entrenched and widespread that special legal focus should be given to this problem. Latinos, in particular, also face negative criminal stereotyping. *See, e.g.,* MANN, *supra* note 39, at 101-02. Although the discussion herein is confined to racial hoaxes, the New Jersey law has other categories, including ethnicity, sexual orientation, and religion. N.J. Assembly Bill 2553, 206th Leg., 2d Sess. (1995), available in WESTLAW, NJ-Bills Database.

151. In February 1996, Gerald Hill, a Black man, was charged in a 1200-count indictment with child abuse. Specifically, Hill was accused of abusing his four children, ages 5 to 12, over a five-year period. The charges allege sexual abuse, injecting the children with cocaine, and feeding them roaches and rats. Just days following the indictment, three of the children stepped forward to recant their allegations, saying that a relative had badgered them into making the allegations. If the charges are false, this case would be an example of a Black-on-Black racial hoax. *Bond in Abuse Case Stands; Judge Not Swayed by Kids' Recantation of Charges,* CHI. TRIB., Feb 10, 1996, at 5.

152. Glidewell, *supra* note 85, at 1.

153. *See, e.g.,* Laure Weber Brooks, *Police Discretionary Behavior,* in CRITICAL ISSUES IN POLICING 140, 154-55 (Roger G. Dunham & Geoffrey P. Alpert eds., 2d ed. 1993).

154. FEDERAL BUREAU OF INVESTIGATION, *supra* note 39, at 235.

155. BUREAU OF JUSTICE STATISTICS, *supra* note 21, at 61.

156. Matsuda, *supra* note 74, at 36.

157. *Id.*

158. Marc Fleischauer, *Teeth for a Paper Tiger: A Proposal to Add Enforceability to Florida's Hate Crimes Act,* 17 FLA. ST. U. L. REV. 697, 703 (1990).

159. *Id.* at 706.

160. 13 S. Ct. 2194 (1993).

161. See *supra* notes 58-62 and accompanying text.

162. A Black man named Willie Bennett was the initial suspect in the Charles Stuart case. See *supra* notes 22-25 and accompanying text.

163. Lawrence, *supra* note 134, at 698.

164. N.J. Assembly Bill 2553, 206th Leg., 2d Sess. (1995), available in WFSTLAW, NJ-Bills Database.

165. This could be reasonably expanded to include Hispanics/Latinos who also have the dubious distinction of symbolizing crime. *See, e.g.,* MANN, *supra* note 39, at 101-02.

166. *Cf.* Tanya Kateri Hernandez, *Bias Crimes Unconscious Racism in the Prosecution of "Racially Motivated Violence,"* 99 YALE L.J. 845, 852-53 (1990) (arguing that prosecutors are less likely to pursue hate crimes with minority victims).

167. See Fleischauer, *supra* note 158, at 703.

168. *Id.* at 707 n.63.

169. *See supra* part I.B.

170. *See, e.g.,* Adarand Constructors v. Pena, 115 S. Ct. 2097 (1995) (mandating heightened legal proof to support a set-aside contract program by requiring the government to demonstrate a narrowly tailored, compelling state interest, based upon clear evidence of past discrimination).

171. *See* MODEL PENAL CODE § 2.02 (1992).

172. N.J. Assembly Bill 2553, 206th Leg., 2d Sess. (1995), available in WESTLAW, NJ-Bills Database.

173. Charles Lawrence, *The Id, the Ego, and Equal Protection: Reckoning with Unconscious Racism,* 39 STAN. L. REV. 317, 322 (1987) (citations omitted).

174. The following are classified as crime index offenses: murder and nonnegligent homicide, burglary, arson, forcible rape, robbery, motor vehicle theft, aggravated assault, and theft. FEDERAL BUREAU OF INVESTIGATION, *supra* note 39, at 380.

175. See N.J. Assembly Bill 2553, 206th Leg., 2d Sess. (1995), available in WESTLAW, NJ-Bills Database.

176. *Id.*

177. Professor Richard Abel has suggested that an apology is an appropriate sanction for hate speech. RICHARD ABEL, SPEECH AND RESPECT 28 (1995). For a critique of this argument, see RICHARD DELGADO & JEAN STEFANCIC, APOLOGIZE AND MOVE ON? (1995).

178. Raspberry, *supra* note 26. Following the George Washington University rape hoax, *see supra* notes 19-21, the school president, in a letter addressed to the university community, wrote, "We must understand that our black students, faculty, staff and neighbors have been given offense and reason to feel concerned and anxious. They were special victims of the hoax." Barras, *supra* note 20, at B4. Smith's brother did issue an apology. *See* Parente, *supra* note 28, at A66.

179. More than one entity could be asked to apologize—for example, the media, the police, the mayor, and the defendant.

180. An educational component would also be useful for the racial hoax. Specifically, a requirement that the perpetrator take a "crash course" on crime statistics. This would include Uniform Crime Reports data on actual arrests, crime rates by race, and the prevalence of intraracial versus interracial crime. Whether this should be legally mandated remains unclear. This could be part of a criminal justice information packet provided upon conviction.

181. Hate Crime Statistics Act, 28 U.S.C. 534 (Supp. V 1993).

182. *Id.*

183. Lawrence, *supra* note 134, at 721.

184. The *Mitchell* court noted that "motive plays the same role under the Wisconsin statute as it does under the federal and state anti-discrimination laws." Wisconsin v. Mitchell, 113 S. Ct. 2194, 2200 (1993); *see also Leading Cases,* 107 HARV. L. REV. 144, 238-39 (1993).

INDEX

About the Editors

Shaun L. Gabbidon is Assistant Professor of Criminal Justice in the School of Public Affairs at Pennsylvania State University, Capital College. He received his bachelor's degree in Government Administration with a specialty in criminal justice from Christopher Newport University in Newport News, Virginia. After receiving an M.S. in Criminal Justice from the University of Baltimore, he received a Ph.D. in Criminology from Indiana University of Pennsylvania. Professor Gabbidon is coauthor (with Helen Taylor Greene) of *African American Criminological Thought* (2000).

Helen Taylor Greene is Associate Professor in the Department of Sociology and Criminal Justice at Old Dominion University. She completed her B.S. in Sociology at Howard University, an M.S. in the Administration of Justice at American University, an M.A. in Political Science, and a Ph.D. in Criminology at the University of Maryland, College Park. She is coauthor with Shaun Gabbidon of *African American Criminological Thought* (2000).

Vernetta D. Young is Associate Professor in the Department of Sociology and Anthropology at Howard University. She completed her B.A. in Sociology at the University of Maryland, College Park, and attended Florida State University before completing her Ph.D. in Criminal Justice at the State University of New York at Albany. She has also taught at American University and the University of Maryland, College Park.

About the Contributors

Elijah Anderson is the Charles and William L. Day Professor of Social Sciences and Professor of Sociology at the University of Pennsylvania. After receiving a B.A. from Indiana University, he received an M.A. from the University of Chicago. He received his Ph.D. in Sociology from Northwestern University in 1976. Anderson is the author of three books: *A Place on the Corner* (1978); *Streetwise: Race, Class, and Change in an Urban Community* (1990); and *Code of the Street* (1999).

Lee P. Brown is currently the mayor of Houston, Texas. Prior to his election as mayor, Brown had a long and distinguished career in law enforcement at the local, state, and federal levels. He received a bachelor's degree from Fresno State University and his master's and doctorate degrees in Criminology from the University of California, Berkeley.

Paul Butler is Professor of Law at George Washington University Law School. He was educated at Yale University (B.A.) and Harvard University (J.D.). Early in his career, he practiced law at both the local and federal levels, most notably in the Justice Department's Public Integrity Section.

W. E. B. Du Bois received bachelor's degrees from both Fisk and Harvard Universities. In 1891, he received a master's degree in History from Harvard University. After 2 years of study at the University of Berlin, he became the first African American to receive a Ph.D. at Harvard University (in History). Along with academic appointments at Wilberforce and Atlanta Universities, DuBois was also a founding member of the National Association for the Advancement of Colored People. A prolific author, he authored several classic works, including *The Suppression* *of the Slave Trade to the United States of America, 1638-1870* (1896); *The Philadelphia Negro* (1899); and *The Souls of Black Folk* (1903).

E. Franklin Frazier was Professor of Sociology at Howard University from the 1930s to the early 1960s. He received a bachelor's degree from Howard University. He also received a master's degree from Clark University and a doctorate from the University of Chicago. He is the author of numerous books, including *The Negro Family in Chicago* (1932), *The Negro Family in the United States* (1939), and *Black Bourgeoisie* (1957).

Daniel E. Georges-Abeyie is Professor of Administration of Justice at Arizona State University West. A geographer by training, Georges-Abeyie's work on petit apartheid has garnered significant scholarly discussion and is the focus of a forthcoming volume. He has degrees from Hope College (B.A.), the University of Connecticut (M.A.), and Syracuse University (Ph.D.). He is the editor of *The Criminal Justice System and Blacks* (1984).

Darnell F. Hawkins is currently Head and Professor of the Department of African American Studies at the University of Illinois at Chicago. He received his bachelor's degree from Kansas State University. He also holds a M.A.T. from Wayne State University and a doctorate in Sociology from the University of Michigan. He later received a law degree from the University of North Carolina at Chapel Hill. Hawkins is the editor of several books, including *Homicide Among Black Americans* (1986); *Ethnicity, Race, and Crime* (1995); *Race, Ethnicity, and Violent Crimes* (in press); and *Crime Control and Social Justice* (in press).

A. Leon Higginbotham, Jr. was first appointed to the federal judiciary by President Lyndon Johnson in 1964. In 1977, he became a judge in the Federal Court of Appeals in Philadelphia and later in 1989 became chief judge. He earned a B.A. at Antioch College and a law degree from Yale in 1952. He taught at Harvard University and practiced law in several cities. He authored *In the Matter of Color* (1978) and *Shades of Freedom* (1996).

Coramae Richey Mann received both her bachelor's and master's degrees from Roosevelt University in Chicago. In 1976, she received a doctorate in Sociology from the University of Illinois at Chicago. She is currently Professor Emeritus at both Florida State University and Indiana University. She has authored several books, including *Female Crime and Delinquency* (1984), *Unequal Justice: A Question of Color* (1993), and *When Women Kill* (1996).

Earl R. Moses received a master's degree in Sociology from the University of Chicago in 1932. He later received a Ph.D. in Sociology from the University of Pennsylvania.

William Oliver is Associate Professor of Criminal Justice in the Department of Criminal Justice at Indiana University. He received his Ph.D. in Criminal Justice from the School of Criminal Justice at the State University of New York at Albany. He is the author of *The Violent Social World of Black Men* (1994).

Katheryn K. Russell is Associate Professor of Criminal Justice at the University of Maryland, College Park. She received a bachelor's degree from the University of California, Berkeley. She is a graduate of the Hastings School of Law in California. Russell is also a graduate of the Ph.D. program in criminology and criminal justice at the University of Maryland, College Park. She is the author and coeditor of *The Color of Crime* (1998) and *Race and Crime* (2000) (with Heather L. Pfeifer and Judith L. Jones).

Robert Staples is Professor Emeritus in the Department of Social and Behavioral Sciences at the University of California, San Francisco. He has degrees from Los Angeles Valley College (A.A.); California State University, Northridge (M.A.); and the University of Minnesota (Ph.D.). He is the author and editor of numerous books, including *The Black Woman in America* (1973), *Introduction to Black Sociology* (1976), *Black Families at the Crossroads* (1993), and *The Black Family* (1994, 5th ed.).

Becky Tatum is Assistant Professor of Criminal Justice in the Department of Criminal Justice at Georgia State University. She received a B.A. from Louisiana Tech University and M.A. and Ph.D. degrees in Criminal Justice from the State University of New York at Albany. She is the author of *Crime, Violence and Minority Youth* (2000).

Ida B. Wells-Barnett was a pioneer in the anti-lynching crusade during the late 19th and early 20th centuries. She was educated a Rust College and Fisk University. She is the author of *Southern Horrors* (1892), *A Red Record* (1895), and *Mob Rule in New Orleans* (1900).

Monroe N. Work was a pioneering sociologist who was educated at the University of Chicago (B.S., 1902, M.S., 1903). He taught at Savannah State University and was appointed director of the research department at Tuskegee Instititue by Booker T. Washington. From 1912 to 1938, he edited the highly acclaimed *The Negro Yearbook.*

CPSIA information can be obtained
at www.ICGtesting.com
Printed in the USA
FFOW04n1737130116
20369FF

9 780761 9243